BIBLICAL HEBREW

An Introductory Grammar

Biblical Hebrew

An Introductory Grammar

Page H. Kelley

WILLIAM B. EERDMANS PUBLISHING COMPANY
GRAND RAPIDS, MICHIGAN

Copyright © 1992 by Wm. B. Eerdmans Publishing Co.
255 Jefferson Ave. S.E., Grand Rapids, Michigan 49503

Printed in the United States of America

Library of Congress Cataloging-in-Publication Data

Kelley, Page H.
Biblical Hebrew : an introductory grammar / Page H. Kelley.
p.   cm.
Includes index.
ISBN 0-8028-0598-1 (pbk.)
1. Hebrew language — Grammar — 1950-   I. Title.
PJ4567.3.K43   1992
492.4'82421 — dc20   92-9728
CIP

Affectionately Dedicated
to
Vernice

CONTENTS

CONTENTS

PREFACE

This grammar has grown out of forty years of classroom experience teaching Biblical Hebrew to seminary students. I have been helped along the way by my own teachers, including Professors John J. Owens, Thomas O. Lambdin, and John Emerton.

My earliest teaching assignment after seminary was in Rio de Janeiro. For a period of seven years I taught Biblical Hebrew in a Brazilian seminary. This experience made me aware of the need for a grammar that was written in simple language, that was as comprehensive as possible, and that contained a wide range of biblically based examples and exercises.

The present work has been prepared with these criteria in mind. If it has any claim to distinction, it is in the design of its examples and exercises. Many hours were spent searching Even-Shoshan's *Hebrew Concordance* for biblical passages that best illustrated the grammatical principles being discussed. Insofar as possible, the choice of passages to be included in a given lesson has been limited to those whose vocabulary and grammar have already been described. A student's ability to handle a lesson's exercises has not been made dependent on the knowledge of subsequent lessons.

A suggested procedure for using the grammar would be for the professor to spend the last part of the class hour highlighting the principal points in the upcoming lesson and assigning all or part of the exercises and vocabulary. Students should be expected to study the lesson carefully, but without attempting to memorize rules. Instead they should move as quickly as possible to the exercises, and then consult the lesson rules and examples as needed to understand the exercises. The opening part of the following class period could be used to correct exercises or to answer any remaining questions students might have. Professors who find such a plan of study too accelerated might prefer to space out the assignments over a longer period of time, especially on the larger lessons. If the course schedule provides time for additional scripture reading assignments, it is suggested that these be made from Genesis, since a deliberate effort has been made to draw materials for exercises and examples from this part of the Hebrew Bible.

It is assumed that students will need to acquire additional tools for use alongside the grammar. A Bible and a lexicon are indispensable. A concordance and a work on syntax are also recommended. The best Bible currently available is *Biblical Hebraica Stuttgartensia*, a critical edition of the Leningrad Manuscript B19^A(L). My choice of lexicons is still *A Hebrew and English Lexicon of the Old Testament*, by F. Brown, S.R. Driver, and C.A. Briggs. While it desperately needs revising, it remains the most versatile tool in its class. My second choice would be an abbreviated version of the Koehler-Baumgartner lexicon prepared by William L. Holladay and titled *A Concise Hebrew and Aramaic Lexicon of the Old Testament*. The best available concordance is *A New Concordance of the Bible*, edited by Abraham Even-Shoshan. The Kautzsch-Cowley edition of *Gesenius' Hebrew Grammar*, although somewhat outdated, still remains useful as a research tool.

I strongly recommend John J. Owen's four-volume *Analytical Key to the Old Testament*, a verse-by-verse analysis of the words and phrases of the Hebrew Bible, all of which are keyed to the Brown, Driver, and Briggs lexicon and translated into into English. Finally, the most comprehensive survey of Hebrew syntax is that recently written by Bruce K. Waltke and M. O'Connor, titled *An Introduction to Biblical Hebrew Syntax*.

This grammar has been used in a number of colleges and seminaries during the course of its preparation. Special thanks is owed to students who struggled through it in its earlier stages, and to professors and instructors who were willing to field-test it and offer suggestions for its improvement. Invaluable assistance and encouragement have come from Joel F. Drinkard, Jr., Gerald L. Keown, Pamela J. Scalise, Thomas G. Smothers, Marvin E. Tate, and John D. W. Watts, my colleagues in the Old Testament Department at The Southern Baptist Theological Seminary. Others who have helped during the course of the preparation of this work include Trent C. Butler, Tim Crawford, Bob Dunston, J. Kenneth Eakins, David M. Fleming, Darlene R. Gautsch, Walter Harrelson, Harry B. Hunt, Jr., Karen Joines, John Laughlin, M. Pierce Matheney, Jr., Ken Matthews, Gregory Mobley, Gerald P. Morris, Ernest W. Nicholson, Robert Owens, Michael Shockley, William P. Steeger, Robert A. Street, John H. Tullock, Ed Rowell, and James W. Watts.

I wish to thank President Roy L. Honeycutt and Dean Larry L. McSwain for providing sabbatical leave time for me to complete this project. My thanks go also to the faculty and staff of Golden Gate Baptist Theological Seminary, especially Dean Robert L. Cate, for providing working space in what is surely one of the most beautiful spots on earth. No one has offered more support and encouragement during the final months of the preparation of the grammar than LeRoy C. King of the staff of Eerdmans. Klaas Wolterstorff, Production Manager for Eerdmans, has rendered invaluable assistance in the final preparation of the Grammar for publication. Finally, I will always be indebted to Terry L. Burden, without whose expertise with a word processor and a laser printer the grammar might never have seen the light of day.

Louisville, Kentucky
February 25, 1992

LESSON I

1. The Alphabet

Name	Form	Final Form	Transliteration	Pronunciation	Modern Script	Block
ʾālĕf	א		ʾ	Silent letter	lc	א
bêt	ב		b	B as in *Boy*	ב	ב
	ב		v	V as in *Vine*	ב	ב
gîmĕl	ג		g	G as in *Go*	c	ג
	ג		g	G as in *Go*	c	ג
dālĕt	ד		d	D as in *Dare*	ד	ד
	ד		d	D as in *Dare*	ד	ד
hēʾ	ה		h	H as in *His*	ה	ה
vāv	ו		v	V as in *Vine*	l	ו
zāyĭn	ז		z	Z as in *Zeal*	ל	ז
ḥêt	ח		ḥ	CH as in *BaCH*	ח	ח
ṭêt	ט		ṭ	T as in *Tall*	ט	ט
yôd	י		y	Y as in *Yes*	י	י
kăf	כ		k	K as in *Keep*	כ	כ
		ך	kh	CH as in *BaCH*	כ	ך
lāmĕd	ל		l	L as in *Let*	ל	ל
mēm	מ	ם	m	M as in *Met*	N	מ
nûn	נ	ן	n	N as in *Net*	J	נ
sāmĕkh	ס		s	S as in *Set*	O	ס
ʿāyĭn	ע		ʿ	Silent letter	ע	ע
pēʾ	פ		p	P as in *Pet*	פ	פ
	פ	ף	f	F as in *Fat*	פ	ף
ṣādê	צ	ץ	ṣ	TS as in *NeTS*	צ	ץ
qôf	ק		q	K as in *Keep*	ק	ק
rêš	ר		r	R as in *Rule*	ר	ר
śîn	ש		ś	S as in *Set*	e	ש
šîn	ש		š	SH as in *SHine*	e	ש
tāv	ת		t	T as in *Tall*	ת	ת
	ת		t	T as in *Tall*	ת	ת

1

Notes:

1.1 The pronunciation recommended here is based upon that used in modern Hebrew. It is known as the Sephardic pronunciation.

1.2 A point is placed under ḥ when it transliterates ח, under ṭ when it transliterates ט, and under ṣ when it transliterates צ. This is to distinguish these letters from others that have similar sounds.

1.3 There are twenty-two letters in the Hebrew alphabet. This number is arrived at by counting שׁ and שׂ as variant forms of the same letter.

1.4 The Hebrew alphabet contains no vowels, but only consonants. This is because ancient Hebrew was written without vowels. Its correct pronunciation was based upon an oral tradition handed down from generation to generation. A written vowel system was devised in the period between A.D. 500 and 1000 for the primary purpose of preserving the oral tradition. A text without vowels is called "an unpointed text." Synagogue scrolls even today are written with an unpointed text, as are most books, magazines, and newspapers printed in Modern Hebrew. The written vowels are of great benefit to the beginning student and will be studied in Lesson 2.

1.5 The first letter in the alphabet is א (ʼālĕf), but it must not be confused with English "*a*" or Greek "*alpha*" (α). The latter two are vowels, while א is always a consonant.

1.6 Hebrew is written and read from right to left. Thus the letters of the alphabet should be written as follows:

א ב ג ד ה ו ז ח ט י כ ל מ נ ס ע פ צ ק ר שׁ שׂ ת

But they should be read as follows: ʼālĕf, bêt, gîmĕl, etc.

1.7 There are no capital letters in Hebrew.

1.8 Each letter in the alphabet represents the initial consonant of the Hebrew name for that letter. The Hebrew names (minus vowels) are as follows:

(1)	אלף	(7)	זין	(13)	מם	(19)	קוף
(2)	בית	(8)	חית	(14)	נון	(20)	ריש
(3)	גימל	(9)	טית	(15)	סמך	(21)	שׁין
(4)	דלת	(10)	יוד	(16)	עין		שׂין
(5)	הא	(11)	כף	(17)	פא	(22)	תו
(6)	וו	(12)	למד	(18)	צדי		

1.9 Six Hebrew consonants, ב, ג, ד, כ, פ, ת, may appear either with or without a dot placed within them. The dot is called a dagesh lene. The dot will normally be required when one of these six consonants begins a new word. It may even be required when one of them begins a new syllable within a word. Rules governing the use of the dagesh lene will be studied later.

A convenient device for remembering the consonants that sometimes accept a dagesh lene is to memorize the artificial words BeGaD KeFaT, where B = ב, G = ג, D = ד, K = כ, F = פ, and T = ת.

In Modern Hebrew pronunciation, the presence or absence of the dagesh lene affects the pronunciation of three of the BeGaD KeFaT letters, namely ב, כ, and פ. With the dagesh lene their pronunciation is hard. Without it their pronunciation is soft. The other three consonants, ג, ד, and ת, are always given a hard sound, regardless of whether or not they have a dagesh lene.

בּ	= b, but	ב	= v	גּ	= g, and	ג	= g
כּ	= k, but	כ	= kh	דּ	= d, and	ד	= d
פּ	= p, but	פ	= f	תּ	= t, and	ת	= t

1.10 Vāv is pronounced like v in "vine." The same is true of the letter bêt without the dagesh lene. Note also that an alternate name for the letter vāv is wāw, pronounced like the letter w in "we."

1.11 Five letters take special forms when they stand at the end of a word. Note that four of the final forms extend below the line, which is not the case with regular consonants, except in the case of ק.

Regular forms   צ פ נ מ כ
Final forms   ץ ף ן ם ך

1.12 Five of the consonants, א, ה, ח, ע, and sometimes ר, are classified as gutturals, because of their having originally been pronounced in the throat. Their distinctive characteristics will be studied later.

1.13 Certain letters are classified as sibilants because of their "s" sounds. They are ז, ס, צ, שׁ, and שׂ. Their presence in certain verb forms influences the writing of these forms (cf. XIV.36.4, p. 110).

1.14 Individual Hebrew letters stand alone and are not joined to each other, except in modern script.

EXERCISES

The exercises included in each lesson are designed to help the student apply the principles studied in that lesson. Examples used in the lessons and exercises will for the most part be taken verbatim from the Hebrew Bible. This will account for the different ways in which the same word may sometimes be written. The style of the author and the demands of the context may alter the form in which a particular word appears.

1. Write a full line of each of the letters of the Hebrew alphabet.

2. Learn to pronounce the letters in proper order from א to ת.

3. Transliterate the following verse (Ezek. 38:12, one of twenty-six verses containing all the letters of the alphabet).

לשלל שלל ולבז בז להשיב ידך על חרבות נושבת ואל עם

מאסף מגוים עשה מקנה וקנין ישבי על טבור הארץ

4. Practice pronouncing the letters in the verse above in the order in which they occur, reading from right to left.

5. Locate and identify all the final forms of letters that occur in the verse above.

6. Transliterate the Hebrew names for all consonants as they appear in paragraph I.1.8, pp. 2f.

        Example: אלף   = 'lf

                           בית   = byt; etc.

7. Certain letters are similar in form and thus easily confused. Examine the following letters and learn to identify each by name.

(1)	ב, כ, פ	(6)	ו, ז, י
(2)	ף, ק	(7)	ם, ס
(3)	ג, נ	(8)	ט, מ
(4)	ך, ן	(9)	ה, ח, ת
(5)	ד, ר	(10)	ע, צ, ץ

8. Certain letters sound alike. Learn to identify these letters by name.

(1)	ס, שׂ – S, as in Set	(4)	ב, ו – V, as in Vine
(2)	כּ, ק – K, as in Keep	(5)	ח, כ – CH, as in BaCH
(3)	ט, ת – T, as in Tall	(6)	א, ע – Silent letters

4

9. What do the letters in each of the following groups have in common with each other?

(1) ‎ב ג ד כ פ ת‎   (3) ‎ך ם ן ף ץ‎

(2) ‎ב כ פ‎   (4) ‎א ה ח ע ר‎

10. Transliterate the following proper names and try to identify them from their consonantal forms. A reference is given to indicate where each may be found in the Hebrew Bible.

(1) ‎בית לחם‎ (Mic. 5:1; Eng. 5:2)   (17) ‎נתן‎ (2 Sam. 7:3)

(2) ‎בלק‎ (Num. 22:2)   (18) ‎סדם‎ (Gen. 13:13)

(3) ‎בנימין‎ (Gen. 42:4)   (19) ‎עשׂו‎ (Gen. 25:25)

(4) ‎גד‎ (Gen. 30:11)   (20) ‎פארן‎ (Deut. 1:1)

(5) ‎גלגל‎ (Josh. 5:9)   (21) ‎קדשׁ‎ (Gen. 14:7)

(6) ‎גשׁן‎ (Gen. 46:28)   (22) ‎רבקה‎ (Gen. 22:23)

(7) ‎דוד‎ (1 Sam. 16:23)   (23) ‎רחל‎ (Gen. 29:6)

(8) ‎הגר‎ (Gen. 16:1)   (24) ‎אברהם‎ (Gen. 17:5)

(9) ‎חזקיה‎ (2 Kgs. 18:1)   (25) ‎שׂרה‎ (Gen. 17:15)

(10) ‎כנען‎ (Gen. 12:5)   (26) ‎שדרך‎ (Dan. 1:7)

(11) ‎ישׂראל‎ (Gen 35:10)   (27) ‎שכם‎ (Judg. 9:6)

(12) ‎כלב‎ (Num. 13:6)   (28) ‎שלמה‎ (2 Sam. 12:24)

(13) ‎לאה‎ (Gen. 29:16)   (29) ‎שם‎ (Gen. 9:23)

(14) ‎לבן‎ (Gen. 24:29)   (30) ‎שפן‎ (2 Kgs. 22:9)

(15) ‎משה‎ (Exod. 2:10)   (31) ‎תל אביב‎ (Ez. 3:15)

(16) ‎נבכדנאצר‎ (2 Kgs. 24:1)   (32) ‎תמר‎ (Gen. 38:6)

11. Practice spelling aloud the names listed above.

Example:

‎בית לחם‎, "bêt–yôd–tāv/lámĕd–ḥēt–(final) mēm."

5

LESSON II

2. Vowels

Ancient Hebrew had no written system of vowels. The language was read and spoken according to an oral tradition handed down from generation to generation.

At an early period in the development of the language certain consonants began to function not only as consonants but also as vowel indicators. Thus א and ה were used to indicate "a" class vowels, י to indicate "e" and "i" class vowels, and ו to indicate "o" and "u" class vowels. Early Hebrew grammarians coined the term *matres lectionis* (literally, "mothers of reading") to designate these letters. The two consonants most frequently used as vowel indicators are י and ו.

Table of Full Vowels

	Name	Sign	Position with Consonant	Sound	Illustration	
1.	qā́mĕṣ	ָ	אָ	ā, as in *car*	אָב	father
2.	pắtăḥ	ַ	אַ	ă, as in *car*	בַּת	daughter
3.	ṣḗrê	ֵ	אֵ	ē, as in *they*	אֵל	God
4.	ṣḗrê-yôd	ֵי	אֵי	ê, as in *they*	בֵּית	house of
5.	sᵉgôl	ֶ	אֶ	ĕ, as in *met*	שֶׁקֶל	shekel
6.	ḥîrĕq-yôd	ִי	אִי	î, as in *marine*	הִיא	she
7.	ḥîrĕq	ִ	אִ	ĭ, as in *sit*	עִם	with
8.	ḥṓlĕm	ֹ	אֹ	ō, as in *row*	לֹא	not
9.	ḥṓlĕm-vāv	וֹ	אוֹ	ô, as in *row*	אוֹר	light
10.	qā́mĕṣ-ḥāṭûf	ָ	אָ	ŏ, as in *cost*	כָּל	all of
11.	šûrĕq	וּ	אוּ	û, as in *rule*	הוּא	he
12.	qĭbbûṣ	ֻ	אֻ	ŭ, as in *pull*	שֻׁלְחָן	table

(A mū́nah appears under the word שֶׁקֶל to indicate the accented syllable. This practice will be followed throughout this grammar whenever a word is accented on a syllable other than the final syllable.)

6

Notes:

2.1 The vowels listed above are designated *full vowels* in order to distinguish them from the *half-vowels*, which will be discussed later.

2.2 For grammatical purposes these vowels are divided into *long vowels* and *short vowels*. This distinction will be especially important for our understanding of the formation of nouns and verbs.

       (1) The long vowels include qāmĕṣ, ṣḗrê, ṣḗrê-yôd, ḥîrĕq-yôd, ḥōlĕm, ḥōlĕm-vāv, and šûrĕq. In order to indicate the long vowels that include one of the vowel letters (*matres lectionis*) a circumflex accent is used in representing their sound. Thus ṣḗrê-yôd (˙˙) is represented as ê, ḥîrĕq-yôd (˙) as î, ḥōlĕm-vāv (˙) as ô, and šûrĕq (˙) as û. These vowels can never be shortened and are therefore said to be characteristically or unchangeably long.

       (2) The short vowels are pătăḥ, sᵉgôl, ḥîrĕq, qāmĕṣ-ḥāṭûf, and qĭbbûṣ. (Note that in Modern Hebrew, pătăḥ is pronounced exactly like qāmĕṣ. In this grammar, however, it is transliterated as "ă" in order to distinguish it from qāmĕṣ, which is transliterated as "ā".)

2.3 The sounds given in the table above only roughly approximate those of spoken Hebrew. Often in the spoken language no noticeable distinction is made between ḥîrĕq-yôd and ḥîrĕq, or between šûrĕq and qĭbbûṣ, just as no distinction is made between qāmĕṣ and pătăḥ.

2.4 Most of the vowels stand directly below the consonants with which they are to be pronounced. The exceptions are ḥōlĕm, ḥōlĕm-vāv, and šûrĕq.

2.5 The vowels were originally designed so that they could be inserted into a consonantal text without actually lengthening the text. In other words, a pointed text (one supplied with vowels) of a given book of the Hebrew Bible should be exactly the same length as the unpointed text of the same book. This means that the yôds in ṣḗrĕ-yôd and ḥîrĕq-yôd, as well as the vāvs in ḥōlĕm-vāv and šûrĕq, were already present in the consonantal text of Hebrew manuscripts (as *matres lectionis*) before they were pointed as vowels. It was the consonants and not the vowels that determined the length of Hebrew texts.

2.6 Qāmĕṣ (ˍ) and qāmĕṣ-ḥāṭûf (ˍ) have the same form, although one represents a long "a" class vowel and the other a short "o" class vowel. The rules for distinguishing between the two will be studied later. It may be of some consolation to know that qāmĕṣ-ḥāṭûf rarely occurs.

2.7 When ḥōlĕm (˙) precedes the letter שׁ, it may combine with the dot over the right hand tip of שׁ to produce a single dot that thus serves a double purpose. Moses' name, for example, is sometimes written as מֹשֶׁה, *Mōšĕh*.

Likewise, whenever ḥôlĕm follows the letter שׂ, it may combine with the dot over the left hand tip of שׂ. The word for "enemy," for example, sometimes appears as שׂנֵא, *śōnēʾ*.

Some printed editions, however, separate the ḥôlĕm from the diacritical points over שׂ and שׁ. The *Biblia Hebraica Stuttgartensia* (BHS) is one such edition. It thus prints "Moses" as מֹשֶׁה and "enemy" as שֹׂנֵא.

2.8 Ḥôlĕm and ḥôlĕm-vāv are often used interchangeably. For example, the masculine plural adjective for "good" may be written either as טֹבִים, *tō-vîm*, or as טוֹבִים, *tô-vîm*.

2.9 One sometimes encounters a pătăḥ-yôd or a qắmĕṣ-yôd at the end of a Hebrew word. These two combinations sound alike and are pronounced somewhat like "ai" in the word "aisle," except the "a" sound is always long.

Whenever the consonant vāv (ו) is added to this ending, as often happens in plural noun endings, the resultant sound is simply that of long "a" followed by "v." Thus the word for "his sons," בָּנָיו (Gen. 9:8), is pronounced bā-nâv. A circumflex accent over the second qắmĕṣ indicates that it has combined with the yôd to form a characteristically long vowel. The following vāv functions as the final consonant in the word.

3. Half-Vowels

In addition to the full vowels listed above, Hebrew makes use of other vowels that could best be described as semi-vowels or half-vowels. They represent full vowels that have been abbreviated for phonetical purposes.

In order to understand half-vowels, we must begin with the *šᵉvāʾ* (שְׁוָא), hereafter referred to as *sheva*.

There are two classes of sheva, the *vocal sheva* and the *silent sheva*. Our concern here is with the former. The vocal sheva is written like a modern colon, except that it is placed below the line. It stands underneath a consonant either at the beginning of a word or at the beginning of a syllable within a word. The first vowel sound in the Hebrew Bible is a vocal sheva, בְּרֵאשִׁית, *bᵉrēʾšît*, "in (the) beginning" (Gen. 1:1).

Note that in this example the vocal sheva is represented in transliteration by a small "e" raised above the line. It has a short, abbreviated sound, pronounced somewhat like the first syllable in the word "severe." The Hebrew word for "covenant," for example, is בְּרִית, (*bᵉrît*), pronounced as if it were written "breet." Likewise, the word for "fruit," פְּרִי (*pᵉrî*), has a pronunciation which sounds like "pree."

The simple vocal sheva may also be combined with three of the short vowels

EXERCISES II

to form compound shevas. Compound shevas are still to be classified as half-vowels and as such they are always vocal and never silent. Compound shevas arose because of the difficulty of pronouncing the gutturals (א, ה, ח, ע, and sometimes ר) with simple vocal shevas. Normally, therefore, a simple vocal sheva will not appear beneath a guttural but will be replaced by one of the three compound shevas.

The three short vowels found in compound shevas are påtăḥ, s^egôl, and qåmĕṣ-ḥāṭûf.

    – plus : equals -: , called ḥăṭĕf-påtăḥ

    ∵ plus : equals ⁖ , called ḥăṭĕf-s^egôl

    T plus : equals T: , called ḥăṭĕf-qåmĕṣ

The ḥăṭĕf-påtăḥ (-:) is sounded like a hurried påtăḥ, the ḥăṭĕf-s^egôl (⁖) as a hurried s^egôl, and the ḥăṭĕf-qåmĕṣ (T:) as a hurried qåmĕṣ-ḥāṭûf. (Please note that T: always represents a half-vowel of the "o" class and never of the "a" class.)

Examples of words written with gutturals followed by compound shevas:

    (1)   אֲנִי   '^ănî, translated "I"

    (2)   אֱנוֹשׁ   '^enôš, translated "man, mankind"

    (3)   חֳלִי   ḥ^ŏlî, translated "sickness"

EXERCISES

1. Write each letter of the alphabet with each of the vowel signs given in the table of full vowels.

    Example: אֳ אֲ אֱ אָ אֹ אוֹ אֻ אִ אֵ אֶ אֲ אַ אָ

                  בְ בַ בָ בִי בְּ   etc.

2. Practice pronouncing the letters with the vowels until you are thoroughly familiar with the sounds.

3. The following combinations of Hebrew letters and vowels sound like English words with which you are familiar. However, the combinations for the most part have no meaning in Hebrew. See if you can discover an English word that matches each of the sounds.

    Example:

    אֶג   = '^eg, pronounced like "egg"

    אָר   = 'ār, pronounced like "are"

    בֵּית   = bêt, pronounced like "bait"

9

(1) אֲג	(9) גֵּיט	(17) טָר	(25) לֵת	(33) סֵף
(2) אָר	(10) דֵּן	(18) טוּל	(26) לִין	(34) סוּן
(3) בֵּית	(11) דּוֹר	(19) יֵט	(27) מֵט	(35) פִּיא
(4) בִּיד	(12) הֵיט	(20) יוֹס	(28) מִין	(36) פֵּט
(5) בּוֹת	(13) הֵג	(21) יֵשׁ	(29) מֵן	(37) רוּת
(6) בֵּל	(14) הוֹל	(22) כֵּק	(30) נִיד	(38) שֹׁל
(7) בֵּן	(15) וִיל	(23) כֹּר	(31) נֹת	(39) שֹׁל
(8) גֵּן	(16) וֵת	(24) כִּיל	(32) נֵט	(40) תּוּל

4. We learned that י and ו can function not only as consonants but also as vowels (*matres lectionis*). See if you can determine which of the following words use ו as a consonant and which use it as a vowel.

(1) לוֹן	(3) וְשֵׁם	(5) מָוֶת	(7) וַיְהִי
(2) רוּת	(4) וִיהִי	(6) בּוֹשׁ	(8) קוּם

5. See if you can determine which of the following words employ י as a consonant and which employ it as a vowel.

(1) יָד   (2) יוֹם   (3) אִישׁ   (4) יֵשׁ   (5) בֵּית   (6) שִׂים

6. Point the following words (supply them with vowels) by consulting a dictionary or word list.

(1) אדמה	(3) חלום	(5) חמור	(7) ערבה
(2) אלהים	(4) חלי	(6) חצי	(8) נחלה

7. Listed below are the letters of the alphabet written in their full Hebrew forms. Transliterate the Hebrew names for these letters and practice pronouncing them.

Example: אָלֶף, *'ālĕf*; בֵּית, *bêt*; etc. [The accent mark used in אָלֶף and elsewhere in this list is explained in 8.1(1).]

(1) אָלֶף	(7) זַיִן	(13) מֵם	(19) קוֹף
(2) בֵּית	(8) חֵית	(14) נוּן	(20) רֵישׁ
(3) גִּימֶל	(9) טֵית	(15) סָמֶךְ	(21) שִׁין
(4) דָּלֶת	(10) יוֹד	(16) עַיִן	שִׂין
(5) הֵא	(11) כַּף	(17) פֵּא	(22) תָּו
(6) וָו	(12) לָמֶד	(18) צָדֵי	

10

8. Here is a similar list of the vowels. Transliterate these and practice pronouncing them.

(1)	קָמֶץ	(5)	סֶגּוֹל	(9)	חוֹלֶם וָו
(2)	פַּתַח	(6)	חִירֶק יוֹד	(10)	קָמֶץ חָטוּף
(3)	צֵרֵי	(7)	חִירֶק	(11)	שׁוּרֶק
(4)	צֵרֵי יוֹד	(8)	חוֹלֶם	(12)	קִבּוּץ

9. Transliterate the proper names listed below and practice pronouncing them in Hebrew.

(1)	בֵּית לֶחֶם	(9)	לָבָן	(17)	שָׂרָה
(2)	גָּד	(10)	מֹשֶׁה	(18)	שְׁכֶם
(3)	גֹּשֶׁן	(11)	נָתָן	(19)	שְׁלֹמֹה
(4)	דָּוִד	(12)	סְדֹם	(20)	שֵׁם
(5)	הָגָר	(13)	עֵשָׂו	(21)	שָׁפָן
(6)	כְּנַעַן	(14)	פָּארָן	(22)	תֵּל אָבִיב
(7)	כָּלֵב	(15)	קָדֵשׁ	(23)	תָּמָר
(8)	לֵאָה	(16)	רָחֵל	(24)	יִשְׂרָאֵל

11

LESSON III

4. Măqqḗf (מַקֵּף)

Măqqḗf is a short horizontal stroke used to join together two or more words within a verse. Words so joined are pronounced as one speech unit, the primary accent falling on the final word in the unit. Another way of stating this is that all words that are not final in such a unit lose their primary accents. They may undergo certain vowel changes on this account. For example, כֹּל, "all," becomes כָּל (with qámĕṣ-ḥāṭûf) when placed before a măqqḗf, as in כָּל־הַיּוֹם (Gen. 6:5). Likewise מָה, "what," becomes מַה when joined to the following word by a măqqḗf, as in מַה־יִּקְרָא־לוֹ (Gen. 2:19).

Most of the occurrences of măqqḗf will be with monosyllabic words such as the following:

(1)	אֶל unto	(5)	לֹא not	(9)	עַד unto
(2)	אִם if	(6)	מָה what	(10)	עַל upon
(3)	גַּם also	(7)	מִי who	(11)	עִם with
(4)	כֹּל all	(8)	מִן from	(12)	פֶּן lest

5. Sign of the Direct Object

A direct object is a word representing a person or thing upon which the action of a verb is performed. The direct object may be either definite or indefinite. If definite, it is usually preceded by the particle אֵת. The particle serves merely as the sign of the direct object and is therefore not to be translated. אֵת may be written alone, or it may be joined by a măqqḗf to the following word. In the latter case ṣḗrê is shortened to sᵉgôl. Thus we find אֵת הַשָּׁמַיִם in Genesis 1:1, but אֶת־הָאוֹר in Genesis 1:4.

6. Dagesh Forte

We studied earlier that dagesh lene is a dot which may be placed in six consonants (ב, ג, ד, כ, פ, ת) in order to indicate when they are to be given a hard pronunciation. Dagesh forte is identical in appearance to dagesh lene, but serves an entirely different purpose. It is a dot that indicates the doubling of the consonant in which it stands. It may be placed in any consonant except the five gutturals (א, ה, ח, ע, ר).

There are three basic rules to follow in distinguishing dagesh lene from dagesh forte.

12

(1) A dot in any letter other than a BeGaD KeFaT letter is a dagesh forte and indicates the doubling of that letter.

(2) A dot in a BeGaD KeFaT letter will be a dagesh lene whenever that letter *is not* immediately preceded by a vowel.

(3) A dot in a BeGaD KeFaT letter will be a dagesh forte whenever that letter *is* immediately preceded by a vowel.

Another way of stating these last two rules is that dagesh lene *never* stands after a vowel, whereas dagesh forte *always* stands immediately after a vowel.

It should also be noted with regard to the six BeGaD KeFaT letters that dagesh forte has the same effect as dagesh lene in hardening their pronunciation.

Thus the dagesh in the word בְּרִית is a dagesh lene (no vowel precedes it), and the pronunciation is hard (be*rît*). On the other hand, the dagesh in הַבֵּן is a dagesh forte (a vowel immediately precedes it), and the pronunciation is also hard (hăb/bén).

7. Silent Sheva

In an earlier study (II.3, pp. 8f.), we learned that Hebrew makes use of semi-vowels, or half-vowels, known as vocal shevas. We learned that there are simple vocal shevas (ְ) and compound vocal shevas (ֲ , ֱ , ֳ).

Hebrew also makes use of the silent sheva, written exactly like the simple vocal sheva (ְ), but serving an entirely different purpose. A vocal sheva, whether simple or compound, will only stand beneath a consonant that *begins* a syllable. The silent sheva, on the other hand, only stands beneath a consonant that *ends* a syllable. The silent sheva, therefore, may also be referred to as a *syllable divider*.

Whenever two shevas stand under adjacent consonants within a word, the first will always be silent and the second will be vocal. In other words, the first marks the end of a syllable, whereas the second stands at the beginning of a new syllable. In יִמְשְׁלוּ (yĭm-šelû), for example, the first sheva (מְ) is silent, whereas the second (שְׁ) is vocal.

A sheva that stands beneath a doubled consonant (one that has a dagesh forte) will always be vocal. In קִטְּלוּ (qĭṭ-ṭelû), for example, where ט is pointed with a dagesh forte, the sheva that follows it (טְ) must be classified as a vocal sheva.

A particularity of the final kāf (ך) is that it is normally pointed with a raised silent sheva (ךְ). This is perhaps to distinguish it from other letters that have final forms.

Examples: לֵךְ, lĕkh; מֶלֶךְ, mĕ-lĕkh.

13

EXERCISES

1. There are BeGaD KeFaT letters in all the words listed below. Add a dagesh lene wherever it belongs in one of these letters. Please note that the shevas are all silent.

(1) אֶכְתֹּב	(5) דָּבָר	(9) מִשְׁכָּב	(13) פָּנִים
(2) בֶּגֶד	(6) יִגְדַּל	(10) קָדוֹשׁ	(14) נֶפֶשׁ
(3) בַּיִת	(7) כֶּסֶף	(11) מִשְׁפָּט	(15) תּוֹרָה
(4) גָּדוֹל	(8) מִדְבָּר	(12) נָבִיא	(16) תִּכְתֹּב

2. Underscore the words in the following list which contain a dagesh forte.

(1) אַתָּה	(4) הִנֵּה	(7) כִּסֵּא	(10) שִׁשִּׁי
(2) גִּבּוֹר	(5) חַיָּה	(8) מִשְׁפָּט	(11) תְּמוּנָה
(3) דִּבֶּר	(6) יַרְדֵּן	(9) שִׁבֵּר	(12) תְּפִלָּה

3. Transliterate the words listed above and practice pronouncing them.

4. Exodus 3:1 is reproduced here.

וּמֹשֶׁה הָיָה רֹעֶה אֶת־צֹאן יִתְרוֹ חֹתְנוֹ
כֹּהֵן מִדְיָן וַיִּנְהַג אֶת־הַצֹּאן אַחַר
הַמִּדְבָּר וַיָּבֹא אֶל־הַר הָאֱלֹהִים חֹרֵבָה:

(1) Copy the three words in which all the letters are gutturals.

(2) Copy the three pairs of words linked together by măqqḗfs.

(3) Copy the word that has both a dagesh lene and a dagesh forte, indicating which is which.

(4) Copy the word that contains a compound sheva.

5. Genesis 2:3 is reproduced here.

וַיְבָרֶךְ אֱלֹהִים אֶת־יוֹם הַשְּׁבִיעִי
וַיְקַדֵּשׁ אֹתוֹ כִּי בוֹ שָׁבַת מִכָּל־
מְלַאכְתּוֹ אֲשֶׁר־בָּרָא אֱלֹהִים לַעֲשׂוֹת:

(1) Copy the two words that contain both a silent sheva and a vocal sheva.

(2) Copy the word that is marked as the direct object of the verb.

(3) Copy the three words that contain dagesh fortes.

(4) Copy the four words that contain compound shevas.

(5) Copy the three words that contain BeGaD KeFaT letters with dagesh lenes.

VOCABULARY

All nouns listed in this and subsequent vocabulary lists will be masculine unless otherwise indicated. All feminine nouns will be indicated by an (f) written beside them.

(1)	אָב	(ʾāv) father	(10)	בַּת	(bắt) (f) daughter
(2)	אָח	(ʾāḥ) brother	(11)	יִשְׂרָאֵל	(yĭś-rā-ʾēl) Israel
(3)	אָחוֹת	(ʾā-ḥôt) (f) sister	(12)	לֵב	(lēv) heart
(4)	אִישׁ	(ʾîš) man	(13)	עִיר	(ʿîr) (f) city
(5)	אִשָּׁה	(ʾĭš-šāh) (f) woman	(14)	עוֹף	(ʿôf) bird(s)
(6)	אֵם	(ʾēm) (f) mother	(15)	עַם	(ʿăm) people
(7)	אָדָם	(ʾā-dām) mạn, mankind	(16)	קוֹל	(qôl) voice
(8)	אֱלֹהִים	(ʾĕlō-hîm) God	(17)	רֹאשׁ	(rōʾš) head
(9)	בֵּן	(bēn) son	(18)	שֵׁם	(šēm) name

LESSON IV

8. Accents

The same scholars who supplied Hebrew texts with vowel pointings also devised a system of accent signs and added these to the vocalized text. Every word in the Hebrew Bible, unless joined to the following word by a măqqḗf, carries a primary accent mark on its tone syllable. Some longer words may receive a secondary accent in addition to the primary accent. In BHS there are twenty-seven prose accents and twenty-one poetic accents, the latter occurring mainly in the books of Psalms, Job, and Proverbs. These accents are about equally divided between those that are written above the word and those that are written below it.

8.1 *Hebrew accents serve a threefold purpose.*

(1) *They mark the tone syllable (accented syllable) in a word.* This will normally be the last syllable in a word, but it may also be the next to the last.

Please note that Hebrew accent signs are not printed in this grammar. However, words accented on any syllable other than the final syllable are marked with a mûnaḥ (ˌ).

Examples: אֶלֶף דָּלֶת זַיִן מֶלֶךְ

If a word appears without a mûnaḥ, it can be assumed that it is accented on the final syllable.

Examples: אַתָּה דָּוִד מֹשֶׁה יִשְׂרָאֵל

(2) *Hebrew accents regulate the chanting of biblical texts in the synagogues.* Note, however, that synagogue scrolls are left unpointed and the vowels and accents are cited from memory.

(3) *Hebrew accents serve as marks of punctuation, showing how sentence structure was perceived at the time the accents were placed in the text.* As marks of punctuations, the accents are either *disjunctive* (separating) or *conjunctive* (joining). They help us to identify the component parts of a Hebrew sentence, and are thus a vital aid to exegesis.

8.2 *There are two major disjunctive accents within each Hebrew verse or sentence.* They indicate where the two halves of the verse end. The accent that marks the end of the first half of the verse is known as the ʾătnāḥ (˄). It is placed below the accented syllable of the last word in the first half of the verse, as in אֱלֹהִים in Genesis 1:1.

The second major disjunctive accent is known as the sĭllûq (ˌ). It is placed below the accented syllable of the last word in the last half of the verse, the word that immediately precedes sôf pāssûq (׃), "end of sentence." See הָאָרֶץ in Genesis 1:1.

16

Note that the two major divisions of a verse are determined not by length but by sense. Thus the two "halves" of a verse may vary greatly in length. Genesis 1:7 is a good example of this. See if you can locate the ʾắtnāḥ and the sīllûq in this verse.

8.3 *A word marked by either ʾátnāḥ or sīllûq (as well as certain other strong disjunctive accents) is said to be "in pause."* This means that there is a break in recitation at this point. (Compare this to the pause that follows commas, semi-colons, and periods in modern languages.) A word in pause must have a long vowel in its accented or tone syllable. If the vowel of the tone syllable is regularly short, it must be lengthened when placed in pause. The rules governing the lengthening of short vowels are complicated and need not be studied at this juncture. At the same time, the student must not be surprised at the vowel changes that frequently occur when words are placed "in pause." These are some common words shown in their regular forms and in their pausal forms.

	Regular Form		Pausal Form	
(1)	אֲנִי	I	אָנִי	(Jer. 17:18)
(2)	אֶרֶץ	earth, land	אָרֶץ	(Exod. 15:12)
(3)	אַתָּה	you	אָתָּה	(Isa. 44:17)
(4)	בַּיִת	house	בָּיִת	(1 Chr. 17:12)
(5)	הֶבֶל	Abel	הָבֶל	(Gen. 4:2)
(6)	יָדְעוּ	they know	יָדָעוּ	(Jer. 4:22)
(7)	יַיִן	wine	יָיִן	(Jer. 35:5)
(8)	יֵשְׁבוּ	they shall dwell	יֵשֵׁבוּ	(Ecc. 10:6)
(9)	לֶחֶם	bread	לָחֶם	(Ps. 37:25)
(10)	מַיִם	water	מָיִם	(Gen. 26:32)

9. Mětěg (מֶתֶג)

9.1 Mětěg is a secondary accent that sometimes appears in addition to the primary accent in a word. It is made exactly like the sīllûq, but the two are easily distinguishable, since sīllûq appears only on the tone syllable of the last word in a verse.

9.2 Mětěg serves several purposes, of which the following are the most important.

(1) It is sometimes used to mark long vowels that stand two or more syllables before the tone syllable of a word, in order to insure that these long vowels

17

are given proper stress in pronunciation.

Examples: לָרָקִיעַ (Gen. 1:8)   לְמִינֵהֶם (Gen. 1:21)

                    הָרֹמֶשֶׂת (Gen. 1:21)

(2) It is often used with short vowels that stand immediately before compound shevas.

Examples: נַעֲשֶׂה (Gen. 1:26)   לַעֲבֹד (Gen. 3:23)

                    תַּעֲבֹד (Exod. 20:9)   וְאֶעֱשֶׂה (Gen. 35:3)

(3) It may also be used with either long or short vowels that stand immediately before simple (vocal) shevas.

Examples: וְחַיְתוֹ (Gen. 1:24)   וַיְהִי (Gen. 1:3)

                    יָלְדָה (Gen. 4:22)   וַיֵּלְכוּ (Gen. 9:23)

(4) It may also be used with unchangeably long vowels that stand before a măqqḗf.

Examples: פְּנֵי־הָאֲדָמָה (Gen. 2:6)   בֵּית־אֵל (Gen. 12:8)

                    כִּי־עָפָר (Gen. 3:19)

9.3 Note that mĕtĕg is normally written to the left of the vowel, as in וַיְהִי (Gen. 1:3). However, in BHS it is sometimes placed to the right of the vowel, as in וַיְהִי (Gen. 1:7). This does not alter its function in any way.

10. Weak Letters

א and ה function as regular consonants at the beginning of syllables. However, at the end of syllables they sometimes become quiescent (silent), losing their consonantal value and remaining only as vowel letters (*matres lectionis*). When this occurs, neither א nor ה is able to close the syllable.

א is always quiescent at the end of a syllable, whether in the middle of a word or at the end of a word. ה is quiescent only when it stands as the consonant that ends a word.

Examples: בְּרֵאשִׁית (Gen. 1:1)   תַּדְשֵׁא (Gen. 1:11)

                    הָיְתָה (Gen. 1:2)   הַיַּבָּשָׁה (Gen. 1:9)

11. Măppíq (מַפִּיק)

Măppíq is a dot that can be inserted in a final ה (הּ) to enable it to retain

its consonantal value, instead of functioning merely as a vowel letter. Final הּ with a
măppîq (הּ) is considered to be a strong guttural, in the same class with ח and ע. It
therefore closes the syllable in which it stands.

Examples: וַיִּגְבַּהּ   (1 Sam. 10:23)   אַרְצָהּ   (Isa. 34:9)

לְמִינָהּ   (Gen. 1:25)

12. Syllables ·

12.1   Every consonant in a Hebrew word, with the exception of final
consonants and of א when it stands at the end of a syllable or is otherwise quiescent
(cf. רֹאשׁ), must be followed by a vowel sound or by a silent sheva. The vowel
sound may be either a full vowel or a half-vowel. The half-vowel may be either
simple or compound.

Examples:

(1)   בְּרֵאשִׁית (Gen. 1:1). א is quiescent at the end of the syllable
and therefore has no vowel or silent sheva following it. ת is final
and likewise has no vowel or silent sheva. The three remaining
consonants all have vowel sounds following them.

(2)   אֱלֹהִים (Gen. 1:1). The first three consonants have vowel
sounds following them. Final ם stands alone, without a vowel or a
silent sheva.

(3)   וַיַּבְדֵּל (Gen. 1:4). This word is a bit more complicated. It
contains five consonants, three vowels, and a silent sheva (syllable
divider). The sheva under ב has to be silent because it is followed
by a BeGaD KeFaT letter with a dagesh lene (דּ). So each of the
letters except the final letter (ל) is supported either by a vowel or a
syllable divider.

12.2   All syllables in a Hebrew word must begin with a consonant, which
may be any consonant in the alphabet. The one seeming exception to this rule occurs
when a word begins with the vowel וּ, as in וּבֵין (Gen. 1:4). Some grammarians
argue that even this is not a true exception, but that the ו in an initial וּ may be
regarded as functioning in a dual capacity, both as consonant and as vowel, i.e, both
as a vāv and as a šûrĕq.

(The word for "Jerusalem" presents special problems. Five times it appears
as יְרוּשָׁלַיִם, which presents no problems. In all other instances, however, it is found
as יְרוּשָׁלַם, i.e., without yôd before the final ḥîrĕq. Perhaps yôd is implied in the
abbreviated form, or perhaps this is a loan word borrowed from another language.)

12.3   A Hebrew syllable must include one (and only one) full vowel.
However, in addition to a full vowel, it may also contain a half-vowel, in which case
the half-vowel will stand beneath the consonant that begins the syllable. The number

19

of syllables in a word is determined by the number of full vowels in that word, irrespective of the number of half-vowels that may be present.

Examples:

(1) בְּרֵא/שִׁית – This word has two full vowels, and thus two syllables. It also has a half-vowel, which stands underneath the consonant that begins the first syllable.

(2) בְּרִית – This word has one full vowel plus a half-vowel and is therefore treated as a one-syllable word.

(3) אֱל/הִים – This word has two full vowels and therefore two syllables. The half-vowel under א does not constitute a separate syllable but attaches itself to the first syllable of the word.

12.4 Hebrew syllables are classified as either open or closed. An open syllable is one that ends in a vowel. The vowel in an open syllable will normally be long. However, it may be short if it is accented or if it is followed by a consonant that is supported by a vocal sheva.

A closed syllable is one that ends in a consonant. Whenever a dagesh forte occurs in a letter, that letter is doubled, and the preceding syllable is always closed. The vowel in a closed syllable will normally be short, but it may be long if it is accented.

Examples:

(1) בְּרֵא/שִׁית – The first syllable is open, because it ends in א, and א never closes a syllable. The second syllable ends in ת and is closed. A final consonant that closes a syllable does not require a syllable divider (silent sheva), except in the case of the final kăf (ךְ).

(2) הַשָּׁמַיִם – There are four full vowels in this word, which indicates that it is made up of four syllables. שׁ is written with a dagesh forte, which indicates that it is doubled. The first syllable, therefore, is הַשׁ. It ends in a consonant, thus making it a closed syllable. The vowel is short, since it stands in an unaccented closed syllable.

The second syllable is שָׁ. It ends in a vowel, and is therefore an open syllable. The vowel is long, which is what one would expect in an unaccented open syllable.

The third syllable is מַ, an open syllable with a short vowel. The short vowel is not what one would expect in an open syllable but it is explained by the fact that the syllable is accented.

The final syllable is יִם, a closed, unaccented syllable with a short vowel. (Note: Do not confuse יִ with ִי . In the first instance, yôd is a regular consonant followed by ḥîrĕq. In the second instance, yôd follows ḥîrĕq and combines with it to form an unchangeable long vowel, ḥîrĕq-yôd.)

20

(3) יַלְדָה - Two full vowels indicate two syllables. The sheva under לְ is a vocal sheva, as determined by the mĕtĕg on the vowel before it and also by the absence of a dagesh lene in the ד that follows it. Therefore, the first syllable is יַ, an open syllable with a long vowel, which requires a mĕtĕg since it is followed by a vocal sheva. The second syllable is לְדָה, which includes a half-vowel under לְ and a full vowel under ד. It is an open syllable, since ה never closes a syllable at the end of a word, unless it carries a mắppîq (הּ). The second syllable is the tone syllable and has a long vowel.

(4) נַעֲשֶׂה - Two full vowels again indicate two syllables. Since compound shevas are always vocal, the division into syllables must come between נַ and עֲ. The first syllable, therefore, is נַ, an open syllable with a short vowel, which requires a mĕtĕg since it precedes a vocal sheva. Although a short vowel does not ordinarily occur in an open syllable, it may do so if it is followed by a consonant with a vocal sheva. The second syllable is עֲשֶׂה. It too is open, since final ה without a mắppîq never closes a syllable. The vowel is short, but this is permitted in an open syllable that serves as the tone syllable of the word.

EXERCISES

1. Turn to Genesis 1:1-5 in a Hebrew Bible and copy the words in each verse that are accented with an ʾắtnāḥ or with a sĭllûq.

Example: Verse 1:   אֱלֹהִים (ʾắtnāḥ),   הָאָרֶץ (sĭllûq)

2. The following words have been divided into syllables. Tell what kind of vowel each has (long or short). Caution: Be careful to distinguish between long "a," qắmĕṣ, and short "o," qắmĕṣ-ḥắṭûf.

Example: חָכְ/מָה

חָכְ - a closed syllable with a short vowel (because it is unaccented).

מָה - an open syllable with a long vowel.

(1)	חָכְ/מָה	(6)	מֹ/שֶׁה
(2)	מַלְ/כָּה	(7)	יְרוּ/שָׁ/לַ/יִם
(3)	שְׁלֹ/מֹה	(8)	אֶ/עֱשֶׂה
(4)	דָּ/וִד	(9)	וַנַ/עֲשֶׂה
(5)	פָּא/רָן	(10)	קָטֵל

21

3. Divide the following words into syllables. Tell what kind of syllable each is (open or closed) and what kind of vowel each has (long or short).

(1) תִּכְתֹּב   (6) הֶעֱמִיד

(2) כָּלָה   (7) יֵשְׁבוּ

(3) יָדַיִם   (8) בַּדֶּרֶךְ

(4) דְּרָכִים   (9) שָׁלוֹם

(5) חֹשֶׁךְ   (10) מָבוֹא

4. There are four silent shevas and eleven vocal shevas in the following list of words. Locate and identify each of these.

Example: בְּרִית – בְּ is vocal

(1) בְּרִית   (6) וְדִבַּרְתִּי

(2) נַעֲבֹד   (7) תִּלְמְדִי

(3) עָבְדוּ   (8) כְּכוֹכְבֵי

(4) יִכְתְּבוּ   (9) בְּדַבְּרִי

(5) לָךְ   (10) בְּגָדִים

5. Take each word in Genesis 1:1, divide it into syllables, and describe each syllable according to the kind of syllable it is and the kind of vowel it has.

6. Practice pronouncing Genesis 1:1.

LESSON V

13. The Gutturals

The gutturals are א, ה, ח, ע, and sometimes ר. They have certain characteristics that distinguish them from other letters of the alphabet.

13.1 *Gutturals cannot be doubled. That is, they reject the dagesh forte.* When this takes place, the preceding short vowel is left in an open, unaccented syllable, and therefore must be lengthened.

        (1) If păthăḥ, it will be lengthened to qāmĕṣ.

        (2) If ḥîrĕq, it will be lengthened to ṣērê.

        (3) If qĭbbûṣ, it will be lengthened to ḥôlĕm.

This is called "compensatory lengthening" of a vowel.

Please note, however, that if the guttural that rejects a dagesh forte is either ה or ח, no lengthening of the preceding short vowel is necessary. Under these circumstances ה and ח are said to be doubled by implication and the preceding syllable is treated as a closed syllable.

13.2 *Gutturals tend to take "a" class vowels before and sometimes after them.* This preference is especially noticeable with the strong gutturals ה, ח, and ע. When one of these gutturals occurs at the end of a word and is preceded by an unchangeably long vowel that is not of the "a" class, then another short "a" sound must be inserted between this vowel and the guttural. This short "a" sound is called a păthăḥ furtive, because of its hurried pronunciation. Păthăḥ furtive is not a full vowel and must not be regarded as increasing the number of syllables in a word. It is represented in transliteration by a raised "a," just as in the case of the ḥātĕf-păthăḥ.
Examples:

    וְרוּחַ (Gen. 1:2), $v^e r\hat{u}^a \dot{h}$ נֹחַ (Gen. 6:9), $n\bar{o}^a \dot{h}$

    רָקִיעַ (Gen. 1:6), $r\bar{a}q\hat{i}^{a}$ גָּבֹהַ (1 Sam. 9:2), $g\bar{a}v\bar{o}^a \dot{h}$

13.3 *Gutturals tend to take compound shevas rather than simple shevas.* This will usually be a ḥātĕf-păthăḥ (ֲ). Initial א, however, often takes a ḥātĕf-sĕgôl (ֱ). Only in rare instances will a guttural appear with a ḥātĕf-qāmĕṣ (ֳ).
Examples of gutturals with compound shevas:

    אֲשֶׁר ʾ$^{\check{a}}\check{s}er$, who, which, what   אֱלֹהִים ʾ$^{\check{e}}l\bar{o}h\hat{i}m$, God

    חֲלוֹם $\dot{h}^{\check{a}}l\hat{o}m$, dream   חֳלִי $\dot{h}^{\bar{o}}l\hat{i}$, sickness

23

The gutturals' preference for compound shevas is so strong that even silent shevas that occur beneath gutturals will usually be changed to compound shevas. Whenever this change takes place, the vowel preceding the guttural will remain short, even though it is now left in an open, unaccented syllable. Sometimes it may receive a mĕtĕg in order to insure its stress in pronunciation. Furthermore, the vowel before the guttural will belong to the same class as the compound sheva that follows the guttural.

Examples:

נַעֲבֹד   nă-ʿăvōd   נַחֲלָה   nă-ḥălāh

מָעֳמָד   mŏ-ʿŏmād   אֶעֱשֶׂה   ʾĕ-ʿĕśĕh

14. The Definite Article

14.1   Hebrew has no indefinite article. It is the absence of the definite article which indicates that a noun is indefinite.

Examples:

אִישׁ   ʾîš, a man   בֵּן   bēn, a son

בַּת   băt, a daughter   יוֹם   yôm, a day

14.2   The definite article never stands alone but is prefixed to the noun whose definiteness it determines. The form of the article is not affected by the gender and number of the noun to which it is prefixed, but is the same for all genders and numbers.

14.3   The principal rules to follow in writing the definite article are these:

(1)   It is usually written · הַ (ה, plus pătăḥ, plus dagesh forte in the first consonant of the noun) before all non-gutturals.

Examples:

יָד   yād, a hand   הַיָּד   hăy-yād, the hand

קוֹל   qôl, a voice   הַקּוֹל   hăq-qôl, the voice

לֵב   lēv, heart   הַלֵּב   hăl-lēv, the heart

(2)   When the article is prefixed to a noun whose initial consonant is a guttural, the form of the article will be modified to compensate for the guttural's refusal to be doubled. The following changes may be noted:

(a)   Before ה and ח, the article is usually written הַ (ה, plus pătăḥ, but *without* the dagesh forte). In this situation, ה and ח are said to be doubled by implication, that is, virtually doubled.

Examples:

חֶרֶב (f) hĕ-rĕv, sword   הַחֶרֶב hă-hĕ-rĕv, the sword

הֵיכָל hê-khāl, temple   הַהֵיכָל hă-hê-khāl, the temple

(b) Before א, ע, and ר, the article is usually written הָ (ה, plus qắmĕṣ). In this case, the guttural's rejection of the dagesh forte causes the preceding short vowel to be lengthened (păṭăḥ to qắmĕṣ). This is known as the compensatory lengthening of a vowel. Without the lengthening, păṭăḥ would have been left as a short vowel in an open, unaccented syllable.

Examples:

רֹאשׁ rō'š, head   הָרֹאשׁ hā-rō'š, the head

אָב 'āv, father   הָאָב hā-'āv, the father

עִיר (f) 'îr, (f) city   הָעִיר hā-'îr, the city

(c) Before ח, and before *unaccented* הָ or *unaccented* עָ, the article is written הֶ (ה, plus sᵉgôl).

Examples:

חָכָם ḥā-khām, wise man   הֶחָכָם hĕ-ḥā-khām, the wise man

עָפָר 'ā-fār, dust   הֶעָפָר hĕ-'ā-fār, the dust

הָרִים hā-rîm, mountains   הֶהָרִים hĕ-hā-rîm, the mountains

(3) When the article is prefixed to a noun whose initial consonant is yôd, followed by a simple sheva (יְ), the article will normally be written הַ (ה, plus păṭăḥ, but without the dagesh forte). The same rule sometimes applies when a noun's initial consonant is מ, followed by a simple sheva (מְ). It does not apply, however, in the case of other letters of the alphabet that occur with a simple sheva.

Examples:

יְלָדִים yᵉlā-dîm, children   הַיְלָדִים hă-yᵉlā-dîm, the children

יְאֹר yᵉ'ōr, river   הַיְאֹר hă-yᵉ'ōr, the river

מְסִלָּה mᵉsĭl-lāh, highway   הַמְסִלָּה hă-mᵉsĭl-lāh, the highway

But note these exceptions with initial מ:

מְלָכִים mᵉlā-khîm, kings   הַמְּלָכִים hăm-mᵉlā-khîm, the kings

מְקֹמוֹת mᵉqō-môt, places   הַמְּקֹמוֹת hăm-mᵉqō-môt, the places

Note the regular manner in which the article is prefixed to consonants other than yôd and mēm when these are supported by a simple sheva.

דְּבָרִים dᵉvā-rîm, words   הַדְּבָרִים hăd-dᵉvā-rîm, the words

זְקֵנִים zᵉqē-nîm, elders   הַזְּקֵנִים hăz-zᵉqē-nîm, the elders

(4) A few nouns in their singular form undergo internal changes when the definite article is prefixed to them. The most important are the following:

אֶרֶץ	ʾé-rĕṣ, earth	הָאָרֶץ	hā-ʾá-rĕṣ, the earth
הַר	hăr, mountain	הָהָר	hā-hār, the mountain
עַם	ʿăm, people	הָעָם	hā-ʿām, the people
גַּן	găn, garden	הַגָּן	hăg-găn, the garden
פַּר	păr, bull	הַפָּר	hăp-pār, the bull
חַג	ḥăg, festival	הֶחָג	hĕ-ḥāg, the festival
אֲרוֹן	ʾărôn, ark	הָאָרוֹן	hā-ʾā-rôn, the ark

EXERCISES

1. A good method for learning a vocabulary is to prepare vocabulary cards. Write the Hebrew on one side of the card and the English translation on the reverse side. Glance at these cards whenever you have a spare moment during the day. Practice pronouncing the Hebrew aloud.

2. Prefix the definite article to the following words.

(1)	יָד	(7)	עָשָׁן	(13)	הֵיכָל
(2)	יְאֹר	(8)	אֶרֶץ	(14)	הַר
(3)	מִדְבָּר	(9)	עַם	(15)	גַּן
(4)	בַּיִת	(10)	חֶרֶב	(16)	חַג
(5)	אִשָּׁה	(11)	רוּחַ	(17)	הָרִים
(6)	עֵת	(12)	בְּרִית	(18)	רֹאשׁ

3. Divide the following words into syllables and specify whether the syllables are open or closed and whether they have long or short vowels.

   Example: הַחֹשֶׁךְ – 1st. syllable (הַח) is closed (ח is doubled by implication) and has a short vowel. 2nd. syllable (ח) is open and has a long vowel. 3rd. syllable (שֶׁךְ) is closed and has a short vowel.

(1)	הַחֹשֶׁךְ	(6)	הָאֱלֹהִים
(2)	הֶעָשִׁיר	(7)	הַשֵּׁם
(3)	הַנָּבִיא	(8)	הַיּוֹם
(4)	הָאָדוֹן	(9)	הַמִּצְוָה
(5)	הֶעָנָן	(10)	הַדְּבָרִים

4.   All the words in the preceding exercise have the definite article. Be prepared to explain why each article was given the form that it has.

5.   Mark the words in the following list that are feminine.

(1)	אוֹר	(7)	חֹשֶׁךְ	(13)	שָׁלוֹם
(2)	אֶרֶץ	(8)	חֶרֶב	(14)	בְּרִית
(3)	אִישׁ	(9)	רֹאשׁ	(15)	רוּחַ
(4)	אִשָּׁה	(10)	עִיר	(16)	אָדָם
(5)	בַּת	(11)	הַר	(17)	מֶלֶךְ
(6)	בֵּן	(12)	שָׁנָה	(18)	בַּיִת

6.   Complete the writing of the definite article with the following nouns.

(1)	הָאֶרֶץ	(7)	הַיְאֹר	(13)	הָראֹשׁ
(2)	היום	(8)	הֶעָנָן	(14)	הַשָּׁלוֹם
(3)	הצאן	(9)	הָהָר	(15)	הַלֵּב
(4)	הָאֹהֶל	(10)	הָאֱלֹהִים	(16)	הָעִיר
(5)	הָעָם	(11)	הַבְּרִית	(17)	הַבַּיִת
(6)	הֶחָג	(12)	הָעֵת	(18)	הַשָּׁנָה

VOCABULARY

(1)	אוֹר	ʾôr, light	(10)	חֶרֶב	(f) ḥĕ-rĕv, sword
(2)	אֶרֶץ	(f) ʾĕ-rĕṣ, earth	(11)	חֹשֶׁךְ	ḥô-šĕkh, darkness
(3)	אֲשֶׁר	ʾăšer, who, which, what	(12)	טוֹב	ṭôv, good
(4)	בַּיִת	bă-yĭt, house	(13)	יָם	yām, sea
(5)	בְּרִית	(f) bĕrît, covenant	(14)	מַיִם	mă-yĭm, water
(6)	גַּן	găn, garden	(15)	מֶלֶךְ	mĕ-lĕkh, king
(7)	דָּבָר	dā-vār, word, thing	(16)	רוּחַ	(f) rûᵃḥ, spirit, wind
(8)	הַר	hăr, mountain	(17)	שָׁלוֹם	šā-lôm, peace
(9)	חַג	ḥăg, feast, festival	(18)	שָׁנָה	(f) šā-nāh, year

LESSON VI

15. Prepositions With Nouns

In comparison with other languages, Hebrew has relatively few prepositions. Some Hebrew prepositions are inseparable and are prefixed to nouns, somewhat like the definite article. Others are independent and function more like English prepositions.

15.1 *Hebrew has three inseparable prepositions:*

בְּ   in, by, with (plus other meanings)

כְּ   as, like, according to (plus other meanings)

לְ   to, for, at (plus other meanings)

These are prefixed to nouns according to the following rules:

(1) *They are written with a simple sheva before consonants that have full vowels, except in some of the instances where they stand before the tone syllable of a word (cf. [5] below).*
Examples:

בְּשֵׁם in a name   כִּדְבָר according to a word   בְּרוּחַ by a spirit

לְשָׁלוֹם for peace   בְּאָב with a father   בְּבֵן with a son

(2) *They are written with a ḥireq* before consonants that have simple (vocal) shevas.* This is because two vocal shevas cannot stand together. The sheva of the preposition, being the first of two vocal shevas in this instance, is changed to ḥireq.
Examples:

כִּבְרִית according to a covenant   לִפְרִי for fruit

בִּדְבָרִים with words   בִּשְׁאוֹל in Sheol

Note, however, that if the preposition is prefixed to a noun whose initial consonant is yod supported by a simple sheva (יְ), other changes also become necessary. First, the sheva of the preposition changes to ḥireq, as in the examples above. This ḥireq then combines with the yod to form a ḥireq-yod. This in turn causes the yod to lose its consonantal value, and the sheva beneath it drops out.

---

*In the following lessons, for simplicity's sake, most of the diacritical marks on transliterated words will be omitted. Only marks necessary for correct pronunciation will be retained.

Examples:

יְרוּשָׁלַיִם plus בְּ = בִּירוּשָׁלַיִם in Jerusalem

יְהוּדָה plus בְּ = בִּיהוּדָה in Judah

(3) *When an inseparable preposition is prefixed to a noun whose initial consonant is supported by a compound sheva, the preposition will take the short vowel that corresponds to that of the compound sheva.* Before ḥatef-pataḥ, it will take pataḥ; before ḥatef-sᵉgol, it will take sᵉgol; before ḥatef-qames, it will take qames-ḥatuf. The vowel before the compound sheva will ordinarily be written with a meteg.

Examples:

כַּאֲשֶׁר according to which, בֶּאֱמֶת in truth, לְחֳלִי for sickness

Note, however, that occasionally before an א that has a ḥatef-sᵉgol (אֱ), the preposition receives a ṣere and the ḥatef-sᵉgol of the א drops out.

Examples:

לֵאלֹהִים = (לְ)אֱלֹהִים for God

לֵאמֹר = (לְ)אֱמֹר to say, saying

(4) *When an inseparable preposition is prefixed to a noun that has the definite article, the* ה *of the article drops out.*

Examples:

1.	אִישׁ	a man	לְאִישׁ	for a man
	הָאִישׁ	the man	לָאִישׁ	for the man
2.	בְּרִית	a covenant	כִּבְרִית	according to a covenant
	הַבְּרִית	the covenant	כַּבְּרִית	according to the covenant
3.	הֵיכָל	a temple	בְּהֵיכָל	in a temple
	הַהֵיכָל	the temple	בַּהֵיכָל	in the temple

(5) *When the inseparable preposition is prefixed to the tone syllable (accented syllable) of a noun, the vowel of the preposition will often be qames.* This rule applies especially to one-syllable words with "a" class vowels.

Examples:

לָעַד to eternity, לָמַיִם to water

15.2 *There are other prepositions, which are referred to as unattached or independent.* They function much like prepositions in English. Some of the more common among these are:

אֶל to, into, toward   לִפְנֵי before, in front of

29

עַל   upon, above, about   מִן   from, out of

עִם   with   תַּחַת   under, instead of

בֵּין   between   אַחֲרֵי   behind, after

עַד   until, unto   אֵצֶל   beside, near

15.3 *The preposition* מִן, *"from, out of," requires further explanation.* The rules for writing it are different from the rules for the other independent prepositions.

(1) *Before nouns with the definite article, the preposition* מִן *appears in its full form and is usually joined to the following word by a maqqef.*

Examples:

מִן־הָאָרֶץ   from the earth   מִן־הַיּוֹם   from the day

מִן־הַבַּיִת   from the house   מִן־הָעֵץ   from the tree

(2) *Before indefinite nouns (nouns without the article) that have a non-guttural as their initial consonant, the preposition* מִן *is written mem, plus ḥireq, plus dagesh forte in the following consonant.*

Examples:

מִן   before   בַּיִת   becomes   מִבַּיִת, from a house

מִן   before   מֶלֶךְ   becomes   מִמֶּלֶךְ, from a king

מִן   before   יוֹם   becomes   מִיּוֹם, from a day

Note, however, that מִן before a yod pointed with a simple sheva contracts to מִי, as in מִיהוּדָה, "from Judah," and מִירוּשָׁלַיִם, "from Jerusalem."

(3) *Before indefinite nouns whose initial consonant is a guttural, the preposition* מִן *is written as mem plus ṣere.* In this case, ḥireq is lengthened to ṣere to compensate for the guttural's refusal to be doubled.

Examples:

מִן   before   אִישׁ   becomes   מֵאִישׁ, from a man

מִן   before   הַר   becomes   מֵהַר, from a mountain

מִן   before   חֶרֶב   becomes   מֵחֶרֶב, from a sword

מִן   before   עִיר   becomes   מֵעִיר, from a city

מִן   before   רֹאשׁ   becomes   מֵרֹאשׁ, from a head

(4) *The preposition* מִן *may also be used to express the comparative.*

Examples:

טוֹב הָאוֹר מִן־הַחֹשֶׁךְ   better (is) the light than the darkness

טוֹב הַבֹּקֶר מִן־הָעֶרֶב   better (is) the morning than the evening

30

16. The Vav Conjunction

The conjunction "and" does not stand alone in Hebrew but is prefixed to the following word. It closely resembles the inseparable prepositions in that its form is determined by the consonants that stand at the beginning of the word to which it is prefixed. The rules for writing the vav conjunction are the following:

16.1 *It is usually written* וְ *(vav plus simple sheva) before consonants pointed with a full vowel, unless the consonants are* בּ, מ, *or* פ. Examples:

וְהָאָרֶץ and the earth, וְחֹשֶׁךְ and darkness, וְלַחֹשֶׁךְ and to the darkness

16.2 *It is written as* וּ *(šureq) before the labials* בּ, מ, *and* פ *(consonants articulated by the lips), and before all consonants pointed with a simple sheva, except when this consonant is a yod.* Examples:

וּנְקֵבָה and female   וּבְרִית and a covenant

וּבֵין and between   וּפְרִי and fruit

וּמִן and from

16.3 *Before* יְ *(yod plus simple sheva) the* וְ *contracts with* יְ *to form* וִי *(vav plus ḥireq-yod).* Examples:

וִירוּשָׁלַיִם becomes וְירוּשָׁלַיִם and Jerusalem

וִיהוּדָה becomes וְיהוּדָה and Judah

וִיהִי becomes וְיְהִי and let there be

16.4 *Before a consonant pointed with a compound sheva, the vav conjunction takes the short vowel that corresponds to that of the compound sheva.* Note that a meteg is usually placed beside the vowel that immediately precedes a compound sheva. Examples:

וַאֲנִי and I (Gen. 6:17)   וָחֳלִי and sickness (Eccl. 6:2)

וֶאֱמֶת and truth (Gen. 24:49)

16.5 *Before monosyllabic words or before the accented syllable of words with two or more syllables, the vav conjunction will often be written* וָ *(vav plus qames).* וָ *usually joins two words of the same class (nearly always nouns) and tends to reflect a close relationship between the two.*

Examples:

טוֹב וָרָע   good and evil (Gen. 2:9)

תֹּהוּ וָבֹהוּ   without form and void (Gen. 1:2)

בְּהֵמָה וָרֶמֶשׂ   cattle and creeping things (Gen. 1:24)

16.6 *Special rules apply when the vav conjunction is prefixed to divine names.*

The two most frequently used designations for deity in the Hebrew Bible are אֱלֹהִים, *ᵉlōhîm*, "God," and יהוה, YHVH, "LORD."

אֱלֹהִים is plural in form, but normally functions as a singular noun. However, it may also function as a plural noun, accompanied by plural modifiers and plural verb forms. This usually occurs when reference is being made to the "gods" of the nations. אֱלֹהִים may occur with or without the definite article (הָאֱלֹהִים).

When the vav conjunction is prefixed to אֱלֹהִים (וֶאֱלֹהִים), the א becomes quiescent (ceases to function as a consonant) and loses its compound sheva, resulting in the form וֵאלֹהִים. Since א never closes a syllable, the preceding vowel, which now stands in an open, unaccented syllable, must be lengthened (sᵉgol to ṣere). The resultant form is וֵאלֹהִים, "and God."

יהוה is the covenant name for Israel's God. At a very early date in Jewish history, it came to be regarded as too sacred to be pronounced. Pious readers avoided pronouncing it by substituting for it the word אֲדֹנָי, *ᵃdō-nāy*, meaning "my Lord." When Masoretic scholars began to supply vowel points to the consonantal text of biblical books, they applied the vowels of אֲדֹנָי to the consonants of יהוה. With the modification of compound sheva to simple sheva under the non-guttural yod, the resultant form was יְהֹוָה (or simply יְהוָה), which was always pronounced as *ᵃdō-nāy*.

If there had been no need to avoid pronouncing יהוה, it would most likely have been pointed as יַהְוֶה and thus read as *Yăhvěh*. The curious attempt to transliterate the hybrid form יְהֹוָה as "Yehovah" (or "Jehovah," since "y" was missing in the German language) was not made until the time of the Protestant Reformation.

Occasionally the two divine names אֲדֹנָי יהוה appear together in the Hebrew text (see Amos 1:8). Since it would have been awkward to read the pair of names as *ᵃdō-nāy ᵃdō-nāy*, Masoretic scholars chose to point יהוה with the modified vowels of אֱלֹהִים. This resulted in the form יֱהֹוִה, later simplified to יְהוִה, which should be pronounced as though it were written אֱלֹהִים, *ᵉlōhîm*. Thus יְהֹוָה (pointed with the modified vowels of אֲדֹנָי) is translated in English versions as "LORD" (note the capital letters), while יְהוִה (pointed with the modified vowels of אֱלֹהִים) is translated as "GOD" (again with capital letters), and אֲדֹנָי יְהוִה is translated as "Lord GOD." Translators, therefore, consistently render any form of יהוה with capital letters, thereby alerting readers to its presence in the Hebrew text.

When the vav conjunction is prefixed to יְהֹוָה, it is written as וַיהֹוָה (see Gen. 19:24), and pronounced as if it were written וַאדֹנָי, *vă-dō-nây* (see 2 Kgs. 7:6).

EXERCISES

1. Prefix the preposition לְ to the following words, first without the article, then with it. Make the necessary changes where BeGaD KeFaT letters are involved. Translate both forms of each word.

Example: בֵּן – לְבֵן to a son   הַבֵּן – לַבֵּן to the son

(1) שָׁלוֹם

(2) דָּבָר

(3) רוּחַ

(4) אִשָּׁה

(5) פְּרִי

(6) בְּרִית

(7) מָקוֹם

(8) אֱמֶת

(9) הֵיכָל

2. Prefix the preposition מִן to the following words.

(1) בַּיִת

(2) הַבַּיִת

(3) אֱמֶת

(4) אִשָּׁה

(5) יְרוּשָׁלַיִם

(6) אֱלֹהִים

(7) פְּרִי

(8) יָד

(9) הַר

(10) רֹאשׁ

(11) אֶרֶץ

(12) הָאָרֶץ

(13) חֹשֶׁךְ

(14) הַחֹשֶׁךְ

(15) הָעִיר

(16) הַהֵיכָל

(17) רוּחַ

(18) הָרוּחַ

3. Place the vav conjunction on the following words or phrases and give a translation of each completed form.

Example: בְּשֵׁם, וּבְשֵׁם "and by a name"

(1) בְּשֵׁם

(2) כִּדְבַר

(3) כַּדְּבַר

(4) בְּרִית

(5) לִבְרִית

(6) יְהוּדָה

(7) בִּיהוּדָה

(8) אֱמֶת

33

(9) מֵאֱמֶת   (14) פְּרִי

(10) לְאִשָּׁה   (15) לְשָׁלוֹם

(11) בַּהֵיכָל   (16) אֱלֹהִים

(12) מִמֶּלֶךְ   (17) בַּלֵּב

(13) מִן־הָעֵץ   (18) הַשָּׁנָה

4. Translate the following phrases:

(1) אִישׁ וְאִשָּׁה

(2) שָׁלוֹם בָּאָרֶץ

(3) הָאוֹר וְהַחֹשֶׁךְ

(4) בֵּין הָאוֹר וּבֵין הַחֹשֶׁךְ

(5) יוֹם וָלַיְלָה

(6) בַּיּוֹם וּבַלַּיְלָה

(7) אָדָם וֵאלֹהִים

(8) מַיִם וּמֵאָרֶץ

(9) אֶל־יְרוּשָׁלַיִם

(10) פְּרִי מִן־הָעֵץ

(11) בָּעִיר וּבַהֵיכָל

(12) בְּאָדָם וּבֵאלֹהִים

(13) אֵצֶל הָהָר

(14) עַד־הָעֶרֶב

(15) יָד וָשֵׁם

(16) שָׁלוֹם וֶאֱמֶת

(17) טוֹב וָרַע

(18) מִבֵּן וּמִבַּת

5. Translate the following clauses.

Example:

אֵין פְּרִי בַּגָּן   "There is no fruit in the garden."

(1) אֵין אִשָּׁה בַּבַּיִת

(2) אֵין אִישׁ בָּעִיר

(3) אֵין בֵּן לְאָדָם

(4) אֵין בְּרִית עִם־הָעָם

34

(5) אֵין שָׁלוֹם בָּאָרֶץ

(6) הָעִיר עַל־הָהָר

(7) אֵין בַּת לָאִשָּׁה

(8) אֵין אוֹר לָעָם

(9) הַגָּן אֵצֶל הַבַּיִת

(10) טוֹב הָאוֹר מִן־הַחֹשֶׁךְ

(11) טוֹב הַיּוֹם מִן־הַלַּיְלָה

(12) אֵין מַיִם בַּמָּקוֹם

VOCABULARY

(1)	אַחֲרֵי	'ă-ḥᵃrê after, behind	(11)	בֹּקֶר	bṓ-qĕr, morning
(2)	אֶל	'ĕl, to, into, toward	(12)	יָד	yād, (f) hand
(3)	בֵּין	bên, between	(13)	יוֹם	yôm, day
(4)	לִפְנֵי	lĭ-fᵉnê, before, in the presence of	(14)	יֵשׁ	yēš, there is
(5)	מִן	mĭn, from, out of	(15)	לֹא	lō', not
(6)	עַד	'ăd, until, unto	(16)	לַיְלָה	lă-yᵉlāh, night
(7)	עִם	'ĭm, with	(17)	מָקוֹם	mā-qôm, place
(8)	עַל	'ăl, upon, above, about	(18)	עֵץ	'ēṣ, tree
(9)	תַּחַת	tă-ḥăt, under, instead of	(19)	עֶרֶב	'é-rĕv, evening
(10)	אֵין	'ên, there is not	(20)	פְּרִי	pᵉrî, fruit

35

LESSON VII

17. Nouns: Derivation

According to their origin or derivation, Hebrew nouns may be divided into three classes.

17.1 *Primitive nouns are those for which no known derivation exists.* The number of such nouns is very small.

Examples:

אָב	father	אֵם	mother	דָּם	blood
יוֹם	day	לַיְלָה	night	פֶּה	mouth
בֵּן	son	יָד	hand	שֵׁם	name

17.2 *The vast majority of Hebrew nouns are derived from verbs.*

דָּבָר	"word," from	דִּבֶּר	"he spoke"
זֶרַע	"seed," from	זָרַע	"he sowed"
מֶלֶךְ	"king," from	מָלַךְ	"he ruled"
עֶבֶד	"servant," from	עָבַד	"he served"
עוֹף	"bird," from	עוּף	"to fly"
פֶּתַח	"door," from	פָּתַח	"he opened"
תִּקְוָה	"hope," from	קָוָה	"he hoped, waited"

17.3 *A few Hebrew nouns are derived from other nouns.* The very first word in Genesis falls within this category. It is the word רֵאשִׁית "beginning," from the noun רֹאשׁ "head." Other examples include the following:

בֹּקֵר	"a herdsman," from	בָּקָר	"a herd"
כֹּרֵם	"a vinedresser," from	כֶּרֶם	"a vineyard"
יִשְׂרְאֵלִי	"Israelite," from	יִשְׂרָאֵל	"Israel"
מִצְרִי	"Egyptian," from	מִצְרַיִם	"Egypt"

18. Nouns: Gender

18.1 *Hebrew nouns are either masculine or feminine.* The only absolute way to determine the gender of a noun is to look it up in a dictionary. Masculine nouns are the most difficult to identify since they do not follow any set pattern.

36

18.2   Feminine nouns are somewhat easier to identify. The following guidelines will provide assistance in this task.

(1)   *Nouns referring to female persons or animals will be feminine.*
Examples:

אֵם   (f) mother   אִשָּׁה   (f) woman

בַּת   (f) daughter   מַלְכָּה   (f) queen   סוּסָה   (f) mare

(2)   *Nouns ending in* הָ *will normally be feminine in gender.*
Examples:

אֲדָמָה   (f) ground, earth   אָכְלָה   (f) food   שָׁנָה   (f) year

בְּהֵמָה   (f) cattle   יַבָּשָׁה   (f) dry land   תּוֹרָה   (f) law, instruction

(3)   *A few nouns are made feminine by the addition of* הָ *to the masculine form of the noun.*
Examples:

מֶלֶךְ   king   מַלְכָּה   (f) queen

נָבִיא   prophet   נְבִיאָה   (f) prophetess

נַעַר   youth, lad   נַעֲרָה   (f) maiden

סוּס   horse   סוּסָה   (f) mare

שַׂר   prince   שָׂרָה   (f) princess

(4)   *Nouns ending in* ת *will ordinarily be feminine.*
Examples:

אָחוֹת   (f) sister   אֱמֶת   (f) truth   בְּרִית   (f) covenant

בַּת   (f) daughter   דֶּלֶת   (f) door   דְּמוּת   (f) likeness

דַּעַת   (f) knowledge   חַטָּאת   (f) sin   מַלְכוּת   (f) kingdom

עֵת   (f) time   קֶשֶׁת   (f) bow   שְׁאֵרִית   (f) remnant

(5)   *Nouns that refer to parts of the body that exist in pairs are usually feminine.*

Examples:

יָד (f) hand   עַיִן (f) eye   רֶגֶל (f) foot

19. Nouns: Number

There are three categories of number to be considered in connection with Hebrew nouns. They are singular, plural, and dual.

37

19.1 Most *singular nouns* are not identifiable by their endings, as can be seen from the examples cited earlier under the discussion of gender.

19.2 *Plural nouns* have special endings that generally correspond to their gender. Unfortunately, plurals are not formed simply by adding special endings to singular forms, but singular forms themselves often undergo changes when plural endings are added. These changes may seem arbitrary to the beginning student but they will become easier to understand as more is learned about the laws that govern the vocalization of words.

(1) *Masculine Plural Endings*

(a) *Most masculine nouns have plurals that end in* ◘ים. (*ḥireq-yod, followed by mem*). The following examples will demonstrate the types of changes that singular forms undergo when plural endings are added.

Singular		Plural	
סוּס	horse	סוּסִים	horses
עֵץ	tree	עֵצִים	trees
הַר	mountain	הָרִים	mountains
דָּבָר	word	דְּבָרִים	words
סֵפֶר	book	סְפָרִים	books
מֶלֶךְ	king	מְלָכִים	kings
אִישׁ	man	אֲנָשִׁים	men
יוֹם	day	יָמִים	days
בֵּן	son	בָּנִים	sons

(b) *A few masculine nouns have plurals that end in* ות (*ḥolem-vav, followed by tav), which is the ending normally used for feminine plurals.*
Examples:

Singular		Plural	
אָב	father	אָבוֹת	fathers
מָקוֹם	place	מְקוֹמוֹת	places
קוֹל	voice	קוֹלוֹת	voices
שֵׁם	name	שֵׁמוֹת	names

(2) *Feminine Plural Endings*

(a) *Most feminine nouns have plurals that end in* ות (*ḥolem-vav, followed by tav).*

38

Examples:

Singular		Plural	
סוּסָה	(f) mare	סוּסוֹת	(f) mares
תּוֹרָה	(f) law	תּוֹרוֹת	(f) laws
מִצְוָה	(f) commandment	מִצְוֹת	(f) commandments
רוּחַ	(f) spirit	רוּחוֹת	(f) spirits
אֵם	(f) mother	אִמּוֹת	(f) mothers
בַּת	(f) daughter	בָּנוֹת	(f) daughters
נֶפֶשׁ	(f) living being	נְפָשׁוֹת	(f) living beings
אֶרֶץ	(f) earth, land	אֲרָצוֹת	(f) lands

(Note that vav serves as both consonant and vowel in מִצְוֹת, "commandments.")

(b) *A few feminine nouns have plurals that end in* יִם *(ḥireq-yod, followed by final mem), which is the ending normally used for the masculine plurals.*
Examples:

Singular		Plural	
אִשָּׁה	(f) woman	נָשִׁים	(f) women
עִיר	(f) city	עָרִים	(f) cities

(3) *Nouns with both Masculine and Feminine Plural Endings*

A few nouns have two plural endings, one is יִם *and one is* וֹת*.*
Examples:

Singular		Plural			
דּוֹר	generation	דּוֹרִים	or	דּוֹרוֹת	generations
שָׁנָה	(f) year	שָׁנִים	or	שָׁנוֹת	years

19.3 *Dual Nouns*

The third number classification for Hebrew nouns is the dual. It is used to designate things that occur in pairs, especially the organs of the body.

(1) *The dual ending is normally written as* יִם *(accented pataḥ, plus yod, plus ḥireq, plus final mem).*

39

Examples:

Singular		Dual	
אֹזֶן	(f) ear	אָזְנַיִם	ears (a pair of)
יָד	(f) hand	יָדַיִם	hands (a pair of)
כָּנָף	(f) wing	כְּנָפַיִם	wings (a pair of)
(no singular)		מֹאזְנַיִם	balances (a pair of)
נַעַל	(f) shoe	נַעֲלַיִם	shoes (a pair of)
עַיִן	(f) eye	עֵינַיִם	eyes (a pair of)
קֶרֶן	(f) horn	קַרְנַיִם	horns (a pair of)
רֶגֶל	(f) foot	רַגְלַיִם	feet (a pair of)
שָׂפָה	(f) lip	שְׂפָתַיִם	lips (a pair of)

(2) *For reasons that are no longer clear, some nouns appear to have a dual ending but without any dual meaning.* Included here are the following:

מַיִם	water	יְרוּשָׁלַיִם	Jerusalem
שָׁמַיִם	sky, heavens	מִצְרַיִם	Egypt

EXERCISES

1. Add the plural endings to the following words and indicate the gender of each.

(1)	אָב	(5)	בַּת	(9)	סוּס
(2)	אִשָּׁה	(6)	דְּבָר	(10)	סוּסָה
(3)	בַּיִת	(7)	הַר	(11)	סֵפֶר
(4)	בֵּן	(8)	מֶלֶךְ	(12)	רוּחַ

2. Translate the following:

(1)   הָאֲנָשִׁים וְהַסוּסִים

(2)   הַמִּצְוֹת אֲשֶׁר בַּסֵּפֶר

(3)   הַנָּשִׁים אֲשֶׁר בַּבַּיִת

(4)   הַמְּלָכִים וְהַנְּבִיאִים

(5)   הַבְּהֵמָה בַּשָּׂדֶה

(6)   הֶעָרִים וְהֶהָרִים

(7)   הַבָּנוֹת וְהָאִמּוֹת

(8)   הַבָּתִּים בֶּעָרִים

(9)   הַדֶּרֶךְ מִן־הָעִיר

(10) הַיָּדַיִם וְהָרַגְלַיִם

3. Add the plural or dual endings to the following words and translate each plural
or dual form.

(1)	אִישׁ	(6)	כָּנָף	
(2)	אֵם	(7)	עַיִן	
(3)	אֶרֶץ	(8)	עִיר	
(4)	יָד	(9)	עֵץ	
(5)	יוֹם	(10)	תּוֹרָה	

4. Translate the following:

(1)   הַמַּיִם בְּתוֹךְ הַיָּם

(2)   הָעוֹף בַּשָּׁמַיִם

(3)   הָאָזְנַיִם וְהָעֵינַיִם

(4)   הַבְּרִית עִם־הַמֶּלֶךְ

(5)   בָּנִים וּבָנוֹת

(6)   הַמִּצְוֺת בַּתּוֹרָה

(7)   עָפָר מִן־הָאֲדָמָה

(8)   בַּיּוֹם וּבַלַּיְלָה

(9)   הַשָּׁמַיִם וְהָאָרֶץ

(10) הַמְּלָכִים מִירוּשָׁלַיִם

(11) הַנָּשִׁים וְהָאֲנָשִׁים

(12) הַסּוּסִים וְהַסּוּסוֹת

41

5. Circle the word that seems to be out of place in each of the following groups.

(1) סוּס בֵּן אָב	(10) אוֹר חֹשֶׁךְ חֶרֶב	
(2) נֶפֶשׁ לַיְלָה יוֹם	(11) לֹא אֵין לִפְנֵי	
(3) מִן פְּרִי בֵּין	(12) אֵצֶל מְאֹד עִם	
(4) עֶרֶב בֹּקֶר עֵץ	(13) דֶּרֶךְ קוֹל דָּבָר	
(5) עָפָר עַיִן יָד	(14) אֲשֶׁר הֵיכָל חַג	
(6) יָם יַבָּשָׁה מַיִם	(15) תּוֹרָה בְּתוֹךְ מִצְוָה	
(7) שָׂדֶה שָׁמַיִם אֲדָמָה	(16) יְהוּדָה יִשְׂרָאֵל לֵב	
(8) אֱלֹהִים יְהוָה אָדָם	(17) רוּחַ עַיִן רֹאשׁ	
(9) הֵיכָל אִשָּׁה עִיר	(18) אָדָם אִישׁ שֵׁם	

VOCABULARY

(1) אֲדָמָה	(f) ground, earth	(10) כִּי — for, that, because
(2) אֲדֹנָי	Lord (pronounced ʾǎdō-nāy)	(11) כֹּל — all
(3) יְהוָה	LORD (also pronounced ʾǎdō-nāy)	(12) כֵּן — thus, so
(4) בְּהֵמָה	(f) cattle	(13) מְאֹד — very, exceedingly
(5) בָּשָׂר	flesh	(14) מִצְוָה — (f) commandment
(6) בְּתוֹךְ	in the midst of	(15) נֶפֶשׁ — (f) soul, living being
(7) גַּם	also	(16) עָפָר — dust
(8) דֶּרֶךְ	(m. and f.) way	(17) שָׂדֶה — field
(9) יַבָּשָׁה	(f) dry ground	(18) שָׁמַיִם — heavens, sky

LESSON VIII

20. Adjectives: Gender and Number

20.1 The function of an adjective is to describe or limit a noun. In comparison with other languages, Hebrew has relatively few adjectives. The most common masculine singular forms are these:

גָּדוֹל	(also גָּדֹל) great, large	עַז	strong
זָקֵן	old (of persons only)	קָדוֹשׁ	(also קָדֹשׁ) holy
חָדָשׁ	new	קָטֹן	small
חָזָק	strong	קָרוֹב	(also קָרֹב) near
חַי	living	קָשֶׁה	hard, difficult, stubborn
חָכָם	wise	רַב	many, much
טוֹב	(also טֹב) good	רָחוֹק	(also רָחֹק) far, distant
יָפֶה	beautiful, fair, handsome	רַע	evil
יָשָׁר	straight, right	תָּמִים	perfect, complete, whole
מַר	bitter		

20.2 The adjectives listed above are all masculine singular forms and can only be used to describe or limit masculine singular nouns. Adjectives describing masculine plural nouns receive a ִים ending. Those describing feminine singular nouns receive a ָה ending. And those describing feminine plural nouns receive a וֹת ending. These adjective endings are consistent and uniform, even when the nouns they describe are irregular in their plural endings.

Examples:

אָב טוֹב	a good father
אָבוֹת טוֹבִים	good fathers (אָבוֹת is an irregular masculine plural)
אִשָּׁה טוֹבָה	a good woman
נָשִׁים טוֹבוֹת	good women (נָשִׁים is an irregular feminine plural)

20.3 There are certain changes that take place in the vocalization and structure of masculine singular adjectives when gender and number endings are added. These changes depend in part upon whether the masculine singular form is monosyllabic or bisyllabic.

(1) *Rules for adding gender and number endings to masculine singular adjectives that are monosyllabic*

(a) Monosyllabic adjectives with unchangeably long vowels (יִ , יֵ , וֹ, or וּ) retain these vowels when gender and number endings are added. Examples:

	(ms)	(mp)	(fs)	(fp)
good	טוֹב	טוֹבִים	טוֹבָה	טוֹבוֹת
empty	רֵיק	רֵיקִים	רֵיקָה	רֵיקוֹת

(b) Monosyllabic adjectives that end in non–gutturals and have short vowels retain their short vowels when gender and number endings are added. Note, however, that when such endings are added, the final consonant of the masculine singular form of the adjective must be doubled (by the addition of dagesh forte).

Examples:

	(ms)	(mp)	(fs)	(fp)
living	חַי	חַיִּים	חַיָּה	חַיּוֹת
strong	עַז	עַזִּים	עַזָּה	עַזּוֹת
many	רַב	רַבִּים	רַבָּה	רַבּוֹת

(c) Monosyllabic adjectives that end in gutturals and also have short vowels must have their short vowels lengthened to long vowels when gender and number endings are added. This is because gutturals refuse to be doubled. Examples:

	(ms)	(mp)	(fs)	(fp)
bitter	מַר	מָרִים	מָרָה	מָרוֹת
evil	רַע	רָעִים	רָעָה	רָעוֹת

(2) *Rules for adding gender and number endings to masculine singular adjectives that are bisyllabic*

(a) All masculine singular adjectives that are bisyllabic will have a qameṣ in their initial syllable. When gender and number endings are added, this initial qameṣ is left two syllables before the tone (accented) syllable and therefore must be volatilized (reduced to a vocal sheva).

(*i*) If the initial consonant of the bisyllabic adjective is a non–guttural, the qameṣ that accompanies it will be reduced to a simple sheva (ְ).

Examples:

	(ms)	(mp)	(fs)	(fp)
great	גָּדוֹל	גְּדוֹלִים	גְּדוֹלָה	גְּדוֹלוֹת
old	זָקֵן	זְקֵנִים	זְקֵנָה	זְקֵנוֹת
right	יָשָׁר	יְשָׁרִים	יְשָׁרָה	יְשָׁרוֹת

(*ii*) However, if the initial consonant of the bisyllabic adjective is a guttural, then the qameṣ that accompanies this consonant must be reduced to a compound sheva (‑ֲ), since gutturals prefer compound shevas.

Examples:

	(ms)	(mp)	(fs)	(fp)
new	חָדָשׁ	חֲדָשִׁים	חֲדָשָׁה	חֲדָשׁוֹת
strong	חָזָק	חֲזָקִים	חֲזָקָה	חֲזָקוֹת
wise	חָכָם	חֲכָמִים	חֲכָמָה	חֲכָמוֹת

(b) The bisyllabic adjective קָטֹן, "small," behaves in an irregular manner. When gender and number endings are added, holem is replaced by pataḥ, and a dagesh forte is placed in the nun.

Examples:

	(ms)	(mp)	(fs)	(fp)
small	קָטֹן	קְטַנִּים	קְטַנָּה	קְטַנּוֹת

(c) Bisyllabic adjectives ending in הֶ will drop the הֶ whenever gender and number endings are added.

Examples:

	(ms)	(mp)	(fs)	(fp)
beautiful	יָפֶה	יָפִים	יָפָה	יָפוֹת
difficult	קָשֶׁה	קָשִׁים	קָשָׁה	קָשׁוֹת

21. Adjectives: Attributive Usage

21.1 An attributive adjective is one that directly describes a noun. Attributive adjectives usually stand after the nouns they describe, although this order may be reversed if the adjective is to be emphasized.

Examples:

אִישׁ טוֹב	a good man	הָאִישׁ הַטּוֹב	the good man
אִשָּׁה טוֹבָה	a good woman	הָאִשָּׁה הַטּוֹבָה	the good woman

21.2 An attributive adjective must agree in gender, number, and definiteness with the noun it describes. To agree in definiteness means that when the noun is definite, the attributive adjective must also be definite; when the noun is indefinite, the attributive adjective must also remain indefinite.
Examples:

מֶלֶךְ גָּדוֹל a great king (indefinite)   הַמֶּלֶךְ הַגָּדוֹל the great king (definite)

מְלָכִים גְּדוֹלִים great kings (indefinite)   הַמְּלָכִים הַגְּדוֹלִים the great kings (definite)

עִיר גְּדוֹלָה a great city (indefinite)   הָעִיר הַגְּדוֹלָה the great city (definite)

עָרִים גְּדוֹלוֹת great cities (indefinite)   הֶעָרִים הַגְּדוֹלוֹת the great cities (definite)

22. Adjectives: Predicative Usage

22.1 Hebrew often makes use of simple sentences consisting of a noun, which functions as subject, and an adjective, which functions as predicate. These are verbless sentences, since the verb "to be" is not written but only implied. It must be supplied in translation.

22.2 A predicate adjective usually stands before its subject noun, but occasionally will stand after it.

22.3 A predicate adjective will agree with its subject noun in gender and number, but will never take the article, even though the subject noun is definite.
Examples:

טוֹב הַדָּבָר   The word (is) good. (1 Kgs. 2:38)

כִּי הַמָּקוֹם קָדשׁ   For the place (is) holy. (Ezek. 42:13)

כִּי־קָדוֹשׁ הַיּוֹם   For the day (is) holy. (Neh. 8:10)

וְהַנַּעֲרָה יָפָה עַד־מְאֹד   And the maiden (was) exceedingly beautiful. (1 Kgs. 1:4)

טוֹבָה הָאָרֶץ מְאֹד מְאֹד   The land (was) exceedingly good. (Num. 14:7)

טוֹב לְיִשְׂרָאֵל אֱלֹהִים   God (is) good to Israel. (Ps. 73:1)

וְהַמֶּלֶךְ זָקֵן מְאֹד   And the king (was) very old. (1 Kgs. 1:15)

וְהָאֲנָשִׁים טֹבִים לָנוּ מְאֹד   And the men were very good to us. (1 Sam. 25:15)

46

22.4 Two predicate adjectives are sometimes used to describe one subject noun.

Examples:

טוֹב־וְיָשָׁר יְהוָה   good and upright (is) the LORD (Ps. 25:8)

כִּי־זָקֵן הָאִישׁ וְכָבֵד   for the man (was) old and heavy (1 Sam. 4:18)

EXERCISES

1. Each of the following entries contains an adjective. In the space marked (a) indicate whether the adjective is used attributively (A) or predicatively (P). In the space marked (b) give the gender of the adjective, and in (c) give its number.

Example:

מֵאֶרֶץ רְחוֹקָה   from a distant land (Josh. 9:6)

    (a)   A   (b)   fem.   (c)   sing.

(1)   נַעֲרָה קְטַנָּה   a little maid (2 Kgs. 5:2)

    (a) _____ (b) _____ (c) _____

(2)   בְּדֶרֶךְ יְשָׁרָה   by a straight way (Ps. 107:7)

    (a) _____ (b) _____ (c) _____

(3)   אֶבֶן גְּדוֹלָה   a great stone (Josh. 24:26)

    (a) _____ (b) _____ (c) _____

(4)   בַּיִת חָדָשׁ   a new house (Deut. 22:8)

    (a) _____ (b) _____ (c) _____

(5)   עִיר גְּדוֹלָה   a great city (Josh. 10:2)

    (a) _____ (b) _____ (c) _____

(6)   קָרוֹב הַיּוֹם   The day is near. (Ezek. 7:7)

    (a) _____ (b) _____ (c) _____

(7)   בְּרִית חֲדָשָׁה   a new covenant (Jer. 31:31)

    (a) _____ (b) _____ (c) _____

(8) נָשִׁים רַבּוֹת many women (Ezek. 16:41)

  (a) _____ (b) _____ (c) _____

(9) אֲבָנִים גְּדֹלוֹת great stones (Josh. 10:18)

  (a) _____ (b) _____ (c) _____

(10) וְרוּחַ גְּדוֹלָה and a great wind (1 Kgs. 19:11)

  (a) _____ (b) _____ (c) _____

(11) טוֹבָה הָאָרֶץ מְאֹד מְאֹד The land was exceedingly good. (Num. 14:7)

  (a) _____ (b) _____ (c) _____

(12) הַדֶּרֶךְ הַטּוֹבָה the good way (2 Chr. 6:27)

  (a) _____ (b) _____ (c) _____

2. Underscore the correct adjectival form in each of the following entries.

(1) מֶלֶךְ (חֲדָשָׁה , חָדָשׁ) עַל־מִצְרַיִם a new king over Egypt (Exod. 1:8)

(2) כִּי אֵל (גָּדוֹל , גְּדוֹלָה) יְהֹוָה For the LORD is a great God. (Ps. 95:3)

(3) בְּיָד (חָזָק , חֲזָקָה) with a strong hand (Deut. 26:8)

(4) רוּחַ (גְּדוֹלָה , גָּדוֹל) a great wind (Jon. 1:4)

(5) עִיר (גְּדוֹלָה , גָּדוֹל) a great city (Jon. 3:3)

(6) אִישׁ (חֲכָמָה , חָכָם) מְאֹד an exceedingly wise man (2 Sam. 13:3)

(7) לֵב (חָכָם , חֲכָמָה) a wise heart (1 Kgs. 3:12)

(8) אִשָּׁה (חָכָם , חֲכָמָה) a wise woman (2 Sam. 14:2)

(9) אֲנָשִׁים (חֲכָמִים , חֲכָמוֹת) wise men (Deut. 1:13)

(10) נָשִׁים (רַבּוֹת , רַבִּים) many women (Judg. 8:30)

(11) עָרִים (רַבּוֹת , רַבִּים) many cities (Zech. 8:20)

(12) (רַבּוֹת , רַבִּים) בָּנוֹת many daughters (Prov. 31:29)

3. Match the following:

( ) מְלָכִים גְּדוֹלִים   (A) And the stone was great. (Gen. 29:2)

( ) יָמִים רַבִּים   (B) a small city (Eccl. 9:14)

( ) רָעָה רַבָּה   (C) many lands (Jer. 28:8)

( ) אֶבֶן גְּדוֹלָה   (D) And the maiden was beautiful. (1 Kgs. 1:4)

( ) אֶרֶץ רְחוֹקָה   (E) many days (Gen. 21:34)

( ) בָּנִים רַבִּים   (F) a beautiful woman (Prov. 11:22)

( ) הָעִיר הַקְּרֹבָה   (G) a new spirit (Ezek. 11:19)

( ) אֲבָנִים גְּדֹלוֹת   (H) a great evil (Eccl. 2:21)

( ) עִיר קְטַנָּה   (I) great kings (Jer. 25:14)

( ) אֲרָצוֹת רַבּוֹת   (J) an evil spirit (Judg. 9:23)

( ) וְהָאֶבֶן גְּדֹלָה   (K) many years (Neh. 9:30)

( ) נַעֲרָה יָפָה   (L) a full (whole) year (Lev. 25:30)

( ) אִשָּׁה יָפָה   (M) the near city (Deut. 21:3)

( ) רוּחַ חֲדָשָׁה   (N) large stones (Josh. 10:18)

( ) רוּחַ רָעָה   (O) a beautiful maiden (1 Kgs. 1:3)

( ) שָׁנָה תְמִימָה   (P) many sons (1 Chr. 4:27)

( ) וְהַנַּעֲרָה יָפָה   (Q) a distant land (2 Chr. 6:36)

( ) שָׁנִים רַבּוֹת   (R) a great stone (Josh. 24:26)

4. Fill in the blanks with the correct translation of the adjectives in the following examples.

(1) בָּתִּים רַבִּים גְּדֹלִים וְטוֹבִים   many houses _____ and _____ (Isa. 5:9)

(2) אִישׁ זָקֵן   an _____ man (Judg. 19:16)

(3) בַּדֶּרֶךְ הַטּוֹבָה וְהַיְשָׁרָה   in the _____ and the _____ way (1 Sam. 12:23)

(4) בְּדֶרֶךְ רָע   into an _____ way (Prov. 28:10)

(5)   בְּיָד חֲזָקָה   by a _____ hand (Exod. 3:19)

(6)   מֶלֶךְ חָכָם   a _____ king (Prov. 20:26)

(7)   שָׁלוֹם רָב   _____ peace (Ps. 119:165)

(8)   עַם גָּדוֹל וָרָב   a people _____ and _____.
(Deut. 2:10)

(9)   בָּנִים רַבִּים   _____ sons (1 Chr. 4:27)

(10)   כְּיוֹם מָר   as a _____ day (Amos 8:10)

(11)   נָשִׁים יָפוֹת   _____ women (Job 42:15)

(12)   אִשָּׁה חֲדָשָׁה   a _____ wife (Deut. 24:5)

5.   Practice pronouncing the Hebrew in the following examples. Cover the English translation and practice translating the Hebrew from sight.

(1)   מֵאָדָם רָע   from an evil man (Ps. 140:2; Eng. 140:1)

(2)   הָאִישׁ מֹשֶׁה גָּדוֹל מְאֹד   The man Moses was very great.
(Exod. 11:3)

(3)   מִי־אֵל גָּדוֹל כֵּאלֹהִים   Who is a great god like God?
(Ps. 77:14; Eng. 77:13)

(4)   כִּי אֵל גָּדוֹל יְהוָה
וּמֶלֶךְ גָּדוֹל עַל־כָּל־
אֱלֹהִים   For the LORD (is) a great God,
and a great King above (over) all
gods. (Ps. 95:3)

(5)   דְּבָרִים רַבִּים   many words (Jer. 36:32)

(6)   עַמִּים רַבִּים   many peoples (Isa. 2:3)

(7)   אִישׁ־יָפֶה   a handsome man (2 Sam. 14:25)

(8)   כְּיוֹם תָּמִים   as a whole day (Josh. 10:13)

(9)   הַשָּׁמַיִם הַחֲדָשִׁים וְהָאָרֶץ
הַחֲדָשָׁה   the new heavens and the new earth
(Isa. 66:22)

(10)   לֵב חָדָשׁ וְרוּחַ חֲדָשָׁה   a new heart and a new spirit (Ezek. 18:31)

(11)   טוֹב־וְיָשָׁר יְהוָה   Good and upright is the LORD. (Ps. 25:8)

(12)   וְדָוִיד זָקֵן   And David was old. (1 Chr. 23:1)

(13)   רוּחַ־רָעָה מֵאֵת יְהוָה   an evil spirit from the LORD
(1 Sam. 16:14)

(14)   שֵׁם רָע   an evil name (Deut. 22:14)

(15)   דְּבָרִים רָעִים   wicked things (2 Kgs. 17:11)

VOCABULARY

(1) גָּדוֹל (גָּדֹל) great, large   (10) קָדוֹשׁ (קָדֹשׁ) holy

(2) זָקֵן old (of persons only)   (11) קָטֹן small

(3) חָדָשׁ new   (12) קָרוֹב (קָרֹב) near

(4) חָזָק strong   (13) קָשֶׁה hard, difficult

(5) חַי living   (14) רַב many, much

(6) חָכָם wise   (15) רָחוֹק (רָחֹק) far, distant

(7) יָפֶה beautiful, fair, handsome   (16) רַע evil, bad

(8) יָשָׁר straight, right, upright   (17) רָעָה (f) (an) evil

(9) מַר bitter   (18) תָּמִים perfect, complete, whole

LESSON IX

23. Independent Personal Pronouns (Subject Pronouns)

23.1 Independent personal pronouns are written as separate forms and may be used as subject pronouns but not as direct objects of a verb or as objects of a preposition. Special pronominal suffixes must be added to verbs, prepositions, and nouns to indicate pronominal relationships other than that of subject. These suffix forms will be introduced in later lessons.

23.2 The forms of the independent personal pronouns are as follows:

אֲנִי, אָנֹכִי	I	(1 cs)	אֲנַחְנוּ, נַחְנוּ, אָנוּ	we	(1 cp)
אַתָּה	you	(2 ms)	אַתֶּם	you	(2 mp)
אַתְּ	you	(2 fs)	אַתֵּן, אַתֵּנָה	you	(2 fp)
הוּא	he/it	(3 ms)	הֵם, הֵמָּה	they	(3 mp)
הִיא	she/it	(3 fs)	הֵן, הֵנָּה	they	(3 fp)

Note: 3 fs = הוא throughout the books of the Pentateuch.

23.3 Sentences that employ independent personal pronouns as subjects will often be verbless sentences (with the verb "to be" understood).
Examples:

אֲנִי יְהוָה	I (am) the LORD. (Gen. 28:13)
אַתָּה הָאִישׁ	You (are) the man. (2 Sam. 12:7)
כִּי־עָפָר אַתָּה	For you (are) dust. (Gen. 3:19)
יְהוָה הוּא הָאֱלֹהִים	The LORD, he (is) God. (1 Kgs. 18:39)
אַחִים אֲנַחְנוּ	We (are) brothers. (Gen. 13:8)
וַאֲנַחְנוּ רַבִּים	And we (are) many. (Ezek. 33:24)
וְהֵמָּה חֲכָמִים	And they (are) wise. (Prov. 30:24)

24. Demonstrative Pronouns

24.1 A demonstrative pronoun is one that indicates something or someone being singled out for attention, as in the case of "*this* man," or "*This* is the man."

24.2 The forms of the demonstrative pronouns are as follows:

Singular			Plural		
masc.	זֶה	this	masc.	אֵלֶּה	these
fem.	זֹאת	this	fem.	אֵלֶּה	these
masc.	הוּא	that	masc.	הֵמָּה (הֵם)	those
fem.	הִיא	that	fem.	הֵנָּה (הֵן)	those

24.3 The demonstrative pronouns have a function in Hebrew parallel to that of adjectives.

(1) *Like adjectives, they may be used attributively. In this case, they agree in gender, number, and definiteness with the nouns to which they refer.*
Examples:

הַמָּקוֹם הַזֶּה	this place (Gen. 28:17)
הָאָרֶץ הַזֹּאת	this land (Gen. 15:7)
בַּיּוֹם הַהוּא	on that day (Gen. 15:18)
בָּעִיר הַהִיא	in that city (Josh. 20:6)
הַדְּבָרִים הָאֵלֶּה	these words (Gen. 29:13)
הֶעָרִים הָאֵלֶּה	these cities (Num. 21:25)
בַּיָּמִים הָהֵם	in those days (Gen. 6:4)

If a noun is modified by an adjective, the demonstrative pronoun will usually stand after the adjective.
Examples:

הַדָּבָר הַגָּדוֹל הַזֶּה	this great thing (1 Sam. 12:16)
הָאָרֶץ הַטּוֹבָה הַזֹּאת	this good land (Deut. 4:22)
הַמִּדְבָּר הַגָּדוֹל הַהוּא	that great wilderness (Deut. 1:19)
הַשָּׁנִים הַטֹּבֹת הָאֵלֶּה	these good years (Gen. 41:35)

Demonstrative pronouns regularly take the definite article when used attributively. Independent personal pronouns, on the other hand, may only be used as subject pronouns, and therefore never take the definite article.

(2) *Demonstrative pronouns may also be used predicatively. Like predicative adjectives, they agree in gender and number with the nouns to which they are linked, but they never take the article.*

Examples:

זֶה הַיּוֹם	This (is) the day. (Judg. 4:14)
זֹאת הָאָרֶץ	This (is) the land. (Num. 34:2)
הוּא הַדָּבָר	That (is) the word. (Gen. 41:28)
הוּא הָעִיר הַגְּדֹלָה	That (is) the great city. (Gen. 10:12)
אֵלֶּה הַדְּבָרִים	These (are) the words. (Deut. 1:1)

EXERCISES

1. Complete the translation of the following entries by filling in the blanks.

(1)   הַשָּׁנִים הַטֹּבֹת הָאֵלֶּה _____ good years (Gen. 41:35)

(2)   צַדִּיק אַתָּה _____ are righteous. (Jer. 12:1)

(3)   כִּי מֶלֶךְ גָּדוֹל אָנִי For _____ (am) a great King. (Mal. 1:14)

(4)   לָעִיר הַגְּדוֹלָה הַזֹּאת to _____ great city (Jer. 22:8)

(5)   כִּי־חֲזָקִים הֵמָּה For _____ (are) strong. (Judg. 18:26)

(6)   חֲכָמִים אֲנַחְנוּ _____ (are) wise. (Jer. 8:8)

(7)   כִּי־חָזָק הוּא For _____ (is) strong. (Num. 13:31)

(8)   כִּי מָרִים הֵם For _____ (were) bitter. (Exod. 15:23)

(9)   הָעִיר הַזֹּאת קְרֹבָה _____ city (is) near. (Gen. 19:20)

(10)   וְאָנֹכִי נַעַר קָטֹן And _____ (am) a little child. (1 Kgs. 3:7)

2. Underscore the correct pronominal form in the following entries.

(1)   (הִיא / הוּא) כִּי קָטֹן For he (is) small. (Amos 7:2)

(2)   (אַתָּה / אַתְּ) כִּי קָשֶׁה that you (are) stubborn (Isa. 48:4)

(3)   מְאֹד (הוּא / הִיא) כִּי־יָפָה For she (was) very beautiful. (Gen. 12:14)

(4)   (אַתְּ / אַתָּה) יָפָה You (are) lovely. (Song of Sol. 6:4)

(5)   (אַתְּ / אַתָּה) תָּמִים You (were) perfect (blameless). (Ezek. 28:15)

(6)   (הַזֶּה / הַזֹּאת) הָרָע הַדָּבָר   this evil word (Exod. 33:4)

(7)   נַעַר (וְהוּא / וְהִיא)   And he (was) a lad. (Gen. 37:2)

(8)   (זֶה / זֹאת) הַדָּבָר   This (is) the word. (Num. 30:2)

(9)   בַּיּוֹם (הַהוּא / הַהוּא)   on that day (Gen. 15:18)

(10) בַּיּוֹם (הַזֹּאת / הַזֶּה)   on this day (Gen. 7:11)

(11) הוּא / זֹאת) זֶה / כִּי   For this (is) he. (1 Sam. 16:12)

(12) (הוּא / הוּא) הָעִיר הַגְּדֹלָה   That (is) the great (chief) city. (Gen. 10:12)

3. Each of the following entries contains either a personal or a demonstrative pronoun. In the space marked (a) indicate whether the pronoun is to be classified as personal (P) or as demonstrative (D). In the space marked (b), give the gender of the pronoun, and in (c) its number.

Example:

יְהוָה הוּא הָאֱלֹהִים   (a)   P
The LORD, he is God. (1 Kgs. 18:39)   (b)   masc.
                                       (c)   sing.

(1)   לֹא בַשָּׁמַיִם הוּא   (a) _____
It (she) is not in the heavens. (Deut. 30:12)   (b) _____
                                       (c) _____

(2)   הַגּוֹי הַגָּדוֹל הַזֶּה   (a) _____
this great nation (Deut. 4:6)   (b) _____
                                       (c) _____

(3)   זֶה הַיּוֹם   (a) _____
This is the day. (Judg. 4:14)   (b) _____
                                       (c) _____

(4)   כִּי אֲנִי יְהוָה   (a) _____
For I am the LORD. (Exod. 7:5)   (b) _____
                                       (c) _____

(5)   הָעָם הַזֶּה הָרָע   (a) _____
this evil people (Jer. 13:10)   (b) _____
                                       (c) _____

(6)   כִּדְבַר הָרָע הַזֶּה

according to this evil word (Deut. 13:12)

(a) _____

(b) _____

(c) _____

4. Practice reading the Hebrew aloud. Cover the English translation and practice translating the Hebrew from sight.

(1)   הָאִישׁ מֹשֶׁה גָּדוֹל מְאֹד

The man Moses was very great. (Exod. 11:3)

(2)   הַדָּבָר הַגָּדוֹל הַזֶּה

this great thing (1 Sam. 12:16)

(3)   כִּי אֵל גָּדוֹל יְהוָה וּמֶלֶךְ
גָּדוֹל עַל־כָּל־אֱלֹהִים

For the LORD is a great God, and a great King above all gods. (Ps. 95:3)

(4)   כִּי קָרוֹב הוּא

For it was near. (Exod. 13:17)

(5)   כִּי־קְרֹבִים הֵם

For they were near (neighbors). (Josh. 9:16)

(6)   וְאָנֹכִי נַעַר קָטֹן

And I am a little child. (1 Kgs. 3:7)

(7)   נֹחַ אִישׁ צַדִּיק

Noah was a righteous man. (Gen. 6:9)

(8)   צַדִּיק וְיָשָׁר הוּא

Righteous and upright is he. (Deut. 32:4)

(9)   לֹא אִישׁ אֵל

God is not man. (Num. 23:19)

(10)   עַם־חָכָם הַגּוֹי הַגָּדוֹל הַזֶּה

A wise people is this great nation. (Deut. 4:6)

VOCABULARY

(1)	אֶבֶן	(f) stone	(10)	מִשְׁפָּט	judgment, justice
(2)	דּוֹר	generation	(11)	מֹשֶׁה	Moses
(3)	יְרוּשָׁלַיִם		(12)	נָבִיא	prophet
	יְרוּשָׁלַם	Jerusalem	(13)	נַעַר	lad, youth
(4)	יֵשׁ	there is, there are	(14)	נַעֲרָה	(f) maiden, young woman
(5)	כֹּה	thus	(15)	סֵפֶר	book
(6)	לֶחֶם	bread	(16)	פֶּן	lest
(7)	מִדְבָּר	wilderness, desert	(17)	רֶגֶל	(f) foot
(8)	מָה	What?	(18)	תּוֹרָה	(f) law, instruction
(9)	מִי	Who?			

LESSON X

25. Nouns: Segholates

Segholates are bisyllabic (two–syllable) nouns that exhibit the following characteristics:

25.1 In the singular they are always accented on the first syllable. The vowels of this syllable may belong to either the "a" class, the "e" class, or the "o" class.

Examples: מָוֶת death   אֶלֶף thousand   אֹהֶל tent

25.2 The second syllable will ordinarily take a s^egol as its vowel, although this may be replaced by a pataḥ whenever the middle or final consonant is a guttural. (Gutturals prefer "a" class vowels around them.)

Examples: מֶלֶךְ king   נַעַר lad   סֵפֶר book   בֹּקֶר morning

25.3 Plural segholates fall into a number of well–defined groups. Some of the more common are these:

(1) *The plurals of masculine nouns that begin with non-gutturals:*

בֶּגֶד	garment	בְּגָדִים	garments
בֹּקֶר	morning	בְּקָרִים	mornings
בַּעַל	Baal, master	בְּעָלִים	Baals, masters
סֵפֶר	book	סְפָרִים	books

Other nouns in this group include:

גֶּפֶן	vine	כֶּרֶם	vineyard	יֶלֶד	child
דֶּרֶךְ	(m. and f.) way	מֶלֶךְ	king	פֶּשַׁע	transgression
זֶבַח	sacrifice	נַעַר	lad	שֶׁמֶן	oil

(2) *The plurals of feminine nouns that begin with non-gutturals:*

דֶּלֶת (f) door   דְּלָתוֹת doors   נֶפֶשׁ (f) soul   נְפָשׁוֹת souls

(3) *The plurals of masculine nouns that begin with gutturals:*

הֶבֶל	vapor, vanity	הֲבָלִים	vapors, vanities
חֶסֶד	mercy	חֲסָדִים	mercies
עֶבֶד	servant	עֲבָדִים	servants

57

(4) *The plurals of feminine nouns that begin with gutturals:*

אֶבֶן	(f) stone	אֲבָנִים	stones
אֶרֶץ	(f) earth, land	אֲרָצוֹת	lands
חֶרֶב	(f) sword	חֲרָבוֹת	swords

(Note: The principle involved in nos. 3 and 4 is that gutturals prefer compound shevas rather than simple shevas.)

(5) *Nouns with dual endings:*

אֹזֶן	(f) ear	אָזְנַיִם	ears
קֶרֶן	(f) horn	קַרְנַיִם	horns
רֶגֶל	(f) foot	רַגְלַיִם	feet

25.4 Some segholates have singular forms but no plural forms. These include the following:

דַּעַת	(f) knowledge	צֶדֶק	righteousness	כֶּסֶף	silver
דֶּשֶׁא	grass	שֶׁמֶשׁ	sun	אֹכֶל	food
לֶחֶם	bread	צֶלֶם	image, likeness	זֶרַע	seed

26. Nouns: Construct Relationship

26.1 *A Hebrew noun has both an absolute state and a construct state.* The singular absolute state is the form under which nouns are listed in lexicons and vocabulary lists. The construct state of a noun represents a shortening of the absolute state, insofar as this is possible. The principles governing the shortening of nouns in the construct state will be explained below.

26.2 *A construct relationship may be defined as the joining together of two (occasionally three, but rarely four) nouns within a sentence. The joining may be either by simple juxtaposition or by the use of a maqqef. The final noun in such a series must remain in the absolute state, while the noun (or nouns) that precedes it must take the form of the construct state.*

26.3 *The function of the construct relationship is to express genitival relationships and the various nuances of meaning associated with the preposition "of."* Since Hebrew lacked such an all-purpose preposition, the construct relationship helped to fill the gap.

26.4 *Nouns joined together in a construct relationship are pronounced as a single speech unit, with the accent falling upon the last noun in the series, i.e., upon*

the noun in the absolute state. The loss of stress upon the initial noun (or nouns) in a construct relationship often causes certain vocalic and/or consonantal changes. The vocalic changes involve the shortening of long vowels left standing in closed, unaccented syllables, and the volatilization of long vowels in open syllables that are two or more syllables before the tone (accented) syllable. Neither shortening nor volatilization will take place in a syllable that has an unchangeably long vowel (יִ ,
 יְ, וֹ, וּ).

(1) For convenience of handling, we will look first at the changes that occur when plural nouns are placed in the construct state.

(a) *When a masculine plural noun in placed in the construct state, its ending is changed from* יִם *(ḥireq-yod, plus final mem) to* יֵ *(ṣere-yod).* Long vowels left standing in open syllables before the יֵ ending are usually reduced to vocal shevas (unless they are unchangeably long).
Examples:

Plural Absolute						Plural Construct	
בָּנִים	sons	→	בְּנֵי	→	בְּנֵי	sons of	
יָמִים	days	→	יְמֵי	→	יְמֵי	days of	
אֱלֹהִים	God (gods)	→			אֱלֹהֵי	God of (gods of)	
סוּסִים	horses	→			סוּסֵי	horses of	

(In the last two examples, ḥolem and šureq are unchangeably long vowels.)

(b) *If the volatilization of the long vowel in an open syllable results in two vocal shevas being placed together at the beginning of the masculine plural construct form, the first of these must be raised to a full vowel.*
Examples:

אֲנָשִׁים	men	→	אֲנְשֵׁי	→	אַנְשֵׁי	men of	
דְּבָרִים	words	→	דְּבְרֵי	→	דִּבְרֵי	words of	
עֲבָדִים	servants	→	עֲבְדֵי	→	עַבְדֵי	servants of	
זְקֵנִים	elders	→	זְקְנֵי	→	זִקְנֵי	elders of	

Examples with unchangeably long vowels:

כּוֹכָבִים	stars	→		כּוֹכְבֵי	stars of
נְבִיאִים	prophets	→		נְבִיאֵי	prophets of

(c) *The dual construct has the same ending (*יֵ*) as the masculine plural construct.* The יֵ takes the place of the dual absolute ending (יִם).

Examples:

Dual Absolute		Dual Construct	
אָזְנַיִם	ears	אָזְנֵי	ears of
רַגְלַיִם	feet	רַגְלֵי	feet of
קַרְנַיִם	horns	קַרְנֵי	horns of

(d) *The feminine plural construct retains the* וֹת *ending of the feminine plural absolute.* This is because holem-vav is unchangeably long. However, certain other changes must be made. These involve volatilizing long vowels (unless unchangeably long) in open syllables, and making certain that two vocal shevas are not left standing side by side. In the event that this occurs, the first of the shevas must be raised to a full vowel. Masculine plural nouns ending in וֹת follow this same pattern.

Examples:

Plural Absolute		Plural Construct	
אָבוֹת	fathers	אֲבוֹת	fathers of
אֲרָצוֹת (f) lands → אֲרָצוֹת →		אַרְצוֹת	lands of

Examples with unchangeably long vowels:

Plural Absolute		Plural Construct	
קוֹלוֹת	voices	קוֹלוֹת	voices of
רוּחוֹת	(f) spirits	רוּחוֹת	spirits of
תּוֹרוֹת	(f) laws	תּוֹרוֹת	laws of

(2) *The rules that govern the formation of singular construct nouns are much more complicated than those that relate to plural construct forms. The only way to be certain about the correct construct form of a particular noun is to consult a lexicon.* The following lists contain many of the most frequently occurring nouns in the Hebrew Bible and illustrate the kinds of changes that take place in the transition from the absolute to the construct state. Special attention is given to the way in which the singular construct is formed. For the formation of the plural construct refer to the rules given above.

(a) *Monosyllabic nouns with unchangeably long vowels have the same form in the singular construct as in the singular absolute, although the plural forms of some of these nouns may be irregular (cf.* רֹאשׁ, עִיר, יוֹם, אִישׁ).

Sing. Abs.		Sing. Const.		Pl. Abs.		Pl. Const.	
אִישׁ	man	אִישׁ	man of	אֲנָשִׁים	men	אַנְשֵׁי	men of
יוֹם	day	יוֹם	day of	יָמִים	days	יְמֵי	days of

60

Sing. Abs.		Sing. Const.		Pl. Abs.		Pl. Const.	
סוּס	horse	סוּס	horse of	סוּסִים	horses	סוּסֵי	horses of
עִיר	(f) city	עִיר	city of	עָרִים	cities	עָרֵי	cities of
קוֹל	voice	קוֹל	voice of	קוֹלוֹת	voices	קוֹלוֹת	voices of
רֹאשׁ	head	רֹאשׁ	head of	רָאשִׁים	heads	רָאשֵׁי	heads of
רוּחַ	(f) spirit	רוּחַ	spirit of	רוּחוֹת	spirits	רוּחוֹת	spirits of

(b) *Monosyllabic nouns with short vowels will also have the same form in the singular construct as in the singular absolute.*

Sing. Abs.		Sing. Const.		Pl. Abs.		Pl. Const.	
בַּת	(f) daughter	בַּת	daughter of	בָּנוֹת	daughters	בְּנוֹת	daughters of
הַר	mountain	הַר	mountain of	הָרִים	mountains	הָרֵי	mountains of
עַם	people	עַם	people of	עַמִּים	peoples	עַמֵּי	peoples of

(c) *Monosyllabic nouns with changeably long vowels in the singular absolute will usually shorten these to form the singular construct.*

Sing. Abs.		Sing. Const.		Pl. Abs.		Pl. Const.	
בֵּן	son	בֶּן (or בֵּן)		בָּנִים		בְּנֵי	
דָּם	blood	דַּם		דָּמִים		דְּמֵי	
יָד	(f) hand	יַד		יָדוֹת		יָדוֹת	
				יָדַיִם	(dual)	יְדֵי	(dual)
שֵׁם	name	שֵׁם (or שֶׁם)		שֵׁמוֹת		שְׁמוֹת	

(d) The monosyllabic nouns אָב and אָח are irregular in the singular construct.

Sing. Abs.		Sing. Const.	Pl. Abs.	Pl. Const.
אָב	father	אֲבִי	אָבוֹת	אֲבוֹת
אָח	brother	אֲחִי	אַחִים	אֲחֵי

(e) *Bisyllabic nouns with the first syllable open and the second closed will form the singular construct by reducing the vowel in the first syllable to a vocal sheva and by shortening the vowel in the second syllable, except when these vowels are unchangeably long (see* הֵיכָל, כּוֹכָב, מָקוֹם, *and* נָבִיא*).*

Sing. Abs.		Sing. Const.	Pl. Abs.	Pl. Const.
דָּבָר	word	דְּבַר	דְּבָרִים	דִּבְרֵי
הֵיכָל	palace	הֵיכַל	הֵיכָלִים	הֵיכְלֵי
כּוֹכָב	star	כּוֹכַב	כּוֹכָבִים	כּוֹכְבֵי
מָקוֹם	place	מְקוֹם	מְקוֹמוֹת	מְקוֹמוֹת
נָבִיא	prophet	נְבִיא	נְבִיאִים	נְבִיאֵי

(f) *Bisyllabic nouns with both syllables closed will form the singular construct by shortening the long vowel in the second syllable (since long vowels cannot stand in closed, unaccented syllables).*

Sing. Abs.		Sing. Const.	Pl. Abs.	Pl. Const.
מִדְבָּר	wilderness	מִדְבַּר	(not used)	(not used)
מִגְדָּל	tower	מִגְדַּל	מִגְדָּלִים	מִגְדְּלֵי
מִסְפָּר	number	מִסְפַּר	מִסְפָּרִים	מִסְפְּרֵי
מִשְׁכָּן	tabernacle	מִשְׁכַּן	מִשְׁכָּנוֹת	מִשְׁכְּנוֹת
מִשְׁפָּט	judgment	מִשְׁפַּט	מִשְׁפָּטִים	מִשְׁפְּטֵי

(Note: Two shevas are allowed to stand side by side in the plural construct forms because the first is silent and only the second is vocal.)

(g) *In the case of segholates, the singular construct has the same form as the singular absolute.*

Sing. Abs.		Sing. Const.	Pl. Abs.	Pl. Const.
אֶרֶץ	(f) land	אֶרֶץ	אֲרָצוֹת	אַרְצוֹת
דֶּרֶךְ	way	דֶּרֶךְ	דְּרָכִים	דַּרְכֵי
מֶלֶךְ	king	מֶלֶךְ	מְלָכִים	מַלְכֵי
נַעַר	lad	נַעַר	נְעָרִים	נַעֲרֵי
נֶפֶשׁ	(f) soul	נֶפֶשׁ	נְפָשׁוֹת	נַפְשׁוֹת
סֵפֶר	book	סֵפֶר	סְפָרִים	סִפְרֵי
עֶבֶד	servant	עֶבֶד	עֲבָדִים	עַבְדֵי

(h) *Feminine nouns ending in* הָ *in the singular absolute will form the singular construct by dropping* ה *and replacing it with* ת, *an old feminine ending, and by shortening* ָ *to* ַ, *because of the closed syllable.*

Sing. Abs.		Sing. Const.	Pl. Abs.	Pl. Const.
מַלְכָּה	queen	מַלְכַּת	מְלָכוֹת	מַלְכוֹת
מִצְוָה	commandment	מִצְוַת	מִצְוֹת	מִצְוֹת
שָׁנָה	year	שְׁנַת	שָׁנִים	שְׁנֵי
				שְׁנוֹת
תּוֹרָה	law	תּוֹרַת	תּוֹרוֹת	תּוֹרוֹת

(Note: אִשָּׁה, "woman," is irregular.)

אִשָּׁה	woman	אֵשֶׁת	נָשִׁים	נְשֵׁי

(i) *Nouns built on the pattern of* בַּיִת , *"house," share certain unique characteristics.*

Sing. Abs.		Sing. Const.	Pl. Abs.	Pl. Const.
בַּיִת	house	בֵּית	בָּתִּים	בָּתֵּי
זַיִת	olive tree	זֵית	זֵיתִים	זֵיתֵי
עַיִן	eye	עֵין	עֵינַיִם	עֵינֵי

26.5 *A noun in the construct state never takes the definite article. Whether it is translated as definite or indefinite depends upon the absolute noun to which it is joined.* If the absolute noun is indefinite, then the construct noun must also be indefinite. If the absolute noun is definite, then the construct noun must also be definite. *Please note that a noun is considered definite when it has the definite article or when it is a proper name.*

Examples:

בֶּן־נָבִיא	a son of a prophet (a prophet's son)
בֶּן־הַמֶּלֶךְ	the son of the king (the king's son)
יוֹם חֹשֶׁךְ	a day of darkness
יוֹם יְהוָה	the day of the LORD
דְּבַר שָׁלוֹם	a word of peace
דְּבַר־אֱלֹהִים	the word of God

26.6 *Nothing is allowed to come between nouns that stand in a construct relationship, not even prepositions or conjunctions.* If either of the nouns is modified by an adjective, which is sometimes the case, the adjective is placed last so as not to separate the nouns. This often makes it difficult to determine precisely which of the nouns the adjective was meant to modify. The ambiguity can usually be resolved by examining the context or by noting agreement in gender and number between the designated noun and its modifying adjective.

Examples:

בֶּן־הָאִשָּׁה הַזֹּאת	the son of this woman (1 Kgs. 3:19)
קוֹל אֱלֹהִים חַיִּים	the voice of the living God (Deut. 5:26)
יַד אֱלֹהֵינוּ הַטּוֹבָה עָלֵינוּ	The good hand of our God (was) upon us. (Ezra 8:18)
קָרוֹב יוֹם־יְהוָה הַגָּדוֹל	The great day of the LORD (is) near. (Zeph. 1:14)
דְּבַר הַמֶּלֶךְ הַגָּדוֹל	the word of the great king (2 Kgs. 18:28)
כְּלֵי בֵית הָאֱלֹהִים הַגְּדֹלִים וְהַקְּטַנִּים	the vessels of the house of God, both great and small (2 Chr. 36:18)

26.7 The various nuances of meaning expressed by the construct relationship include the following:

(1) *It may indicate the location or origin of a person or thing.*
Examples:

עָרֵי יְהוּדָה	the cities of Judah (location)
אַנְשֵׁי יְרוּשָׁלַͅם	the men of Jerusalem (origin)

(2) *It may serve as a further description or identification of a person or thing.*
Examples:

יוֹם חֹשֶׁךְ	a day of darkness (kind of day)
סוּסֵי אֵשׁ	horses of fire (kind of horses)
סֵפֶר הַבְּרִית	the book of the covenant (which book?)
אֶרֶץ מִצְרַיִם	the land of Egypt (which land?)

(3) *Most frequently it will be used to show possession or ownership.*
Examples:

בֶּן־הָאִשָּׁה	the son of the woman
דְּבַר אֱלֹהִים	the word of God
שְׂדֵה נָבוֹת	the field of Naboth
רוּחַ אֱלֹהִים	the spirit of God

(4) *Other nuances of meaning will be noted as one begins to read the Hebrew Bible.*

EXERCISES

1. Fill in the blanks in order to complete the following construct relationships:

(1) הָאָרֶץ _____ the people of the earth (Jer. 37:2)

(2) יִשְׂרָאֵל _____ the sons of Israel (Gen. 42:5)

(3) יְהוּדָה _____ the cities of Judah (2 Sam. 2:1)

(4) יְרוּשָׁלַםִ _____ the king of Jerusalem (Josh. 10:1)

(5) יִשְׂרָאֵל _____ the land of Israel (1 Sam. 13:19)

(6) הַמִּדְבָּר _____ the way of the wilderness (Exod. 13:18)

(7) הָעָם _____ the soul of the people (1 Sam. 30:6)

(8) הַמֶּלֶךְ _____ the servants of the king (2 Sam. 16:6)

(9) הָאֱלֹהִים _____ the servant of God (1 Chr. 6:34)

(10) מֹשֶׁה _____ בְּסֵפֶר in the book of the law of Moses (Josh. 8:31)

(11) יִשְׂרָאֵל _____ the house of Israel (Exod. 16:31)

(12) סֵפֶר הַתּוֹרָה _____ the words of the book of the law (2 Kgs. 22:11)

2. Translate the following:

(1) מִיַּד הָאִשָּׁה (Gen. 38:20)

(2) יוֹם הַשַּׁבָּת (Exod. 20:11)

(3) בֶּן־אָדָם (Ezek. 2:1)

(4) מִבְּנֵי־הַנְּבִיאִים (2 Kgs. 2:7)

(5) וּמִבְּנֵי יִשְׂרָאֵל (1 Kgs. 9:22)

(6) בְּנוֹת אַנְשֵׁי הָעִיר (Gen. 24:13)

(7) בְּשֵׁם הַמֶּלֶךְ (Est. 3:12)

(8) רָאשֵׁי הֶהָרִים (Gen. 8:5)

(9) וְאֵלֶּה מַלְכֵי הָאָרֶץ (Josh. 12:1)

(10)   בְּאֶרֶץ בְּנֵי יִשְׂרָאֵל   (Josh. 11:22)

(11)   עַבְדֵי הַמֶּלֶךְ   (1 Sam. 22:17)

(12)   מֹשֶׁה עֶבֶד יְהוָה   (Josh. 1:15)

[Watch for the proper names in #5, 10, and 12.]

3.   Practice pronouncing each of the phrases in #1.

4.   Translate the following:

(1)   כָּל־יְמֵי הָאָרֶץ   (Gen. 8:22)

(2)   דַּם־כָּל־בָּשָׂר   (Lev. 17:14)

(3)   וְלֹא בֶן־נָבִיא אָנֹכִי   (Amos 7:14)

(4)   אִישׁ מִבְּנֵי יִשְׂרָאֵל   (Lev. 17:13)

(5)   בְּהַר צִיּוֹן וּבִירוּשָׁלִַם   (Isa. 10:12)

(6)   שֵׁם אֵשֶׁת־אַבְרָם שָׂרָי   (Gen. 11:29)

(7)   וְאֵלֶּה שְׁמוֹת בְּנֵי יִשְׂרָאֵל   (Exod. 1:1)

(8)   אֶת־דֶּרֶךְ עֵץ הַחַיִּים   (Gen. 3:24)

(9)   בְּתוֹרַת מֹשֶׁה עֶבֶד־הָאֱלֹהִים   (Dan. 9:11)

(10)   כִּי בַת־מֶלֶךְ הִיא   (2 Kgs. 9:34)

2.   Match the following:

( )   כְּכוֹכְבֵי הַשָּׁמַיִם   (A)   For they are merciful kings.
(1 Kgs. 20:31)

( )   בְּנוֹת אַנְשֵׁי הָעִיר   (B)   the book of the law of
the LORD (2 Chr. 17:9)

( )   כִּי מִצְוַת הַמֶּלֶךְ הִיא   (C)   The voice is the voice of Jacob.
(Gen. 27:22)

( )   מִנְּשֵׁי בְנֵי־הַנְּבִיאִים   (D)   and the houses of the kings of
Judah (Jer. 19:13)

( )   וְזֹאת תּוֹרַת הָאָדָם   (E)   the daughters of the men of
the city (Gen. 24:13)

( )   זֹאת תּוֹרַת הַבָּיִת   (F)   as the stars of the heavens
(Gen. 26:4)

( )   סֵפֶר תּוֹרַת יְהוָה   (G)   in the way of the kings of
Israel (2 Kgs. 8:18)

( )   דִּבְרֵי הַנָּבִיא הַהוּא   (H)   from the wives of the sons of
the prophets (2 Kgs. 4:1)

( )   דִּבְרֵי שָׁלוֹם וֶאֱמֶת   (I)   men from the elders of Israel
                                         (Ezek. 14:1)

( )   לְכָל־זִקְנֵי הָאָרֶץ   (J)   the words of that prophet
                                         (Deut. 13:4)

( )   וּדְבַר יְהוָה מִירוּשָׁלָ͏ִם   (K)   words of peace and truth
                                         (Est. 9:30)

( )   וְאֵלֶּה דִּבְרֵי הַסֵּפֶר   (L)   This is the law of the house.
                                         (Ezek. 43:12)

( )   אֲנָשִׁים מִזִּקְנֵי יִשְׂרָאֵל   (M)   concerning the houses of this
                                         city (Jer. 33:4)

( )   עַל־בָּתֵּי הָעִיר הַזֹּאת   (N)   to all the elders of the land
                                         (1 Kgs. 20:7)

( )   וּבָתֵּי מַלְכֵי יְהוּדָה   (O)   and the word of the LORD from
                                         Jerusalem (Isa. 2:3)

( )   בְּדֶרֶךְ מַלְכֵי יִשְׂרָאֵל   (P)   And these are the words of
                                         the book. (Jer. 29:1)

( )   כִּי מַלְכֵי חֶסֶד הֵם   (Q)   For it is the commandment of
                                         the king. (Isa. 36:21)

( )   הֲקֹל קוֹל יַעֲקֹב   (R)   And this is the law of the man.
                                         (2 Sam. 7:19)

6.   Practice pronouncing the Hebrew phrases listed in the previous exercise. Cover
the English translation and practice translating the Hebrew phrases from sight.

VOCABULARY

(1)	אֹהֶל	tent		(10)	כּוֹכָב	star
(2)	אֱמֶת	(f) truth		(11)	כֶּסֶף	silver
(3)	אֵשׁ	(f) fire		(12)	מַלְכָּה	(f) queen
(4)	דָּם	blood		(13)	מִצְרַיִם	Egypt
(5)	זָהָב	gold		(14)	סוּס	horse
(6)	חַיָּה	(f) living thing, animal		(15)	עֵת	(f) time
(7)	חָכְמָה	(f) wisdom		(16)	רֵעַ	friend
(8)	חֶסֶד	goodness, kindness		(17)	פֶּה	mouth
(9)	יַיִן	wine		(18)	תְּהוֹם	(f) great deep, abyss

LESSON XI

27. Pronominal Suffixes on Prepositions and Particles

Pronominal suffixes are shortened forms of personal pronouns (cf. IX.23, p. 52). They may be attached directly to the end of prepositions, particles, nouns, and verbs. When attached directly to prepositions, they serve as objects of the preposition. When attached to particles, they may express a variety of relationships, depending upon the function of the particles. When attached to nouns, they function as possessive pronouns. When affixed to verbs, they normally serve as direct objects of the verbs.

27.1 *Pronominal Suffixes with Prepositions*

(1) The pronominal suffixes for the inseparable prepositions בְּ and לְ are as follows:

1 cs	יִ	me	1 cp	נוּ	us
2 ms	ךָ	you	2 mp	כֶם	you
2 fs	ךְ	you	2 fp	כֶן	you
3 ms	וֹ	him	3 mp	הֶם	them
3 fs	הָ	her	3 fp	הֶן	them

These suffixes should be memorized, since with only minor variations they are the same for all other prepositions and particles.

(a) בְּ "in, by, with"

1 cs	בִּי	with me	1 cp	בָּנוּ	with us
2 ms	בְּךָ	with you	2 mp	בָּכֶם	with you
2 fs	בָּךְ	with you	2 fp	בָּכֶן	with you
3 ms	בּוֹ	with him	3 mp	בָּהֶם	with them
3 fs	בָּהּ	with her	3 fp	בָּהֶן	with them

(b) לְ "to, for, at"

1 cs	לִי	to me	1 cp	לָנוּ	to us
2 ms	לְךָ	to you	2 mp	לָכֶם	to you
2 fs	לָךְ	to you	2 fp	לָכֶן	to you
3 ms	לוֹ	to him	3 mp	לָהֶם	to them
3 fs	לָהּ	to her	3 fp	לָהֶן	to them

(2) The inseparable preposition כְּ is irregular.

1 cs	כָּמוֹנִי	like me	1 cp	כָּמוֹנוּ	like us
2 ms	כָּמוֹךָ	like you	2 mp	כָּכֶם	like you
2 fs			2 fp		
3 ms	כָּמוֹהוּ	like him	3 mp	כָּהֶם	like them
3 fs	כָּמוֹהָ	like her	3 fp	כָּהֵן	like them

(3) Some prepositions take a dagesh forte in the final consonant before pronominal suffixes. (Some of these prepositions also have alternate forms without the dagesh forte.)

(a) אֵת "with" (not to be confused with the particle אֵת, sign of the direct object)

1 cs	אִתִּי, אוֹתִי	with me	1 cp	אִתָּנוּ, אוֹתָנוּ	with us
2 ms	אִתְּךָ, אוֹתְךָ	with you	2 mp	אִתְּכֶם, אֶתְכֶם	with you
2 fs	אִתָּךְ, אוֹתָךְ	with you	2 fp		
3 ms	אִתּוֹ, אוֹתוֹ	with him	3 mp	אִתָּם, אוֹתָם	with them
3 fs	אִתָּהּ	with her	3 fs		

(b) לְבַד "alone, by oneself, by itself" (made up of the preposition לְ, "to," plus the noun בַד, "separation, aloneness," its literal meaning being "in separation, alone")

1 cs	לְבַדִּי	by myself	1 cp		
2 ms	לְבַדְּךָ	by yourself	2 mp	לְבַדְּכֶם	by yourselves
2 fs			2 fp		
3 ms	לְבַדּוֹ	by himself	3 mp	לְבַדָּם	by themselves
3 fs	לְבַדָּהּ	by herself	3 fp	לְבַדְּהֶן	by themselves

(c) עִם "with"

1 cs	עִמָּדִי, עִמִּי	with me	1 cp	עִמָּנוּ	with us
2 ms	עִמָּךְ, עִמְּךָ	with you	2 mp	עִמָּכֶם	with you
2 fs			2 fp		
3 ms	עִמּוֹ	with him	3 ms	עִמָּם, עִמָּהֶם	with them
3 fs	עִמָּהּ	with her	3 fp		

69

(4)   The preposition מִן, "from, away from, more than," is actually duplicated before some of the pronominal suffixes. For example, the first common singular form, מִמֶּנִּי, is made up of מִן־מֶן־נִי, literally "from, from me." The two final nuns are assimilated into the following letters by means of the two dagesh fortes.

1 cs	מִמֶּנִּי	from me	1 cp	מִמֶּנּוּ	from us
2 ms	מִמְּךָ	from you	2 mp	מִכֶּם	from you
2 fs	מִמֵּךְ	from you	2 fp	מִכֶּן	from you
3 ms	מִמֶּנּוּ	from him	3 mp	מֵהֶם	from them
3 fs	מִמֶּנָּה	from her	3 fp	מֵהֶן	from them

Not all of the forms have a duplicated מִן. In some it is only partially duplicated (2 ms, 2 fs), and in others not at all (2 mp, 2 fp, 3 mp, 3 fp). The final nuns are assimilated in all instances except before ה (3 mp, 3 fp). Since ה is a guttural and therefore cannot receive a dagesh forte, the vowel before it must be lengthened (ḥireq to ṣere).

Two of the forms (3 ms and 1 cp) are identical. Only the context makes it possible to distinguish between them.

(5)   A few prepositions take pronominal suffixes that are the same as those that appear on plural nouns. Two of the most common of these prepositions are לִפְנֵי, "before, in front of, in the presence of," and אֶל, "to, unto."

(a)   לִפְנֵי   This form is made up of פְּנֵי, the plural construct form of פָּנִים, which though plural in form is translated simply as "face," plus the preposition לְ, "to." "To the face of" means "before." Compare also עַל־פְּנֵי, "upon the face of."

1 cs	לְפָנַי	before me	1 cp	לְפָנֵינוּ	before us
2 ms	לְפָנֶיךָ	before you	2 mp	לִפְנֵיכֶם	before you
2 fs	לְפָנַיִךְ	before you	2 fp		
3 ms	לְפָנָיו	before him	3 mp	לִפְנֵיהֶם	before them
3 fs	לְפָנֶיהָ	before her	3 fp		

(b)   אֶל   "to, unto"

1 cs	אֵלַי	unto me	1 cp	אֵלֵינוּ	unto us
2 ms	אֵלֶיךָ	unto you	2 mp	אֲלֵיכֶם	unto you
2 fs	אֵלַיִךְ	unto you	2 fp	אֲלֵיכֶן	unto you
3 ms	אֵלָיו	unto him	3 mp	אֲלֵיהֶם	unto them
3 fs	אֵלֶיהָ	unto her	3 fp	אֲלֵיהֶן	unto them

27.2 *Pronominal Suffixes with Particles*

(1) אֵת   the sign of the direct object.

1 cs	אוֹתִי	me	1 cp	אוֹתָנוּ	us
2 ms	אוֹתְךָ	you	2 mp	אֶתְכֶם	you
2 fs	אוֹתָךְ	you	2 fp	אֶתְכֶן	you
3 ms	אוֹתוֹ	him	3 mp	אוֹתָם	them
3 fs	אוֹתָהּ	her	3 fp	אוֹתָן	them

(2) הִנֵּה   "Behold!"

1 cs	הִנְנִי, הִנֵּנִי	behold, I	1 cp	הִנְנוּ, הִנֵּנוּ	behold, we
2 ms	הִנְּךָ	behold, you	2 mp	הִנְּכֶם	behold, you
2 fs	הִנָּךְ	behold, you	2 fp		
3 ms	הִנּוֹ	behold, he	3 mp	הִנָּם	behold, they
3 fs			3 fp		

28. Pronominal Suffixes on Nouns

Pronominal suffixes are affixed to the ends of nouns to show possession. Only nouns in the construct state may receive pronominal suffixes. Thus דְּבָרִי, "my word," is formed of the singular construct דְּבַר and the pronominal ending of the first person common singular, the literal meaning of which is "word of me." Likewise, דְּבָרַי, "my words," is formed of the plural construct דִּבְרֵי and the first person common singular pronominal suffix, the literal meaning of which is "words of me."

A construct noun with a pronominal suffix will always be treated as definite, even though it never takes the definite article. For this reason any attributive adjective placed after such a form must be written with the definite article.

28.1 *Pronominal Suffixes for Singular Nouns (Masculine or Feminine)*

1 cs	ִי	my	1 cp	ֵנוּ	our
2 ms	ְךָ	your	2 mp	ְכֶם	your
2 fs	ֵךְ	your	2 fp	ְכֶן	your
3 ms	וֹ	his	3 mp	ָם	their
3 fs	ָהּ	her	3 fp	ָן	their

Examples:

(a) קוֹל   masculine singular absolute, "voice"

קוֹל   masculine singular construct, "voice of"

1 cs	קוֹלִי	my voice		1 cp	קוֹלֵנוּ	our voice
2 ms	קוֹלְךָ	your voice		2 mp	קוֹלְכֶם	your voice
2 fs	קוֹלֵךְ	your voice		2 fp	קוֹלְכֶן	your voice
3 ms	קוֹלוֹ	his voice		3 mp	קוֹלָם	their voice
3 fs	קוֹלָהּ	her voice		3 fp	קוֹלָן	their voice

(b) תּוֹרָה   feminine singular absolute, "law"

תּוֹרַת   feminine singular construct, "law of"

1 cs	תּוֹרָתִי	my law		1 cp	תּוֹרָתֵנוּ	our law
2 ms	תּוֹרָתְךָ	your law		2 mp	תּוֹרַתְכֶם	your law
2 fs	תּוֹרָתֵךְ	your law		2 fp	תּוֹרַתְכֶן	your law
3 ms	תּוֹרָתוֹ	his law		3 mp	תּוֹרָתָם	their law
3 fs	תּוֹרָתָהּ	her law		3 fp	תּוֹרָתָן	their law

28.2 *Pronominal Suffixes for Plural Nouns (Masculine or Feminine)*

1 cs	ַי	my		1 cp	ֵינוּ	our
2 ms	ֶיךָ	your		2 mp	ֵיכֶם	your
2 fs	ַיִךְ	your		2 fp	ֵיכֶן	your
3 ms	ָיו	his		3 mp	ֵיהֶם	their
3 fs	ֶיהָ	her		3 fp	ֵיהֶן	their

Examples:

(a) אֱלֹהִים   masculine plural absolute, "God, gods"

אֱלֹהֵי   masculine plural construct, "God of, gods of"

1 cs	אֱלֹהַי	my God		1 cp	אֱלֹהֵינוּ	our God
2 ms	אֱלֹהֶיךָ	your God		2 mp	אֱלֹהֵיכֶם	your God
2 fs	אֱלֹהַיִךְ	your God		2 fp	אֱלֹהֵיכֶן	your God
3 ms	אֱלֹהָיו	his God		3 mp	אֱלֹהֵיהֶם	their God
3 fs	אֱלֹהֶיהָ	her God		3 fp	אֱלֹהֵיהֶן	their God

(b)   תּוֹרוֹת   feminine plural absolute, "laws"

        תּוֹרוֹת   feminine plural construct, "laws of"

1 cs	תּוֹרוֹתַי	my laws	1 cp	תּוֹרוֹתֵינוּ	our laws
2 ms	תּוֹרוֹתֶיךָ	your laws	2 mp	תּוֹרוֹתֵיכֶם	your laws
2 fs	תּוֹרוֹתַיִךְ	your laws	2 fp	תּוֹרוֹתֵיכֶן	your laws
3 ms	תּוֹרוֹתָיו	his laws	3 mp	תּוֹרוֹתֵיהֶם	their laws
3 fs	תּוֹרוֹתֶיהָ	her laws	3 fp	תּוֹרוֹתֵיהֶן	their laws

28.3 *Further Examples of Pronominal Suffixes on Nouns, both Regular and Irregular*

(1)   בֵּן   m.s. abs., "son"   בָּנִים   m.p.abs., "sons"

     בֶּן   m.s. const., "son of"   בְּנֵי   m.p.const., "sons of"

1 cs	בְּנִי	my son	1 cs	בָּנַי	my sons
2 ms	בִּנְךָ	your son	2 ms	בָּנֶיךָ	your sons
2 fs	בְּנֵךְ	your son	2 fs	בָּנַיִךְ	your sons
3 ms	בְּנוֹ	his son	3 ms	בָּנָיו	his sons
3 fs	בְּנָהּ	her son	3 fs	בָּנֶיהָ	her sons
1 cp	בְּנֵנוּ	our son	1 cp	בָּנֵינוּ	our sons
2 mp			2 mp	בְּנֵיכֶם	your sons
2 fs			2 fp		
3 mp			3 mp	בְּנֵיהֶם	their sons
3 fp			3 fp	בְּנֵיהֶן	their sons

(2)   אָב   m.s.abs., "father"   אָבוֹת   m.p.abs., "fathers"

     אֲבִי   m.s.const., "father of"   אֲבוֹת   m.p.const., "fathers of"

1 cs	אָבִי	my father	1 cs	אֲבוֹתַי	my fathers
2 ms	אָבִיךָ	your father	2 ms	אֲבוֹתֶיךָ	your fathers
2 fs	אָבִיךְ	your father	2 fs		
3 ms	אָבִיהוּ, אָבִיו	his father	3 ms	אֲבוֹתָיו	his fathers
3 fs	אָבִיהָ	her father	3 fs		

73

1 cp	אָבִינוּ	our father	1 cp	אֲבוֹתֵינוּ	our fathers
2 mp	אֲבִיכֶם	your father	2 mp	אֲבוֹתֵיכֶם	your fathers
2 fp	אֲבִיכֶן	your father	2 fp		
3 mp	אֲבִיהֶם	their father	3 mp	אֲבוֹתֵיהֶם אֲבוֹתָם	their fathers
3 fp	אֲבִיהֶן	their father	3 fp		

(3)	בַּת	f.s.abs., "daughter"	בָּנוֹת	f.p.abs., "daughters"	
	בַּת	f.s.const., "daughter of"	בְּנוֹת	f.p.const., "daughters of"	

1 cs	בִּתִּי	my daughter	1 cs	בְּנוֹתַי	my daughters
2 ms	בִּתְּךָ	your daughter	2 ms	בְּנוֹתֶיךָ	your daughters
2 fs			2 fs	בְּנוֹתַיִךְ	your daughters
3 ms	בִּתּוֹ	his daughter	3 ms	בְּנוֹתָיו	his daughters
3 fs	בִּתָּהּ	her daughter	3 fs	בְּנוֹתֶיהָ	her daughters
1 cp	בִּתֵּנוּ	our daughter	1 cp	בְּנוֹתֵינוּ	our daughters
2 mp	בִּתְּכֶם	your daughter	2 mp	בְּנוֹתֵיכֶם	your daughters
2 fp			2 fp	בְּנוֹתֵיכֶן	your daughters
3 mp			3 mp	בְּנוֹתֵיהֶם	their daughters
3 fp			3 fp	בְּנוֹתֵיהֶן	their daughters

(4)	בַּיִת	m.s.abs., "house"	בָּתִּים	m.p.abs., "houses"	
	בֵּית	m.s.const., "house of"	בָּתֵּי	m.p.const., "houses of"	

1 cs	בֵּיתִי	my house	1 cs	בָּתַּי	my houses
2 ms	בֵּיתְךָ	your house	2 ms	בָּתֶּיךָ	your houses
2 fs	בֵּיתֵךְ	your house	2 fs	בָּתַּיִךְ	your houses
3 ms	בֵּיתוֹ	his house	3 ms	בָּתָּיו	his houses
3 fs	בֵּיתָהּ	her house	3 fs	בָּתֶּיהָ	her houses

1 cp		our houses	1 cp	בָּתֵּינוּ	our houses	
2 mp	בֵּיתְכֶם	your house	2 mp	בָּתֵּיכֶם	your houses	
2 fp			2 fp			
3 mp	בֵּיתָם	their house	3 mp	בָּתֵּיהֶם	their houses	
3 fp			3 fp	בָּתֵּיהֶן	their houses	

(5)   יָד f.s.abs., "hand"   יָדַיִם f.dual abs., "hands"
      יַד_ f.s.const., "hand of"   יְדֵי f.dual const., "hands of"

1 cs	יָדִי	my hand	1 cs	יָדַי	my hands
2 ms	יָדְךָ	your hand	2 ms	יָדֶיךָ	your hands
2 fs	יָדֵךְ	your hand	2 fs	יָדַיִךְ	your hands
3 ms	יָדוֹ	his hand	3 ms	יָדָיו	his hands
3 fs	יָדָהּ	her hand	3 fs	יָדֶיהָ	her hands
1 cp	יָדֵנוּ	our hand	1 cp	יָדֵינוּ	our hands
2 mp	יֶדְכֶם	your hand	2 mp	יְדֵיכֶם	your hands
2 fp			2 fp		
3 mp	יָדָם	their hand	3 mp	יְדֵיהֶם	their hands
3 fp			3 fp	יְדֵיהֶן	their hands

(6)   דָּבָר m.s.abs., "word"   דְּבָרִים m.p.abs., "words"
      דְּבַר m.s.const., "word of"   דִּבְרֵי m.p.const., "words of"

1 cs	דְּבָרִי	my word	1 cs	דְּבָרַי	my words
2 ms	דְּבָרְךָ	your word	2 ms	דְּבָרֶיךָ	your words
2 fs	דְּבָרֵךְ	your word	2 fs	דְּבָרַיִךְ	your hands
3 ms	דְּבָרוֹ	his word	3 ms	דְּבָרָיו	his words
3 fs			3 fs	דְּבָרֶיהָ	her words
1 cp	דְּבָרֵנוּ	our word	1 cp		
2 mp			2 mp	דִּבְרֵיכֶם	your words
2 fp			2 fp		
3 mp			3 mp	דִּבְרֵיהֶם	their words
3 fp			3 fp		

EXERCISES

1. Match the following:

( ) מִדַּרְכּוֹ הָרָעָה   (A) I am your son. (Gen. 27:32)

( ) גָּדוֹל שְׁמוֹ   (B) Our father is old. (Gen. 19:31)

( ) כִּי־גָדוֹל אֱלֹהֵינוּ   (C) You are my God. (Ps. 31:15; Eng. 31:14)

( ) בִּשְׁמִי הַגָּדוֹל   (D) You are my father. (Ps. 89:27; Eng. 89:26)

( ) וְתוֹרַת־יְהוָה אִתָּנוּ   (E) His name is great. (Ps. 76:2; Eng. 76:1)

( ) תָּמִים דַּרְכּוֹ   (F) For the ways of the LORD are right. (Hos. 14:10; Eng. 14:9)

( ) תָּמִים אַתָּה בִּדְרָכֶיךָ   (G) He is my brother. (Gen. 20:5)

( ) כִּי־יָשָׁר דְּבַר־יְהוָה   (H) from his evil way (Jer. 26:3)

( ) כִּי יְשָׁרִים דַּרְכֵי יְהוָה   (I) For God is with us. (Isa. 8:10)

( ) אָבִינוּ זָקֵן   (J) And the law of the LORD is with us. (Jer. 8:8)

( ) יֶשׁ־לָנוּ אָב זָקֵן   (K) For our God is great. (2 Chr. 2:4)

( ) אִישָׁהּ זָקֵן   (L) For I will be with you. (Gen. 26:24)

( ) אֱלֹהַי אַתָּה   (M) His way is perfect. (Ps. 18:31; Eng. 18:30)

( ) אָחִי הוּא   (N) Perfect are you in your ways. (Ezek. 28:15)

( ) כִּי עִמָּנוּ אֵל   (O) We have an old father. (Gen. 44:20)

( ) כִּי־אִתְּךָ אָנֹכִי   (P) by my great name (Jer. 44:26)

( ) אֲנִי בִנְךָ   (Q) For the word of the LORD is upright. (Ps. 33:4)

( ) אָבִי אַתָּה   (R) Her husband was old. (2 Kgs. 4:14)

2. Translate the following:

(1)   אַתָּה אָבִינוּ   (Isa. 63:16)

(2)   מִיַּד הָאִשָּׁה   (Num. 5:25)

(3)   בְּנֵי יִשְׂרָאֵל   (Josh. 9:26)

(4)   בְּיַד עַמִּי יִשְׂרָאֵל   (Ezek. 25:14)

(5)   בְּיַד־נְבִיאֶיךָ   (Neh. 9:30)

(6)   בְּיַד עֲבָדֶיךָ   (Ezra 9:11)

(7)   כִּי לִי כָּל־הָאָרֶץ   (Exod. 19:5)

(8)   וְכָל־אַנְשֵׁי בֵיתוֹ   (Gen. 17:27)

(9)   וּדְבַר אֱלֹהֵינוּ   (Isa. 40:8)

(10)   אֱלֹהֵי אָבִי אַבְרָהָם   (Gen. 32:10)

3. Supply the correct pronouns in order to translate the following entries:

(1)   יְהוָה צְבָאוֹת עִמָּנוּ The LORD of hosts is with _____.
(Ps. 46:12; Eng. 46:11)

(2)   בְּיַד עֲבָדָיו הַנְּבִיאִים by the hand of _____ servants the prophets
(2 Kgs. 24:2)

(3)   מִימֵי אֲבֹתֵינוּ from the days of _____ fathers (Ezra 9:7)

(4)   לָכֶם וְלַאֲבוֹתֵיכֶם to _____ and to _____ fathers
(Jer. 7:14)

(5)   הֵמָּה וַאֲבוֹתָם _____ and _____ fathers (Jer. 9:15;
Eng. 9:16)

(6)   אֱלֹהֵי אֲבוֹתֵיהֶם the God of _____ fathers (1 Chr. 5:25)

(7)   כָּל־בָּנָיו וְכָל־בְּנֹתָיו all _____ sons and all _____
daughters (Gen. 37:35)

(8)   מִפְּרִי יָדֶיהָ from the fruit of _____ hands (Prov. 31:31)

(9)   וְהִנֵּה יָדִי עִמָּךְ Behold, _____ hand is with _____.
(2 Sam. 3:12)

(10)   הִנֵּה כָל־אֲשֶׁר־לוֹ בְּיָדֶךָ Behold, all that _____ has is in
_____ hand. (Job 1:12)

(11)   יָדַי וְרַגְלָי _____ hands and _____ feet (Ps. 22:17; Eng. 22:16)

(12)   אַתֶּם וּבְנֵיכֶם _____ and _____ sons (Deut. 12:12)

4.   Practice reading aloud the Hebrew examples. Cover the English translation and practice translating the Hebrew from sight.

(1)   בְּנִי אַבְשָׁלוֹם בְּנִי בְנִי   My son, Absalom, my son, my son! (2 Sam. 19:5)

(2)   כִּי אֲנִי יְהוָה אֱלֹהֵיכֶם   For I am the LORD your God. (Exod. 6:7)

(3)   כִּי אֵין לָהּ אָב וָאֵם   For she had no father or mother. (Est. 2:7)

(4)   כֵּן אַתֶּם בְּיָדִי בֵּית יִשְׂרָאֵל   So are you in my hand, O house of Israel. (Jer. 18:6)

(5)   הוּא אֲבִי־יִשַׁי אֲבִי דָוִד   He was the father of Jesse, the father of David. (Ruth 4:17)

(6)   וְעַתָּה יְהוָה אָבִינוּ אָתָּה   And now, O LORD, you are our father. (Isa. 64:7)

(7)   עַמֵּךְ עַמִּי וֵאלֹהַיִךְ אֱלֹהָי   Your people shall be my people, and your God my God. (Ruth 1:16)

(8)   אַתָּה אֱלֹהִים לְבַדֶּךָ   You are God alone. (Ps. 86:10)

(9)   בֵּן אֵין לָהּ וְאִישָׁהּ זָקֵן   She has no son, and her husband is old. (2 Kgs. 4:14)

(10)   וּבְבֵיתִי אֵין לֶחֶם   And there is no bread in my house. (Isa. 3:7)

(11)   לִי הַכֶּסֶף וְלִי הַזָּהָב   Mine is the silver, and mine is the gold. (Hag. 2:8)

(12)   וַיהוָה אֱלֹהֵי צְבָאוֹת עִמּוֹ   For the LORD, the God of hosts, was with him. (2 Sam. 5:10)

(13)   כִּי אֲנִי־אֵל וְאֵין עוֹד   For I am God, and there is no other. (Isa. 45:22)

(14) כִּי־לִי בְנֵי־יִשְׂרָאֵל עֲבָדִים
עֲבָדַי הֵם מֵאֶרֶץ מִצְרָיִם
אֲנִי יְהוָה אֱלֹהֵיכֶם

For to me the children of Israel are servants; they are my servants from the land of Egypt; I am the LORD your God. (Lev. 25:55)

(15) יְהוָה אֲדֹנֵינוּ מָה־אַדִּיר
שִׁמְךָ בְּכָל־הָאָרֶץ

O LORD, our Lord, how excellent is your name in all the earth! (Ps. 8:2; Eng. 8:1)

VOCABULARY

(1)	אָהַב	he loved	(11)	עוֹד	again, yet, still
(2)	אָמַר	he said	(12)	עַל־פְּנֵי	over, above
(3)	בָּרָא	he created	(13)	עַתָּה	now
(4)	הָיָה	he was, became	(14)	פֹּה	here
(5)	הָלַךְ	he walked, went	(15)	צְבָאוֹת	hosts, armies
(6)	יָדַע	he knew	(יְהוָה צְבָאוֹת	LORD of hosts)
(7)	יַחְדָּו	together	(16)	שַׁבָּת	(m. and f.) sabbath
(8)	יֶלֶד	child	(17)	שָׁם	there
(9)	כָּבוֹד	glory, honor	(18)	שְׁנֵיהֶם	the two of them
(10)	תֵּבָה	(f) ark			

LESSON XII

29. Verbs: General Characteristics*

29.1 The simplest form for most Hebrew verbs, the form under which they are listed in the lexicon, is the Qal perfect third masculine singular. The word Qal (קַל) comes from קָלַל and means "he (it) was light," i.e., "not heavy." It designates the *simple active stem* of the verb.

29.2 The Qal perfect third masculine singular form of the verb normally has three consonants accompanied by two vowels, thus making it a bisyllabic form. The accent falls on the second syllable. The first syllable is open and always has qameṣ as its vowel. The second syllable is closed, except when it ends in א or ה. When closed, it has pataḥ as its vowel. When open, i.e., when it ends in א or ה, pataḥ is lengthened to qameṣ.

Examples:

(1) אָכַל he ate   (4) יָשַׁב he sat

(2) אָמַר he said   (5) נָשָׂא he took up, lifted up

(3) הָיָה he was   (6) עָשָׂה he did, made

29.3 An exception to this rule occurs in the case of some verbs classified as "stative" verbs. These are verbs that describe a condition or state of being. Most of these follow the same vowel pattern as the verbs listed in the preceding paragraph. However, some appear with either ṣere or ḥolem as the second stem vowel.

Examples:

(1) גָּדַל he was great   (5) זָקֵן he was old

(2) חָזַק he was strong   (6) יָרֵא he was afraid

(3) קָדַשׁ he was holy   (7) יָכֹל he was able

(4) קָרַב he was near   (8) קָטֹן he was small

29.4 In addition to the bisyllabic verbs we have considered thus far, there are also a number of monosyllabic verbs. These originally had either a yod or a vav as the middle consonant. However, in the course of the development of the language, the yod or vav contracted with a preceding vowel to form a diphthong (an unchangeably long vowel) and thus ceased to function as a consonant. Because these verbs are considered as no longer having a middle consonant, they are sometimes referred to as "hollow" verbs. Others describe them as "middle vowel" verbs, or as "middle yod/middle vav" verbs. The form listed in the lexicon as the root for these verbs is the Qal infinitive construct, rather than the Qal perfect third masculine singular.

---

*Refer to Verb Chart 1, pp. 400f., for the conjugation of the strong verb.

Examples:

(1) בּוֹא to go, enter   (4) רוּם to be high, exalted

(2) מוּת to die   (5) שִׂים to put, place

(3) קוּם to arise   (6) שׁוּב to turn, return

In the case of a few verbs ending in ה or ח, the middle yods and middle vavs failed to contract with preceding vowels and therefore continued to function as regular consonants.

Examples:

(1) הָיָה he, it was   (4) קָוָה he waited, hoped

(2) חָיָה he, it lived   (5) רָוַח he revived, was refreshed

(3) צָוָה he commanded

29.5 Hebrew verbs are classified as either "strong" ("sound") or "weak." A strong verb must have three consonants in its Qal perfect third masculine singular form, the form under which it is listed in the lexicon. This automatically requires that middle vowel verbs be classified as weak verbs, since in their lexical form they have only two consonants. Furthermore, a verb is considered weak if one or more of its consonants is a guttural (א, ה, ח, ע, and sometimes ר). A verb is also weak if it begins with either י, ו, or נ, or if its second and third consonants are identical. Subclasses of weak verbs include those that end with ה, and those that either begin or end with א.

29.6 All strong verbs are grouped together in one class. Weak verbs on the other hand, fall into ten separate classes, and grammarians have had to devise names descriptive of each of these classes.

Early grammarians named the various classes of weak verbs on the basis of a paradigm verb chosen for this purpose. They might have chosen any triliteral verb as a basis for the names, but the one they favored was פָּעַל, translated "he did, made." Weak verbs were then organized into separate classes on the basis of how their weak consonants were positioned in relation to the three consonants of the paradigm verb. Thus a verb with an initial guttural was called a Pe guttural; one with a middle guttural, an 'Ayin guttural; one with a final guttural, a Lamed guttural, etc. Many modern grammarians prefer to designate these simply as I-guttural, II-guttural, III-guttural, etc. The following table will demonstrate both the traditional and the modern systems for naming the various classes of weak verbs.

Traditional System				Modern Alternative			
לַ	עֲ	פְּ	Paradigm Verb	III	II	I	Numerical Designation
(1)	ד מַ עֲ		Pe Guttural	(1)	ד מַ עֲ		I – Guttural
(2)	ל אַ שֵׁ		ʿAyin Guttural	(2)	ל אַ שֵׁ		II – Guttural
(3)	ח לַ שָׁ		Lamed Guttural	(3)	ח לַ שָׁ		III – Guttural
(4)	ל כַ אָ		Pe ʾAlef	(4)	ל כַ אָ		I –ʾAlef
(5)	א צָ מָ		Lamed ʾAlef	(5)	א צָ מָ		III – ʾAlef
(6)	ה נָ בָּ		Lamed He	(6)	ה נָ בָּ		III – He
(7)	ל פַ נָ		Pe Nun	(7)	ל פַ נָ		I – Nun
(8)	ב וּ שֵׁ		ʿAyin Vav/ʿAyin	(8)	ב וּ שֵׁ		II – Vav/II – Yod
	ם יֵ שֵׂ		Yod		ם יֵ שֵׂ		(or Hollow Verbs)
(9)	ב שֵׁ יָ		Pe Vav/Pe Yod	(9)	ב שֵׁ יָ		I-Vav/I-Yod
(10)	ב בַ סָ		Double ʿAyin	(10)	ב בַ סָ		Geminate Verbs

29.7 Weak verbs may have more than one weak consonant, thus causing them to exhibit the peculiarities of more than one class of weak verbs. Here are some examples of verbs that are doubly weak:

- (1) חָיָה   Pe Guttural *and* Lamed He (note that yod serves as a regular consonant)
- (2) חָטָא   Pe Guttural *and* Lamed ʾAlef
- (3) נָכָה   Pe Nun *and* Lamed He
- (4) הָלַל   Pe Guttural *and* Double ʿAyin
- (5) יָשַׁע   Pe Vav/Pe Yod *and* Lamed Guttural

29.8 In contrast to weak verbs, a strong verb is one that has no weak letters among its consonants. Compare this representative list of strong verbs with the weak verbs listed above.

- (1) כָּרַת   he cut
- (2) כָּשַׁל   he stumbled
- (3) כָּתַב   he wrote
- (4) מָשַׁל   he ruled
- (5) פָּקַד   he visited, appointed
- (6) קָטַל   he killed
- (7) שָׁכַב   he lay down
- (8) שָׁמַר   he kept

(Note: In two of these verbs — כָּרַת and שָׁמַר — ר does not function as a guttural but as a regular consonant.)

29.9 Time (tense) is not inherent in the form of a Hebrew verb, but is determined by the context in which it stands. Therefore, the same verb form may be translated as past in one context, as present in another, and as future in still another.

The translation suggested for isolated verb forms in this grammar is only for purposes of illustration, and is not meant to preclude the possibility of other translations in other more specific contexts. Isolated perfects, for example, for the sake of consistency, will usually be translated in past time. However, if their contexts were provided, they might just as readily be translated as present or as future.

30. Verbs: The Qal Perfect of the Strong Verb

30.1 Hebrew verbs have two full inflections that cover all possible variations of person, gender, and number. They are known as the perfect inflection and the imperfect inflection. They are terms designed to reflect the state of action of verb forms, and not their time (tense). Perfect verb forms reflect a completed state of action, and imperfect verb forms an incompleted state.

30.2 To form the Qal perfect inflection, one should begin with the verb root (Qal perfect, 3 ms), adding to it a fixed set of pronominal suffixes, and making the changes in vocalization demanded by the addition of the suffixes. The suffixes are remnants of personal pronouns and serve as indicators of person, gender, and number in the verb forms of which they are a part. The same perfect suffixes are used for all stems of all verbs, both weak and strong. *This makes it absolutely imperative that beginning students master the Qal perfect inflection in all its forms. It will serve as the model for all other perfect inflections.*

The suffixes for the Qal perfect are as follows:

3 ms	(none)	he	3 cp	וּ	they
3 fs	הָ	she			
2 ms	תָּ	you	2 mp	תֶּם	you
2 fs	תְּ	you	2 fp	תֶּן	you
1 cs	תִּי	I	1 cp	נוּ	we

[The abbreviation "c" indicates a "common" gender, one that covers both masculine and feminine subjects.]

30.3 The addition of these suffixes to the third masculine singular form of the Qal perfect of שָׁמַר, "he kept," gives these results:

3 ms	שָׁמַר	he kept	3 cp	שָׁמְרוּ	they kept
3 fs	שָׁמְרָה	she kept			
2 ms	שָׁמַרְתָּ	you kept	2 mp	שְׁמַרְתֶּם	you kept
2 fs	שָׁמַרְתְּ	you kept	2 fp	שְׁמַרְתֶּן	you kept
1 cs	שָׁמַרְתִּי	I kept	1 cp	שָׁמַרְנוּ	we kept

30.4 An explanation of the vocalization changes taking place here will aid the student in writing the perfect inflections for other stems of this and other verbs.

(1) The first step in forming the Qal perfect inflection is to begin with the third masculine singular form and prepare to add the various suffixes to it.

(2) The second step is to divide the suffixes into two groups, those that begin with a vowel (vocalic suffixes) and those that begin with a consonant (consonantal suffixes). The vocalization changes will be determined by the kind of suffix a form takes.

(3) There are two vocalic suffixes in the perfect inflections of verbs. They are הָ in the third feminine singular and וּ in the third common plural.

All vocalic suffixes, including even those for the imperfect and imperative inflections, share a common characteristic: *Unless they are preceded by an unchangeably long vowel, they draw the accent to themselves and away from its original position on the second stem syllable.* When the accent shifts to the suffix, the nearest preceding vowel in an open syllable will volatilize (be reduced to a vocal sheva). Furthermore, if a long vowel stands immediately before the vocal sheva, the long vowel must be marked with a secondary accent called a meteg (cf. IV.9, pp. 17–18).

Thus when the vocalic suffix הָ is added to שָׁמַר, "he kept," the resultant form is שָׁמְרָה. Since ר has been pulled away from the preceding syllable to begin a new syllable, the preceding syllable has changed from a closed syllable (מַר) to an open syllable (מַ). Since the accent is on the new syllable (רָה), the vowel in the nearest preceding open syllable (מַ) must volatilize (מַ becomes מְ). And since the vowel immediately preceding the vocal sheva is long, it must receive a meteg. The resultant form for Qal perfect, third feminine singular is שָׁמְרָה, "she kept." By the same process the resultant form for Qal perfect, third common plural is שָׁמְרוּ, "they kept."

(4) All the remaining suffixes begin with a consonant and so are classified as consonantal suffixes. A silent sheva must be placed under the third consonant of שָׁמַר, the Qal perfect third masculine singular form, when consonantal suffixes are added to it. The silent sheva functions as a syllable divider (cf. III.7, p. 13). Thus when the consonantal suffix תָּ (2 ms) is added to שָׁמַר, it is first written שָׁמַרתָּ, and then with the addition of the silent sheva under the third stem consonant it becomes שָׁמַרְתָּ. This form must be accented on the second syllable (שָׁמַרְתָּ) since the only consonantal suffixes that draw the accent to themselves are תֶּם and תֶּן.

The following forms follow a similar pattern:

שָׁמַרְתְּ	(2 fs) becomes	שָׁמַרְתְּ
שָׁמַרְתִּי	(1 cs) becomes	שָׁמַרְתִּי
שָׁמַרְנוּ	(1 cp) becomes	שָׁמַרְנוּ

Among the consonantal suffixes, only תֶּם (2 mp) and תֶּן (2 fp) take the accent. Since the shift in accent to the suffix syllable causes the nearest preceding vowel in an open syllable to volatilize, the following changes must be made in the תֶּם and תֶּן forms.

שְׁמַרְתֶּם   becomes   שְׁמַרְתֶּם

שְׁמַרְתֶּן   becomes   שְׁמַרְתֶּן

Can you explain why the first stem vowel was volatilized and not the second? Can you anticipate what might have happened to the simple vocal sheva if the initial stem consonant had been a guttural instead of a regular consonant?

30.5 The rules for writing the Qal perfect inflection of the verb שָׁמַר are applicable to all other strong verbs. Two further examples will suffice:

The Qal Perfect Inflection of מָשַׁל

3 ms	מָשַׁל	he ruled	3 cp	מָשְׁלוּ	they ruled
3 fs	מָשְׁלָה	she ruled			
2 ms	מָשַׁלְתָּ	you ruled	2 mp	מְשַׁלְתֶּם	you ruled
2 fs	מָשַׁלְתְּ	you ruled	2 fp	מְשַׁלְתֶּן	you ruled
1 cs	מָשַׁלְתִּי	I ruled	1 cp	מָשַׁלְנוּ	we ruled

The Qal Perfect Inflection of פָּקַד

3 ms	פָּקַד	he visited	3 cp	פָּקְדוּ	they visited
3 fs	פָּקְדָה	she visited			
2 ms	פָּקַדְתָּ	you visited	2 mp	פְּקַדְתֶּם	you visited
2 fs	פָּקַדְתְּ	you visited	2 fp	פְּקַדְתֶּן	you visited
1 cs	פָּקַדְתִּי	I visited	1 cp	פָּקַדְנוּ	we visited

31. Verbs: The Meaning of the Perfect

31.1 There are several ways in which the Hebrew perfect may be translated, depending upon the context in which it is used and the kind of action or state of being represented by the verb itself.

(1) A perfect may be translated as a simple action completed in past time.

Examples:

(a)   עַל־כֵּן קָרְאָה שְׁמוֹ דָּן   Therefore she *called* his name Dan. (Gen. 30:6)

(b)   הוּא נָתְנָה־לִּי מִן־הָעֵץ   She *gave* to me from the tree. (Gen. 3:12)

(c)   בְּרֵאשִׁית בָּרָא אֱלֹהִים   In the beginning God *created*. (Gen. 1:1)

(2)   A perfect may be translated as a past perfect, i.e., as an action completed prior to a point of reference in past time.

Examples:

(a)   וַיהוָה פָּקַד אֶת־שָׂרָה כַּאֲשֶׁר אָמָר   And the LORD visited Sarah as *he had said*. (Gen. 21:1)

(b)   נָתְנוּ לוֹ אֶת־הָעִיר אֲשֶׁר שָׁאָל   They gave to him the city which *he had asked*. (Josh. 19:50)

(3)   A perfect may be translated in the present tense when it represents a verb of perception, attitude, disposition, or mental or physical state of being.

Examples:

(a)   וְדֶרֶךְ שָׁלוֹם לֹא יָדָעוּ   And the way of peace *they do not know*. (Isa. 59:8)

(b)   הִנֵּה אַתָּה זָקַנְתָּ   Behold, *you are old*. (1 Sam. 8:5)

(c)   אָהַבְתִּי אֶתְכֶם אָמַר יְהוָה   I *love* (or *have loved*) you, *says* the LORD. (Mal. 1:2)

(4)   A perfect prefixed with vav conjunction will usually be translated in the future tense (cf. XXI.63.2 [2])..

Examples:

(a)   וְשָׁמְרוּ בְנֵי־יִשְׂרָאֵל   And the people of Israel *shall keep*
אֶת־הַשַּׁבָּת   the sabbath. (Exod. 31:16)

(b)   וְשָׁכַבְתִּי עִם־אֲבֹתַי   And I *shall lie down* with my fathers. (Gen. 47:30)

31.2   Note that there is agreement in person, gender, and number between Hebrew verbs and their subjects. This rule applies to all perfects, imperfects, and imperatives.

Examples:

(1)   זֶה־הַיּוֹם עָשָׂה יְהוָה   This (is) the day the LORD made. (Ps. 118:24)

(2)   וְאָמְרָה הָאִשָּׁה אָמֵן אָמֵן   And the woman shall say, "Amen! Amen!" (Num. 5:22)

(3)   וְכָל־הָעָם אָמְרוּ אָמֵן   And all the people said, "Amen!" (Deut. 27:15)

31.3 Pronominal subjects need not be written separately since they are inherent in the verb forms themselves. When subject pronouns are used in addition to verb forms, it is for the sake of clarity or for emphasis.

Examples:

(1)	הוּא נָתְנָה־לִּי מִן־הָעֵץ	*She* (emphatic) gave to me from the tree. (Gen. 3:12)
(2)	וַאֲנִי יָדַעְתִּי גֹּאֲלִי חָי	*And I* (emphatic) know my redeemer lives. (Job 19:25)
(3)	כִּי אַתָּה הַדַּעַת מָאַסְתָּ	Because *you* (emphatic) have rejected knowledge. (Hos. 4:6)

32. Verbs: Word Order in Verbal Sentences

32.1 The normal word order in a Hebrew verbal sentence is first the verb, then the subject (plus any modifiers), and finally the object (plus any modifiers). Note, however, that the negative particle לֹא is placed before the verb.

Examples:

(1)	נָפְלוּ אֲבוֹתֵינוּ בֶּחָרֶב	Our fathers have fallen by the sword. (2 Chr. 29:9)
(2)	לֹא־שָׁמְרוּ אֲבוֹתֵינוּ אֶת־דְּבַר יְהוָה	Our fathers did not keep the word of the LORD. (2 Chr. 34:21)
(3)	אָמַר נָבָל בְּלִבּוֹ אֵין אֱלֹהִים	The fool says in his heart, "There is no God." (Ps. 53:2; Eng. 53:1)

32.2 When a different word order from the one described above is used, it is to emphasize the part of speech that is placed first.

Examples:

(1)	יְהוָה נָתַן וַיהוָה לָקַח	*The LORD* (emphatic) gave, and *the LORD* (emphatic) has taken away. (Job 1:21)
(2)	לֶחֶם לֹא אָכַלְתִּי	*Bread* (emphatic) I have not eaten. (Deut. 9:9)
(3)	דֶּרֶךְ שָׁלוֹם לֹא יָדָעוּ	*The way of peace* (emphatic) they do not know. (Isa. 59:8)
(4)	יְהוָה אֱלֹהֵינוּ כָּרַת עִמָּנוּ בְּרִית בְּחֹרֵב	*The LORD our God* (emphatic) cut (made) with us a covenant in Horeb. (Deut. 5:2)
(5)	וּבִירוּשָׁלַ͏ִם מָלַךְ עַל־כָּל־יִשְׂרָאֵל	*And in Jerusalem* (emphatic) he ruled over all Israel. (2 Sam. 5:5)

33. Verbs: The Use of the Lexicon in the Location and Translation of Verbs

It is important from the very beginning for the student to be able to make an analysis of any new verb form that may be encountered in reading. *The first step* in this process is to isolate and identify all prefixes and suffixes that may be present. *The second step* is to reconstruct the verb root. This will be the Qal perfect third masculine singular form in the case of bisyllabic verbs, and the Qal infinitive construct in the case of monosyllabic verbs. *The third step* is to find the root form in a reliable lexicon in order to determine its meaning. *The fourth step* is to identify the stem to which this particular verb form belongs (we have studied only the Qal stem thus far), and to ascertain whether it is a form of the perfect, the imperfect, the imperative, the infinitives, or the participles (again we have studied only the perfect thus far). Where applicable, the verb form being analyzed must also be identified as to person, gender, and number. Finally on the basis of all this information, the location and translation of the verb form should be written out in full. All the examples given here are Qal perfect forms of bisyllabic verbs.

Examples:

(1)   וְעָבְדוּ אֶת יְהוָה אֱלֹהֵיהֶם (Jer. 30:9)

The verb is the first word in this sentence. If we begin by removing the vav conjunction prefix (וְ) and the suffix (וּ), we are left with three consonants עבד, from which we may make a tentative reconstruction of the verb root. Based on the analogy of other similar verb roots, it should be עָבַד. When we look this root up in Brown, Driver, and Briggs *Hebrew Lexicon* (hereafter referred to simply as *BDB*), we find it listed on pp. 712f. as a verb meaning "to work, serve." Therefore, this form is to be located and translated as follows:

וְעָבְדוּ   Qal pf. (for perfect), 3 cp, plus vav conjunction,
from עָבַד, "he served." Translation: "and they served."

The entire sentence is to be translated: "And they served the LORD their God."

(2)   וְלֹא שָׁמַעְנוּ בְּקוֹל יְהוָה אֱלֹהֵינוּ (Jer. 3:25)

The verb is the second word in this sentence. It has no prefix but does have a suffix (נוּ) which we can readily identify as that of the perfect, first common plural. The reconstructed verb root is שָׁמַע, listed in *BDB*, pp. 1033f., as a verb meaning "to hear." The form is to be located and translated as follows:

שָׁמַעְנוּ   Qal pf., 1 cp, from שָׁמַע, "he heard."
Translation: "we heard."

The sentence is to be translated: "We did not hear (or, listen to) the voice of the LORD our God."

(3)   הִנֵּה שָׁלַחְתִּי לְךָ כֶּסֶף וְזָהָב   (2 Chr. 16:3)

The verb is the second word in this sentence. It has no prefix but does have תִי as its suffix. This can readily be identified as the perfect, first common singular suffix. The reconstructed verb root is שָׁלַח, listed in *BDB*, pp. 1018f., as a verb meaning "to send." The form may be located and translated as follows:

שָׁלַחְתִּי   Qal pf., 1 cs, from שָׁלַח, "he sent."
Translation: "I sent."

The sentence can therefore be translated: "Behold, I sent to you silver and gold."

EXERCISES

1. Write the Qal perfect inflection of מָשַׁל, "he ruled."

3 ms	משל	3 cp	משל
3 fs	משל		
2 ms	משל	2 mp	משל
2 fs	משל	2 fp	משל
1 cs	משל	1 cp	משל

2. Indicate beside each of the following verbs whether it is weak (W) or strong (S).

( )	אָכַל	he ate	( )	מָלַךְ	he reigned
( )	בּוֹא	to go, enter	( )	מָשַׁל	he ruled
( )	בָּרָא	he created	( )	נָתַן	he gave
( )	גָּדַל	he was great	( )	עָשָׂה	he did, made
( )	יָדַע	he knew	( )	קָטַל	he killed
( )	יָשַׁב	he sat, dwelled	( )	שִׂים	to put, place
( )	כָּתַב	he wrote	( )	שָׁכַב	he lay down
( )	לָבַשׁ	he put on, wore	( )	שָׁלַח	he sent
( )	לָקַח	he took	( )	שָׁמַע	he heard, obeyed

3. Each of the following entries contains a Qal perfect form of a verb. Give the correct translation of the verb form by filling in the blank. In the space marked (a) give the person, gender, and number of the verb form; in the space marked (b) give its root.

Example:

וְאֶת־אֲשֶׁר בַּשָּׂדֶה לָקָחוּ   (a)   3 cp

And that which was in the field they __took__.   (b)   לָקַח

(Gen. 34:28)

(1)   וְלֹא־הָלְכוּ בְתוֹרָתִי   (a) _____

And they did not _____ in my law. (Jer. 44:10)   (b) _____

(2)   כִּי שָׁמַעְנוּ אֱלֹהִים עִמָּכֶם   (a) _____

For we have _____ that God is with you. (Zech. 8:23)   (b) _____

(3)   וְלַחֹשֶׁךְ קָרָא לָיְלָה   (a) _____

And to the darkness he _____ night. (Gen. 1:5)   (b) _____

(4)   כָּל־הָעָם אָמְרוּ אָמֵן   (a) _____

All the people _____, "Amen!" (Deut. 27:15)   (b) _____

(5)   אֵשׁ אֱלֹהִים נָפְלָה מִן־הַשָּׁמַיִם   (a) _____

The fire of God _____ from the heavens. (Job 1:16)   (b) _____

(6)   בְּכָל־כֹּחִי עָבַדְתִּי אֶת־אֲבִיכֶן   (a) _____

With all my strength I _____ your father. (Gen. 31:6)   (b) _____

(7)   הָלְכוּ בְנֵי יִשְׂרָאֵל בַּמִּדְבָּר   (a) _____

The people of Israel _____ in the wilderness.   (b) _____

(Josh. 5:6)

(8)   מָצָאנוּ מָיִם   (a) _____

We have _____ water. (Gen. 26:32)   (b) _____

(9)   אָהַבְתָּ רָע מִטּוֹב   (a) _____

You _____ evil more than good. (Ps. 52:5; Eng. 52:3)   (b) _____

(10)   עֲבָדִים מָשְׁלוּ בָנוּ   (a) _____

Servants _____ over us. (Lam. 5:8)   (b) _____

(11)   וְשָׁמְרוּ בְנֵי־יִשְׂרָאֵל אֶת־הַשַּׁבָּת   (a) _____

And the people of Israel shall _____ the sabbath.   (b) _____

(Exod. 31:16)

(12) כַּסְפִּי וּזְהָבִי לְקַחְתֶּם   (a) _____

You have _____ my silver and my gold.   (b) _____
(Joel 4:5; Eng. 3:5)

4. Complete the translation of each entry by supplying the missing pronouns.

(1) וְאֶת־קֹלוֹ שָׁמַעְנוּ And _____ heard _____ voice. (Deut. 5:24)

(2) אֶת־קֹלְךָ שָׁמַעְתִּי בַּגָּן _____ heard _____ voice in the garden.
(Gen. 3:10)

(3) וְאָבִיו וְאִמּוֹ לֹא יָדָעוּ But _____ father and _____ mother
did not know. (Judg. 14:4)

(4) לֹא שָׁמַרְתָּ אֶת־מִצְוַת יְהוָה אֱלֹהֶיךָ _____ have not kept the
commandment of the LORD _____ God. (1 Sam. 13:13)

(5) לֹא־שָׁמְרוּ תוֹרָתֶךָ _____ did not keep _____ law. (Ps. 119:136)

(6) שָׁמַעְתִּי אֶת־תְּפִלָּתְךָ _____ have heard _____ prayer.
(1 Kgs. 9:3)

(7) לֹא שָׁמַעְתָּ בְּקוֹל יְהוָה אֱלֹהֶיךָ _____ have not listened to
the voice of the LORD _____ God. (Deut. 28:45)

(8) וְלֹא שָׁמְעוּ בְּקוֹלִי And _____ have not listened to (obeyed)
_____ voice. (Num. 14:22)

(9) וְלָקַחְתָּ אִשָּׁה לִבְנִי And _____ shall take a wife for _____ son.
(Gen. 24:4)

(10) כִּי־אֹתוֹ אָהַב אֲבִיהֶם For _____ father loved _____. (Gen. 37:4)

5. Translate the following:

(1) כִּי שָׁמַע אֱלֹהִים אֶל־קוֹל הַנַּעַר (Gen. 21:17)
(2) כֹּה־אָמַר יְהוָה אֱלֹהֵי יִשְׂרָאֵל (Exod. 5:1)
(3) וּבִירוּשָׁלַ͏ִם מָלַךְ עַל כָּל־יִשְׂרָאֵל (2 Sam. 5:5)
(4) וּלְכָל־בְּנֵי יִשְׂרָאֵל הָיָה אוֹר (Exod. 10:23)
(5) וּמֹשֶׁה עָלָה אֶל־הָאֱלֹהִים (Exod. 19:3)
(6) כִּי־שָׁכַב דָּוִד עִם־אֲבֹתָיו (1 Kgs. 11:21)
(7) וּדְבָרָיו שָׁמַעְתָּ מִתּוֹךְ הָאֵשׁ (Deut. 4:36)
(8) לֹא שָׁמְרוּ בְּרִית אֱלֹהִים (Ps. 78:10)
(9) לֹא שָׁמְרוּ אֲבוֹתֵינוּ אֶת־דְּבַר יְהוָה (2 Chr. 34:21)
(10) וְלֹא־שָׁמַע עַמִּי לְקוֹלִי (Ps. 81:12; Eng. 81:11)

6. Match the following:

( )   אֹתִי שָׁלַח יְהוָה   (A)   And I shall lie down with my fathers. (Gen. 47:30)

( )   וַיהוָה פָּקַד אֶת־שָׂרָה   (B)   as a sign upon your hand (Exod. 13:9)

( )   וְלַחֹשֶׁךְ קָרָא לָיְלָה   (C)   and the word of the LORD from Jerusalem (Isa. 2:3)

( )   וְשָׁכַבְתִּי עִם־אֲבֹתַי   (D)   the book of the law of the LORD (2 Chr. 34:14)

( )   כִּי־פָּקַד יְהוָה אֶת־עַמּוֹ   (E)   according to the word of the man of God (2 Kgs. 5:14)

( )   לְאוֹת עַל־יָדְךָ   (F)   The LORD visited Sarah. (Gen. 21:1)

( )   כָּל־יְמֵי אָדָם   (G)   that the LORD had visited his people (Ruth 1:6)

( )   כִּדְבַר אִישׁ הָאֱלֹהִים   (H)   the words of that prophet (Deut. 13:4)

( )   וּדְבַר יְהוָה מִירוּשָׁלַ͏ִם   (I)   the God of our fathers (Deut. 26:7)

( )   דִּבְרֵי הַנָּבִיא הַהוּא   (J)   The LORD sent me. (1 Sam. 15:1)

( )   אֶת־סֵפֶר תּוֹרַת־יְהוָה   (K)   all the days of Adam (Gen. 5:5)

( )   אֱלֹהֵי אֲבֹתֵינוּ   (L)   But the darkness he called night. (Gen. 1:5)

7. Practice reading the Hebrew entries aloud. Cover the English translation and practice translating the Hebrew from sight.

(1)   בְּצֶלֶם אֱלֹהִים בָּרָא אֹתוֹ   In the image of God he created him. (Gen. 1:27)

(2)   וּבְנֵי יִשְׂרָאֵל הָלְכוּ בַיַּבָּשָׁה   But (and) the people (sons) of Israel walked on the dry ground. (Exod. 14:29)

(3)   וְקָרָא זֶה אֶל־זֶה וְאָמַר קָדוֹשׁ   And this one called to this one
        קָדוֹשׁ קָדוֹשׁ יְהוָה צְבָאוֹת   and said, "Holy, holy, holy is the LORD of hosts." (Isa. 6:3)

(4)   סֵפֶר נָתַן לִי חִלְקִיָּה הַכֹּהֵן   Hilkiah the priest gave me a book. (2 Kgs. 22:10)

92

(5)   הֵן הָאָדָם הָיָה כְּאַחַד מִמֶּנּוּ   Behold, the man is (has become) like one of us. (Gen. 3:22)

(6)   וְאֵין־דַּעַת אֱלֹהִים בָּאָרֶץ   There is no knowledge of God in the land. (Hos. 4:1)

(7)   עַל־כֵּן קָרְאוּ־לוֹ עִיר דָּוִיד   Therefore they called it the city of David. (1 Chr. 11:7)

(8)   בְּרֵאשִׁית בָּרָא אֱלֹהִים אֵת הַשָּׁמַיִם וְאֵת הָאָרֶץ   In (the) beginning God created the heavens and the earth. (Gen. 1:1)

(9)   אָכֵן יֵשׁ יְהוָה בַּמָּקוֹם הַזֶּה וְאָנֹכִי לֹא יָדָעְתִּי   Surely the LORD is in this place, but I did not know. (Gen. 28:16)

(10)   וְהָאָדָם יָדַע אֶת־חַוָּה אִשְׁתּוֹ   And the man knew Eve his wife. (Gen. 4:1)

(11)   וּמִמִּצְרַיִם קָרָאתִי לִבְנִי   And from Egypt have I called my son. (Hos. 11:1)

(12)   אֶת־קֹלְךָ שָׁמַעְתִּי בַּגָּן   I heard your voice in the garden. (Gen. 3:10)

VOCABULARY

(1)   אוֹ   or
(2)   אוֹת   sign
(3)   אֵל   God
(4)   הִנֵּה , הֵן   behold
(5)   זֶרַע   seed
(6)   חֲצִי   half
(7)   לָקַח   he took
(8)   מָלַךְ   he reigned, became king
(9)   מָצָא   he found

(10)   נָפַל   he fell
(11)   עָבַד   he served
(12)   עָלָה   he went up
(13)   פָּקַד   he visited, appointed
(14)   קָרָא   he called
(15)   שָׁכַב   he lay down
(16)   שָׁלַח   he sent
(17)   שָׁמַע   he heard, obeyed
(18)   שָׁמַר   he kept

LESSON XIII

34. Interrogative Sentences

34.1 A simple yes-or-no question is normally introduced by the interrogative הֲ, which is prefixed to the first word in the sentence. The rules for writing interrogative הֲ are these:

(1) Before non-gutturals supported by a full vowel, interrogative הֲ is pointed הֲ.

Examples:

(a) הֲזֶה אֲחִיכֶם הַקָּטֹן Is this your youngest brother? (Gen. 43:29)

(b) הֲלֹא־חֹשֶׁךְ יוֹם יְהוָה Is not the day of the LORD darkness? (Amos 5:20)

(c) הֲכֶלֶב אָנֹכִי Am I a dog? (1 Sam. 17:43)

(d) הֲיֵשׁ לָכֶם אָח Is there to you a brother? (Do you have a brother?) (Gen. 43:7)

(2) Before gutturals supported by a full vowel (other than qameṣ or qameṣ-ḥaṭuf), interrogative הֲ is written הַ.

Examples:

(a) הַעוֹד לָכֶם אָח Is there yet to you a brother? (Do you have another brother?) (Gen. 43:6)

(b) הַאֵין פֹּה נָבִיא Is there no prophet here? (2 Kgs. 3:11)

(c) הַעֶבֶד יִשְׂרָאֵל Is Israel a slave? (Jer. 2:14)

(d) הַאַתָּה אִישׁ־הָאֱלֹהִים Are you the man of God? (1 Kgs. 13:14)

(3) Before gutturals supported by either a qameṣ or a qameṣ-ḥaṭuf, interrogative הֲ is pointed הֶ.

Examples:

(a) כִּי־אֶל־אֵל הֶאָמַר For has one said to God? (Job 34:31)

(b) הֶאָנֹכִי הָרִיתִי אֵת כָּל־ Did I conceive (from הָרָה)
הָעָם הַזֶּה all this people? (Num. 11:12)

(c) הֶחָזָק הוּא Is he strong? (Num. 13:18)

(4) Before all consonants supported by a vocal sheva, whether simple or compound, interrogative הֲ is written הַ.

Examples:

(a) הַבְרָכָה אַחַת הִוא־לְךָ   Do you have one blessing,
אָבִי   my father? (Gen. 27:38)

(b) הַאֱלֹהִים אָנִי   Am I God? (2 Kgs. 5:7)

(c) הַמְעַט הָעָם אִם־רָב   Are the people few or many?
(Num. 13:18)

34.2 Questions may also be introduced by the interrogative pronouns מִי (who?) and מָה (what?). The first refers to people and the second to things. Neither of these is inflected for gender or number.

(1) מִי usually stands alone, but is sometimes joined to the following word by a maqqef. Its form remains the same in either case.

Examples:

(a) מִי אַתָּה בְּנִי   Who are you, my son? (Gen. 27:18)

(b) מִי הָאֲנָשִׁים הָאֵלֶּה   Who are these men? (Num. 22:9)

(c) מִי־אֵל כָּמוֹךָ   Who is a God like you? (Mic. 7:18)

(d) מִי־לִי בַשָּׁמַיִם   Whom have I (who is to me?)
in heaven? (Ps. 73:25)

(2) מָה occasionally stands alone, but is more likely to be joined to the following word by a maqqef. When joining occurs, it usually alters the pointing of מָה. The following rules will cover most of the changes.

(a) Before non-gutturals, it is written מַה־, followed by a dagesh forte in the first consonant of the next word.

Examples:

מַה־שְּׁמֶךָ   What is your name? (Gen. 32:28)

מַה־זֹּאת   What is this? (Exod. 13:14)

מַה־יֶּשׁ־לָךְ בַּבָּיִת   What is there to you in the house?
(What do you have in the house?)
(2 Kgs. 4:2)

וּמַה־שֶּׁם־בְּנוֹ   And what is his son's name?
(Prov. 30:4)

(b) Before the gutturals א, ה, and ר, it is usually written either as מָה or מָה־. (Note, however, that before ה it is sometimes written as מַה־.)

Examples:

מָה־הַדָּבָר הַזֶּה   What is this thing? (Exod. 18:14)

מָה אַרְצֶךָ   What is your land (country)? (Jon. 1:8)

95

מָה הֶעָרִים הָאֵלֶּה   What are these cities? (1 Kgs. 9:13)

מַה־הִיא   What is it? (Zech. 5:6)

מָה־אָדָם   What is man? (Ps. 144:3)

      (c) Before the gutturals ח and ע, the interrogative מָה is usually written as מֶה־ or מֶה.
Examples:

מֶה־עֲוֹנִי וּמֶה־חַטָּאתִי   What is my iniquity, and what is my sin? (1 Sam. 20:1)

וּמֶה עַז מֵאֲרִי   And what is stronger than a lion? (Judg. 14:18)

מֶה עַבְדֶּךָ   What is your servant? (2 Sam. 9:8)

34.3 Questions may also be introduced by interrogative adverbs. Some of the more common are these:

(1)	אֵי	Where?	(6)	אֵיךְ	How?	
(2)	אַיֵּה	Where?	(7)	אָנָה, אָן	Whither? To what place?	
(3)	אֵיפֹה	Where?	(8)	(לָמָה, לָמֶה)	Why? To what purpose?	
(4)	מֵאַיִן	Whence? From where?		(מַה plus ל)		
(5)	אֵי־מִזֶּה	Whence? From where?	(9)	מַדּוּעַ	Why?	

(אֵי plus מִן plus זֶה)

Examples:

(a)   אֵי הֶבֶל אָחִיךָ   Where is Abel your brother? (Gen. 4:9)

(b)   אַיֵּה שָׂרָה אִשְׁתֶּךָ   Where is Sarah your wife? (Gen. 18:9)

(c)   אֵיפֹה שְׁמוּאֵל וְדָוִד   Where are Samuel and David? (1 Sam. 19:22)

(d)   אַחַי מֵאַיִן אַתֶּם   My brothers, where are you from? (Gen. 29:4)

(e)   מַדּוּעַ אַתָּה לְבַדֶּךָ   Why are you alone? (1 Sam. 21:2)

35. The Numerals

35.1 The following tables include the cardinal numerals from 1 to 10 and the ordinal numerals from 1st to 10th. A cardinal numeral is used in counting, as *one*, *two*, *three*, etc. An ordinal numeral expresses consecution or position in a series,, as *first*, *second*, *third*, etc.

	Cardinals				Ordinals		
	Masculine		Feminine			Masculine	Feminine
	Absolute	Construct	Absolute	Construct			
1	אֶחָד	אַחַד	אַחַת	אַחַת	1st	רִאשׁוֹן	רִאשׁוֹנָה
2	שְׁנַיִם	שְׁנֵי	שְׁתַּיִם	שְׁתֵּי	2nd	שֵׁנִי	שֵׁנִית
3	שָׁלוֹשׁ	שְׁלֹשׁ	שְׁלֹשָׁה	שְׁלֹשֶׁת	3rd	שְׁלִישִׁי	שְׁלִישִׁית
4	אַרְבַּע	אַרְבַּע	אַרְבָּעָה	אַרְבַּעַת	4th	רְבִיעִי	רְבִיעִית
5	חָמֵשׁ	חֲמֵשׁ	חֲמִשָּׁה	חֲמֵשֶׁת	5th	חֲמִישִׁי	חֲמִישִׁית
6	שֵׁשׁ	שֵׁשׁ	שִׁשָּׁה	שֵׁשֶׁת	6th	שִׁשִּׁי	שִׁשִּׁית
7	שֶׁבַע	שֶׁבַע	שִׁבְעָה	שִׁבְעַת	7th	שְׁבִיעִי	שְׁבִיעִית
8	שְׁמֹנֶה	שְׁמֹנֶה	שְׁמֹנָה	שְׁמֹנַת	8th	שְׁמִינִי	שְׁמִינִית
9	תֵּשַׁע	תְּשַׁע	תִּשְׁעָה	תִּשְׁעַת	9th	תְּשִׁיעִי	תְּשִׁיעִית
10	עֶשֶׂר	עֶשֶׂר	עֲשָׂרָה	עֲשֶׂרֶת	10th	עֲשִׂירִי	עֲשִׂירִית

(1) The numeral *one* (m. אֶחָד, f. אַחַת) is classified as an adjective. It follows the noun it modifies and agrees with it in gender.

Examples: יוֹם אֶחָד one day, תּוֹרָה אַחַת one law.

(2) The numerals 2 – 10 also function as adjectives, although they are classified as nouns. In their absolute forms, they may stand either before or after the nouns they modify. In their construct forms, however, they must stand before the nouns they modify.

Examples:

(a) שְׁנַיִם אֲנָשִׁים two men   שְׁנֵי אֲנָשִׁים two men

(b) נָשִׁים שְׁתַּיִם two women (wives)   שְׁתֵּי נָשִׁים two women (wives)

(3) The numeral *two* agrees in gender with the noun it modifies (see the examples given above). The numerals 3 – 10, however, follow a different pattern. When they modify masculine nouns they take the feminine form; when they modify feminine nouns, they take the masculine form. There is no satisfactory explanation for this phenomenon. Note that this rule does not apply to ordinals, since they regularly agree in gender with the nouns they modify.

Examples:

(a) שְׁנֵי בָנִים two sons   שְׁתֵּי בָנוֹת two daughters
(nouns and numerals *agree* in gender)

(b) שְׁלֹשָׁה בָנִים three sons   שָׁלוֹשׁ בָּנוֹת three daughters
(nouns and numerals *disagree* in gender)

(4) The absolute and construct forms of numerals can be used interchangeably, with no apparent difference in meaning.

Examples:

(a)   שְׁלֹשָׁה יָמִים   three days   שְׁלֹשֶׁת יָמִים   three days

(b)   שְׁלֹשָׁה אֲנָשִׁים   three men   שְׁלֹשֶׁת אֲנָשִׁים   three men

(c)   אַרְבָּעָה בָנִים   four sons

(d)   וְאַרְבַּעַת בָּנָיו עִמּוֹ   and his four sons with him

(5) Because numerals are nouns, the numerals from 2 – 10 may receive pronominal suffixes. Suffixes can only be added to the construct forms of the numerals. Most of these occur with the numeral 2.

Examples:

(a)   שְׁנֵינוּ   the two of us (Gen. 31:37)

(b)   שְׁנֵיכֶם   the two of you (Gen. 27:45)

(c)   שְׁנֵיהֶם   the two of them (Gen. 2:25)

35.2 *Cardinal Numerals From 11 to 19*

	With Masculine Nouns	With Feminine Nouns
11	אַחַד עָשָׂר	אַחַת עֶשְׂרֵה
	עַשְׁתֵּי עָשָׂר	עַשְׁתֵּי עֶשְׂרֵה
12	שְׁנֵים עָשָׂר	שְׁתֵּים עֶשְׂרֵה
	שְׁנֵי עָשָׂר	שְׁתֵּי עֶשְׂרֵה
13	שְׁלֹשָׁה עָשָׂר	שְׁלֹשׁ עֶשְׂרֵה
14	אַרְבָּעָה עָשָׂר	אַרְבַּע עֶשְׂרֵה
15	חֲמִשָּׁה עָשָׂר	חֲמֵשׁ עֶשְׂרֵה
16	שִׁשָּׁה עָשָׂר	שֵׁשׁ עֶשְׂרֵה
17	שִׁבְעָה עָשָׂר	שְׁבַע עֶשְׂרֵה
18	שְׁמֹנָה עָשָׂר	שְׁמֹנֶה עֶשְׂרֵה
19	תִּשְׁעָה עָשָׂר	תְּשַׁע עֶשְׂרֵה

(1) The units (1,2,3 etc.) are placed before the word for ten, which in the masculine is עָשָׂר and in the feminine עֶשְׂרֵה.

(2) The numerals from 11 to 19 agree in gender with the nouns to which they refer. They also normally occur with plural forms of nouns, although a few nouns (e.g., אִישׁ, "man," יוֹם, "day," שָׁנָה, "year," נֶפֶשׁ, "soul, self, being") may remain in their singular forms when they stand after these numerals.

Examples:

    (a)   אַחַד עָשָׂר יוֹם, "11 days"

    (b)   אַחַד עָשָׂר אִישׁ, "11 men"

    (c)   אַחַת עֶשְׂרֵה שָׁנָה, "11 years"

35.3 *Cardinal Numerals From 20 to 99*

20	עֶשְׂרִים	(the plural of ten, עֶשֶׂר)
21 (m)	עֶשְׂרִים וְאֶחָד	(or אֶחָד וְעֶשְׂרִים
(f)	עֶשְׂרִים וְאַחַת	(or אַחַת וְעֶשְׂרִים
22 (m)	עֶשְׂרִים וּשְׁנַיִם	

23–29 (like the above)

30	שְׁלֹשִׁים	(From 30 through 90, the tens are the plural forms of the units 3 through 9.)

31 (m)	שְׁלֹשִׁים וְאֶחָד

32 – 39 (like the above)

40	אַרְבָּעִים

41–49 (like the above)

50	חֲמִשִּׁים

51 – 59 (like the above)

60	שִׁשִּׁים

61 – 69 (like the above)

70	שִׁבְעִים

71–79 (like the above)

80	שְׁמֹנִים

81–89 (like the above)

90	תִּשְׁעִים

91 – 99 (like the above)

35.4 *Cardinal Numerals Above 99*

100	מֵאָה	(always feminine; construct form is מְאַת; plural form is מֵאוֹת, "hundreds")

200	מָאתַיִם	(dual: lit., "a pair, or couple of hundreds")
300	שְׁלֹשׁ מֵאוֹת	(note the masc. const. שְׁלֹשׁ)
400	אַרְבַּע מֵאוֹת	
500 – 900 (like the above)		
1000	אֶלֶף	(masc.) (plural אֲלָפִים)
2000	אַלְפַּיִם	(dual)
3000	שְׁלֹשֶׁת אֲלָפִים	(note the fem. const. שְׁלֹשֶׁת)
4000	אַרְבַּעַת אֲלָפִים	etc.

35.5 *The Numeral Values of the Letters of the Alphabet (a post-biblical development)*

א = 1	ב = 2	ג = 3	ד = 4	ה = 5
ו = 6	ז = 7	ח = 8	ט = 9	י = 10
יא = 11	יב = 12	יג = 13	יד = 14	טו = 15

(ט = 9; ו = 6: 9 + 6 = 15. This method of counting was used in order to avoid writing יה and יו, both of which were used as abbreviations of the divine name יהוה)

טז = 16	יז = 17	יח = 18	יט = 19
כ = 20	כא – כט	= 21 – 29	
ל = 30	לא – לט	= 31 – 39	
מ = 40	מא – מט	= 41 – 49	
נ = 50	נא – נט	= 51 – 59	
ס = 60	סא – סט	= 61 – 69	
ע = 70	עא – עט	= 71 – 79	
פ = 80	פא – פט	= 81 – 89	
צ = 90	צא – צט	= 91 – 99	
ק = 100	קא – קט	= 101 – 109	
קי = 110	קיא–קיט	= 111 – 119	

etc.

EXERCISES

1. Fill in the blanks with the correct pronouns.

(1)   מַה־הַדָּבָר הָרָע הַזֶּה   _____ is _____ evil thing? (Neh. 13:17)

(2)   אַיֵּה כְבוֹדִי   Where is _____ glory (honor)? (Mal. 1:6)

(3)   וּמִי כָמוֹךָ בְּיִשְׂרָאֵל   And _____ is like _____ in Israel?
(1 Sam. 26:15)

(4)   הֲלֹא יְהוָה אֱלֹהֵיכֶם עִמָּכֶם   Is not the LORD _____ God with
_____? (1 Chr. 22:18)

(5)   הֲלֹא כָל־הָאָרֶץ לְפָנֶיךָ   Is not all the land before _____?
(Gen. 13:9)

(6)   מִי אַתָּה בְּנִי   _____ are _____, _____ son?
(Gen. 27:18)

(7)   מִי־אָתָּה   _____ are _____? (Gen. 27:32)

(8)   לְמִי־אַתָּה   _____ are _____? (Gen. 32:18; Eng. 32:17)

(9)   מַה־שְּׁמֶךָ   _____ is _____ name? (Gen. 32:28)

(10)   מִי הָאֲנָשִׁים הָאֵלֶּה עִמָּךְ   _____ are _____ men with
_____? (Num. 22:9)

(11)   מַזֶּה בְיָדֶךָ   _____ is _____ in _____ hand? (Exod. 4:2)

(12)   הֲזֶה אֲחִיכֶם הַקָּטֹן   Is _____ _____ youngest brother?
(Gen. 43:29)

(13)   אַחַי מֵאַיִן אַתֶּם   _____ brothers, where are _____ from?
(Gen. 29:4)

(14)   וְאַיֵּה נְבִיאֵיכֶם   And where are _____ prophets? (Jer. 37:19)

(15)   אֲחֹתִי הוּא   _____ is _____ sister. (Gen. 26:9)

2. Match the following:

( )   מַה־שֶּׁם־בְּנוֹ   (A)   Where is Sarah your wife? (Gen. 18:9)

( )   הֲלֹא הוּא אָבִיךָ   (B)   Where is your God? (Ps. 42:4; Eng. 42:3)

( )   מִי זֶה מֶלֶךְ הַכָּבוֹד   (C)   the LORD God of your fathers
(Deut. 1:21)

( )　　אַיֵּה שָׂרָה אִשְׁתֶּךָ　　　(D) What is his son's name? (Prov. 30:4)

( )　　אַיֵּה אֱלֹהֵיהֶם　　　　(E) Do they not belong to us? (Gen. 34:23)

( )　　אַיֵּה אֱלֹהֶיךָ　　　　(F) in the days of your fathers (Joel 1:2)

( )　　יְהוָה אֱלֹהֵי אֲבֹתֶיךָ　(G) Is he not your father? (Deut. 32:6)

( )　　יְהוָה אֱלֹהֵי אֲבוֹתָיו　(H) Was not this my word? (Jon. 4:2)

( )　　בִּימֵי אֲבֹתֵיכֶם　　　(I) you and your fathers (Jer. 44:3)

( )　　הֲלוֹא־זֶה דְבָרִי　　　(J) Who is this king of glory? (Ps. 24:8)

( )　　אַתֶּם וַאֲבֹתֵיכֶם　　　(K) Where is their God? (Joel 2:17)

( )　　הֲלוֹא לָנוּ הֵם　　　　(L) the LORD God of his fathers
　　　　　　　　　　　　　　　　(2 Chr. 30:19)

3. Match the following:

( )　　שְׁנֵיהֶם יַחְדָּו　　　(A) in one day (Isa. 10:17)

( )　　בֵּין שְׁנֵיהֶם　　　　(B) on the fifth day (Num. 7:36)

( )　　שְׁנֵיהֶם לְבַדָּם　　(C) on the sixth day (Exod. 16:5)

( )　　בֵּין שְׁנֵינוּ　　　　(D) on the tenth day (Num. 7:66)

( )　　בַּיּוֹם הַשְּׁמִינִי　　(E) on the second day (Num. 7:18)

( )　　בַּיּוֹם אֶחָד　　　　(F) the two of them alone (1 Kgs. 11:29)

( )　　בַּיּוֹם הַשִּׁשִּׁי　　(G) on the ninth day (Num. 7:60)

( )　　בַּיּוֹם הַשֵּׁנִי　　　(H) on the third day (Gen. 22:4)

( )　　בַּיּוֹם הַחֲמִישִׁי　　(I) between the two of us (Gen. 31:37)

( )　　בַּיּוֹם הָעֲשִׂירִי　　(J) on the seventh day (Exod. 16:27)

( )　　בַּיּוֹם הָרִאשׁוֹן　　(K) between the two of them
　　　　　　　　　　　　　　　　(Exod. 22:10; Eng. 22:11)

( )　　בַּיּוֹם הַשְּׁלִישִׁי　　(L) on the fourth day (Num. 7:30)

( )　　בַּיּוֹם הַשְּׁבִיעִי　　(M) on the first day (Exod. 12:15)

( )　　בַּיּוֹם הָרְבִיעִי　　(N) on the eighth day (Exod. 22:29;
　　　　　　　　　　　　　　　　Eng. 22:30)

( )　　בַּיּוֹם הַתְּשִׁיעִי　　(O) the two of them together (Gen. 22:6)

4. Answer the following questions by translating the Hebrew phrases.

Example:

On which day did God rest?

בַּיּוֹם הַשְּׁבִיעִי (Gen. 2:2)

Answer: "on the seventh day"

(1)   What was the total length of David's reign?

אַרְבָּעִים שָׁנָה (2 Sam. 5:4)

Answer:

(2)   How long did David reign in Hebron?

שֶׁבַע שָׁנִים וְשִׁשָּׁה חֳדָשִׁים (2 Sam. 5:5)

Answer:

(3)   How long did David reign in Jerusalem?

שְׁלֹשִׁים וְשָׁלֹשׁ שָׁנָה (2 Sam. 5:5)

Answer:

(4)   How long did it rain?

אַרְבָּעִים יוֹם וְאַרְבָּעִים לָיְלָה (Gen. 7:12)

Answer:

(5)   How long did Adam live?

תְּשַׁע מֵאוֹת שָׁנָה וּשְׁלֹשִׁים שָׁנָה (Gen. 5:5)

Answer:

(6)   How long did Methuselah live?

תֵּשַׁע וְשִׁשִּׁים שָׁנָה וּתְשַׁע מֵאוֹת שָׁנָה (Gen. 5:27)

Answer:

(7)   How long did Abraham live?

מְאַת שָׁנָה וְשִׁבְעִים שָׁנָה וְחָמֵשׁ שָׁנִים (Gen. 25:7)

Answer:

(8)   How long did Sarah live?

מֵאָה שָׁנָה וְעֶשְׂרִים שָׁנָה וְשֶׁבַע שָׁנִים (Gen. 23:1)

Answer:

(9)   How long did the Israelites remain in Egypt?

שְׁלֹשִׁים שָׁנָה וְאַרְבַּע מֵאוֹת שָׁנָה (Exod. 12:40)

Answer:

(10)   How many faithful Israelites had not bowed the knee to Baal?

שִׁבְעַת אֲלָפִים (1 Kgs. 19:18)

Answer:

(11)   How many men participated in the exodus from Egypt?

שֵׁשׁ־מֵאוֹת אֶלֶף (Exod. 12:37)

Answer:

(12)   How many sons and daughters were born to Job?

שִׁבְעָה בָנִים וְשָׁלוֹשׁ בָּנוֹת (Job 1:2)

Answer:

(13)   How many sheep did Job own?

אַרְבָּעָה עָשָׂר אֶלֶף (Job 42:12)

Answer:

(14)   How many camels did Job own?

שֵׁשֶׁת אֲלָפִים (Job 42:12)

Answer:

(15)   When was Passover celebrated?

בְּאַרְבָּעָה עָשָׂר לַחֹדֶשׁ הָרִאשׁוֹן (2 Chr. 35:1)

Answer:

(16)   How old was Abram when he left Haran?

חָמֵשׁ שָׁנִים וְשִׁבְעִים שָׁנָה (Gen. 12:4)

Answer:

(17)   How many trained warriors did Abram have in his household?

שְׁמֹנָה עָשָׂר וּשְׁלֹשׁ מֵאוֹת (Gen. 14:14)

Answer:

(18)   How many sons were born to Jacob?

שְׁנֵים עָשָׂר (Gen. 35:22)

Answer:

5. Each of the following entries contains a Qal perfect form of a Hebrew verb. Complete the translation of the verb forms by filling in the blanks. In the space marked (a) give the person, gender, and number of the form, and in (b) give its root (Qal perfect 3 ms).

Example:

וּקְרָאתֶם בְּשֵׁם אֱלֹהֵיכֶם And you shall ___call___   (a) ___2 mp___

on the name of your gods. (1 Kgs. 18:24)   (b) ___קָרָא___

(1) וּמִמִּצְרַיִם קָרָאתִי לִבְנִי And from Egypt I _____   (a) _____

my son. (Hos. 11:1)   (b) _____

(2) עַל־כֵּן קָרְאָה שְׁמוֹ יְהוּדָה Therefore she _____   (a) _____

his name Judah. (Gen. 29:35)   (b) _____

(3) אֵיךְ כָּתַבְתָּ אֵת כָּל־הַדְּבָרִים הָאֵלֶּה How did you   (a) _____

_____ all these words? (Jer. 36:17)   (b) _____

(4) לָמָּה לֹא־הָלַכְתָּ עִמִּי Why did you not _____   (a) _____

with me? (2 Sam. 19:26)   (b) _____

(5) לָמָה אָמַרְתָּ אֲחֹתִי הִוא Why did you _____, "She   (a) _____

is my sister"? (Gen. 12:19)   (b) _____

(6) אֵיךְ נָפַלְתָּ מִשָּׁמַיִם How you have _____ from   (a) _____

heaven! (Isa. 14:12)   (b) _____

(7) לֹא יָדַעְתִּי אֵי מִזֶּה הֵמָּה I do not _____ where   (a) _____

they are from. (1 Sam. 25:11)   (b) _____

(8) מַה־יָּדַעְתָּ What do you _____? (Job 15:9)   (a) _____

   (b) _____

(9) וְאָמְרוּ־לִי מַה־שְּׁמוֹ And they shall _____ to   (a) _____

me, "What is his name?" (Exod. 3:13)   (b) _____

(10) הֲלֹא יְדַעְתֶּם מָה־אֵלֶּה Do you not _____ what   (a) _____

these are? (Ezek. 17:12)   (b) _____

(11) לֹא יָדַעְנוּ מֶה־הָיָה לוֹ We do not _____ what   (a) _____

has become of him. (Exod. 32:1)   (b) _____

(12) וּשְׁנֵיהֶם עָמְדוּ עַל־הַיַּרְדֵּן And the two of them   (a) _____

_____ beside the Jordan. (2 Kgs. 2:7)   (b) _____

6. Practice reading the Hebrew aloud.   Cover the English and practice translating from sight.

(1)   יְהוָה אֱלֹהֵינוּ יְהוָה אֶחָד

The LORD our God, the LORD is one.

(Deut. 6:4)

(2)   הֲשָׁלוֹם לָךְ הֲשָׁלוֹם לְאִישֵׁךְ הֲשָׁלוֹם לַיָּלֶד

Is it well with you? Is it well with your husband? Is it well with the child? (2 Kgs. 4:26)

(3)   יְהוָה אֱלֹהֵינוּ עִמָּנוּ

The LORD our God is with us. (1 Kgs. 8:57)

(4)   וְכָל־מִצְוֹתֶיךָ אֱמֶת

And all your commandments are true. (Ps. 119:151)

(5)   מִי הָאֲנָשִׁים הָאֵלֶּה עִמָּךְ

Who are these men with you? (Num. 22:9)

(6)   הֲלוֹא־אָח עֵשָׂו לְיַעֲקֹב

Was not Esau brother to Jacob? (Mal. 1:2)

(7)   הֲלוֹא אָב אֶחָד לְכֻלָּנוּ

Is there not one father to all of us? (Mal. 2:10)

(8)   לָמָּה גָּנַבְתָּ אֶת־אֱלֹהָי

Why have you stolen my gods? (Gen. 31:30)

(9)   וְלָמָּה לֹא־שָׁמַעְתָּ בְּקוֹל יְהוָה

And why have you not listened to the voice of the LORD? (1 Sam. 15:19)

(10)   מַה־זֹּאת עָשָׂה אֱלֹהִים לָנוּ

What is this that God has done to us? (Gen. 42:28)

(11)   כִּי לֹא יָדְעוּ מַה־הוּא

For they did not know what it was. (Exod. 16:15)

(12)   כִּי מִי עָמַד בְּסוֹד יְהוָה

For who has stood in the council of the LORD? (Jer. 23:18)

(13)   טוֹבִים הַשְּׁנַיִם מִן־הָאֶחָד

Two are better than one. (Eccl. 4:9)

(14)   וּמָלַךְ יְהוָה עֲלֵיהֶם בְּהַר צִיּוֹן

And the LORD will reign over them on Mount Zion. (Mic. 4:7)

(15)   עַל־כֵּן קָרְאוּ־לוֹ עִיר דָּוִיד

Therefore they called it the city of David. (1 Chr. 11:7)

VOCABULARY

(1)	אָכַל	he ate	(10)	לָכֵן	therefore	
(2)	גָּנַב	he stole	(11)	מַלְכוּת	(f) kingdom	
(3)	דְּמוּת	(f) likeness, image	(12)	נֶגֶב	Negev, dry country, south	
(4)	דַּעַת	(f) knowledge	(13)	נָתַן	he gave	
(5)	הַיּוֹם	today	(14)	עָמַד	he stood	
(6)	הֵיכָל	temple	(15)	עָשָׂה	he did, made	
(7)	חֹדֶשׁ	new moon, month	(16)	צֹאן	flock, sheep	
(8)	חוֹמָה	(f) wall	(17)	צַדִּיק	righteous one	
(9)	כָּתַב	he wrote	(18)	צֶלֶם	image, likeness	

LESSON XIV

36. Verbs: The Remaining Stems

The seven stems of Hebrew verbs are Qal, Nif‘al, Pi‘el, Pu‘al, Hitpa‘el, Hif‘il, and Hof‘al. Qal (קַל) comes from the verb root קָלַל, "he (it) was light (not heavy)." As its name indicates, it is the simple active stem.

The names of the remaining stems are derived from the verb root פָּעַל, "he did, made." These names, unlike that of Qal, are in no way descriptive of the nature and function of the stems themselves. They are merely the names given to them when פָּעַל was still being used as the paradigm form for Hebrew verbs. The decision by early grammarians to use it for this purpose was an unfortunate one, since it had a guttural as its middle consonant and thus fell within the category of weak verbs. For this reason, later grammarians stopped using it, and substituted in its place strong verbs such as כָּתַב, "he wrote," מָשַׁל, "he ruled," פָּקַד, "he visited, appointed," קָטַל, "he killed," and שָׁמַר, "he kept." However, most modern grammarians continue to refer to the verb stems by their traditional names, names assigned to them when פָּעַל was still being used as the paradigm verb. (We learned earlier that the traditional names for the various classes of weak verbs were also derived from פָּעַל.) The following list gives the names of the verb stems, written first in Hebrew and then transliterated.

(1)　　　קַל　　Qal (Simple Active)

(2)　　נִפְעַל　　Nif‘al (Simple Passive or Reflexive)

(3)　　פִּעֵל　　Pi‘el (Intensive Active or Causative)

(4)　　פֻּעַל　　Pu‘al (Intensive Passive)

(5)　　הִתְפַּעֵל　　Hitpa‘el (Reflexive)

(6)　　הִפְעִיל　　Hif‘il (Causative Active)

(7)　　הָפְעַל　　Hof‘al (Causative Passive)

For the sake of convenience, verb charts appearing in this grammar will designate Nif‘al forms as passive and Pi‘el forms as intensive active.

36.1 *Nif‘al* (נִפְעַל)

(1) In most verb roots the Nif‘al functions as the simple passive, in contrast to Qal, which functions as the simple active.
Examples:

Qal (3 ms)		Nif‘al (3 ms)	
לָכַד	he captured	נִלְכַּד	he was captured
שָׁבַר	he broke	נִשְׁבַּר	he was broken
שָׁמַע	he heard	נִשְׁמַע	he was heard

108

(2) In a few verb roots, Nif‘al expresses a reflexive action, an action the subject performs upon himself/herself.

Examples:

Qal (3 ms)		Nif‘al (3 ms)	
סָתַר	he hid (something)	נִסְתַּר	he hid himself
שָׁמַר	he kept (something)	נִשְׁמַר	he kept himself

(3) In some verb roots, where there are no Qal forms, the Nif‘al has a meaning quite similar to the Qal.

Examples:

Nif‘al (3 ms)

נִלְחַם	he fought	נִשְׁבַּע	he swore

36.2 *Pi‘el* (פִּעֵל)

Pi‘el, Pu‘al, and Hitpa‘el are classified as *intensive* stems. Pi‘el is active (or causative), Pu‘al is passive, and Hitpa‘el is reflexive. The feature that these three stems share in common is the doubling of the middle consonant of the verb root, except when this consonant is a guttural.

(1) The most common use of the Pi‘el is as the intensification of the Qal.

Examples:

Qal (3 ms)		Pi‘el (3 ms)	
נָשַׁק	he kissed	נִשֵּׁק	he kissed repeatedly
שָׁבַר	he broke	שִׁבֵּר	he shattered

(2) A surprisingly large number of verbs are used in the Pi‘el to express the causative sense, much like the Hif‘il. Most of these are either stative verbs or weak verbs, which explains the occurrence of pataḥ as the second vowel in the 3 ms form.

Examples:

Qal (3 ms)		Pi‘el (3 ms)	
אָבַד	he perished	אִבַּד	he destroyed
גָּדַל	he was great	גִּדַּל	he exalted (made great)
לָמַד	he learned	לִמַּד	he taught
קָדֵשׁ	he was holy	קִדַּשׁ	he consecrated

(3) In some verbs, where there are no Qal forms, the Pi‘el is used without any apparent causative or intensive force, i.e., as the simple active. Several

of the verbs listed here are weak verbs.
Examples:

Pi'el (3 ms)

בִּקֵּשׁ   he sought   דִּבֶּר   he spoke   הִלֵּל   he praised

36.3 *Pu'al* (פֻּעַל)

Pu'al is the passive of Pi'el, and like Pi'el, has a dagesh forte in the middle consonant of the verb root (except, of course, when the middle consonant is a guttural, in which case the preceding vowel has to be lengthened).

Since Pu'al is the passive of Pi'el, its meaning is more uniform and more predictable than that of the other stems.
Examples:

Pi'el (3 ms)		Pu'al (3 ms)	
בִּקֵּשׁ	he sought	בֻּקַּשׁ	he was sought
הִלֵּל	he praised	הֻלַּל	he was praised
לִמַּד	he taught	לֻמַּד	he was taught
קִדַּשׁ	he consecrated	קֻדַּשׁ	he was consecrated

36.4 *Hitpa'el* (הִתְפָּעֵל)

Hitpa'el forms can be identified by their longer prefixes and by the doubling of the middle consonant of their verb roots.

(1) Hitpa'el forms normally express a reflexive action, i.e., an action performed by the subject upon himself/herself.
Examples:

Qal (3 ms)		Hitpa'el (3 ms)	
אָמֵץ	he was strong	הִתְאַמֵּץ	he strengthened himself
נָפַל	he fell	הִתְנַפֵּל	he prostrated himself
נָשָׂא	he lifted, took up	הִתְנַשֵּׂא	he exalted himself
קָדַשׁ	he was holy	הִתְקַדֵּשׁ	he sanctified himself

(2) Some Hitpa'el verb forms are similar in meaning to those of the Qal stem, i.e., they are translated as simple active.
Examples:

Hitpa'el (3 ms)

הִתְהַלֵּךְ	he walked to and fro	הִתְפַּלֵּל	he prayed, interceded
הִתְחַנֵּן	he implored, entreated	הִתְנַבֵּא	he prophesied, raved
הִתְיַצֵּב	he took his stand		

(3) When the prefix of any Hitpaʿel form precedes the sibilants ס, צ, שׂ, or שׁ, the ת of the prefix and the sibilant itself will change positions in the word. The change is made in order to facilitate pronunciation of the form.

Examples:

הִתְשַׁמֵּר, "he took heed to himself," becomes הִשְׁתַּמֵּר

הִתְסַתֵּר, "he hid himself,"   becomes הִסְתַּתֵּר

A further change takes place when the sibilant is a צ. In this case the ת of the prefix and the צ of the verb root not only change positions within the word but the ת is also changed to ט.

Example:

הִתְצַדֵּק, "he justified himself," becomes first הִצְתַּדֵּק

and finally הִצְטַדֵּק

A further change takes place when the ת of the prefix precedes ד, ט, or another ת. In this case the ת of the prefix is assimilated into the following consonant by means of a dagesh forte.

Examples:

הִתְטַהֵר, "he purified himself," becomes הִטַּהֵר

הִתְטַמֵּא, "he defiled himself,"   becomes הִטַּמֵּא

36.5 Hifʿil (הִפְעִיל)

The Hifʿil stem has a prefixed ה throughout the perfect inflection.

(1) Hifʿil verbs normally serve as the causative of the Qal. Note the weak verbs in the list below.

Qal (3 ms)		Hifʿil (3 ms)	
יָדַע	he knew	הוֹדִיעַ	he caused to know
יָצָא	he went out	הוֹצִיא	he brought out
עָבַר	he passed over	הֶעֱבִיר	he brought over
עָמַד	he stood	הֶעֱמִיד	he caused to stand
שָׁכַן	he dwelled	הִשְׁכִּין	he caused to dwell
שָׁמַע	he heard	הִשְׁמִיעַ	he proclaimed, announced

(2) Hifʿil verbs are sometimes used in a declaratory sense. The subject of the verb declares someone else to be in a certain condition or state of being.

111

Examples:

	Qal (3 ms)		Hif'il (3 ms)
צָדֵק	he was righteous, just	הִצְדִּיק	he declared righteous, just; he justified
רָשַׁע	he was unjust, wicked	הִרְשִׁיעַ	he declared unjust, guilty; he condemned

(3)   Some Hif'il verbs have a meaning that is more like the simple active of the Qal stem than the causative. Brackets indicate verb roots that do not usually occur in the Qal stem.

Examples:

	Qal (3 ms)		Hif'il (3 ms)
[יֹשַׁע]	he saved	הוֹשִׁיעַ	he saved, delivered
כָּרַת	he cut off	הִכְרִית	he cut off, destroyed
[סתר]	he hid, concealed	הִסְתִּיר	he hid, concealed
שָׂכַל	he was prudent, wise	הִשְׂכִּיל	he was wise, prudent, prosperous, successful
[שׁכם]	he arose early	הִשְׁכִּים	he arose early, started (doing something) early
[שׁלך]	he cast, threw	הִשְׁלִיךְ	he cast, threw
[שׁמד]	he destroyed	הִשְׁמִיד	he destroyed, exterminated

(4)   Some Hif'il verbs do not seem to fit into any of the above categories. Their meaning can best be understood by a careful examination of the context in which they stand.

36.6 *Hof'al* (הָפְעַל)

The Hof'al stem, like the Hif'il, has a prefixed ה in all perfects. The Hof'al is the passive of the Hif'il. Most of the verbs listed below are weak verbs. This is because very few of the strong verbs appear in the Hof'al stem.

Examples:

	Hif'il (3 ms)		Hof'al (3 ms)
הֵבִיא	he brought (בּוֹא)	הוּבָא	he (it) was brought
הִגִּיד	he announced, told [נגד]	הֻגַּד	it was announced, told
הִכָּה	he smote [נכה]	הֻכָּה	he was smitten
הֵמִית	he killed (מוּת)	הוּמַת	he was killed

112

הִמְלִיךְ   he made (someone) king   הָמְלַךְ   he was made king
(מָלַךְ)

הִצִּיל   he delivered, rescued   הֻצַּל   he was delivered,
[נצל]   rescued

37. Verbs: The Remaining Perfects of the Strong Verb

The Qal perfect of the strong verb was presented in an earlier lesson (XII.30, pp. 83–85). There it was stressed that the Qal perfect furnished the pattern for the perfects of the other six stems of the verb.

This is illustrated in the tables that follow.

Table 1

	Qal (קַל) Perfect			Nif‘al (נִפְעַל) Perfect		
3 ms	מָשַׁל		he ruled	נִמְשַׁל		he was ruled
3 fs	מָ שְׁלָה		she ruled	נִמְ שְׁלָה		she was ruled
2 ms	מָ שַׁלְתָּ		you ruled	נִמְ שַׁלְתָּ		you were ruled
2 fs	מָ שַׁלְתְּ		you ruled	נִמְ שַׁלְתְּ		you were ruled
1 cs	מָ שַׁלְתִּי		I ruled	נִמְ שַׁלְתִּי		I was ruled
3 cp	מָ שְׁלוּ		they ruled	נִמְ שְׁלוּ		they were ruled
2 mp	מָ שַׁלְתֶּם		you ruled	נִמְ שַׁלְתֶּם		you were ruled
2 fp	מָ שַׁלְתֶּן		you ruled	נִמְ שַׁלְתֶּן		you were ruled
1 cp	מָ שַׁלְנוּ		we ruled	נִמְ שַׁלְנוּ		we were ruled

Notes:

(A) The spaces left between the first and second stem consonants are merely for the purpose of pointing out the similarities as well as the differences between the Qal perfect and the Nif‘al perfect.

(B) Note that the Nif‘al perfect third masculine singular form has the same vowels as are found in the name of the stem (נִמְשַׁל → נִפְעַל).

(C) The prefix נ combines with the first stem consonant to form a closed syllable (נִמְ) and this continues unchanged throughout the Nif‘al perfect inflection of מָשַׁל.

(D) In all other respects Nif‘al perfect forms are identical to Qal perfect forms. This can be seen by comparing what lies left of the spaces placed in the Qal perfect and the Nif‘al perfect. *Once again, this underscores the importance of mastering the Qal perfect inflection of the strong verb.*

Table 2

	Qal (קַל) Perfect			Piʿel (פִּעֵל) Perfect		
3 ms	מָשַׁל		he ruled	מִשֵּׁל		he ruled (with force)
3 fs	מָ שְׁלָה		she ruled	מִ שְּׁלָה		she ruled (with force)
2 ms	מָ שַׁלְתָּ		you ruled	מִ שַּׁלְתָּ		you ruled (with force)
2 fs	מָ שַׁלְתְּ		you ruled	מִ שַּׁלְתְּ		you ruled (with force)
1 cs	מָ שַׁלְתִּי		I ruled	מִ שַּׁלְתִּי		I ruled (with force)
3 cp	מָ שְׁלוּ		they ruled	מִ שְּׁלוּ		they ruled (with force)
2 mp	מְ שַׁלְתֶּם		you ruled	מִ שַּׁלְתֶּם		you ruled (with force)
2 fp	מְ שַׁלְתֶּן		you ruled	מִ שַּׁלְתֶּן		you ruled (with force)
1 cp	מָ שַׁלְנוּ		we ruled	מִ שַּׁלְנוּ		we ruled (with force)

Notes:

(A)   Piʿel has no prefix in the perfect. The three stems that have no prefix in the perfect are Qal, Piʿel, and Puʿal.

(B)   Piʿel perfect third masculine singular form has the same vowels as are found in the name of the stem (מִשֵּׁל ← פִּעֵל).

(C)   Note that ḥireq, which stands beneath the first stem consonant of the Piʿel perfect third masculine singular form, continues unchanged throughout the entire Piʿel perfect inflection.

(D)   The second stem vowel in the Piʿel perfect third masculine singular form is ṣere. In all other forms of the Piʿel perfect, however, this vowel reverts to pataḥ, just as in the corresponding forms of the Qal perfect.

(E)   Note that there is a dagesh forte in the middle consonant of the verb root in all Piʿel verb forms. This is true of all strong verbs throughout the Piʿel stem.

(F)   Except for the doubling of the middle stem consonant and the placing of the ḥireq under the first stem consonant, all Piʿel perfect forms are patterned after the corresponding forms of the Qal perfect. This can be seen by comparing the Piʿel perfect with the Qal perfect in the table given above.

Table 3

	Qal (קַל) Perfect			Puʿal (פֻּעַל) Perfect		
3 ms	מָשַׁל		he ruled	מֻשַּׁל		he was ruled (with force)
3 fs	מָ שְׁלָה		she ruled	מֻ שְּׁלָה		she was ruled (with force)
2 ms	מָ שַׁלְתָּ		you ruled	מֻ שַּׁלְתָּ		you were ruled (with force)
2 fs	מָ שַׁלְתְּ		you ruled	מֻ שַּׁלְתְּ		you were ruled (with force)
1 cs	מָ שַׁלְתִּי		I ruled	מֻ שַּׁלְתִּי		I was ruled (with force)

3 cp	מֻ	שְׁלוּ	they ruled	מֻ	שְׁלוּ	they were ruled (with force)
2 mp	מֻ	שַׁלְתֶּם	you ruled	מֻ	שַׁלְתֶּם	you were ruled (with force)
2 fp	מֻ	שַׁלְתֶּן	you ruled	מֻ	שַׁלְתֶּן	you were ruled (with force)
1 cp	מֻ	שַׁלְנוּ	we ruled	מֻ	שַׁלְנוּ	we were ruled (with force)

Notes:

(A) Puʻal has no prefix in the perfect.

(B) Puʻal perfect, third masculine singular has the same vowels as are found in the name of the stem (פֻּעַל → מֻשַּׁל).

(C) Qibbuṣ appears under the first stem consonant in all forms of the Puʻal perfect.

(D) The middle stem consonant is doubled throughout the Puʻal perfect inflection.

(E) In all other aspects the Puʻal perfect is patterned after the Qal perfect.

(F) Puʻal forms of the verb are intensive passive, as over against the intensive active of the Piʻel.

Table 4

	Qal (קַל) Perfect			Hitpaʻel (הִתְפַּעֵל) Perfect	
3 ms	מָשַׁל		he ruled	הִתְמַשֵּׁל	he ruled himself
3 fs	מָ	שְׁלָה	she ruled	הִתְמַ שְּׁלָה	she ruled herself
2 ms	מָ	שַׁלְתָּ	you ruled	הִתְמַ שַּׁלְתָּ	you ruled yourself
2 fs	מָ	שַׁלְתְּ	you ruled	הִתְמַ שַּׁלְתְּ	you ruled yourself
1 cs	מָ	שַׁלְתִּי	I ruled	הִתְמַ שַּׁלְתִּי	I ruled myself
3 cp	מָ	שְׁלוּ	they ruled	הִתְמַ שְּׁלוּ	they ruled themselves
2 mp	מְ	שַׁלְתֶּם	you ruled	הִתְמַ שַּׁלְתֶּם	you ruled yourselves
2 fp	מְ	שַׁלְתֶּן	you ruled	הִתְמַ שַּׁלְתֶּן	you ruled yourselves
1 cp	מָ	שַׁלְנוּ	we ruled	הִתְמַ שַּׁלְנוּ	we ruled ourselves

Notes:

(A) All Hitpaʻel perfect forms are prefixed with הִתְ, which is a closed syllable. It is the longest prefix of any of the verb stems.

(B) The third masculine singular form of Hitpaʻel perfect has the same vowels as are found in the name of the stem (הִתְפַּעֵל → הִתְמַשֵּׁל).

(C) The pataḥ under the first stem consonant of the third masculine singular form is continued in all other forms of the Hitpaʻel perfect.

(D) The doubling in the middle stem consonant in all Hitpaʻel forms is characteristic of this stem.

(E) In all other aspects Hitpaʻel perfects are patterned after Qal perfects.

(F) Hitpaʻel is normally reflexive in meaning.

Table 5

	Qal (קַל) Perfect			Hif‘il (הִפְעִיל) Perfect		
3 ms	מָשַׁל		he ruled	הִמְשִׁיל		he caused to rule
3 fs	מָ שְׁלָה		she ruled	הִמְ שִׁילָה		she caused to rule
2 ms	מָ שַׁלְתָּ		you ruled	הִמְ שַׁלְתָּ		you caused to rule
2 fs	מָ שַׁלְתְּ		you ruled	הִמְ שַׁלְתְּ		you caused to rule
1 cs	מָ שַׁלְתִּי		I ruled	הִמְ שַׁלְתִּי		I caused to rule
3 cp	מָ שְׁלוּ		they ruled	הִמְ שִׁילוּ		they caused to rule
2 mp	מְ שַׁלְתֶּם		you ruled	הִמְ שַׁלְתֶּם		you caused to rule
2 fp	מְ שַׁלְתֶּן		you ruled	הִמְ שַׁלְתֶּן		you caused to rule
1 cp	מָ שַׁלְנוּ		we ruled	הִמְ שַׁלְנוּ		we caused to rule

Notes:

(A)   All Hif‘il perfects are prefixed with הִ (he plus ḥireq). This combines with the first stem consonant to form a closed syllable (הִמְ) and this continues unchanged throughtout the Hif‘il perfect inflection.

(B)   The third masculine singular form of Hif‘il perfect has the same vowels as are found in the name of the stem (הִמְשִׁיל ← הִפְעִיל).

(C)   We learned earlier that vocalic afformatives draw the accent to themselves, causing the nearest preceding vowel in an open syllable to volatilize (be reduced to a vocal sheva). The only exception to this is the Hif‘il stem of the verb. Vocalic afformatives of the Hif‘il stem do not draw the accent to themselves. This is because the vowel before vocalic afformatives in the Hif'il stem is ḥireq–yod, which, because it is unchangeably long and thus cannot be volatilized, must retain the accent. This affects the writing of Hif‘il perfect third feminine singular, and Hif‘il perfect third common plural.

(D)   In all other respects, Hif‘il perfects are patterned after Qal perfects.

Table 6

	Qal (קַל) Perfect			Hof‘al (הֻפְעַל) Perfect		
3 ms	מָשַׁל		he ruled	הֻמְשַׁל		he was caused to rule
3 fs	מָ שְׁלָה		she ruled	הָמְ שְׁלָה		she was caused to rule
2 ms	מָ שַׁלְתָּ		you ruled	הָמְ שַׁלְתָּ		you were caused to rule
2 fs	מָ שַׁלְתְּ		you ruled	הָמְ שַׁלְתְּ		you were caused to rule
1 cs	מָ שַׁלְתִּי		I ruled	הָמְ שַׁלְתִּי		I was caused to rule

3 cp	מָ שְׁלוּ		they ruled	הָמְ שְׁלוּ	they were caused to rule
2 mp	מְ שַׁלְתֶּם		you ruled	הָמְ שַׁלְתֶּם	you were caused to rule
2 fp	מְ שַׁלְתֶּן		you ruled	הָמְ שַׁלְתֶּן	you were caused to rule
1 cp	מָ שַׁלְנוּ		we ruled	הָמְ שַׁלְנוּ	we were caused to rule

Notes:

(A) All Hof'al perfects are prefixed with הָ (he plus qames–hatuf). This combines with the first stem consonant to form a closed syllable (הָמְ) and this continues unchanged throughout the Hof'al perfect inflection.

(B) The third masculine singular form of Hof'al perfect has the same vowels as are found in the name of the stem (הָמְשַׁל → הָפְעַל).

(C) In all other respects, Hof'al perfects are patterned after Qal perfects.

38. Verbs: Locating and Translating Perfect Forms of the Hebrew Verb

There are certain guidelines that help to simplify the task of locating and translating perfect forms of Hebrew verbs.

38.1 The first step is to determine whether or not there are any prefixes on the verb form under consideration. Remember that only the Nif'al, Hitpa'el, Hif'il, and Hof'al stems carry prefixes in the perfect. Remember also that a vav conjunction, "and," may be prefixed to any verb form of any stem.

38.2 If there is no prefix on the perfect, except perhaps a vav conjunction, then the form is either Qal, Pi'el, or Pu'al, because these are the only stems that are not prefixed in the perfect. Once it has been determined that the form is not prefixed, it is relatively easy to determine whether it is Qal (simple active), Pi'el (intensive active), or Pu'al (intensive passive), since both Pi'el and Pu'al have a dagesh forte in the middle consonant.

38.3 If the perfect form is prefixed, then the prefix must be isolated from the three consonants of the verb root and identified as to its stem.

(1)   נ   is the prefix for the Nif'al perfect.

(2)   הִת   is the prefix for the Hitpa'el perfect.

(3)   הִ   is the prefix for the Hif'il perfect.

(4)   הָ   is the prefix for the Hof'al perfect.

38.4 Having isolated and identified the prefix of a perfect form and having identified the stem to which it belongs, the next step is to isolate and analyze the suffixes to determine the person, gender, and number of the form. The only form of the perfect that has no suffix is the third masculine singular. The other suffixes are these:

(1)	הָ	(3 fs)	(5)	וּ	(3 cp)
(2)	תָ	(2 ms)	(6)	תֶּם	(2 mp)
(3)	תְּ	(2 fs)	(7)	תֶּן	(2 fp)
(4)	תִּי	(1 cs)	(8)	נוּ	(1 cp)

38.5 The next step is to reconstruct the verb root from the consonants that remain after all prefixes and suffixes have been removed. In all strong verbs, and even in most weak verbs, there will be three consonants left over from which to reconstruct the verb root.

38.6 The final step is to find the verb root in *BDB* (or some other reliable Hebrew lexicon) to determine its meaning in the stem to which this particular form belongs.

These steps having been completed, it is possible to write out a full location and translation of the verb form under consideration.

Examples:

(1) בִּקֵּשׁ אֶת־יְהוָה אֱלֹהֵי יִשְׂרָאֵל

The verb in this clause is בִּקֵּשׁ. It has no prefix and must therefore belong either to the Qal, the Piʿel, or the Puʿal stem. Doubling in the middle consonant indicates it is intensive and the vowels used in it indicate that it is Piʿel. It has no afformative and therefore must be the third masculine singular form. The three stem consonants are בקשׁ, which are listed in *BDB*, p. 134, as [בָּקַשׁ], bracketed to show that the verb root is not used in the Qal stem in the Hebrew Bible. The meaning given for the verb root is "to seek."

בִּקֵּשׁ   Piʿel pf. 3 ms from [בקשׁ], "he sought"
Translation: "he sought"
Translation of the entire clause:
"He sought the LORD, the God of Israel."

(2) וּבִקְשׁוּ שָׁלוֹם

The verb is וּבִקְשׁוּ. It is prefixed with vav conjunction but has no stem prefix. This means it is either Qal, Piʿel, or Puʿal. It cannot be Qal, otherwise the vowels would be different (and also because [בקשׁ] is not used in the Qal stem). But if it were Piʿel or Puʿal, we would expect to find a dagesh forte in the middle consonant. However, dagesh forte tends to drop out whenever the consonant in which it is placed is supported by a vocal sheva. This is what has occurred in the present situation and the verb does in fact belong to the Piʿel stem. The ending indicates that it is third person common plural.

וּבִקְשׁוּ Piʻel pf. 3 cp, plus vav conjunction,
from [בקשׁ], "he sought"
Translation: "and they sought"
Translation of the entire clause: "And they sought
peace."

(3) הִבְדַּלְתִּי אֶתְכֶם מִן־הָעַמִּים

The verb in this clause is הִבְדַּלְתִּי. It is prefixed with הִ, which is the prefix for Hifʻil perfect. The suffix is תִּי, which fixes the person, gender, and number as first person common singular. The remaining consonants are בדל, listed in *BDB*, p. 95, as [בָּדַל], bracketed to show that it does not appear in the Qal stem in the Hebrew Bible. The verb root means "to be divided, separate."

הִבְדַּלְתִּי Hifʻil pf. 1 cs, from [בדל], "he divided, separated"
Translation: "I separated, divided"
Translation of the entire clause: "I separated
you from the peoples."

(4) הִמְלִיךְ אֶת־שָׁאוּל עַל־יִשְׂרָאֵל

The verb in this clause is הִמְלִיךְ. The prefix is הִ, the prefix of the Hifʻil perfect. The form has no suffix and therefore has to be classified as third masculine singular. The verb root is מָלַךְ, listed on p. 573 of *BDB* as a denominative verb, i.e., a verb derived from a noun (מֶלֶךְ, "king"). The verb signifies "to become king, to reign." In the Hifʻil it has a causative force and means "to cause (someone) to be king," or "to cause (someone) to reign."

הִמְלִיךְ Hifʻil pf. 3 ms, from מָלַךְ, "he reigned"
Translation: "he caused to reign"
Translation of the entire clause: "He caused Saul
to reign over Israel."

(5) אֶת־אֱלֹהִים הִתְהַלֶּךְ־נֹחַ

The verb הִתְהַלֶּךְ has a הִת prefix, which is the prefix of the Hitpaʻel perfect. It has no suffix, thus indicating that it is a third masculine singular form. The verb root is הָלַךְ (*BDB*, pp. 229ff.), "to go, come, walk." The Hitpaʻel (pp. 235f.) means "to walk, to walk to and fro."

הִתְהַלֶּךְ Hitpaʻel pf. 3 ms., from הָלַךְ, "he walked"
Translation: "he walked (to and fro)"
Translation of clause: "With God walked Noah,"
or "Noah walked with God."

(6) הִכְרַתִּי אֹתוֹ מִקֶּרֶב עַמּוֹ

The verb הִכְרַתִּי has a הִ prefix, which is the Hif'il perfect prefix. It also has a תִּי suffix, indicating that it is a first person common singular form. At first glance this would appear to leave only two consonants from which to reconstruct the verb root, namely, כ and ר. However, closer examination reveals that the dagesh in תּ is a dagesh forte, since תּ is preceded by a vowel. The root, therefore, is listed on pp. 503f. of *BDB* as כָּרַת, meaning "to cut off, cut down." The rule is that where the final root consonant is the same as the consonant that begins the suffix, these are written as a doubled consonant with a dagesh forte.

הִכְרַתִּי   Hif'il pf. 1 cs, from כָּרַת, "he cut off"
Translation: "I cut off"
Translation of clause: "I cut him off from
the midst of his people."

(7) נָתַנּוּ אֶת־בְּנֹתֵינוּ לָכֶם

The verb is נָתַנּוּ. The initial consonant is נ, but it is not pointed like a prefix and therefore must be considered as part of the verb root. The suffix is נוּ, which identifies this as a first person common plural form. The dagesh forte in the נ means that it is doubled and that the verb root is נָתַן. The rule applied here is the same as in the example given above: When the final root consonant is the same as that which begins the suffix, the two consonants are combined into one by means of a dagesh forte. Since נָתַנּוּ has no prefix, it must be either Qal, Pi'el, or Pu'al, and since it is not doubled in the middle consonant, it has to be Qal. The verb root נָתַן is listed on p. 687 of *BDB* as meaning "to give, put, set."

נָתַנּוּ   Qal pf. 1 cp, from נָתַן, "he gave"
Translation: "we gave"
Translation of clause: "We gave our daughters to you."

(8) כִּי קוֹל יְהוָה נִשְׁמַע מִירוּשָׁלַיִם

The verb נִשְׁמַע has a נִ prefix and must therefore be classified as a Nif'al perfect. The fact that it has no suffix means that it is third person masculine singular. The verb root is שָׁמַע, listed in *BDB*, p. 1033, with the meaning "to hear."

נִשְׁמַע   Nif'al pf. 3 ms, from שָׁמַע, "he heard"
Translation: "he (it) was heard"
Translation of clause: "For the voice of the LORD
was heard (is heard) from Jerusalem."

EXERCISES

1. Write the full perfect inflection of the verb מָשַׁל , "he ruled," in each of the following stems, indicating the person, gender, and number of each form.

    (1) Qal   (3) Pi‛el   (2) Nif‛al   (4) Hif‛il

2. Indicate the three root consonants in each of the following perfects.

    Example: הִקְטִיל   ___קטל___

    (1)   הִמְשִׁילוּ   _____   (10) נִלְחַם   _____
    (2)   נָתְנָה   _____   (11) הָקְטַלְתֶּן   _____
    (3)   שְׁמַרְתָּ   _____   (12) רֻדְּפוּ   _____
    (4)   גָּדְלָה   _____   (13) נָפְלוּ   _____
    (5)   דִּבַּרְנוּ   _____   (14) הִזְכַּרְתִּי   _____
    (6)   הִתְקַדְּשָׁה   _____   (15) הִכְשַׁלְתָּ   _____
    (7)   הִכְשַׁלְתֶּם   _____   (16) קֻדַּשְׁנוּ   _____
    (8)   נִשְׁבְּרוּ   _____   (17) הִתְפַּקְדוּ   _____
    (9)   הִמְשַׁלְתִּי   _____   (18) הֻבְרַכְתֶּם   _____

3. Indicate the stem to which each of the following perfects belongs.

    Example: מְשַׁלְתֶּם   ___Qal___

    (1)   בִּקֵּשׁ   _____   (10) נִלְכְּדָה   _____
    (2)   הִבְדַּלְתִּי   _____   (11) לֻמַּדְתָּ   _____
    (3)   דִּבְּרוּ   _____   (12) הָשְׁבַּרְתִּי   _____
    (4)   שָׁמַעְתִּי   _____   (13) הִכְשַׁלְתֶּם   _____
    (5)   הִשְׁמִיד   _____   (14) נִמְכַּרְנוּ   _____
    (6)   לָקַח   _____   (15) סִפֵּר   _____
    (7)   נִכְרַת   _____   (16) נִסְתְּרָה   _____
    (8)   הִכְבַּדְתִּי   _____   (17) הִסְתִּיר   _____
    (9)   קִדַּשְׁתִּי   _____   (18) הִבְדִּיל   _____

121

4. Vocabulary Review: Match the following words so that opposites are paired.
For example, the opposite of זָכָר, "male," is נְקֵבָה, "female," therefore the letter E
(E) is placed in the block opposite זָכָר.

(E)	זָכָר		(A)	נָתַן
( )	מִלְחָמָה		(B)	אִשָּׁה
( )	בֹּקֶר		(C)	רָחֹק
( )	מֶלֶךְ		(D)	רוּחַ
( )	אֶרֶץ		(E)	נְקֵבָה
( )	אוֹר		(F)	רַע
( )	יוֹם		(G)	אָב
( )	אִישׁ		(H)	קָטֹן
( )	טוֹב		(I)	בָּנִים
( )	אֵשׁ		(J)	הִיא
( )	לָקַח		(K)	לַיְלָה
( )	אָח		(L)	עֶרֶב
( )	גָּדוֹל		(M)	אָחוֹת
( )	הוּא		(N)	עֶבֶד
( )	קָרֹב		(O)	שָׁלוֹם
( )	בָּנוֹת		(P)	מַיִם
( )	בָּשָׂר		(Q)	שָׁמַיִם
( )	אֵם		(R)	חֹשֶׁךְ

5. Each of the following entries contains a perfect form of a Hebrew verb. Supply
the proper translation of the verb form by filling in the blank. In the space marked
(a) give its stem, in (b) its person, gender, and number (abbreviated), and in (c) its
root.

Example:

וְנִכְרַת מֵעַמָּיו   (a) __Nifʻal__

He shall be __cut off__ from his people.   (b) __3 ms__

(Exod. 30:33)   (c) __כָּרַת__

(1)   מִי־בִקֵּשׁ זֹאת מִיֶּדְכֶם   (a) _____

Who has _____ this from your hand? (Isa. 1:12)   (b) _____

                                                         (c) _____

122

(2)   לֶחֶם לֹא אָכַלְתִּי   (a) _____

I have not _____ bread. (Deut. 9:9)   (b) _____

                                            (c) _____

(3)   כִּי מִמֶּנָּה לֻקָּחְתָּ   (a) _____

For from it you were _____. (Gen. 3:19)   (b) _____

                                            (c) _____

(4)   הֲלֹא כָתַבְתִּי לְךָ   (a) _____

Have I not _____ to (for) you? (Prov. 22:20)   (b) _____

                                            (c) _____

(5)   וְאָנֹכִי עָמַדְתִּי בָהָר   (a) _____

And I _____ on the mountain. (Deut. 10:10)   (b) _____

                                            (c) _____

(6)   לֹא־שָׁלַחְתִּי אֶת־הַנְּבִאִים   (a) _____

I did not _____ the prophets. (Jer. 23:21)   (b) _____

                                            (c) _____

(7)   כִּי־מָצָאתָ חֵן בְּעֵינָי   (a) _____

For you have _____ favor in my eyes.   (b) _____

(Exod. 33:17)   (c) _____

(8)   נִמְצְאוּ דְבָרֶיךָ   (a) _____

Your words were _____. (Jer. 15:16)   (b) _____

                                            (c) _____

(9)   וְהִנֵּה נָפְלוּ אֲבוֹתֵינוּ בֶּחָרֶב   (a) _____

And behold, our fathers have _____ by   (b) _____

the sword. (2 Chr. 29:9)   (c) _____

(10)   פָּקַד יְהוָה אֶת־עַמּוֹ   (a) _____

The LORD had _____ his people. (Ruth 1:6)   (b) _____

                                            (c) _____

(11)   שָׁלַחְתִּי אֲלֵיכֶם אֵת הַמִּצְוָה הַזֹּאת   (a) _____

I have _____ to you this commandment.   (b) _____

(Mal. 2:4)   (c) _____

(12)   דִּבַּרְנוּ אֵלֶיךָ בְמִצְרַיִם   (a) _____

We _____ to you in Egypt. (Exod. 14:12)   (b) _____

                                            (c) _____

6. Fill in the blanks with the correct pronouns.

(1)   הִבְדַּלְתִּי אֶתְכֶם מִן־הָעַמִּים _____ have separated _____ from the peoples. (Lev. 20:24)

(2)   מָצָאתִי דָּוִד עַבְדִּי _____ have found David _____ servant. (Ps. 89:21; Eng. 89:20)

(3)   וּבִקְשׁוּ אֶת־יְהוָה אֱלֹהֵיהֶם And _____ shall seek the LORD _____ God. (Hos. 3:5)

(4)   לֹא אֶת־אֲבֹתֵינוּ כָּרַת יְהוָה אֶת־הַבְּרִית הַזֹּאת כִּי אִתָּנוּ Not with _____ fathers did the LORD make (cut) _____ covenant, but with _____. (Deut. 5:3)

(5)   וְהִכְרַתִּי אֹתָהּ מִקֶּרֶב עַמָּהּ And _____ will cut _____ off from the midst of _____ people. (Lev. 17:10)

(6)   וְהִכְרַתִּי סוּסֶיךָ מִקִּרְבֶּךָ And _____ will cut off _____ horses from the midst of _____. (Mic. 5:9; Eng. 5:10)

(7)   אֵיךְ כָּתַבְתָּ אֶת־כָּל־הַדְּבָרִים הָאֵלֶּה מִפִּיו How did _____ write all _____ words from _____ mouth? (Jer. 36:17)

(8)   וְאֶת־אִשְׁתּוֹ לָקַחְתָּ And _____ wife _____ have taken. (2 Sam. 12:9)

(9)   וְנָפַלְתָּ אַתָּה וִיהוּדָה עִמָּךְ And _____ shall fall, and Judah with _____. (2 Chr. 25:19)

(10) וַעֲבַדְתֶּם אֹתָנוּ And _____ shall serve _____. (1 Sam. 17:9)

(11) וְשָׁכַבְתִּי עִם־אֲבֹתַי And _____ will lie down with _____ fathers. (Gen. 47:30)

(12) וְשִׁלַּחְתִּי־אֵשׁ בְּעָרָיו And _____ will send fire upon _____ cities. (Hos. 8:14)

(13) דִּבַּרְנוּ אֵלֶיךָ בְמִצְרַיִם _____ spoke to _____ in Egypt. (Exod. 14:12)

(14) דִּבְּרוּ אֶחָיו אִתּוֹ _____ brothers spoke with _____. (Gen. 45:15)

7. Practice reading the Hebrew aloud. Then cover the English and practice translating from sight.

(1) אֱמֶת הָיָה הַדָּבָר אֲשֶׁר שָׁמַעְתִּי בְּאַרְצִי

The word was true which I heard in my country. (1 Kgs. 10:6)

(2) אִישׁ הָיָה בְאֶרֶץ עוּץ אִיּוֹב שְׁמוֹ

There was a man in the land of Uz; Job was his name. (Job 1:1)

(3) כִּי אֲמַרְתֶּם כָּרַתְנוּ בְרִית אֶת־מָוֶת

For you say, "We have made (cut) a covenant with death." (Isa. 28:15)

(4) וְנִכְרְתָה קֶשֶׁת מִלְחָמָה וְדִבֶּר שָׁלוֹם לַגּוֹיִם

And the war bow shall be cut off, and he will speak peace to the nations. (Zech. 9:10)

(5) עֵשָׂו לָקַח אֶת־נָשָׁיו מִבְּנוֹת כְּנָעַן

Esau took his wives from the daughters of Canaan. (Gen. 36:2)

(6) וַיהוָה נִחָם כִּי־הִמְלִיךְ אֶת־שָׁאוּל עַל־יִשְׂרָאֵל

And the LORD repented that he had made Saul king over Israel. (1 Sam. 15:35)

(7) וְעַתָּה יְהוָה אֱלֹהַי אַתָּה הִמְלַכְתָּ אֶת־עַבְדְּךָ תַּחַת דָּוִד אָבִי וְאָנֹכִי נַעַר קָטֹן

And now, O LORD my God, you have made your servant to be king instead of David my father, and I am a little child. (1 Kgs. 3:7)

(8) מָצָא חִלְקִיָּהוּ הַכֹּהֵן אֶת־סֵפֶר תּוֹרַת־יְהוָה בְּיַד־מֹשֶׁה

Hilkiah the priest found the book of the law of the LORD by the hand of Moses. (2 Chr. 34:14)

(9) לֹא־נָפַל דָּבָר אֶחָד מִכֹּל הַדְּבָרִים הַטּוֹבִים אֲשֶׁר דִּבֶּר יְהוָה אֱלֹהֵיכֶם עֲלֵיכֶם

Not one word has fallen (failed) from all the good words which the LORD your God spoke to you. (Josh. 23:14)

(10) יַחְדָּיו נָפְלוּ שְׁנֵיהֶם

Together the two of them have fallen. (Jer. 46:12)

(11) בַּיּוֹם הַשְּׁמִינִי שִׁלַּח אֶת־הָעָם On the eighth day he sent the people away. (1 Kgs. 8:66)

(12) כִּי עַתָּה שֻׁלַּחְתִּי אֵלֶיךָ For now I have been sent to you. (Dan. 10:11)

(13) [כֵּן דִּבֶּר] נָתָן אֶל־דָּוִד אַתָּה הָאִישׁ Thus spoke Nathan to David, "You are the man!" (2 Sam. 12:7)

(14) מַה־זֹּאת עָשָׂה אֱלֹהִים לָנוּ What is this God has done to us? (Gen. 42:28)

(15) אָמַרְתִּי לַיהוָה אֵלִי אַתָּה I say to the LORD, "You are my God." (Ps. 140:7)

VOCABULARY

(1)	אֶחָד	one	(10)	כֶּרֶם	vineyard
(2)	אֵת	with	(11)	כָּרַת	he cut, cut off
(3)	[בדל]	he separated, divided	(12)	מִין	species, kind
(4)	בָּנָה	he built	(13)	מִלְחָמָה	(f) war, battle
(5)	[בקשׁ]	he sought	(14)	נְחֹשֶׁת	copper, bronze
(6)	בַּרְזֶל	iron	(15)	נְקֵבָה	(f) female
(7)	[דבר]	(Piʿel) he spoke	(16)	עָנָן	cloud
(8)	זָכָר	male	(17)	פַּר	young bull
(9)	כֹּהֵן	priest	(18)	קֶרֶב	midst

LESSON XV

39. Verbs: Qal Imperfect of the Strong Verb*

39.1 The Qal imperfect is formed by taking the Qal infinitive construct (infinitive construct for מָשַׁל is מְשֹׁל) and adding to it a fixed set of prefixes and suffixes. One must also make the necessary changes in vocalization that these additions demand. As was the case with the perfect suffixes, the imperfect prefixes and suffixes are remnants of personal pronouns and thus serve to indicate changes in person, gender, and number from one verb form to another.

39.2 The following table shows the prefixes and suffixes used to form the Qal imperfect of the strong verb. The X marks are used to show the position of the prefixes and suffixes in relation to the three consonants of the verb root.

3 ms	יXXX	3 mp	יXXXוּ
3 fs	תXXX	3 fp	תXXXנָה
2 ms	תXXX	2 mp	תXXXוּ
2 fs	תXXXִי	2 fp	תXXXנָה
1 cs	אXXX	1 cp	נXXX

(1) The singular prefixes are yod, three tavs, and ʼalef.

(2) The plural prefixes are yod, three tavs, and nun.

(3) The prefix vowel for the Qal imperfect appears as ḥireq after all prefixes except ʼalef (1 cs). Because ʼalef is a guttural, it requires a sᵉgol rather than a ḥireq.

(4) The only singular suffix that occurs in the imperfect inflection of the verb is ḥireq-yod (ִי), which is found in the second person feminine singular.

(5) The first four forms of the plural imperfect inflection have suffixes and these follow the pattern of וּ, נָה, וּ, נָה. The first person common plural form has no suffix.

(6) The forms for the third person feminine singular and the second person masculine singular are identical. The same is true for the third person feminine plural and the second person feminine plural. The context will almost always enable the student to distinguish between these identical forms.

---

*Refer to Verb Chart 1, pp. 400f. for the conjugation of the strong verb.

39.3 The resultant forms for the Qal imperfect of מָשַׁל are these:

3 ms	יִמְשֹׁל	3 mp	יִמְשְׁלוּ
3 fs	תִּמְשֹׁל	3 fp	תִּמְשֹׁלְנָה
2 ms	תִּמְשֹׁל	2 mp	תִּמְשְׁלוּ
2 fs	תִּמְשְׁלִי	2 fp	תִּמְשֹׁלְנָה
1 cs	אֶמְשֹׁל	1 cp	נִמְשֹׁל

(1) The preformative syllable is closed, thus requiring that the sheva under the first stem consonant be silent. If the second stem consonant had been a BeBaD KeFaT letter, it would have been pointed with a dagesh lene (cf. כָּתַב in the example below).

(2) The rule that vocalic afformatives draw the accent to themselves applies here as well as in the perfect inflection (cf. XII.30.4 [3], p. 84). The forms of the imperfect affected by this rule are second person feminine singular, third person masculine plural, and second person masculine plural. The shift of accent to the suffix syllable causes the nearest preceding vowel in an open syllable to volatilize. In the three forms listed above, holem is reduced to a vocal sheva.

2 fs	תִּמְשֹׁלִי	becomes	תִּמְשְׁלִי
3 mp	יִמְשֹׁלוּ	becomes	יִמְשְׁלוּ
2 mp	תִּמְשֹׁלוּ	becomes	תִּמְשְׁלוּ

(3) The rule for consonantal suffixes is that only the heavy suffixes תֶּם and תֶּן, used in the perfect inflection of the verb (cf. XII.30.4 [4], pp. 84f.), draw the accent to themselves. This means that the consonantal suffix נָה, used in the imperfect third person feminine plural and second person feminine plural, is not accented. In these forms the accent remains on the next to the last syllable and so must be marked. Furthermore, a syllable divider must be placed under the third stem consonant when it is followed by a consonantal afformative.

3 fp, 2 fp	תִּמְשֹׁלְנָה	becomes	תִּמְשֹׁלְנָה

(4) Sometimes the suffix for the third person masculine plural and the second person masculine plural may appear as וּן, thus occasionally יִמְשְׁלוּ may appear as יִמְשְׁלוּן, or תִּמְשְׁלוּ as תִּמְשְׁלוּן. The addition of a final nun to an imperfect form does not change the meaning of the form.

39.4 The Qal imperfect inflection of כָּתַב, "he wrote," follows the same pattern as מָשַׁל.

3 ms	יִכְתֹּב	3 mp	יִכְתְּבוּ
3 fs	תִּכְתֹּב	3 fp	תִּכְתֹּבְנָה
2 ms	תִּכְתֹּב	2 mp	תִּכְתְּבוּ
2 fs	תִּכְתְּבִי	2 fp	תִּכְתֹּבְנָה
1 cs	אֶכְתֹּב	1 cp	נִכְתֹּב

39.5 Other strong verbs that are inflected like מָשַׁל include the following:

(1)	זָכַר	he remembered	(6)	שָׁבַר	he broke in pieces
(2)	כָּתַב	he wrote	(7)	שָׁבַת	he rested, ceased
(3)	מָלַךְ	he reigned	(8)	שָׁמַר	he kept, watched
(4)	קָטַל	he killed	(9)	שָׁפַט	he judged
(5)	פָּקַד	he visited, attended to			

39.6 Some stative verbs have the stem vowel of the Qal imperfect as pataḥ instead of ḥolem.

Example: Qal imperfect of כָּבֵד, "he was heavy, honored"

3 ms	יִכְבַּד	3 mp	יִכְבְּדוּ
3 fs	תִּכְבַּד	3 fp	תִּכְבַּדְנָה
2 ms	תִּכְבַּד	2 mp	תִּכְבְּדוּ
2 fs	תִּכְבְּדִי	2 fp	תִּכְבַּדְנָה
1 cs	אֶכְבַּד	1 cp	נִכְבַּד

40. Verbs: The Meaning of the Imperfect

Imperfect verbs may be used in a variety of senses and the context must often be consulted in order to determine the sense that is intended. However, there are some uses of the imperfect that seem to be fairly clear. The following examples are by no means intended to cover all these uses. They are merely designed to illustrate some of the more common uses.

40.1 One of the most common uses of the imperfect is to describe a simple action in future time.

Examples:

(1)	כִּי־מֶלֶךְ יִמְלֹךְ עָלֵינוּ	For a king shall reign over us. (1 Sam. 12:12)
(2)	אֲנִי אֶכְרֹת אִתְּךָ בְּרִית	I will make (cut) a covenant with you. (2 Sam. 3:13)

129

(3)	וְאַתָּה תִּמְלֹךְ עַל־יִשְׂרָאֵל	And you shall reign over Israel. (1 Sam. 23:17)
(4)	לֹא־אֶמְשֹׁל אֲנִי בָּכֶם	I will not rule over you. (Judg. 8:23)
(5)	בִּי מְלָכִים יִמְלֹכוּ	By me kings shall reign. (Prov. 8:15)

40.2   A second use of the imperfect is to express repeated, habitual, or customary actions, whether in the past, the present, or the future. This is sometimes referred to as the frequentative use of the imperfect.

(1) Examples of repeated, habitual, or customary actions in past time

(a)	וְאֵד יַעֲלֶה מִן־הָאָרֶץ	And a mist went up (used to go up) from the earth. (Gen. 2:6)
(b)	וְכֵן יַעֲשֶׂה שָׁנָה בְשָׁנָה	And so he did year by year. (1 Sam. 1:7)

(2) Examples of repeated, habitual, or customary actions in present time

(a)	לְמַעַן אֶשְׁמֹר דְּבָרֶךְ	In order that I may keep your word. (Ps. 119:101)
(b)	וּתְפִלַּת צַדִּיקִים יִשְׁמָע	But the prayer of the righteous he hears. (Prov. 15:29)
(c)	בֵּן יְכַבֵּד אָב	A son honors (Piʿel) (his) father. (Mal. 1:6)

(3) Examples of repeated, habitual, or customary actions in future time

(a)	יִזְכֹּר לְעוֹלָם בְּרִיתוֹ	He will remember his covenant forever. (Ps. 111:5)
(b)	יְהוָה יִמְלֹךְ לְעֹלָם וָעֶד	The LORD will reign forever and ever. (Exod. 15:18)
(c)	אֶשְׁכָּן־שָׁם בְּתוֹךְ בְּנֵי־יִשְׂרָאֵל לְעוֹלָם	I will dwell there in the midst of the children (sons) of Israel forever. (Ezek. 43:7)

40.3   The imperfect is frequently used to express actions that are contingent or dependent upon other factors in the context. The possibilities of translation are many and these often involve the use of modal auxiliaries such as "may, can, shall, might, could, should, would, etc."

The forms included in this category may be dependent upon a variety of factors. Sometimes they reflect the will, desire, judgment, premonition, or permission of the speaker. Sometimes they are dependent upon a prior action demanding response or reaction. Their sense is often determined by the preceding use of conditional particles such as אִם, "if, though," and אוּלַי, "perhaps." These forms of the imperfect are also common after particles expressing end or purpose, such as לְמַעַן, "in order that," כִּי, "for, because," אֲשֶׁר, "that," and פֶּן, "lest." Finally, they may often appear after interrogative pronouns or adverbs such as אֵיךְ, "how," מָה, "what," מִי, "who," and לָמָה, "why."

Examples:

(1)	אוּלַי יִשְׁמְעוּ בֵּית יְהוּדָה	Perhaps the house of Judah will hear. (Jer. 36:3)
(2)	מִי יְהוָה אֲשֶׁר אֶשְׁמַע בְּקֹלוֹ	Who is the LORD that I should listen to (obey) his voice? (Exod. 5:2)
(3)	פֶּן־תִּשְׁכַּח אֶת־יְהוָה אֱלֹהֶיךָ	Lest you forget the LORD your God. (Deut. 6:12)
(4)	לָמָה זֶּה תִּשְׁאַל לִשְׁמִי	Why is it that you ask my name? (Gen. 32:30)
(5)	אֶת־מִי אֶשְׁלַח	Whom shall I send? (Isa. 6:8)

41. Verbs: The Jussive and Cohortative

Two further functions of the imperfect remain to be noted. These functions are designated as the jussive and the cohortative.

41.1 The jussive involves only imperfect forms, third person singular and third person plural. A jussive may appear in any of the verb stems. In strong verbs the jussive takes the same form as the imperfect and therefore must be identified by its context. In weak verbs it is often represented by a shortened form of the imperfect, which may involve either the shortening of a long vowel or the dropping of the final syllable.

The jussive is used to express the speaker's desire, wish, or command where a third person is the subject of the action. It is represented in translation by the modal auxiliaries "may" and "let."

The particle נָא is sometimes added after jussives and cohortatives, perhaps to make them more emphatic. It is usually classified as a particle of entreaty, translated "I pray!"

Examples of the use of the jussive:

(a)	יִזְכָּר־נָא הַמֶּלֶךְ אֶת־יְהוָה אֱלֹהֶיךָ	Pray let the king remember the LORD your God. (2 Sam. 14:11)
(b)	אַל־יִמְשְׁלוּ־בִי	Let them not have dominion (rule) over me. (Ps. 19:14; Eng. 19:13)
(c)	יִשְׁפֹּט יְהוָה בֵּינִי וּבֵינֶיךָ	May the LORD judge between me and between you. (Gen. 16:5)

131

41.2 The cohortative involves first person imperfect forms, both singular and plural. A cohortative may appear in any of the verb stems. In contrast to the jussive, which sometimes appears as a shortened form of the imperfect, the cohortative is sometimes lengthened by the addition of הָ as a suffix. Since this is a vocalic suffix, it draws the accent to itself, causing the preceding vowel, now left in an open unaccented syllable, to volatilize. Volatilization will not take place, of course, if the preceding vowel is unchangeably long. Instead, unchangeably long vowels will retain their accents.

The cohortative is used to express the speaker's desire, intention, self-encouragement, or determination to perform a certain action.

Examples of the use of the cohortative:

(a) נִכְרְתָה בְרִית אֲנִי וָאֶתָּה Let us make (cut) a covenant, you and I (suffix הָ added to נִכְרֹת, from כָּרַת, "he cut"). (Gen. 31:44)

(b) וְאֶשְׁמְרָה תוֹרָתְךָ תָמִיד And I will keep thy law continually (suffix הָ added to אֶשְׁמֹר, from שָׁמַר, "he kept"). (Ps. 119:44)

(c) וְאֶכְרְתָה לָכֶם בְּרִית עוֹלָם And I will make for you an everlasting covenant (suffix הָ added to אֶכְרֹת, from כָּרַת, "he cut"). (Isa. 55:3)

(d) וְעַתָּה נִכְרָת־בְּרִית לֵאלֹהֵינוּ And now, let us make (cut) a covenant with our God. (Ezra 10:3)

EXERCISES

1. Write the Qal imperfect of כָּתַב, "he wrote." Translate each of the forms.

3 ms	כתב	3 mp	כתב
3 fs	כתב	3 fp	כתב
2 ms	כתב	2 mp	כתב
2 fs	כתב	2 fp	כתב
1 cs	כתב	1 cp	כתב

2. Match the following:

( )   יְכַבְּדוּ בָנָיו   (A)   In order that you may learn.
                                                  (Deut. 14:23)

( )   לְמַעַן תִּזְכְּרוּ   (B)   I shall keep your flock. (Gen. 30:31)

( )   אֲנִי אֶמְלֹךְ   (C)   They shall lie down together.
                                                  (Isa. 43:17)

( )   שָׁאוּל יִמְלֹךְ עָלֵינוּ   (D)   The LORD will rule over you.
                                                  (Judg. 8:23)

( )   לְמַעַן תִּלְמַד   (E)   And you shall keep my
                                                  commandments. (Lev 26:3)

( )   יַחְדָּו יִשְׁכָּבוּ   (F)   These things I remember.
                                                  (Ps. 42:5; Eng. 42:4)

( )   צֹאנְךָ אֶשְׁמֹר   (G)   I shall reign. (1 Kgs. 1:5)

( )   וְאֶת־מִצְוֹתַי תִּשְׁמֹרוּ   (H)   And you shall keep his
                                                  commandments. (Deut. 13:5)

( )   וְאֶת־מִצְוֹתָיו תִּשְׁמֹרוּ   (I)   His sons are honored. (Job 14:21)

( )   אֶשְׁפֹּט אֶתְכֶם   (J)   I shall judge you. (Ezek. 11:11)

( )   אֵלֶּה אֶזְכְּרָה   (K)   In order that they may learn.
                                                  (Deut. 31:12)

( )   יְהוָה יִמְשֹׁל בָּכֶם   (L)   In order that you may remember.
                                                  (Num. 15:40)

( )   אֶזְכְּרָה אֱלֹהִים   (M)   I will remember God.
                                                  (Ps. 77:4; Eng. 77:3)

( )   לְמַעַן יִלְמְדוּ   (N)   Perhaps the LORD will hear.
                                                  (Isa. 37:4)

( )   אוּלַי יִשְׁמַע יְהוָה   (O)   Saul shall reign over us.
                                                  (1 Sam. 11:12)

3. Fill in the blanks with the correct pronouns.

(1)   פֶּן־תִּשְׁכַּח אֶת־יְהוָה אֱלֹהֶיךָ   Lest _____ forget the LORD _____
God. (Deut. 8:11)

(2)   כִּי־תִשְׁמֹר אֶת־כָּל־הַמִּצְוָה הַזֹּאת   For _____ shall keep all
_____ commandment. (Deut. 19:9)

(3)   אִם־יִשְׁמְרוּ בָנֶיךָ בְּרִיתִי   If _____ sons keep _____ covenant.
(Ps. 132:12)

(4)   נִשְׁלְחָה אֲנָשִׁים לְפָנֵינוּ   Let _____ send men before _____.
(Deut. 1:22)

(5)   וְלֹא אֶשְׁמַע אֲלֵיהֶם   And _____ will not listen to _____.
(Jer. 11:11)

(6)   לֹא־אֶמְשֹׁל אֲנִי בָּכֶם   _____ will not rule over _____.
(Judg. 8:23)

(7)   נִכְרְתָה בְרִית אֲנִי וָאָתָּה   Let _____ make (cut) a covenant,
_____ and _____. (Gen. 31:44)

(8)   וְאַתָּה אֶת־בְּרִיתִי תִשְׁמֹר   But _____ shall keep
_____ covenant. (Gen. 17:9)

(9)   הֲיִכְרֹת בְּרִית עִמָּךְ   Will _____ make (cut) a covenant with
_____? (Job. 40:28; Eng. 41:4)

(10)   וְנִכְרְתָה בְרִית עִמָּךְ   And let _____ make a covenant with
_____. (Gen. 26:28)

(11)   וַיִּכְרְתוּ אִתְּךָ בְּרִית   And _____ shall make a covenant with
_____. (2 Sam. 3:21)

(12)   כִּי־שְׁלֹמֹה בְנֵךְ יִמְלֹךְ אַחֲרַי   For Solomon _____ son shall reign
after _____. (1 Kgs. 1:13)

(13)   אֶשְׁמְרָה דְרָכַי   _____ will guard _____ ways. (Ps. 39:2;
Eng. 39:1)

(14)   אֶשְׁמְרָה תוֹרָתְךָ תָמִיד   _____ will keep _____ law
continually. (Ps. 119:44)

(15)   וְאֵיךְ נִגְנֹב מִבֵּית אֲדֹנֶיךָ כֶּסֶף אוֹ זָהָב   For how shall _____
steal silver or gold from the house of _____ master (lord)? (Gen. 44:8)

4. Each of the following entries contains a Qal imperfect form of a Hebrew verb. Give its correct translation by filling in the blank. In the space marked (a) give its person, gender, and number, and in (b) its root (i.e., its Qal perfect 3 ms form).

(1) לֹא תִגְנֹב You shall not _____. (Exod. 20:15)   (a) _____
(b) _____

(2) לֹא תִגְנֹבוּ You shall not _____. (Lev. 19:11)   (a) _____
(b) _____

(3) וְחַטֹּאתֶיךָ לֹא אֶזְכֹּר And your sins I will not   (a) _____
_____. (Isa. 43:25)   (b) _____

(4) לְמַעַן תִּזְכְּרִי In order that you may _____.   (a) _____
(Ezek. 16:63)   (b) _____

(5) אַל־תִּזְכְּרוּ רִאשֹׁנוֹת _____ not the former   (a) _____
things. (Isa. 43:18)   (b) _____

(6) וְאַתָּה תִּמְלֹךְ עַל־יִשְׂרָאֵל And you shall _____   (a) _____
over Israel. (1 Sam. 23:17)   (b) _____

(7) כִּי אֶשְׁבֹּר אֶת־עֹל מֶלֶךְ בָּבֶל For I will   (a) _____
_____ the yoke of the king of Babylon.   (b) _____
(Jer. 28:4)

(8) וְהוּא יִשְׁפֹּט־תֵּבֵל בְּצֶדֶק And he will _____   (a) _____
the world with righteousness. (Ps. 9:9; Eng. 9:8)   (b) _____

(9) הֲתִשְׁפֹּט אֹתָם בֶּן־אָדָם Will you _____   (a) _____
them, son of man? (Ezek. 20:4)   (b) _____

(10) וּמִצְוֹתַי לֹא יִשְׁמֹרוּ And they do not _____   (a) _____
my commandments. (Ps. 89:32; Eng. 89:31)   (b) _____

(11) וְיִזְכֹּר אֶת־יְמֵי הַחֹשֶׁךְ But let him _____   (a) _____
the days of darkness. (Eccl. 11:8)   (b) _____

(12) וּמִצְרַיִם לֹא תִזְכְּרִי־עוֹד And you shall _____   (a) _____
Egypt no more. (Ezek. 23:27)   (b) _____

(13) אֶפְקֹד אֶתְכֶם I will _____ you. (Jer. 29:10)   (a) _____
(b) _____

(14) לְמַעַן אֶלְמַד חֻקֶּיךָ In order that I may _____   (a) _____
your statutes. (Ps. 119:71)   (b) _____

(15)   כָּכָה אֶשְׁבֹּר אֶת־הָעָם הַזֶּה וְאֶת־הָעִיר הַזֹּאת   (a) _____

So will I _____ this people and this city.   (b) _____

(Jer. 19:11)

5. Practice reading the Hebrew aloud. Cover the English translation and practice translating from sight.

(1)   פֶּן־נִשְׂרֹף אוֹתָךְ וְאֶת־בֵּית אָבִיךְ בָּאֵשׁ
Lest we burn you and your father's house with fire. (Judg. 14:15)

(2)   אַל־תִּשְׁלַח יָדְךָ אֶל־הַנַּעַר
Do not lay (send) your hand upon the lad. (Gen. 22:12)

(3)   יוֹמָם וָלַיְלָה תִּכְבַּד עָלַי יָדֶךָ
Day and night your hand was heavy upon me. (Ps. 32:4)

(4)   וַאֲנַחְנוּ נִכְרֹת עֵצִים מִן־הַלְּבָנוֹן
And we will cut timber (trees) from Lebanon. (2 Chr. 2:15; Eng. 2:16)

(5)   בְּיָד חֲזָקָה אֶמְלוֹךְ עֲלֵיכֶם
I will reign over you with a mighty hand. (Ezek. 20:33)

(6)   הִנֵּה בֶן־הַמֶּלֶךְ יִמְלֹךְ כַּאֲשֶׁר דִּבֶּר יְהוָה עַל־בְּנֵי דָוִיד
Behold, the king's son! Let him reign, as the LORD spoke concerning the sons of David. (2 Chr. 23:3)

(7)   יִזְכֹּר עֲוֹנָם וְיִפְקֹד חַטֹּאתָם
He will remember their iniquity and he will punish (visit) their sins. (Jer. 14:10)

(8)   וְלֹא־יִלְמְדוּן עוֹד מִלְחָמָה
And they shall learn war no more. (Mic. 4:3)

(9)   וְקֶשֶׁת וְחֶרֶב וּמִלְחָמָה אֶשְׁבּוֹר מִן־הָאָרֶץ
And the bow, the sword, and war I will abolish (break) from the land. (Hos. 2:20; Eng. 2:18)

(10)   וַעֲבָדַי יִשְׁכְּנוּ־שָׁמָּה
And my servants shall dwell there. (Isa. 65:9)

(11)   כִּי־מִי יִשְׁפֹּט אֶת־עַמְּךָ הַזֶּה הַגָּדוֹל
For who can judge this great people of yours? (2 Chr. 1:10)

(12) אָמַרְתִּי אֲנִי בְּלִבִּי אֶת־הַצַּדִּיק
וְאֶת־הָרָשָׁע יִשְׁפֹּט הָאֱלֹהִים

I said in my heart, "God will judge the righteous and the wicked." (Eccl. 3:17)

(13) אֱלֹהֵי אַבְרָהָם וֵאלֹהֵי
נָחוֹר יִשְׁפְּטוּ בֵינֵינוּ

Let the God of Abraham and the God of Nahor judge between us. (Gen. 31:53)

(14) זֶה מִשְׁפַּט הַמֶּלֶךְ אֲשֶׁר
יִמְלֹךְ עֲלֵיכֶם

This will be the practice (custom) of the king who will reign over you. (1 Sam. 8:11)

(15) מִי־יִשְׁכֹּן בְּהַר קָדְשֶׁךָ

Who shall dwell on your holy mountain? (Ps. 15:1)

VOCABULARY

(1)	אַיִל	ram	(10)	שָׂפָה	(f) lip, speech, edge
(2)	בּוֹא	to come, go	(11)	שָׁאַל	he asked
(3)	זָכַר	he remembered	(12)	שָׁבַר	he broke in pieces
(4)	חָיָה	he lived, revived	(13)	שׁוּב	to turn, return
(5)	מָשַׁל	he ruled	(14)	שׁוֹפָר	ram's horn, trumpet
(6)	עֶבֶד	servant, slave	(15)	שָׁכַח	he forgot
(7)	עָבַר	he passed over, through	(16)	שָׁפַט	he judged, delivered
(8)	עוֹלָם	eternity	(17)	תָּמִיד	continuously
(9)	קוּם	to arise, stand	(18)	תְּפִלָּה	(f) prayer

LESSON XVI

42. Verbs: The Imperfects of the Remaining Verb Stems*

Imperfect forms of the verb occur not only in the Qal stem but in the other six stems as well. It is important for one to learn the imperfect forms for all stems of the strong verb since the imperfect forms of the weak verbs are based upon them.

The imperfect prefixes and suffixes have the same consonants in all stems of the verb. This rule applies to both strong verbs and weak verbs. The vowels of the suffixes are also the same for all stems. However, the vowels of the prefixes differ from stem to stem and so must be memorized.

Examples:

	Qal Imperfect	Nif'al Imperfect	Pi'el Imperfect
3 ms	יְ ____	יִ ____	יְ ____
3 fs	תְ ____ ִ	תִ ____ ִ	תְ ____ ִ
2 ms	תְ ____ ִ	תִ ____ ִ	תְ ____ ִ
2 fs	תְ ____ ִ י	תִ ____ ִ י	תְ ____ ִ י
1 cs	אֶ ____	אֶ ____	אֲ ____
3 mp	יְ ____ וּ	יִ ____ וּ	יְ ____ וּ
3 fp	תְ ____ נָה	תִ ____ נָה	תְ ____ נָה
2 mp	תְ ____ וּ	תִ ____ וּ	תְ ____ וּ
2 fp	תְ ____ נָה	תִ ____ נָה	תְ ____ נָה
1 cp	נְ ____	נִ ____	נְ ____

This same pattern is continued throughout the remaining stems of the verb.

The prefix vowels will be the same for all imperfect forms in any given stem, except in the first person common singular form, where the prefix consonant is א. Whenever ḥireq stands after the א prefix, it is changed to seghol (אִ → אֶ); and whenever a simple sheva stands after the א prefix, it is changed to ḥatef-pataḥ (אְ → אֲ).

---

*Refer to Verb Chart 1, pp. 400f. for the conjugation of the strong verb.

42.1 *The Nif'al Imperfect of* כָּתַב *and* מָשַׁל

3 ms	יִמָּשֵׁל	יִכָּתֵב
3 fs	תִּמָּשֵׁל	תִּכָּתֵב
2 ms	תִּמָּשֵׁל	תִּכָּתֵב
2 fs	תִּמָּשְׁלִי	תִּכָּתְבִי
1 cs	אֶמָּשֵׁל	אֶכָּתֵב
3 mp	יִמָּשְׁלוּ	יִכָּתְבוּ
3 fp	תִּמָּשַׁלְנָה	תִּכָּתַבְנָה
2 mp	תִּמָּשְׁלוּ	תִּכָּתְבוּ
2 fp	תִּמָּשַׁלְנָה	תִּכָּתַבְנָה
1 cp	נִמָּשֵׁל	נִכָּתֵה

(1)   The prefix vowel for the Nif'al imperfect is ḥireq in all forms except first person common singular, where it is s^egol.

(2)   A dagesh forte is placed in the first consonant of the verb root in the Nif'al imperfect. This consonant is therefore doubled. The doubling occurs because an original נ has dropped out. יִנְמָשֵׁל has become יִמָּשֵׁל. *Whenever* נ *closes a syllable within a Hebrew word and is followed by a syllable divider (silent sheva), it is assimilated into the following consonant by means of a dagesh forte.*

(3)   There are three vocalic suffixes (2 fs, 3 mp, and 2 mp). These draw the accent to themselves, causing the nearest preceding vowel in an open syllable to be volatilized.

2 fs	תִּמָּשֵׁלִי	becomes	תִּמָּשְׁלִי
3 mp	יִמָּשֵׁלוּ	becomes	יִמָּשְׁלוּ
2 mp	תִּמָּשֵׁלוּ	becomes	תִּמָּשְׁלוּ

(Note that a meteg is placed beside a long vowel standing immediately before a vocal sheva.)

(4)   The stem vowel that stands in the syllable before the נָה endings of the imperfect (3 fp and 2 fp) will be ḥolem in the Qal stem, pataḥ in the Nif'al, Pu'al, and Hof'al stems, and ṣere in the Pi'el, Hitpa'el, and Hif'il stems. This same rule applies to most of the weak verbs. The exceptions will be noted as they occur.

(5)   The Nif'al imperfect may be used in a variety of ways, just as is true of imperfects in general. It is often passive in meaning, although it may also be reflexive.

(a) The Nif'al imperfect sometimes describes a simple action in future time.

Examples:

בָּאֵשׁ יִשָּׂרֵף	With fire it shall be burned. (Lev. 7:19)
וְשָׁם אֶקָּבֵר	And there I will be buried. (Ruth 1:17)
מֵי הַיַּרְדֵּן יִכָּרֵתוּן	The waters of the Jordan shall be cut off. (Josh. 3:13)

(b) The Nif'al imperfect is sometimes used in a frequentative sense, expressing repeated, habitual, or customary actions.

Examples:

וּשְׁמוֹ לֹא־יִזָּכֵר עוֹד	And his name shall not be remembered again. (Jer. 11:19)
וְאַתֶּם כֹּהֲנֵי יְהוָה תִּקָּרֵאוּ	And you shall be called the priests of the LORD. (Isa. 61:6)

(c) The Nif'al imperfect is sometimes used to express actions that are contingent upon other elements in the context. The possibilities of translation are manifold and the context must be relied upon to determine which is more accurate. Jussives and cohortatives are included here.

Examples:

אוּלַי יִמָּצְאוּן שָׁם אַרְבָּעִים [אֲנָשִׁים]	Suppose there should be found there forty [men]. (Gen. 18:29)
יִשָּׁפְטוּ גוֹיִם עַל־פָּנֶיךָ	Let the nations be judged before you. (Ps. 9:20; Eng. 9:19)

42.2 *The Pi'el Imperfect of* מָשַׁל *and* דָּבַר

3 ms	יִמְשֵׁל	יְדַבֵּר
3 fs	תִּמְשֵׁל	תְּדַבֵּר
2 ms	תִּמְשֵׁל	תְּדַבֵּר
2 fs	תִּמְשְׁלִי	תְּדַבְּרִי
1 cs	אֲמַשֵּׁל	אֲדַבֵּר
3 mp	יְמַשְׁלוּ	יְדַבְּרוּ
3 fp	תְּמַשֵּׁלְנָה	תְּדַבֵּרְנָה
2 mp	תְּמַשְׁלוּ	תְּדַבְּרוּ
2 fp	תְּמַשֵּׁלְנָה	תְּדַבֵּרְנָה
1 cp	נְמַשֵּׁל	נְדַבֵּר

(1) The two distinguishing characteristics of the Pi'el imperfect are the sheva after the prefix consonant (normally ְ , but ֲ after א), and the doubling of the middle consonant of the verb root. Note also that the stem vowel in the syllable before the נָה endings (3 fp and 2 fp) is ṣere, as in all active stems (except Qal).

(2) The Pi'el imperfect also may be translated in a variety of ways. It is sometimes intensive in meaning, but often it is rendered as simple active, much like the Qal imperfect, or even as causative active, much like the Hif'il imperfect.

(a) The Pi'el imperfect is sometimes translated as a simple action in future time.
Examples:

כִּי יְדַבֵּר שָׁלוֹם אֶל־עַמּוֹ   For he will speak peace to his people. (Ps. 85:9; Eng. 85:8)

אֲשֶׁר יְדַבֵּר יְהוָה אֹתוֹ אֲדַבֵּר   What the LORD speaks, that will I speak. (Num. 24:13)

(b) The Pi'el imperfect is often used in a frequentative sense, expressing repeated, habitual, or customary actions.
Examples:

פֶּה־לָהֶם וְלֹא יְדַבֵּרוּ   They have a mouth, but they do not speak. (Ps. 135:16)

קֶשֶׁת יְשַׁבֵּר   He breaks the bow. (Ps. 46:10; Eng. 46:9)

מַה־תְּבַקֵּשׁ   What are you seeking? (Gen. 37:15)

(c) The Pi'el imperfect may also be used to express actions that are contingent upon other factors in the context. Jussives and cohortatives are included here.
Examples:

אֲדַבְּרָה־נָּא אֶל־הַמֶּלֶךְ   Let me speak, I pray, to the king. (2 Sam. 14:15)

לָמָה יְבַקֵּשׁ זֹאת אֲדֹנִי   Why should my lord seek (require) this? (1 Chr. 21:3)

42.3 *The Puʻal Imperfect of* כָּתַב *and* מָשַׁל

3 ms	יְמֻשַּׁל	יְכֻתַּב
3 fs	תְּמֻשַּׁל	תְּכֻתַּב
2 ms	תְּמֻשַּׁל	תְּכֻתַּב
2 fs	תְּמֻשְּׁלִי	תְּכֻתְּבִי
1 cs	אֲמֻשַּׁל	אֲכֻתַּב
3 mp	יְמֻשְּׁלוּ	יְכֻתְּבוּ
3 fp	תְּמֻשַּׁלְנָה	תְּכֻתַּבְנָה
2 mp	תְּמֻשְּׁלוּ	תְּכֻתְּבוּ
2 fp	תְּמֻשַּׁלְנָה	תְּכֻתַּבְנָה
1 cp	נְמֻשַּׁל	נְכֻתַּב

(1)   The distinguishing characteristics of the Puʻal imperfect are the sheva after the prefix consonant (normally ְ , but ֲ after א), the qibbuṣ after the first root consonant, and the doubling of the middle root consonant.

(2)   The Puʻal imperfect is the passive of the Piʻel imperfect. Examples:

וּמַלְאָךְ יְשֻׁלַּח־בּוֹ	And a messenger (angel) will be sent to him. (Prov. 17:11)
לָכֵן בְּזֹאת יְכֻפַּר עֲוֹן־יַעֲקֹב	Therefore by this the iniquity (guilt) of Jacob will be expiated (covered). (Isa. 27:9)
וְחַטָּאתְךָ תְּכֻפָּר	And your sin is forgiven (covered). (Isa. 6:7)

42.4 *The Hitpaʻel Imperfect of* מָשַׁל *and* הָלַךְ, *"he walked, went"*

3 ms	יִתְמַשֵּׁל	יִתְהַלֵּךְ
3 fs	תִּתְמַשֵּׁל	תִּתְהַלֵּךְ
2 ms	תִּתְמַשֵּׁל	תִּתְהַלֵּךְ
2 fs	תִּתְמַשְּׁלִי	תִּתְהַלְּכִי
1 cs	אֶתְמַשֵּׁל	אֶתְהַלֵּךְ
3 mp	יִתְמַשְּׁלוּ	יִתְהַלְּכוּ
3 fp	תִּתְמַשֵּׁלְנָה	תִּתְהַלֵּכְנָה
2 mp	תִּתְמַשְּׁלוּ	תִּתְהַלְּכוּ
2 fp	תִּתְמַשֵּׁלְנָה	תִּתְהַלֵּכְנָה
1 cp	נִתְמַשֵּׁל	נִתְהַלֵּךְ

(1) The distinguishing characteristics of the Hitpa‛el imperfect are the longer prefix and the doubling of the middle consonant of the verb root.

(2) The Hitpa‛el imperfect is normally reflexive in meaning but sometimes is almost parallel in meaning to the Qal imperfect, expressing a simple action in the active voice.

(a) The Hitpa‛el imperfect normally expresses an action that is repeated, customary, or habitual in nature.
Examples:

וְהַמֶּלֶךְ יִתְגַּדֵּל עַל־כָּל־אֵל And the king shall exalt himself above every god. (Dan. 11:36)

אֶתְהַלֵּךְ לִפְנֵי יְהוָה בְּאֶרֶץ חַיִּים I walk before the LORD in the land of the living. (Ps. 116:9)

וּבִשְׁמוֹ יִתְהַלָּכוּ And they shall walk in his name. (Zech. 10:12)

(b) Hitpa‛el imperfects are sometimes used to express actions that are contingent upon other factors in the context. These include imperfects used as jussives or cohortatives others whose translation requires one of the modal auxiliaries.
Examples:

אָמַרְתִּי בֵּיתְךָ וּבֵית אָבִיךָ I promised (said) that your house and

יִתְהַלְּכוּ לְפָנַי עַד־עוֹלָם The house of your father should walk before me forever. (1 Sam. 2:30)

יִתְקַדְּשׁוּ [הַכֹּהֲנִים] Let [the priests] sanctify themselves. (Exod. 19:22)

42.5 *The Hif‛il Imperfect of* מָשַׁל *and* סָתַר, *"he hid, concealed"*

3 ms	יַמְשִׁיל	יַסְתִּיר
3 fs	תַּמְשִׁיל	תַּסְתִּיר
2 ms	תַּמְשִׁיל	תַּסְתִּיר
2 fs	תַּמְשִׁילִי	תַּסְתִּירִי
1 cs	אַמְשִׁיל	אַסְתִּיר
3 mp	יַמְשִׁילוּ	יַסְתִּירוּ
3 fp	תַּמְשֵׁלְנָה	תַּסְתֵּרְנָה
2 mp	תַּמְשִׁילוּ	תַּסְתִּירוּ
2 fp	תַּמְשֵׁלְנָה	תַּסְתֵּרְנָה
1 cp	נַמְשִׁיל	נַסְתִּיר

(1)   The Hif'il imperfect is characterized by pataḥ in the prefix syllable and ḥireq-yod in the second syllable.

(2)   Ḥireq-yod is unchangeably long and cannot be reduced to a vocal sheva before vocalic suffixes (2 fs, 3 mp, and 2 mp). It is therefore retained in each of these forms and the syllable in which it stands continues to bear the accent. Hif'il is the only stem in which the accent does not shift before a vocalic suffix (cf. XII.30.4 [3], p. 84; XV.39.3 [2], p. 128).

(3)   The נָה suffixes (3 fp, 2 fp) do not draw the accent to themselves. Like the Pi'el and Hitpa'el imperfects, Hif'il imperfect has a ṣere in the root syllable before נָה suffixes (cf. XV.39.3 [3], p. 128).

(4)   The Hif'il imperfect normally serves as the causative of the Qal imperfect. However, this may vary from verb to verb. Often the meaning of a form can only be determined by a careful analysis of the context in which it stands.

(a)   A Hif'il imperfect sometimes describes a simple action in future time.

Examples:

אַכְרִית אֶת־שְׁמוֹת הָעֲצַבִּים מִן־הָאָרֶץ	I will cut off the names of the idols from the land. (Zech. 13:2)
שָׁלוֹשׁ עָרִים תַּבְדִּיל לָךְ בְּתוֹךְ אַרְצֶךְ	Three cities you shall set apart (separate) for yourself in your land. (Deut. 19:2)
וְאֶת בָּנָיו תַּקְרִיב	And his sons you shall bring (cause to draw near). (Exod. 29:8)
הוּא־יַשְׁמִיד אֶת־הַגּוֹיִם הָאֵלֶּה מִלְּפָנֶיךָ	He [emphatic] will destroy these nations before you. (Deut. 31:3)

(b)   Often the Hif'il imperfect is used to express repeated, habitual, or customary actions.

Examples:

אֶל־פֶּתַח אֹהֶל מוֹעֵד יַקְרִיב אֹתוֹ	At the door of the tent of meeting he shall offer it (bring it near). (Lev. 1:3)
אַזְכִּירָה שִׁמְךָ בְּכָל־דֹּר וָדֹר	I will cause your name to be celebrated (remembered) in all generations. (Ps. 45:18; Eng. 45:17)

42.6 *The Hofʻal Imperfect of* מָשַׁל

3 ms	יָמְשַׁל	3 mp	יָמְשְׁלוּ
3 fs	תָּמְשַׁל	3 fp	תָּמְשַׁלְנָה
2 ms	תָּמְשַׁל	2 mp	תָּמְשְׁלוּ
2 fs	תָּמְשְׁלִי	2 fp	תָּמְשַׁלְנָה
1 cs	אָמְשַׁל	1 cp	נָמְשַׁל

(1)   The distinguishing characteristics of the Hofʻal imperfect are qameṣ-ḥaṭuf as the prefix vowel and pataḥ as the vowel between the second and third consonants of the verb root. This pataḥ is continued before the נָה suffixes, as in the Nifʻal and Puʻal imperfects.

(2)   The Hofʻal imperfect is the passive of the Hifʻil imperfect. Its occurrences in the Hebrew Bible are relatively infrequent, so that the examples given here are necessarily drawn from weak verbs.

Examples:

	Hifʻil Imperfect 3 ms	Hofʻal Imperfect 3 ms
(a)	יָבִיא, "he will bring,"	יוּבָא, "he will be brought"
	from בּוֹא, "to go"	(see 2 Kgs. 12:5,17)
(b)	יָמִית, "he will kill,"	יוּמַת, "he will be killed"
	from מוּת, "to die"	(see Exod. 19:12; 21:15)

43. Verbs: Imperfects with Vav Consecutive

43.1   The vav consecutive is a special form of the conjunction which can be prefixed to imperfect forms of Hebrew verbs to express the narrated past. A passage narrating consecutive events in past time will often begin with a perfect, and then be continued by a series of imperfects with vav consecutive. Because both perfects and imperfects in such a sequence are normally translated in the past tense, it is common for grammarians to refer to the vav consecutive as the "vav conversive" and to claim that it "converts" imperfect forms of the verb into perfects. It would be simpler to say that imperfects prefixed with vav consecutives represent consecutive actions that from the reader's viewpoint took place in past time. They may be understood as either sequential ("and then") or consequential ("and so"), although it is not always possible to draw a sharp line of distinction between these two meanings, nor is it always necessary to express the distinction in translation.

43.2   The vav consecutive is written ·וַ (vav, plus pataḥ, plus dagesh forte in the following consonant). The rules for its pointing are similar to those for the definite article (see V.14, pp. 24ff.). If, for example, the vav consecutive is prefixed to the first person singular form of the imperfect, which begins with א, the dagesh forte is rejected by א and the preceding vowel has to be lengthened (pataḥ to qameṣ). Examples:

וָאֶזְכֹּר   "and I remembered" (Exod. 6:5)

וָאֶכְתֹּב   "and I wrote" (Jer. 32:10)

The dagesh forte is also rejected by certain non-gutturals that are accompanied by vocal shevas. This happens most frequently when a vav consecutive is prefixed to a word that begins with יְ (yod, supported by a vocal sheva).

43.3 The Qal imperfect third person masculine singular form of אָמַר, "he said," without vav consecutive, is written יֹאמַר. However, with vav consecutive, it is changed to וַיֹּאמֶר, translated, "and (then) he said." This form occurs so frequently in the Hebrew Bible that it should be committed to memory.

43.4 Examples of imperfects with vav consecutive:

(a) וַיִּכְתֹּב בְּשֵׁם הַמֶּלֶךְ   And he wrote in the name of the king. (Est. 8:10)

(b) וַתִּכְתֹּב אֶסְתֵּר הַמַּלְכָּה   Then Esther the queen wrote. (Est. 9:29)

(c) וַיַּמְלִיכוּ אֹתוֹ   And they made him king
עַל־כָּל־יִשְׂרָאֵל   over all Israel. (1 Kgs. 12:20)

(d) וַיְדַבֵּר שְׁלֹשֶׁת   And he spoke three thousand
אֲלָפִים מָשָׁל   proverbs. (1 Kgs. 5:12)

44. He-Directive (הָ)

Hebrew frequently makes use of the suffix הָ to indicate "direction toward" or "motion toward."

44.1 He-directive may be added to both common and proper nouns, and also to adverbs of direction. It is never accented, and must not be confused with the feminine singular ending of nouns.

44.2 Common nouns having the He-directive suffix may appear either with or without the article.

44.3 The vowel and accent changes that occur when He-directive is added to nouns and adverbs are unpredictable, so that each form must be learned individually. Some of the more common occurrences are these:

146

(1) He-directive with common nouns:

(a)   אֶרֶץ   ground, earth   אַרְצָה   to the ground (2 Sam. 14:11)

(b)   הַבַּיִת   the house   הַבַּיְתָה   to the house (Gen. 43:26)

(c)   הָהָר   the mountain   הָהָרָה   to the mountain (Deut. 10:1)

(2) He-directive with proper nouns:

(a)   מִצְרַיִם   Egypt   מִצְרַיְמָה   toward Egypt (Gen. 41:57)

(b)   בָּבֶל   Babylon   בָּבֶלָה   toward Babylon (Jer. 29:20)

(c)   יְרוּשָׁלַיִם   Jerusalem   יְרוּשָׁלַיְמָה   toward Jerusalem
(2 Chr. 32:9)

(3) He-directive with directional adverbs:

(a)   שָׁם   there   שָׁמָּה   thither, to there (Gen. 24:8)

(b)   אָן   where?   אָנָה   whither? to where?
(Ps. 139:7)

(c)   צָפוֹן   north   צָפוֹנָה   northward (Gen. 13:14)

(d)   תֵּימָן   south   תֵּימָנָה   southward (Deut. 3:27)

(e)   קֶדֶם   east   קֵדְמָה   eastward (Gen. 13:14)

(f)   יָם   west   יָמָּה   westward (Gen. 13:14)

45. Conjunctive Dagesh Forte

A dagesh forte is sometimes placed in the initial consonant of a word in order to link it to the preceding word. This always happens when the first word is זֶה or מַה and they are joined to the following words by a maqqef. It also happens when the first word ends in qames, qames-he, or segol-he, and the second word is monosyllabic. Some grammarians prefer to call the conjunctive dagesh forte the "euphonic dagesh forte." The phonetic value of this dagesh is not certain.

Examples:

(a)   אֲדַבְּרָה־נָּא אֶל־הַמֶּלֶךְ   Let me speak, I pray, to the king.
(2 Sam. 14:15)

(b)   זֶה־שְּׁמִי לְעֹלָם   This is my name forever. (Exod. 3:15)

(c)   מַה־זֹּאת עָשָׂה   What is this (that) God has
אֱלֹהִים לָנוּ   done to us? (Gen. 42:28)

147

EXERCISES

1. Write the following inflections:

        (1) Qal imperfect of מָשַׁל

        (2) Nifʻal imperfect of קָבַר

        (3) Piʻel imperfect of דִּבֶּר

        (4) Puʻal imperfect of כָּתַב

        (5) Hitpaʻel imperfect of הָלַךְ

        (6) Hifʻil imperfect of סָתַר

        (7) Hofʻal imperfect of שָׁלַח

2. Each of the following examples contains an imperfect form of a Hebrew verb. Complete the translation by supplying the meaning of the verb form. In the space marked (a) give its stem, in (b) its person, gender, and number, and in (c) its root.

     Example:

וַיְגַנֵּב אַבְשָׁלוֹם אֶת־לֵב אַנְשֵׁי יִשְׂרָאֵל   (a) ___Piʻel___

Absalom ___stole___ the heart of the men   (b) ___3 ms___

of Israel. (2 Sam. 15:6)   (c) ___גָּנַב___

(1)   וַיִּכְתֹּב בַּסֵּפֶר   (a) _____

And he _____ in the book. (1 Sam. 10:25)   (b) _____

    (c) _____

(2)   אֶת־פָּנֶיךָ יְהוָה אֲבַקֵּשׁ   (a) _____

Your face, O LORD, I will _____. (Ps. 27:8)   (b) _____

    (c) _____

(3)   וַיִּכְרְתוּ בְרִית בִּבְאֵר שָׁבַע   (a) _____

And they _____ a covenant at Beer-sheba.   (b) _____

(Gen. 21:32)   (c) _____

(4)   וּרְשָׁעִים מֵאֶרֶץ יִכָּרֵתוּ   (a) _____

But the wicked will be _____ from the land.   (b) _____

(Prov. 2:22)   (c) _____

(5)   וָאֶזְכֹּר אֶת־בְּרִיתִי   (a) _____

And I _____ my covenant. (Exod. 6:5)   (b) _____

    (c) _____

(6) וַיִּזְכֹּר בְּרִיתוֹ

And he _____ his covenant. (Ps. 106:45)

(a) _____
(b) _____
(c) _____

(7) וְלֹא יִזָּכְרוּ עוֹד

And they shall not be _____ again. (Zech. 13:2)

(a) _____
(b) _____
(c) _____

(8) בֵּן יְכַבֵּד אָב וְעֶבֶד אֲדֹנָיו

A son _____ (his) father and a servant
his master. (Mal. 1:6)

(a) _____
(b) _____
(c) _____

(9) וְאֶת־בְּנֵיהֶם יְלַמֵּדוּן

And they shall _____ their children (sons).
(Deut. 4:10)

(a) _____
(b) _____
(c) _____

(10) יְהוָה יִלָּחֵם לָכֶם

The LORD shall _____ for you. (Exod. 14:14)

(a) _____
(b) _____
(c) _____

(11) וָאֲמַלֵּא אֹתוֹ רוּחַ אֱלֹהִים

And I have _____ him (with) the Spirit of God.
(Exod. 31:3)

(a) _____
(b) _____
(c) _____

(12) אַסְתִּירָה פָנַי מֵהֶם

I will _____ my face from them. (Deut. 32:20)

(a) _____
(b) _____
(c) _____

(13) וְשָׁם תִּקָּבֵר

And there you shall be _____. (Jer. 20:6)

(a) _____
(b) _____
(c) _____

(14) פֶּן־נִשְׂרֹף אוֹתָךְ וְאֶת־בֵּית אָבִיךְ בָּאֵשׁ

Lest we _____ you and your father's house
with fire. (Judg. 14:15)

(a) _____
(b) _____
(c) _____

(15) יְדַבֶּר־נָא אֲדֹנִי הַמֶּלֶךְ

Let my lord the king _____. (2 Sam. 14:18)

(a) _____
(b) _____
(c) _____

3. Fill in the blanks with the correct pronouns.

(1) וַתֹּאמֶר מִי־אַתְּ בִּתִּי And _____ said, "_____ are _____, _____ daughter?" (Ruth 3:16)

(2) וַיֹּאמֶר לִי מִי־אָתָּה And _____ said to _____, "_____ are _____?" (2 Sam. 1:8)

(3) מַה־נֹּאמַר לַאדֹנִי מַה־נְּדַבֵּר _____ shall _____ say to _____ lord? _____ shall _____ speak? (Gen. 44:16)

(4) וְשָׁם אֲדַבֵּר אוֹתָךְ And there _____ will speak with _____. (Ezek. 3:22)

(5) וְלֹא־אֲדַבֵּר עוֹד בִּשְׁמוֹ _____ will speak no more in _____ name. (Jer. 20:9)

(6) וַיִּשְׂרְפוּ אוֹתָהּ וְאֶת־אָבִיהָ בָּאֵשׁ And _____ burned _____ and _____ father with fire. (Judg. 15:6)

(7) בֵּיתְךָ נִשְׂרֹף בָּאֵשׁ _____ house _____ will burn with fire. (Judg. 12:1)

(8) אַל־תַּסְתֵּר מִמֶּנִּי מִצְוֹתֶיךָ Do not hide _____ commandments from _____. (Ps. 119:19)

(9) וְאַתָּה לֹא תִמָּלֵט מִיָּדוֹ But _____ shall not escape (be delivered) from _____ hand. (Jer. 34:3)

(10) וּמִפָּנֶיךָ אֶסָּתֵר And from _____ face _____ shall be hidden. (Gen. 4:14)

(11) וְלֹא־תִלָּחֲמוּ עִם־אֲחֵיכֶם And _____ shall not fight against _____ brothers. (2 Chr. 11:4)

(12) יְהַלְלוּ שְׁמוֹ Let _____ praise _____ name. (Ps. 149:3)

4. Complete the translation of the following entries by filling in the blanks.

(1) וַיִּשְׁכַּב דָּוִד עִם־אֲבֹתָיו Then David lay down with _____ _____. (1 Kgs. 2:10)

(2) בְּיָדְךָ אַפְקִיד רוּחִי Into _____ _____ I commit _____ _____. (Ps. 31:6; Eng. 31:5)

(3) וַיִּשְׁמֹר מִצְוֹתָיו But he _____ his _____. (2 Kgs. 18:6)

(4)   הֲלוֹא אֲבַקֵּשׁ אֶת־דָּמוֹ מִיֶּדְכֶם   Shall I not _____ his _____ from your _____? (2 Sam. 4:11)

(5)   עַתָּה יִזְכֹּר עֲוֺנָם   Now he will _____ their _____. (Jer. 14:10)

(6)   וַיְשַׁבֵּר אֹתָם   And he _____ _____. (Exod. 32:19)

(7)   יִשָּׁפְטוּ גוֹיִם עַל־פָּנֶיךָ   Let the _____ be _____ before you. (Ps. 9:20; Eng. 9:19)

(8)   וַעֲבָדַי יִשְׁכְּנוּ־שָׁמָּה   And my _____ shall _____ there. (Isa. 65:9)

(9)   וְלֹא־יִזָּכְרוּ עוֹד   And _____ shall be _____ no more. (Zech. 13:2)

(10)   יִזָּכֵר עֲוֺן אֲבֹתָיו   May the iniquity of his _____ be _____. (Ps. 109:14)

(11)   וַיִּכְתֹּב בְּשֵׁם הַמֶּלֶךְ   And he _____ in the _____ of the _____. (Est. 8:10)

(12)   וְלֹא־יִזָּכֵר שֵׁם־יִשְׂרָאֵל עוֹד   Let the _____ of Israel be _____ no more. (Ps. 83:5; Eng. 83:4)

5. Practice pronouncing the Hebrew. Cover the English translation and practice translating from sight.

(1)   אַכְרִית אֶת־שְׁמוֹת [הַנְּבִיאִים] מִן־הָאָרֶץ וְלֹא יִזָּכְרוּ עוֹד   I will cut off the names of [the prophets] from the earth, and they shall be remembered no more. (Zech. 13:2)

(2)   כֹּל אֲשֶׁר־יִקְרָא בְּשֵׁם יְהוָה יִמָּלֵט   Whoever calls on the name of the LORD shall be delivered. (Joel 3:5)

(3)   וַיִּשְׁכֹּן כְּבוֹד־יְהוָה עַל־הַר סִינַי   The glory of the LORD abode on Mount Sinai. (Exod. 24:16)

(4)   וַיְלַמְּדוּ סֵפֶר תּוֹרַת יְהוָה בְּכָל־עָרֵי יְהוּדָה   And they taught the book of the law of the LORD in all the cities of Judah. (2 Chr. 17:9)

(5)   בְּנֵי יִשְׂרָאֵל אַל־תִּלָּחֲמוּ עִם־יְהוָה אֱלֹהֵי־אֲבֹתֵיכֶם   O sons of Israel, do not fight against (with) the LORD, the God of your fathers. (2 Chr. 13:12)

(6)   וַיִּקָּבֵר עִם־אֲבֹתָיו בְּעִיר דָּוִד   And he was buried with his fathers in the city of David. (1 Kgs. 14:31)

(7)   וַיִּשְׂרֹף אֶת־בֵּית־יְהֹוָה
       וְאֶת־בֵּית הַמֶּלֶךְ וְאֵת
       כָּל־בָּתֵּי יְרוּשָׁלַם

He burned the house of the LORD
and the house of the king and all
the houses of Jerusalem. (2 Kgs. 25:9)

(8)   אֶשְׁפּוֹךְ אֶת־רוּחִי עַל־
       כָּל־בָּשָׂר

I will pour out my spirit upon all flesh.
(Joel 3:1)

(9)   אֶת־הַדָּבָר אֲשֶׁר־אֲדַבֵּר
       אֵלֶיךָ אֹתוֹ תְדַבֵּר

The word that I speak unto you, that
shall you speak. (Num. 22:35)

(10)   וְלֹא יִקָּרֵא עוֹד אֶת־שִׁמְךָ
       אַבְרָם

And your name shall no more be
called Abram. (Gen. 17:5)

(11)   כִּי בֵיתִי בֵּית־תְּפִלָּה יִקָּרֵא
       לְכָל־הָעַמִּים

For my house shall be called a house of
prayer for all peoples. (Isa. 56:7)

(12)   וַיִּתְהַלֵּךְ חֲנוֹךְ אֶת־הָאֱלֹהִים

And Enoch walked with God. (Gen. 5:24)

(13)   אֶתְהַלֵּךְ לִפְנֵי יְהֹוָה בְּאֶרֶץ
       חַיִּים

I walk before the LORD in the
land of the living. (Ps. 116:9)

(14)   עַד־אָנָה תַּסְתִּיר אֶת־פָּנֶיךָ
       מִמֶּנִּי

How long will you hide your face
from me? (Ps. 13:2; Eng. 13:1)

(15)   וַיִּזְכֹּר אֱלֹהִים אֶת־נֹחַ

And then God remembered Noah.
(Gen. 8:1)

VOCABULARY

(1)   בֶּטֶן   (f) belly, body, womb
(2)   [ברך]   he blessed
(3)   גָּאַל   he redeemed
(4)   הָלַל   he praised
(5)   חַטָּאת   (f) sin
(6)   [לחם]   he fought
(7)   לָמַד   he learned
(8)   מָלֵא   he was full
(9)   מָלַט   he escaped

(10)   נָשָׂא   he lifted, carried
(11)   סָתַר   he concealed
(12)   עָוֹן   iniquity, guilt
(13)   פֶּשַׁע   rebellion, transgression
(14)   קָבַר   he buried
(15)   רָאָה   he saw
(16)   רָקִיעַ   expanse, firmament
(17)   שָׂרַף   he burned
(18)   שָׁפַךְ   he poured out

LESSON XVII

46. Verbs: Pronominal Suffixes with Perfects

46.1 A transitive verb is any verb that may take a direct object. When the object of a transitive verb is a pronoun, this may be expressed in either of two ways. The pronominal suffix may be joined to אֵת, the sign of the direct object (see XI.27.2 [1], p. 71), and placed either before or after the verb. Or the pronominal suffix may be joined directly to the end of the verb of which it serves as object. There is no difference in meaning between these two ways of expressing the pronominal object.

Examples:

יְהוָה שְׁלָחַנִי	The LORD sent me. (Jer. 26:12)
אֹתִי שָׁלַח יְהוָה	The LORD sent me [emphatic]. (1 Sam. 15:1)
אֹתִי עָזָבוּ	They have forsaken me [emphatic]. (Jer. 2:13)
בָּנַיִךְ עֲזָבוּנִי	Your sons have forsaken me. (Jer. 5:7)
וְהִכְרַתִּיו מִתּוֹךְ עַמִּי	And I will cut him off from the midst of my people. (Ez. 14:8)
וְהִכְרַתִּי אֹתוֹ מִקֶּרֶב עַמּוֹ	And I will cut him off from the midst of his people. (Lev. 20:3)
בֵּרַכְנוּ אֶתְכֶם בְּשֵׁם יְהוָה	We bless you in the name of the LORD. (Ps. 129:8)
בֵּרַכְנוּכֶם מִבֵּית יְהוָה	We bless you from the house of the LORD. (Ps. 118:26)

46.2 The pronominal suffixes for perfects that end in vowels are the same for all stems of the verb. They are as follows:

1 cs	נִי	me	1 cp	נוּ	us
2 ms	ךָ	you	2 mp	כֶם	you
2 fs	ךְ	you	2 fp	כֶן	you
3 ms	הוּ, וֹ	him	3 mp	הֶם, ם	them
3 fs	הָ	her	3 fp	ן	them

153

(1) Example: Pronominal suffixes added to שָׁמְרוּ, Qal perfect, 3 cp, from שָׁמַר, "he kept," translated "they kept."

שְׁמָרוּנִי	they kept me	שְׁמָרוּנוּ	they kept us
שְׁמָרוּךָ	they kept you	שְׁמָרוּכֶם	they kept you
שְׁמָרוּךְ	they kept you	שְׁמָרוּכֶן	they kept you
שְׁמָרוּהוּ	they kept him	שְׁמָרוּם	they kept them
שְׁמָרוּהָ	they kept her	שְׁמָרוּן	they kept them

(A) Only the strong pronominal suffixes כֶם, כֶן, and הֶם draw the accent to themselves. Before all other suffixes, the accent is placed on the syllable beginning with the final stem consonant of the verb.

(B) The addition of a pronominal suffix to a verb form having a vocal sheva under the second stem consonant will cause the sheva to be restored to its original form (patah), and then to be lengthened to qames (open unaccented syllables require long vowels). Further, the qames under the initial stem consonant, now left in an open syllable two syllables removed from the accented syllable, must be volatilized (reduced to a vocal sheva). Note, however, that these changes do not take place with vowels in closed syllables or with vowels that are unchangeably long. These rules are illustrated in the examples given above.

(2) Example: Pronominal suffixes added to בִּקְּשׁוּ, Pi‘el perfect, 3 ms, from [בקשׁ], "he sought," translated "they sought."

בִּקְשׁוּנִי	they sought me	בִּקְשׁוּנוּ	they sought us
בִּקְשׁוּךָ	they sought you	בִּקְשׁוּכֶם	they sought you
בִּקְשׁוּךְ	they sought you	בִּקְשׁוּכֶן	they sought you
בִּקְשׁוּהוּ	they sought him	בִּקְשׁוּהֶם	they sought them
בִּקְשׁוּהָ	they sought her	בִּקְשׁוּן	they sought them

(ק loses its dagesh forte because it is supported by a vocal sheva.)

(3) Example: Pronominal suffixes added to הִכְרִיתוּ, Hif‘il perfect, 3 cp, from כָּרַת "he cut off," translated "they cut off."

הִכְרִיתוּנִי	they cut me off	הִכְרִיתוּנוּ	they cut us off
הִכְרִיתוּךָ	they cut you off	הִכְרִיתוּכֶם	they cut you off
הִכְרִיתוּךְ	they cut you off	הִכְרִיתוּכֶן	they cut you off
הִכְרִיתוּהוּ	they cut him off	הִכְרִיתוּם	they cut them off
הִכְרִיתוּהָ	they cut her off	הִכְרִיתוּן	they cut them off

46.3 Pronominal suffixes for perfects ending in consonants are also the same for all verb stems. They are as follows:

1 cs	נִי ָ	(pausal נִי ָ)	me	1 cp	נוּ ָ	us
2 ms	ךָ ְ	(pausal ךָ ֶ)	you	2 mp	כֶם ְ	you
2 fs	ךְ ָ or ךְ ֵ		you	2 fp	כֶן ְ	you
3 ms	הוּ ָ or וֹ		him	3 mp	ם ָ	them
3 fs	הּ ָ		her	3 fp	ן ָ	them

      (1) Example: Pronominal suffixes added to שָׁמַר, Qal perfect, 3 ms, translated "he kept."

שְׁמָרַנִי	he kept me	שְׁמָרָנוּ	he kept us
שְׁמָרְךָ	he kept you	שְׁמַרְכֶם	he kept you
שְׁמָרֵךְ	he kept you	שְׁמַרְכֶן	he kept you
שְׁמָרוֹ	he kept him (it)	שְׁמָרָם	he kept them
שְׁמָרָהּ	he kept her (it)	שְׁמָרָן	he kept them

(A) A connecting vowel is used to join pronominal suffixes to verb forms ending in a consonant. Perfects tend to prefer pataḥ or qameṣ as the connecting vowel, whereas imperfects prefer ṣere (cf. XVII.47.2, pp. 157f.).

(B) The vocalization changes that take place when pronominal suffixes are added to Qal perfect ending in a consonant are the same as those for forms ending in a vowel. This means that the vowel in the first syllable is volatilized and the vowel in the second syllable is raised to a qameṣ. This qameṣ receives a meteg whenever it precedes a vocal sheva. This occurs in 2 ms, 2 mp, and 2 fp (see above).

      (2) Example: Pronominal suffixes added to הִכְרִית, Hifʿil perfect, 3 ms from כָּרַת, "he cut off."

הִכְרִיתַנִי	he cut me off	הִכְרִיתָנוּ	he cut us off
הִכְרִיתְךָ	he cut you off	הִכְרִיתְכֶם	he cut you off
הִכְרִיתֵךְ	he cut you off	הִכְרִיתְכֶן	he cut you off
הִכְרִיתוֹ	he cut him off	הִכְרִיתָם	he cut them off
הִכְרִיתָהּ	he cut her off	הִכְרִיתָן	he cut them off

No vowel changes take place when pronominal suffixes are added to הִכְרִית. This is because the first syllable of this Hifʿil form is a closed syllable and therefore its vowel cannot be volatilized. Likewise, the vowel of the second syllable is unchangeably long and therefore cannot be shortened.

46.4   There are additional forms of the perfect inflection that undergo certain internal changes when pronominal suffixes are added to them. Such forms are relatively rare and the following examples need only be noted for future reference.

(1)   When pronominal suffixes are to be added to a perfect 3 fs, the הָ ending of the form is replaced by ת_ , an old feminine ending. Examples:

שָׁמְרָה   (Qal) becomes ־שָׁמְרַת

בִּקְשָׁה   (Pi‹el) becomes ־בִּקְשַׁת

הִשְׁמִידָה   (Hif‹il) becomes ־הִשְׁמִידַת

Pronominal suffixes are then added to the resultant form in this manner:

שְׁמָרַתְנִי   she kept me

שְׁמָרַתְךָ   she kept you

etc.

(2)   When pronominal suffixes are added to the perfect 2 fs (שָׁמַרְתְּ) the final תְּ becomes תִי־. The resultant form (־שְׁמַרְתִּי) is identical to the perfect 1 cs and only the context can be relied upon to distinguish between the two forms.

(3)   When pronominal suffixes are added to the perfect 2 mp (שְׁמַרְתֶּם) the final mem is dropped and the preceding seḡol is changed to šureq. The resultant form to which suffixes are added is ־שְׁמַרְתּוּ.

46.5   In summary, the forms of the Qal perfect used before pronominal suffixes are as follows:

3 ms	־שְׁמָר		
3 fs	־שְׁמָרַת	3 cp	־שְׁמָרוּ
2 ms	־שְׁמָרְת	2 mp	־שְׁמַרְתּוּ
2 fs	־שְׁמַרְתִּי	2 fp	־שְׁמַרְתּוּ
1 cs	־שְׁמַרְתִּי	1 cp	־שְׁמַרְנוּ

47. Verbs: Pronominal Suffixes with Imperfects

47.1   Pronominal suffixes for imperfects ending in vowels are the same as those for perfects ending in vowels. They are the following:

1 cs	נִי	me	1 cp	נוּ	us
2 ms	ךָ	you	2 mp	כֶם	you
2 fs	ךְ	you	2 fp	כֶן	you
3 ms	הוּ, וֹ	him	3 mp	ם	them
3 fs	הָ	her	3 fp	ן	them

(1) Example: Pronominal suffixes added to יִשְׁמְרוּ, Qal imperfect, 3 mp, from שָׁמַר, "he kept," translated "they will keep"

יִשְׁמְרוּנִי	they will keep me	יִשְׁמְרוּנוּ	they will keep us
יִשְׁמְרוּךָ	they will keep you	יִשְׁמְרוּכֶם	they will keep you
יִשְׁמְרוּךְ	they will keep you	יִשְׁמְרוּכֶן	they will keep you
יִשְׁמְרוּהוּ	they will keep him (it)	יִשְׁמְרוּם	they will keep them
יִשְׁמְרוּהָ	they will keep her (it)	יִשְׁמְרוּן	they will keep them

An alternate form sometimes occurs when a pronominal suffix stands after an imperfect ending in šureq. The šureq is sometimes written defectively, i.e., as a qibbuṣ. The fact that qibbuṣ in such instances bears the accent indicates that it is still regarded as a long vowel. Changes of this sort will normally take place before the third masculine singular pronominal suffix.

Examples:

וַיַּמְלִיכֵהוּ תַחַת־אָבִיו   And they make him king instead of his father. (2 Chr. 36:1)

וַיְבַקְשֻׁהוּ וְלֹא נִמְצָא   And they sought him, but he could not be found. (1 Sam. 10:21)

(2) Example: Pronominal suffixes added to יְשַׁלְּחוּ, Pi‘el imperfect 3 mp, from שָׁלַח, "he sent," translated "they will send"

יְשַׁלְּחוּנִי	they will send me	יְשַׁלְּחוּנוּ	they will send us
יְשַׁלְּחוּךָ	they will send you	יְשַׁלְּחוּכֶם	they will send you
יְשַׁלְּחוּךְ	they will send you	יְשַׁלְּחוּכֶן	they will send you
יְשַׁלְּחֻהוּ	they will send him	יְשַׁלְּחוּם	they will send them
יְשַׁלְּחוּהָ	they will send her	יְשַׁלְּחוּן	they will send them

(Some Pi‘el forms retain the dagesh forte in middle consonants supported by a vocal sheva, as is the case with לְ in the examples used here.)

47.2 Pronominal suffixes for imperfects ending in consonants are the same for all verb stems. A connecting vowel is needed between the suffix and the verb form. Imperfects prefer ṣere, or another vowel of the "e" class (ֵ or ֶ), as the connecting vowel.

1 cs	נִי	me	1 cp	נוּ	us
2 ms	ךָ	(pausal ךְָ) you	2 mp	כֶם	you
2 fs	ךְ	you	2 fp	כֶן	you
3 ms	הוּ	him (it)	3 mp	ם	them
3 fs	הָ , הָ	her (it)	3 fp	ן	them

(1) Example: Pronominal suffixes added to יִשְׁמֹר, Qal imperfect 3 ms, from שָׁמַר, "he kept," translated "he will keep"

יִשְׁמְרֵנִי	he will keep me	יִשְׁמְרֵנוּ	he will keep us
יִשְׁמָרְךָ	he will keep you	יִשְׁמָרְכֶם	he will keep you
יִשְׁמְרֵךְ	he will keep you	יִשְׁמָרְכֶן	he will keep you
יִשְׁמְרֵהוּ	he will keep him (it)	יִשְׁמְרֵם	he will keep them
יִשְׁמְרֶהָ	he will keep her (it)	יִשְׁמְרֵן	he will keep them

The ḥolem in the second syllable of יִשְׁמֹר is shortened to qameṣ ḥatuf before the pronominal suffixes ךָ (2 ms), כֶם (2 mp), and כֶן (2 fp). Before all other pronominal suffixes ḥolem is reduced to a vocal sheva.

(2) Example: Pronominal suffixes added to יְבַקֵּשׁ, Piʻel imperfect 3 ms, from [בקשׁ], "he sought," translated "he will seek"

יְבַקְשֵׁנִי	he will seek me	יְבַקְשֵׁנוּ	he will seek us
יְבַקֶּשְׁךָ	he will seek you	יְבַקֶּשְׁכֶם	he will seek you
יְבַקְשֵׁךְ	he will seek you	יְבַקֶּשְׁכֶן	he will seek you
יְבַקְשֵׁהוּ	he will seek him (it)	יְבַקְשֵׁם	he will seek them
יְבַקְשֶׁהָ	he will seek her (it)	יְבַקְשֵׁן	he will seek them

In three of the examples listed above, the vocal sheva that should have been placed beneath ק, the middle consonant of the verb root, is changed to seʻgol. The three examples are 2 ms, 2 mp, and 2 fp. The rule that has been applied here is that whenever two vocal shevas stand adjacent to each other within a word, the first of the shevas must be changed to a full vowel.

(2 ms)	יְבַקְשְׁךָ	becomes	יְבַקֶּשְׁךָ
(2 mp)	יְבַקְשְׁכֶם	becomes	יְבַקֶּשְׁכֶם
(2 fp)	יְבַקְשְׁכֶן	becomes	יְבַקֶּשְׁכֶן

(3) Example: Pronominal suffixes added to יַקְרִיב, Hif'il imperfect 3 ms, from קָרַב, "he drew near," translated "he will bring near"

יַקְרִיבֵנִי	he will bring me near	יַקְרִיבֵנוּ	he will bring us near
יַקְרִיבְךָ	he will bring you near	יַקְרִיבְכֶם	he will bring you near
יַקְרִיבֵךְ	he will bring you near	יַקְרִיבְכֶן	he will bring you near
יַקְרִיבֵהוּ	he will bring him (it) near	יַקְרִיבֵם	he will bring them near
יַקְרִיבֶהָ	he will bring her (it) near	יַקְרִיבֵן	he will bring them near

There is no volatilization before pronominal suffixes in this verb form since the initial syllable is closed and the vowel of the second syllable (יִ) is unchangeably long.

47.3 Sometimes a variant form of the pronominal suffix occurs with verbs ending in consonants. It involves the insertion of an additional nun between the verb form and the suffix.

(1) The following forms are found in the Hebrew Bible:

1 cs	ַנִּי	(for ַנְנִי)	1 cp	ַנּוּ	(for ַנְנוּ)
2 ms	ַךָּ	(for ַנְךָ)			
3 ms	ַנּוּ	(for ַנְנוּ)			
3 fs	ַנָּה	(for ַנְנָה)			

(A) There is no change in meaning between a suffix which has the additional nun and one which does not have it.

(B) Whenever nun is supported by a silent sheva (syllable divider), nun is assimilated into the following consonant by means of a dagesh forte. This accounts for the unusual forms listed above. Note especially the dagesh forte in the final kaf of the 2 ms suffix (ַךָּ).

(C) The suffix for third person masculine singular is identical to that for first person common plural. Only the context will enable the reader to distinguish between the two.

(2) Example: Alternate forms of pronominal suffixes attached to יְבַקֵּשׁ, Pi'el imperfect 3 ms, from [בקשׁ], "he sought," translated "he will seek"

יְבַקְשֵׁנִי	he will seek me	יְבַקְשֶׁנָּה	he will seek her (it)
יְבַקֶּשְׁךָ	he will seek you	יְבַקְשֵׁנוּ	he will seek us
יְבַקְשֶׁנּוּ	he will seek him (it)		

EXERCISES

1. Match the following:

( )   וַיִּשְׂרְפָהּ בָּאֵשׁ   (A)   They seek him with all the heart.
                                    (Ps. 119:2)

( )   שָׁמָּה תִּקְבְּרֵנִי   (B)   They did not kill them. (Josh. 9:26)

( )   עַל־הָאָרֶץ תִּשְׁפְּכֶנּוּ   (C)   And they clothed them. (2 Chr. 28:15)

( )   בְּכָל־לֵב יִדְרְשׁוּהוּ   (D)   You shall pour it out upon the earth.
                                    (Deut. 12:16)

( )   וְלֹא הֲרַגְתִּיךָ   (E)   I will honor him. (Ps. 91:15)

( )   וְלֹא הֲרַגְתָּנִי   (F)   And he clothed them. (Gen. 3:21)

( )   וְלֹא הֲרָגוּם   (G)   There you shall bury me. (Gen. 50:5)

( )   וַיַּלְבִּשׁוּם   (H)   You shall sacrifice (offer) it.
                                    (Lev. 19:5)

( )   וַיַּלְבִּשֵׁם   (I)   I did not kill you.
                                    (1 Sam. 24:12; Eng. 24:11)

( )   תִּזְבָּחֵהוּ   (J)   You shall honor (glorify) me.
                                    (Ps. 50:15)

( )   אֲכַבְּדֵךְ   (K)   They shall glorify you. (Isa. 25:3)

( )   תְּכַבְּדֵנִי   (L)   And he burned it with fire.
                                    (1 Kgs. 9:16)

( )   אֲכַבְּדֵהוּ   (M)   And they clothed him. (Zech. 3:5)

( )   יְכַבְּדוּךָ   (N)   I will honor you. (Num. 22:17)

( )   וַיַּלְבִּשֻׁהוּ   (O)   You did not kill me.
                                    (1 Sam. 24:19; Eng. 24:18)

2. Fill in the blanks with the correct pronouns in the following phrases and sentences.

(1)   יְהוָה יִשְׁמָרְךָ מִכָּל־רָע   The LORD will keep _____ from all evil.
      (Ps. 121:7)

(2)   מָה־אֱנוֹשׁ כִּי־תִזְכְּרֶנּוּ   What is man that you remember _____?
      (Ps. 8:5; Eng. 8:4)

(3)   אַךְ טוֹב וָחֶסֶד יִרְדְּפוּנִי   Surely goodness and mercy shall pursue
      _____. (Ps. 23:6)

(4) וַיְשַׁלְּחֵהוּ יְהוָה אֱלֹהִים מִגַּן־עֵדֶן And the LORD God sent _____ out of the garden of Eden. (Gen. 3:23)

(5) תְּבַקְשֵׁם וְלֹא תִמְצָאֵם You shall seek _____ but you shall not find _____. (Isa. 41:12)

(6) וְכָל־עֲבָדָיו אֲהֵבוּךְ And all _____ servants love _____. (1 Sam. 18:22)

(7) יִרְאַת יְהוָה אֲלַמֶּדְכֶם The fear of the LORD I will teach _____. (Ps. 34:12; Eng. 34:11)

(8) יְהוָה אֱלֹהֵי הַשָּׁמַיִם אֲשֶׁר לְקָחַנִי מִבֵּית אָבִי the LORD, the God of the heavens, who took _____ from the house of _____ father (Gen. 24:7)

(9) וַיִּשְׁלָחֵנִי אֱלֹהִים לִפְנֵיכֶם And God sent _____ before _____. (Gen. 45:7)

(10) וַאֲנִי לֹא שְׁלַחְתִּיו But _____ did not send _____. (Jer. 29:31)

(11) וַאֲנִי לֹא־שְׁלַחְתִּים But _____ did not send _____. (Jer. 14:15)

(12) וַיִּרְדְּפֵם יִשְׂרָאֵל And Israel pursued _____. (1 Kgs. 20:20)

3. Supply the correct translation of the verb forms by filling in the blanks. In the space marked (a) give the stem of the verb, in (b) its form (perfect, imperfect), in (c) its person, gender, and number, and in (d) its root.

Example:

וּנְבַקְשֶׁנּוּ עִמָּךְ Let us __seek__ him with you. (Song of Sol. 6:1)

   (a) __Pi‛el__ (b) imperfect (c) __1 cp__ (d) [בקשׁ]

(1) וְלֹא בִקְשֻׁהוּ בְּכָל־זֹאת Yet they do not _____ him, for all this. (Hos. 7:10)

   (a) _____ (b) _____ (c) _____ (d) _____

(2) יְהַלְלוּהוּ שָׁמַיִם וָאָרֶץ Let heavens and earth _____ him. (Ps. 69:35; Eng. 69:34)

   (a) _____ (b) _____ (c) _____ (d) _____

(3) אִם־תְּבַקְשֶׁנָּה כַכָּסֶף If you _____ it like silver. (Prov. 2:4)

   (a) _____ (b) _____ (c) _____ (d) _____

161

(4)   עַל־כֵּן אֶזְכָּרְךָ מֵאֶרֶץ יַרְדֵּן   Therefore I _____ you from the land of
the Jordan. (Ps. 42:7; Eng. 42:6)

    (a) _____ (b) _____ (c) _____ (d) _____

(5)   יַבְדִּילַנִי יְהוָה מֵעַל עַמּוֹ   The LORD will _____ me from his people.
(Isa. 56:3)

    (a) _____ (b) _____ (c) _____ (d) _____

(6)   וָאֲשַׁבְּרֵם לְעֵינֵיכֶם   And I _____ them before your eyes. (Deut. 9:17)

    (a) _____ (b) _____ (c) _____ (d) _____

(7)   וּמִתּוֹרָתְךָ תְלַמְּדֶנּוּ   And out of your law you _____ him. (Ps. 94:12)

    (a) _____ (b) _____ (c) _____ (d) _____

(8)   שֶׁבַע בַּיּוֹם הִלַּלְתִּיךָ   I _____ you seven times in the day.
(Ps. 119:164)

    (a) _____ (b) _____ (c) _____ (d) _____

(9)   בְּצֵל כְּנָפֶיךָ תַּסְתִּירֵנִי   You will _____ me in the shadow of
your wings. (Ps. 17:8)

    (a) _____ (b) _____ (c) _____ (d) _____

(10)   אַל־נָא תִקְבְּרֵנִי בְּמִצְרָיִם   Do not _____ me in Egypt. (Gen. 47:29)

    (a) _____ (b) _____ (c) _____ (d) _____

(11)   וַיִּקְבְּרֻהוּ בְּבֵיתוֹ בָּרָמָה   And they _____ him in his house at Ramah.
(1 Sam. 25:1)

    (a) _____ (b) _____ (c) _____ (d) _____

(12)   אֲנִי יְדַעְתִּיךָ בַּמִּדְבָּר   I _____ you in the wilderness. (Hos. 13:5)

    (a) _____ (b) _____ (c) _____ (d) _____

4.   Read the Hebrew sentences and phrases aloud. Then cover the English and
practice translating the Hebrew from sight.

(1)   מָה־אֱנוֹשׁ כִּי־תִזְכְּרֶנּוּ וּבֶן־   What is man that you are mindful of
אָדָם כִּי תִפְקְדֶנּוּ   him, and the son of man that you
care for him? (Ps. 8:5; Eng. 8:4)

(2)   אַךְ טוֹב וָחֶסֶד יִרְדְּפוּנִי   Surely goodness and mercy shall pursue
כָּל־יְמֵי חַיָּי   me all the days of my life. (Ps. 23:6)

162

(3)   וַיִּתְהַלֵּךְ חֲנוֹךְ אֶת־הָאֱלֹהִים וְאֵינֶנּוּ כִּי־לָקַח אֹתוֹ אֱלֹהִים

And Enoch walked with God; and he was not, for God took him. (Gen. 5:24)

(4)   יְהוָה יִשְׁמָרְךָ מִכָּל־רָע יִשְׁמֹר אֶת־נַפְשֶׁךָ

The LORD will keep you from all evil; he will keep your soul. (Ps. 121:7)

(5)   אֵלִי אֵלִי לָמָה עֲזַבְתָּנִי

My God, my God, why have you forsaken me? (Ps. 22:2; Eng., 22:1)

(6)   אָהַבְתִּי אֶתְכֶם אָמַר יְהוָה וַאֲמַרְתֶּם בַּמָּה אֲהַבְתָּנוּ

I have loved you, says the LORD; but you say, How have you loved us? (Mal. 1:2)

(7)   וְזֶה־לְּךָ הָאוֹת כִּי אָנֹכִי שְׁלַחְתִּיךָ

And this will be the sign for you that I have sent you. (Exod. 3:12)

(8)   אֹתִי עָזְבוּ מְקוֹר מַיִם חַיִּים

Me they have forsaken, the fountain of living waters. (Jer. 2:13)

(9)   כִּי אַתָּה הִמְלַכְתַּנִי עַל־עַם רַב כַּעֲפַר הָאָרֶץ

For you have made me king over a people as many (numerous) as the dust of the earth. (2 Chr. 1:9)

(10)   יְהוָה אֱלֹהֵי הָעִבְרִים שְׁלָחַנִי אֵלֶיךָ

The LORD, the God of the Hebrews, sent me to you. (Exod. 7:16)

(11)   וַיְשַׁלְּחֵהוּ יְהוָה אֱלֹהִים מִגַּן־עֵדֶן

And the LORD God sent him from the garden of Eden. (Gen. 3:23)

(12)   כִּי־אָבִי וְאִמִּי עֲזָבוּנִי

For my father and my mother have forsaken me. (Ps. 27:10)

(13)   וַיִּכְתְּבֵם עַל־שְׁנֵי לֻחוֹת אֲבָנִים

And he wrote them upon two tablets of stone. (Deut. 4:13)

(14)   תַּמְשִׁילֵהוּ בְּמַעֲשֵׂי יָדֶיךָ

You made him to rule (have dominion) over the works of your hands. (Ps. 8:7; Eng. 8:6)

(15)   וְקֶשֶׁת וְחֶרֶב וּמִלְחָמָה אֶשְׁבּוֹר מִן־הָאָרֶץ וְהִשְׁכַּבְתִּים לָבֶטַח

And I will break the bow, the sword and warfare from the land; and I will make them lie down in safety. (Hos. 2:20; Eng. 2:18)

VOCABULARY

(1) בָּטַח   he trusted

(2) גָּדַל   he was (became) great

(3) דָּרַשׁ   he sought, inquired

(4) דֶּשֶׁא   grass

(5) הָרַג   he killed, slew

(6) זָבַח   he sacrificed

(7) חָזַק   he was (became) strong

(8) חָשַׁב   he thought, devised, reckoned

(9) כָּבֵד   he was (became) heavy; (Piʿel) he was honored, glorified

(10) כָּנָף   (f) wing, skirt

(11) [כפר]   (Piʿel) he covered, made atonement

(12) לָבַשׁ   he put on, wore

(13) נַחַל   torrent valley, wadi

(14) עָזַב   he abandoned, left, forsook

(15) קָרַב   he drew near, approached; (Hifʿil) offered

(16) רָדַף   he pursued, persecuted

(17) שֵׁבֶט   rod, staff, scepter, tribe

(18) שָׁכַן   he settled, dwelt

LESSON XVIII

48. Verbs: Qal Imperative*

Hebrew imperatives occur only in second person forms (masculine and feminine, singular and plural). They are used only to express positive commands and never to express prohibitions. Imperatives never appear in the Puʻal or Hofʻal stems, since these stems are always passive in meaning.

The Qal imperatives may be described as shortened forms of the Qal imperfect. The shortening involves the dropping of the preformatives from the imperfect second person forms (masculine and feminine, singular and plural).

The dropping of the Qal imperfect preformatives causes two vocal shevas to be left together at the beginning of two of the forms, the second feminine singular and the second masculine plural. Since two vocal shevas can never stand together, the first sheva in each of these forms is changed to a ḥireq.

48.1 *Examples of the Qal imperative of some representative strong verbs:*

(1) שָׁמַר he kept, watched

	Imperfect				Imperative
2 ms	תִּשְׁמֹר	→		→	שְׁמֹר
2 fs	תִּשְׁמְרִי	→	שִׁמְרִי	→	שִׁמְרִי
2 mp	תִּשְׁמְרוּ	→	שִׁמְרוּ	→	שִׁמְרוּ
2 fp	תִּשְׁמֹרְנָה	→		→	שְׁמֹרְנָה

(2) שָׁפַט he judged

	Imperfect				Imperative
2 ms	תִּשְׁפֹּט	→		→	שְׁפֹט
2 fs	תִּשְׁפְּטִי	→	שִׁפְטִי	→	שִׁפְטִי
2 mp	תִּשְׁפְּטוּ	→	שִׁפְטוּ	→	שִׁפְטוּ
2 fp	תִּשְׁפֹּטְנָה	→		→	שְׁפֹטְנָה

(3) שָׁכַב he lay down

	Imperfect				Imperative
2 ms	תִּשְׁכַּב	→		→	שְׁכַב
2 fs	תִּשְׁכְּבִי	→	שִׁכְבִי	→	שִׁכְבִי
2 mp	תִּשְׁכְּבוּ	→	שִׁכְבוּ	→	שִׁכְבוּ
2 fp	תִּשְׁכַּבְנָה	→		→	שְׁכַבְנָה

---

*Refer to Verb Chart 1, pp. 400f. for the conjugation of the strong verb.

48.2 *Examples of the Qal imperative of some representative classes of weak verbs:*

(1) עָמַד he stood (Pe Guttural)

2 ms	עֲמֹד	2 mp	עִמְדוּ
2 fs	עִמְדִי	2 fp	עֲמֹדְנָה

(2) אָכַל he ate (Pe ʾAlef)

2 ms	אֱכֹל	2 mp	אִכְלוּ
2 fs	אִכְלִי	2 fp	אֱכֹלְנָה

(3) שָׁמַע he heard (Lamed Guttural)

2 ms	שְׁמַע	2 mp	שִׁמְעוּ
2 fs	שִׁמְעִי	2 fp	שְׁמַעְנָה

(4) עָלָה he went up (Pe Guttural and Lamed He)

2 ms	עֲלֵה	2 mp	עֲלוּ
2 fs	עֲלִי	2 fp	עֲלֶינָה

(5) מָצָא he found (Lamed ʾAlef)

2 ms	מְצָא	2 mp	מִצְאוּ
2 fs	מִצְאִי	2 fp	מְצֶאנָה

(6) נָתַן he gave (Pe Nun)

2 ms	תֵּן	2 mp	תְּנוּ
2 fs	תְּנִי	2 fp	תֵּנָּה

(7) יָשַׁב he sat, dwelt (Pe Vav/Pe Yod)

2 ms	שֵׁב	2 mp	שְׁבוּ
2 fs	שְׁבִי	2 fp	שֵׁבְנָה

(8) יָדַע he knew (Pe Vav/Pe Yod and Lamed Guttural)

2 ms	דַּע	2 mp	דְּעוּ
2 fs	דְּעִי	2 fp	דַּעְנָה

(9) הָלַךְ he walked, went (Pe Guttural, inflected as Pe Vav/Pe Yod)

2 ms	לֵךְ	2 mp	לְכוּ
2 fs	לְכִי	2 fp	לֵכְנָה

(10) סָבַב he surrounded (Double ʿAyin)

2 ms	סֹב	2 mp	סֹבּוּ
2 fs	סֹבִּי	2 fp	סֻבֶּינָה

(11) קוּם to arise (ʿAyin Vav/ʿAyin Yod)

2 ms	קוּם	2 mp	קוּמוּ
2 fs	קוּמִי	2 fp	קוּמֶינָה (קֻמְנָה)

48.3 *Examples of the use of the Qal imperative:*

(1)	וַיֹּאמֶר אֵלַי בֶּן־אָדָם עֲמֹד עַל־רַגְלֶיךָ	And he said to me, "Son of man, stand upon your feet!" (Ezek. 2:1)
(2)	שְׁמַע יִשְׂרָאֵל יְהוָה אֱלֹהֵינוּ יְהוָה אֶחָד	Hear, O Israel, the LORD our God is one LORD. (Deut. 6:4)
(3)	לֵב טָהוֹר בְּרָא־לִי אֱלֹהִים	Create in me (for me, to me) a clean heart, O God (Ps. 51:12; Eng. 51:10)
(4)	שִׁמְעוּ אֶת־הַדָּבָר הַזֶּה	Hear this word! (Amos 3:1)
(5)	אֶרֶץ אֶרֶץ אָרֶץ שִׁמְעִי דְּבַר־יְהוָה	O earth, earth, earth, hear the word of the LORD. (Jer. 22:29)

48.4 *Qal imperative with pronominal suffixes:* (Note: Pronominal suffixes with imperatives follow the same pattern as pronominal suffixes with imperfects [cf. XVII.47, pp. 156–159]).

(1)	שָׁפְטֵנִי יְהוָה	Judge me, O LORD! (Ps. 7:9)
(2)	כָּתְבֵם עַל־לוּחַ לִבֶּךָ	Write them on the tablet of your heart! (Prov. 3:3)
(3)	עָזְרֵנִי יְהוָה אֱלֹהָי	Help me, O LORD my God! (Ps. 109:26)
(4)	עָזְרֵנוּ יְהוָה אֱלֹהֵינוּ	Help us, O LORD our God! (2 Chr. 14:10)
(5)	יְהוָה זָכְרֵנִי וּפָקְדֵנִי	O LORD, remember me and visit me! (Jer. 15:15)

167

49. Verbs: The Nif'al Imperative

The Nif'al imperative is formed by isolating the four second person forms of the imperfect and by changing the תּ prefix of these forms to a הּ prefix.

49.1 *Examples of the Nif'al imperative of some representative verbs:*

(1) שָׁמַר   he kept, watched

	Imperfect		Imperative
2 ms	תִּשָּׁמֵר	→	הִשָּׁמֵר
2 fs	תִּשָּׁמְרִי	→	הִשָּׁמְרִי
2 mp	תִּשָּׁמְרוּ	→	הִשָּׁמְרוּ
2 fp	תִּשָּׁמַרְנָה	→	הִשָּׁמַרְנָה

(2) [שׁבע]   he swore (Lamed Guttural)

	Imperfect		Imperative
2 ms	תִּשָּׁבַע	→	הִשָּׁבַע
2 fs	תִּשָּׁבְעִי	→	הִשָּׁבְעִי
2 mp	תִּשָּׁבְעוּ	→	הִשָּׁבְעוּ
2 fp	תִּשָּׁבַעְנָה	→	הִשָּׁבַעְנָה

49.2 *Examples of the use of the Nif'al imperative:*

(1) וְעַתָּה הִשָּׁבְעוּ־נָא לִי בַּיהוָה   And now, swear to me by the LORD. (Josh. 2:12)

(2) הִשָּׁמֶר לְךָ פֶּן־תִּשְׁכַּח אֶת־יְהוָה   Take heed to yourself lest you forget the LORD. (Deut. 6:12)

(3) הִשָּׁמְרוּ לָכֶם פֶּן־תִּשְׁכְּחוּ אֶת־בְּרִית יְהוָה אֱלֹהֵיכֶם   Take heed to yourselves lest you forget the covenant of the LORD your God. (Deut. 4:23)

(4) וְהִלָּחֵם מִלְחֲמוֹת יְהוָה   And fight the LORD's battles. (1 Sam. 18:17)

(5) וְהִלָּחֲמוּ עַל־אֲחֵיכֶם בְּנֵיכֶם וּבְנֹתֵיכֶם נְשֵׁיכֶם וּבָתֵּיכֶם   And fight for your brothers, your sons, and your daughters, your wives, and your homes (houses). (Neh. 4:8)

50. Verbs: The Piᶜel Imperative

Like the Qal imperative, the Piᶜel imperative is a shortened form of the imperfect. The shortening results from the dropping of the preformatives from all second person imperfect forms.

50.1 *Examples of the Piᶜel imperative of some representative verbs:*

(1) [דבר] (Piᶜel, to speak)

	Imperfect		Imperative
2 ms	תְּדַבֵּר	→	דַּבֵּר
2 fs	תְּדַבְּרִי	→	דַּבְּרִי
2 mp	תְּדַבְּרוּ	→	דַּבְּרוּ
2 fp	תְּדַבֵּרְנָה	→	דַּבֵּרְנָה

When the imperative form begins with a BeGaD KeFaT letter, that letter must receive a dagesh lene.

(2) לָמַד he learned (Piᶜel, to teach)

	Imperfect		Imperative
2 ms	תְּלַמֵּד	→	לַמֵּד
2 fs	תְּלַמְּדִי	→	לַמְּדִי
2 mp	תְּלַמְּדוּ	→	לַמְּדוּ
2 fp	תְּלַמֵּדְנָה	→	לַמֵּדְנָה

(3) הָלַל he was boastful (Piᶜel, to praise)

	Imperfect		Imperative
2 ms	תְּהַלֵּל	→	הַלֵּל
2 fs	תְּהַלְלִי	→	הַלְלִי
2 mp	תְּהַלְלוּ	→	הַלְלוּ
2 fp	תְּהַלֵּלְנָה	→	הַלֵּלְנָה

The dagesh forte drops out of ל, the middle consonant of הלל, whenever it is followed by a vocal sheva. This occurs in Piᶜel imperfect, 2 fs and 2 mp, and in Piᶜel imperative, 2 fs and 2 mp.

50.2 *Examples of the use of the Piᶜel imperative:*

(1) הַלְלוּ־יָהּ הַלְלִי נַפְשִׁי Praise the LORD! Praise the LORD,
      אֶת־יְהוָה O my soul! (Ps. 146:1)

(2) כַּבֵּד אֶת־אָבִיךָ וְאֶת־אִמֶּךָ   Honor your father and your mother! (Deut. 5:16)

(3) גַּדְּלוּ לַיהוָה אִתִּי   O, magnify the LORD with me! (Ps. 34:4; Eng. 34:3)

(4) דַּבְּרוּ עַל־לֵב יְרוּשָׁלַם   Speak to the heart of Jerusalem! (Isa. 40:2)

(5) מַלֵּא קַרְנְךָ שֶׁמֶן   Fill your horn with oil! (1 Sam. 16:1)

(6) סַפְּרוּ בַגּוֹיִם אֶת־כְּבוֹדוֹ   Declare his glory among the nations! (1 Chr. 16:24)

50.3 *The Pi‘el imperative with pronominal suffixes:*

(1) וְלַמְּדָהּ אֶת־בְּנֵי־יִשְׂרָאֵל   And teach it to the children of Israel! (Deut. 31:19)

(2) לַמְּדֵנִי חֻקֶּיךָ   Teach me thy statutes! (Ps. 119:12)

(3) אֱלֹהַי פַּלְּטֵנִי מִיַּד רָשָׁע   Rescue me, O my God, from the hand of the wicked! (Ps. 71:4)

51. Verbs: The Hitpa‘el Imperative

The Hitpa‘el imperative, like the Nif‘al imperative, is formed by isolating the second person forms of the imperfect and then changing the תִ of the prefix to a הִ. No other changes are needed to arrive at the completed forms.

51.1 *Examples of the Hitpa‘el imperative of some representative verbs:*

(1) קָדַשׁ   he consecrated, set apart

	Imperfect		Imperative
2 ms	תִּתְקַדֵּשׁ	→	הִתְקַדֵּשׁ
2 fs	תִּתְקַדְּשִׁי	→	הִתְקַדְּשִׁי
2 mp	תִּתְקַדְּשׁוּ	→	הִתְקַדְּשׁוּ
2 fp	תִּתְקַדֵּשְׁנָה	→	הִתְקַדֵּשְׁנָה

(2) [פלל]   he interposed, intervened, prayed

	Imperfect		Imperative
2 ms	תִּתְפַּלֵּל	→	הִתְפַּלֵּל
2 fs	תִּתְפַּלְלִי	→	הִתְפַּלְלִי
2 mp	תִּתְפַּלְלוּ	→	הִתְפַּלְלוּ
2 fp	תִּתְפַּלֵּלְנָה	→	הִתְפַּלֵּלְנָה

170

51.2 *Examples of the use of the Hitpaʿel imperative:*

(1) הִתְקַדְּשׁוּ וְקַדְּשׁוּ אֶת־בֵּית יְהוָה
Sanctify yourselves, and sanctify the house of the LORD! (2 Chr. 29:5)

(2) הִתְקַדְּשׁוּ אַתֶּם וַאֲחֵיכֶם
Sanctify yourselves, you and your brethren! (1 Chr. 15:12)

(3) הִתְפַּלֵּל בְּעַד־עֲבָדֶיךָ אֶל־יְהוָה אֱלֹהֶיךָ
Pray on behalf of your servants to the LORD your God! (1 Sam. 12:19)

(4) הִתְהַלְּכוּ בָאָרֶץ
Walk about in the earth (patrol the earth)! (Zech. 6:7)

52. Verbs: The Hif‘il Imperative

The Hif‘il imperative is formed after the same pattern as the imperative of the Nif‘al and Hitpaʿel stems. The ת of the prefix of the second person imperfect forms is changed to ה. In addition, the vowel in the final syllable of the second person masculine singular form is changed from ḥireq-yod to ṣere. No other changes are necessary.

52.1 *Examples of the Hif‘il imperative of some representative verbs:*

(1) [סתר] he hid

	Imperfect			Imperative
2 ms	תַּסְתִּיר	→	הַסְתִּיר →	הַסְתֵּר
2 fs	תַּסְתִּירִי		→	הַסְתִּירִי
2 mp	תַּסְתִּירוּ		→	הַסְתִּירוּ
2 fp	תַּסְתֵּרְנָה		→	הַסְתֵּרְנָה

(2) [שלך] he threw, cast

	Imperfect		Imperative
2 ms	תַּשְׁלִיךְ	→	הַשְׁלֵךְ
2 fs	תַּשְׁלִיכִי	→	הַשְׁלִיכִי
2 mp	תַּשְׁלִיכוּ	→	הַשְׁלִיכוּ
2 fp	תַּשְׁלֵכְנָה	→	הַשְׁלֵכְנָה

52.2 *Examples of the use of the Hif‘il imperative:*

(1) הַסְתֵּר פָּנֶיךָ מֵחֲטָאָי
Hide your face from my sins! (Ps. 51:11; Eng. 51:9)

(2) הַשְׁלִיכוּ אֹתוֹ אֶל־הַבּוֹר הַזֶּה
Cast him into this pit! (Gen. 37:22)

171

(3) וּבִירוּשָׁלַ͏ִם הַשְׁמִיעוּ   And announce (cause to be heard)
in Jerusalem! (Jer. 4:5)

52.3 *The Hif‘il imperative with pronominal suffixes:*

(1) הַזְכִּירֵנִי   Cause me to remember. (Isa. 43:26)

(2) הַקְרִיבֵהוּ נָא לְפֶחָתֶךָ   Offer it now to your governor. (Mal. 1:8)

(3) הַשְׁמִיעֵנִי בַבֹּקֶר חַסְדֶּךָ   Cause me to hear thy steadfast
love in the morning! (Ps. 143:8)

53. Verbs: Imperatives with הַ Suffix

The הַ suffix is often added to the second masculine singular form of the
imperative. It may occur in any of the verb stems that have imperatives. It is
identical in form to the cohortative הַ suffix (cf. XV.41.2, p. 132) Unlike the
cohortative suffix, however, it seems to have little or no influence upon the meaning
of the form, except perhaps to make it more emphatic. The addition of this suffix to
an imperative will cause certain vocalization changes, as indicated in the examples
that follow.

53.1 *Examples of* הַ *suffix added to 2 ms imperatives:*

(1)	שְׁפֹט	(Qal)	שָׁפְטָה	judge!	(from שָׁפַט)
(2)	שְׁמֹר	(Qal)	שָׁמְרָה	keep!	(from שָׁמַר)
(3)	שְׁכַב	(Qal)	שִׁכְבָה	lie down!	(from שָׁכַב)
(4)	שְׁלַח	(Qal)	שִׁלְחָה	send!	(from שָׁלַח)
(5)	שְׁמַע	(Qal)	שִׁמְעָה	hear!	(from שָׁמַע)
(6)	תֵּן	(Qal)	תְּנָה	give!	(from נָתַן)
(7)	הִשָּׁבַע	(Nif‘al)	הִשָּׁבְעָה	swear!	(from [שבע])
(8)	סַפֵּר	(Pi‘el)	סַפְּרָה	tell!	(from [ספר])

53.2 *Examples of the use of the* הַ *suffix on imperatives:*

(1) אֱלֹהִים שָׁפְטָה הָאָרֶץ   O God, judge the earth! (Ps. 82:8)

(2) שָׁמְרָה נַפְשִׁי   Oh guard my life (soul)! (Ps. 25:20)

(3) שִׁכְבָה עִמִּי   Lie with me! (Gen. 39:7)

(4) שִׁלְחָה אֵלַי אֶת־דָּוִד בִּנְךָ   Send to me David your son!
(1 Sam. 16:19)

(5) יְהוָה שִׁמְעָה תְפִלָּתִי   O LORD, hear my prayer! (Ps. 84:9;
Eng. 84:8)

(6)   וְעַתָּה הִשָּׁבְעָה לִּי בַּיהוָה   And now, swear to me by the LORD!
(1 Sam. 24:22)

(7)   סַפְּרָה־נָא לִי אֵת כָּל־   Tell me, I pray, all the great things
הַגְּדֹלוֹת אֲשֶׁר־עָשָׂה אֱלִישָׁע   that Elisha has done. (2 Kgs. 8:4)

54. Verbs: Imperatives with the Particle נָא

The particle נָא, which is sometimes used with jussives and cohortatives (cf. XV.41.1, p. 131), may also be used with imperatives. The function of the particle is to make the imperative more emphatic or more urgent. It is not always possible to translate the particle into English.

Examples of the use of the particle נָא with imperatives:

(1)   שִׁפְטוּ־נָא בֵּינִי וּבֵין כַּרְמִי   Judge, I pray, between me and
(between) my vineyard! (Isa. 5:3)

(2)   יְהוָה פְּקַח־נָא אֶת־עֵינָיו   O LORD, open his eyes! (2 Kgs. 6:17)

(3)   וְעַתָּה דַּבֶּר־נָא אֶל־הַמֶּלֶךְ   And now, speak to the king!
(2 Sam. 13:13)

55. Verbs: Negative Commands or Prohibitions

The imperative is not used in Hebrew to express negative commands or prohibitions. Instead, these are expressed either by לֹא with the imperfect or by אַל with the jussive (cf. XV.41.1, p. 131).

When לֹא is used with the imperfect, it expresses an absolute or categorical prohibition. It is used, for example, for the prohibitions of the Ten Commandments.

When אַל is used with the jussive, it expresses a milder form of the prohibition, more on the order of a negative wish or dissuasion. The particle נָא is sometimes added to אַל in a negative command, further emphasizing its milder nature.

55.1 *Examples of the use of* לֹא *with the imperfect to express absolute prohibitions:*

(1)   לֹא תִשְׁמַע אֶל־דִּבְרֵי   You shall not listen to the words of
הַנָּבִיא הַהוּא   that prophet! (Deut. 13:4)

(2)   לֹא תִּגְנֹב   You shall not steal! (Exod. 20:15)

(3)   לֹא־תִכְרֹת לָהֶם   You shall not make a covenant with
וְלֵאלֹהֵיהֶם בְּרִית   them or with their gods! (Exod. 23:32)

(4)   לֹא תִנָּבֵא עַל־יִשְׂרָאֵל   You shall not prophecy against Israel!
(Amos 7:16)

173

55.2 *Examples of the use of* אַל *with the jussive to express a negative wish, a negative exhortation, or a dissuasion:*

(1) בְּנִי תּוֹרָתִי אַל־תִּשְׁכָּח   My son, do not forget my law (teaching). (Prov. 3:1)

(2) אַל־תַּסְתֵּר פָּנֶיךָ מִמֶּנִּי   Hide not thy face from me. (Ps. 27:9)

(3) אַל־תַּשְׁלִיכֵנִי מִלְּפָנֶיךָ   Cast me not away from thy presence. (Ps. 51:13; Eng. 51:11)

(4) וְאַתָּה אַל־תִּתְפַּלֵּל בְּעַד־ הָעָם הַזֶּה   But as for you, do not pray on behalf of this people. (Jer. 11:14)

(5) אַל־נָא תִקְבְּרֵנִי בְּמִצְרָיִם   Do not bury me in Egypt. (Gen. 47:29)

EXERCISES

1. Locate fully the following imperatives:

   Example: דַּבֵּר   Pi'el impv., 2 ms from [דבר], "he spoke"
   Translation: "Speak!"

   (1) קִרְאוּ   (3) הִשָּׁמֶר   (5) שִׁמְעִי   (7) מְשֹׁל   (9) הִתְפַּלְלוּ

   (2) כִּתְבוּ   (4) הַלְלוּ   (6) לַמֵּדְנָה   (8) פַּלְּטוּ   (10) הַסְתֵּר

2. Fill in the imperative form that appears in the Hebrew Bible in each of the following sentences or clauses. Be prepared to translate each sentence or clause and to locate the imperative form found in it.

   (1) פָּנֶיךָ מֵחֲטָאָי   _____   (Ps. 51:11; Eng. 51:9)

   (2) הָרִים אֶת־רִיב יְהוָה   _____   (Mic. 6:2)

   (3) אֶל־בְּנֵי יִשְׂרָאֵל   _____   (Lev. 18:2)

   (4) אֱלֹהַיִךְ צִיּוֹן   _____   (Ps. 147:12)

   (5) אַתֶּם וַאֲחֵיכֶם   _____   (1 Chr. 15:12)

   (6) תּוֹרַת מֹשֶׁה עַבְדִּי   _____   (Mal. 3:22)

   (7) לָכֶם אֶת־הַשִּׁירָה הַזֹּאת   _____   (Deut. 31:19)

   (8) וּמִשְׁפָּטֶיךָ   _____   (Ps. 119:108)

   (9) לִי   _____   וַיֹּאמֶר   (Gen. 47:31)

3. Write the imperatives for the following verbs in the stems indicated:

Examples: Qal imperative of שָׁמַר, "he kept"

	2 ms	שְׁמֹר	2 mp	שִׁמְרוּ
	2 fs	שִׁמְרִי	2 fp	שְׁמֹרְנָה

    (1)   Qal imperative of שָׁפַט, "he judged"

    (2)   Nif'al imperative of שָׁמַר, "he kept"

    (3)   Pi'el imperative of לָמַד, "he learned" (Pi'el, "taught")

    (4)   Hitpa'el imperative of [פלל], "he prayed"

    (5)   Hif'il imperative of [שלך], "he threw, cast"

4. Fill in the blanks with the correct imperatives based on the imperfect forms found in parentheses. Check the scripture references for the accuracy of your work, but only after the blanks have been filled in.

(1) _____ (תַּסְתֵּר) (Ps. 51:11)   (6) _____ (תִּלָּחֵם) (1 Sam. 18:17)

(2) _____ (תִּתְקַדְּשׁוּ) (1 Chr. 15:12)   (7) _____ (תִּקְרְבוּ) (Isa. 48:16)

(3) _____ (תְּהַלְלוּ) (Ps. 113:1)   (8) _____ (תִּשְׁכְּבִי) (2 Sam. 13:11)

(4) _____ (תְּבַקֵּשׁ) (Ps. 34:15)   (9) _____ (תַּשְׁלִיכוּ) (Gen. 37:22)

(5) _____ (תִּזְכְּרוּ) (Mal. 3:22)   (10) _____ (תִּשָּׁבְעוּ) (Josh. 2:12)

5. Match the following imperatives with the proper translation:

( )	עָבְדֵהוּ (1 Chr. 28:9)	(A)	send me
( )	לַמְּדֵנִי (Ps. 119:108)	(B)	seek me
( )	לַמְּדָהּ (Deut. 31:19)	(C)	judge me
( )	שְׁלָחֵנִי (Isa. 6:8)	(D)	cause me to hear
( )	הַשְׁמִיעֵנִי (Ps. 143:8)	(E)	teach me
( )	הַלְלוּהוּ (Ps. 150:1)	(F)	remember me
( )	בַּקְשׁוּנִי (Isa. 45:19)	(G)	write them
( )	כָּתְבֵם (Prov. 3:3)	(H)	teach it (f)
( )	שָׁפְטֵנִי (Ps. 43:1)	(I)	help me
( )	רְפָאֵנִי (Jer. 17:14)	(J)	praise him
( )	זָכְרֵנִי (Jer. 15:15)	(K)	serve him
( )	עָזְרֵנִי (Ps. 109:26)	(L)	heal me

6. Fill in the blanks with the correct pronouns.

(1) שִׁכְבִי עִמִּי אֲחוֹתִי   Lie with _____, _____ sister. (2 Sam. 13:11)

(2) מְשָׁל־בָּנוּ גַּם־אַתָּה גַּם־בִּנְךָ   Rule over _____, both _____ and _____ son. (Judg. 8:22)

(3) שָׁמְרֵם בְּתוֹךְ לְבָבֶךָ   Keep _____ within _____ heart. (Prov. 4:21)

(4) כָּתְבֵם עַל־לוּחַ לִבֶּךָ   Write _____ on the tablet of _____ heart. (Prov. 3:3)

(5) וּמַלְּטִי אֶת־נַפְשֵׁךְ וְאֶת־נֶפֶשׁ בְּנֵךְ שְׁלֹמֹה   Save _____ life and the life of _____ son Solomon. (1 Kgs. 1:12)

(6) וּקְבֹר אֶת־אָבִיךָ כַּאֲשֶׁר הִשְׁבִּיעֶךָ   And bury _____ father, as he caused _____ to swear. (Gen. 50:6)

(7) קִבְרוּ אֹתִי אֶל־אֲבֹתָי   Bury _____ with _____ fathers. (Gen. 49:29)

(8) זִבְחוּ לֵאלֹהֵיכֶם בָּאָרֶץ   Sacrifice to _____ God in the land. (Exod. 8:21)

(9) כַּבְּדֵנִי נָא נֶגֶד זִקְנֵי־עַמִּי   Honor _____ now before the elders of _____ people. (1 Sam. 15:30)

(10) רִדְפוּ אַחֲרֵי אֹיְבֵיכֶם   Pursue after _____ enemies. (Josh. 10:19)

(11) וְעִבְדוּ אֹתוֹ וְעַמּוֹ   Serve _____ and _____ people. (Jer. 27:12)

(12) וְעַתָּה בְנִי שְׁמַע בְּקֹלִי   And now, _____ son, hear _____ voice. (Gen. 27:8)

(13) שְׁמַע־נָא וְאָנֹכִי אֲדַבֵּר   Hear now, and _____ will speak. (Job. 42:4)

(14) שִׁמְעָה עַמִּי וַאֲדַבֵּרָה   Hear, O _____ people, and _____ will speak. (Ps. 50:7)

(15) שִׁמְעוּ־נָא דְבָרָי   Hear now _____ words. (Num. 12:6)

(16) וְעִבְדֻהוּ לְבַדּוֹ   And serve _____ only. (1 Sam. 7:3)

7. Verb review

(1) Write the Qal perfect forms for מָשַׁל.

(2) Write the Qal imperfect forms for מָשַׁל.

(3) Write the Qal imperative forms for מָשַׁל.

(4) Write the Pi‛el perfect forms for [דבר].

(5) Write the Pi‛el imperfect forms for [דבר].

(6) Write the Pi‛el imperative form for [דבר].

8. Practice reading these sentences aloud. Then cover the English and practice translating them from sight.

(1)	הַלְלוּ יָהּ הַלְלוּ־אֵל בְּקָדְשׁוֹ	Praise the LORD! Praise God in his sanctuary (holy place)! (Ps. 150:1)
(2)	בַּקֵּשׁ שָׁלוֹם וְרָדְפֵהוּ	Seek peace and pursue it. (Ps. 34:15; Eng. 34:14)
(3)	וְדִרְשׁוּ אֶת־שְׁלוֹם הָעִיר וְהִתְפַּלְלוּ בַעֲדָהּ אֶל־יְהוָה כִּי בִשְׁלוֹמָהּ יִהְיֶה לָכֶם שָׁלוֹם	And seek the peace (welfare) of the city and pray to the LORD on its behalf, for in its peace (welfare) you will find your peace (welfare). (Jer. 29:7)
(4)	שִׁמְרוּ כָּל־מִצְוֺת יְהוָה	Keep all the commandments of the LORD. (1 Chr. 28:8)
(5)	וּכְתֹב עָלֶיהָ אֵת כָּל־הַדְּבָרִים הָרִאשֹׁנִים	And write upon it all the former words. (Jer. 36:28)
(6)	הִתְהַלְּכוּ בָאָרֶץ וְכִתְבוּ אוֹתָהּ	Walk through the land and write (about) it. (Josh. 18:8)
(7)	זְכֹר יְהוָה מֶה־הָיָה לָנוּ	Remember, O LORD, what has happened to us. (Lam. 5:1)
(8)	בַּקְּשׁוּ פָנָיו תָּמִיד	Seek his presence (face) continually. (Ps. 105:4)
(9)	זָכְרֵנִי נָא וְחַזְּקֵנִי נָא	Remember me, I pray, and strengthen me, I pray. (Judg. 16:28)

177

(10)   לַמֵּדְנָה בְּנוֹתֵיכֶם   Teach your daughters. (Jer. 9:19)

(11)   הַלְלוּהוּ שֶׁמֶשׁ וְיָרֵחַ   Praise him, sun and moon. (Ps. 148:3)

(12)   וְקִבְרוּהָ כִּי בַת־מֶלֶךְ הִיא   Bury her, for she is a king's daughter. (2 Kgs. 9:34)

(13)   הַקְרֵב אֶת־מַטֵּה לֵוִי   Bring near the tribe of Levi. (Num. 3:6)

(14)   דַּבֶּר־נָא בְּאָזְנֵי הָעָם   Speak in the ears of the people. (Exod. 11:2)

(15)   וּסְפֹר הַכּוֹכָבִים   And count the stars. (Gen. 15:5)

VOCABULARY

(1)   יוֹמָם   daily

(2)   יָצָא   he went out

(3)   יָרֵא   he feared

(4)   יָשַׁב   he sat, dwelt

(5)   [יָשַׁע]   (Hifʿil) he saved, delivered

(6)   מוּת   to die

(7)   [נצל]   (Hifʿil) he delivered

(8)   [ספר]   he counted; (Piʿel) he told, related

(9)   עָזַר   he helped

(10)   עָנָה   he answered, replied

(11)   [פלל]   (Hitpaʿel) he prayed

(12)   פָּרָה   he (it) was fruitful

(13)   [צוה]   (Piʿel) he commanded

(14)   רָבָה   he became many, multiplied

(15)   שִׂים   to put, place

(16)   שָׂמַח   he rejoiced, was glad

(17)   [שבע]   (Nifʿal) he swore

(18)   [שלך]   (Hifʿil) he cast, threw

178

LESSON XIX

56. Verbs: The Infinitive Construct*

There are two infinitives in the Hebrew verb system, the infinitive construct and the infinitive absolute. Infinitives are "infinite" in the sense that they express the basic idea of the verb root without the limitations of person, gender, and number. Perfects, imperfects, and imperatives, on the other hand, are limited to a specific person (first, second, or third), gender (masculine or feminine), and number (singular or plural). For this reason they are known as "finite" verbs.

Infinitives are actually verbal nouns, which means that they behave as both verbs and nouns. They are like verbs in that they express the basic idea of the verb root, as in the infinitives בּוֹא, "to go," שָׁפֹט, "to judge," דַּבֵּר (Pi'el), "to speak," etc. On the other hand, they sometimes function like the English gerund, and may be translated as "going," "judging," "speaking," etc. The latter function is especially characteristic of the infinitive absolute. The infinitive construct also functions as a noun by sometimes having a gerundial meaning and by sometimes receiving prepositional prefixes and pronominal suffixes.

56.1 *Forming the Infinitive Construct*

The infinitive construct of any given stem of the verb is identical in form to the imperative 2 ms form of the same stem. In the Qal stem, for example, the imperative 2 ms of מָשַׁל is מְשֹׁל. The Qal infinitive construct is also מְשֹׁל.

The sole exception to this rule is in the Hif'il stem. The Hif'il imperative 2 ms of מָשַׁל is הַמְשֵׁל, but the Hif'il infinitive construct for this verb is הַמְשִׁיל, a substitution of ḥireq-yod for ṣere.

(1) The following table illustrates the parallels between the imperatives 2 ms and the infinitives construct for the various stems of מָשַׁל, "he ruled." Parentheses indicate verb forms that do not usually occur in the Hebrew Bible.

	Qal	Nif'al	Pi'el	Pu'al	Hitpa'el	Hif'il	Hof'al
Impv. 2 ms	מְשֹׁל	הִמָּשֵׁל	מַשֵּׁל		הִתְמַשֵּׁל	הַמְשֵׁל	
Inf. Const.	מְשֹׁל	הִמָּשֵׁל	(מַשֵּׁל) מַשֵּׁל	הִתְמַשֵּׁל	הַמְשִׁיל	(הָמְשַׁל)

(2) The infinitives construct of other representative strong verbs are listed below. Each form is also shown with the preposition לְ prefixed to it. The usage of infinitives construct with prefixed prepositions will be explained later.

---

*Refer to Verb Chart 1, pp. 400f. for the conjugation of the strong verb.

179

(a)   Pi‘el inf. const.   בַּקֵּשׁ (לְבַקֵּשׁ)   "to seek"

(b)   Pi‘el inf. const.   דַּבֵּר (לְדַבֵּר)   "to speak"

(c)   Qal inf. const.   לְמֹד (לִלְמֹד)   "to learn"

(d)   Pi‘el inf. const.   לַמֵּד (לְלַמֵּד)   "to teach"

(e)   Qal inf. const.   קְרֹב (לִקְרֹב)   "to draw near"

(f)   Hif‘il inf. const. הַקְרִיב (לְהַקְרִיב)   "to bring near"

(g)   Qal inf. const.   שְׁכַב (לִשְׁכַּב)   "to lie down"

(h)   Qal inf. const.   שְׁפֹט (לִשְׁפֹט)   "to judge"

(3) The infinitives construct of representative weak verbs are included here for comparison with those of strong verbs. They are listed only for the stems in which they actually occur. Note that some of these verbs are doubly weak.

(a) עָבַד (Pe Guttural)

Qal inf. const. עֲבֹד (לַעֲבֹד) "to serve"

Hif‘il inf. const. הַעֲבִיד (לְהַעֲבִיד) "to cause to serve"

(b) שָׁמַע (Lamed Guttural)

Qal inf. const. שְׁמֹעַ (לִשְׁמֹעַ) "to hear"

Hif‘il inf. const. הַשְׁמִיעַ (לְהַשְׁמִיעַ) "to cause to hear"

(c) אָכַל (Pe ʾAlef)

Qal inf. const. אֱכֹל (לֶאֱכֹל) "to eat"

(d) אָמַר (Pe ʾAlef)

Qal inf. const. אֱמֹר (לֵאמֹר) "to say"

(e) יָדַע (Pe Vav/Pe Yod; Lamed Guttural)

Qal inf. const. דַּעַת (לָדַעַת) "to know"

Hif‘il inf. const. הוֹדִיעַ (לְהוֹדִיעַ) "to cause to know"

(f) יָרַד (Pe Vav/Pe Yod; ‘Ayin Guttural)

Qal inf. const. רֶדֶת (לָרֶדֶת) "to go down"

Hif‘il inf. const. הוֹרִיד (לְהוֹרִיד) "to cause to go down"

(g) [יָשַׁע] (Pe Vav/Pe Yod; Lamed Guttural)

Hif‘il inf. const. הוֹשִׁיעַ (לְהוֹשִׁיעַ) "to save"

(h) [נכה] (Pe Nun; Lamed He)

Hif‘il inf. const. הַכּוֹת (לְהַכּוֹת) "to smite"

180

(i)   נָתַן (Pe Nun)

Qal inf. const. תֵּת (לָתֵת)   "to set, place, give"

Nif'al inf. const. הִנָּתֵן (לְהִנָּתֵן)   "to be placed, given"

(j)   בָּנָה (Lamed He)

Qal inf. const. בְּנוֹת (לִבְנוֹת)   "to build"

Nif'al inf. const. הִבָּנוֹת (לְהִבָּנוֹת)   "to be built"

(k)   הָיָה (Pe Guttural; Lamed He)

Qal inf. const. הֱיוֹת (לִהְיוֹת)   "to be"

(l)   עָשָׂה (Pe Guttural; Lamed He)

Qal inf. const. עֲשׂוֹת (לַעֲשׂוֹת)   "to do, make"

(m)   מוּת ('Ayin Vav/'Ayin Yod)

Qal inf. const. מוּת (לָמוּת)   "to die"

Hif'il inf. const. הָמִית (לְהָמִית)   "to kill, put to death"

(n)   שׁוּב ('Ayin Vav/'Ayin Yod)

Qal inf. const. שׁוּב (לָשׁוּב)   "to turn, return, repent"

Hif'il inf. const. הָשִׁיב (לְהָשִׁיב)   "to bring back, restore"

(o)   Special attention should be given to the weak verb קָרָא "he met, encountered." (This is to be distinguished from another verb root with the same consonants, קָרָא, meaning "he called, read aloud.") The Qal infinitive construct is קְרַאת, although it never occurs in the Hebrew Bible without the prefixed preposition לְ, as לִקְרַאת, meaning "to meet, encounter." It occurs often (121 times), and therefore should be learned.

56.2 *The Function of the Infinitive Construct*

(1)   The infinitive construct may be used without prefixes or suffixes, much like the infinitive is used in the English language.
Examples:

(a)   הִנֵּה לֹא־יָדַעְתִּי דַּבֵּר   Behold, I do not know (how) to speak. (Jer. 1:6)

(b)   לֹא־טוֹב הֱיוֹת הָאָדָם לְבַדּוֹ   It is not good for the man to be alone. (The man's being alone is not good.) (Gen. 2:18)

(2)   The infinitive construct often follows a preposition or a prepositional prefix.

(a)   An infinitive construct prefixed with the preposition בְּ may be translated as a temporal clause (expressing *when* an action took place), or as a causal clause (expressing *why* an action took place).

(i)   בִּהְיוֹת יְהוֹשֻׁעַ בִּירִיחוֹ   while Joshua was in Jericho (Josh. 5:13)

(ii)   בְּהַכְרִית אִיזֶבֶל אֵת   when Jezebel cut off the prophets
         נְבִיאֵי יְהוָה   of the LORD (1 Kgs. 18:4)

(b)   An infinitive construct prefixed with the preposition כְּ is also translated as a temporal clause, to be understood as "when," "as," "just as," or "as soon as."

Examples:

(i)   כִּשְׁכַב אֲדֹנִי־הַמֶּלֶךְ   when my lord the king lies down with
         עִם־אֲבֹתָיו   his fathers (1 Kgs. 1:21)

(ii)   כְּדַבֵּר אִישׁ הָאֱלֹהִים   when the man of God had spoken to
         אֶל־הַמֶּלֶךְ   the king (2 Kgs. 7:18)

(c)   The preposition most frequently prefixed to infinitives construct is לְ. It may be used to introduce a purpose clause, a result clause, or a temporal clause. Other usages will be noted as the student gains facility in reading the language.

Examples:

(i)   כִּי־יָצָא שָׁאוּל לְבַקֵּשׁ   For Saul had gone out to seek his
         אֶת־נַפְשׁוֹ   life (soul). (1 Sam. 23:15)

(ii)   וְעֵת לִדְרוֹשׁ אֶת־יְהוָה   For it is time to seek the LORD.
         (Hos. 10:12)

Special attention should be given to the preposition לְ when it is prefixed to the Qal infinitive construct אֱמֹר, "to say." One would expect the לְ to take the short vowel corresponding to the compound sheva under א, resulting in לֶאֱמֹר. However, because of the weak nature of א, this changes to לֵאמֹר, the א having become quiescent. לֵאמֹר is used to mark direct discourse, somewhat as quotation marks are used in modern languages. This form should be memorized.

(d)   The preposition מִן is sometimes prefixed to infinitives construct, especially after verbs denoting the idea of withholding, restraining, or refusing to grant a privilege. It is also used occasionally to express the comparative. Sometimes it may simply mean "from."

Examples:

(i)   וַיָּשָׁב שָׁאוּל מִרְדֹף אַחֲרֵי דָוִד   And Saul returned from pursuing after David. (1 Sam. 23:28)

(ii)   הִשָּׁמֶר לְךָ מִדַּבֵּר עִם־יַעֲקֹב   Guard yourself from speaking with Jacob. (Gen. 31:29)

(iii) גָּדוֹל עֲוֹנִי מִנְּשֹׂא   My punishment (iniquity) is too great to bear. (Gen. 4:13)

(iv)   וַיִּמְאָסְךָ יְהוָה מִהְיוֹת מֶלֶךְ עַל־יִשְׂרָאֵל   For the LORD has rejected you from being king over Israel. (1 Sam. 15:26)

(3)   The infinitive construct is often used with a pronominal suffix. Such a suffix may function either as the subject or as the object of the infinitive.

(a) Pronominal suffixes as subjects of the infinitive construct

(i)   בְּשָׁכְבְּךָ תִּשְׁמֹר עָלֶיךָ   When you lie down, she will watch over (keep) you. (Prov. 6:22)

(ii)   בְּזָכְרֵנוּ אֶת־צִיּוֹן   when we remember Zion (Ps. 137:1)

(iii) כְּקָרָבְכֶם אֶל־הַמִּלְחָמָה   when you draw near to the battle (warfare) (Deut. 20:2)

(b) Pronominal suffixes as objects of the infinitive construct

(i)   לִשְׁמָרְךָ בְּכָל־דְּרָכֶיךָ   to keep you in all your ways (Ps. 91:11)

(ii)   לִרְדָפְךָ וּלְבַקֵּשׁ אֶת־נַפְשֶׁךָ   to pursue you and to seek your life (1 Sam. 25:29)

(iii) מֶלֶךְ לְשָׁפְטֵנוּ כְּכָל־הַגּוֹיִם   a king to rule (judge) us, like all the nations (1 Sam. 8:5)

(4)   A negative infinitive clause is formed by placing לְבִלְתִּי, "so as not," or "in order not," before the infinitive construct. Thus לְבִלְתִּי functions somewhat as לֹא does in other constructions.

Examples:

(a)   לְבִלְתִּי שְׁמֹר מִצְוֹתָיו   so as not to keep his commandments (Deut. 8:11)

(b)   לְבִלְתִּי אֲכֹל הַדָּם   so as not to eat the blood (Deut. 12:23)

(c)   לְבִלְתִּי שְׂרֹף אֶת־הַמְּגִלָּה   not to burn the scroll (Jer. 36:25)

183

57. Verbs: The Infinitive Absolute

Unlike the infinitives construct, the infinitive absolute never takes pre-positional prefixes or pronominal suffixes. However, it may have a prefixed vav conjunction.

57.1 *A comparison of the infinitive construct and the infinitive absolute for the verb* מָשַׁל, *"he ruled":*

	Qal	Nif‘al	Pi‘el	Pu‘al	Hitpa‘el	Hif‘il	Hof‘al
Inf. Const.	מְשֹׁל	הִמָּשֵׁל	מַשֵּׁל	(מֻשַּׁל)	הִתְמַשֵּׁל	הַמְשִׁיל	(הָמְשַׁל)
Inf. Abs.	מָשׁוֹל	הִמָּשֵׁל	מַשֵּׁל	מֻשַּׁל	הִתְמַשֵּׁל	הַמְשֵׁל	הָמְשֵׁל
	נִמְשֹׁל	מַשֵּׁל					

57.2 *The infinitives absolute of some of the more frequently occurring strong and weak verbs (listed only for the stems in which they actually occur):*

(1)	לָמַד	he learned	Qal inf. abs.	לָמוֹד
(2)	קָרַב	he drew near	Qal inf. abs.	קָרוֹב
			Hif‘il inf. abs.	הַקְרֵב
(3)	שָׁכַב	he lay down	Qal inf. abs.	שָׁכוֹב
(4)	עָמַד	he stood	Qal inf. abs.	עָמוֹד
(5)	אָכַל	he ate	Qal inf. abs.	אָכוֹל
(6)	אָמַר	he said	Qal inf. abs.	אָמוֹר
(7)	הָלַךְ	he went, walked	Qal inf. abs.	הָלוֹךְ
(8)	נָפַל	he fell	Qal inf. abs.	נָפוֹל
(9)	נָתַן	he gave, set	Qal inf. abs.	נָתוֹן
			Nif‘al inf. abs.	הִנָּתוֹן
(10)	הָיָה	he was	Qal inf. abs.	הָיֹה (הָיוֹ)

57.3 *Some of the more common uses of the infinitive absolute:*

The infinitive absolute functions primarily in an adverbial sense, although it has other usages as well. It has few parallels in English grammar, and its nuances of meaning are often too subtle for the beginning student to grasp. Precise translation equivalencies are difficult to achieve. Only the more common uses are listed here.

(1)   It is sometimes used in a gerundial sense, somewhat like the –ing endings for verb forms in English.

Example:

וְהִנֵּה שָׂשׂוֹן וְשִׂמְחָה   and behold, joy and gladness,

הָרֹג בָּקָר וְשָׁחֹט צֹאן   slaying oxen and killing sheep,

אָכֹל בָּשָׂר וְשָׁתוֹת יָיִן   eating flesh and drinking wine (Isa. 22:13)

(2)   The infinitive absolute often stands immediately before its cognate verb, thus serving to strengthen, reinforce, and intensify the verbal idea.

Examples:

(a) זָכֹר תִּזְכֹּר אֵת אֲשֶׁר־ עָשָׂה יְהוָה אֱלֹהֶיךָ   You shall surely remember what the LORD your God did. (Deut. 7:19)

(b) שָׁמוֹר תִּשְׁמְרוּן אֶת־ מִצְוֹת יְהוָה אֱלֹהֵיכֶם   You shall diligently keep the commandments of the LORD your God. (Deut. 6:17)

(c) וֵאלֹהִים פָּקֹד יִפְקֹד אֶתְכֶם   And God will surely visit you. (Gen. 50:24)

(3)   The infinitive absolute sometimes stands after its cognate verb, in which case it serves to emphasize the duration or continuation of the verbal idea.

Examples:

(a) שִׁמְעוּ שָׁמוֹעַ וְאַל־ תָּבִינוּ וּרְאוּ רָאוֹ וְאַל־תֵּדָעוּ   Keep on hearing, but do not understand; keep on seeing, but do not perceive. (Isa. 6:9)

(b) לַשָּׁוְא צָרַף צָרוֹף   In vain one goes on refining. (Jer. 6:29)

(4)   The infinitive absolute is sometimes used as a substitute for a finite verb form.

Examples:

(a) זָכוֹר אֶת־יוֹם הַשַּׁבָּת לְקַדְּשׁוֹ   Remember [imperative] the sabbath day, to keep it holy. (Exod. 20:8)

(b) הָלוֹךְ וְדִבַּרְתָּ אֶל־דָּוִד   Go [imperative] and say to David. (2 Sam. 24:12)

(c) שָׁמוֹר אֶת־יוֹם הַשַּׁבָּת לְקַדְּשׁוֹ   Keep [imperative] the sabbath day to make it holy. (Deut. 5:12)

185

EXERCISES

1. Write the Qal infinitives for the following verbs:

	Verb	Infinitive Construct	Infinitive Absolute
(1)	שָׁפַט	_____	_____
(2)	לָמַד	_____	_____
(3)	קָרַב	_____	_____
(4)	שָׁכַב	_____	_____
(5)	מָשַׁל	_____	_____
(6)	פָּקַד	_____	_____
(7)	קָטַל	_____	_____

2. Each of the following entries contains an infinitive construct. Complete the translation by giving the meaning of the infinitive. In the space marked (a) give the stem of the infinitive and in (b) give its root. If it has a pronominal suffix, give the person, gender, and number of the suffix in (c), and indicate whether it is used as subject or object in (d).

כְּהַזְכִּירוֹ אֶת־אֲרוֹן הָאֱלֹהִים   when he __mentioned__ the ark of God
(1 Sam. 4:18)

(a) ___Hif'il___ (b) ___זָכַר___ (c) ___3 ms___ (d) ___subject___

(1) לִשְׁכַּב אֶת־בַּת־יַעֲקֹב   to _____ with the daughter of Jacob
(Gen. 34:7)
(a) _____ (b) _____

(2) לִשְׁמֹר אֶת־דֶּרֶךְ עֵץ הַחַיִּים   to _____ the way of the tree of life
(Gen. 3:24)
(a) _____ (b) _____

(3) בְּכָתְבוֹ אֶת־הַדְּבָרִים הָאֵלֶּה   when he _____ these words (Jer. 45:1)
(a) _____ (b) _____ (c) _____ (d) _____

(4) לִשְׁפֹּט אֶת־הָעָם   to _____ the people (Exod. 18:13)
(a) _____ (b) _____

(5) לְלַמְּדָם מִלְחָמָה   to _____ them war (Judg. 3:2)
(a) _____ (b) _____ (c) _____ (d) _____

(6) לְהִלָּחֵם עִם־יִשְׂרָאֵל   to _____ with Israel (Josh. 11:5)
(a) _____ (b) _____

186

(7)   לְקָבְרָהּ   to _____ her (2 Kgs. 9:35)

        (a) _____ (b) _____ (c) _____ (d) _____

(8)   לְשָׂרְפוֹ בָאֵשׁ   to _____ it with fire (Judg. 9:52)

        (a) _____ (b) _____ (c) _____ (d) _____

(9)   בִּשְׁפָּכְךָ אֶת־חֲמָתְךָ עַל־יְרוּשָׁלַם   when you _____ your wrath upon Jerusalem (Ezek. 9:8)

        (a) _____ (b) _____ (c) _____ (d) _____

(10)   לִדְרוֹשׁ אֶת־תּוֹרַת יְהוָה   to _____ the law of the LORD (Ezr. 7:10)

        (a) _____ (b) _____

(11)   וַיְבַקֵּשׁ לַהֲרֹג אֶת־מֹשֶׁה   And he sought to _____ Moses. (Exod. 2:15)

        (a) _____ (b) _____

(12)   וּבֶגֶד לִלְבֹּשׁ   and clothing to _____ (Gen. 28:20)

        (a) _____ (b) _____

3. Fill in the blanks with the correct pronouns.

(1)   יְהוָה יִשְׁמַע בְּקָרְאִי אֵלָיו   The LORD hears when _____ call to _____. (Ps. 4:4; Eng. 4:3)

(2)   וַיָּקָם הַמֶּלֶךְ לִקְרָאתָהּ   And the king rose to meet _____. (1 Kgs. 2:19)

(3)   וְאֵלֶּה יָצְאוּ מִן־הָעִיר לִקְרָאתָם   And these went forth from the city to meet _____. (Josh. 8:22)

(4)   בְּבָרְחוֹ מִפְּנֵי אַבְשָׁלוֹם בְּנוֹ   when _____ fled from Absalom _____ son (Ps. 3:1; Eng. title)

(5)   כִּי אִתְּכֶם אָנִי לְהוֹשִׁיעַ אֶתְכֶם   For _____ am with _____ to deliver _____. (Jer. 42:11)

(6)   עַד שׁוּבִי בְשָׁלוֹם   until _____ return in peace (2 Chr. 18:26)

(7)   עִמּוֹ זְרוֹעַ בָּשָׂר וְעִמָּנוּ יְהוָה אֱלֹהֵינוּ לְעָזְרֵנוּ וּלְהִלָּחֵם מִלְחֲמֹתֵנוּ

With _____ is an arm of flesh; but with _____ is the LORD _____ God, to help _____ and to fight _____ battles. (2 Chr. 32:8)

(8)   וַיֹּאמְרוּ לוֹ אֶחָיו הֲמָלֹךְ תִּמְלֹךְ עָלֵינוּ And _____ brothers said to _____, "Shall _____ indeed reign over _____?" (Gen. 37:8)

(9)   הִנֵּה יָצָא לְהִלָּחֵם אִתָּךְ Behold, _____ has come forth to fight with _____. (2 Kgs. 19:9)

(10)   לֹא יִקְרַב לְהַקְרִיב לֶחֶם אֱלֹהָיו _____ shall not draw near to offer the bread of _____ God. (Lev. 21:17)

(11)   וַיִּשְׁמַע יְהוָה אֶת־קוֹל דִּבְרֵיכֶם בְּדַבֶּרְכֶם אֵלָי And the LORD heard _____ words when _____ spoke to _____. (Deut. 5:28)

(12)   וּכִשְׁמֹעַ אֶת־דִּבְרֵי רִבְקָה אֲחֹתוֹ when _____ heard the words of Rebekah _____ sister (Gen. 24:30)

4. Translate the following:

(1)   לִשְׁמֹר אֶת־מִצְוֹת יְהוָה   (Deut. 4:2)

(2)   לְבַקֵּשׁ אֶת־יְהוָה צְבָאוֹת בִּירוּשָׁלָ͏ִם   (Zech. 8:22)

(3)   לְהַבְדִּיל בֵּין הַיּוֹם וּבֵין הַלָּיְלָה   (Gen. 1:14)

(4)   לִשְׁפֹּט אֶת־עַמְּךָ   (1 Kgs. 3:9)

(5)   לְהַלֵּל אֶת־יְהוָה   (Ezr. 3:10)

(6)   לְמַלֵּא אֶת־דְּבַר יְהוָה   (1 Kgs. 2:27)

(7)   לִקְבֹּר אֶת־אָבִיו   (Gen. 50:7)

(8)   לִדְרֹשׁ אֶת־יְהוָה   (Gen. 25:22)

(9)   לִרְדֹּף אַחֲרֵיהֶם   (Josh. 8:16)

(10)   לִרְדָּפְךָ וּלְבַקֵּשׁ אֶת־נַפְשֶׁךָ   (1 Sam. 25:29)

(11)   לְדַבֵּר בִּשְׁמֶךָ   (Exod. 5:23)

(12)   לְדַבֵּר דָּבָר בִּשְׁמִי   (Deut. 18:20)

5. Match the numbers on the following words so that those that express similar actions or states of being are paired:

( )	בּוֹא	(A)	דָּרַשׁ
( )	שָׁתָה	(B)	שָׁכַן
( )	עָלָה	(C)	בִּין
( )	רָבָה	(D)	בָּרָא
( )	יָדַע	(E)	הָלַךְ
( )	[בקשׁ]	(F)	[ישׁע]
( )	יָשַׁב	(G)	קוּם
( )	עָשָׂה	(H)	מָשַׁל
( )	מָלַךְ	(I)	אָכַל
( )	[נצל]	(J)	גָּדַל

6. In each of the following examples an infinitive absolute stands before a finite verb of the same root and serves to intensify the action of the finite verb. Try to think of other ways the sentences might be translated in order to express the intensification. Consult at least two modern translations to see how they have rendered these sentences. In the space marked (a) give the stem of the infinitive absolute, and in (b) give its root.

(1) אִם־מָשׁוֹל תִּמְשֹׁל בָּנוּ   (a) _____
Will you indeed rule over us? (Gen. 37:8)   (b) _____

(2) הַבְדֵּל יַבְדִּילַנִי יְהוָה מֵעַל עַמּוֹ   (a) _____
The LORD will surely separate me from his people.   (b) _____
(Isa. 56:3)

(3) זָכֹר אֶזְכְּרֶנּוּ עוֹד   (a) _____
I still remember him. (Jer. 31:20)   (b) _____

(4) אִם־לָמֹד יִלְמְדוּ אֶת־דַּרְכֵי עַמִּי   (a) _____
if they will diligently learn the ways of my people   (b) _____
(Jer. 12:16)

(5) וְאָנֹכִי הַסְתֵּר אַסְתִּיר פָּנַי בַּיּוֹם הַהוּא   (a) _____
And I will surely hide my face in that day.   (b) _____
(Deut. 31:18)

(6) כִּי־קָבוֹר תִּקְבְּרֶנּוּ בַּיּוֹם הַהוּא   (a) _____

You shall certainly bury him on that (same) day.   (b) _____
(Deut. 21:23)

(7) דָּרֹשׁ דָּרַשׁ מֹשֶׁה   (a) _____

Moses searched diligently. (Lev. 10:16)   (b) _____

(8) כִּי־כַבֵּד אֲכַבֶּדְךָ מְאֹד   (a) _____

For I will surely honor you greatly. (Num. 22:17)   (b) _____

(9) יָדַעְתִּי כִּי־דַבֵּר יְדַבֵּר הוּא   (a) _____

I know that he can speak well. (Exod. 4:14)   (b) _____

(10) אִם־שָׁמוֹעַ תִּשְׁמְעוּ בְּקֹלִי   (a) _____

if you truly hearken to my voice (Exod. 19:5)   (b) _____

7. Practice reading the Hebrew aloud. Then cover the English and practice translating from sight.

(1) כְּדַבְּרָהּ אֶל־יוֹסֵף יוֹם יוֹם
וְלֹא־שָׁמַע אֵלֶיהָ לִשְׁכַּב
אֶצְלָהּ

As she spoke to Joseph day by day he did not listen to her, to lie with her. (Gen. 39:10)

(2) כִּי הִנָּתֹן יִנָּתֵן צִדְקִיָּהוּ בְּיַד
מֶלֶךְ־בָּבֶל

For Zedekiah shall surely be given into the hand of the king of Babylon. (Jer. 32:4)

(3) אֵלֶּה דִבְרֵי הַבְּרִית אֲשֶׁר־צִוָּה
יְהוָה אֶת־מֹשֶׁה לִכְרֹת אֶת־
בְּנֵי יִשְׂרָאֵל

These are the words of the covenant which the LORD commanded Moses to make (cut) with the children (sons) of Israel. (Deut. 28:69)

(4) וְהָמָן עָמַד לְבַקֵּשׁ עַל־נַפְשׁוֹ
מֵאֶסְתֵּר הַמַּלְכָּה

And Haman remained (stood) to beg (seek) his life from Esther the queen. (Est. 7:7)

(5) עִמּוֹ זְרוֹעַ בָּשָׂר וְעִמָּנוּ יְהוָה
אֱלֹהֵינוּ לְעָזְרֵנוּ וּלְהִלָּחֵם
מִלְחֲמֹתֵנוּ

With him is an arm of flesh; but with us is the LORD our God, to help us and to fight our battles. (2 Chr. 32:8)

190

(6)   יְהוָה יִשְׁמַע בְּקָרְאִי אֵלָיו   The LORD hears when I call to him. (Ps. 4:4; Eng. 4:3)

(7)   אָמַרְתִּי כַּבֵּד אֲכַבֶּדְךָ   I said, "I will certainly honor you." (Num. 24:11)

(8)   וַתִּשְׁלַח בְּגָדִים לְהַלְבִּישׁ אֶת־מָרְדֳּכַי   She sent garments to clothe Mordecai. (Est. 4:4)

(9)   לִמְּדוּ לְשׁוֹנָם דַּבֶּר־שֶׁקֶר   They have taught their tongue to speak falsehood. (Jer. 9:4; Eng. 9:5)

(10)   וּבְדַבְּרִי אוֹתְךָ אֶפְתַּח אֶת־פִּיךָ   But when I speak with you, I will open your mouth. (Ezek. 3:27)

(11)   וּמֹשֶׁה בֶּן־שְׁמֹנִים שָׁנָה וְאַהֲרֹן בֶּן־שָׁלֹשׁ וּשְׁמֹנִים שָׁנָה בְּדַבְּרָם אֶל־פַּרְעֹה   Moses was eighty years old, and Aaron was eighty–three years old, when they spoke to Pharaoh. (Exod. 7:7)

(12)   וּבְדַבְּרוֹ עִמִּי אֶת־הַדָּבָר הַזֶּה עָמַדְתִּי   While he was speaking this word to me, I stood up. (Dan. 10:11)

(13)   לִזְכֹּר בְּרִית עוֹלָם בֵּין אֱלֹהִים וּבֵין כָּל־נֶפֶשׁ חַיָּה   to remember the everlasting covenant between God and every living being (Gen. 9:16)

(14)   לִכְתֹּב אֶת־דִּבְרֵי הַתּוֹרָה־הַזֹּאת עַל־סֵפֶר   to write the words of this law in a book (Deut. 31:24)

(15)   לְהַלֵּל לַיהוָה בְּקוֹל גָּדוֹל   to praise the LORD with a loud (great) voice (2 Chr. 20:19)

VOCABULARY

(1) אָבַד   he perished

(2) אָסַף   he gathered

(3) בִּין   to understand, discern

(4) בָּרַח   he fled

(5) חָדַל   he ceased

(6) חָטָא   he sinned, missed the mark

(7) יָכֹל   he was able

(8) יָלַד   he begot (children)

(9) יָסַף   he added

(10) יָרַד   he went down

(11) יָרַשׁ   he possessed, subdued

(12) כּוּן   to be fixed, firm, established

(13) כָּלָה   he (it) was completed, finished

(14) [מאן]   (Piʻel) he refused

(15) מָאַס   he rejected, despised

(16) מָכַר   he sold

(17) [נגד]   (Hifʻil) he told, declared

(18) נָטָה   he stretched out, extended

(19) [נכה]   (Hifʻil) he struck, killed

(20) רוּם   to be high, exalted

(21) רָפָא   he healed, cured

(22) רָצָה   he was gracious, took delight in

(23) שָׂנֵא   he hated

(24) שָׁתָה   he drank

192

LESSON XX

58. Verbs: Introduction to Participles*

58.1 An English participle is defined as "a verb form used as an adjective," or "an adjective derived from a verb, and therefore used to describe participation in the action or state of the verb."

English participles do not reflect person, gender, or number by the forms they take. Hebrew participles likewise do not reflect person, but they do reflect both gender and number. They may be either masculine or feminine, and either singular or plural.

58.2 Participles in Hebrew, as well as in English, may be in either the active or the passive voice (writing – written; sending – sent; redeeming – redeemed; making – made; seeking – sought; etc.).

In Hebrew, only the Qal stem has both active and passive participles, the latter probably standing as the only remnants of a lost Qal passive conjugation. Voice is determined in the remaining stems by the nature of the stems themselves. For example, active stems (Pi'el and Hif'il) will have active participles, reflexive stems (Hitpa'el, and sometimes Nif'al) reflexive participles, and the passive stems (Nif'al, Pu'al, and Hof'al) passive participles. Participles in the active stems far outnumber those in the reflexive and passive stems.

58.3 Qal participles (both active and passive) occur without prefixes. Participles of the remaining stems all have prefixes. Nif'al participles are prefixed with nun (נ), while the participles of all other stems are prefixed with mem (מ). These rules apply to both strong verbs and weak verbs.

59. Verbs: The Forms of Participles

The forms that Hebrew participles take will vary according to the various classes of strong and weak verbs. The following lists will illustrate some of the variations. They should be used by the student as a reference in identifying participial forms as they are encountered in reading.

59.1 *Synopsis of Qal active participles of representative strong and weak verbs:*

	Root	Masc.Sing.	Masc.Pl.	Fem.Sing.	Fem.Pl.
(1)	מָשַׁל	מֹשֵׁל (A)	מֹשְׁלִים	מֹשֶׁלֶת	מֹשְׁלוֹת
(2)	כָּתַב	כֹּתֵב (A)	כֹּתְבִים	כֹּתְבָה (B) כֹּתֶבֶת	כֹּתְבוֹת

---

*Refer to Verb Chart 1, pp. 400f. for the conjugation of the strong verb.

	Root	Masc.Sing.	Masc.Pl.	Fem.Sing.	Fem.Pl.
(3)	יָשַׁב	(A)יוֹשֵׁב	יוֹשְׁבִים	יוֹשֶׁבֶת	יוֹשְׁבוֹת
(4)	יָצָא	(A)יוֹצֵא	יוֹצְאִים	(C)יוֹצֵאת	יוֹצְאוֹת
(5)	קָרָא	(A)קוֹרֵא	קֹרְאִים	(C)קֹרֵאת	קֹרְאוֹת
(6)	שָׁמַע	(D)שֹׁמֵעַ	שֹׁמְעִים	(E)שֹׁמַעַת	שֹׁמְעוֹת
(7)	יָדַע	(D)יוֹדֵעַ	יוֹדְעִים	(E)יוֹדַעַת	יוֹדְעוֹת
(8)	בָּנָה	(F)בֹּנֶה	(G)בֹּנִים	בֹּנָה	(G)בֹּנוֹת
(9)	רָאָה	(F)רֹאֶה	(G)רֹאִים	רֹאָה	(G)רֹאוֹת
(10)	בּוֹא	(H)בָּא	(H)בָּאִים	(H)בָּאָה	(H)בָּאוֹת

(A) The initial ḥolem appears in all forms of the Qal active participle (except for verbs like בּוֹא, "to go;" see number 10), but it may be written either full (ḥolem plus vav) or defective (ḥolem without vav). Pe Vav/Pe Yod verbs (see numbers 3, 4, 7) prefer the full ḥolem.

(B) The feminine singular form of the Qal active participle may end either in הָ or some form of ת (תְ, תֶ, or simple ת). The ת endings probably represent an old construct ending.

(C) In the Qal active feminine singular participial form of triliteral verb roots ending in ʾalef (א), the ʾalef becomes quiescent, needing no vowel beneath it, and the preceding sᵉgol is lengthened to ṣere.

(D) A pataḥ furtive (cf. V.13.2, p. 23) is inserted before the strong gutturals ה, ח, and ע when they stand as final consonants in a word and are not preceded by an "a" class vowel.

(E) The characteristic form for the Qal active feminine singular participial form for verb roots ending in a strong guttural (ה, ח, ע) can be seen in שֹׁמַעַת and יוֹדַעַת. Note that these forms result from the fact that gutturals prefer "a" class vowels around them.

(F) Verb roots ending in ה always have sᵉgol as the final vowel in the masculine singular participial forms, with the exception of the Qal passive form. This rule applies not only to the Qal stem, but to all other stems as well.

(G) In the formation of the Qal active masculine plural and feminine plural participial forms of verb roots ending in ה, the final ה is dropped before the plural endings are added.

(H) Qameṣ, rather than ḥolem, is used as the initial vowel in Qal active participial forms of בּוֹא.

59.2 *Synopsis of Qal passive participles of representative strong and weak verbs:*

	Root	Masc.Sing.	Masc.Pl.	Fem.Sing.	Fem.Pl.
(1)	מָשַׁל	מָשׁוּל (A)	מְשׁוּלִים	מְשׁוּלָה	מְשׁוּלוֹת
(2)	כָּתַב	כָּתוּב	כְּתוּבִים	כְּתוּבָה	כְּתוּבוֹת
(3)	שָׁלַח	שָׁלוּחַ (B)	שְׁלוּחִים	שְׁלוּחָה	שְׁלוּחוֹת
(4)	אָהַב	אָהוּב	אֲהוּבִים (C)	אֲהוּבָה (C)	אֲהוּבוֹת (C)
(5)	בָּנָה	בָּנוּי (D)	בְּנוּיִים (D)	בְּנוּיָה (D)	בְּנוּיוֹת (D)
(6)	עָשָׂה	עָשׂוּי (D)	עֲשׂוּיִים (C)	עֲשׂוּיָה (C)	עֲשׂוּיוֹת (C)
(7)	אָרַר	אָרוּר	אֲרוּרִים (C)	אֲרוּרָה (C)	אֲרוּרוֹת (C)

(A) All forms of the Qal passive participle are written with šureq between the second and third consonants of the verb root.

(B) A pataḥ furtive is placed before a final strong guttural when it is not preceded by an "a" class vowel.

(C) Gutturals prefer compound shevas rather than simple shevas.

(D) For verb roots ending in ה, Qal passive participles (masculine and feminine, singular and plural) are formed by substituting י for ה. Otherwise, the forms are regular, despite their unusual appearance.

59.3 *Synopsis of Nifʻal participles of representative strong and weak verbs:*

	Root	Masc.Sing.	Masc.Pl.	Fem.Sing.	Fem.Pl.
(1)	מָשַׁל	נִמְשָׁל (A)	נִמְשָׁלִים	נִמְשֶׁלֶת	נִמְשָׁלוֹת
(2)	שָׁאַר	נִשְׁאָר	נִשְׁאָרִים	נִשְׁאֶרֶת	נִשְׁאָרוֹת
(3)	שָׁמַע	נִשְׁמָע	נִשְׁמָעִים	נִשְׁמַעַת (B)	נִשְׁמָעוֹת
(4)	עָשָׂה	נַעֲשֶׂה (C)	נַעֲשִׂים (C)	נַעֲשָׂה (C)	נַעֲשׂוֹת (C)
(5)	[אמן]	נֶאֱמָן (C)	נֶאֱמָנִים (C)	נֶאֱמָנָה (C)	נֶאֱמָנוֹת (C)
(6)	נָשָׂא	נִשָּׂא (D)	נִשָּׂאִים (D)	נִשָּׂאָה (D)	נִשָּׂאוֹת (D)

(A) The nun prefix is characteristic of all Nifʻal participial forms.

(B) The Nifʻal feminine singular participle for verb roots ending in a strong guttural is formed by substituting pataḥ for sᵉgol in each of the two final syllables.

195

(C) Gutturals prefer compound shevas. In the Nifʻal participial forms this will be ḥaṭef-pataḥ with עַ, and ḥaṭef-sᵉgol with אַ. Whenever either of these compound shevas is used after the nun prefix, the nun is pointed with the corresponding short vowel and marked with the secondary accent meteg (cf. IV.9, pp. 17f.).

(D) Whenever nun is supported by a syllable divider, the nun drops out and is assimilated into the following consonant by means of a dagesh forte. Thus the original form נִנְשָׂא has become נִשָּׂא, נִנְשָׂאִים has become נִשָּׂאִים, etc.

59.4 *Synopsis of Piʻel participles of representative strong and weak verbs:*

	Root	Masc.Sing.	Masc.Pl.	Fem.Sing.	Fem.Pl.
(1)	מָשַׁל	מְמַשֵּׁל(A)	מְמַשְּׁלִים	מְמַשֶּׁלֶת	מְמַשְּׁלוֹת
(2)	[בקשׁ]	מְבַקֵּשׁ	מְבַקְּשִׁים	מְבַקֶּשֶׁת	מְבַקְּשׁוֹת
(3)	[דבר]	מְדַבֵּר	מְדַבְּרִים	מְדַבְּרָה(B)	מְדַבְּרוֹת
(4)	[ברך]	מְבָרֵךְ(C)	מְבָרְכִים(C)	מְבָרְכָה(C)	מְבָרְכוֹת(C)
(5)	[צוה]	מְצַוֶּה(D)	מְצַוִּים(D)	מְצַוָּה(D)	מְצַוּוֹת(D)

(A) The characteristics of the Piʻel participles are the מְ prefix and the doubling in the middle root consonant.

(B) This is the alternate form of the feminine singular participle.

(C) Because the guttural ר refuses to be doubled, the preceding vowel is lengthened from pataḥ to qameṣ.

(D) Vav acts as a regular consonant in the verb [צוה]. Therefore, it is a doubled consonant in the Piʻel participial forms, and should not be confused with šureq.

59.5 *Synopsis of Puʻal participles of representative strong and weak verbs:*

	Root	Masc.Sing.	Masc.Pl.	Fem.Sing.	Fem.Pl.
(1)	מָשַׁל	מְמֻשָּׁל(A)	מְמֻשָּׁלִים	מְמֻשָּׁלָה	מְמֻשָּׁלוֹת
(2)	עָנָה	מְעֻנֶּה	מְעֻנִּים	מְעֻנָּה	מְעֻנּוֹת
(3)	[ברך]	מְבֹרָךְ(B)	מְבֹרָכִים(B)	מְבֹרָכָה(B)	מְבֹרָכוֹת(B)

(A) The characteristics that distinguish Puʻal participles are the מְ prefix, the qibbuṣ under the initial root consonant, and the doubling of the middle root consonant.

(B) Because the guttural ר refuses to be doubled, the preceding vowel is lengthened from qibbuṣ to ḥolem.

59.6 *Synopsis of Hitpaʻel participles of representative strong and weak verbs:*

	Root	Masc.Sing.	Masc.Pl.	Fem.Sing.	Fem.Pl.
(1)	מָשַׁל	(A)מִתְמַשֵּׁל	מִתְמַשְּׁלִים	מִתְמַשֶּׁלֶת	מִתְמַשְּׁלוֹת
(2)	הָלַךְ	מִתְהַלֵּךְ	מִתְהַלְּכִים	מִתְהַלֶּכֶת	מִתְהַלְּכוֹת
(3)	קָדַשׁ	מִתְקַדֵּשׁ	מִתְקַדְּשִׁים	מִתְקַדֶּשֶׁת	מִתְקַדְּשׁוֹת
(4)	[אוה]	(B)מִתְאַוֶּה	(B)מִתְאַוִּים	(B)מִתְאַוָּה	(B)מִתְאַוֹּת

(A)   The distinguishing characteristics of the Hitpaʻel participles are the מִת prefix and the doubling of the middle root consonant.

(B)   Because vav acts as a regular consonant in the verb אָוָה, "he desired, longed after," it serves as a doubled middle consonant in the Hitpaʻel participial forms and should not be confused with šureq.

59.7 *Synopsis of Hifʻil participles of representative strong and weak verbs:*

	Root	Masc.Sing.	Masc.Pl.	Fem.Sing.	Fem.Pl.
(1)	מָשַׁל	(A)מַמְשִׁיל	(A)מַמְשִׁילִים	(A)מַמְשִׁילָה	(A)מַמְשִׁילוֹת
(2)	שָׁמַע	(B)מַשְׁמִיעַ	מַשְׁמִיעִים	מַשְׁמִיעָה	מַשְׁמִיעוֹת
(3)	עָלָה	(C)מַעֲלֶה	(C)מַעֲלִים	(C)מַעֲלָה	(C)מַעֲלוֹת
(4)	יָדַע	(B)(D)מוֹדִיעַ	(D)מוֹדִיעִים	(D)מוֹדִידָה	(D)מוֹדִיעוֹת
(5)	[נגד]	(E)מַגִּיד	(E)מַגִּידִים	(E)מַגִּידָה	(E)מַגִּידוֹת
(6)	[נכה]	(F)מַכֶּה	(F)מַכִּים	מַכָּה	(F)מַכּוֹת
(7)	בּוֹא	(G)מֵבִיא	מְבִיאִים	מְבִיאָה	מְבִיאוֹת

(A)   Hifʻil participles of strong verbs are to be identified by the מ prefix and the ḥireq-yod stem vowel. Some weak verbs also follow this pattern, although most will have alternate forms.

(B)   When a strong guttural is final in a word and is not preceded by an "a" class vowel, a pataḥ furtive must be inserted before it.

(C)   Gutturals prefer compound shevas.

(D)   The yod in יָדַע appears as vav in prefixed forms. The Hifʻil participles of this and all similar verb roots point vav as ḥolem-vav after the mem prefix.

(E)   Nun, when supported by a syllable divider is assimilated into the following consonant. Thus the original מַנְגִּיד become מַגִּיד, and similar changes take place in

197

the remaining Hifʻil participial forms of Pe Nun verbs.

(F)   The verb [נכה], "he smote," is doubly weak because it has both an initial nun and a final ה. Therefore, its Hifʻil participial forms reflect the characteristics of initial nun verb roots as well as final ה verb roots. The loss of a nun supported by a syllable divider accounts for the doubling in the middle consonant (מַנְכֶּה became מַכֶּה), while the ה ֶ ending in the masculine singular form and the dropping of ה in the masculine plural and feminine plural forms are characteristic of all verb roots ending in ה.

(G)   The distinguishing mark of the Hifʻil participle for בּוֹא , and other middle vowel verbs, is the use of מֵ rather than מַ as the prefix.

59.8 *Synopsis of Hofʻal participles of representative strong and weak verbs:*

	Root	Masc.Sing.	Masc.Pl.	Fem.Sing.	Fem.Pl.
(1)	מָשַׁל	מָמְשָׁל(A)	מָמְשָׁלִים	מָמְשָׁלָה	מָמְשָׁלוֹת
(2)	שָׁלַךְ	מֻשְׁלָךְ	מֻשְׁלָכִים	מֻשְׁלֶכֶת	מֻשְׁלָכוֹת
(3)	גָּלָה	מֻגְלֶה(B)	מֻגְלִים(B)	מֻגְלָה(B)	מֻגְלוֹת(B)
(4)	[נכה]	מֻכֶּה(C)	מֻכִּים(C)	מֻכָּה(C)	מֻכּוֹת(C)
(5)	נָגַשׁ	מֻגָּשׁ	מֻגָּשִׁים	מֻגָּשָׁה	מֻגָּשׁוֹת
(6)	עָמַד	מָעֳמָד(D)	מָעֳמָדִים(D)	מָעֳמָדָה(D)	מָעֳמָדוֹת(D)
(7)	יָדַע	מוּדָע(E)	מוּדָעִים(E)	מוּדַעַת(E)	מוּדָעוֹת(E)

(A)   Hofʻal participles are characterized by the "o" and "u" class vowels accompanying the מ prefix. The vowels are either qameṣ–ḥaṭuf, qibbuṣ, or šureq.

(B)   These forms are to be explained by the fact that the verb root has a final ה.

(C)   These forms are to be explained by the fact that the verb root has both an initial נ and a final ה.

(D)   Gutturals prefer compound shevas, and the preceding prefix is pointed with the corresponding short vowel, in this case qameṣ–ḥaṭuf.

(E)   The yod of יָדַע appears as vav in prefixed verb forms. In the Hofʻal participial forms of this verb, vav stands after the mem prefix and is pointed as šureq.

60. Verbs: The Functions of Participles

Participles have three principal functions in Hebrew. They may be employed as adjectives, as verbs, or as nouns.

60.1 *Participles as Adjectives*

The rules that govern ordinary adjectives also apply to participles that are used as adjectives (cf. VIII.20, 21, 22; pp. 43–47).

(1) The attributive use of participial adjectives

Participial adjectives, like other adjectives, may be used either attributively or predicatively. When used attributively, they usually follow the nouns they describe and agree with them in gender, number, and definiteness (a definite noun requiring a definite adjective, an indefinite noun an indefinite adjective). Participial adjectives, when used attributively, are usually translated as relative clauses, with such relative pronouns as "who," "which," or "that" being supplied by the translator.

Examples:

(a) כִּי כֹה אָמַר־יְהוָה אֶל־ שַׁלֻּם הַמֹּלֵךְ תַּחַת יֹאשִׁיָּהוּ אָבִיו
For thus says the LORD concerning Shallum, who reigned instead of Josiah his father. (Jer. 22:11)

(b) הָאִישׁ הַשֹּׁכֵב עִם־ הָאִשָּׁה
the man who lay with the woman (Deut. 22:22)

(c) לֻחֹת אֶבֶן כְּתֻבִים בְּאֶצְבַּע אֱלֹהִים
tables of stone, (which were) written with the finger of God (Exod. 31:18)

(d) כָּל־הָאָלוֹת הַכְּתוּבוֹת עַל־הַסֵּפֶר
all the curses that are written in the book (2 Chr. 34:24)

(e) כָּל־הָאֲנָשִׁים הַמְבַקְשִׁים אֶת־נַפְשֶׁךָ
all the men who were seeking your life (Exod. 4:19)

Compare the example given above (e) with the relative clause introduced by אֲשֶׁר in Jeremiah 38:16:

הָאֲנָשִׁים הָאֵלֶּה אֲשֶׁר   these men who
מְבַקְשִׁים אֶת־נַפְשֶׁךָ   are seeking your life

(2) The predicative use of participial adjectives

A predicate participial adjective is one used in the predicate position in the sentence. It describes or modifies the subject and is usually joined to it by some form of the verb "to be," although this is seldom written and so must be inferred from the context.

It is often difficult to distinguish between a participle used as a predicate adjective and one used as a verb. The line of demarcation between the two is very thin.

Predicate participial adjectives may stand before or after the nouns (or pronouns) they describe. They agree with them in gender and number, but never take the definite article.

Examples:

(a) בָּרוּךְ אַתָּה בָּעִיר

Blessed shall you be in the city. (Deut. 28:3)

(b) אָרוּר אַתָּה מִכָּל־הַבְּהֵמָה

Cursed are you above all cattle. (Gen. 3:14)

(c) וְהִנֵּה אִשָּׁה שֹׁכֶבֶת מַרְגְּלֹתָיו

And behold, a woman was lying at his feet! (Ruth 3:8)

(d) עָרֵיכֶם שְׂרֻפוֹת אֵשׁ

Your cities are burned with fire. (Isa. 1:7)

60.2 *Participles as Verbs*

Participles used as verbs are normally preceded by an expressed subject, with which they must agree in gender and number. However, participles used as verbs do not take the definite article.

Participial verbs in and of themselves are timeless, and time can only be determined by the context in which they stand. They describe continuous action in the time of the context, which may be either past, present, or future. Thus they represent what was going on in the past, what is going on in the present, or what is to take place in the future. Past participles are made even more explicit when preceded by the verb הָיָה. Future participles often refer to the immediate future, especially when introduced by the demonstrative particle הִנֵּה, "Behold!"

(1) Examples of participial verbs in past time:

(a) וְאַבְרָהָם עוֹדֶנּוּ עֹמֵד
לִפְנֵי יְהוָה

And Abraham was still standing before the LORD. (Gen. 18:22)

(b) שְׂרָפִים עֹמְדִים מִמַּעַל לוֹ

Seraphim were standing above him. (Isa. 6:2)

(c) וּשְׁמוּאֵל שֹׁכֵב בְּהֵיכַל
יְהוָה

And Samuel was lying down in the temple of the LORD. (1 Sam. 3:3)

(d) וְהִנֵּה הַסְּנֶה בֹּעֵר בָּאֵשׁ

And behold, the bush was burning with fire. (Exod. 3:2)

200

(2) Examples of participial verbs in present time:

(a)   כִּי אֲנִי יְהוָה אֹהֵב מִשְׁפָּט   For I the LORD love justice. (Isa. 61:8)

(b)   אֶת־אַחַי אָנֹכִי מְבַקֵּשׁ   I am seeking my brothers. (Gen. 37:16)

(c)   הַמָּקוֹם אֲשֶׁר אַתָּה עוֹמֵד
עָלָיו אַדְמַת־קֹדֶשׁ הוּא   The place upon which you are standing is holy ground. (Exod. 3:5)

(d)   הַשָּׁמַיִם מְסַפְּרִים
כְּבוֹד־אֵל   The heavens declare the glory of God. (Ps. 19:2; Eng. 19:1)

(3) Examples of participial verbs in future time:

(a)   הִנְּךָ שֹׁכֵב עִם־אֲבֹתֶיךָ   Behold, you are about to sleep (lie down) with your fathers. (Deut. 31:16)

(b)   כִּי־שֹׁפֵט אֲנִי אֶת־בֵּיתוֹ
עַד־עוֹלָם   For I am about to punish (judge) his house forever. (1 Sam. 3:13)

(c)   הִנֵּה אָנֹכִי הֹרֵג אֶת־בִּנְךָ   Behold, I will slay (kill) your son. (Exod. 4:23)

60.3 *Participles as Nouns*

Participles as nouns indicate the "one who" or the "ones who" are performing a certain action or exist in a certain state or condition. Such nouns may be definite or indefinite, masculine or feminine, singular or plural, depending on the person or persons to whom they refer.

Participial nouns may be used in all the ways nouns are normally used, including subject, predicate, direct object, object of the preposition, and in apposition to other nouns. Being verbal nouns, they may also take a direct object, either in the form of another noun or a pronominal suffix.

Participial nouns are simply listed in *BDB* under the verb roots from which they are derived. Some of these are so widely used, however, that more recent lexicons and concordances have begun to provide them with separate entries. These are the verbal nouns that describe a person's major or vocationally identifying activity. They include such forms as גֹּאֵל, "redeemer," יוֹשֵׁב, "inhabitant," יוֹצֵר, "potter," מוֹשִׁיעַ, "savior, deliverer," סֹפֵר, "scribe," רֹאֶה, "seer," רֹעֶה, "shepherd," and שֹׁפֵט, "judge." These might be compared to English words such as "commander," "counselor," "farmer," "miller," "sailor," and "teacher."

Participial nouns may occur in either the absolute state or the construct state. The rules for determining their construct state are basically the same as for other nouns (cf. X.26, pp. 58-64). Special attention should be given, however, to masculine singular absolute forms ending in הֶ . In the construct state, these endings will become הֵ . This is because the construct form loses its accent, and when seǥol is left in an unaccented open syllable (final ה never closes the syllable), it must be lengthened to ṣere.

(1) Examples of participial nouns in the absolute state:

(a) וְעָמְדוּ שְׁנֵי־הָאֲנָשִׁים
     לִפְנֵי הַשֹּׁפְטִים
     And two of the men stood before the judges. (Deut. 19:17)

(b) וְהָלְכוּ שָׁם גְּאוּלִים
     And the redeemed shall go (walk) there. (Isa. 35:9)

(c) שָׁלַח הַמֶּלֶךְ אֶת־שָׁפָן
     הַסֹּפֵר בֵּית יְהוָה
     The king sent Shaphan the scribe to the house of the LORD. (2 Kgs. 22:3)

(2) Examples of participial nouns in the construct state:

(a) Construct participial nouns without pronominal suffixes

(i) הֲשֹׁמֵר אָחִי אָנֹכִי
     Am I the keeper of my brother? (Gen. 4:9)

(ii) לְשֹׁמְרֵי בְרִיתוֹ
     to the ones keeping his covenant (Ps. 103:18)

(iii) בְּיַד מְבַקְשֵׁי נַפְשׁוֹ
     into the hand of those who seek his life (Jer. 44:30)

(b) Construct participial nouns with pronominal suffixes

(i) יַד־אֱלֹהֵינוּ עַל־כָּל־מְבַקְשָׁיו
     The hand of our God is upon all who seek him. (Ezr. 8:22)

(ii) וְגֹאֲלֵךְ קְדוֹשׁ יִשְׂרָאֵל
     And your Redeemer is the Holy One of Israel. (Isa. 41:14)

(iii) כִּי־מְכַבְּדַי אֲכַבֵּד
     For those who honor me I will honor. (1 Sam. 2:30)

61. Verbs: Synopsis of the Strong Verb

Introduction of the participle completes the study of the strong verb. It is now possible to write a synopsis of the entire verb. The student should master the forms of the synopsis. Nothing short of this is adequate.

	Qal	Nif'al	Pi'el	Pu'al	Hitpa'el	Hif'il	Hof'al
Perf. 3 ms	מָשַׁל	נִמְשַׁל	מִשֵּׁל	מֻשַּׁל	הִתְמַשֵּׁל	הִמְשִׁיל	הָמְשַׁל
Impf. 3 ms	יִמְשֹׁל	יִמָּשֵׁל	יְמַשֵּׁל	יְמֻשַּׁל	יִתְמַשֵּׁל	יַמְשִׁיל	יָמְשַׁל
Impv. 2 ms	מְשֹׁל	הִמָּשֵׁל	מַשֵּׁל		הִתְמַשֵּׁל	הַמְשֵׁל	
Inf. const.	מְשֹׁל	הִמָּשֵׁל	מַשֵּׁל	(מֻשַּׁל)	הִתְמַשֵּׁל	הַמְשִׁיל	(הָמְשַׁל)
Inf. Abs.	מָשׁוֹל	הִמָּשֵׁל נִמְשֹׁל	מַשֵּׁל מַשֹּׁל	מֻשַּׁל	הִתְמַשֵּׁל	הַמְשֵׁל	הָמְשֵׁל
Part. Act. ms	מֹשֵׁל		מְמַשֵּׁל		מִתְמַשֵּׁל	מַמְשִׁיל	
Part. Act. fs	מֹשְׁלָה מֹשֶׁלֶת		מְמַשֶּׁלֶת		מִתְמַשֶּׁלֶת	מַמְשִׁילָה	
Part. Pass. ms	מָשׁוּל	נִמְשָׁל		מְמֻשָּׁל			מָמְשָׁל
Part. Pass. fs	מְשׁוּלָה	נִמְשֶׁלֶת		מְמֻשָּׁלָה			מָמְשֶׁלֶת

(Nif'al participles may be reflexive as well as passive.)

EXERCISES

1. Write the synopsis for the verb כָּתַב.

2. Fill in the blanks with the correct pronouns.

   (1)   וְאַתָּה מוֹשֵׁל בַּכֹּל   _____ rule over all. (1 Chr. 29:12)

   (2)   וּזְרֹעוֹ מֹשְׁלָה לוֹ   _____ arm rules for _____. (Isa. 40:10)

   (3)   אַל־יָנוּם שֹׁמְרֶךָ   The one keeping _____ will not slumber. (Ps. 121:3)

   (4)   לְאֹהֲבָיו וּלְשֹׁמְרֵי מִצְוֺתָיו   to those who love _____ and keep _____ commandments (Dan. 9:4)

   (5)   וְלֹא אִתְּכֶם לְבַדְּכֶם אָנֹכִי כֹּרֵת אֶת־הַבְּרִית הַזֹּאת   And not with _____ alone am _____ making (cutting) _____ covenant. (Deut. 29:13; Eng. 29:14)

   (6)   הִנֵּה בְנִי מְבַקֵּשׁ אֶת־נַפְשִׁי   Behold, _____ son is seeking _____ life. (2 Sam. 16:11)

   (7)   כָּל־מְבַקְשֶׁיהָ   all who seek _____ (Jer. 2:24)

(8) אֶת־חֲטָאַי אֲנִי מַזְכִּיר הַיּוֹם _____ sins _____ remember today. (Gen. 41:9)

(9) הֲלוֹא דָוִד מִסְתַּתֵּר עִמָּנוּ Is not David hiding among _____? (1 Sam. 23:19)

(10) וְהַשֹּׂרֵף אֹתָם יְכַבֵּס בְּגָדָיו And the one burning _____ shall wash _____ garments. (Lev. 16:28)

(11) הִיא שֹׁפְטָה אֶת־יִשְׂרָאֵל בָּעֵת הַהִיא _____ was judging Israel at _____ time. (Judg. 4:4)

(12) לָמָּה זֶּה אֲדֹנִי רֹדֵף אַחֲרֵי עַבְדּוֹ Why is _____ lord pursuing after _____ servant? (1 Sam. 26:18)

3. Underscore the correct form of the participle in each of the following sentences and phrases. Check the scripture references for accuracy, but only after completing the assignment.

(1) וְחַנָּה הִיא (מְדַבֵּר / מְדַבֶּרֶת) עַל־לִבָּהּ
And Hannah was speaking in her heart. (1 Sam. 1:13)

(2) הָאִישׁ (הַשֹּׁכֵב / הַשֹּׁכֶבֶת) עִמָּהּ
the man who lay with her (Deut. 22:29)

(3) הֲלֹא־הִיא (כָתוּב / כְתוּבָה) עַל־סֵפֶר הַיָּשָׁר
Is this not written in the Book of Jashar? (Josh. 10:13)

(4) (בָּרוּךְ / בְּרוּכָה) אַתְּ לַיהוָה בִּתִּי
May you be blessed by the LORD, my daughter. (Ruth 3:10)

(5) (בְּרוּכִים / בְּרוּכוֹת) אַתֶּם לַיהוָה
May you be blessed by the LORD. (1 Sam. 23:21)

(6) זִבְחֵי אֱלֹהִים רוּחַ (נִשְׁבָּר / נִשְׁבָּרָה)
The sacrifices of God are a broken spirit. (Ps. 51:19; Eng. 51:17)

(7) עִיר (שֹׁפֵךְ / שֹׁפֶכֶת) דָּם בְּתוֹכָהּ
a city shedding blood in her midst (Ezek. 22:3)

(8) וְיָדַיִם (שֹׁפְכִים / שֹׁפְכוֹת) דָּם־נָקִי
and hands shedding innocent blood (Prov. 6:17)

(9) (וּבָרוּךְ / וּבְרוּכָה) אַתָּה בַּשָּׂדֶה
And blessed shall you be in the field. (Deut. 28:3)

(10) וְהִנֵּה [הָעִיר] (שָׂרוּף / שְׂרוּפָה) בָּאֵשׁ
Behold, [the city] was burned with fire. (1 Sam. 30:3)

(11) וָאֶשְׁמַע אֶת־הָאִישׁ (לְבֻשׁ / לְבוּשָׁה) הַבַּדִּים
And I heard the man clothed in linen. (Dan. 12:7)

(12) כָּל־הָעִיר (עָזוּב / עֲזוּבָה)
Every city is forsaken. (Jer. 4:29)

(13) (עֲזוּבִים / עֲזֻבוֹת) עָרֵי עֲרֹעֵר
The cities of Aroer are forsaken. (Isa. 17:2)

(14) אַחֲרֵי מִי אַתָּה (רֹדֵף / רֹדְפָה)
After whom are you pursuing? (1 Sam. 24:15; Eng. 24:14)

(15) מָה אֲדֹנִי (מְדַבֵּר / מְדַבֶּרֶת) אֶל־עַבְדּוֹ
What is my lord saying to his servant? (Josh. 5:14)

(16) חָמֵשׁ עָרִים בְּאֶרֶץ מִצְרַיִם (מְדַבְּרִים / מְדַבְּרוֹת) שְׂפַת כְּנַעַן
five cities in the land of Egypt which speak the language of Canaan
(Isa. 19:18)

(17) וַיֹּאמֶר מָה־אַתָּה (רֹאֶה / רֹאָה) עָמוֹס
And he said, "What do you see, Amos?" (Amos 8:2)

(18) הֵם (הַמְדַבְּרִים / הַמְדַבְּרוֹת) אֶל־פַּרְעֹה מֶלֶךְ־מִצְרַיִם
It was they who spoke to Pharaoh king of Egypt. (Exod. 6:27)

4. Each of the following entries contains a participial form. In the space marked (a) give its stem, in (b) its voice (active or passive), in (c) its gender and number, and in (d) its root.
Example:

אָכֵן אַתָּה אֵל מִסְתַּתֵּר Truly, you are a God who hides yourself.
(Isa. 45:15)

(a) __Hitpaʿel__ (b) __active__ (c) __ms__ (d) __[סתר]__

(1) וּשְׁמוּאֵל שֹׁכֵב בְּהֵיכַל יְהוָה And Samuel was lying down in the temple
of the LORD. (1 Sam. 3:3)

(a) _____ (b) _____ (c) _____ (d) _____

(2) וּשְׁלֹמֹה הָיָה מוֹשֵׁל בְּכָל־הַמַּמְלָכוֹת Solomon ruled over all the
kingdoms. (1 Kgs. 5:1; Eng. 4:21)

(a) _____ (b) _____ (c) _____ (d) _____

(3)   שׁוֹמֵר יִשְׂרָאֵל   he who keeps Israel (Ps. 121:4)

    (a) _____ (b) _____ (c) _____ (d) _____

(4)   הֲשֹׁמְרִים הֵם אֶת־דֶּרֶךְ יְהוָה   Are they keeping the way of the LORD?
(Judg. 2:22)

    (a) _____ (b) _____ (c) _____ (d) _____

(5)   כַּאֲשֶׁר כָּתוּב בְּתוֹרַת מֹשֶׁה   as it is written in the law of Moses
(Dan. 9:13)

    (a) _____ (b) _____ (c) _____ (d) _____

(6)   כִּי אַתָּה אַתֶּם מְבַקְשִׁים   For that is what you seek (what you desire).
(Exod. 10:11)

    (a) _____ (b) _____ (c) _____ (d) _____

(7)   בְּיַד מְבַקְשֵׁי נַפְשָׁם   into the hand of those who seek their life (Jer. 46:26)

    (a) _____ (b) _____ (c) _____ (d) _____

(8)   קָרוֹב יְהוָה לְנִשְׁבְּרֵי־לֵב   The LORD is near to the broken-hearted.
(Ps. 34:19; Eng. 34:18)

    (a) _____ (b) _____ (c) _____ (d) _____

(9)   מַשְׁבִּית מִלְחָמוֹת עַד־קְצֵה הָאָרֶץ   who makes wars to cease to the end
of the earth (Ps. 46:10; Eng. 46:9)

    (a) _____ (b) _____ (c) _____ (d) _____

(10)   מְלַמֵּד יָדַי לַמִּלְחָמָה   who teaches (trains) my hands for war (2 Sam. 22:35)

    (a) _____ (b) _____ (c) _____ (d) _____

(11)   הַנִּסְתָּרֹת לַיהוָה אֱלֹהֵינוּ   The hidden things belong to the LORD our God.
(Deut. 29:28; Eng. 29:29)

    (a) _____ (b) _____ (c) _____ (d) _____

(12)   הַמַּסְתִּיר פָּנָיו מִבֵּית יַעֲקֹב   who is hiding his face from the house
of Jacob (Isa. 8:17)

    (a) _____ (b) _____ (c) _____ (d) _____

(13)   כִּי יְהוָה שֹׁפְטֵנוּ   For the LORD is our judge. (Isa. 33:22)

    (a) _____ (b) _____ (c) _____ (d) _____

(14)   יְהַלְלוּ יְהוָה דֹּרְשָׁיו   Those who seek him shall praise the LORD. (Ps. 22:27;
Eng. 22:26)

    (a) _____ (b) _____ (c) _____ (d) _____

(15) רַבִּים רֹדְפָי Many are my pursuers (persecutors). (Ps. 119:157)

(a) _____ (b) _____ (c) _____ (d) _____

5. Each of the following sentences contains one or more participial forms. Practice reading the sentences aloud. Then cover the English and practice translating from sight.

(1) וַיִּשְׁמְעוּ אֶת־קוֹל יְהוָה אֱלֹהִים מִתְהַלֵּךְ בַּגָּן לְרוּחַ הַיּוֹם

And they heard the sound (voice) of the LORD God walking in the garden in the cool of the day. (Gen. 3:8)

(2) שֹׁפֵךְ דַּם הָאָדָם בָּאָדָם דָּמוֹ יִשָּׁפֵךְ כִּי בְּצֶלֶם אֱלֹהִים עָשָׂה אֶת־הָאָדָם

One shedding the blood of man, by man his blood shall be shed; for in the image of God he made man. (Gen. 9:6)

(3) וַעֲתַלְיָה מֹלֶכֶת עַל־הָאָרֶץ

Athaliah reigned over the land. (2 Kgs. 11:3)

(4) וְקָרְאוּ לָהֶם עַם־הַקֹּדֶשׁ גְּאוּלֵי יְהוָה

And they shall call them the holy people, the redeemed of the LORD. (Isa. 62:12)

(5) הֲשֹׁפֵט כָּל־הָאָרֶץ לֹא יַעֲשֶׂה מִשְׁפָּט

Shall not the judge of all the earth do justice? (Gen. 18:25)

(6) כִּי לֹא־עָזַבְתָּ דֹרְשֶׁיךָ יְהוָה

For you, O LORD, have not forsaken those who seek you. (Ps. 9:11; Eng. 9:10)

(7) וְהוּא נִכְבָּד מִכֹּל בֵּית אָבִיו

Now he was honored above all his father's household. (Gen. 34:19)

(8) וּקְבַרְתֶּם אֹתִי בַּקֶּבֶר אֲשֶׁר אִישׁ הָאֱלֹהִים קָבוּר בּוֹ

And you shall bury me in the tomb in which the man of God is buried. (1 Kgs. 13:31)

(9) רֹדֵף צְדָקָה וָחָסֶד יִמְצָא חַיִּים צְדָקָה וְכָבוֹד

He who pursues righteousness and mercy will find life, righteousness, and honor. (Prov. 21:21)

(10) תְּהוֹם־אֶל־תְּהוֹם קוֹרֵא

Deep calls unto deep. (Ps. 42:8; Eng. 42:7)

(11) הֲשָׁמַע עָם קוֹל אֱלֹהִים
מְדַבֵּר מִתּוֹד־הָאֵשׁ כַּאֲשֶׁר־
שָׁמַעְתָּ אַתָּה

Has a people heard the voice of God speaking from the midst of the fire as you have heard? (Deut. 4:33)

(12) כִּי כָל־בֵּיתָהּ לָבֻשׁ שָׁנִים

For all her household is clothed in scarlet. (Prov. 31:21)

(13) וּמְהַלְלִים לַיהוָה יוֹם בְּיוֹם
הַלְוִיִּם וְהַכֹּהֲנִים

The Levites and the priests praised the LORD day by day. (2 Chr. 30:21)

(14) בָּרוּךְ אַתָּה בְּנִי דָוִד

Blessed be you, my son David! (1 Sam. 26:25)

(15) שִׁמְעוּ אֵלַי רֹדְפֵי צֶדֶק
מְבַקְשֵׁי יְהוָה

Hearken to me, you who pursue justice, you who seek the LORD. (Isa. 51:1)

VOCABULARY

(1) [אמן] (Nifʻal) he was faithful (Hifʻil) he believed

(2) אָרַר he cursed

(3) גּוֹאֵל redeemer

(4) גָּלָה he uncovered, revealed

(5) גָּמָל camel

(6) יוֹשֵׁב inhabitant

(7) יוֹצֵר potter

(8) יָצַר he formed

(9) מוֹשִׁיעַ savior, deliverer

(10) מַלְאָךְ angel, messenger

(11) נָגַע he touched, smote

(12) נָגַשׁ he approached

(13) נָהָר river

(14) סוֹפֵר scribe

(15) פָּדָה he ransomed, redeemed

(16) פָּשַׁע he rebelled, transgressed

(17) רוֹאֶה seer, prophet

(18) רוֹעֶה shepherd

(19) רָעָה he pastured, tended

(20) שַׂר prince, ruler

(21) שָׁאַר he was left, left over

(22) שׁוֹפֵט judge

(23) שָׁקָה he drank, (Hifʻil) he watered

(24) תּוֹעֵבָה (f) abomination

LESSON XXI

62. Verbs: The Pointing of Vav Conjunction with Verb Forms

Attention has already been given to the form and function of the vav consecutive (·וַ) on Hebrew imperfects (cf. XVI.43, pp. 145–146). While the vav consecutive occurs only on imperfect forms of the verb, the vav conjunction may be used on all verb forms, including imperfects.

The rules for pointing the vav conjunction before verb forms are the same as those for pointing it before nouns and other parts of speech (cf. VI.16, pp. 30–32). They are repeated here for review purposes.

62.1 וְ before consonants with full vowels, unless these consonants are בּ, מ, or פּ, or unless they belong to the tone syllable of the word (cf. XXI.62.5 below)
Examples:

(1)	וְכָתַבְתָּ	(Jer. 36:2)	(3)	וְהָיוּ	(Gen. 1:14)
(2)	וְלָקַח	(Gen. 3:22)	(4)	וְיִשְׁמְרֶךָ	(Num. 6:24)

62.2 וּ before בּ, מ, or פּ
Examples:

(1)	וּבָנִינוּ	(Neh. 2:18)	(3)	וּמִלְאוּ	(Gen. 9:1)
(2)	וּמְבָרַכֶיךָ	(Gen. 27:29)	(4)	וּפָנָה	(Mal. 3:1)

62.3 וּ before all consonants with simple shevas (except יְ, הְ, and חְ)
Examples:

(1)	וּשְׂרָפָה	(Jer. 21:10)	(3)	וּנְמִיתֶם	(1 Sam. 11:12)
(2)	וּתְחִי	(Isa. 55:3)	(4)	וּדְעוּ	(Ps. 46:11)

62.4 וִ before יְ, הְ, חְ
Examples:

(1)	וִיגְדַּל	(from וְיִגְדַּל)	(1 Kgs. 1:47)
(2)	וִיהִי	(from וְיִהִי)	(Gen. 1:6)
(3)	וִהְיִיתֶם	(from וְהְיִיתֶם)	(Zech. 8:13)
(4)	וִחְיוּ	(from וְחְיוּ)	(Gen. 42:18)

62.5 וָ sometimes found before the tone syllable, especially in mono-syllabic words
Examples:

(1)	וָבֹשְׁתְּ	(Ezek. 16:63)	(3)	וָמֵתוּ	(Exod. 9:19)
(2)	וָבֹא	(1 Kgs. 3:7)	(4)	וָמֵת	(Job 2:9)

62.6 וַ, וְ before consonants supported by ḥaṭef-pataḥ or ḥaṭef-seᵉgol
Examples:

(1) וַאֲכַלְתֶּם (Ezek. 39:17)

(2) וַעֲשֵׂה (1 Chr. 22:16)

(3) וֶאֱכֹל (1 Kgs. 13:15)

63. Verbs: Coordinate Relationship.
A Study of Hebrew Verb Sequences

A coordinate relationship consists of two or more verb forms linked together by means of vav conjunction or vav consecutive. The verb that stands first in such a sequence functions as the governing verb and determines both the time (past, present, or future) and the mode (indicative, subjunctive, or imperative) of the verbs linked to it. This literary device gave writers greater flexibility in expressing their thoughts, even though they worked with a limited number of verb forms.

The presentation here is not meant to be exhaustive. Coordinate relationships are not always so easy to identify as those presented here. However, the consistencies far outweigh the inconsistencies and prove that the emerging patterns must be taken seriously.

63.1 *Coordinate Relationships Involving a Perfect as the Governing Verb*

A perfect may serve as the governing verb when it stands in sequence with another perfect or with an imperfect. Its usage seems to be limited to these two categories.

(1) Perfect + Perfect Sequence

The linking of two perfects is the simplest form of the coordinate relationship. The first perfect in such a sequence does not alter the time and mode of the second, since the two are already essentially alike. Examples of the perfect plus perfect sequence are surprisingly rare in the Hebrew Bible.
Examples:

(a) דָּבָר שָׁלַח אֲדֹנָי
     בְּיַעֲקֹב וְנָפַל
     בְּיִשְׂרָאֵל

The Lord has sent a word against Jacob, and it has fallen upon Israel.
(Isa. 9:7; Eng. 9:8)

(b) אֶרֶץ יָרְאָה וְשָׁקָטָה

The earth feared and was still.
(Ps. 76:9; Eng. 76:8)

210

(c)   אָבִיךָ הֲלוֹא אָכַל   Did not your father eat and drink
וְשָׁתָה וְעָשָׂה מִשְׁפָּט   and do justice and righteousness?
וּצְדָקָה   (Jer. 22:15)

(2) Perfect + Imperfect Sequence

This is one of the most frequently occurring verb sequences in the
Hebrew Bible. It is a true narrative sequence, as noted earlier in the grammar (cf.
XVI.43, pp. 147-148). It is marked by the vav consecutive (·וַ), the special form of
the conjunction linking the imperfect to its governing perfect. The vav consecutive
(·וַ) is used nowhere else in the Hebrew verb system except here, not even on
imperfects placed in sequence with other verb forms. Furthermore, in the perfect +
imperfect sequence, one rarely encounters an imperfect prefixed with vav conjunction
(וְ).

An imperfect prefixed with vav consecutive will customarily be
translated in past time and in the indicative mode. It may describe an action
resulting from a previous action (consequence) or an action subsequent to a previous
action (sequence).

Examples:

(a)   וְהָאָדָם יָדַע אֶת־חַוָּה   Now the man knew Eve his wife,
אִשְׁתּוֹ וַתַּהַר וַתֵּלֶד   and she conceived and bore Cain.
אֶת־קַיִן   (Gen. 4:1)

(b)   זָכָר וּנְקֵבָה בְּרָאָם   Male and female he created them,
וַיְבָרֶךְ אֹתָם וַיִּקְרָא   and he blessed them, and he called
אֶת־שְׁמָם אָדָם   their name Adam. (Gen. 5:2)

(c)   זָכַרְתִּי בַלַּיְלָה שִׁמְךָ   I have remembered thy name in the
יְהוָה וָאֶשְׁמְרָה   night, O LORD, and I have kept
תּוֹרָתֶךָ   thy law. (Ps. 119:55)

The narrative use of imperfects with vav consecutive became so
commonplace that they were often used in this sense even without a preceding
governing perfect, especially with imperfect forms of the verb הָיָה, "he was."

Examples:

(i)   וַיְהִי דְבַר־יְהוָה   And the word of the LORD came
אֶל־יוֹנָה   (was) to Jonah. (Jon. 1:1)

(ii)   וַיְהִי אַחַר הַדְּבָרִים   And it came to pass after
הָאֵלֶּה   these things. (Gen. 22:1)

211

63.2 *Relationships Involving an Imperfect as the Governing Verb*

Imperfects may serve as governing verbs when they are placed in sequence with other imperfects or with perfects.

(1) Imperfect + Imperfect Sequence

The conjunction used in this sequence will be the ordinary form of the vav conjunction, pointed according to the rules given in XXI.62, pp. 209f. The second verb in this sequence sometimes expresses the outcome or purpose of the action of the first verb. There are no objective criteria for determining when this is the case. The reader must decide whether this was the author's intended meaning. The work of the translator becomes both an art and a science.

Examples:

(a)   יְבָרֶכְךָ יהוה וְיִשְׁמְרֶךָ   May the LORD bless you, and may he keep you. (Num. 6:24)

(b)   נִשְׁלְחָה אֲנָשִׁים לְפָנֵינוּ   Let us send men before us, that
וְיַחְפְּרוּ־לָנוּ אֶת־הָאָרֶץ   they may explore the land for us. (Deut. 1:22)

(c)   וַאֲנִי אֶשְׁמַע מִן־הַשָּׁמַיִם   And I will hear from heaven, and
וְאֶסְלַח לְחַטָּאתָם וְאֶרְפָּא   I will forgive their sin, and I
אֶת־אַרְצָם   will heal their land. (2 Chr. 7:14)

(2) Imperfect + Perfect Sequence

The conjunction used in this sequence will also be the normal form of the vav conjunction, pointed according to the rules given in XXI.62, pp. 209f. This sequence is used with all the various meanings and in all the various modes of the imperfect. It should be noted that when perfects are prefixed with vav conjunction the accent shifts to the final syllable in the 2 ms and 1 cs forms, except in the case of Lamed He verbs.

Examples:

(a)   אָמַרְתָּ   (Isa. 14:13), but   וְאָמַרְתָּ   (Gen. 32:19)

(b)   הָלַכְתִּי   (Jer. 2:23), but   וְהָלַכְתִּי   (Judg. 1:3)

(c)   בָּנִיתִי   (1 Kgs. 8:27), and   וּבָנִיתִי   (Jer. 42:10)

(a) Indicative Imperfect + Perfect Sequence
Examples:

(*i*)   הוּא יִשְׁלַח מַלְאָכוֹ   He will send his angel before you,
לְפָנֶיךָ וְלָקַחְתָּ אִשָּׁה   and you shall take a wife for my son
לִבְנִי מִשָּׁם   from there. (Gen. 24:7)

212

(ii) וְאֵד יַעֲלֶה מִן־הָאָרֶץ וְהִשְׁקָה אֶת־כָּל־פְּנֵי־ הָאֲדָמָה

And a mist used to go up from the earth, and it used to water all the face of the ground. (Gen. 2:6)

(iii) בְּיַד מֶלֶךְ־בָּבֶל תִּנָּתֵן וּשְׂרָפָהּ בָּאֵשׁ

It shall be given into the hand of the king of Babylon, and he shall burn it with fire. (Jer. 34:2)

(b) Jussive Imperfect + Perfect Sequence
Examples:

(i) וַיֹּאמֶר אֱלֹהִים יְהִי מְאֹרֹת בִּרְקִיעַ הַשָּׁמַיִם וְהָיוּ לְאֹתֹת וּלְמוֹעֲדִים וּלְיָמִים וְשָׁנִים

And God said, Let there be lights in the firmament of the heavens, and let them be for signs and for seasons and for days and years. (Gen. 1:14)

(ii) וְאֵל שַׁדַּי יְבָרֵךְ אֹתְךָ וְיַפְרְךָ וְיַרְבֶּךָ וְהָיִיתָ לִקְהַל עַמִּים

May God Almighty bless you and may he make you fruitful, and may he multiply you, and may you become a company of peoples. (Gen. 28:3)

(c) Cohortative Imperfect + Perfect Sequence
Examples:

(i) וַיֹּאמֶר עָלֹה נַעֲלֶה וְיָרַשְׁנוּ אֹתָהּ

And he said, Let us go up at once, and let us possess it. (Num. 13:30)

(ii) וַיֹּאמְרוּ נָקוּם וּבָנִינוּ

And they said, Let us rise up, and let us build. (Neh. 2:18)

(iii) וְעַתָּה לְכָה נִכְרְתָה בְרִית אֲנִי וְאָתָּה וְהָיָה לְעֵד בֵּינִי וּבֵינֶךָ

And now, come, let us make (cut) a covenant, I and you, and let it be for a witness between me and between you. (Gen. 31:44)

(d) Subjunctive Imperfect + Perfect Sequence
Examples:

(i) פֶּן־יִנָּחֵם הָעָם וְשָׁבוּ מִצְרָיְמָה

Lest the people repent, and (lest) they return to Egypt. (Exod. 13:17)

(ii) לְמַעַן תִּזְכְּרִי וָבֹשְׁתְּ

In order that you may remember, and that you may be confounded (ashamed). (Ezek. 16:63)

(iii) וַיִּדַּר יַעֲקֹב נֶדֶר לֵאמֹר
אִם־יִהְיֶה אֱלֹהִים עִמָּדִי
וּשְׁמָרַנִי בַּדֶּרֶךְ הַזֶּה
וְנָתַן־לִי לֶחֶם לֶאֱכֹל
וּבֶגֶד לִלְבֹּשׁ

And Jacob vowed a vow, saying, If God will be with me, and (if) he will keep me in this way, and (if) he will give me bread to eat and clothing to wear. (Gen. 28:20)

(iv) פֶּן־יִשְׁלַח יָדוֹ וְלָקַח גַּם
מֵעֵץ הַחַיִּים

Lest he put forth his hand, and (lest) he take also from the tree of life. (Gen. 3:22)

63.3 *Relationships Involving an Imperative as the Governing Verb*

An imperative may serve as a governing verb when it is placed in sequence with a perfect, an imperfect, or another imperative. The conjunction used in this sequence will also be the vav conjunction, pointed according to the rules given in XXI.62, pp. 209f. When an imperative functions as the governing verb, the verb that follows it sometimes expresses the notion of purpose or result. It is not always clear which meaning the writer had in mind. In such cases the translator must exercise his or her judgment.

(1) Imperative + Perfect Sequence

The perfect in this coordinate relationship must be translated as an imperative. It is instructive in this respect to compare the similar commands given in Jeremiah 36:2 and 36:28, the first involving an Imperative + Perfect sequence and the second involving an Imperative + Imperative sequence.

(36:2)   קַח־לְךָ מְגִלַּת־סֵפֶר
וְכָתַבְתָּ אֵלֶיהָ

Take a scroll and write on it.

(36:28)   קַח־לְךָ מְגִלָּה אַחֶרֶת
וּכְתֹב עָלֶיהָ

Take another scroll and write on it.

The conclusion to be drawn from these two passages is that placing an imperative in sequence with a perfect has the same effect as placing it in sequence with an imperative. Both provide a continuation of the initial command.

Examples of Imperative + Perfect Sequence:

(a)   שׁוּבוּ אֶל־הַמֶּלֶךְ אֲשֶׁר־
שָׁלַח אֶתְכֶם וְדִבַּרְתֶּם
אֵלָיו

Return to the king who sent you, and say to him. (2 Kgs. 1:6)

(b)   קוּם וְיָרַדְתָּ בֵּית הַיּוֹצֵר

Arise, and go down to the house of the potter. (Jer. 18:2)

(c) שִׁמְעוּ אֶת־דִּבְרֵי הַבְּרִית   Hear the words of this covenant,
הַזֹּאת וַעֲשִׂיתֶם אוֹתָם   and do them. (Jer. 11:6)

(2) Imperative + Imperfect Sequence

An imperfect in coordinate relationship with an imperative sometimes expresses purpose or result.

Examples:

(a) לְכוּ וְנִבְנֶה אֶת־חוֹמַת   Come, let us build the wall of
יְרוּשָׁלָ͏ִם   Jerusalem. (Neh. 2:17)

(b) קוּמוּ וְנַעֲלֶה צִיּוֹן   Arise, and let us go up to Zion.
(Jer. 31:6)

(c) תְּנָה־לָּנוּ בָשָׂר וְנֹאכֵלָה   Give to us flesh (meat), that we
may eat. (Num. 11:13)

(d) פְּקַח־נָא אֶת־עֵינָיו   Open his eyes, that he may see.
וְיִרְאֶה   (2 Kgs. 6:17)

(3) Imperative + Imperative Sequence

The second imperative in this sequence often expresses purpose or result. The translator must decide whether or not this is the case. Support may sometimes be drawn from other ancient versions.

(a) סוּר מֵרָע וַעֲשֵׂה־טוֹב   Depart from evil and do good.
(Ps. 34:15; Eng. 34:14)

(b) בַּקֵּשׁ שָׁלוֹם וְרָדְפֵהוּ   Seek peace, and pursue it.
(Ps. 34:15; Eng.34:14)

(c) בָּרֵךְ אֱלֹהִים וָמֻת   Curse (bless) God, and die.
(Job. 2:9)

(d) עִמְדוּ וּרְאוּ אֶת־יְשׁוּעַת   Stand still, and see the salvation
יְהוָה   of the LORD. (2 Chr. 20:17)

63.4 *Infinitive Absolute + Perfect Sequence*

The infinitive absolute may sometimes be used with the force of an imperative (on the various uses of infinitive absolute, cf. XIX.57, pp. 184ff.). A perfect may be placed in sequence with an infinitive absolute used in this manner, in which case the perfect must also be translated as an imperative.

Examples:

(1) הָלוֹךְ וְדִבַּרְתָּ אֶל־דָּוִד   Go and say to David. (2 Sam. 24:12)

215

(2)   הָלוֹךְ וְרָחַצְתָּ   Go and bathe seven times in the
שֶׁבַע־פְּעָמִים בַּיַּרְדֵּן   Jordan. (2 Kgs. 5:10)

(3)   שָׁמֹעַ בֵּין־אֲחֵיכֶם   Hear (cases) between your brethren,
וּשְׁפַטְתֶּם צֶדֶק   and judge righteously. (Deut. 1:16)

63.5 *Participle + Perfect Sequence*

The participle is often used to describe an impending action, something destined to take place in the near future. This is especially true when the participle is introduced by the demonstrative particle הִנֵּה, "behold!" (cf. XX.60, pp. 198–202). When a perfect is placed in sequence with such a participle, it too is translated in future time.

Examples:

(a)   וְאַתֶּם עֹבְרִים וִירִשְׁתֶּם   And you shall cross over and shall
אֶת־הָאָרֶץ הַטּוֹבָה הַזֹּאת   take possession of that good land.
(Deut. 4:22)

(b)   הִנְנִי שֹׁלֵחַ מַלְאָכִי   Behold, I will send my messenger,
וּפִנָּה־דֶרֶךְ לְפָנָי   and he will prepare a way before me.
(Mal. 3:1)

EXERCISES

1. In the following clauses and sentences, identify (a) the verb sequence, (b) the verb stems, and (c) the verb roots.

Example:

קַח־לְךָ מְגִלַּת־סֵפֶר   Take a scroll and write on it. (Jer. 36:2)
וְכָתַבְתָּ אֵלֶיהָ

(a) Imperative + Perfect sequence (b) ___Qal___ , ___Qal___
(c) ___לָקַח___ , ___כָּתַב___

(1)   שַׁלַּח אֶת־עַמִּי וְיַעַבְדֻנִי   Send my people out, that they may
serve me. (Exod. 7:26; Eng. 8:1)

(a) _____ + _____ sequence (b) _____ , _____
(c) _____ , _____

(2)   בְּנֵה־לְךָ בַיִת בִּירוּשָׁלַ͏ִם   Build yourself a house in Jerusalem,
וְיָשַׁבְתָּ שָׁם   and dwell there. (1 Kgs. 2:36)

(a) _____ + _____ sequence (b) _____ , _____
(c) _____ , _____

216

(3) הִנָּבֵא בֶן־אָדָם וְאָמַרְתָּ אֶל־הָרוּחַ
Prophesy, son of man, and say to the wind (breath). (Ezek. 37:9)

(a) _____ + _____ sequence (b) _____ , _____

(c) _____ , _____

(4) וְלֹא יִקָּרֵא עוֹד שִׁמְךָ אַבְרָם וְהָיָה שִׁמְךָ אַבְרָהָם
No longer shall your name be called Abram, but your name shall be Abraham (Gen. 17:5)

(a) _____ + _____ sequence (b) _____ , _____

(c) _____ , _____

(5) כִּי תִשְׁמֹר אֶת־מִצְוֹת יְהוָה אֱלֹהֶיךָ וְהָלַכְתָּ בִּדְרָכָיו
if you keep the commandments of the LORD your God, and walk in his ways (Deut. 28:9)

(a) _____ + _____ sequence (b) _____ , _____

(c) _____ , _____

(6) נִבְנֶה־לָּנוּ עִיר וְנַעֲשֶׂה־לָּנוּ שֵׁם
Let us build for ourselves a city, and let us make for ourselves a name. (Gen. 11:4)

(a) _____ + _____ sequence (b) _____ , _____

(c) _____ , _____

(7) יִקְרָאֵנִי וְאֶעֱנֵהוּ
He will call to me, and I will answer him. (Ps. 91:15)

(a) _____ + _____ sequence (b) _____ , _____

(c) _____ , _____

(8) קְרַב עַד־הֵנָּה וַאֲדַבְּרָה אֵלֶיךָ
Come near, that I may speak to you. (2 Sam. 20:16)

(a) _____ + _____ sequence (b) _____ , _____

(c) _____ , _____

(9) פְּקַח־נָא אֶת־עֵינָיו וְיִרְאֶה
Open his eyes, that he may see. (2 Kgs. 6:17)

(a) _____ + _____ sequence (b) _____ , _____

(c) _____ , _____

(10) תְּנוּ־לָנוּ מַיִם וְנִשְׁתֶּה
Give to us water, that we may drink. (Exod. 17:2)

(a) _____ + _____ sequence (b) _____ , _____

(c) _____ , _____

217

(11)   שִׂנְאוּ־רָע וְאֶהֱבוּ טוֹב   Hate evil and love good.
       (Amos 5:15)

   (a) _____ + _____ sequence (b) _____ , _____

                (c) _____ , _____

(12) שִׁמְרוּ מִשְׁפָּט וַעֲשׂוּ צְדָקָה   Keep justice, and do righteousness.
       (Isa. 56:1)

   (a) _____ + _____ sequence (b) _____ , _____

                (c) _____ , _____

2. Translate the following clauses and sentences, and locate fully all verb forms, following the guidelines given in XIV.38, pp. 117ff.

(1)   זָכַרְתִּי בַלַּיְלָה שִׁמְךָ וָאֶשְׁמְרָה תּוֹרָתֶךָ   (Ps. 119:55)

(2)   וַיֹּאמֶר צֵא וְעָמַדְתָּ בָהָר לִפְנֵי יְהוָה   (1 Kgs. 19:11)

(3)   כִּי־יִצְעַק אֵלַי וְשָׁמַעְתִּי   (Exod. 22:26)

(4)   וַיִּזְכֹּר אֱלֹהִים אֶת־בְּרִיתוֹ אֶת־אַבְרָהָם   (Exod. 2:24)

3. Match each of these weak verbs with its proper classification, according to the traditional classification system.

( )   מָדַד   (A)   Pe Nun

( )   עָזַב   (B)   Lamed Guttural

( )   פָּנָה   (C)   Lamed ʾAlef

( )   קוּם   (D)   ʿAyin Guttural

( )   נָתַן   (E)   Pe ʾAlef

( )   שָׁמַע   (F)   ʿAyin Vav

( )   בִּין   (G)   Lamed He

( )   מָצָא   (H)   Pe Guttural

( )   יָלַד   (I)   ʿAyin Yod

( )   זָעַק   (J)   Double ʿAyin

( )   אָבַד   (K)   Pe Vav/Pe Yod

4. Copy the infinitives in the following examples and give (a) the stem, and (b) the root of each.

Example:

לֶחֶם לֶאֱכֹל וּבֶגֶד לִלְבֹּשׁ

bread to eat, and clothes to wear
(Gen. 28:20)

Inf. לֶאֱכֹל

(a) Qal (b) אָכַל

Inf. לִלְבֹּשׁ

(a) Qal (b) לָבַשׁ

(2) הָלוֹךְ וְדִבַּרְתָּ אֶל־דָּוִד

Go and say to David. (2 Sam. 24:12)

Inf. _____

(a) _____ (b) _____

(3) לְהַבְדִּיל בֵּין הַיּוֹם וּבֵין הַלָּיְלָה

to separate between the day and between the night (Gen. 1:14)

Inf. _____

(a) _____ (b) _____

(4) וַיִּשְׁאַל דָּוִד בַּיהוָה לֵאמֹר

And David inquired (asked) of the LORD, saying: (1 Sam. 23:2)

Inf. _____

(a) _____ (b) _____

(5) אֲשֶׁר עֵינַיִם לָהֶם לִרְאוֹת וְלֹא רָאוּ אָזְנַיִם לָהֶם לִשְׁמֹעַ וְלֹא שָׁמֵעוּ

who have eyes to see, but see not; who have ears to hear, but hear not (Ezek. 12:2)

Inf. _____

(a) _____ (b) _____

Inf. _____

(a) _____ (b) _____

(6) לֹא אֵדַע צֵאת וָבֹא

I do not know (how) to go out or to come in. (1 Kgs. 3:7)

Inf. _____

(a) _____ (b) _____

Inf. _____

(a) _____ (b) _____

(7) וְלִמְשֹׁל בַּיּוֹם וּבַלָּיְלָה

to rule over the day and over the night (Gen. 1:18)

Inf. _____

(a) _____ (b) _____

(8) לִדְרוֹשׁ אֶת־תּוֹרַת יְהוָה וְלַעֲשֹׂת וּלְלַמֵּד בְּיִשְׂרָאֵל חֹק וּמִשְׁפָּט

to seek the law of the LORD, and to do (it); and to teach statutes and ordinances in Israel (Ezra 7:10)

Inf. _____

(a) _____ (b) _____

Inf. _____

(a) _____ (b) _____

Inf. _____

(a) _____ (b) _____

(9) וַיַּנִּחֵהוּ בְגַן־עֵדֶן לְעָבְדָהּ וּלְשָׁמְרָהּ

And he placed him in the garden of Eden
to tend it and to keep it. (Gen. 2:15)

Inf. _____

(a) _____ (b) _____

Inf. _____

(a) _____ (b) _____

(10) לֹא־טוֹב הֱיוֹת הָאָדָם לְבַדּוֹ

It is not good for the man to be alone.
(Gen. 2:18)

Inf. _____

(a) _____ (b) _____

5. Practice pronouncing the Hebrew aloud. Then cover the English and practice translating the Hebrew from sight.

(1) וְהָאֶבֶן הַזֹּאת אֲשֶׁר־שַׂמְתִּי
מַצֵּבָה יִהְיֶה בֵּית אֱלֹהִים
וְכֹל אֲשֶׁר תִּתֶּן־לִי עַשֵּׂר
אֲעַשְּׂרֶנּוּ לָךְ

And this stone, which I have set up
as a pillar, shall be the house of God;
and of all that you give to me I will
without fail give the tenth part
to you. (Gen. 28:22)

(2) שְׁמַע יִשְׂרָאֵל יְהוָה אֱלֹהֵינוּ
יְהוָה אֶחָד וְאָהַבְתָּ אֵת
יְהוָה אֱלֹהֶיךָ בְּכָל־
לְבָבְךָ וּבְכָל־נַפְשְׁךָ
וּבְכָל־מְאֹדֶךָ

Hear, O Israel: The LORD our God is
one LORD; and you shall love the
LORD your God with all your heart,
and with all your soul, and with all
your might. (Deut. 6:4–5)

(3) אַךְ טוֹב וָחֶסֶד יִרְדְּפוּנִי
כָּל־יְמֵי חַיָּי

Surely goodness and mercy shall
follow me all the days of my life.
(Ps. 23:6)

(4) יִשְׁלַח דְּבָרוֹ וְיִרְפָּאֵם

He sends forth his word, and heals
them. (Ps. 107:20)

(5) טַעֲמוּ וּרְאוּ כִּי־טוֹב יְהוָה

Taste and see that the LORD is good.
(Ps. 34:9; Eng. 34:8)

(6) פְּרוּ וּרְבוּ וּמִלְאוּ אֶת־הָאָרֶץ

Be fruitful, and multiply, and fill
up the earth. (Gen. 9:1)

(7) הוֹשִׁיעֵנוּ אֱלֹהֵי יִשְׁעֵנוּ
וְקַבְּצֵנוּ וְהַצִּילֵנוּ מִן־הַגּוֹיִם

Save us, O God of our salvation, and
gather us, and deliver us from the
nations. (1 Chr. 16:35)

(8)   יְהוָה יִשְׁמָר־צֵאתְךָ וּבוֹאֶךָ   The LORD will keep your going out
מֵעַתָּה וְעַד־עוֹלָם   and your coming in from now on and
for evermore. (Ps. 121:8)

(9)   יִקָּווּ הַמַּיִם אֶל־מָקוֹם אֶחָד   Let the waters be gathered together
וְתֵרָאֶה הַיַּבָּשָׁה   in one place, and let the dry land
appear (be seen). (Gen. 1:9)

(10)   הַקְהֶל־לִי אֶת־הָעָם   Gather the people to me, that I may
וְאַשְׁמִעֵם אֶת־דְּבָרִי   cause them to hear my words.
(Deut. 4:10)

VOCABULARY

(1) בּוֹשׁ to be ashamed, confounded

(2) דָּבַק he cleaved, clung to

(3) הָרָה (she) conceived, became pregnant

(4) סוּר to turn aside

(5) פָּנָה he turned towards, faced, prepared

(6) רָחַץ he washed

(7) אֹזֶן (f) ear

(8) אֱנוֹשׁ man, mankind

(9) בֶּגֶד garment

(10) בְּרָכָה (f) blessing

(11) גּוֹרָל lot, portion, share

(12) גֶּפֶן (f) vine

(13) גֶּשֶׁם rain, shower

(14) זְרֹעַ (f) arm, strength

(15) מוֹעֵד appointed time, place

(16) עֵד a witness, testimony, evidence

(17) עַיִן (f) eye, fountain

(18) שֶׁקֶר deception, falsehood

221

LESSON XXII

64. Weak Verbs: Their Classification

The various classes of weak verbs were introduced in a previous lesson (cf. XII.29, pp. 80ff.). They are simply listed here for review purposes.

(1)	עָזַב	Pe Guttural (I–Guttural)
(2)	זָעַק	ʿAyin Guttural (II–Guttural)
(3)	שָׁמַע	Lamed Guttural (III–Guttural)
(4)	אָבַד	Pe ʾAlef (I–ʾAlef)
(5)	מָצָא	Lamed ʾAlef (III–ʾAlef)
(6)	פָּנָה	Lamed He (III–He)
(7)	נָתַן	Pe Nun (I–Nun)
(8)	בִּין, קוּם	ʿAyin Vav/ʿAyin Yod (II–Vav/II–Yod)
(9)	יָלַד	Pe Vav/Pe Yod (I–Vav/I–Yod)
(10)	מָדַד	Double ʿAyin (Geminate Verbs)

65. Characteristics of Gutturals

The various characteristics of gutturals were given in a previous lesson (cf. V.13, pp. 23f.). They are repeated here in order to show how they apply to the inflection of verb forms where there is at least one guttural among the consonants of the verb root. (Note especially the first three classes of weak verbs in the list given above.)

The gutturals include א, ה, ח, ע, and sometimes ר. They exhibit three distinct characteristics that set them apart from other letters of the Hebrew alphabet.

65.1 *Gutturals cannot be doubled.*

This refusal on the part of the guttural to accept a dagesh forte calls for the compensatory lengthening of the preceding vowel, which otherwise would be left as a short vowel in an unaccented open syllable (cf. IV.12, pp. 19ff.). The normal pattern for compensatory lengthening is as follows:

(1) Pataḥ is lengthened to Qameṣ (ַ to ָ).
(2) Ḥireq is lengthened to Ṣere (ִ to ֵ).
(3) Qibbuṣ is lengthened to Ḥolem (ֻ to ֹ).

222

65.2 *Gutturals usually take "a" class vowels.*

If the guttural has a vowel following it, the vowel will normally be pataḥ. Certain strong gutturals, when situated as the final consonant in a word, also demand an "a" class vowel immediately *before* them. These gutturals include ה (he with mappiq; cf. IV.11, p.18), ח, and ע. In the event that the vowel before one of these final gutturals is unchangeably long (ִי , ֵי , ֹו , ֹו), a pataḥ furtive (cf. V.13.2, p. 23) must be inserted between this vowel and the final guttural.

65.3 *Gutturals usually take compound shevas rather than simple shevas.*

Simple shevas must therefore be changed to compound shevas when placed after gutturals. This rule applies even to silent shevas (cf. III.7. p. 13) when they stand after a guttural at the end of the first syllable of a prefixed form of a Pe Guttural verb.

66. Weak Verbs: Pe Guttural Verbs*

66.1 *Definition*

A Pe Guttural verb is one whose initial consonant is either ה, ח, ע, or ר. A verb whose initial consonant is א may also belong to the Pe Guttural class, or it may differ so widely from other verbs of this class that it must be assigned to a class all its own, the Pe 'Alef class.

Some of the more common Pe Guttural verbs are these:

(a)	אָהַב	he loved	(j)	עָבַד	he served, worked
(b)	[אמן]	(Nif.) he was trust-worthy, faithful; (Hif.) he believed, trusted	(k)	עָבַר	he crossed over, transgressed
(c)	הָפַךְ	he overturned, changed	(l)	עָזַב	he forsook, left
(d)	הָרַג	he killed	(m)	עָזַר	he helped
(e)	הָרַס	he broke down, destroyed	(n)	עָמַד	he stood
(f)	חָגַר	he bound, girded	(o)	עָנָה	he answered
(g)	חָזַק	he was strong, firm	(p)	עָרַךְ	he arranged, set in order
(h)	חָפֵץ	he took delight in, desired	(q)	רָאָה	he saw; (Nif.) he appeared; (Hif.) he revealed, showed
(i)	חָשַׁב	he thought, reckoned, imputed	(r)	רָפָא	he healed

*Refer to Verb Chart 2, pp. 402f., for the conjugation of the Pe Guttural verb.

223

66.2 Pe Guttural verbs are written like strong verbs in the Pi'el, Pu'al, and Hitpa'el stems.

Examples:

	Strong Verb	Pe Guttural
Pi'el Perfect 3 ms	מָשַׁל	עָמַד
etc.		
Pu'al Perfect 3 ms	מֻשַּׁל	עֻמַּד
etc.		
Hitpa'el Perfect 3 ms	הִתְמַשֵּׁל	הִתְעַמֵּד
etc.		

66.3 Pe Guttural verbs differ from strong verbs in some of the Qal and Nif'al forms and in all of the Hif'il and Hof'al stems.

These differences may be divided into three groups:

(1) Some differences are due to the fact that the initial guttural verb cannot be doubled. In the forms where doubling would normally have been expected in the initial root consonant but cannot occur because of the guttural nature of this consonant, compensatory lengthening of the preceding vowel (the preformative vowel) becomes necessary (cf. Verb Chart 1, pp. 400f., Verb Chart 2, pp. 402f.). Otherwise, a short vowel would be left standing in an open unaccented syllable.

These changes occur only in Nif'al forms that are prefixed and would normally have a dagesh forte in the initial root consonant. This includes all Nif'al imperfects and imperatives, as well as the infinitive construct. In these forms the preformative vowel before the guttural is lengthened from hireq to sere. Sere in turn is pointed with a meteg, since it stands in an open syllable which is two syllables removed from the accented syllable.

Examples:

			Strong Verb	Pe Guttural
(a)	Nif'al Imperfect	3 ms	יִמָּשֵׁל	יֵעָמֵד
		3 fs	תִּמָּשֵׁל	תֵּעָמֵד
		etc.		
(b)	Nif'al Imperative	2 ms	הִמָּשֵׁל	הֵעָמֵד
		2 fs	הִמָּשְׁלִי	הֵעָמְדִי
		etc.		
(c)	Nif'al Infinitive Construct		הִמָּשֵׁל	הֵעָמֵד

(2) Other differences result from the fact that gutturals generally take compound shevas.

(a) The shevas that stands after initial gutturals in non–prefixed verb forms must be compound shevas. This rule applies to only five Pe Guttural forms, all of which occur in the Qal stem, and all of which take the ḥatef-pataḥ (‑ֲ). The forms included here are as follows:

Examples:

		Strong Verb	Pe Guttural
(i)	Qal Perfect 2 mp	מְשַׁלְתֶּם	עֲמַדְתֶּם
(ii)	Qal Perfect 2 fp	מְשַׁלְתֶּן	עֲמַדְתֶּן
(iii)	Qal Imperative 2 ms	מְשֹׁל	עֲמֹד
(iv)	Qal Imperative 2 fp	מְשֹׁלְנָה	עֲמֹדְנָה
(v)	Qal Infinitive Construct	מְשֹׁל	עֲמֹד

(b) A silent sheva which would close the initial syllable (the prefix syllable) of a strong verb is changed to a compound sheva in the corresponding form of a Pe Guttural verb. The prefix vowel standing immediately before such a compound sheva becomes the short vowel corresponding to the vowel of the compound sheva. The prefix vowel normally receives a meteg. This produces the following combinations: (ַ‑ֲ), (ֶ‑ֱ), (ָ‑ֳ).

(i) The first of these combinations (ַ‑ֲ) is found in the Qal imperfect (although a few Pe Gutturals take ֶ‑ֱ), Nifʼal infinitive absolute, Hifʼil imperfect, Hifʼil imperative, Hifʼil infinitives (construct and absolute) and Hifʼil participle.

Examples:

Qal Imperfect

	Strong Verb	Pe Guttural	Pe Guttural
3 ms	יִמְשֹׁל	יַעֲמֹד	יֶחֱזַק
3 fs	תִּמְשֹׁל	תַּעֲמֹד	תֶּחֱזַק
2 ms	תִּמְשֹׁל	תַּעֲמֹד	תֶּחֱזַק
2 fs	תִּמְשְׁלִי	תַּעַמְדִי	תֶּחֶזְקִי
1 cs	אֶמְשֹׁל	אֶעֱמֹד	אֶחֱזַק
3 mp	יִמְשְׁלוּ	יַעַמְדוּ	יֶחֶזְקוּ
3 fp	תִּמְשֹׁלְנָה	תַּעֲמֹדְנָה	תֶּחֱזַקְנָה
2 mp	תִּמְשְׁלוּ	תַּעַמְדוּ	תֶּחֶזְקוּ
2 fp	תִּמְשֹׁלְנָה	תַּעֲמֹדְנָה	תֶּחֱזַקְנָה
1 cp	נִמְשֹׁל	נַעֲמֹד	נֶחֱזַק

Hif'il Imperfect

	Strong Verb	Pe Guttural
3 ms	יַמְשִׁיל	יַעֲמִיד
3 fs	תַּמְשִׁיל	תַּעֲמִיד
2 ms	תַּמְשִׁיל	תַּעֲמִיד
2 fs	תַּמְשִׁילִי	תַּעֲמִידִי
1 cs	אַמְשִׁיל	אַעֲמִיד
3 mp	יַמְשִׁילוּ	יַעֲמִידוּ
3 fp	תַּמְשֵׁלְנָה	תַּעֲמֵדְנָה
2 mp	תַּמְשִׁילוּ	תַּעֲמִידוּ
2 fp	תַּמְשֵׁלְנָה	תַּעֲמֵדְנָה
1 cp	נַמְשִׁיל	נַעֲמִיד

Hif'il Imperative

	Strong Verb	Pe Guttural
2 ms	הַמְשֵׁל	הַעֲמֵד
2 fs	הַמְשִׁילִי	הַעֲמִידִי
	etc.	

Hif'il Infinitive

	Strong Verb	Pe Guttural
Construct	הַמְשִׁיל	הַעֲמִיד
Absolute	הַמְשֵׁל	הַעֲמֵד

Hif'il Participle

	Strong Verb	Pe Guttural
ms	מַמְשִׁיל	מַעֲמִיד

(*ii*) The second combination of vowels (ֱ ֶ) is found in the Qal imperfect of a few verbs (see above), but appears regularly in the Nif'al perfect, the Nif'al participle, and the Hif'il perfect of Pe Gutturals.

226

Nif'al Perfect

	Strong Verb	Pe Guttural
3 ms	נִמְשַׁל	נֶעֱמַד
3 fs	נִמְשְׁלָה	נֶעֶמְדָה
2 ms	נִמְשַׁלְתָּ	נֶעֱמַדְתָּ
2 fs	נִמְשַׁלְתְּ	נֶעֱמַדְתְּ
1 cs	נִמְשַׁלְתִּי	נֶעֱמַדְתִּי
3 cp	נִמְשְׁלוּ	נֶעֶמְדוּ
2 mp	נִמְשַׁלְתֶּם	נֶעֱמַדְתֶּם
2 fp	נִמְשַׁלְתֶּן	נֶעֱמַדְתֶּן
1 cp	נִמְשַׁלְנוּ	נֶעֱמַדְנוּ

Nif'al Participle

	Strong Verb	Pe Guttural
ms	נִמְשָׁל	נֶעֱמָד

Hif'il Perfect

	Strong Verb	Pe Guttural
3 ms	הִמְשִׁיל	הֶעֱמִיד
3 fs	הִמְשִׁילָה	הֶעֱמִידָה
2 ms	הִמְשַׁלְתָּ	הֶעֱמַדְתָּ
2 fs	הִמְשַׁלְתְּ	הֶעֱמַדְתְּ
1 cs	הִמְשַׁלְתִּי	הֶעֱמַדְתִּי
3 cp	הִמְשִׁילוּ	הֶעֱמִידוּ
2 mp	הִמְשַׁלְתֶּם	הֶעֱמַדְתֶּם
2 fp	הִמְשַׁלְתֶּן	הֶעֱמַדְתֶּן
1 cp	הִמְשַׁלְנוּ	הֶעֱמַדְנוּ

(*iii*) The third combination of vowels (ֱ ָ) is found in all forms of the Hof'al stem of Pe Gutturals.
Example:

Hofʻal Perfect

	Strong Verb	Pe Guttural
3 ms	הָמְשַׁל etc.	הָעֳמַד

Hofʻal Imperfect

	Strong Verb	Pe Guttural
3 ms	יָמְשַׁל etc.	יָעֳמַד

Hofʻal Infinitive

	Strong Verb	Pe Guttural
Construct	הָמְשַׁל	הָעֳמַד
Absolute	הָמְשֵׁל	הָעֳמַד

Hofʻal Participle

	Strong Verb	Pe Guttural
ms	מָמְשָׁל	מָעֳמָד

(3) Another change that takes place in the inflection of Pe Gutturals involves forms that have vocalic afformatives and in which there is the juxtaposition of two vocal shevas. Since two vocal shevas cannot stand together within a word (cf. XVIII.48, pp. 165ff.), the first of these must be raised to a full vowel. The full vowel that takes the place of a compound sheva must be the short vowel that corresponds to the vowel of the compound sheva. Thus

— Ḥatef-Pataḥ becomes Pataḥ (ֲ to ַ).

— Ḥatef-Sᵉgol becomes Sᵉgol (ֱ to ֶ).

— Ḥatef-Qameṣ becomes Qameṣ-Ḥaṭuf (ֳ to ָ).

The Pe Guttural forms affected by this rule are as follows:

(a) Qal Imperfect

2 fs (תַּעֲמְדִי) becomes תַּעַמְדִי

3 mp (יַעֲמְדוּ) becomes יַעַמְדוּ

2 mp (תַּעֲמְדוּ) becomes תַּעַמְדוּ

228

(b) Nif'al Perfect

    3 fs (נֶעֶמְדָה) becomes נֶעֶמְדָה)

    3 cp (נֶעֶמְדוּ) becomes נֶעֶמְדוּ)

(c) Hof'al Perfect

    3 fs (הָעֶמְדָה) becomes הָעֶמְדָה)

    3 cp (הָעֶמְדוּ) becomes הָעֶמְדוּ)

(d) Hof'al Imperfect

    2 fs (תָּעֶמְדִי) becomes תָּעֶמְדִי)

    3 mp (יָעֶמְדוּ) becomes יָעֶמְדוּ)

    2 mp (תָּעֶמְדוּ) becomes תָּעֶמְדוּ)

EXERCISES

1. Write the synopsis of עָבַד, "he served," in the Qal, Nif'al, Pi'el, Hif'il, and Hof'al stems.

	Qal	Nif'al	Pi'el	Hif'il	Hof'al
Perf. 3 ms					
Impf. 3 ms					
Impv. 2 ms					X X X
Inf. Const.					
Inf. Abs.					
Part. Act. (ms)		X X X			X X X
Part. Pass. (ms)			X X X	X X X	

229

2. Write the full inflection of the perfect of עָבַד, "he served," in the Qal, Nifʻal, Piʻel, and Hifʻil stems.

	Qal	Nifʻal	Piʻel	Hifʻil
3 ms				
3 fs				
2 ms				
2 fs				
1 cs				
3 cp				
2 mp				
2 fp				
1 cp				

3. Each of the following sentences contains a perfect form of a Pe Guttural verb. In the space numbered (a) give the perfect's stem, in (b) its person, gender, and number, and in (c) its root.

Example:

נַחֲלָתֵנוּ נֶהֶפְכָה לְזָרִים   (a) __Nifʻal__

Our inheritance has been turned over to strangers.   (b) __3 fs__

(Lam. 5:2)   (c) __הָפַךְ__

(1)   אֵיפֹה הָאֲנָשִׁים אֲשֶׁר הֲרַגְתֶּם בְּתָבוֹר   (a) _____

Where are the men whom you killed at Tabor? (Judg. 8:18)   (b) _____

(c) _____

(2)   וַעֲבַדְתֶּם אֶת־יְהוָה בְּכָל־לְבַבְכֶם   (a) _____

And you shall serve the LORD with all your heart.   (b) _____

(1 Sam. 12:20)   (c) _____

(3)   וְהוּא הֶעֱבִיר אֶת־בָּנָיו בָּאֵשׁ   (a) _____

And he caused his sons to pass through the fire.   (b) _____

(2 Chr. 33:6)   (c) _____

(4)   אֵלִי אֵלִי לָמָה עֲזַבְתָּנִי   (a) _____

My God, my God, why have you forsaken me? (Ps. 22:2;   (b) _____
Eng. 22:1)   (c) _____

(5)   בָּנַיִךְ עֲזָבוּנִי   (a) _____

Your children (sons) have forsaken me. (Jer. 5:7)   (b) _____
                                               (c) _____

(6)   בְּיוֹם יְשׁוּעָה עֲזַרְתִּיךָ   (a) _____

In a day of salvation I have helped you. (Isa. 49:8)   (b) _____
                                               (c) _____

(7)   וְהֶעֱמִיד הַכֹּהֵן אֶת־הָאִשָּׁה לִפְנֵי יְהוָה   (a) _____

And the priest shall set the woman (shall cause the woman   (b) _____
to stand) before the LORD. (Num. 5:18)   (c) _____

(8)   בַּמָּה אֲהַבְתָּנוּ   (a) _____

In what (wherein) have you loved us? (Mal. 1:2)   (b) _____
                                               (c) _____

(9)   וְלֹא הֶאֱמִין לָהֶם גְּדַלְיָהוּ   (a) _____

But Gedaliah did not believe them. (Jer. 40:14)   (b) _____
                                               (c) _____

(10) לָמָה זֶּה עֲזַבְתֶּן אֶת־הָאִישׁ   (a) _____

Why is it that you have left the man? (Exod. 2:20)   (b) _____
                                               (c) _____

4. Each of the following sentences contains an imperfect form of a Pe Guttural verb. In the space numbered (a) give the imperfect's stem, in (b) its person, gender, and number, and in (c) its root.
   Example:

       וַיַּחֲלֹם יוֹסֵף חֲלוֹם   (a)   Qal

       And Joseph dreamed a dream. (Gen. 37:5)   (b)   3 ms

                                                 (c)   חָלַם

(1)   הֲיַהֲפֹךְ כּוּשִׁי עוֹרוֹ   (a) _____

Can the Ethiopian change his skin? (Jer. 13:23)   (b) _____
                                               (c) _____

(2)   הַשֶּׁמֶשׁ יֵהָפֵךְ לְחֹשֶׁךְ

The sun shall be turned to darkness. (Joel 3:4)

(a) _____
(b) _____
(c) _____

(3)   וַיַּהֲרֹג יְהוָה כָּל־בְּכוֹר בְּאֶרֶץ מִצְרָיִם

And the LORD killed all the firstborn in the land of Egypt.
(Exod. 13:15)

(a) _____
(b) _____
(c) _____

(4)   זִקְנֵיכֶם חֲלֹמוֹת יַחֲלֹמוּן

Your old men shall dream dreams. (Joel 3:1)

(a) _____
(b) _____
(c) _____

(5)   גַּם־אֲנַחְנוּ נַעֲבֹד אֶת־יְהוָה כִּי־הוּא אֱלֹהֵינוּ

We also will serve the LORD, for he is our God.
(Josh. 24:18)

(a) _____
(b) _____
(c) _____

(6)   וַיַּעֲבֹד יִשְׂרָאֵל אֶת־יְהוָה כֹּל יְמֵי יְהוֹשֻׁעַ

And Israel served the LORD all the days of Joshua.
(Josh. 24:31)

(a) _____
(b) _____
(c) _____

(7)   לֹא תַעַבְדוּ אֶת־מֶלֶךְ בָּבֶל

You shall not serve the king of Babylon. (Jer. 27:9)

(a) _____
(b) _____
(c) _____

(8)   כִּי־תַעֲבֹר בַּמַּיִם אִתְּךָ־אָנִי

When you pass through the waters, I will be with you.
(Isa. 43:2)

(a) _____
(b) _____
(c) _____

(9)   אֲנִי אַעֲבִיר כָּל־טוּבִי עַל־פָּנֶיךָ

I will cause all my goodness to pass before you (before
your face). (Exod. 33:19)

(a) _____
(b) _____
(c) _____

(10)   תַּעֲרֹךְ לְפָנַי שֻׁלְחָן נֶגֶד צֹרְרָי

You prepare a table before me in the presence of my
harassers. (Ps. 23:5)

(a) _____
(b) _____
(c) _____

(11)   וַיֶּחֱזַק הָרָעָב בְּאֶרֶץ מִצְרָיִם

For the famine was severe (strong) in the land of Egypt.
(Gen. 41:56)

(a) _____
(b) _____
(c) _____

(12)   וַיֶּאֱהַב גַּם־אֶת־רָחֵל מִלֵּאָה

And he loved Rachel more than Leah. (Gen. 29:30)

(a) _____
(b) _____
(c) _____

5. Each of the following sentences contains an imperative form of a Pe Guttural verb. In the space numbered (a) give the imperative's stem, in (b) its person, gender, and number, and in (c) its root.

(1) הַאֲמִינוּ בִנְבִיאָיו

Believe (in) his prophets. (2 Chr. 20:20)

(a) _____
(b) _____
(c) _____

(2) עֲבֹר אֶת־הַיַּרְדֵּן הַזֶּה

Cross over this Jordan. (Josh. 1:2)

(a) _____
(b) _____
(c) _____

(3) בֶּן־אָדָם עֲמֹד עַל־רַגְלֶיךָ

Son of man, stand upon your feet. (Ezek. 2:1)

(a) _____
(b) _____
(c) _____

(4) עֲלֵה רֹאשׁ הַפִּסְגָּה

Go up to the top of Pisgah. (Deut. 3:27)

(a) _____
(b) _____
(c) _____

6. Each of the following contains an infinitive construct of a Pe Guttural verb. Give the stem (a) and root (b) of each. (The verb יוּכַל, used in 3, 4, 5 below is from יָכֹל, a Pe Vav/Pe Yod verb.)

(1) בַּהֲרֹג אִיזֶבֶל אֵת נְבִיאֵי יְהוָה

when Jezebel killed the prophets of the LORD
(1 Kgs. 18:13)

(a) _____
(b) _____

(2) וְאָדָם אַיִן לַעֲבֹד אֶת־הָאֲדָמָה

And there was no man to till the ground. (Gen. 2:5)

(a) _____
(b) _____

(3) לֹא־יוּכַל הַנַּעַר לַעֲזֹב אֶת־אָבִיו

The lad is not able to leave his father. (Gen. 44:22)

(a) _____
(b) _____

(4) אָמְרוּ הֲיוּכַל אֵל לַעֲרֹךְ שֻׁלְחָן בַּמִּדְבָּר

They said, "Can God spread a table in the wilderness?"
(Ps. 78:19)

(a) _____
(b) _____

(5) מִי יוּכַל לַעֲמֹד לִפְנֵי יְהוָה

Who is able to stand before the LORD? (1 Sam. 6:20)

(a) _____
(b) _____

(6) וּלְהַעֲמִיד אֶת־יְרוּשָׁלָם

and to establish (cause to stand) Jerusalem (1 Kgs. 15:4)

(a) _____
(b) _____

7. Each of the following contains a participle of a Pe Guttural verb. Indicate the stem (a), root (b), gender (c), and number (d) of each.

חַטַּאת יְהוּדָה חֲרוּשָׁה עַל־לוּחַ לִבָּם

The sin of Judah is engraved upon the tablet of their heart. (Jer. 17:1)

(a) ___Qal___ (b) ___חָרַשׁ___ (c) ___Fem.___ (d) ___Sing.___

(1)   וְלֹא־רָאִיתִי צַדִּיק נֶעֱזָב

And I have not seen a righteous man forsaken. (Ps. 37:25)

(a) _____ (b) _____ (c) _____ (d) _____

(2)   כִּי עַזָּה עֲזוּבָה תִהְיֶה

For Gaza shall be forsaken. (Zeph. 2:4)

(a) _____ (b) _____ (c) _____ (d) _____

(3)   כִּי הַמָּקוֹם אֲשֶׁר אַתָּה עוֹמֵד עָלָיו אַדְמַת־קֹדֶשׁ הוּא

For the place where you are standing is holy ground. (Exod. 3:5)

(a) _____ (b) _____ (c) _____ (d) _____

(4)   לֹא־יִמָּצֵא בְךָ מַעֲבִיר בְּנוֹ־וּבִתּוֹ בָּאֵשׁ

There shall not be found among you one causing his son or his daughter to pass through the fire. (Deut. 18:10)

(a) _____ (b) _____ (c) _____ (d) _____

(5)   בְּכָל־בֵּיתִי נֶאֱמָן הוּא

In all my house he is faithful. (Num. 12:7)

(a) _____ (b) _____ (c) _____ (d) _____

8. Practice pronouncing the Hebrew, noting especially Pe Guttural forms. Cover the English and practice translating the Hebrew from sight.

(1)   וַיֵּהָפְכוּ כָּל־הַמַּיִם אֲשֶׁר בַּיְאֹר לְדָם

And all the waters which were in the Nile were changed to blood. (Exod. 7:20)

(2)   וְאַתֶּם חֲשַׁבְתֶּם עָלַי רָעָה אֱלֹהִים חֲשָׁבָהּ לְטֹבָה

You devised evil against me; God devised it for good. (Gen. 50:20)

(3)   וַיֹּאמֶר אֶעֱבָדְךָ שֶׁבַע שָׁנִים בְּרָחֵל בִּתְּךָ הַקְּטַנָּה

And he said, "I will serve you seven years for Rachel your younger daughter." (Gen. 29:18)

234

(4) וְאִם רַע בְּעֵינֵיכֶם לַעֲבֹד
אֶת־יְהוָה בַּחֲרוּ לָכֶם
הַיּוֹם אֶת־מִי תַעֲבֹדוּן וְאָנֹכִי
וּבֵיתִי נַעֲבֹד אֶת־יְהוָה

And if (it seem) evil in your eyes
to serve the LORD, (then) choose for
yourselves today whom you will serve;
but (as for) me and my house, we
will serve the LORD. (Josh. 24:15)

(5) וַיַּעַבְדוּ אֶת־הַבְּעָלִים
וַיַּעַזְבוּ אֶת־יְהוָה וְלֹא
עֲבָדוּהוּ

And they served the Baals; but they
forsook the LORD and did not serve
him. (Judg. 10:6)

(6) וְאַתֶּם עֲזַבְתֶּם אוֹתִי וַתַּעַבְדוּ
אֱלֹהִים אֲחֵרִים

But you have forsaken me, and you
have served other gods. (Judg. 10:13)

(7) בָּקַע יָם וַיַּעֲבִירֵם

He divided the sea, and caused
them to pass over. (Ps. 78:13)

(8) וְאַתָּה בְּרַחֲמֶיךָ הָרַבִּים
לֹא עֲזַבְתָּם בַּמִּדְבָּר

But you in your great mercies did
not forsake them in the wilderness.
(Neh. 9:19)

(9) וַתֹּאמֶר צִיּוֹן עֲזָבַנִי יְהוָה
וַאדֹנָי שְׁכֵחָנִי

And Zion said, "The LORD has
forsaken me; and my LORD has
forgotten me." (Isa. 49:14)

(10) וְאִם תַּעַזְבֻהוּ יַעֲזֹב אֶתְכֶם

And if you forsake him, he will
forsake you. (2 Chr. 15:2)

(11) וַיְחַזֵּק יְהוָה אֶת־לֵב פַּרְעֹה
וְלֹא שָׁמַע אֲלֵהֶם

And the LORD hardened the heart of
Pharaoh, and he did not listen
to them. (Exod. 9:12)

(12) אֵלֶּה יַעַמְדוּ לְבָרֵךְ אֶת־
הָעָם עַל־הַר גְּרִזִים

These shall stand to bless the people
upon Mount Gerizim. (Deut. 27:12)

(13) וְאַתָּה פֹּה עֲמֹד עִמָּדִי
וַאֲדַבְּרָה אֵלֶיךָ

But you, stand here with me, so
that I may speak to you. (Deut. 5:31)

(14) וַיֹּאמֶר שְׁמָעוּנִי יְהוּדָה
וְיֹשְׁבֵי יְרוּשָׁלַם הַאֲמִינוּ
בַּיהוָה אֱלֹהֵיכֶם וְתֵאָמֵנוּ

And he said, "Hear me, Judah and
inhabitants of Jerusalem! Believe
in the LORD your God, and you will
be established." (2 Chr. 20:20)

(15) אִם לֹא תַאֲמִינוּ כִּי לֹא
תֵאָמֵנוּ

If you do not believe, surely
you shall not be established. (Isa. 7:9)

VOCABULARY

(1) אָחַז   he seized, took possession; (Nif.) he was caught

(2) גָּנַב   he stole

(3) הָפַךְ   he overturned, changed, (Nif.) he was changed, overthrown

(4) הָרַס   he broke down, destroyed

(5) חָגַר   he bound, girded

(6) [חדשׁ]   (Pi.) he renewed, repaired

(7) חָפֵץ   he took delight in, desired

(8) עָרַךְ   he arranged, set in order

(9) אָז   then

(10) אַךְ   surely, only

(11) אֱמוּנָה   (f) faithfulness, fidelity

(12) בְּאֵר   (f) well

(13) בְּכוֹר   first-born, oldest

(14) דְּבַשׁ   honey

(15) חֹק   (f) statute

(16) לָשׁוֹן   tongue

(17) מָוֶת   death

(18) מִזְבֵּחַ   altar, place of sacrifice

LESSON XXIII

67. Weak Verbs: Pe ʾAlef Verbs*

67.1 Strictly speaking, a Pe ʾAlef verb is any verb whose initial root consonant is א. However, most of the verbs that fall within this category are inflected exactly like other Pe Guttural verbs. This is true of the following verbs:

(1)	אָבַל	he mourned
(2)	אָהֵב	he loved
(3)	[אמן]	(Nif.) he was trustworthy, faithful; (Hif.) he believed, trusted
(4)	אָסַף	he gathered
(5)	אָסַר	he bound

The verbs listed above all have sᵉgol as the preformative vowel in the Qal imperfect, regardless of the stem vowel. However, when the addition of vocalic afformatives results in the juxtaposition of two vocal shevas within a word, the first of the shevas converts to pataḥ (with meteg), and the preformative vowel likewise changes from sᵉgol to pataḥ.

Examples:

(1) אָבַל "he mourned"
- (a) Qal Imperfect 3 ms: יֶאֱבַל
- (b) Qal Imperfect 3 mp: יַאַבְלוּ ← יֶאַבְלוּ ← יֶאֱבְלוּ

(2) אָסַף "he gathered"
- (a) Qal Imperfect 3 ms: יֶאֱסֹף
- (b) Qal Imperfect 3 mp: יַאַסְפוּ ← יֶאַסְפוּ ← יֶאֱסְפוּ

(3) אָסַר "he bound"
- (a) Qal Imperfect 3 ms: יֶאֱסֹר
- (b) Qal Imperfect 3 mp: יַאַסְרוּ ← יֶאַסְרוּ ← יֶאֱסְרוּ

67.2 In addition to the verbs listed above, there is a second group of Pe ʾAlef verbs that differ considerably from regular Pe Guttural verbs in the way they are inflected in the Qal imperfect.

The characteristics of these verbs are three. *First,* א becomes quiescent after Qal imperfect preformatives, thus ceasing to function as a consonant. As a result, any BeGaD KeFaT letter coming immediately after א loses its dagesh lene. *Second,* the preformative vowel for Qal imperfect forms appears as holem. *Third,* the stem vowel for Qal imperfect forms appears as pataḥ.

---

*Refer to Verb Chart 3, pp. 404f., for the conjugation of the Pe ʾAlef verb.

67.3 The three principal verbs in this group are:

(1) אָבַד   he perished, was lost   (3) אָמַר   he said

(2) אָכַל   he ate

Two other verbs sometimes grouped with these are אָבָה, "he was willing," and אָפָה, "he baked." However, since both end in ה, and are therefore doubly weak, they will be examined along with other Lamed He verbs. It should also be noted that the verb אָחַז, "he seized, took possession," presents a mixture of forms in the Qal imperfect, sometimes following the regular pattern for Pe Guttural verbs, and at other times following the pattern for the three special Pe ʾAlef verbs listed above.

67.4 Qal Imperfect inflection of אָבַד and אָכַל

3 ms	יֹאבַד	יֹאכַל
3 fs	תֹּאבַד	תֹּאכַל
2 ms	תֹּאבַד	תֹּאכַל
2 fs	תֹּאבְדִי	תֹּאכְלִי
1 cs	אֹבַד	אֹכַל
3 mp	יֹאבְדוּ	יֹאכְלוּ
3 fp	תֹּאבַדְנָה	תֹּאכַלְנָה
2 mp	תֹּאבְדוּ	תֹּאכְלוּ
2 fp	תֹּאבַדְנָה	תֹּאכַלְנָה
1 cp	נֹאבַד	נֹאכַל

(A) Because א ceases to function as a consonant, both ב and כ are in effect preceded by a vowel (ḥolem) and therefore lose the dagesh lene that would otherwise appear in them.

(B) A meteg appears under the first syllable of the 2 fs, 3 mp, and 2 mp forms, since א has become quiescent, thus placing the long preformative vowel ḥolem immediately before a vocal sheva (cf. IV.9, pp. 17f.).

(C) The א of the preformative has combined with the א of the verb root in the 1 cs forms of these two verbs. Thus אֹאבַד has been shortened to אֹבַד, and אֹאכַל to אֹכַל.

67.5 Qal Imperfect inflection of אָמַר (also with Vav Consecutive)

3 ms	יֹאמַר	וַיֹּאמֶר
3 fs	תֹּאמַר	וַתֹּאמֶר
2 ms	תֹּאמַר	וַתֹּאמֶר
2 fs	תֹּאמְרִי	וַתֹּאמְרִי
1 cs	אֹמַר	וָאֹמַר

238

3 mp	וַיֹּאמְרוּ	יֹאמְרוּ	
3 fp	וַתֹּאמַרְנָה	תֹּאמַרְנָה	
2 mp	וַתֹּאמְרוּ	תֹּאמְרוּ	
2 fp	וַתֹּאמַרְנָה	תֹּאמַרְנָה	
1 cp	וַנֹּאמֶר	נֹאמַר	

(A) The Qal imperfect forms of אָמַר that have no afformatives undergo certain changes when they are prefixed with the vav consecutive.

In 3 ms, 3 fs, 2 ms, and 1 cp, the accent shifts from the final syllable to the next to the final syllable, that is, from the stem syllable with pataḥ to the preformative syllable with ḥolem. This normally causes pataḥ to be attenuated to sᵉgol, although there will be no shift in accent and no attenuation of pataḥ if the form is marked with an atnaḥ (cf. IV.8.2, pp. 16f.). Examples of both forms can be seen in Numbers 23:11,12.

The 1 cs form follows the normal rule for lengthening the vowel of the vav consecutive when it stands before א, since א refuses to be doubled (cf. XVI.43.2, pp. 145f.).

(B) In all other respects the Qal imperfect of אָמַר is formed like that of אָבַד and אָכַל.

67.6 The remaining Qal forms of אָמַר

(1) Qal Imperative

2 ms	אֱמֹר	2 mp	אִמְרוּ
2 fs	אִמְרִי	2 fp	אֱמֹרְנָה

(A) א is not quiescent at the beginning of a word (or at the beginning of a syllable within a word). In the Qal imperative forms, therefore, it functions as a consonant.
(B) The sheva under the initial consonant of 2 ms and 2 fp becomes a compound sheva because it follows a guttural. א prefers ḥatef-sᵉgol as its compound sheva.
(C) The 2 fs and 2 mp forms are inflected after the pattern of strong verbs.

(2) Qal Infinitive Construct

(a) אֱמֹר (the same form as Qal imperative 2 ms)

(b) When the inseparable preposition לְ is added to אֱמֹר, it first becomes לְאֱמֹר, then לֶאֱמֹר, and finally לֵאמֹר (cf. לְאֱלֹהִים → לֵאלֹהִים). No other preposition causes this change when attached to the infinitive construct (cf. בֶּאֱמֹר, Deut. 4:10; כֶּאֱמֹר, Josh. 6:8). Furthermore, לְ does not produce this change when added to the infinitive construct of any other Pe ʾAlef verb (cf. לֶאֱהֹב, Eccl. 3:8; לֶאֱכֹל, Gen. 28:20; לֶאֱסֹף, Zeph. 3:8).

(3) Qal Infinitive Absolute

אָמוֹר

(4) Qal Active Participle

(a) Masculine Singular אוֹמֵר   (c) Feminine Singular אוֹמְרָה or אוֹמֶרֶת

(b) Masculine Plural אוֹמְרִים   (d) Feminine Plural אוֹמְרוֹת

(5) Qal Passive Participle (not used in the verb אָמַר)

68. Pausal Forms of Heavily Accented Words

When a Hebrew word is marked with a strong disjunctive accent (cf. IV.8.3, p. 17), it is said to be "in pause." A word that normally has a short vowel in its accented syllable will have this vowel lengthened when it is in pause. The following list will illustrate the types of changes that take place in words that are placed in pause. Included here are a number of pausal forms in which the accent has shifted from the final syllable to the vocal sheva preceding it, resulting in the conversion of the vocal sheva to a full vowel and thus adding an extra syllable to the word.

68.1 *Nouns*

(1) Segholates

(a)	אֶרֶץ	to	אָרֶץ	(Exod. 15:12)
(b)	הַדֶּבֶר	to	הַדָּבֶר	(Jer. 29:17)
(c)	בַּדֶּרֶךְ	to	בַּדָּרֶךְ	(Ezr. 8:22)
(d)	הֶבֶל	to	הָבֶל	(Gen. 4:2)
(e)	בְּחֶרֶב	to	בֶּחָרֶב	(Amos 7:9)
(f)	לֶחֶם	to	לָחֶם	(Ps. 37:25)

(2) Others

(a)	הַבַּיִת	to	הַבָּיִת	(2 Chr. 7:3)
(b)	בֵּיתְךָ	to	בֵּיתֶךָ	(2 Sam. 11:11)
(c)	בַּבְּעַל	to	בַּבָּעַל	(Jer. 23:27)
(d)	דְּבְרֵי	to	דְּבָרֵי	(Jer. 18:2)
(e)	הַשָּׁמַיִם	to	הַשָּׁמָיִם	(Deut. 7:24)
(f)	חַיַּי	to	חַיָּי	(Ps. 23:6)
(g)	יֵין	to	יָיִן	(Jer. 35:5)

(h)   יְרוּשָׁלַםִ   to   יְרוּשָׁלָםִ   (1 Chr. 9:34)

(i)   מֶיִם   to   מָיִם   (1 Kgs. 13:9)

(j)   מִצְרַיִם   to   מִצְרָיִם   (Ps. 106:21)

(k)   פְּנֵי   to   פָנָי   (Gen. 44:23)

68.2 *Pronouns*

(1)   אֲנִי   ("I")   to   אָנִי   (Jer. 17:18)

(2)   אָנֹכִי   ("I")   to   אָנֹכִי   (Gen. 4:9)

(3)   אַתָּה   ("you")   to   אָתָּה   (Isa. 44:17)

(4)   אֲנַחְנוּ   ("we")   to   אֲנָחְנוּ   (Gen. 13:8)

68.3 *Verbs*

(1) Vocal shevas raised to full vowels

(a)   יְבָרְכוּ   to   יְבָרֵכוּ   (Ps. 62:5; Eng. 62:4)

(b)   יָדְעוּ   to   יָדָעוּ   (Jer. 4:22)

(c)   יִכְרְתוּ   to   יִכָּרֵתוּ   (Isa. 11:13)

(d)   יִשְׂמְחוּ   to   יִשְׂמָחוּ   (Ps. 34:3; Eng. 34:2)

(e)   יֵשְׁבוּ   to   יֵשֵׁבוּ   (Zeph. 1:13)

(f)   שָׁמְעוּ   to   שָׁמָעוּ   (Ezek. 12:2)

(2) Imperfects with vav consecutive

(a)   וַיֹּאמֶר   to   וַיֹּאמַר   (Exod. 5:22)

(b)   וַתֹּאמֶר   to   וַתֹּאמַר   (1 Sam. 2:1)

(c)   וָאֹכֵל   to   וָאֹכֵל   (Gen. 3:12)

(3) Other verb forms

(a)   יֹאכֵל   to   יֹאכֵל   (Isa. 65:22)

(b)   לְשֶׁבֶת   to   לָשֶׁבֶת   (Josh. 21:2)

(c)   פְּשָׁעַתְּ   to   פָּשָׁעַתְּ   (Jer. 3:13)

(d)   שְׁכַב   to   שְׁכָב   (1 Sam. 3:6)

(e)   תִּשְׁכַּח   to   תִּשְׁכָּח   (Prov. 3:1)

(f)   תִּשְׁמַע   to   תִּשְׁמָע   (Neh. 9:27)

EXERCISES

1. Underline the participial form that belongs in each of the following entries.

(1) וּמְפִיבֹשֶׁת (יָשַׁב / יֹשֵׁב / יָשְׁבָה) בִּירוּשָׁלַ͏ִם כִּי עַל־שֻׁלְחַן הַמֶּלֶךְ תָּמִיד הוּא (אֹכֵל / אֹכֶלֶת)

So Mephibosheth dwelt in Jerusalem; for he ate always at the king's table. (2 Sam. 9:13)

(2) וְהָאֹכֵל / וְהָאֹכְלִים) בַּבַּיִת יְכַבֵּס אֶת־בְּגָדָיו

And he who eats in the house shall wash his clothes. (Lev. 14:47)

(3) כִּי יְהוָה אֱלֹהֶיךָ אֵשׁ (אֹכֵל / אֹכְלָה) הוּא

For the LORD your God is a devouring fire. (Deut. 4:24)

(4) וּמַרְאֵה כְּבוֹד יְהוָה כְּאֵשׁ (אֹכֶלֶת , אוֹכְלוֹת) בְּרֹאשׁ הָהָר

Now the appearance of the glory of the LORD was like a devouring fire on the top of the mountain. (Exod. 24:17)

(5) אֶרֶץ (אֹכֵל , אֹכֶלֶת) יוֹשְׁבֶיהָ הוּא

It is a land that devours its inhabitants. (Num. 13:32)

(6) אֲשֶׁר לֹא־נְטַעְתֶּם אַתֶּם (אֹכְלִים , אוֹכְלוֹת)

That which you did not plant you are eating. (Josh. 24:13)

(7) וּבָנָיו וּבְנֹתָיו (אוֹכְלוֹת , אֹכְלִים) וְשֹׁתִים יַיִן בְּבֵית אֲחִיהֶם הַבְּכוֹר

And his sons and his daughters were eating and drinking wine in the house of their elder brother. (Job 1:13)

(8) וְזֹאת (אֹמֶרֶת , אוֹמְרוֹת)

But this one said. (1 Kgs. 3:26)

(9) הָאֹמְרָה , הָאֹמֵר) בִּלְבָבָהּ

the one saying in her heart (Isa. 47:8)

(10) כֵּן נַעֲשֶׂה כַּאֲשֶׁר אַתָּה (אֹמֶרֶת , אֹמֵר)

Thus we will do according as you are saying. (Neh. 5:12)

(11) וָאֶשְׁמַע אֶת־קוֹל אֲדֹנָי (אֹמֵר , אֹמְרָה)

And I heard the voice of the Lord saying. (Isa. 6:8)

(12) וְרִבְקָה (אֹהֵב , אֹהֶבֶת) אֶת־יַעֲקֹב

And Rebekah loved Jacob. (Gen. 25:28)

2. Each of the following entries contains a Pe ʾAlef verb form. In the space marked (a) identify the stem, in (b) the form (perfect, imperfect, imperative, etc.), in (c) the person, gender, and number, and in (d) the root. Ignore verb forms that are not Pe ʾAlef.

הוא נָתְנָה־לִי מִן־הָעֵץ וָאֹכֵל   she gave to me from the tree, and I ate. (Gen. 3:12)

    (a) ___Qal___   (b) ___Imperfect___ (c) ___1 cs___   (d) ___אָכַל___

(2)   וַתֹּאמֶר הָאִשָּׁה אֶל־הַנָּחָשׁ   And the woman said to the serpent. (Gen. 3:2)

    (a) _____   (b) _____   (c) _____   (d) _____

(3)   מִפְּרִי עֵץ־הַגָּן נֹאכֵל   From the fruit of the tree(s) of the garden we may eat. (Gen. 3:2)

    (a) _____   (b) _____   (c) _____   (d) _____

(4)   תֹּאכְלֶנּוּ בַּמָּקוֹם אֲשֶׁר יִבְחַר יְהוָה   You shall eat it in the place that the LORD chooses. (Deut. 12:18)

    (a) _____   (b) _____   (c) _____   (d) _____

(5)   וְשָׁם תֹּאכְלוּ אֹתוֹ וְאֶת־הַלֶּחֶם   And there you shall eat it and the bread. (Lev. 8:31)

    (a) _____   (b) _____   (c) _____   (d) _____

(6)   אַהֲרֹן וּבָנָיו יֹאכְלֻהוּ   Aaron and his sons shall eat it. (Lev. 8:31)

    (a) _____   (b) _____   (c) _____   (d) _____

(7)   הֶאֱכַלְתִּי אֶתְכֶם בַּמִּדְבָּר   I fed you (caused you to eat) in the wilderness. (Exod. 16:32)

    (a) _____   (b) _____   (c) _____   (d) _____

(8)   בְּבַיִת אֶחָד יֵאָכֵל   In one house it shall be eaten. (Exod. 12:46)

    (a) _____   (b) _____   (c) _____   (d) _____

(9)   וַיַּאֲכִלְךָ אֶת־הַמָּן   And he fed you with manna. (Deut. 8:3)

    (a) _____   (b) _____   (c) _____   (d) _____

(10)   וַיְהִי דְבַר־יְהוָה אֵלַי לֵאמֹר   And the word of the LORD came (was) to me saying. (Jer. 18:5)

    (a) _____   (b) _____   (c) _____   (d) _____

(11) בְּאָמְרִי לָרָשָׁע מוֹת תָּמוּת when I say (in my saying) to the wicked, "You shall surely die." (Ezek. 3:18)

     (a) _____ (b) _____ (c) _____ (d) _____

(12) בְּאָמְרָם אֵלַי כָּל־הַיּוֹם אַיֵּה אֱלֹהֶיךָ through their saying to me all the day (every day), "Where is your God?" (Ps. 42:11; Eng. 42:10)

     (a) _____ (b) _____ (c) _____ (d) _____

(13) כֹּל אֲשֶׁר־תֹּאמְרִי [אֵלַי] אֶעֱשֶׂה־לָּךְ All that you say [to me], I will do to you. (Ruth 3:11)

     (a) _____ (b) _____ (c) _____ (d) _____

(14) וַתֹּאמַרְנָה הֲזֹאת נָעֳמִי And they said, "Is this Naomi?" (Ruth 1:19)

     a) _____ (b) _____ (c) _____ (d) _____

(15) אֱמֹר לִבְנֵי־יִשְׂרָאֵל אֲנִי יְהוָה Say to the sons of Israel, "I am the LORD." (Exod. 6:6)

     (a) _____ (b) _____ (c) _____ (d) _____

(16) אִמְרִי לְעָרֵי יְהוּדָה הִנֵּה אֱלֹהֵיכֶם Say to the cities of Judah, "Behold your God!" (Isa. 40:9)

     (a) _____ (b) _____ (c) _____ (d) _____

(17) אִמְרוּ בַגּוֹיִם יְהוָה מָלָךְ Say among the nations, "The LORD reigns" (Ps. 96:10)

     (a) _____ (b) _____ (c) _____ (d) _____

(18) אֶת־הָאֹבֶדֶת אֲבַקֵּשׁ And I will seek that which is lost. (Ezek. 34:16)

     (a) _____ (b) _____ (c) _____ (d) _____

(19) כִּי לֹא־תֹאבַד תּוֹרָה מִכֹּהֵן For the law shall not perish from the priest. (Jer. 18:18)

     (a) _____ (b) _____ (c) _____ (d) _____

(20) וְאַתְּ וּבֵית־אָבִיךְ תֹּאבֵדוּ But you and your father's house shall perish. (Est. 4:14)

     (a) _____ (b) _____ (c) _____ (d) _____

(21) וַיְשַׁלְּחֵם בִּיהוּדָה לְהַאֲבִידוֹ And he sent them against Judah to destroy it. (2 Kgs. 24:2)

     (a) _____ (b) _____ (c) _____ (d) _____

3. Each of the following entries contains a plural construct form of a participle. Match each entry with its correct translation.

( ) אֹהֲבַי (A) those who eat it (Lev. 17:14)

( ) אֹהֲבֶיךָ (B) all who seek you (Ps. 40:17; Eng. 40:16)

( ) אֹהֲבָיו (C) all who serve (worship) him (2 Kgs. 10:19)

( ) אֹהֲבֶיהָ (D) all who forsake you (Jer. 17:13)

( ) אֹכְלֶיךָ (E) all who help her (Ezek. 30:8)

( ) אֹכְלָיו (F) from those that pursue (persecute) me (Ps. 142:7; Eng. 142:6)

( ) מְבַקְשֵׁי נַפְשָׁם (G) those who love me (Prov. 8:17)

( ) מְבַקְשֵׁי נַפְשֶׁךָ (H) all those who seek her (Jer. 2:24)

( ) כָּל־מְבַקְשֶׁיךָ (I) those who devour you (Jer. 30:16)

( ) כָּל־מְבַקְשָׁיו (J) all those that pursue her (Lam. 1:3)

( ) כָּל־מְבַקְשֶׁיהָ (K) those who love you (Jer. 20:6)

( ) כָּל־עֹבְדָיו (L) those that pursue us (Lam. 4:19)

( ) כָּל־עֹזְבֶיךָ (M) those who seek your life (soul) (Jer. 22:25)

( ) כָּל־עֹזְבָיו (N) those who love him (Ps. 145:20)

( ) כָּל־עֹזְרֶיהָ (O) those who seek their life (soul) (Jer. 19:7)

( ) מֵרֹדְפַי (P) all who seek him (Ezr. 8:22)

( ) כָּל־רֹדְפֶיהָ (Q) all who forsake him (Ezr. 8:22)

( ) רֹדְפֵינוּ (R) those who love her (it) (Prov. 18:21)

4. In the following clauses and sentences, identify (a) the verb sequence (cf. XXI.63, pp. 210–216), (b) the verb stems, and (c) the verb roots.

   Example:

   הֵמָּה כָּשְׁלוּ וְנָפָלוּ They shall stumble and fall. (Ps. 27:2)

   (a) __Perfect__ + __Perfect__ Sequence (b) __Qal__ , __Qal__

   (c) __נָפַל__ , __כָּשַׁל__

(1) שָׁמְעָה וַתִּשְׂמַח צִיּוֹן Zion heard and was glad. (Ps. 97:8)

   (a) _____ + _____ Sequence (b) _____ , _____

   (c) _____ , _____

(2) יִזְכֹּר עֲוֺנָם וְיִפְקֹד חַטֹּאתָם He will remember their iniquity and punish (visit) their sins. (Jer. 14:10)

   (a) _____ + _____ Sequence (b) _____ , _____

   (c) _____ , _____

(3) נִמְצָא־חֵן בְּעֵינֵי אֲדֹנִי וְהָיִינוּ עֲבָדִים לְפַרְעֹה Let us find favor in the eyes of my lord, and let us become slaves (servants) to Pharaoh. (Gen. 47:25)

   (a) _____ + _____ Sequence (b) _____ , _____

   (c) _____ , _____

(4) לֹא־תִשְׂנָא אֶת־אָחִיךָ בִּלְבָבֶךָ וְאָהַבְתָּ לְרֵעֲךָ כָּמוֹךָ You shall not hate your brother in your heart, but you shall love your neighbor as yourself. (Lev. 19:17,18)

   (a) _____ + _____ Sequence (b) _____ , _____

   (c) _____ , _____

(5) בַּקֵּשׁ שָׁלוֹם וְרָדְפֵהוּ Seek peace and pursue it. (Ps. 34:15; Eng. 34:14)

   (a) _____ + _____ Sequence (b) _____ , _____

   (c) _____ , _____

(6) שִׂנְאוּ־רָע וְאֶהֱבוּ טוֹב Hate evil, and love good. (Amos 5:15)

   (a) _____ + _____ Sequence (b) _____ , _____

   (c) _____ , _____

(7) שְׁמַע בְּקוֹלָם וְהִמְלַכְתָּ לָהֶם מֶלֶךְ Hearken to their voice, and make for them a king. (1 Sam. 8:22)

   (a) _____ + _____ Sequence (b) _____ , _____

   (c) _____ , _____

(8) שַׁלַּח אֶת־עַמִּי וְיַעַבְדֻנִי Send my people away, that they may serve me.
(Exod. 7:26)

(a) _____ + _____ Sequence (b) _____ , _____

(c) _____ , _____

(9) הָלוֹךְ וְדִבַּרְתָּ אֶל־דָּוִד Go and speak to David. (2 Sam. 24:12)

(a) _____ + _____ Sequence (b) _____ , _____

(c) _____ , _____

(10) הוּא נָתְנָה־לִּי מִן־הָעֵץ וָאֹכֵל She gave to me from the tree, and I ate.
(Gen. 3:12)

(a) _____ + _____ Sequence (b) _____ , _____

(c) _____ , _____

5. Practice pronouncing the Hebrew, noting especially Pe ʾAlef verb forms. Cover
the English and practice translating the Hebrew from sight.

(1)
מִכֹּל עֵץ־הַגָּן אָכֹל תֹּאכֵל
וּמֵעֵץ הַדַּעַת טוֹב וָרָע לֹא
תֹאכַל מִמֶּנּוּ כִּי בְּיוֹם
אֲכָלְךָ מִמֶּנּוּ מוֹת תָּמוּת

From every tree of the garden you
may freely eat, but from the tree of
the knowledge of good and evil you
shall not eat, for in the day of your
eating from it you shall surely die.
(Gen. 2:15f.)

(2)
וַיֹּאמֶר אֶל־הָאִשָּׁה אַף
כִּי־אָמַר אֱלֹהִים לֹא תֹאכְלוּ
מִכֹּל עֵץ הַגָּן

And he said to the woman, "Has God
indeed said, 'You shall not eat from
all the trees of the garden'?" (Gen. 3:1)

(3)
וַתִּקַּח מִפִּרְיוֹ וַתֹּאכַל וַתִּתֵּן
גַּם־לְאִישָׁהּ עִמָּהּ וַיֹּאכַל

And she took (לָקַח) from its fruit,
and she ate, and she gave (נָתַן) also
to her husband with her, and he ate.
(Gen. 3:6)

(4)
וְעָפָר תֹּאכַל כָּל־יְמֵי חַיֶּיךָ

And dust shall you eat all the days
of your life. (Gen. 3:14)

(5)
כָּל־זָכָר בַּכֹּהֲנִים יֹאכְלֶנּוּ
בְּמָקוֹם קָדוֹשׁ יֵאָכֵל

Every male among the priests shall
eat it; in a holy place it shall
be eaten. (Lev. 7:6)

(6)   לַחְמֵנוּ נֹאכֵל רַק יִקָּרֵא
                  שִׁמְךָ עָלֵינוּ

Our bread we will eat, only let your name be called upon us. (Isa. 4:1)

(7)   וְהַאֲכַלְתִּים אֶת־בְּשַׂר בְּנֵיהֶם
            וְאֵת בְּשַׂר בְּנֹתֵיהֶם

And I will cause them to eat the flesh of their sons and the flesh of their daughters. (Jer. 19:9)

(8)   וָאֶשְׁאַל אֹתָהּ וָאֹמַר בַּת־מִי
         אַתְּ וַתֹּאמֶר בַּת־בְּתוּאֵל
                  בֶּן־נָחוֹר

And I asked her, and I said, "Whose daughter are you?" And she said, "The daughter of Bethuel, the son of Nahor." (Gen. 24:47)

(9)   אֵיכָה תֹאמְרוּ חֲכָמִים
         אֲנַחְנוּ וְתוֹרַת יְהוָה אִתָּנוּ

How can you say, "We are wise, and the law of the LORD is with us?" (Jer. 8:8)

(10)   וַיֹּאמֶר אֵלַי אֱמֹר כֹּה־אָמַר
       יְהוָה כֵּן אֲמַרְתֶּם בֵּית יִשְׂרָאֵל

And he said to me, "Say, thus says the LORD, thus you have said, O house of Israel." (Ezek. 11:5)

(11)   לָמָּה יֹאמְרוּ הַגּוֹיִם אַיֵּה
                 אֱלֹהֵיהֶם

Why do the nations say, "Where is their God?" (Ps. 79:10)

(12)   וַיֹּאמְרוּ אֵלָיו אַיֵּה שָׂרָה
       אִשְׁתֶּךָ וַיֹּאמֶר הִנֵּה בָאֹהֶל

And they said to him, "Where is Sarah your wife?" And he said, "Behold, in the tent!" (Gen. 18:9)

(13)   וַיֹּאמֶר לֹא יַעֲקֹב יֵאָמֵר עוֹד
         שִׁמְךָ כִּי אִם־יִשְׂרָאֵל

And he said, "Your name shall no more be called Jacob, but Israel." (Gen. 32:29)

(14)   וְהָיָה בִמְקוֹם אֲשֶׁר־יֵאָמֵר לָהֶם
       לֹא־עַמִּי אַתֶּם יֵאָמֵר לָהֶם
                בְּנֵי אֵל־חָי

And it shall come to pass that in the place where it was said to them, "You are not my people," it shall be said to them, "Sons of the living God." (Hos. 2:1; Eng. 1:10)

(15)   כִּי־יוֹדֵעַ יְהוָה דֶּרֶךְ צַדִּיקִים
         וְדֶרֶךְ רְשָׁעִים תֹּאבֵד

For the LORD knows the way of the righteous, but the way of the wicked shall perish. (Ps. 1:6)

VOCABULARY

(1)	אָבָה	he was willing	(11)	חוּץ	a place outside the house, the outdoors, a street	
(2)	אָבַל	he mourned				
(3)	[אזן]	he listened, heard	(12)	מֵאָה	(f) hundred	
(4)	אָמֵץ	he was strong, firm, bold	(13)	פָּנִים	face (faces)	
(5)	אָסַר	he bound, imprisoned	(14)	קֹדֶשׁ	holiness, holy thing, sanctuary	
			(15)	שְׁנַיִם	two	
(6)	אָפָה	he baked		שְׁתַּיִם	(f)	
(7)	אָרַךְ	he prolonged	(16)	שָׁלֹשׁ	three	
(8)	אָשֵׁם	he committed a wrong, was quilty		שְׁלֹשָׁה	(f)	
			(17)	אַרְבַּע	four	
(9)	אֶלֶף	ox, thousand		אַרְבָּעָה	(f)	
(10)	גּוֹי	nation	(18)	חָמֵשׁ	five	
				חֲמִשָּׁה	(f)	

LESSON XXIV

69. Weak Verbs: ʿAyin Guttural Verbs*

69.1 An ʿAyin Guttural verb is one whose middle consonant is a guttural. Some of the most frequently occurring ʿAyin Guttural verbs are these:

(a) בָּחַן   he tested

(b) בָּחַר   he chose

(c) בָּעַר   he burned, consumed

(d) [בּרך]   he blessed

(e) גָּאַל   he redeemed

(f) גָּעַר   he rebuked

(g) זָעַק   he cried out

(h) [מאן]   (Piʿel) he refused

(i) מָאַס   he refused, rejected

(j) [מהר]   he made haste

(k) נָחַל   he took possession, inherited

(l) [נחם]   he was sorry, had compassion, grieved, repented

(m) פָּעַל   he made, did

(n) פָּרַד   he divided, separated

(o) צָחַק   he laughed, made sport

(p) צָעַק   he cried out

(q) קָטַל   he killed

(r) קָרַב   he came near; (Hifʿil) he offered

(s) רָחַץ   he washed

(t) שָׂחַק   he laughed

(u) שָׁאַל   he asked, prayed

(v) שָׁחַט   he slaughtered

69.2 The three characteristics of gutturals all come into play in the inflection of ʿAyin Guttural verbs.

(1) Gutturals cannot be doubled.

Strong verbs have their middle consonants doubled in the Piʿel, Puʿal, and Hitpaʿel stems. It is in these three stems, therefore, that substantive changes take place in ʿAyin Guttural verbs.

(a) When א and ר (and occasionally ע) appear in ʿAyin Guttural verbs and reject the dagesh forte, the preceding vowel must be lengthened. In all other respects these forms are like their counterparts in the strong verb. The rules for vowel lengthening are these:

— Pataḥ is lengthened to Qameṣ (_ to ָ).
— Ḥireq is lengthened to Ṣere (. to ..).
— Qibbuṣ is lengthened to Ḥolem (ֻ to ֹ)

---

*Refer to Verb Chart 4, pp. 406f., for the conjugation of the ʿAyin Guttural verb.

Examples:

(i)   וַאֲנַחְנוּ נְבָרֵךְ יָהּ   But we will bless the LORD. (Ps. 115:18)

(נְבָרֵךְ becomes נְבַרֵךְ)

(ii)   הִנֵּה בֵּרַכְתִּי אֹתוֹ   Behold, I will bless him. (Gen. 17:20)

(בֵּרַכְתִּי becomes בֵּרַכְתִּי)

(iii)   יְהִי שֵׁם יְהוָה מְבֹרָךְ   May the name of the LORD be blessed.

(מְבֹרָךְ becomes מְבֹרָךְ)   (Ps. 113:2)

(b)   When ה and ח appear in 'Ayin Guttural verbs and reject the dagesh forte, the vowel in the preceding syllable remains short, since ה and ח are considered to be doubled by implication (practically doubled). This rule ordinarily applies also to ע.

Examples:

(i)   וַיְמַהֵר אַבְרָהָם הָאֹהֱלָה   And Abraham hastened into the tent

אֶל־שָׂרָה   to Sarah. (Gen. 18:6)

(ii)   וַיְצַחֵק לִפְנֵיהֶם   And he made sport before them.
                                        (Judg. 16:25)

(iii) וּבִעֵר עָלֶיהָ הַכֹּהֵן עֵצִים   And the priest shall burn wood (trees)
                                        upon it. (Lev. 6:5; Eng. 6:12)

(2)   Gutturals generally take "a" class vowels.

(a) This rule, when applied to 'Ayin Guttural verbs, often causes the stem vowel of Qal imperfect and Qal imperative forms to appear as pataḥ instead of ḥolem, as in the strong verb.

Examples:

(i)   וַיִּבְחַר אֶת־שֵׁבֶט יְהוּדָה   And he chose the tribe of Judah.

(יִבְחֹר instead of יִבְחַר)   (Ps. 78:68)

(ii)   בְּחַר־לָנוּ אֲנָשִׁים   Choose for us men. (Exod. 17:9)

(בְּחֹר instead of בְּחַר)

(iii)   כְּאֵשׁ תִּבְעַר־יָעַר   as fire consumes a forest (Ps. 83:15;

(תִּבְעֹר instead of תִּבְעַר)   Eng. 83:14)

(iv)   וַנִּצְעַק אֶל־יְהוָה   And we cried unto the LORD.

(נִצְעֹק instead of נִצְעַק)   (Num. 20:16)

(v)   שְׁאַל־לְךָ אוֹת מֵעִם יְהוָה   Ask a sign from the LORD your God.

אֱלֹהֶיךָ   (Isa. 7:11)

(שְׁאֹל instead of שְׁאַל)

251

(b) Pi'el perfect 3 ms forms sometimes appear with pataḥ instead of ṣere as the second stem vowel.

Examples:

(i)   וַיהוָה בֵּרַךְ אֶת־אַבְרָהָם   And the LORD blessed Abraham.
(בֵּרַךְ instead of בֵּרֵךְ)   (Gen. 24:1)

(ii)   וְהָאִישׁ מִהַר   Then the man hastened. (1 Sam. 4:14)
(מִהַר instead of מִהֵר)

(3) Gutturals generally take compound shevas.

(a)   This rule applies throughout 'Ayin Guttural verbs with all gutturals except ר. Since a vocal sheva normally stands beneath the middle root consonant of all verb forms having vocalic afformatives (except in the Hif'il stem), and since in 'Ayin guttural verbs the middle root consonant is a guttural, then in verbs of this class any vocal sheva in this position must be a compound sheva. Usually this will be ḥatef-pataḥ (ֲ).

(b)   In each of the seven stems, vocalic afformatives occur in the following forms:

> Perfect: 3 fs, 3 cp
>
> Imperfect: 2 fs, 3 mp, 2 mp
>
> Imperative: 2 fs, 2 mp

A comparison of the Qal stems of the strong verb מָשַׁל and the weak verb בָּחַר will illustrate the changes that 'Ayin Guttural verbs must undergo before all vocalic afformatives (except in the Hif'il stem).

	מָשַׁל	בָּחַר
Qal Perfect 3 fs	מָשְׁלָה	בָּחֲרָה
Qal Perfect 3 cp	מָשְׁלוּ	בָּחֲרוּ
Qal Imperfect 2 fs	תִּמְשְׁלִי	תִּבְחֲרִי
Qal Imperfect 3 mp	יִמְשְׁלוּ	יִבְחֲרוּ
Qal imperfect 2 mp	תִּמְשְׁלוּ	תִּבְחֲרוּ
Qal Imperative 2 fs	מָשְׁלִי	בַּחֲרִי
Qal Imperative 2 mp	מָשְׁלוּ	בַּחֲרוּ

Note: The Qal imperative forms of בָּחַר listed above are irregular in that they have pataḥ instead of ḥireq as the vowel under the initial consonant. This came about through the dropping of the preformatives of the Qal imperfect 2 fs and 2 mp forms.

Since this resulted in two vocal shevas being left at the beginning of each of these shortened forms, the first of the shevas in each case was raised to pataḥ, since it came before a ḥatef–pataḥ.

תִּבְחֲרִי ← בְּחֲרִי ← בְּחֲרִי

תִּבְחֲרוּ ← בְּחֲרוּ ← בְּחֲרוּ

Examples:

(i) בַּחֲרוּ לָכֶם הַיּוֹם אֶת־מִי תַעֲבֹדוּן
Choose this day whom you will serve. (Josh. 24:15)

(ii) לְכוּ וְזַעֲקוּ אֶל־הָאֱלֹהִים אֲשֶׁר בְּחַרְתֶּם בָּם
Go and cry to the gods whom you have chosen. (Judg. 10:14)

69.3 A Synopsis of בָּחַר, "he chose"

	Qal	Nifʿal	Piʿel	Puʿal	Hitpaʿel	Hifʿil	Hofʿal
Perf. 3 ms	בָּחַר	נִבְחַר	בִּחַר	בֻּחַר	הִתְבַּחֵר	הִבְחִיר	הָבְחַר
Impf. 3 ms	יִבְחַר	יִבָּחֵר	יְבַחֵר	יְבֻחַר	יִתְבַּחֵר	יַבְחִיר	יָבְחַר
Impv. 2 ms	בְּחַר	הִבָּחֵר	בַּחֵר		הִתְבַּחֵר	הַבְחֵר	
Inf. Const.	בְּחֹר	הִבָּחֵר	בַּחֵר	בֻּחַר	הִתְבַּחֵר	הַבְחִיר	הָבְחַר
Inf. Abs.	בָּחוֹר	נִבְחֹר	בַּחֵר	בֻּחַר	הִתְבַּחֵר	הַבְחֵר	הָבְחֵר
Part. Act.	בֹּחֵר		מְבַחֵר		מִתְבַּחֵר	מַבְחִיר	
Part. Pass.	בָּחוּר	נִבְחָר		מְבֻחָר			מָבְחָר

69.4 A Synopsis of גָּאַל, "he redeemed"

	Qal	Nifʿal	Piʿel	Puʿal	Hitpaʿel	Hifʿil	Hofʿal
Perf. 3 ms	גָּאַל	נִגְאַל	גֵּאַל	גֹּאַל	הִתְגָּאֵל	הִגְאִיל	הָגְאַל
Impf. 3 ms	יִגְאַל	יִגָּאֵל	יְגָאֵל	יְגֹאַל	יִתְגָּאֵל	יַגְאִיל	יָגְאַל
Impv. 2 ms	גְּאַל	הִגָּאֵל	גָּאֵל		הִתְגָּאֵל	הַגְאֵל	
Inf. Const.	גְּאֹל	הִגָּאֵל	גָּאֵל	גֹּאַל	הִהְגָּאֵל	הַגְאִיל	הָגְאַל
Inf. Abs.	גָּאוֹל	נִגְאֹל	גָּאֵל	גֹּאַל	הִתְגָּאֵל	הַגְאֵל	הָגְאֵל
Part. Act.	גֹּאֵל		מְגָאֵל		מִתְגָּאֵל	מַגְאִיל	
Part. Pass.	גָּאוּל	נִגְאָל		מְגֹאָל			מָגְאָל

69.5 A Comparison of Strong Verbs and ʿAyin Guttural Verbs in the Qal,

Piᶜel, and Puᶜal Stems (with ʿAyin Guttural Forms in parentheses differing from the corresponding Strong Verb forms)

	Qal (Strong)	Qal (Weak)	Piᶜel (Strong)	Piᶜel (Weak)	Puᶜal (Strong)	Puᶜal (Weak)
PERFECT	קָטַל	בָּחַר	שָׁבַּר	בָּרַךְ	שָׁבַּר	בָּרַךְ
3 ms	קָטַל	בָּחַר	שִׁבֵּר	(בֵּרֵךְ)	שֻׁבַּר	(בֹּרַךְ)
3 fs	קָטְלָה	(בָּחֲרָה)	שִׁבְּרָה	(בֵּרְכָה)	שֻׁבְּרָה	(בֹּרְכָה)
2 ms	קָטַלְתָּ	בָּחַרְתָּ	שִׁבַּרְתָּ	(בֵּרַכְתָּ)	שֻׁבַּרְתָּ	(בֹּרַכְתָּ)
2 fs	קָטַלְתְּ	בָּחַרְתְּ	שִׁבַּרְתְּ	(בֵּרַכְתְּ)	שֻׁבַּרְתְּ	(בֹּרַכְתְּ)
1 cs	קָטַלְתִּי	בָּחַרְתִּי	שִׁבַּרְתִּי	(בֵּרַכְתִּי)	שֻׁבַּרְתִּי	(בֹּרַכְתִּי)
3 cp	קָטְלוּ	(בָּחֲרוּ)	שִׁבְּרוּ	(בֵּרְכוּ)	שֻׁבְּרוּ	(בֹּרְכוּ)
2 mp	קְטַלְתֶּם	בְּחַרְתֶּם	שִׁבַּרְתֶּם	(בֵּרַכְתֶּם)	שֻׁבַּרְתֶּם	(בֹּרַכְתֶּם)
2 fp	קְטַלְתֶּן	בְּחַרְתֶּן	שִׁבַּרְתֶּן	(בֵּרַכְתֶּן)	שֻׁבַּרְתֶּן	(בֹּרַכְתֶּן)
1 cp	קָטַלְנוּ	בָּחַרְנוּ	שִׁבַּרְנוּ	(בֵּרַכְנוּ)	שֻׁבַּרְנוּ	(בֹּרַכְנוּ)
IMPERFECT						
3 ms	יִקְטֹל	(יִבְחַר)	יְשַׁבֵּר	(יְבָרֵךְ)	יְשֻׁבַּר	(יְבֹרַךְ)
3 fs	תִּקְטֹל	(תִּבְחַר)	תְּשַׁבֵּר	(תְּבָרֵךְ)	תְּשֻׁבַּר	(תְּבֹרַךְ)
2 ms	תִּקְטֹל	(תִּבְחַר)	תְּשַׁבֵּר	(תְּבָרֵךְ)	תְּשֻׁבַּר	(תְּבֹרַךְ)
2 fs	תִּקְטְלִי	(תִּבְחֲרִי)	תְּשַׁבְּרִי	(תְּבָרְכִי)	תְּשֻׁבְּרִי	(תְּבֹרְכִי)
1 cs	אֶקְטֹל	(אֶבְחַר)	אֲשַׁבֵּר	(אֲבָרֵךְ)	אֲשֻׁבַּר	(אֲבֹרַךְ)
3 mp	יִקְטְלוּ	(יִבְחֲרוּ)	יְשַׁבְּרוּ	(יְבָרְכוּ)	יְשֻׁבְּרוּ	(יְבֹרְכוּ)
3 fp	תִּקְטֹלְנָה	(תִּבְחַרְנָה)	תְּשַׁבֵּרְנָה	(תְּבָרֵכְנָה)	תְּשֻׁבַּרְנָה	(תְּבֹרַכְנָה)
2 mp	תִּקְטְלוּ	(תִּבְחֲרוּ)	תְּשַׁבְּרוּ	(תְּבָרְכוּ)	תְּשֻׁבְּרוּ	(תְּבֹרְכוּ)
2 fp	תִּקְטֹלְנָה	(תִּבְחַרְנָה)	תְּשַׁבֵּרְנָה	(תְּבָרֵכְנָה)	תְּשֻׁבַּרְנָה	(תְּבֹרַכְנָה)
1 cp	נִקְטֹל	(נִבְחַר)	נְשַׁבֵּר	(נְבָרֵךְ)	נְשֻׁבַּר	(נְבֹרַךְ)
IMPERATIVE						
2 ms	קְטֹל	(בְּחַר)	שַׁבֵּר	(בָּרֵךְ)		
2 fs	קִטְלִי	(בַּחֲרִי)	שַׁבְּרִי	(בָּרְכִי)		
2 mp	קִטְלוּ	(בַּחֲרוּ)	שַׁבְּרוּ	(בָּרְכוּ)		
2 fp	קְטֹלְנָה	(בְּחַרְנָה)	שַׁבֵּרְנָה	(בָּרֵכְנָה)		

254

	Qal		Pi'el		Pu'al	
INFINITIVE CONSTRUCT						
	קְטֹל	בְּחֹר	שַׁבֵּר	(בָּרֵךְ)	שֻׁבַּר	(בֹּרַךְ)
INFINITIVE ABSOLUTE						
	קָטוֹל	בָּחוֹר	שַׁבֵּר	(בָּרֵךְ)	שֻׁבַּר	
PARTICIPLES						
Active ms	קֹטֵל	בֹּחֵר	מְשַׁבֵּר	(מְבָרֵךְ)		
Active mp	קֹטְלִים	(בֹּחֲרִים)	מְשַׁבְּרִים	(מְבָרְכִים)		
Active fs	קֹטֶלֶת	(בֹּחֲרָה)	מְשַׁבֶּרֶת	(מְבָרְכָה)		
Active fp	קֹטְלוֹת	(בֹּחֲרוֹת)	מְשַׁבְּרוֹת	(מְבָרְכוֹת)		
Passive ms	קָטוּל	בָּחוּר		מְשֻׁבָּר	(מְבֹרָךְ)	
Passive mp	קְטוּלִים	בְּחוּרִים		מְשֻׁבָּרִים	(מְבֹרְכִים)	
Passive fs	קְטוּלָה	בְּחוּרָה		מְשֻׁבֶּרֶת	(מְבֹרְכָה)	
Passive fp	קְטוּלוֹת	בְּחוּרוֹת		מְשֻׁבָּרוֹת	(מְבֹרְכוֹת)	

EXERCISES

1. Observe the ʻAyin Guttural verb forms as they occur in the following sentences. Fill in the blanks with the correct pronouns.

(1) אָז יִזְעֲקוּ אֶל־יְהוָה וְלֹא יַעֲנֶה אוֹתָם Then _____ cried to the LORD, but he did not answer _____. (Mic. 3:4)

(2) וַיִּמְאֲסוּ אֶת־חֻקָּיו וְאֶת־בְּרִיתוֹ אֲשֶׁר כָּרַת אֶת־אֲבוֹתָם And _____ rejected _____ statutes and _____ covenant which _____ made with _____ fathers. (2 Kgs. 17:15)

(3) וַנִּצְעַק אֶל־יְהוָה וַיִּשְׁמַע קֹלֵנוּ Then _____ cried to the LORD, and he heard _____ voice. (Num. 20:16)

(4) וְרָחֲצוּ יְדֵיהֶם וְרַגְלֵיהֶם And _____ shall wash _____ hands and _____ feet (Exod. 30:21)

(5) אַל־תַּעַזְבֵנִי יְהוָה אֱלֹהָי Do not forsake _____, O LORD _____ God. (Ps. 38:22; Eng. 38:21)

(6) וּבֵרַכְתָּ אֶת־יְהוָה אֱלֹהֶיךָ And _____ shall bless the LORD _____ God. (Deut. 8:10)

(7) בֵּרַכְנוּ אֶתְכֶם בְּשֵׁם יְהוָה _____ bless _____ in the name of the LORD. (Ps. 129:8)

(8) בֵּרַכְנוּכֶם מִבֵּית יְהוָה _____ bless _____ from the house of the LORD. (Ps. 118:26)

(9) וַאֲבָרֶכְךָ וַאֲגַדְּלָה שְׁמֶךָ And _____ will bless _____, and _____ will make _____ name great. (Gen. 12:2)

(10) יְבָרְכֵנוּ אֱלֹהִים אֱלֹהֵינוּ May God _____ God bless _____. (Ps. 67:7; Eng. 67:6)

(11) זָכָר וּנְקֵבָה בְּרָאָם וַיְבָרֶךְ אֹתָם וַיִּקְרָא אֶת־שְׁמָם אָדָם Male and female _____ created _____, and _____ blessed _____, and _____ called _____ name Adam (Mankind). (Gen. 5:2)

(12) כִּי נִחַמְתִּי כִּי עֲשִׂיתִים For _____ am sorry that _____ have made _____. (Gen. 6:7)

2. Each of the following sentences contains a form of an ʿAyin Guttural verb. In the space numbered (a) identify the verb form (perfect, imperfect, etc.), in (b) the verb stem (Qal, Nifʿal, etc.), in (c) the person, gender, and number of the form, and in (d) the verb root.

Example:

וַיִּזְעֲקוּ אִישׁ אֶל־אֱלֹהָיו And they cried, each unto his God. (Jon. 1:5)

(a) __Imperfect__ (b) __Qal__ (c) __3 mp__ (d) __זָעַק__

(1) וְעַתָּה הִנֵּה הַמֶּלֶךְ אֲשֶׁר בְּחַרְתֶּם And now behold the king whom you have chosen. (1 Sam. 12:13)

(a) _____ (b) _____ (c) _____ (d) _____

(2) אֶחָד מֵאֶחָיו יִגְאָלֶנּוּ One of his brothers shall redeem him. (Lev. 25:48)

(a) _____ (b) _____ (c) _____ (d) _____

(3) וְלֹא־זָעֲקוּ אֵלַי בְּלִבָּם But they do not cry to me with (in) their heart. (Hos. 7:14)

(a) _____ (b) _____ (c) _____ (d) _____

(4) וַיִּזְעַק הַמֶּלֶךְ קוֹל גָּדוֹל בְּנִי אַבְשָׁלוֹם אַבְשָׁלוֹם בְּנִי בְנִי And the king cried with a loud voice, "O my son Absalom, O Absalom, my son, my son." (2 Sam. 19:5; Eng. 19:4)

    (a) _____ (b) _____ (c) _____ (d) _____

(5) גַּם־אֲנִי אֶמְאַס בְּכָל־זֶרַע יִשְׂרָאֵל Also I will reject all the seed (descendants) of Israel. (Jer. 31:37)

    (a) _____ (b) _____ (c) _____ (d) _____

(6) וְאִשָּׁה צָעֲקָה אֵלָיו And a woman cried out to him. (2 Kgs. 6:26)

    (a) _____ (b) _____ (c) _____ (d) _____

(7) וַיִּצְעֲקוּ בְנֵי־יִשְׂרָאֵל אֶל־יְהוָה And the children (sons) of Israel cried out to the LORD. (Exod. 14:10)

    (a) _____ (b) _____ (c) _____ (d) _____

(8) וַיִּרְחֲצוּ רַגְלֵיהֶם And they washed their feet. (Gen. 43:24)

    (a) _____ (b) _____ (c) _____ (d) _____

(9) וָאֶשְׁאַל אֹתָהּ בַּת־מִי אַתְּ And I asked her, "Whose daughter are you?" (Gen. 24:47)

    (a) _____ (b) _____ (c) _____ (d) _____

(10) שַׁאֲלוּ שְׁלוֹם יְרוּשָׁלָ͏ִם Pray (ask) for the peace of Jerusalem. (Ps. 122:6)

    (a) _____ (b) _____ (c) _____ (d) _____

(11) יְהוָה יְבָרֵךְ אֶת־עַמּוֹ בַשָּׁלוֹם May the LORD bless his people with peace! (Ps. 29:11)

    (a) _____ (b) _____ (c) _____ (d) _____

(12) וַאֲנַחְנוּ נְבָרֵךְ יָהּ מֵעַתָּה וְעַד־עוֹלָם But we will bless the LORD from now until eternity. (Ps. 115:18)

    (a) _____ (b) _____ (c) _____ (d) _____

(13) וַיְבָרֲכוּ אֱלֹהִים בְּנֵי יִשְׂרָאֵל And the people (sons) of Israel blessed God. (Josh. 22:33)

    (a) _____ (b) _____ (c) _____ (d) _____

(14) בָּרֲכִי נַפְשִׁי אֶת־יְהוָה Bless the LORD, O my soul! (Ps. 103:1)

    (a) _____ (b) _____ (c) _____ (d) _____

(15) וַיְנַחֵם דָּוִד אֵת בַּת־שֶׁבַע אִשְׁתּוֹ And David comforted Bathsheba his
wife. (2 Sam. 12:24)

 (a) _____ (b) _____ (c) _____ (d) _____

(16) שִׁבְטְךָ וּמִשְׁעַנְתֶּךָ הֵמָּה יְנַחֲמֻנִי Your rod and your staff, they comfort me.
(Ps. 23:4)

 (a) _____ (b) _____ (c) _____ (d) _____

(17) וּבְתוֹךְ בְּנֵי יִשְׂרָאֵל לֹא יִנְחֲלוּ נַחֲלָה And among (in the midst of) the
people (sons) of Israel they shall not receive (inherit) an inheritance.
(Num. 18:23)

 (a) _____ (b) _____ (c) _____ (d) _____

(18) וְהִתְנַחַלְתֶּם אֶת־הָאָרֶץ בְּגוֹרָל And you shall inherit the land by lot.
(Num. 33:54)

 (a) _____ (b) _____ (c) _____ (d) _____

3. Each of the following sentences contains an infinitive construct. In the space
numbered (a) list its stem, and in (b) its root.

(1) וְאָכַלְתָּ לִפְנֵי יְהוָה אֱלֹהֶיךָ בַּמָּקוֹם אֲשֶׁר־יִבְחַר לְשַׁכֵּן שְׁמוֹ שָׁם
And you shall eat before the LORD your God in the place which he will
choose, to make his name dwell there.
(Deut. 14:23)   (a) _____ (b) _____

(2) וָאֶבְחַר בִּירוּשָׁלַם לִהְיוֹת שְׁמִי שָׁם
But I have chosen Jerusalem in order that
my name might be there. (2 Chr. 6:6)   (a) _____ (b) _____

(3) וְאִם רַע בְּעֵינֵיכֶם לַעֲבֹד אֶת־יְהוָה בַּחֲרוּ לָכֶם הַיּוֹם אֶת־מִי תַעֲבֹדוּן
And if it be evil in your eyes to serve the LORD, choose for yourselves
this day whom you will serve. (Josh. 24:15)
       (a) _____ (b) _____

(4) כִּי־אֹתִי מָאֲסוּ מִמְּלֹךְ עֲלֵיהֶם
But they have rejected me from being
king over them. (1 Sam. 8:7)   (a) _____ (b) _____

(5) אֵלֶּה יַעַמְדוּ לְבָרֵךְ אֶת־הָעָם עַל־הַר גְּרִזִים
These shall stand upon Mount Gerizim
to bless the people. (Deut. 27:12)   (a) _____ (b) _____

(6)   כִּי לֹא אָדָם הוּא לְהִנָּחֵם

For he is not a man, that he should repent.
(1 Sam. 15:29)   (a) _____ (b) _____

(7)   וַיְמָאֵן לְהִתְנַחֵם

But he refused to be comforted.
(Gen. 37:35)   (a) _____ (b) _____

(8)   כָּבֵד לֵב פַּרְעֹה מֵאֵן לְשַׁלַּח הָעָם

Pharaoh's heart is hardened; he refuses
to let the people go. (Exod. 7:14)   (a) _____ (b) _____

(9)   מֵאֲנוּ לָשׁוּב

They refuse to return (repent). (Jer. 5:3)   (a) _____ (b) _____

(10)   וַיְמָאֲנוּ הָעָם לִשְׁמֹעַ בְּקוֹל שְׁמוּאֵל

And the people refused to harken (listen)
to the voice of Samuel. (1 Sam. 8:19)   (a) _____ (b) _____

4. Each of the following sentences contains a participle. In the space numbered (a) write the participle, in (b) give its stem, in (c) its gender and number, and in (d) its root.

Example:

וּבָעֲרוּ שְׁנֵיהֶם יַחְדָּו וְאֵין מְכַבֶּה And both of them shall burn together, and no one quenching (them). (Isa. 1:31)

     (a) _מְכַבֶּה_ (b) Pi'el (c) ms (d) _כָּבָה_

(1)   וְהָיָה בְלִבִּי כְּאֵשׁ בֹּעֶרֶת And there is in my heart as a burning fire (as if it were a burning fire). (Jer. 20:9)

     (a) _____ (b) _____ (c) _____ (d) _____

(2)   וְהִנֵּה יִצְחָק מְצַחֵק אֵת רִבְקָה אִשְׁתּוֹ And behold, Isaac was fondling Rebekah his wife. (Gen. 26:8)

     (a) _____ (b) _____ (c) _____ (d) _____

(3)   וַיְהִי מֶלֶךְ יִשְׂרָאֵל עֹבֵר עַל־הַחֹמָה And the king of Israel was passing by upon the wall. (2 Kgs. 6:26)

     (a) _____ (b) _____ (c) _____ (d) _____

(4)   מֶה עָשִׂיתָ קוֹל דְּמֵי אָחִיךָ צֹעֲקִים אֵלַי מִן־הָאֲדָמָה What have you done? The voice of your brother's blood(s) is crying out to me from the ground. (Gen. 4:10)

     (a) _____ (b) _____ (c) _____ (d) _____

(5) וְדָוִד וְכָל־יִשְׂרָאֵל מְשַׂחֲקִים לִפְנֵי הָאֱלֹהִים בְּכָל־עֹז   And David and all Israel were making merry (celebrating) before God with all their might. (1 Chr. 13:8)

(a) _____ (b) _____ (c) _____ (d) _____

(6) וַאֲבָרֲכָה מְבָרֲכֶיךָ   And I will bless the ones who bless you. (Gen. 12:3)

(a) _____ (b) _____ (c) _____ (d) _____

(7) כִּי יָדַעְתִּי אֵת אֲשֶׁר־תְּבָרֵךְ מְבֹרָךְ   For I know that the one whom you bless is blessed. (Num. 22:6)

(a) _____ (b) _____ (c) _____ (d) _____

(8) אֵין מְנַחֵם לָהּ   There is no comforter for her. (Lam. 1:9)

(a) _____ (b) _____ (c) _____ (d) _____

(9) מֵאַיִן אֲבַקֵּשׁ מְנַחֲמִים לָךְ   Whence shall I seek comforters for you? (Nah. 3:7)

(a) _____ (b) _____ (c) _____ (d) _____

(10) אָנֹכִי אָנֹכִי הוּא מְנַחֶמְכֶם   I, I am he that comforts you. (Isa. 51:12)

(a) _____ (b) _____ (c) _____ (d) _____

5. Practice pronouncing the Hebrew, noting especially ʿAyin Guttural verb forms. Cover the English and practice translating the Hebrew from sight.

(1) וַיַּעֲבֵר יִשַׁי שִׁבְעַת בָּנָיו לִפְנֵי שְׁמוּאֵל וַיֹּאמֶר שְׁמוּאֵל אֶל־יִשַׁי לֹא־בָחַר יְהוָה בָּאֵלֶּה
And Jesse made seven of his sons pass before Samuel. And Samuel said to Jesse, "The LORD has not chosen these." (1 Sam. 16:10)

(2) וַיִּבְחַר יְהוָה אֱלֹהֵי יִשְׂרָאֵל בִּי מִכֹּל בֵּית־אָבִי לִהְיוֹת לְמֶלֶךְ עַל־יִשְׂרָאֵל לְעוֹלָם
And the LORD God of Israel chose me above all my father's house to be king over Israel for ever. (1 Chr. 28:4)

(3) וְאִם־לֹא יִגְאַל אֶת־הַשָּׂדֶה וְאִם־מָכַר אֶת־הַשָּׂדֶה לְאִישׁ אַחֵר לֹא יִגָּאֵל עוֹד
But (and) if he does not redeem the field, or if he has sold the field to another man, it shall not be redeemed again. (Lev. 27:20)

(4) אֶזְעַק אֵלֶיךָ חָמָס וְלֹא תוֹשִׁיעַ
I cry out to you, "Violence!" but you do not save. (Hab. 1:2)

260

(5) וַיִּזְעַק שְׁמוּאֵל אֶל־יְהוָה בְּעַד יִשְׂרָאֵל וַיַּעֲנֵהוּ יְהוָה

And Samuel cried to the LORD on behalf of Israel, and the LORD answered him. (1 Sam. 7:9)

(6) וַיְצַחֵק לִפְנֵיהֶם וַיַּעֲמִידוּ אוֹתוֹ בֵּין הָעַמּוּדִים

And he made sport before them, and they caused him to stand between the pillars. (Judg. 16:25)

(7) וַיִּשְׁחַט מֶלֶךְ בָּבֶל אֶת־בְּנֵי צִדְקִיָּהוּ בְּרִבְלָה לְעֵינָיו

The king of Babylon slew the sons of Zedekiah at Riblah before his eyes. (Jer. 39:6)

(8) וְאֶת־בָּרוּךְ שָׁאֲלוּ לֵאמֹר אֵיךְ כָּתַבְתָּ אֶת־כָּל־הַדְּבָרִים הָאֵלֶּה מִפִּיו

And they asked Baruch (saying), "How did you write all these words from his mouth (at his dictation)?" (Jer. 36:17)

(9) יְבָרֶכְךָ יְהוָה וְיִשְׁמְרֶךָ

May the LORD bless you, and may he keep you. (Num. 6:24)

(10) עַל־כֵּן בֵּרַךְ יְהוָה אֶת־יוֹם הַשַּׁבָּת וַיְקַדְּשֵׁהוּ

Therefore the LORD blessed the sabbath day and hallowed it (made it holy). (Exod. 20:11)

(11) וַיְבָרֶךְ אֱלֹהִים אֶת־יוֹם הַשְּׁבִיעִי וַיְקַדֵּשׁ אֹתוֹ

And God blessed the seventh day and hallowed it. (Gen. 2:3)

(12) וַיִּצְעַק צְעָקָה גְּדֹלָה וּמָרָה עַד־מְאֹד וַיֹּאמֶר לְאָבִיו בָּרֲכֵנִי גַם־אָנִי אָבִי

And he cried out (with) a great and exceedingly bitter cry, and said to his father, "Bless me, even me also, my father!" (Gen. 27:34)

(13) נִחַמְתִּי כִּי־הִמְלַכְתִּי אֶת־שָׁאוּל

I repent that I have made Saul king. (1 Sam. 15:11)

(14) כְּאִישׁ אֲשֶׁר אִמּוֹ תְּנַחֲמֶנּוּ כֵּן אָנֹכִי אֲנַחֶמְכֶם וּבִירוּשָׁלַםִ תְּנֻחָמוּ

As one whom his mother comforts (him), so I will comfort you; and in Jerusalem you shall be comforted. (Isa. 66:13)

(15) יְהִי שֵׁם יְהוָה מְבֹרָךְ מֵעַתָּה וְעַד־עוֹלָם

May the name of the LORD be blessed, rom henceforth and forever. (Ps. 113:2)

VOCABULARY

(1) בָּחַן   he tested

(2) בָּחַר   he chose

(3) בָּעַר   he (it) burned

(4) זָעַק   he cried out

(5) [מהר]   he hastened

(6) נָחַל   he took possession, inherited

(7) [נחם]   he was sorry, had compassion, suffered grief, repented

(8) צָחַק   he laughed

(9) צָעַק   he cried out

(10) שָׂחַק   he laughed, jested

(11) שָׁחַט   he killed, slaughtered

(12) אַחֵר   another, other

(13) אַחַר   behind, after

(14) אֹיֵב   enemy

(15) בָּקָר   herd, cattle

(16) מִגְדָּל   tower, fortress

(17) זֶבַח   sacrifice

(18) מִנְחָה   (f) offering, gift, tribute

LESSON XXV

70. Weak Verbs: Lamed Guttural Verbs*

70.1 *Definition*

A Lamed Guttural verb is one whose final root consonant is either ה (rarely used), ח, or ע. Final ר does not behave as a guttural but as a strong consonant (cf. שָׁמַר, "he kept"). Verbs ending in א or ה behave so differently that they are treated as separate classes of weak verbs.

70.2 *A List of Some of the Most Frequently Occurring Lamed Guttural Verbs*

(a)	בָּטַח	he trusted	(l)	פָּשַׁע	he rebelled
(b)	בָּלַע	he swallowed	(m)	פָּתַח	he opened
(c)	בָּקַע	he split	(n)	קָרַע	he tore
(d)	בָּרַח	he fled	(o)	רָצַח	he killed
(e)	גָּבַה	he was high, exalted	(p)	שָׂבַע	he was satisfied, sated
(f)	זָבַח	he sacrificed	(q)	שָׂמַח	he rejoiced, made merry
(g)	זָרַע	he sowed	(r)	שָׁכַח	he forgot
(h)	כָּרַע	he knelt, bowed down	(s)	שָׁלַח	he sent; (Pi.) he set free
(i)	מָשַׁח	he anointed	(t)	שָׁמַע	he heard
(j)	סָלַח	he forgave	(u)	תָּקַע	he struck, thrust (a weapon into someone), he blew (a trumpet), he pitched (a tent)
(k)	פָּגַע	he met, interceded			

70.3 *Distinctive Characteristics of Lamed Guttural Verbs*

(1) When a Lamed Guttural verb form has no suffix (afformative), and thus ends in ה, ח, or ע, the final guttural must be preceded by either pataḥ (lengthened to qames in masculine singular forms of passive participles) or pataḥ furtive (cf. V.13.2, p. 23).

---

*Refer to Verb Chart 5, pp. 408f., for the conjugation of the Lamed Guttural verb.

(a) If a form of the strong verb has a pataḥ or qameṣ as its stem vowel, then the corresponding form of a Lamed Guttural verb will follow suit. Examples:

	Strong Verb	Lamed Guttural
Nifʾal Perf. 3 ms	נִמְשַׁל	נִשְׁמַע
Nifʿal Part. ms	נִמְשָׁל	נִשְׁמָע
Puʾal Impf. 3 ms	יְמֻשַּׁל	יְשֻׁמַּע
Puʾal Part. ms	מְמֻשָּׁל	מְשֻׁמָּע

(b) If a form of the perfect, the imperfect, the imperative, or the infinitive construct (except Qal infinitive construct) of the strong verb has a stem vowel which is not of the "a" class, this vowel must be changed to pataḥ in the corresponding form of a Lamed Guttural verb. This rule applies to all stems except the Hifʿil. Note the transposition of ת and שׁ in the Hitpaʿel of שָׁמַע (cf. XIV.36.4 [3], p. 111).

Examples:

	Strong Verb	Lamed Guttural
Qal Impf. 3 ms	יִמְשֹׁל	יִשְׁמַע
Qal Impv. 2 ms	מְשֹׁל	שְׁמַע
Nifʾal Impf. 3 ms	יִמָּשֵׁל	יִשָּׁמַע
Nifʾal Impv. 2 ms	הִמָּשֵׁל	הִשָּׁמַע
Nifʿal Inf. Const.	הִמָּשֵׁל	הִשָּׁמַע
Piʿel Perf. 3 ms	מִשֵּׁל	שִׁמַּע
Piʿel Impf. 3 ms	יְמַשֵּׁל	יְשַׁמַּע
Piʿel Impv. 2 ms	מַשֵּׁל	שַׁמַּע
Piʿel Inf. Const.	מַשֵּׁל	שַׁמַּע
Hitpaʿel Perf. 3 ms	הִתְמַשֵּׁל	הִשְׁתַּמַּע
Hitpaʿel Impf. 3 ms	יִתְמַשֵּׁל	יִשְׁתַּמַּע

(c) If the stem vowel of a strong verb form is unchangeably long (יִ , וֹ, וּ), the corresponding form of a Lamed Guttural verb will retain the unchangeably long vowel as its stem vowel, but will have a pataḥ furtive inserted between this vowel and the final guttural. This rule applies in Qal infinitive absolute, Qal passive participle (ms), and in all Hifʿil forms having יִ as the stem vowel.

Examples:

	Strong Verb	Lamed Guttural
Qal Inf. Abs.	מָשׁוֹל	שָׁמוֹעַ
Qal Pass. Part. (ms)	מָשׁוּל	שָׁמוּעַ
Hif‘il Perf. 3 ms	הִמְשִׁיל	הִשְׁמִיעַ
Hif‘il Impf. 3 ms	יַמְשִׁיל	יַשְׁמִיעַ
Hif‘il Inf. Const.	הַמְשִׁיל	הַשְׁמִיעַ
Hif‘il Part. (ms)	מַמְשִׁיל	מַשְׁמִיעַ

(d)   Although ḥolem and ṣere are not normally considered to be unchangeably long vowels, they function as such in certain forms of Lamed Guttural verbs. In all such forms, a pataḥ furtive is inserted between the stem vowel and the final guttural. In the case of ḥolem, this rule applies to Qal infinitive construct, Nif‘al infinitive absolute, Pu‘al infinitive absolute, and Hitpa‘el infinitive absolute. In the case of ṣere, it applies to Qal active participle (ms), Pi‘el infinitive absolute, Pi‘el participle (ms), Hitpa‘el Participle (ms), Hif‘il infinitive absolute, and Hof‘al infinitive absolute.

Examples:

	Strong Verb	Lamed Guttural
Qal Inf. Const.	מְשֹׁל	שְׁמֹעַ
Nif‘al Inf. Abs.	נִמְשֹׁל	נִשְׁמֹעַ
Pu‘al Inf. Abs.	מֻשֹׁל	שֻׁמֹעַ
Hitpa‘el Inf. Abs.	הִתְמַשֹּׁל	הִשְׁתַּמֹּעַ
Qal Act. Part. (ms)	מֹשֵׁל	שֹׁמֵעַ
Pi‘el Inf. Abs.	מַשֵּׁל	שַׁמֵּעַ
Pi‘el Part. (ms)	מְמַשֵּׁל	מְשַׁמֵּעַ
Hitpa‘el Part. (ms)	מִתְמַשֵּׁל	מִשְׁתַּמֵּעַ
Hif‘il Inf. Abs.	הַמְשֵׁל	הַשְׁמֵעַ
Hof‘al Inf. Abs.	הָמְשֵׁל	הָשְׁמֵעַ

(2)   When suffixes (afformatives) are added to Lamed Guttural verb forms, the forms are pointed like their counterparts in the strong verb, except in two instances.

265

(a)   The stem vowel before all נָה suffixes will be pataḥ, regardless of whether the stem is active or passive. This contrasts to the pattern found in strong verbs where the stem vowel before נָה suffixes is ḥolem in the Qal imperfect and imperative, ṣere in all other active stems (Piʻel, Hitpaʻel, and Hifʻil), and pataḥ in all passive stems (Nifʻal, Puʻal, and Hofʻal).

Examples:

	Strong Verb	Lamed Guttural
Qal Impf. 3 fp, 2fp	תִּמְשֹׁלְנָה	תִּשְׁמַעְנָה
Qal Impv. 2 fp	מְשֹׁלְנָה	שְׁמַעְנָה
Piʻel Impf. 3 fp, 2 fp	תְּמַשֵּׁלְנָה	תְּשַׁמַּעְנָה
Piʻel Impv. 2 fp	מַשֵּׁלְנָה	שַׁמַּעְנָה
Hifʻil Impf. 3 fp, 2 fp	תַּמְשֵׁלְנָה	תַּשְׁמַעְנָה
Hifʻil Impv. 2 fp	הַמְשֵׁלְנָה	הַשְׁמַעְנָה

(b)   The second instance in which Lamed Gutturals differ from strong verbs when suffixes are added is in the 2 fs form of the perfect in all stems. While in the case of strong verbs a silent sheva stands beneath the final root consonant in these forms, a pataḥ replaces the silent sheva in corresponding forms of Lamed Guttural verbs. Since the accent does not shift to the added syllable, it must be marked at its original position in the word.

Examples:

	Strong Verb	Lamed Guttural
Qal Perf. 2 fs	מָשַׁלְתְּ	שָׁמַעַתְּ
Nifʻal Perf. 2 fs	נִמְשַׁלְתְּ	נִשְׁמַעַתְּ
Piʻel Perf. 2 fs	מִשַּׁלְתְּ	שִׁמַּעַתְּ
Puʻal Perf. 2 fs	מֻשַּׁלְתְּ	שֻׁמַּעַתְּ
Hitpaʻel Perf. 2 fs	הִתְמַשַּׁלְתְּ	הִשְׁתַּמַּעַתְּ
Hifʻil Perf. 2 fs	הִמְשַׁלְתְּ	הִשְׁמַעַתְּ
Hofʻal Perf. 2 fs	הֻמְשַׁלְתְּ	הֻשְׁמַעַתְּ

266

70.4 *A Synopsis of* שָׁמַע*, "he heard"*

	Qal	Nif'al	Pi'el	Pu'al	Hitpa'el	Hif'il	Hof'al
Perf. 3 ms	שָׁמַע	נִשְׁמַע	שִׁמַּע	שֻׁמַּע	הִשְׁתַּמַּע	הִשְׁמִיעַ	הָשְׁמַע
Impf. 3 ms	יִשְׁמַע	יִשָּׁמַע	יְשַׁמַּע	יְשֻׁמַּע	יִשְׁתַּמַּע	יַשְׁמִיעַ	יָשְׁמַע
Impv. 2 ms	שְׁמַע	הִשָּׁמַע	שַׁמַּע		הִשְׁתַּמַּע	הַשְׁמַע	
Inf. Const.	שְׁמֹעַ	הִשָּׁמַע	שַׁמַּע	שֻׁמַּע	הִשְׁתַּמַּע	הַשְׁמִיעַ	הָשְׁמַע
Inf. Abs.	שָׁמוֹעַ	נִשְׁמֹעַ	שַׁמֵּעַ	שֻׁמֹּעַ	הִשְׁתַּמֹּעַ	הַשְׁמֵעַ	הָשְׁמֵעַ
Part. Act. (ms)	שֹׁמֵעַ		מְשַׁמֵּעַ		מִשְׁתַּמֵּעַ	מַשְׁמִיעַ	
Part. Pass. (ms)	שָׁמוּעַ	נִשְׁמָע		מְשֻׁמָּע			מֻשְׁמָע

EXERCISES

1. Fill in the blanks with the proper verb translations.

(1) וַיְמָאֲנוּ הָעָם לִשְׁמֹעַ בְּקוֹל שְׁמוּאֵל And the people _____ to _____ to the voice of Samuel. (1 Sam. 8:19)

(2) וּכְשָׁמְעִי אֶת־הַדָּבָר הַזֶּה קָרַעְתִּי אֶת־בִּגְדִי And when I _____ this word, I _____ my garment. (Ezr. 9:3)

(3) בָּרוּךְ הַגֶּבֶר אֲשֶׁר יִבְטַח בַּיהוָה _____ is the man who _____ in the LORD. (Jer. 17:7)

(4) כִּי־יָדְעוּ הָאֲנָשִׁים כִּי־מִלִּפְנֵי יְהוָה הוּא בֹרֵחַ For the men _____ that he was _____ from the presence of the LORD. (Jon. 1:10)

(5) אֶשְׁלַח אֵלֶיךָ אִישׁ מֵאֶרֶץ בִּנְיָמִן I will _____ to you a man from the land of Benjamin. (1 Sam. 9:16)

(6) לֹא אֶשְׁכַּח דְּבָרֶךָ I will not _____ your word. (Ps. 119:16)

(7) בְּרִית עוֹלָם לֹא תִשָּׁכֵחַ An everlasting covenant (which) shall not be _____. (Jer. 50:5)

(8) וְשֵׁשׁ שָׁנִים תִּזְרַע אֶת־אַרְצֶךָ For six years you shall _____ your land. (Exod. 23:10)

(9) כִּי כִגְבֹהַּ שָׁמַיִם עַל־הָאָרֶץ for as the heavens are _____ above
the earth (Ps. 103:11)

(10) כִּי בַּיהוָה אֱלֹהַיִךְ פָּשָׁעַתְּ For you have _____ against the LORD
your God. (Jer. 3:13)

2. Each of the following sentences contains a perfect form of a Lamed Guttural verb.
In the space marked (a) give its stem, in (b) its person, gender, and number, and in
(c) its root.

(1) הֵן בְּנֵי־יִשְׂרָאֵל לֹא־שָׁמְעוּ אֵלַי   (a) _____
Behold, the people of Israel have not listened to me.   (b) _____
(Exod. 6:12)   (c) _____

(2) אֲשֶׁר שָׁלַחְתִּי מִירוּשָׁלַם בָּבֶלָה   (a) _____
whom I sent from Jerusalem to Babylon (Jer. 29:20)   (b) _____
          (c) _____

(3) יְהוָה אֱלֹהֵי הָעִבְרִים שְׁלָחַנִי אֵלֶיךָ   (a) _____
The LORD God of the Hebrews has sent me to you.   (b) _____
(Exod. 7:16)   (c) _____

(4) כַּאֲשֶׁר שָׁכְחוּ אֲבוֹתָם אֶת־שְׁמִי בַּבָּעַל   (a) _____
just as their fathers forgot my name for Baal (Jer. 23:27)   (b) _____
          (c) _____

(5) וְגַם־בְּזֹאת לֹא שָׂבָעַתְּ   (a) _____
And even with this you were not satisfied. (Ezek. 16:29)   (b) _____
          (c) _____

3. Each of the following entries contains an imperfect form of a Lamed Guttural
verb. In the space marked (a) give its stem, in (b) its person, gender, and number,
and in (c) its root.

(1) וְגַם אֶת־יִשְׂרָאֵל לֹא אֲשַׁלֵּחַ   (a) _____
And moreover I will not set Israel free (let Israel go).   (b) _____
(Exod. 5:2)   (c) _____

(2) וְאֵיךְ יִשְׁמַע אֵלַי פַּרְעֹה   (a) _____
How then shall Pharaoh listen to me? (Exod. 6:30)   (b) _____
          (c) _____

(3) כִּי נִשְׁמַע בְּקוֹל יְהוָה אֱלֹהֵינוּ

For we will listen to (obey) the voice of the LORD our
God. (Jer. 42:6)

(a) _____
(b) _____
(c) _____

(4) וְלֹא־יִשָּׁמַע בָּהּ עוֹד קוֹל בְּכִי

There shall no more be heard in her (it) the voice (sound)
of weeping. (Isa. 65:19)

(a) _____
(b) _____
(c) _____

(5) לְךָ־אֶזְבַּח זֶבַח תּוֹדָה

To you I will sacrifice a sacrifice of thanksgiving.
(Ps. 116:17)

(a) _____
(b) _____
(c) _____

(6) וָאֶשְׁלַח לְפָנֶיךָ אֶת־מֹשֶׁה אַהֲרֹן וּמִרְיָם

And I sent before you Moses, Aaron, and Miriam.
(Mic. 6:4)

(a) _____
(b) _____
(c) _____

(7) וְלֹא יְשַׁלַּח אֶת־הָעָם

And he will not let the people go (set the people free).
(Exod. 4:21)

(a) _____
(b) _____
(c) _____

(8) בְּנִי תּוֹרָתִי אַל־תִּשְׁכָּח

My son, do not forget my law (my instruction). (Prov. 3:1)

(a) _____
(b) _____
(c) _____

(9) כִּי לֹא לָנֶצַח יִשָּׁכַח אֶבְיוֹן

For the needy shall never be forgotten. (Ps. 9:19; Eng. 9:18)

(a) _____
(b) _____
(c) _____

(10) וְהַמֶּלֶךְ יִשְׂמַח בֵּאלֹהִים

But the king shall rejoice in God. (Ps. 63:12; Eng. 63:11)

(a) _____
(b) _____
(c) _____

(11) וְיַיִן יְשַׂמַּח לְבַב־אֱנוֹשׁ

And wine shall gladden the heart of man. (Ps. 104:15)

(a) _____
(b) _____
(c) _____

(12) וַיִּגְבַּה יְהוָה צְבָאוֹת בַּמִּשְׁפָּט

But the LORD of hosts is exalted in justice. (Isa. 5:16)

(a) _____
(b) _____
(c) _____

4. Each of the following entries contains an imperative form of a Lamed Guttural verb. In the space marked (a) give its stem, in (b) its person, gender, and number, and in (c) its root.

(1) אֱלֹהִים שְׁמַע תְּפִלָּתִי   (a) _____
O God, hear my prayer. (Ps. 54:4; Eng. 54:2)   (b) _____
                                              (c) _____

(2) כִּי־שְׁמַעְנָה נָשִׁים דְּבַר־יְהוָה   (a) _____
Hear, O women, the word of the LORD! (Jer. 9:19; (b) _____
Eng. 9:20)   (c) _____

(3) אֶרֶץ אֶרֶץ אָרֶץ שִׁמְעִי דְּבַר־יְהוָה   (a) _____
O earth, earth, earth, hear the word of the LORD! (b) _____
(Jer. 22:29)   (c) _____

(4) הַשְׁמִיעִינִי אֶת־קוֹלֵךְ   (a) _____
Let me hear (cause me to hear) your voice.   (b) _____
(Song of Sol. 2:14)   (c) _____

(5) בְּטַח אֶל־יְהוָה בְּכָל־לִבֶּךָ   (a) _____
Trust in the LORD with all your heart. (Prov. 3:5) (b) _____
                                              (c) _____

(6) סְלַח־נָא לַעֲוֹן הָעָם הַזֶּה   (a) _____
Forgive the iniquity of this people. (Num. 14:19) (b) _____
                                              (c) _____

(7) וְאַתֶּם שִׁמְעוּ דְבַר־יְהוָה   (a) _____
Hear the word of the LORD! (Jer. 29:20)   (b) _____
                                              (c) _____

(8) וְעַתָּה שְׁלַח־לִי אִישׁ־חָכָם   (a) _____
And now send me a wise man (a skilled man).   (b) _____
(2 Chr. 2:6; Eng. 2:7)   (c) _____

(9) שַׁלַּח אֶת־עַמִּי וְיַעַבְדֻנִי בַּמִּדְבָּר (a) _____
Let my people go (send my people) that they may serve (b) _____
(worship) me in the wilderness. (Exod. 7:16)   (c) _____

(10) חֲכַם בְּנִי וְשַׂמַּח לִבִּי   (a) _____
Be wise, my son, and make my heart glad. (Prov. 27:11) (b) _____
                                              (c) _____

270

5. Each of the following entries contains either an infinitive construct or an infinitive absolute from a Lamed Guttural verb. In the space marked (a) indicate whether it is construct or absolute, in (b) give its stem, and in (c) its root.

(1) וַיְהִי כִשְׁמֹעַ הָעָם אֶת־קוֹל הַשּׁוֹפָר

(a) _____

and so it was that when the people heard the sound of the trumpet (Josh. 6:20)

(b) _____

(c) _____

(2) אָזְנַיִם לָהֶם לִשְׁמֹעַ וְלֹא שָׁמֵעוּ

(a) _____

They have ears to hear, but they do not hear. (Ezek. 12:2)

(b) _____

(c) _____

(3) מִי יְהוָה אֲשֶׁר אֶשְׁמַע בְּקֹלוֹ לְשַׁלַּח אֶת־יִשְׂרָאֵל

(a) _____

Who is the LORD that I should obey (listen to) his voice to let Israel go? (Exod. 5:2)

(b) _____

(c) _____

(4) שִׁמְעוּ שָׁמוֹעַ אֵלַי וְאִכְלוּ־טוֹב

(a) _____

Hearken diligently to me, and eat what is good. (Isa. 55:2)

(b) _____

(c) _____

(5) אִם־שָׁמוֹעַ תִּשְׁמַע לְקוֹל יְהוָה אֱלֹהֶיךָ

(a) _____

if you will diligently hearken to the voice of the LORD your God (Exod. 15:26)

(b) _____

(c) _____

(6) שַׁלֵּחַ תְּשַׁלַּח אֶת־הָאֵם

(a) _____

You shall surely let the mother go free. (Deut. 22:7)

(b) _____

(c) _____

(7) וְהָיָה אִם־שָׁכֹחַ תִּשְׁכַּח אֶת־יְהוָה אֱלֹהֶיךָ

(a) _____

and it shall be (that) if you totally forget the LORD your God (Deut. 8:19)

(b) _____

(c) _____

(8) הַחֹשְׁבִים לְהַשְׁכִּיחַ אֶת־עַמִּי שְׁמִי בַּחֲלוֹמֹתָם

(a) _____

the ones thinking (intending) to cause my people to forget my name through their dreams (Jer. 23:27)

(b) _____

(c) _____

(9) כִּי כִגְבֹהַּ שָׁמַיִם עַל־הָאָרֶץ

(a) _____

for as the heavens are high above the earth (Ps. 103:11)

(b) _____

(c) _____

(10) לִזְבֹּחַ לַיהוָה אֱלֹהֶיךָ בַּגִּלְגָּל

(a) _____

to sacrifice to the LORD your God in Gilgal (1 Sam. 15:21)

(b) _____

(c) _____

6. Each of the following entries contains a participle from a Lamed Guttural verb. In the space marked (a) give its stem, in (b) its gender and number, and in (c) its root.

(1) וַיֹּאמֶר שְׁמוּאֵל דַּבֵּר כִּי שֹׁמֵעַ עַבְדֶּךָ

And Samuel said, "Speak, for your servant is listening." (1 Sam. 3:10)

(a) _____
(b) _____
(c) _____

(2) בְּזֹאת אֲנִי בוֹטֵחַ

(Even) in this I will trust (be confident). (Ps. 27:3)

(a) _____
(b) _____
(c) _____

(3) מִפְּנֵי שָׂרַי גְּבִרְתִּי אָנֹכִי בֹּרַחַת

I am fleeing from Sarai my mistress. (Gen. 16:8)

(a) _____
(b) _____
(c) _____

(4) בֶּן־אָדָם שׁוֹלֵחַ אֲנִי אוֹתְךָ אֶל־בְּנֵי יִשְׂרָאֵל

Son of man, I am sending you to the people (sons) of Israel. (Ezek. 2:3)

(a) _____
(b) _____
(c) _____

(5) הִנְנִי מְשַׁלֵּחַ בָּם אֶת־הַחֶרֶב אֶת־הָרָעָב וְאֶת־הַדָּבֶר

Behold, I am sending against them sword, famine, and pestilence. (Jer. 29:17)

(a) _____
(b) _____
(c) _____

7. Practice pronouncing the Hebrew, noting especially Lamed Guttural verb forms. Cover the English and practice translating the Hebrew from sight.

(1) וָאֶשְׁמַע אֶת־קוֹל אֲדֹנָי אֹמֵר
אֶת־מִי אֶשְׁלַח וּמִי יֵלֶךְ־לָנוּ
וָאֹמַר הִנְנִי שְׁלָחֵנִי

And I heard the voice of the LORD saying, "Whom shall I send, and who will go for us?" And I said, "Here am I; send me!" (Isa. 6:8)

(2) וּבְעֵת צָרָתָם יִצְעֲקוּ אֵלֶיךָ
וְאַתָּה מִשָּׁמַיִם תִּשְׁמָע

And in the time of their trouble they cried to you, and you heard from heaven. (Neh. 9:27)

(3) מַה־נָּאווּ עַל־הֶהָרִים רַגְלֵי
מְבַשֵּׂר מַשְׁמִיעַ שָׁלוֹם מְבַשֵּׂר
טוֹב מַשְׁמִיעַ יְשׁוּעָה אֹמֵר
לְצִיּוֹן מָלַךְ אֱלֹהָיִךְ

How beautiful (from נָאָה) upon the mountains are the feet of the proclaimers of good news, the announcers of peace, the proclaimers of good news of good, the announcers of salvation, the ones saying to Zion, "Your God reigns!" (Isa. 52:7)

272

(4) וַיִּמְשַׁח אֶת־שְׁלֹמֹה וַיִּתְקְעוּ
בַּשּׁוֹפָר וַיֹּאמְרוּ כָּל־הָעָם
יְחִי הַמֶּלֶךְ שְׁלֹמֹה

And he anointed Solomon, and they blew the trumpet, and all the people said, "Long live king Solomon!" (1 Kgs. 1:39)

(5) וַיִּשְׁמְעוּ פְלִשְׁתִּים כִּי־נִמְשַׁח
דָוִיד לְמֶלֶךְ עַל־כָּל־יִשְׂרָאֵל

And the Philistines heard that David had been anointed as king over all Israel. (1 Chr. 14:8)

(6) בִּי נִשְׁבַּעְתִּי כִּי־לִי תִּכְרַע
כָּל־בֶּרֶךְ תִּשָּׁבַע כָּל־לָשׁוֹן

By myself I have sworn that to me every knee shall bow, every tongue shall swear. (Isa. 45:23)

(7) וַיִּשְׁלַח יְהוָה אֱלֹהֵי אֲבוֹתֵיהֶם
עֲלֵיהֶם בְּיַד מַלְאָכָיו
הַשְׁכֵּם וְשָׁלוֹחַ

And the LORD God of their fathers sent to them persistently (lit., to rise early and to send) by the hand of his messengers. (2 Chr. 36:15)

(8) הִנֵּה אָנֹכִי שֹׁלֵחַ מַלְאָךְ
לְפָנֶיךָ לִשְׁמָרְךָ בַּדָּרֶךְ

Behold, I am sending an angel (messenger) before you to guard (protect) you on the way. (Exod. 23:20)

(9) וַיְחַזֵּק יְהוָה אֶת־לֵב פַּרְעֹה
וְלֹא־שִׁלַּח אֶת־בְּנֵי־יִשְׂרָאֵל
מֵאַרְצוֹ

And the LORD hardened Pharaoh's heart, and he would not let the people of Israel go from his land. (Exod. 11:10)

(10) וַיְשַׁלְּחֵהוּ יְהוָה אֱלֹהִים
מִגַּן־עֵדֶן לַעֲבֹד אֶת־הָאֲדָמָה
אֲשֶׁר לֻקַּח מִשָּׁם

And the LORD God sent him from the garden of Eden to till (serve) the ground from which he had been taken. (Gen. 3:23)

(11) הֲתִשְׁכַּח אִשָּׁה בֶּן־בִּטְנָהּ
גַּם־אֵלֶּה תִשְׁכַּחְנָה וְאָנֹכִי
לֹא אֶשְׁכָּחֵךְ

Will a woman forget the son of her womb? Even these may forget, but I will not forget you. (Isa. 49:15)

(12) זֶה־הַיּוֹם עָשָׂה יְהוָה נָגִילָה
וְנִשְׂמְחָה בוֹ

This is the day the LORD made; let us exult and be glad in it. (Ps. 118:24)

(13) אֵין־טוֹב לָאָדָם תַּחַת
הַשֶּׁמֶשׁ כִּי אִם־לֶאֱכוֹל
וְלִשְׁתּוֹת וְלִשְׂמוֹחַ

There is nothing good for man under the sun but to eat and drink, and to make merry. (Eccl. 8:15)

(14) וַיִּתְקַע יוֹאָב בַּשּׁוֹפָר וַיַּעַמְדוּ
כָּל־הָעָם

And Joab blew the trumpet, and all the people stood. (2 Sam. 2:28)

(15) כִּי־גָבְהוּ שָׁמַיִם מֵאֶרֶץ כֵּן
גָּבְהוּ דְרָכַי מִדַּרְכֵיכֶם

For as the heavens are higher than the earth, so are my ways higher than your ways. (Isa. 55:9)

VOCABULARY

(1) בָּלַע he swallowed, consumed

(2) בָּקַע he split open

(3) גָּבַה he was high, proud

(4) זָרַע he sowed

(5) כָּרַע he knelt, bowed down

(6) מָשַׁח he anointed

(7) סָלַח he forgave

(8) פָּגַע he met, interceded

(9) פָּתַח he opened

(10) קָרַע he tore

(11) רָצַח he killed, murdered

(12) שָׂבַע he was satisfied, sated

(13) בָּמָה (f) high place

(14) צוּר rock

(15) קֵץ end

(16) שֻׁלְחָן table

(17) שֶׁמֶשׁ sun

(18) תּוֹלְדוֹת (f) generations

LESSON XXVI

71. Weak Verbs: Lamed 'Alef Verbs*

71.1 *Definition*

A Lamed 'Alef verb is one whose final consonant is an 'alef. This includes a number of stative verbs, as well as some that are doubly weak.

71.2 *A List of the Most Frequently Occurring Lamed 'Alef Verbs*

(1) Regular Lamed 'Alef verbs

    (a)   בָּרָא   he created

    (b)   מָצָא   he found

    (c)   קָרָא   he called, announced, read

    (d)   רָפָא   he healed

(2) Stative Lamed 'Alef verbs

    (a)   יָרֵא   he was afraid

    (b)   מָלֵא   he (it) was full

    (c)   צָמֵא   he was thirsty

    (d)   שָׂנֵא   he hated

    (e)   טָמֵא   he was unclean

(3) Doubly weak Lamed 'Alef verbs

    (a)   [חבא]   he hid

    (b)   חָטָא   he sinned, missed the mark

    (c)   יָצָא   he went out

    (d)   [נבא]   he prophesied

    (e)   נָשָׂא   he lifted up, carried

71.3 *Distinctive Characteristics of Lamed 'Alef Verbs*

(1) א always becomes quiescent (ceases to function as a consonant) at the end of a syllable. Any syllable, therefore, that ends in א becomes an open syllable, and must have a long vowel. If the vowel before quiescent א is already long, it is allowed to stand as it is. However, if it is short, it must be lengthened. In actual practice, this always involves the lengthening of the stem vowel pataḥ to qameṣ.

---

*Refer to Verb Chart 6, pp. 410f., for the conjugation of the Lamed 'Alef verb.

Examples:

	Qal Perfect	Nifʿal Perfect	Piʿel Perfect	Puʿal Perfect
Strong Verb 3 ms	מָשַׁל	נִמְשַׁל	מִשֵּׁל	מֻשַּׁל
Lamed ʾAlef 3 ms	מָצָא	נִמְצָא	מִצֵּא	מֻצָּא

(2) א becomes quiescent not only when it is final in a verb form, but also when it stands before a consonantal afformative. When it stands before a vocalic afformative, however, it continues to function as a consonant.

Examples:

Qal Perfect

3 ms	מָצָא	quiescent (final in the form)
3 fs	מָצְאָה	not quiescent (before a vocalic afformative)
3 cp	מָצְאוּ	not quiescent (before a vocalic afformative)
1 cp	מָצָאנוּ	quiescent (before a consonantal afformative)

(3) A BeGaD KeFaT letter standing immediately after quiescent א loses its dagesh lene (cf. I.1.9, pp. 2f.; III.6, pp. 12f.).

Examples:

	Qal Perfect 2 ms	Qal Perfect 1 cs	Qal Perfect 2 mp
Strong Verb	מָשַׁלְתָּ	מָשַׁלְתִּי	מְשַׁלְתֶּם
Lamed ʾAlef	מָצָאתָ	מָצָאתִי	מְצָאתֶם

(4) In the Qal perfect and Hofʿal perfect of Lamed ʾAlef verbs the stem vowel before consonantal afformatives is qameṣ.

Examples:

	Qal Perfect	Hofʿal Perfect
2 ms	מָצָאתָ	הֻמְצֵאתָ
2 fs	מָצָאת	הֻמְצֵאת
1 cs	מָצָאתִי	הֻמְצֵאתִי
2 mp	מְצָאתֶם	הֻמְצֵאתֶם
2 fp	מְצָאתֶן	הֻמְצֵאתֶן
1 cp	מָצָאנוּ	הֻמְצֵאנוּ

(5) In all stems except Qal and Hofʿal, the stem vowel before consonantal afformatives in the perfect is ṣere.

Examples:

	Nif'al Perfect	Pi'el Perfect	Pu'al Perfect	Hif'il Perfect
2 ms	נִמְצֵאתָ	מֻצֵּאתָ	מֻצֵּאתָ	הֻמְצֵאתָ
2 fs	נִמְצֵאת	מֻצֵּאת	מֻצֵּאת	הֻמְצֵאת
1 cs	נִמְצֵאתִי	מֻצֵּאתִי	מֻצֵּאתִי	הֻמְצֵאתִי
2 mp	נִמְצֵאתֶם	מֻצֵּאתֶם	מֻצֵּאתֶם	הֻמְצֵאתֶם
2 fp	נִמְצֵאתֶן	מֻצֵּאתֶן	מֻצֵּאתֶן	הֻמְצֵאתֶן
1 cp	נִמְצֵאנוּ	מֻצֵּאנוּ	מֻצֵּאנוּ	הֻמְצֵאנוּ

(6) The stem vowel before quiescent א in all forms of the Qal imperfect, except 3 fp and 2 fp, changes from ḥolem in the strong verb to qameṣ in the Lamed 'Alef verb. This change is also carried over to the Qal imperative 2 ms. Examples:

	(מָשַׁל)	(מָצָא)
Qal Imperfect 3 ms	יִמְשֹׁל	יִמְצָא
Qal Imperfect 3 fs	תִּמְשֹׁל	תִּמְצָא
Qal Imperfect 2 ms	תִּמְשֹׁל	תִּמְצָא
Qal Imperfect 1 cs	אֶמְשֹׁל -	אֶמְצָא
Qal Imperfect 1 cp	נִמְשֹׁל	נִמְצָא
Qal Imperative 2 ms	מְשֹׁל	מְצָא

(7) The stem vowel before נָה endings in the imperfect 3 fp and 2 fp, and in the imperative 2 fp, is s^egol in all stems of Lamed 'Alef verbs. Examples:

	Qal	Nif'al	Pi'el	Pu'al	Hitpa'el	Hif'il	Hof'al
Impf. 3 fp, 2 fp	תִּמְצֶאנָה	תִּמָּצֶאנָה	תְּמַצֶּאנָה	תְּמֻצֶּאנָה	תִּתְמַצֶּאנָה	תַּמְצֶאנָה	תֻּמְצֶאנָה
Impv. 2 fs	מְצֶאנָה	הִמָּצֶאנָה	מַצֶּאנָה		הִתְמַצֶּאנָה	הַמְצֶאנָה	

(8) The preformative vowel of all Hof'al forms of Lamed 'Alef verbs is generally regarded to be qibbuṣ rather than qameṣ-ḥaṭuf, although the number of attested Hof'al forms is too small to prove that this is so.

Examples:

	(מְשֵׁל)	(מְצָא)
Hofʿal Perfect 3 ms	הָמְשַׁל	הֻמְצָא
Hofʿal Imperfect 3 ms	יָמְשַׁל	יֻמְצָא
Hofʿal Inf. Const.	הָמְשַׁל	הֻמְצָא
Hofʿal Inf. Abs.	הָמְשֵׁל	הֻמְצֵא
Hofʿal Part. (ms)	מָמְשָׁל	מֻמְצָא

(9) The participles of Lamed ʾAlef verbs are patterned after those of strong verbs, except that the segholate form of the feminine singular participle has ṣere as its stem vowel, and also drops the vowel after א (מֹצֵאת becomes מֹצֵאת).

Examples:

	Qal (Active)	Nifʿal	Piʿel	Hifʿil
ms	מֹצֵא	נִמְצָא	מְמַצֵּא	מַמְצִיא
mp	מֹצְאִים	נִמְצָאִים	מְמַצְּאִים	מַמְצִיאִים
fs	מֹצֵאת	נִמְצֵאת	מְמַצֵּאת	מַמְצִיאָה
		נִמְצָאָה	מְמַצְּאָה	
fp	מֹצְאוֹת	נִמְצָאוֹת	מְמַצְּאוֹת	מַמְצִיאוֹת

(10) All other forms of Lamed ʾAlef verbs are patterned after the corresponding forms of strong verbs.

71.4 *A Synopsis of* מָצָא, *"he found"*

	Qal	Nifʿal	Piʿel	Puʿal	Hitpaʿel	Hifʿil	Hofʿal
Perf. 3 ms	מָצָא	נִמְצָא	מִצֵּא	מֻצָּא	הִתְמַצֵּא	הִמְצִיא	הֻמְצָא
Impf. 3 ms	יִמְצָא	יִמָּצֵא	יְמַצֵּא	יְמֻצָּא	יִתְמַצֵּא	יַמְצִיא	יֻמְצָא
Impv. 2 ms	מְצָא	הִמָּצֵא	מַצֵּא		הִתְמַצֵּא	הַמְצֵא	
Inf. Const.	מְצֹא	הִמָּצֵא	מַצֵּא	מֻצָּא	הִתְמַצֵּא	הַמְצִיא	הֻמְצָא
Inf. Abs.	מָצוֹא	נִמְצֹא	מַצֵּא	מֻצָּא	הִתְמַצֵּא	הַמְצֵא	הֻמְצֵא
Part. Act.	מֹצֵא		מְמַצֵּא		מִתְמַצֵּא	מַמְצִיא	
Part. Pass.	מָצוּא	נִמְצָא		מְמֻצָּא			מֻמְצָא

278

71.5 Stative Lamed ᾿Alef verbs differ from other Lamed ᾿Alef verbs in three important aspects.

(1) The stem vowel before consonantal afformatives in the Qal perfect is ṣere rather than qameṣ.
Examples:

Qal Perfect

	Regular	Stative	Stative	Stative
3 ms	מָצָא	מָלֵא	יָרֵא	שָׂנֵא
2 ms	מָצָאתָ	מָלֵאתָ	יָרֵאתָ	שָׂנֵאתָ
2 fs	מָצָאת	מָלֵאת	יָרֵאת	שָׂנֵאת
1 cs	מָצָאתִי	מָלֵאתִי	יָרֵאתִי	שָׂנֵאתִי
2 mp	מְצָאתֶם	מְלֵאתֶם	יְרֵאתֶם	שְׂנֵאתֶם
2 fp	מְצָאתֶן	מְלֵאתֶן	יְרֵאתֶן	שְׂנֵאתֶן
1 cp	מָצָאנוּ	מָלֵאנוּ	יָרֵאנוּ	שָׂנֵאנוּ

(2) In some verbs of this class the Qal active participle (ms) has the same form as the Qal perfect 3 ms.
Examples:

יָרֵא "he feared"   מָלֵא "he was full"

Qal Perfect 3 ms	יָרֵא	מָלֵא
Qal Active Part. (ms)	יָרֵא	מָלֵא

(3) In some verbs of this class infinitive construct forms sometimes end in ה ָ or ת.
Examples:

Qal Inf. Const.   Piᵉel Inf. Const.

			Qal Inf. Const.	Piᵉel Inf. Const.
(a)	יָרֵא	"he feared"	יִרְאָה	
(b)	מָלֵא	"he was full"	מְלֹאת	מַלֵּאת
(c)	טָמֵא	"he was unclean"	טָמְאָה	
			טָמֵאת	

279

EXERCISES

1. Fill in the blanks with the correct translation for the verbs in the following entries, noting especially Lamed 'Alef verbs as they occur.

(1) אָמַרְתִּי אֶשְׁמְרָה דְרָכַי מֵחֲטוֹא בִלְשׁוֹנִי I _____, "I will _____ my ways, that I might not _____ with my tongue." (Ps. 39:2; Eng. 39:1)

(2) רְפָאָה נַפְשִׁי כִּי־חָטָאתִי לָךְ _____ my soul, for I have _____ against thee. (Ps. 41:5; Eng. 41:4)

(3) וַאֲנִי אֶשְׁמַע מִן־הַשָּׁמַיִם וְאֶסְלַח לְחַטָּאתָם וְאֶרְפָּא אֶת־אַרְצָם And I will _____ from heaven, and I will _____ their sin, and I will _____ their land. (2 Chr. 7:14)

(4) קוֹל אֹמֵר קְרָא וְאָמַר מָה אֶקְרָא A voice saying, "_____!" And he _____, "What shall I _____?" (Isa. 40:6)

(5) וְדֶרֶךְ הַקֹּדֶשׁ יִקָּרֵא לָהּ And it shall be _____ the holy way. (Isa. 35:8)

(6) יְהוָה יִשְׁמַע בְּקָרְאִי אֵלָיו The LORD will _____ when I _____ to him. (Ps. 4:4)

(7) סֵפֶר הַתּוֹרָה מָצָאתִי בְּבֵית יְהוָה I have _____ the book of the law in the house of the LORD. (2 Kgs. 22:8)

(8) וַיִּקְרָא אֶת־שְׁמָם אָדָם בְּיוֹם הִבָּרְאָם And he _____ their name Adam (Mankind) in the day they were _____. (Gen. 5:2)

(9) מָה אוֹת כִּי־יִרְפָּא יְהוָה לִי What is the sign that the LORD will _____ me? (2 Kgs. 20:8)

(10) בְּצֵל יָדוֹ הֶחְבִּיאָנִי In the shadow (shade) of his hand he _____ me. (Isa. 49:2)

(11) וְהִנֵּה מָלֵא כְבוֹד־יְהוָה הַבָּיִת And behold the glory of the LORD _____ the house. (Ezek. 43:5)

(12) מַלֵּא קַרְנְךָ שֶׁמֶן _____ your horn with oil. (1 Sam. 16:1)

(13) עֵת לֶאֱהֹב וְעֵת לִשְׂנֹא a time to _____ and a time to _____ (Eccl. 3:8)

(14) שָׂנֵאתָ כָּל־פֹּעֲלֵי אָוֶן You _____ all workers of iniquity (evil).
(Ps. 5:6; Eng. 5:5)

(15) חָטָאנוּ כִּי־דִבַּרְנוּ בַיהוָה וָבָךְ We have _____ for we have
_____ against the LORD and against you. (Num. 21:7)

(16) וְהֶחֱטִיאָם חֲטָאָה גְדוֹלָה And he caused them to _____ a great sin.
(2 Kgs. 17:21)

2. Fill in the blanks with the correct pronouns, noting especially Lamed 'Alef verb forms as they occur.

(1) פֶּן־יַחֲטִיאוּ אֹתְךָ לִי Lest _____ cause _____ to sin against
_____ . (Exod. 23:33)

(2) חָטָאתִי לַיהוָה אֱלֹהֵיכֶם וְלָכֶם _____ have sinned against the
LORD _____ God and against _____ . (Exod. 10:16)

(3) כִּי־יָרֵא אָנֹכִי אֹתוֹ For _____ fear _____ . (Gen. 32:12;
Eng. 32:11)

(4) הוּא יִקְרָא בִשְׁמִי וַאֲנִי אֶעֱנֶה אֹתוֹ _____ will call on _____
name and _____ will answer _____ . (Zech. 13:9)

(5) יִקְרָאֵנִי וְאֶעֱנֵהוּ _____ will call on _____ and _____ will
answer _____ (Ps. 91:15)

(6) וְקָרָאת שְׁמוֹ עִמָּנוּ אֵל And _____ shall call _____ name
Immanuel. (Isa. 7:14)

(7) וַתִּקְרָא לְאַנְשֵׁי בֵיתָהּ And _____ called to the men of _____
house. (Gen. 39:14)

(8) קְרָאתִיו וְלֹא עָנָנִי _____ called _____ but _____ did not
answer _____ . (Song of Sol. 5:6)

(9) בִּקַּשְׁתִּיו וְלֹא מְצָאתִיו _____ sought _____ but did not find
_____ . (Song of Sol. 3:1)

(10) וְגַם־מָצָאתָ חֵן בְּעֵינִי And also _____ have found favor in
_____ eyes. (Exod. 33:12)

(11) וּבִקַּשְׁתֶּם אֹתִי וּמְצָאתֶם (אֹתִי) And _____ shall seek _____ ,
and _____ shall find (_____). (Jer. 29:13)

(12) זָכָר וּנְקֵבָה בְּרָאָם וַיְבָרֶךְ אֹתָם Male and female _____ created
_____ , and _____ blessed _____ . (Gen. 5:2)

281

(13) וּמִלֵּאתִי אֶת־הַבַּיִת הַזֶּה כָּבוֹד   And _____ will fill _____ house with glory. (Hag. 2:7)

(14) אֶת־מִסְפַּר יָמֶיךָ אֲמַלֵּא   _____ will fulfil the number of _____ days. (Exod. 23:26)

(15) כָּל־רָעָתָם בַּגִּלְגָּל כִּי־שָׁם שְׂנֵאתִים   All _____ evil is in Gilgal, for there _____ have hated _____. (Hos. 9:15)

(16) וַיֹּאמֶר אָבִיהָ אָמֹר אָמַרְתִּי כִּי־שָׂנֹא שְׂנֵאתָהּ   And _____ father said, "_____ surely said that _____ utterly hated _____." (Judg. 15:2)

(17) יָרֵא אֲנִי אֶת־אֲדֹנִי הַמֶּלֶךְ   _____ fear _____ lord the king. (Dan. 1:10)

(18) לְמַעַן לֹא אֶחֱטָא־לָךְ   In order that _____ might not sin against _____. (Ps. 119:11)

3. Each of the following entries contains a participle from a Lamed 'Alef verb. In the space marked (a) give its stem, in (b) tell whether it is *active* or *passive*, in (c) give its gender and number, and in (d) list its root.

(1) כִּי־הִנְנִי בוֹרֵא שָׁמַיִם חֲדָשִׁים   For behold, I am creating new heavens. (Isa. 65:17)

   (a) _____ (b) _____ (c) _____ (d) _____

(2) הָרֹפֵא לִשְׁבוּרֵי לֵב   the one healing the broken hearted (Ps. 147:3)

   (a) _____ (b) _____ (c) _____ (d) _____

(3) שֹׂנְאֵי טוֹב וְאֹהֲבֵי רָע   those who hate good and love evil (Mic. 3:2)

   (a) _____ (b) _____ (c) _____ (d) _____

(4) הָאַחַת אֲהוּבָה וְהָאַחַת שְׂנוּאָה   the one loved, and the one hated (Deut. 21:15)

   (a) _____ (b) _____ (c) _____ (d) _____

(5) הֲלוֹא־מְשַׂנְאֶיךָ יְהוָה אֶשְׂנָא   O LORD, do I not hate the ones hating you? (Ps. 139:21)

   (a) _____ (b) _____ (c) _____ (d) _____

(6) וְאֶת־יְהוָה אֱלֹהֵי הַשָּׁמַיִם אֲנִי יָרֵא   And the LORD God of the heavens I fear. (Jon. 1:9)

   (a) _____ (b) _____ (c) _____ (d) _____

(7) וְשׁוּלָיו מְלֵאִים אֶת־הַהֵיכָל And his skirts were filling the temple. (Isa. 6:1)

       (a) _____ (b) _____ (c) _____ (d) _____

(8) הוֹי גּוֹי חֹטֵא Woe to the nation that sins (the sinful nation). (Isa. 1:4)

       (a) _____ (b) _____ (c) _____ (d) _____

(9) הַנֶּפֶשׁ הַחֹטֵאת הִיא תָמוּת The soul that sins, it shall die. (Ezek. 18:4)

       (a) _____ (b) _____ (c) _____ (d) _____

(10) תְּהוֹם־אֶל־תְּהוֹם קוֹרֵא Deep calls unto deep. (Ps. 42:8; Eng. 42:7)

       (a) _____ (b) _____ (c) _____ (d) _____

4. Each of the following entries contains a verb form from a Lamed 'Alef verb. In (a) identify the form (perfect, imperfect, or imperative), in (b) give its stem, in (c) its person, gender, and number, and in (d) its root.

(1) קְרָא שְׁמוֹ לֹא עַמִּי Call his name "Not–My–People." (Hos. 1:9)

       (a) _____ (b) _____ (c) _____ (d) _____

(2) לֹא־יִקָּרֵא שִׁמְךָ עוֹד יַעֲקֹב Your name shall no longer be called Jacob. (Gen. 35:10)

       (a) _____ (b) _____ (c) _____ (d) _____

(3) אֲנִי יְהוָה קְרָאתִיךָ בְצֶדֶק I the LORD have called you in righteousness. (Isa. 42:6)

       (a) _____ (b) _____ (c) _____ (d) _____

(4) וַתִּקְרֶאנָה שְׁמוֹ עוֹבֵד הוּא אֲבִי־יִשַׁי אֲבִי דָוִד And they called his name Obed; he was the father of Jesse, the father of David. (Ruth 4:17)

       (a) _____ (b) _____ (c) _____ (d) _____

(5) הַמְצָאתַנִי אֹיְבִי Have you found me, O my enemy? (1 Kgs. 21:20)

       (a) _____ (b) _____ (c) _____ (d) _____

(6) אוּלַי יִמָּצְאוּן שָׁם אַרְבָּעִים Perhaps forty shall be found there. (Gen. 18:29)

       (a) _____ (b) _____ (c) _____ (d) _____

(7) אֲנִי יְהוָה בְּרָאתִיו I the LORD have created it. (Isa. 45:8)

       (a) _____ (b) _____ (c) _____ (d) _____

(8) לֵב טָהוֹר בְּרָא־לִי אֱלֹהִים   Create for me a clean heart, O God!
(Ps. 51:12)

     (a) _____ (b) _____ (c) _____ (d) _____

(9) וְהַבַּיִת יִמָּלֵא עָשָׁן   And the house was filled with smoke. (Isa. 6:4)

     (a) _____ (b) _____ (c) _____ (d) _____

(10) וָאֲמַלֵּא אֹתוֹ רוּחַ אֱלֹהִים   And I have filled him (with) the spirit of God.
(Exod. 31:3)

     (a) _____ (b) _____ (c) _____ (d) _____

(11) וְאֶת־עֵשָׂו שָׂנֵאתִי   But Esau have I hated. (Mal. 1:3)

     (a) _____ (b) _____ (c) _____ (d) _____

(12) חָדְשֵׁיכֶם וּמוֹעֲדֵיכֶם שָׂנְאָה נַפְשִׁי   Your new moon (festivals) and your
appointed feasts my soul hates. (Isa. 1:14)

     (a) _____ (b) _____ (c) _____ (d) _____

5. Practice pronouncing the Hebrew, noting especially Lamed 'Alef verb forms.
Cover the English and practice translating the Hebrew from sight.

(1) כִּי אֵין אָדָם אֲשֶׁר לֹא־יֶחֱטָא   For there is no man who does not sin.
(1 Kgs. 8:46)

(2) וְקָרָא זֶה אֶל־זֶה וְאָמַר קָדוֹשׁ   And this one called unto this one and
קָדוֹשׁ קָדוֹשׁ יְהוָה צְבָאוֹת   said, "Holy, holy, holy is the LORD
of hosts." (Isa. 6:3)

(3) כִּי בֵיתִי בֵּית־תְּפִלָּה יִקָּרֵא   For my house shall be called a house of
לְכָל־הָעַמִּים   prayer for all the peoples. (Isa. 56:7)

(4) וְטָמֵא טָמֵא יִקְרָא   And he shall cry, "Unclean, unclean!"
(Lev. 13:45)

(5) וְהָיָה כֹּל אֲשֶׁר־יִקְרָא בְּשֵׁם   And it shall be that everyone who calls
יְהוָה יִמָּלֵט   upon the name of the LORD shall be
delivered. (Joel 3:5)

(6) דִּרְשׁוּ יְהוָה בְּהִמָּצְאוֹ קְרָאֻהוּ   Seek the LORD in his being found
בִּהְיוֹתוֹ קָרוֹב   (while he may be found); call on him
in his being near (while he is near).
(Isa. 55:6)

(7) וְנֹחַ מָצָא חֵן בְּעֵינֵי יְהוָה   But Noah found favor in the eyes of
the LORD. (Gen. 6:8)

(8) וַיִּמְצָא יוֹסֵף חֵן בְּעֵינָיו   And Joseph found favor in his eyes. (Gen. 39:4)

(9) וּבָעֵת הַהִיא יִמָּלֵט עַמְּךָ כָּל־הַנִּמְצָא כָּתוּב בַּסֵּפֶר   And in that time your people shall be delivered, everyone found written in the book. (Dan. 12:1)

(10) הֲלוֹא אָב אֶחָד לְכֻלָּנוּ הֲלוֹא אֵל אֶחָד בְּרָאָנוּ   Is there not one father to all of us? Did not one God create us? (Mal. 2:10)

(11) וַיִּבְרָא אֱלֹהִים אֶת־הָאָדָם בְּצַלְמוֹ בְּצֶלֶם אֱלֹהִים בָּרָא אֹתוֹ זָכָר וּנְקֵבָה בָּרָא אֹתָם   And God created the man (mankind) in his image; in the image of God he created him; male and female he created them. (Gen. 1:27)

(12) וְלֹא יָדְעוּ כִּי רְפָאתִים   But they did not know that I healed them. (Hos. 11:3)

(13) רְפָאֵנִי יְהוָה וְאֵרָפֵא   Heal me, O LORD, so that I may be healed. (Jer. 17:14)

(14) לֹא־תִשְׂנָא אֶת־אָחִיךָ בִּלְבָבֶךָ וְאָהַבְתָּ לְרֵעֲךָ כָּמוֹךָ אֲנִי יְהוָה   You shall not hate your brother in your heart, but you shall love your neighbor as yourself; I am the LORD. (Lev. 19:17,18)

(15) שִׂנְאוּ־רָע וְאֶהֱבוּ טוֹב   Hate evil, and love good. (Amos 5:15)

VOCABULARY

(1) [חבא]   he hid

(2) טָמֵא   he was unclean

(3) [נבא]   he prophesied

(4) צָמֵא   he was thirsty

(5) קָבַץ   he collected, gathered

(6) קָדַשׁ   he was holy

(7) [שחת]   he destroyed, corrupted

(8) שָׁלֵם   he was whole, complete

(9) כְּלִי   tool, weapon, vessel

(10) נְאֻם   utterance, oracle

(11) סָבִיב   around, surrounding

(12) עֶשֶׂר   ten

(13) עֲשָׂרָה   (f) ten

(14) צֶדֶק   righteousness

(15) צְדָקָה   (f) righteousness

(16) שֶׁבַע   seven

(17) שִׁבְעָה   (f) seven

(18) שַׁעַר   gate

LESSON XXVII

72. Weak Verbs: Lamed He Verbs*

72.1 *Definition*

A Lamed He verb is one whose final root consonant is ה. There is evidence, however, that at an earlier stage in the development of the language the final root consonant was י (yod), which later evolved into ה. This earlier yod reappears in many of the forms of Lamed He verbs.

72.2 *A List of Some of the Most Frequently Occurring Lamed He Verbs*

(1) Regular Lamed He verbs

(a) בָּכָה   he wept

(b) בָּנָה   he built

(c) גָּלָה   he uncovered, revealed, went into exile

(d) זָנָה   he committed adultery or fornication

(e) כָּלָה   he was completed, finished

(f) כָּסָה   he covered, concealed

(g) פָּדָה   he redeemed, ransomed

(h) פָּנָה   he turned, prepared

(i) [צִוָּה]   (Pi‛el) he commanded

(j) צָפָה   he kept watch, spied

(k) קָנָה   he took possession, bought, acquired

(l) רָבָה   he was many, became numerous, multiplied

(m) שָׁתָה   he drank

(n) רָצָה   he was pleased

(2) Doubly Weak Lamed He verbs

(a) אָבָה   he was willing

(b) אָפָה   he baked

(c) הָיָה   he was

(d) חָזָה   he saw (as in a vision)

(e) חָיָה   he lived

(f) חָלָה   he was sick, weak

(g) חָנָה   he encamped

(h) חָרָה   it (anger) was hot, burned

(i) [ידה]   he praised, thanked, confessed

(j) יָרָה   he taught

(k) נָטָה   he stretched forth

(l) [נכה]   he smote, killed

(m) עָלָה   he went up

(n) עָנָה   (#1) he answered, replied

(o) עָנָה   (#2) he was bowed down, afflicted

(p) עָשָׂה   he did, made

(q) רָאָה   he saw

(r) רָעָה   he fed, tended, shepherded

(s) [שחה]   he bowed down, worshipped, confessed

---

*Refer to Verb Chart 7, pp. 412f., for the conjugation of the Lamed He verb.

72.3 *Distinctive Characteristics of Lamed He Verbs*

(1) A remarkably uniform pattern of stem vowels can be observed in all Lamed He verb forms without afformatives.

(a) All perfects without affirmatives end in הָ .

(b) All imperfects without afformatives end in הֶ .

(c) All imperatives without afformatives end in הֵ .

(d) All infinitives construct drop final ה together with the vowel that precedes it and replace them with וֹת.

(e) Infinitives absolutes end either in הֹ (ḥolem + he) (Qal, Nifʻal, Piʻel, Puʻal, and Hitpaʻel stems), or הֵ (ṣere + he) (Hifʻil, Hofʻal, and sometimes Piʻel stems).

(f) All masculine singular participles (except Qal passive) end in הֶ (sᵉgol + he), which is changed to הֵ (ṣere + he) in the construct state.

(g) Qal passive participle (ms) is patterned after the strong verb, except that yod (י) takes the place of the final he (ה). Thus בָּנוּה becomes בָּנוּי .

The synopsis of בָּנָה , "he built," illustrates the changes in Lamed He forms without afformatives.

Synopsis

	Qal	Nifʻal	Piʻel	Puʻal	Hitpaʻel	Hifʻil	Hofʻal
Perf. 3 ms	בָּנָה	נִבְנָה	בִּנָּה	בֻּנָּה	הִתְבַּנָּה	הִבְנָה	הָבְנָה
Impf. 3 ms	יִבְנֶה	יִבָּנֶה	יְבַנֶּה	יְבֻנֶּה	יִתְבַּנֶּה	יַבְנֶה	יָבְנֶה
Impv. 2 ms	בְּנֵה	הִבָּנֵה	בַּנֵּה		הִתְבַּנֵּה	הַבְנֵה	
Inf. Const.	בְּנוֹת	הִבָּנוֹת	בַּנּוֹת	בֻּנּוֹת	הִתְבַּנּוֹת	הַבְנוֹת	הָבְנוֹת
Inf. Abs.	בָּנֹה	נִבְנֹה	בַּנֹּה	בֻּנֹּה	הִתְבַּנֹּה	הַבְנֵה	הָבְנֵה
Part. Act. ms	בּוֹנֶה		מְבַנֶּה		מִתְבַּנֶּה	מַבְנֶה	
Part. Pass. ms	בָּנוּי	נִבְנֶה		מְבֻנֶּה			מָבְנֶה

(2) Uniform changes also take place when afformatives or pronominal suffixes are added to Lamed He verb forms. Verb forms with *vocalic* afformatives undergo the following changes.

(a) The perfect 3 fs in all stems of Lamed He verbs is formed by substituting the old feminine תּ for the final ה of the verb root and adding הָ, the 3 fs afformative.

Examples of Perfect 3 fs forms of בָּנָה

Qal	בָּנְתָה	becomes	בָּנְתָה
Nifʿal	נִבְנְתָה	becomes	נִבְנְתָה
Piʿel	בִּנְּתָה	becomes	בִּנְּתָה
Puʿal	בֻּנְּתָה	becomes	בֻּנְּתָה
Hitpaʿel	הִתְבַּנְּתָה	becomes	הִתְבַּנְּתָה
Hifʿil	הִבְנְתָה	becomes	הִבְנְתָה
Hofʿal	הָבְנְתָה	becomes	הָבְנְתָה

(b) All other forms with vocalic afformatives are simply shortened by the dropping of ה together with the vowel or vocal sheva that precedes it. This applies to all stems of the verb and involves the shortening of all perfects 3 cp, all imperfects 2 fs, 3 mp, and 2 mp, and all imperatives 2 fs and 2 mp.

Examples:

Qal Perfect 3 cp	בָּנְהוּ	becomes	בָּנוּ
Nifʿal Perfect 3 cp	נִבְנְהוּ	becomes	נִבְנוּ
Piʿel Perfect 3 cp	בִּנְּהוּ	becomes	בִּנּוּ
Qal Imperfect 2 fs	תִּבְנְהִי	becomes	תִּבְנִי
Qal Imperative 2 mp	בָּנְהוּ	becomes	בְּנוּ

(2) Lamed He verb forms with *consonantal* aformatives consistently drop the ה of the verb root and substitute י in its place. This י in turn combines with the preceding vowel to form a diphthong.

(a) This results in a יִ (ḥireq-yod) before perfect consonantal afformative in all *active* stems (Qal, Piʿel, Hitpaʾel, Hifʿil).

Examples:

	Qal	Piʿel	Hifʿil
Perfect 2 ms	בָּנִיתָ	בִּנִּיתָ	הִבְנִיתָ
Perfect 2 fs	בָּנִית	בִּנִּית	הִבְנִית
Perfect 1 cs	בָּנִיתִי	בִּנִּיתִי	הִבְנִיתִי
Perfect 2 mp	בְּנִיתֶם	בִּנִּיתֶם	הִבְנִיתֶם
Perfect 2 fp	בְּנִיתֶן	בִּנִּיתֶן	הִבְנִיתֶן
Perfect 1 cp	בָּנִינוּ	בִּנִּינוּ	הִבְנִינוּ

(b) The vowel before perfect consonantal afformatives in all *passive* stems (Nifʿal, Puʿal, and Hofʿal) is יִ (ṣere-yod).

Examples:

	Nifʿal	Puʿal	Hofʿal
Perfect 2 ms	נִבְנֵיתָ	בֻּנֵּיתָ	הָבְנֵיתָ
Perfect 2 fs	נִבְנֵית	בֻּנֵּית	הָבְנֵית
Perfect 1 cs	נִבְנֵיתִי	בֻּנֵּיתִי	הָבְנֵיתִי
Perfect 2 mp	נִבְנֵיתֶם	בֻּנֵּיתֶם	הָבְנֵיתֶם
Perfect 2 fp	נִבְנֵיתֶן	בֻּנֵּיתֶן	הָבְנֵיתֶן
Perfect 1 cp	נִבְנֵינוּ	בֻּנֵּינוּ	הָבְנֵינוּ

(c) The vowel before imperfect and imperative consonantal afformatives in all stems is יֶ (sᵉgol-yod). This involves all forms with נָה endings (imperfect 3 fp and 2 fp; imperative 2 fp).

Examples:

	Qal	Nifʿal	Hifʿil
Imperfect 3 fp, 2 fp	תִּבְנֶינָה	תִּבָּנֶינָה	תַּבְנֶינָה
Imperative 2 fp	בְּנֶינָה	הִבָּנֶינָה	הַבְנֶינָה

72.4 *Inflection of the Qal Stem of* גָּלָה, *"he uncovered, revealed, went into exile"*

	Perfect		Imperfect		Imperative
3 ms	גָּלָה	3 mp	יִגְלֶה		
3 fs	גָּלְתָה	3 fp	תִּגְלֶה		
2 ms	גָּלִיתָ	2 mp	תִּגְלֶה	2 ms	גְּלֵה
2 fs	גָּלִית	2 fp	תִּגְלִי	2 fs	גְּלִי
1 cs	גָּלִיתִי	1 cp	אֶגְלֶה		
		3 mp	יִגְלוּ		
3 cp	גָּלוּ	3 fp	תִּגְלֶינָה		
2 mp	גְּלִיתֶם	2 mp	תִּגְלוּ	2 mp	גְּלוּ
2 fp	גְּלִיתֶן	2 fp	תִּגְלֶינָה	2 fp	גְּלֶינָה
1 cp	גָּלִינוּ	1 cp	נִגְלֶה		

Infinitive Construct	גְּלוֹת	Participle Active ms	גֹּלֶה
Infinitive Absolute	גָּלֹה	Participle Passive ms	גָּלוּי

72.5 *Inflection of the Qal Stem of* אָבָה, *"he was willing," a doubly weak verb (Pe ʾAlef and Lamed He)*

	Perfect		Imperfect		Imperative
3 ms	אָבָה	3 ms	יֹאבֶה		
3 fs	אָבְתָה	3 fs	תֹּאבֶה		
2 ms	אָבִיתָ	2 ms	תֹּאבֶה	2 ms	אֲבֵה
2 fs	אָבִית	2 fs	תֹּאבִי	2 fs	אֲבִי
1 cs	אָבִיתִי	1 cs	אֹבֶה		
3 cp	אָבוּ	3 mp	יֹאבוּ		
		3 fp	תֹּאבֶינָה		
2 mp	אֲבִיתֶם	2 mp	תֹּאבוּ	2 mp	אֲבוּ
2 fp	אֲבִיתֶן	2 fp	תֹּאבֶינָה	2 fp	אֲבֶינָה
1 cp	אָבִינוּ	1 cp	נֹאבֶה		

Infinitive Construct	אֲבוֹת	Participle Active ms	אֹבֶה
Infinitive Absolute	אָבֹה	Participle Passive ms	אָבוּי

72.6 *Inflection of the Qal Stem of* עָשָׂה, *"he did, made," a doubly weak verb (Pe Guttural, Lamed He)*

	Perfect		Imperfect		Imperative
3 ms	עָשָׂה	3 ms	יַעֲשֶׂה		
3 fs	עָשְׂתָה	3 fs	תַּעֲשֶׂה		
2 ms	עָשִׂיתָ	2 ms	תַּעֲשֶׂה	2 ms	עֲשֵׂה
2 fs	עָשִׂית	2 fs	תַּעֲשִׂי	2 fs	עֲשִׂי
1 cs	עָשִׂיתִי	1 cs	אֶעֱשֶׂה		
3 cp	עָשׂוּ	3 mp	יַעֲשׂוּ		
		3 fp	תַּעֲשֶׂינָה		
2 mp	עֲשִׂיתֶם	2 mp	תַּעֲשׂוּ	2 mp	עֲשׂוּ
2 fp	עֲשִׂיתֶן	2 fp	תַּעֲשֶׂינָה	2 fp	עֲשֶׂינָה
1 cp	עָשִׂינוּ	1 cp	נַעֲשֶׂה		

Infinitive Construct	עֲשׂוֹת	Participle Active ms	עוֹשֶׂה
Infinitive Absolute	עָשׂוֹ	Participle Active mp	עוֹשִׂים
	עָשֹׂה	Participle Active fs	עוֹשָׂה
		Participle Active fp	עוֹשׂוֹת
		Participle Passive ms	עָשׂוּי

72.7 *Inflection of* הָיָה, *"he was," in the Qal Stem and Nifʻal Stem (attested occurrences only)*

Qal

	Perfect		Imperfect		Imperative
3 ms	הָיָה	3 ms	יִהְיֶה		
3 fs	הָיְתָה	3 fs	תִּהְיֶה		
2 ms	הָיִיתָ	2 ms	תִּהְיֶה	2 ms	הֱיֵה
2 fs	הָיִית	2 fs	תִּהְיִי	2 fs	הֲיִי *(once)*
1 cs	הָיִיתִי	1 cs	אֶהְיֶה		
3 cp	הָיוּ	3 mp	יִהְיוּ		
		3 fp	תִּהְיֶינָה		
2 mp	הֱיִיתֶם	2 mp	תִּהְיוּ	2 mp	הֱיוּ
2 fp	הֱיִיתֶן	2 fp	תִּהְיֶינָה	2 fp	הֱיֶינָה
1 cp	הָיִינוּ	1 cp	נִהְיֶה		

Infinitive Construct	הֱיוֹת	Participle Active ms	הוֹיֶה
Infinitive Absolute	הָיוֹ	Participle Active fs	הוֹיָה
	הָיֹה		

Nifʻal Perfect

3 ms	נִהְיָה
3 fs	נִהְיְתָה
2 ms	נִהְיֵיתָ
1 cs	נִהְיֵיתִי

Note: There are no other attested forms of this important verb in this or any other verb stem.

291

72.8 Imperfects of Lamed He verbs that have no afformatives, and thus have ה as their final consonant, often appear in apocopated (shortened) form. This occurs when they function as jussives (cf. XV.41, pp. 131f.), or when they are prefixed with vav consecutive (cf. XVI.43, pp. 145f.). Apocopation involves the loss of the final ה and the vowel that precedes it. Other vocalization changes may also be demanded by the shortening of the imperfect forms. The following table illustrates the way apocopation takes place in representative Lamed He verbs.

	Root	Meaning	Stem/Person	Imperfect	With ַו	Jussive	With וְ
(1)	בָּנָה	he built	Qal 3 ms	יִבְנֶה	וַיִּבֶן	יִבֶן	וְיִבֶן
(2)	גָּלָה	he revealed	Qal 3 ms	יִגְלֶה	וַיִּגֶל	יִגֶל	וְיִגֶל
(3)	פָּנָה	he turned	Qal 3 ms	יִפְנֶה	וַיִּפֶן	יִפֶן	וְיִפֶן
(4)	רָבָה	he was many	Qal 3 ms	יִרְבֶּה	וַיִּרֶב	יִרֶב	וְיִרֶב
			Hif. 3 ms	יַרְבֶּה	וַיֶּרֶב	יֶרֶב	וְיֶרֶב
(5)	כָּסָה	he covered	Pi‘el 3 ms	יְכַסֶּה	וַיְכַס		
(6)	בָּכָה	he wept	Qal 3 ms	יִבְכֶּה	וַיֵּבְךְּ	יֵבְךְּ	
(7)	שָׁתָה	he drank	Qal 3 ms	יִשְׁתֶּה	וַיֵּשְׁתְּ	יֵשְׁתְּ	וְיֵשְׁתְּ
(8)	הָיָה	he was	Qal 3 ms	יִהְיֶה	וַיְהִי	יְהִי	וִיהִי
			Qal 2 ms	תִּהְיֶה	וַתְּהִי	תְּהִי	וּתְהִי
			Qal 1 cs	אֶהְיֶה	וָאֱהִי		וֶאֱהִי
(9)	חָיָה	he lived	Qal 3 ms	יִחְיֶה	וַיְחִי	יְחִי	וִיחִי
(10)	רָאָה	he saw	Qal 3 ms	יִרְאֶה	וַיַּרְא	יֵרֶא	וְיֵרֶא
			Nif. 3 ms	יֵרָאֶה	וַיֵּרָא	יֵרָא	וְיֵרָא
			Hif. 3 ms	יַרְאֶה	וַיַּרְא		
(11)	עָלָה	he went up	Qal 3 ms	יַעֲלֶה	וַיַּעַל	יַעַל	וְיַעַל
			Hif. 3 ms	יַעֲלֶה	וַיַּעַל	יַעַל	וְיַעַל
(12)	עָנָה	he answered	Qal 3 ms	יַעֲנֶה	וַיַּעַן	יַעַן	
(13)	עָשָׂה	he made	Qal 3 ms	יַעֲשֶׂה	וַיַּעַשׂ	יַעַשׂ	וְיַעַשׂ
			Qal 2 ms	תַּעֲשֶׂה	וַתַּעַשׂ	תַּעַשׂ	
			Qal 1 cs	אֶעֱשֶׂה	וָאַעַשׂ		
(14)	[צוה]	he commanded	Pi‘el 3 ms	יְצַוֶּה	וַיְצַו	יְצַו	

Use the following as a pattern for the translation of the forms above.

בָּנָה			הָיָה		
(a)	יִבְנֶה	he will build	(a)	יִהְיֶה	he will be
(b)	וַיִּבֶן	and he built	(b)	וַיְהִי	and he (it) was
(c)	יִבֶן	let him build	(c)	יְהִי	let there be
(d)	וְיִבֶן	and let him build	(d)	וִיהִי	and let there be

EXERCISES

1. Each of the following entries contains a Lamed He verb form. In the space marked (a) give its stem, in (b) its form (perfect, imperfect, or imperative), in (c) its person, gender, and number, and in (d) its root. *Ignore all verb forms that are not Lamed He.*

(1)   וַיֹּאמְרוּ כֹּל אֲשֶׁר־דִּבֶּר יְהוָה נַעֲשֶׂה וְנִשְׁמָע   And they said, "All that the LORD has spoken we will do, and we will obey (listen)." (Exod. 24:7)

(a) _____ (b) _____ (c) _____ (d) _____

(2)   בְּטַח בַּיהוָה וַעֲשֵׂה־טוֹב   Trust in the LORD and do good. (Ps. 37:3)

(a) _____ (b) _____ (c) _____ (d) _____

(3)   לָמָּה לֹא־בְנִיתֶם לִי בֵּית אֲרָזִים   Why have you not built for me a house of cedar (cedars)? (2 Sam. 7:7)

(a) _____ (b) _____ (c) _____ (d) _____

(4)   וַיַּעֲלוּ עֹלוֹת וּשְׁלָמִים   And they offered up (caused to go up) whole burnt offerings and peace offerings. (Judg. 21:4)

(a) _____ (b) _____ (c) _____ (d) _____

(5)   וַיִּבֶן נֹחַ מִזְבֵּחַ לַיהוָה   And Noah built an altar to the LORD. (Gen. 8:20)

(a) _____ (b) _____ (c) _____ (d) _____

(6)   בֵּיתִי יִבָּנֶה בָּהּ   My house shall be built in her (it). (Zech. 1:16)

(a) _____ (b) _____ (c) _____ (d) _____

(7)   כֻּלָּם לְדַרְכָּם פָּנוּ   They have all turned to their (own) way. (Isa. 56:11)

   (a) _____ (b) _____ (c) _____ (d) _____

(8)   בְּנוֹת יִשְׂרָאֵל אֶל־שָׁאוּל בְּכֶינָה   Daughters of Israel, weep over Saul.
   (2 Sam. 1:24)

   (a) _____ (b) _____ (c) _____ (d) _____

(9)   צִיּוֹן בְּמִשְׁפָּט תִּפָּדֶה   Zion shall be redeemed in justice. (Isa. 1:27)

   (a) _____ (b) _____ (c) _____ (d) _____

(10)   וְנִגְלָה כְּבוֹד יְהוָה   And the glory of the LORD shall be revealed.
   (Isa. 40:5)

   (a) _____ (b) _____ (c) _____ (d) _____

(11)   וְרָאוּ כָל־בָּשָׂר יַחְדָּו   And all flesh shall see it together. (Isa. 40:5)

   (a) _____ (b) _____ (c) _____ (d) _____

(12)   אֶרֶץ אַל־תְּכַסִּי דָמִי   O earth, do not cover my blood! (Job 16:18)

   (a) _____ (b) _____ (c) _____ (d) _____

(13)   וְיִתְכַּסּוּ שַׂקִּים הָאָדָם וְהַבְּהֵמָה   And let them cover themselves with
   sackcloth, both men and cattle. (Jon. 3:8)

   (a) _____ (b) _____ (c) _____ (d) _____

(14)   כְּרֹעֶה עֶדְרוֹ יִרְעֶה   Like a shepherd he will feed his flock. (Isa. 40:11)

   (a) _____ (b) _____ (c) _____ (d) _____

(15)   לֶחֶם לֹא אָכַלְתִּי וּמַיִם לֹא שָׁתִיתִי   I did not eat bread, and I did not
   drink water. (Deut. 9:9)

   (a) _____ (b) _____ (c) _____ (d) _____

(16)   וַתֹּאמֶר שְׁתֵה אֲדֹנִי   And she said, "Drink, my lord." (Gen. 24:18)

   (a) _____ (b) _____ (c) _____ (d) _____

(17)   וְתֵרָאֶה הַיַּבָּשָׁה   And let dry land appear (be seen). (Gen. 1:9)

   (a) _____ (b) _____ (c) _____ (d) _____

(18)   יְהוָה הֶעֱלִיתָ מִן־שְׁאוֹל נַפְשִׁי   O LORD, you have brought up (caused
   to go up) my soul from Sheol. (Ps. 30:4; Eng. 30:3)

   (a) _____ (b) _____ (c) _____ (d) _____

2. Each of the following entries contains a Qal form of הָיָה, "he was." In the space marked (a) identify each form (perfect, imperfect, etc.), in (b) give its person, gender, and number, and if the verb form has a prefixed vav, indicate in (c) whether it is a vav conjunction (vav conj.) or a vav consecutive (vav cons.). *Ignore verb forms not derived from* הָיָה.

(1)   וְהָאָרֶץ הָיְתָה תֹהוּ וָבֹהוּ   Now the earth was without form and empty.
(Gen. 1:2)   (a) _____   (b) _____

(2)   וַיֹּאמֶר אֱלֹהִים יְהִי אוֹר   And god said, "Let there be light." (Gen. 1:3)
                              (a) _____   (b) _____

(3)   וַיְהִי־אוֹר   And there was light. (Gen. 1:3)
              (a) _____ (b) _____ (c) _____

(4)   וְהָיוּ לְאֹתֹת וּלְמוֹעֲדִים וּלְיָמִים וְשָׁנִים   And let them be for signs and for appointed seasons, and for days and years. (Gen. 1:14)
              (a) _____ (b) _____ (c) _____

(5)   לֹא־טוֹב הֱיוֹת הָאָדָם לְבַדּוֹ   It is not good for the man to be alone.
(Gen. 2:18)   (a) _____

(6)   וְהָיֵה־לָּנוּ לְאָב וּלְכֹהֵן   And be to us a father and a priest. (Judg. 18:19)
              (a) _____ (b) _____ (c) _____

(7)   וַיֹּאמֶר אֱלֹהִים אֶל־מֹשֶׁה אֶהְיֶה אֲשֶׁר אֶהְיֶה   And God said to Moses, "I am who I am" (or, "I will be who I will be"). (Exod. 3:14)
                              (a) _____   (b) _____

(8)   תְּהִי נָא יָדְךָ בִּי וּבְבֵית אָבִי   I pray, let your hand be upon me and upon my father's house. (2 Sam. 24:17)   (a) _____   (b) _____

(9)   כִּי־תִהְיֶינָה לְאִישׁ שְׁתֵּי נָשִׁים   if there shall be two wives to a man (if a man has two wives) (Deut. 21:15) (a) _____ (b) _____

(10)   וַיִּהְיוּ שְׁנֵיהֶם עֲרוּמִּים הָאָדָם וְאִשְׁתּוֹ   And the two of them were naked, the man and his wife. (Gen. 2:25)
              (a) _____ (b) _____ (c) _____

(11)   נְטֵה יָדְךָ עַל־הַשָּׁמַיִם   Stretch out your hand toward the heavens.
(Exod. 10:21)   (a) _____ (b) _____ (c) _____

(12)   וְהָיוּ לְבָשָׂר אֶחָד   And they shall become (be) one flesh. (Gen. 2:24)
              (a) _____ (b) _____ (c) _____

(13) וְאַתֶּם תִּהְיוּ־לִי מַמְלֶכֶת כֹּהֲנִים וְגוֹי קָדוֹשׁ And you shall be to me
a kingdom of priests and a holy nation. (Exod. 19:6)

(a) _____ (b) _____

(14) הֱיֵה־עֹזֵר לִי Be my helper (be a helper to me). (Ps. 30:11; Eng. 30:10)

(a) _____ (b) _____

(15) הִתְחַזְּקוּ וִהְיוּ לַאֲנָשִׁים Make yourselves strong and be men! (1 Sam. 4:9)

(a) _____ (b) _____ (c) _____

(16) וַתְּהִי־לִי לְאִשָּׁה And she became my wife. (Gen. 20:12)

(a) _____ (b) _____ (c) _____

(17) לְמַעַן תִּהְיֶה תּוֹרַת יְהוָה בְּפִיךָ In order that the law of the LORD
may be in your mouth. (Exod. 13:9) (a) _____ (b) _____

(18) לִהְיוֹת־שְׁמִי שָׁם עַד־עוֹלָם that my name may be there for ever
(2 Chr. 7:16) (a) _____

3. Each of the following entries contains a participle of a Lamed He verb.
Underscore the correct form for each entry.

(1) הַבַּיִת הַזֶּה אֲשֶׁר־אַתָּה (בֹּנֶה / בָּנָה)
the house which you are building (1 Kgs. 6:12)

(2) וַיֹּאמֶר חֲזָאֵל מַדּוּעַ אֲדֹנִי (בֹּכֶה / בּוֹכִים)
And Hazael said, "Why is my lord weeping?" (2 Kgs. 8:12)

(3) רָחֵל (מְבַכֶּה / מְבַכָּה) עַל־בָּנֶיהָ
Rachel weeping for her children (Jer. 31:15)

(4) וְיַעֲקֹב (רֹעֶה / רֹעִים) אֶת־צֹאן לָבָן
And Jacob was tending the flock of Laban. (Gen. 30:36)

(5) מָה־אַתָּה (רֹאָה / רֹאֶה) עָמוֹס
What are you seeing, Amos? (Amos 7:8)

(6) כַּאֲשֶׁר אַתֶּם (רֹאִים / רֹאֶה) בְּעֵינֵיכֶם
as you are seeing with your (own) eyes (2 Chr. 29:8)

(7) וַיֹּאמֶר אֶל־הַשֹּׁפְטִים רְאוּ מָה־אַתֶּם (עֹשֶׂה / עֹשִׂים)
And he said to the judges, "See (consider) what you are doing." (2 Chr. 19:6)

(8) עֲבָדֶיךָ יַעֲשׂוּ כַּאֲשֶׁר אֲדֹנִי (מְצַוֶּה / מְצַוִּים)
Your servants will do as my lord commands. (Num. 32:25)

(9) מִי זֹאת (עֹלֶה / עֹלָה) מִן־הַמִּדְבָּר

Who is this going up from the desert? (Song of Sol. 3:6)

(10) וְהִנֵּה מִן־הַיְאֹר (עֹלִים / עֹלֹת) שֶׁבַע פָּרוֹת

And behold, seven cows were coming up out of the Nile (river). (Gen. 41:2)

(11) וַיְהִי שְׁמוּאֵל (מַעֲלֶה / מַעֲלָה) הָעוֹלָה

And Samuel was offering up the whole burnt offering. (1 Sam. 7:10)

(12) כִּי אֲנִי יְהוָה (הַמַּעֲלֶה / הַמַּעֲלִים) אֶתְכֶם מֵאֶרֶץ מִצְרַיִם

For I (am) the LORD, the one bringing you up from the land of Egypt. (Lev. 11:45)

(13) וַיִּהְיוּ (מַעֲלִים / מַעֲלוֹת) עֹלוֹת בְּבֵית־יְהוָה תָּמִיד

And they were offering up whole burnt offerings in the house of the LORD continually. (2 Chr. 24:14)

(14) וַיֹּאמֶר אֲלֵיהֶם הַכֹּהֵן מָה אַתֶּם (עֹשֶׂה / עֹשִׂים)

And the priest said to them, "What are you doing?" (Judg. 18:18)

(15) הוֹי (הַמַּרְבֶּה / הַמַּרְבָּה) לֹא־לוֹ

Woe to the one heaping up (making much, multiplying) what is not his own. (Hab. 2:6)

4. Supply the correct pronouns in the translations of the Hebrew in the following examples of Lamed He verbs.

(1) וַיֹּאמְרוּ אֵלָיו מַה־זֹּאת עָשִׂיתָ And _____ said to _____, "What is this _____ have done?" (Jon. 1:10)

(2) וְאָמְרוּ לֶהָרִים כַּסּוּנוּ And _____ shall say to the mountains, "Cover _____!" (Hos. 10:8)

(3) וָאֹמַר אֲלֵיהֶם שְׁתוּ־יָיִן And _____ said to _____, "Drink wine!" (Jer. 35:5)

(4) וַיַּרְא אֹתָם אֶת־בֶּן־הַמֶּלֶךְ And _____ showed _____ the king's son. (2 Kgs. 11:4)

(5) וַיַּרְאוּם אֶת־פְּרִי הָאָרֶץ And _____ showed _____ the fruit of the land. (Num. 13:26)

(6) וַיֹּאמַר הַרְאֵנִי נָא אֶת־כְּבֹדֶךָ And _____ said, "Show _____ _____ glory." (Exod. 33:18)

297

(7)   לֹא־תִרְאֶה אֶת־פָּנַי _____ shall not see _____ face.
(2 Sam. 3:13)

(8)   לַעֲשׂוֹת כְּכֹל אֲשֶׁר צִוִּיתִיךָ to do according to all that _____
commanded _____ (1 Kgs. 9:4)

(9)   וּכְבוֹדוֹ עָלַיִךְ יֵרָאֶה And _____ glory will be seen upon _____.
(Isa. 60:2)

(10)   עָשִׂיתִי כְּכֹל אֲשֶׁר צִוִּיתָנִי _____ have done according to all that
_____ commanded _____. (Deut. 26:14)

(11)   וְלָהּ אָמַר עֲלִי לְשָׁלוֹם לְבֵיתֵךְ And _____ said to _____,
"Go up in peace to _____ house." (1 Sam. 25:35)

(12)   וַיֹּאמְרוּ זֶה אֱלֹהֶיךָ אֲשֶׁר הֶעֶלְךָ מִמִּצְרָיִם And _____ said, "This is
_____ God who brought _____ up from Egypt." (Neh. 9:18)

(13)   וַיֹּאמְרוּ אֵלֶּה אֱלֹהֶיךָ אֲשֶׁר הֶעֱלוּךָ מֵאֶרֶץ מִצְרָיִם And _____ said,
"_____ are _____ gods which brought _____ up from the land
of Egypt." (Exod. 32:4)

(14)   וָאֶקְרָא לָהֶם וְלֹא עָנוּ And _____ called to _____ but
_____ did not answer. (Jer. 35:17)

(15)   עַמִּי מֶה־עָשִׂיתִי לְךָ עֲנֵה בִי O _____ people, what have _____
done to _____? Answer _____! (Mic. 6:3)

(16)   עֲשֵׂה־לָנוּ אֱלֹהִים אֲשֶׁר יֵלְכוּ לְפָנֵינוּ Make for _____ gods which
shall go before _____. (Exod. 32:1)

(17)   וַיֹּאמֶר לוֹ עֲשֵׂה כָּל־אֲשֶׁר בִּלְבָבֶךָ And _____ said to _____,
"Do all that is in _____ heart." (1 Sam. 14:7)

(18)   וְלֹא אָבִיתִי לִשְׁלֹחַ יָדִי בִּמְשִׁיחַ יְהוָה And _____ was not willing
to put forth _____ hand against the LORD's anointed. (1 Sam. 26:23)

5. Practice pronouncing the Hebrew, noting especially Lamed He verbs. Cover the English translation and practice translating from sight.

(1)   וַיַּעֲשֵׂהוּ כְּלִי אַחֵר כַּאֲשֶׁר   And he made it another vessel, as it was
יָשַׁר בְּעֵינֵי הַיּוֹצֵר לַעֲשׂוֹת   right in the eyes of the potter to do.
(Jer. 18:4)

(2) וַיֹּאמֶר יַעֲקֹב אֶל־יוֹסֵף
אֵל שַׁדַּי נִרְאָה־אֵלַי
בְּאֶרֶץ כְּנַעַן וַיְבָרֶךְ אֹתִי

And Jacob said to Joseph, "El Shaddai appeared to me in the land of Canaan and blessed me." (Gen. 48:3)

(3) וְהַבַּיִת אֲשֶׁר־אֲנִי בוֹנֶה
גָּדוֹל כִּי־גָדוֹל אֱלֹהֵינוּ
מִכָּל־הָאֱלֹהִים

And the house which I am building is great, for greater is our God than all the gods. (2 Chr. 2:4)

(4) וָאֶבְחַר בִּירוּשָׁלַם לִהְיוֹת
שְׁמִי שָׁם וָאֶבְחַר בְּדָוִיד
לִהְיוֹת עַל־עַמִּי יִשְׂרָאֵל

And I chose Jerusalem so that my name might be there; and I chose David so that he might be over my people Israel. (2 Chr. 6:6)

(5) וַיֹּאמְרוּ נִבְנֶה־לָּנוּ עִיר
וּמִגְדָּל וְרֹאשׁוֹ בַשָּׁמַיִם
וְנַעֲשֶׂה־לָּנוּ שֵׁם

And they said, "Let us build for ourselves a city, and a tower whose top is in the heavens, and let us make for ourselves a name." (Gen. 11:4)

(6) כֻּלָּנוּ כַּצֹּאן תָּעִינוּ
אִישׁ לְדַרְכּוֹ פָּנִינוּ וַיהוָה
הִפְגִּיעַ בּוֹ אֵת עֲוֹן כֻּלָּנוּ

All of us like a flock have wandered; we have turned each to his own way; but the LORD has caused the iniquity of all of us to strike him. (Isa. 53:6)

(7) וַיַּעֲנוּ אֶת־יְהוֹשֻׁעַ לֵאמֹר
כֹּל אֲשֶׁר־צִוִּיתָנוּ נַעֲשֶׂה

And they answered Joshua saying, "All that you commanded us we will do." (Josh. 1:16)

(8) וְהָיוּ־לִי לְעָם וְאָנֹכִי
אֶהְיֶה לָהֶם לֵאלֹהִים

And they shall be to me for a people, and I will be to them for God. (Jer. 24:7)

(9) כֹּה תֹאמַר לִבְנֵי יִשְׂרָאֵל
אֶהְיֶה שְׁלָחַנִי אֲלֵיכֶם

Thus you shall say to the sons of Israel, "I AM has sent me to you." (Exod. 3:14)

(10) יְהִי יְהוָה אֱלֹהֵינוּ עִמָּנוּ
כַּאֲשֶׁר הָיָה עִם־אֲבֹתֵינוּ

May the LORD our God be with us, according as he was with our fathers. (1 Kgs. 8:57)

(11) וַיְחַזֵּק יְהוָה אֶת־לֵב
פַּרְעֹה וְלֹא אָבָה לְשַׁלְּחָם

And the LORD hardened (strengthened) the heart of Pharaoh, and he was not willing to let them go (to send them). (Exod. 10:27)

(12) כִּי תִמָּלֵא הָאָרֶץ לָדַעַת
אֶת־כְּבוֹד יְהוָה כַּמַּיִם
יְכַסּוּ עַל־יָם

For the earth shall be filled with the knowledge of the glory of the LORD as the waters cover the sea. (Hab. 2:14)

(13)   וַיַּרְא אֱלֹהִים אֶת־כָּל־אֲשֶׁר
עָשָׂה וְהִנֵּה־טוֹב מְאֹד

And God saw all that he had made, and behold, (it was) very good. (Gen. 1:31)

(14)   וָאֵרָא אֶל־אַבְרָהָם
אֶל־יִצְחָק וְאֶל־יַעֲקֹב
בְּאֵל שַׁדָּי

And I appeared (was seen) unto Abraham, unto Isaac, and unto Jacob as in El Shaddai. (Exod. 6:3)

(15)   עַל נַהֲרוֹת בָּבֶל שָׁם
יָשַׁבְנוּ גַּם־בָּכִינוּ בְּזָכְרֵנוּ
אֶת־צִיּוֹן

By the rivers of Babylon, there we sat down; also we wept when we remembered Zion. (Ps. 137:1)

(16)   וַיְכַל אֱלֹהִים בַּיּוֹם הַשְּׁבִיעִי
מְלַאכְתּוֹ אֲשֶׁר עָשָׂה וַיִּשְׁבֹּת
בַּיּוֹם הַשְּׁבִיעִי מִכָּל־מְלַאכְתּוֹ
אֲשֶׁר עָשָׂה

And God finished on the seventh day his work that he had done, and he rested on the seventh day from all his work that he had done. (Gen. 2:2)

(17)   בִּשְׁתַּיִם יְכַסֶּה פָנָיו
וּבִשְׁתַּיִם יְכַסֶּה רַגְלָיו

With two he covered his face, and with two he covered his feet. (Isa. 6:2)

(18)   וְרָאוּ כָּל־אַפְסֵי־אָרֶץ
אֵת יְשׁוּעַת אֱלֹהֵינוּ

And all the ends of the earth shall see the salvation of our God. (Isa. 52:10)

VOCABULARY

(1)   בָּכָה   he wept

(2)   זָנָה   he committed adultery, fornication

(3)   חָזָה   he saw (as in a vision)

(4)   חָלָה   he was sick, weak

(5)   חָנָה   he encamped

(6)   חָרָה   it (anger) was hot, burned

(7)   יָרָה   he taught

(8)   כָּסָה   he covered, concealed

(9)   עָנָה   he was bowed down, afflicted

(10)   צָפָה   he kept watch, spied

(11)   קָנָה   he took possession, acquired, bought

(12)   [שׁחה]   he bowed down, worshipped

(13)   אַמָּה   (f) cubit

(14)   מַחֲנֶה   (m and f) camp, encampment

(15)   מַטֶּה   staff, rod, branch, tribe

(16)   מַעֲשֶׂה   work, deed

(17)   מִשְׁפָּחָה   (f) family, clan

(18)   עֹלָה   (f) whole burnt offering

300

LESSON XXVIII

73. Weak Verbs: Pe Nun Verbs*

73.1 *Definition*

A Pe Nun verb is one whose initial root consonant is נ .

(1) Regular Pe Nun Verbs

(a) [נבט] (Hif.) he saw, looked upon

(b) [נגד] (Hif.) he told, declared

(c) נָגַף he struck, smote

(d) נָגַשׁ he drew near, approached

(e) נָדַר he vowed

(f) נָטַשׁ he left, forsook

(g) נָפַל he fell

(h) [נצב] (Nif.) he stationed himself, took his stand, (Hif.) he stationed, set, caused to stand

(i) [נצל] (Hif.) he took away, rescued, delivered

(j) נָצַר he watched, guarded, kept

(k) נָקַם he avenged, took vengeance

(l) [נשׂג] (Hif.) he reached, overtook, attained

(m) נָתַךְ he poured out

(n) נָתַץ he pulled down, broke down

(2) Doubly Weak Verbs: Pe Nun and Lamed ʼAlef

(a) [נבא] (Nif.) he prophesied

(b) נָשָׂא he lifted up, carried, took away

(3) Doubly Weak Verbs: Pe Nun and Lamed He

(a) נָזָה he (it) spurted, spattered; (Hif.) he sprinkled

(b) נָטָה he stretched out, spread out, turned aside

(c) [נכה] (Hif.) he struck, smote, killed

(d) [נסה] (Pi.) he tested, tried

(e) נָקָה he was clean, innocent, guiltless

(f) נָשָׁה (1) he lent, borrowed

(g) נָשָׁה (2) he forgot

---

*Refer to Verb Chart 8, pp. 414f., for the conjugation of the Pe Nun verb.

(4) Doubly Weak Verbs: Pe Nun and Lamed Guttural

(a) נָגַע   he touched, smote   (d) נָסַע   he set out, departed,
(b) נָדַח   he drove out, banished,   journeyed
     expelled   (e) נָפַח   he breathed, blew
(c) נָטַע   he planted

Note: לָקַח, "he took," also follows the pattern of a doubly weak verb of the Pe Nun/ Lamed Guttural class.

(5) Doubly Weak Verb: Pe Nun and Lamed Nun

Only one verb falls within this category, the frequently occurring נָתַן, "he gave, put, set, paid, permitted."

73.2 *Distinctive Characteristics of Pe Nun Verbs*

(1) When נ is the final consonant in a syllable other than the last syllable of the word, it is assimilated into the following consonant by means of a dagesh forte.

(2) However, if the following consonant is a guttural, and therefore cannot to be doubled, נ is ordinarily allowed to stand as an unassimilated consonant. This is the case in such verbs as נָאַץ, "he despised, reviled," נָהַג, "he drove, led," and נָחַל, "he inherited, took possession." An exception to this rule is the verb [נחם], "he was sorry, repented, consoled himself," which has the assimilated nun in the Nif‘al perfect and Nif'al participle.
Examples:

(a) Qal imperfect 3 ms of נָחַל: יִנְחַל
(b) Nif‘al perfect 3 ms of [נחם]: נִנְחַם becomes נִחַם
     (ח doubled by implication)
(c) Nif‘al participle (ms) of [נחם]: נִנְחָם becomes נִחָם
     (ח doubled by implication)

(3) The assimilation of the נ of Pe Nun verbs, apart from the exceptions mentioned above, occurs in all forms of Qal imperfect, Nif‘al perfect, and Nif‘al participle. In addition to this, it occurs throughout the entire Hif‘il and Hof‘al inflections. In the Pi‘el, Pu‘al, and Hitpa‘el stems, regular Pe Nun verbs follow the same pattern as strong verbs.

302

Examples:

    (a) Qal imperfect of נָפַל, "he fell"

        3 ms   יִנְפֹּל becomes יִפֹּל

        3 fs   תִּנְפֹּל becomes תִּפֹּל

               etc.

    (b) Nifʻal perfect of נָגַשׁ, "he approached, drew near"

        3 ms   נִנְגַּשׁ becomes נִגַּשׁ

        3 fs   נִנְגְּשָׁה becomes נִגְּשָׁה

               etc.

    (c) Hifʻil perfect of [נצל], "he took away, rescued, delivered"

        3 ms   הִנְצִיל becomes הִצִּיל

        3 fs   הִנְצִילָה becomes הִצִּילָה

        2 ms   הִנְצַלְתָּ becomes הִצַּלְתָּ

               etc.

    (d) Hifʻil imperfect of נָגַשׁ, "he approached, drew near;" (Hif.) "he brought near"

        3 ms   יַנְגִּישׁ becomes יַגִּישׁ

        3 fs   תַּנְגִּישׁ becomes תַּגִּישׁ

               etc.

    (4) The stem vowel for Qal imperfect and Qal imperative forms of Pe Nun verbs exhibits the following variations.

    (a) The stem vowel is ḥolem in most of the regular Pe Nun verbs. Examples:

Qal Imperfect

נָפַל, "he fell"		נָטַשׁ, "he left, forsook"	
3 ms	יִפֹּל	3 ms	יִטֹּשׁ
3 fs	תִּפֹּל	3 fs	תִּטֹּשׁ
2 fs	תִּפְּלִי	2 fs	תִּטְּשִׁי
1 cs	אֶפֹּל	1 cs	אֶטֹּשׁ
2 mp	תִּפְּלוּ	2 mp	תִּטְּשׁוּ
2 fp	תִּפֹּלְנָה	2 fp	תִּטֹּשְׁנָה
1 cp	נִפֹּל	1 cp	נִטֹּשׁ

Qal Imperative

2 ms	נְפֹל	2 ms	נְטֹשׁ
2 fs	נִפְלִי	2 fs	נִטְשִׁי
2 mp	נִפְלוּ	2 mp	נִטְשׁוּ
2 fp	נְפֹלְנָה	2 fp	נְטֹשְׁנָה

(b)   The stem vowel is pataḥ in a few regular Pe Nun verbs (cf. נָגַשׁ, נָתַךְ), in all doubly weak Pe Nun/Lamed Guttural verbs, and in the verb לָקַח, "he took," a verb that exhibits the characteristics of Pe Nun/Lamed Guttural verbs.

Examples of Qal imperfect forms:

3 ms	יִגַּשׁ	from	נָגַשׁ
3 ms	יִגַּע	from	נָגַע
3 ms	יִטַּע	from	נָטַע
3 ms	יִסַּע	from	נָסַע
3 ms	יִקַּח	from	לָקַח

The Pe Nun verbs in this category form the Qal imperative by dropping the initial נ altogether.

Examples of the Qal imperative of representative verbs in this category:

נָגַשׁ, "he drew near"   נָגַע, "he touched"   לָקַח, "he took"

2 ms	גַּשׁ	גַּע	קַח
2 fs	גְּשִׁי	גְּעִי	קְחִי
2 mp	גְּשׁוּ	גְּעוּ	קְחוּ
2 fp	גַּשְׁנָה	גַּעְנָה	קַחְנָה

(c)   The stem vowel is ṣere in the Qal imperfect and Qal imperative of the doubly weak Pe Nun/Lamed Nun verb נָתַן, "he gave."

Examples:

	Qal Imperfect		Qal Imperative
3 ms	יִתֵּן	2 ms	תֵּן
3 fs	תִּתֵּן	2 fs	תְּנִי
2 ms	תִּתֵּן	2 mp	תְּנוּ
2 fs	תִּתְּנִי	2 fp	תֵּנָּה (תֵּנְנָה) becomes
1 cs	אֶתֵּן		(תֵּנָּה)
	etc.		

(d) The stem vowel is qameṣ in the Qal imperfect and Qal imperative 2 ms of the doubly weak Pe Nun/Lamed ʾAlef verb נָשָׂא, "he lifted up." Examples:

	Qal Imperfect		Qal Imperative
3 ms	יִשָּׂא	2 ms	שָׂא
3 fs	תִּשָּׂא	2 fs	שְׂאִי
2 ms	תִּשָּׂא	2 mp	שְׂאוּ
2 fs	תִּשְׂאִי	2 fp	שֶׂאנָה
1 cs	אֶשָּׂא		
	etc.		

(5) In Pe Nun verbs that do not have ḥolem as the stem vowel in the Qal imperfect, the Qal infinitive construct is formed by dropping the initial נ and adding a final ת to form a segholate. This rule applies also to לָקַח. The doubly weak נָתַן forms the Qal infinitive construct by dropping the initial נ and by substituting ת for the final נ, thus arriving at the form תֵּת.

When a preposition is prefixed to one of the segholate infinitive construct forms or to one of the monosyllabic forms, it is pointed with qameṣ, since it stands before the stressed, or accented, syllable of the word. Examples:

	Verb Root	Qal Infinitive Construct	With Preposition
(a)	נָגַשׁ	גֶּשֶׁת	לָגֶשֶׁת
(b)	נָגַע	גַּעַת	לָגַעַת
(c)	נָטַע	טַעַת (נְטֹעַ)	לָטַעַת
(d)	נָשָׂא	שְׂאֵת	לָשְׂאֵת
(e)	נָתַן	תֵּת	לָתֵת
(f)	לָקַח	קַחַת	לָקַחַת

(6) The verb נָתַן also assimilates the final נ when it stands at the end of a syllable before a consonantal afformative. Examples:

	Qal Perfect		
2 ms	נָתַנְתָּ	becomes	נָתַתָּ (נָתַתָּה)
2 fs	נָתַנְתְּ	becomes	נָתַתְּ
1 cs	נָתַנְתִּי	becomes	נָתַתִּי
2 mp	נְתַנְתֶּם	becomes	נְתַתֶּם
1 cp	נָתַנּוּ	becomes	נָתַנּוּ

305

Qal Imperfect

3 fp, 2 fp	תִּגְתַּנְּגָה becomes תִּתֵּנָּה

Qal Imperative

2 fp	תִּנְגְנָה becomes תֵּנָּה

(7) Doubly weak verbs that are both Pe Nun and Lamed He present special problems for the beginning student. Not only is the initial נ assimilated according to the rules given above, but also the weakness of the final ה sometimes results in apocopated verb forms, especially when these are used as jussives or when they are prefixed with vav consecutive. The inflection of the Hifʾil stem of נָכָה will illustrate the peculiar characteristics of this class of verbs.

Hifʾil Stem of נָכָה, "he struck, smote, killed"

	Perfect		Imperfect	Jussive	Impf. + ·וַ
3 ms	הִכָּה	3 ms	יַכֶּה	יַךְ	וַיַּךְ
3 fs	הִכְּתָה	3 fs	תַּכֶּה		וַתַּךְ
2 ms	הִכִּיתָ	2 ms	תַּכֶּה		
2 fs	הִכִּית	2 fs	תַּכִּי		
1 cs	הִכֵּיתִי	1 cs	אַכֶּה		וָאַךְ
3 cp	הִכּוּ	3 mp	יַכּוּ	יַכּוּ	וַיַּכּוּ
		3 fp	תַּכֶּינָה		
2 mp	הִכִּיתֶם	2 mp	תַּכּוּ		
2 fp	הִכִּיתֶן	2 fp	תַּכֶּינָה		
1 cp	הִכִּינוּ	1 cp	נַכֶּה		וַנַּךְ

Imperative

2 ms	הַךְ (הַכֵּה)
2 fs	הַכִּי
2 mp	הַכּוּ
2 fp	הַכֶּינָה

Infinitive Construct	Infinitive Absolute	Participle	
הַכּוֹת (לְהַכּוֹת)	הַכֵּה	ms	מַכֶּה (construct מַכֵּה)
		mp	מַכִּים

(8) The Qal Stem of לָקַח, "he took"

	Perfect		Imperfect		Imperative
3 ms	לָקַח	3 ms	יִקַּח		
3 fs	לָקְחָה	3 fs	תִּקַּח		
2 ms	לָקַחְתָּ	2 ms	תִּקַּח	2 ms	קַח
2 fs	לָקַחַתְּ	2 fs	תִּקְחִי	2 fs	קְחִי
1 cs	לָקַחְתִּי	1 cs	אֶקַּח		
3 cp	לָקְחוּ	3 mp	יִקְחוּ		
		3 fp	תִּקַּחְנָה		
2 mp	לְקַחְתֶּם	2 mp	תִּקְחוּ	2 mp	קְחוּ
2 fp	לְקַחְתֶּן	2 fp	תִּקַּחְנָה	2 fp	קַחְנָה
1 cp	לָקַחְנוּ	1 cp	נִקַּח		

Infinitive Construct	(לָקַחַת) קַחַת	Participle Active	ms	לֹקֵחַ
Infinitive Absolute	לָקוֹחַ		mp	לוֹקְחִים
			Construct	לוֹקְחֵי
		Participle Passive	ms	לָקוּחַ
			mp	לְקוּחִים

(9) The Synopsis of נָגַשׁ, "he drew near, approached"

	Qal	Nif'al	Pi'el	Pu'al	Hitpa'el	Hif'il	Hof'al
Perf. 3 ms	נָגַשׁ	נִגַּשׁ	נִגֵּשׁ	נֻגַּשׁ	הִתְנַגֵּשׁ	הִגִּישׁ	הֻגַּשׁ
Impf. 3 ms	יִגַּשׁ	יִנָּגֵשׁ	יְנַגֵּשׁ	יְנֻגַּשׁ	יִתְנַגֵּשׁ	יַגִּישׁ	יֻגַּשׁ
Impv. 2 ms	גַּשׁ	הִנָּגֵשׁ	נַגֵּשׁ		הִתְנַגֵּשׁ	הַגֵּשׁ	
Inf. Const.	גֶּשֶׁת	הִנָּגֵשׁ	נַגֵּשׁ	נֻגַּשׁ	הִתְנַגֵּשׁ	הַגִּישׁ	הֻגַּשׁ
Inf. Abs.	נָגוֹשׁ	הִנָּגֵשׁ	נַגֵּשׁ	נֻגַּשׁ	הִתְנַגֵּשׁ	הַגֵּשׁ	הֻגַּשׁ
Part. Act.	נֹגֵשׁ		מְנַגֵּשׁ		מִתְנַגֵּשׁ	מַגִּישׁ	
Part. Pass.	נָגוּשׁ	נִגָּשׁ		מְנֻגָּשׁ			מֻגָּשׁ

307

EXERCISES

1. Each of the following entries contains a Pe Nun verb form. Supply the correct translation of the verb form. In the space marked (a) give its stem, in (b) the identification of the form (perfect, imperfect, etc.), in (c) its person, gender, and number, and in (d) its root. *Ignore verb forms that are not Pe Nun, except for* לָקַח, "*he took.*"

(1) לֹא־יִשָּׂא גוֹי אֶל־גּוֹי חֶרֶב Nation shall not _____ _____ sword against nation. (Isa. 2:4)

　　　(a) _____ (b) _____ (c) _____ (d) _____

(2) כִּי אֶת־כָּל־הָאָרֶץ אֲשֶׁר אַתָּה רֹאֶה לְךָ אֶתְּנֶנָּה For all the land that you see, to you I will _____ it. (Gen. 13:15)

　　　(a) _____ (b) _____ (c) _____ (d) _____

(3) שְׂאוּ שְׁעָרִים רָאשֵׁיכֶם _____ up your heads, O gates! (Ps. 24:7)

　　　(a) _____ (b) _____ (c) _____ (d) _____

(4) וַיִּפֹּל הַגּוֹרָל עַל־יוֹנָה And the lot _____ upon Jonah. (Jon. 1:7)

　　　(a) _____ (b) _____ (c) _____ (d) _____

(5) וְיִתְפַּלֵּל אֵלָיו וְיֹאמַר הַצִּילֵנִי כִּי אֵלִי אָתָּה And he prays to it and says, "_____ me, for you are my god." (Isa. 44:17)

　　　(a) _____ (b) _____ (c) _____ (d) _____

(6) לָמָה לֹא־הִגַּדְתָּ לִּי כִּי אִשְׁתְּךָ הִוא Why did you not _____ me that she was your wife? (Gen. 12:18)

　　　(a) _____ (b) _____ (c) _____ (d) _____

(7) וַיִּשְׁלַח יְהוָה אֶת־יָדוֹ וַיַּגַּע עַל־פִּי And the LORD put forth (sent) his hand and _____ my mouth. (Jer. 1:9)

　　　(a) _____ (b) _____ (c) _____ (d) _____

(8) וַיֹּאמֶר יְהוָה אֵלַי הִנֵּה נָתַתִּי דְבָרַי בְּפִיךָ And the LORD said to me, "Behold, I have _____ my words in your mouth." (Jer. 1:9)

　　　(a) _____ (b) _____ (c) _____ (d) _____

(9) וַיִּטַּע יְהוָה אֱלֹהִים גַּן־בְּעֵדֶן And the LORD God _____ a garden in Eden. (Gen. 2:8)

　　　(a) _____ (b) _____ (c) _____ (d) _____

308

(10) הַבֵּט מִשָּׁמַיִם וּרְאֵה _____ from heaven and see! (Isa. 63:15)

(a) _____ (b) _____ (c) _____ (d) _____

(11) וּבַמָּקוֹם הַזֶּה אֶתֵּן שָׁלוֹם And in this place I will _____ peace. (Hag. 2:9)

(a) _____ (b) _____ (c) _____ (d) _____

(12) וְהִכֵּיתִי כָל־בְּכוֹר בְּאֶרֶץ מִצְרַיִם And I will _____ all the firstborn in the the land of Egypt. (Exod. 12:12)

(a) _____ (b) _____ (c) _____ (d) _____

(13) וְרוּחַ קָדְשְׁךָ אַל־תִּקַּח מִמֶּנִּי And _____ not your holy spirit from me. (Ps. 51:13; Eng. 51:11)

(a) _____ (b) _____ (c) _____ (d) _____

(14) וַתִּקַּח מִפִּרְיוֹ וַתֹּאכַל And she _____ from its fruit, and she ate. (Gen. 3:6)

(a) _____ (b) _____ (c) _____ (d) _____

(15) יִשָּׂא יְהוָה פָּנָיו אֵלֶיךָ May the LORD _____ _____ his countenance (face) upon you. (Num. 6:26)

(a) _____ (b) _____ (c) _____ (d) _____

2. Each of the following entries contains an infinitive form from a Pe Nun verb. In the space marked (a) give its stem, in (b) tell whether it is *construct* or *absolute*, and in (c) give its root.

(1) לָתֵת לָהֶם לֵב אֶחָד

to give to them one heart (2 Chr. 30:12)

(a) _____
(b) _____
(c) _____

(2) וַיְבַקְשׁוּ אֶת־נַפְשִׁי לְקַחְתָּהּ

And they seek my soul (life) to take it. (1 Kgs. 19:10)

(a) _____
(b) _____
(c) _____

(3) וְעַתָּה אָרוּר אָתָּה מִן־הָאֲדָמָה אֲשֶׁר פָּצְתָה אֶת־פִּיהָ
לָקַחַת אֶת־דְּמֵי אָחִיךָ מִיָּדֶךָ

And now cursed are you from the ground which has opened its mouth to receive (take) the blood (bloods) of your brother from your hand. (Gen. 4:11)

(a) _____
(b) _____
(c) _____

309

(4)   בִּנְטֹתִי אֶת־יָדִי עַל־מִצְרָיִם   (a) _____

when I stretch out my hand against Egypt (Exod. 7:5)   (b) _____

(c) _____

(5)   וַיְמָאֵן הָאִישׁ לְהַכֹּתוֹ   (a) _____

But the man refused to smite him. (1 Kgs. 20:35)   (b) _____

(c) _____

(6)   וַיֹּאמְרוּ אֶל־בָּרוּךְ הַגֵּיד נַגִּיד לַמֶּלֶךְ אֵת כָּל־הַדְּבָרִים   (a) _____

הָאֵלֶּה   (b) _____

And they said to Baruch, "We must surely report (declare)   (c) _____
all these words to the king." (Jer. 36:16)

(7)   לְהַגִּיד לְיַעֲקֹב פִּשְׁעוֹ וּלְיִשְׂרָאֵל חַטָּאתוֹ   (a) _____

to declare to Jacob his transgression and to Israel his sin   (b) _____

(Mic. 3:8)   (c) _____

(8)   כִּי־אִתְּךָ אֲנִי לְהַצִּלֶךָ   (a) _____

For I am with you to deliver you. (Jer. 1:8)   (b) _____

(c) _____

(9)   וְאַל־יַבְטַח אֶתְכֶם חִזְקִיָּהוּ אֶל־יְהוָה לֵאמֹר הַצֵּל   (a) _____

יַצִּילֵנוּ יְהוָה   (b) _____

And do not let Hezekiah cause you to trust in the LORD   (c) _____
saying, "The LORD will surely deliver us." (Isa. 36:15)

(10)   וְשָׁאוּל חָשַׁב לְהַפִּיל אֶת־דָּוִד בְּיַד־פְּלִשְׁתִּים   (a) _____

And Saul thought to make David fall by the hand of the   (b) _____
Philistines. (1 Sam. 18:25)   (c) _____

(11)   הַכֵּה תַכֶּה אֶת־יֹשְׁבֵי הָעִיר הַהִוא לְפִי־חָרֶב   (a) _____

You shall surely smite the inhabitants of that city   (b) _____
by the edge (mouth) of the sword. (Deut. 13:16)   (c) _____

3. Fill in the blanks with the correct pronouns.

(1)   אֶשָּׂא עֵינַי אֶל־הֶהָרִים   _____ will lift up _____ eyes to the
mountains. (Ps. 121:1)

(2)   וְרוּחַ יְהוָה יִשָּׂאֲךָ   And the spirit of the LORD shall lift _____ up.
(1 Kgs. 18:12)

310

(3) וְאַתָּה נָשָׂאתָ עֲוֹן חַטָּאתִי But _____ have forgiven (lifted up) the iniquity of _____ sin. (Ps. 32:5)

(4) אָכֵן חֳלָיֵנוּ הוּא נָשָׂא Surely _____ has carried (lifted up) _____ sicknesses. (Isa. 53:4)

(5) וָאֶפֹּל עַל־פָּנָי And _____ fell on _____ face. (Ezek. 3:23)

(6) וְהִפַּלְתִּים בַּחֶרֶב לִפְנֵי אֹיְבֵיהֶם And _____ caused _____ to fall by the sword before _____ enemies. (Jer. 19:7)

(7) כִּי הִצַּלְתָּ נַפְשִׁי מִמָּוֶת For _____ delivered _____ soul from death. (Ps. 56:14; Eng. 56:13)

(8) לְמַעַן הַצִּיל אֹתוֹ מִיָּדָם In order to deliver _____ from _____ hand. (Gen. 37:22)

(9) בְּצִדְקָתְךָ תַּצִּילֵנִי In _____ righteousness _____ will deliver _____. (Ps. 71:2)

(10) וַיֹּאמֶר מִי הִגִּיד לְךָ כִּי עֵירֹם אָתָּה And _____ said, "_____ told _____ that _____ were naked?" (Gen. 3:11)

(11) וְהִגִּידוּ אֶת־כְּבוֹדִי בַּגּוֹיִם And _____ shall declare _____ glory among the nations. (Isa. 66:19)

(12) וַיַּכּוּ אֹתוֹ וְאֶת־בָּנָיו וְאֶת־כָּל־עַמּוֹ And _____ smote _____ and _____ sons and all _____ people. (Num. 21:35)

(13) וְנָטִיתִי אֶת־יָדִי עֲלֵיהֶם And _____ will stretch out _____ hand against _____. (Ezek. 6:14)

(14) הַטּוּ אָזְנְכֶם וּלְכוּ אֵלַי שִׁמְעוּ וּתְחִי נַפְשְׁכֶם Incline (stretch out) _____ ears and come to _____; hear that _____ soul may live. (Isa. 55:3)

(15) תְּנָה־לָּנוּ מֶלֶךְ לְשָׁפְטֵנוּ Give to _____ a king to judge _____. (1 Sam. 8:6)

4. Each of the following entries contains an imperative form of a Pe Nun verb. Fill in the correct translation for each form. In the space marked (a) give its stem, in (b) its person, gender, and number, and in (c) its root. *Ignore verb forms that are not Pe Nun.*

(1) שָׂא נָא עֵינֶיךָ וּרְאֵה מִן־הַמָּקוֹם אֲשֶׁר־אַתָּה שָׁם   (a) _____

_____ up your eyes and look from the place where   (b) _____

you are. (Gen. 13:14)   (c) _____

(2) וְעַתָּה הַצִּילֵנוּ מִיַּד אֹיְבֵינוּ   (a) _____

And now _____ us from the hand of our enemies.   (b) _____

(1 Sam. 12:10)   (c) _____

(3) הַגֵּד אֶת־כָּל־אֲשֶׁר־אַתָּה רֹאֶה לְבֵית יִשְׂרָאֵל   (a) _____

_____ all that you are seeing to the house of Israel.   (b) _____

(Ezek. 40:4)   (c) _____

(4) וַיֹּאמֶר הַגִּידָה־נָּא שְׁמֶךָ   (a) _____

And he said, "_____ me, I pray, your name!"   (b) _____

(Gen. 32:30)   (c) _____

(5) וַיֹּאמֶר אֵלָיו יִצְחָק אָבִיו גְּשָׁה־נָּא וַיִּגַּשׁ   (a) _____

And Isaac his father said to him, "_____ _____,   (b) _____

and he drew near." (Gen. 27:26–27)   (c) _____

(6) שְׁלַח־נָא יָדְךָ וְגַע בְּכָל־אֲשֶׁר־לוֹ   (a) _____

Put forth (send) your hand and _____ all that   (b) _____

which is his. (Job 1:11)   (c) _____

(7) וַיֹּאמֶר הַבֶּט־נָא הַשָּׁמַיְמָה   (a) _____

And he said, "_____ to the heavens." (Gen. 15:5)   (b) _____

    (c) _____

(8) וַיֹּאמְרוּ תְּנוּ־לָנוּ מַיִם וְנִשְׁתֶּה   (a) _____

And they said, "_____ us water that we may drink."   (b) _____

(Exod. 17:2)   (c) _____

(9) לֹא לָנוּ יְהוָה לֹא לָנוּ כִּי־לְשִׁמְךָ תֵּן כָּבוֹד   (a) _____

"Not to us, O LORD, not to us, but to your name   (b) _____

_____ glory." (Ps. 115:1)   (c) _____

(10) תְּנָה־אֶת־בִּתְּךָ לִבְנִי לְאִשָּׁה   (a) _____

_____ your daughter to my son for a wife.   (b) _____

(2 Kgs. 14:9)   (c) _____

(11) וַיֹּאמֶר יְהוָה אֶל־מֹשֶׁה אֱמֹר אֶל־אַהֲרֹן נְטֵה אֶת־מַטֶּךָ   (a) _____

And the LORD said to Moses, "Say to Aaron, _____   (b) _____

out your rod." (Exod. 8:12; Eng. 8:16)   (c) _____

(12) וְעַתָּה יְהוָה קַח־נָא אֶת־נַפְשִׁי מִמֶּנִּי כִּי טוֹב מוֹתִי מֵחַיָּי   (a) _____

And now, O LORD, _____ from me my soul (life),   (b) _____

for better is my death than my life. (Jon. 4:3)   (c) _____

(13) וְעַתָּה קְחוּ לָכֶם שְׁנֵי עָשָׂר אִישׁ מִשִּׁבְטֵי יִשְׂרָאֵל   (a) _____

And now _____ for you twelve men from the tribes   (b) _____

of Israel. (Josh. 3:12)   (c) _____

(14) הַצִּילֵנִי נָא מִיַּד אָחִי מִיַּד עֵשָׂו   (a) _____

_____, me, I pray, from the hand of my brother,   (b) _____

from the hand of Esau. (Gen. 32:12)   (c) _____

(15) הַגִּידָה לִּי מֶה עָשִׂיתָה   (a) _____

_____ me what you have done. (1 Sam. 14:43)   (b) _____

    (c) _____

5. Practice pronouncing the Hebrew, noting especially Pe Nun verb forms. Cover the English translation and practice translating from sight.

(1) וַיִּקָּחֵנִי יְהוָה מֵאַחֲרֵי הַצֹּאן וַיֹּאמֶר אֵלַי יְהוָה לֵךְ הִנָּבֵא אֶל־עַמִּי יִשְׂרָאֵל

And the LORD took me from behind the flock, and the LORD said to me, "Go, prophesy to my people Israel." (Amos 7:15)

(2) לֹא תִשָּׂא אֶת־שֵׁם־יְהוָה אֱלֹהֶיךָ לַשָּׁוְא

You shall not take up (lift, bear) the name of the LORD your God in vain (to vanity). (Exod. 20:7)

(3) שִׁבְטְךָ וּמִשְׁעַנְתֶּךָ הֵמָּה יְנַחֲמֻנִי

You rod and your staff, they comfort me. (Ps. 23:4)

(4) וָאֶרְאֶה אֶת־אֲדֹנָי יֹשֵׁב עַל־כִּסֵּא רָם וְנִשָּׂא

And I saw the LORD sitting upon a throne that was high and lifted up. (Isa. 6:1)

(5) וַיֹּאמְרוּ לְכוּ וְנַפִּילָה גוֹרָלוֹת וַיַּפִּלוּ גּוֹרָלוֹת וַיִּפֹּל הַגּוֹרָל עַל־יוֹנָה

And they said, "Come and let us cast lots." And they cast lots, and the lot fell upon Jonah. (Jon. 1:7)

(6) וַיֹּאמֶר דָּוִד יְהוָה אֲשֶׁר הִצִּלַנִי
מִיַּד הָאֲרִי וּמִיַּד הַדֹּב יַצִּילֵנִי
מִיַּד הַפְּלִשְׁתִּי הַזֶּה

And David said, "The LORD who delivered me from the hand (power) of the lion and from the hand of the bear will deliver me from the hand of this Philistine." (1 Sam. 17:37)

(7) הַשָּׁמַיִם מְסַפְּרִים כְּבוֹד־אֵל
וּמַעֲשֵׂה יָדָיו מַגִּיד הָרָקִיעַ

The heavens are reciting the glory of God, and the work of his hands the firmament is declaring. (Ps. 19:2; Eng. 19:1)

(8) וַיִּגְּשׁוּ עֲבָדָיו וַיְדַבְּרוּ אֵלָיו
וַיֹּאמְרוּ אָבִי דָּבָר גָּדוֹל הַנָּבִיא
דִּבֶּר אֵלֶיךָ הֲלוֹא תַעֲשֶׂה

Then his servants approached him, and they said, "My father, (if) the prophet had spoken a great word (thing) to you, would you not have done (it)?" (2 Kgs. 5:13)

(9) הַבִּיטוּ אֶל־אַבְרָהָם אֲבִיכֶם
כִּי־אֶחָד קְרָאתִיו וַאֲבָרְכֵהוּ
וְאַרְבֵּהוּ

Look to Abraham your father, for (when he was) one I called him, and I blessed him, and I multiplied him (caused him to be many). (Isa. 51:2)

(10) וַיֹּאמֶר יְהוָה אֶל־מֹשֶׁה רְאֵה
נְתַתִּיךָ אֱלֹהִים לְפַרְעֹה
וְאַהֲרֹן אָחִיךָ יִהְיֶה נְבִיאֶךָ

And the LORD said to Moses, "See, I have set (given) you as God to Pharaoh, and Aaron your brother shall be your prophet." (Exod. 7:1)

(11) רְאֵה נָתַתִּי לְפָנֶיךָ הַיּוֹם
אֶת־הַחַיִּים וְאֶת־הַטּוֹב
וְאֶת־הַמָּוֶת וְאֶת־הָרָע

See, I have set (given) before you today life and good and death and evil. (Deut. 30:15)

(12) אֵת אוּרִיָּה הַחִתִּי הִכִּיתָ
בַחֶרֶב וְאֶת־אִשְׁתּוֹ לָקַחְתָּ
לְךָ לְאִשָּׁה

Uriah the Hittite you have slain with the sword, and his wife you have taken as a wife to you (as your wife). (2 Sam. 12:9)

(13) יוֹמָם הַשֶּׁמֶשׁ לֹא־יַכֶּכָּה וְיָרֵחַ
בַּלָּיְלָה

The sun shall not smite you by day, nor the moon by night. (Ps. 121:6)

(14) וַיִּשְׁלַח אַבְרָהָם אֶת־יָדוֹ וַיִּקַּח
אֶת־הַמַּאֲכֶלֶת לִשְׁחֹט אֶת־בְּנוֹ

And Abraham put forth (sent) his hand and took the knife to slay his son. (Gen. 22:10)

(15) יְהוָה נָתַן וַיהוָה לָקַח יְהִי
שֵׁם יְהוָה מְבֹרָךְ

The LORD gave, and the LORD has taken away; may the name of the LORD be blessed. (Job 1:21)

VOCABULARY

(1) [נבט] (Hif.) he saw, looked upon

(2) נָגַף he smote, struck

(3) נָדַח he drove out, banished, expelled

(4) נָדַר he vowed

(5) [נהל] (Pi.) he led, guided, refreshed

(6) נָזָה he (it) spurted, spattered; (Hif.) he sprinkled

(7) נָטַע he planted

(8) נָטַשׁ he left, forsook

(9) [נסה] (Pi.) he tested, tried

(10) נָסַע he set out, departed, journeyed

(11) [נצב] (Nif.) he stationed himself, took his stand; (Hif.) he stationed, set, caused to stand

(12) נָצַר he watched, guarded, kept

(13) [נקה] he was clean, innocent, guiltless

(14) [נקם] he avenged, took vengeance

(15) [נשג] (Hif.) he reached, overtook, attained

(16) נָתַץ he pulled down, broke down

(17) הַיִל strength, wealth, army

(18) נַחֲלָה (f) possession, inheritance

LESSON XXIX

74. Weak Verbs: ʿAyin Vav/ʿAyin Yod Verbs*

74.1 *Definition*

ʿAyin Vav/ʿAyin Yod verbs may also be referred to as "Middle Vowel verbs," "II–Vav/II–Yod verbs," or "Hollow verbs." Whatever the designation, this class of weak verbs includes those in which middle vav or middle yod lost its consonantal character and either dropped out of verb forms altogether or else combined with the preceding vowel to form ְי , וֹ, or וּ. In either case the resultant verb forms are essentially biliteral.

A few verbs with middle consonants in vav or yod resisted these changes and maintained their triliteral character. The most important among these are גָּוַע, "he expired, died," [צָוָה], "he commanded," קָוָה, "he waited for, hoped for," הָיָה, "he was," and חָיָה, "he lived."

In the inflection of the Qal perfect of ʿAyin Vav/ʿAyin Yod verbs, middle vav and middle yod completely disappear. For this reason Hebrew lexicons list as the root for these verbs the Qal infinitive construct rather than the customary Qal perfect 3 ms.

74.2 *A List of Some of the Most Frequently Occurring ʿAyin Vav/ʿAyin Yod Verbs*

(1) Verbs with וּ as the middle vowel

(a)	גוּר	to sojourn	(g)	נוּעַ	(doubly weak) to quiver, stagger, tremble
(b)	כוּן	to be firm, fixed, established	(h)	סוּר	to turn aside
(c)	מוּל	to circumcise	(i)	עוּר	to awaken, arouse oneself
(d)	מוּת	to die	(j)	פוּץ	to be scattered, dispersed
(e)	נוּחַ	(doubly weak) to come to rest, to be at rest	(k)	קוּם	to arise, to stand, establish
			(l)	רוּם	to be high, exalted
(f)	נוּס	to flee	(m)	רוּץ	to run
			(n)	שׁוּב	to turn, return, repent

(2) Verbs with וֹ as the middle vowel

(a)	בּוֹא	(doubly weak) to come, go, enter	(b)	בּוֹשׁ	to be ashamed

---

*Refer to Verb Chart 9, pp. 416–419, for the conjugation of the ʿAyin Vav/ʿAyin Yod verb.

(3) Verbs with ֖י as the middle vowel

(a)	בִּין	to discern	(d)	רִיב	to strive
(b)	גִּיל	to rejoice	(e)	שִׁיר	to sing
(c)	דִּין	to judge	(f)	שִׁית	to put, place, set

(4) Verbs with either ֖י or וּ as the middle vowel

(a)	חוּל/חִיל	to whirl, dance, writhe
(b)	לוּן/לִין	to lodge, pass the night, abide
(c)	שׂוּם/שִׂים	to put, place, appoint

74.3 *The Qal Inflection of Representative ʿAyin Vav/ʿAyin Yod Verbs*

(1) קוּם "to arise"

	Perfect		Imperfect		Imperative
3 ms	קָם	3 ms	יָקוּם		
3 fs	קָמָה	3 fs	תָּקוּם		
2 ms	קַמְתָּ	2 ms	תָּקוּם	2 ms	קוּם
2 fs	קַמְתְּ	2 fs	תָּקוּמִי	2 fs	קוּמִי
1 cs	קַמְתִּי	1 cs	אָקוּם		
3 cp	קָמוּ	3 mp	יָקוּמוּ		
		3 fp	תְּקוּמֶינָה		
2 mp	קַמְתֶּם	2 mp	תָּקוּמוּ	2 mp	קוּמוּ
2 fp	קַמְתֶּן	2 fp	תְּקוּמֶינָה	2 fp	קֹמְנָה
1 cp	קַמְנוּ	1 cp	נָקוּם		

Infinitive Construct	קוּם	Participle Active	ms	קָם
Infinitive Absolute	קוֹם	Participle Active	mp	קָמִים
			fs	קָמָה
			fp	קָמוֹת
		Participle Passive	(Not used)	

(A) Almost all ʿAyin Vav/ʿAyin Yod verbs follow the pattern of קוּם in the inflection of the Qal perfect. The exceptions include the doubly weak בּוֹא, "to go," and the two stative verbs, בּוֹשׁ, "to be ashamed," and מוּת, "to die."

(B) The Qal perfect 3 ms and the Qal active participle (ms) are identical in form. The context alone will enable the reader to distinguish between the two.

(C) The only difference between the Qal perfect 3 fs and the Qal active participle (fs) is the manner in which these two forms are accented. The perfect form is accented on the initial syllable; the participial form is accented on the final syllable.

Root	Qal Perfect 3 fs	Qal Active Participle (fs)
קוּם	קָ֫מָה	קָמָה
בּוֹא	בָּ֫אָה	בָּאָה
מוּת	מֵ֫תָה	מֵתָה
נוּחַ	נָ֫חָה	נָחָה

(D) Vocalic afformatives normally draw the accent to themselves, except when they come immediately after an unchangeably long stem vowel (cf. XII.30.4[3], p. 83). This does not occur, however, in the two Qal perfect forms with vocalic afformatives. Before both the הָ afformative of the 3 fs and the וּ affformative of the 3 cp, the accent remains on the stem vowel. The resultant forms are קָ֫מָה a n d קָ֫מוּ. Only in the Hofʿal stem of ʿAyin Vav/ʿAyin Yod verbs do vocalic afformatives draw the accent to themselves.

(E) In the Qal inflection of קוּם, the middle vav appears in the imperfect, the imperative, and the infinitive construct as וּ, and in the infinitive absolute as וֹ. Practically all ʿAyin Vav verbs follow the same pattern, two notable exceptions being בּוֹא, "to go, come, enter," and בּוֹשׁ, "to be ashamed," both of which substitute וֹ in the place of וּ.

(F) The preformative vowels of the Qal imperfect, the Nifʿal perfect, and the Nifʿal participle, as well as those used throughout the Hifʿil and Hofʿal stems of ʿAyin Vav/ʿAyin Yod verbs all stand in open syllables and therefore must be long. These vowels normally occur in the following patterns:

> (a) Qameṣ in Qal imperfect, Nifʿal perfect, Nifʿal participle, Hifʿil imperfect, Hifʿil imperative, Hifʿil infinitive construct, and Hifʿil infinitive absolute.

> (b) Ṣere in Hifʿil perfect and Hifʿil participle.

> (c) Šureq in all forms of the Hofʿal stem.

(G) A linking vowel is usually inserted before the נָה endings of the Qal imperfect and before all consonantal afformatives of the Nifʿal perfect and the Hifʿil perfect of ʾAyin Vav/ʿAyin Yod verbs. The linking vowel is יֶ in the Qal imperfect and וֹ in the Nifʿal perfect and Hifʿil perfect. The linking vowels always draw the accent to themselves, except before the heavy consonantal afformatives תֶּם and תֶּן. This results in the volatilization of the nearest preceding changeably long vowel in an open syllable. Thus תָּקוּמֶינָה becomes תָּקוּמֶינָה.

(2) שׂוּם/שִׂים, "to put, place"

	Perfect		Imperfect		Imperative
3 ms	שָׂם	3 ms	יָשִׂים		
3 fs	שָׂמָה	3 fs	תָּשִׂים		
2 ms	שַׂמְתָּ	2 ms	תָּשִׂים	2 ms	שִׂים
2 fs	שַׂמְתְּ	2 fs	תָּשִׂימִי	2 fs	שִׂימִי
1 cs	שַׂמְתִּי	1 cs	אָשִׂים		
3 cp	שָׂמוּ	3 mp	יָשִׂימוּ		
		3 fp	תְּשִׂימֶינָה		
2 mp	שַׂמְתֶּם	2 mp	תָּשִׂימוּ	2 mp	שִׂימוּ
2 fp	שַׂמְתֶּן	2 fp	תְּשִׂימֶינָה	2 fp	שִׂמְנָה
1 cp	שַׂמְנוּ	1 cp	נָשִׂים		

Infinitive Construct	שׂוּם/שִׂים	Participle Active	ms	שָׂם
Infinitive Absolute	שׂוֹם		mp	שָׂמִים
			fs	שָׂמָה
			fp	שָׂמוֹת

(A) Except for the presence of יְ in the imperfect, imperative, and infinitive construct forms of this verb, it follows the same pattern as that of the Qal inflection of קוּם. It is only the presence of יְ that indicates that this is an ʿAyin Yod verb.
(B) There is no difference between the form of ʿAyin Yod verbs in the Qal imperfect and the Hifʿil imperfect. Example: יָשִׂים may be either Qal imperfect 3 ms or Hifʿil imperfect 3 ms. Sometimes it is necessary to consult a lexicon or concordance to determine the correct location of this and similar forms.

(3) מוּת, "to die"

	Perfect		Imperfect		Imperative
3 ms	מֵת	3 ms	יָמוּת		
3 fs	מֵתָה	3 fs	תָּמוּת		
2 ms	מַתָּה	2 ms	תָּמוּת	2 ms	מוּת
2 fs	מַתְּ	2 fs	תָּמוּתִי	2 fs	מוּתִי
1 cs	מַתִּי	1 cs	אָמוּת		

319

3 cp	מֵתוּ	3 mp	יָמוּתוּ			
		3 fp	תְּמוּתֶינָה			
2 mp	מַתֶּם	2 mp	תָּמוּתוּ	2 mp	מוּתוּ	
2 fp	מַתֶּן	2 fp	תְּמוּתֶינָה	2 fp	מֹתְנָה	
1 cp	מַתְנוּ	1 cp	נָמוּת			

Infinitive Construct	מוּת	Participle Active	ms	מֵת
Infinitive Absolute	מוֹת		mp	מֵתִים
			fs	מֵתָה
			fp	מֵתוֹת

(A) The stem vowel for this stative verb is ṣere in all third person forms of the Qal perfect and in all forms of the participle.

(B) The dagesh forte in תּ of the Qal perfect 2 ms, 2 fs, 1 cs, 2 mp, and 2 fp forms indicates that the ת of the verb root has been combined with the ת of the consonantal afformatives. The rule involved here is that when the final root consonant is the same as the initial consonant of the afformative the two consonants are combined by doubling (cf. XIV.38.6[6], [7], p. 120).

מֵתְתָ   becomes   מֵתָה

מֵתְתְ   becomes   מַתְּ

etc.

(C) The Qal imperative 2 fs is apparently derived from an alternate form of the Qal imperfect 2 fp (תְּמֹתְנָה; cf. תֵּבֹשְׁנָה).

(4) בּוֹשׁ, "to be ashamed"

	Perfect		Imperfect		Imperative	
3 ms	בּוֹשׁ	3 ms	יֵבוֹשׁ			
3 fs	בּוֹשָׁה	3 fs	תֵּבוֹשׁ			
2 ms	בֹּשְׁתָ	2 ms	תֵּבוֹשׁ	2 ms	בּוֹשׁ	
2 fs	בֹּשְׁתְּ	2 fs	תֵּבוֹשִׁי	2 fs	בּוֹשִׁי	
1 cs	בֹּשְׁתִּי	1 cs	אֵבוֹשׁ			

320

3 cp	בֹּושׁוּ	3 mp	יֵבֹושׁוּ		
		3 fp	תֵּבֹושְׁנָה		
2 mp	בָּשְׁתֶּם	2 mp	תֵּבֹושׁוּ	2 mp	בֹּושׁוּ
2 fp	בָּשְׁתֶּן	2 fp	תֵּבֹושְׁנָה	2 fp	בֹּשְׁנָה
1 cp	בֹּשְׁנוּ	1 cp	נֵבֹושׁ		

Infinitive Construct	בֹּושׁ	Participle Active	ms	בֹּושׁ	
Infinitive Absolute	בֹּושׁ		mp	בֹּושִׁים	
			fs	בֹּושָׁה	
			fp	בֹּושֹׁות	

(A) The stem vowel in the Qal perfect 2 mp and 2 fp forms is not to be identified as qameṣ but as qameṣ-ḥaṭuf, shortened from ḥolem. It has to be short for it stands in an unaccented closed syllable.

(B) The preformative vowel of the Qal imperfect forms of בֹּושׁ is ṣere rather than qameṣ.

(5) בֹּוא, "to come, go, enter"

	Perfect		Imperfect		Imperative
3 ms	בָּא	3 ms	יָבֹוא		
3 fs	בָּאָה	3 fs	תָּבֹוא		
2 ms	בָּאתָ	2 ms	תָּבֹוא	2 ms	בֹּוא
2 fs	בָּאת	2 fs	תָּבֹואִי	2 fs	בֹּואִי
1 cs	בָּאתִי	1 cs	אָבֹוא		
3 cp	בָּאוּ	3 mp	יָבֹואוּ		
		3 fp	תָּבֹואנָה		
2 mp	בָּאתֶם	2 mp	תָּבֹואוּ	2 mp	בֹּואוּ
2 fp	בָּאתֶן	2 fp	תָּבֹואנָה	2 fp	בֹּואנָה
1 cp	בָּאנוּ	1 cp	נָבֹוא		

Infinitive Construct	בֹּוא	Participle Active	ms	בָּא	
Infinitive Absolute	בֹּוא		ms	בָּאִים	
			fs	בָּאָה	
			fp	בָּאֹות	

(A) The verb בּוֹא is doubly weak and exhibits the characteristics of ʿAyin Vav/ʿAyin Yod verbs as well as those of Lamed ʾAlef verbs.

(B) Since א never closes the syllable, the vowel preceding it must be long. The vowel is qameṣ in all Qal perfect and Qal participle forms, and holem in all other forms of the Qal stem.

(6) נוּחַ, "to rest, come to rest, abide"

	Perfect		Imperfect		Imperative
3 ms	נָח	3 ms	יָנוּחַ		
3 fs	נָחָה	3 fs	תָּנוּחַ		
2 ms	נַחְתָּ	2 ms	תָּנוּחַ	2 ms	-----
2 fs	נַחְתְּ	2 fs	תָּנוּחִי	2 fs	-----
1 cs	נַחְתִּי	1 cs	אָנוּחַ		
3 cp	נָחוּ	3 mp	יָנוּחוּ		
		3 fp	-----		
2 mp	נַחְתֶּם	2 mp	-----	2 mp	-----
2 fp	נַחְתֶּן	2 fp	-----	2 fp	-----
1 cp	נַחְנוּ	1 cp	-----		

Infinitive Construct	נוּחַ/נוֹחַ	Participle Active	ms	נָח
Infinitive Absolute	נוֹחַ		ms	נָחִים
			fs	נָחָה
			fp	נָחוֹת

(A) This doubly weak verb exhibits the characteristics of both ʿAyin Vav/ʿAyin Yod and Lamed Guttural verbs.

(B) When ח is final in a verb form it must be preceded by an "a" class vowel. This is qameṣ in Qal perfect 3 ms and Qal active participle (ms). However, when final ח is preceded by וּ or וֹ, both of which are unchangeably long vowels, a pataḥ furtive (cf. V.13.2, p. 23) must be inserted between final ח and the preceding vowel.

74.4 *The Nifʿal Inflection of* [כּוּן]*, which in the Nifʿal signifies "to be firm, established, fixed, prepared, ready"*

	Perfect		Imperfect		Imperative
3 ms	נָכוֹן	3 ms	יִכּוֹן		
3 fs	נָכוֹנָה	3 fs	תִּכּוֹן		
2 ms	נְכוּנוֹתָ	2 ms	תִּכּוֹן	2 ms	הִכּוֹן
2 fs	נְכוּנוֹת	2 fs	תִּכּוֹנִי	2 fs	הִכּוֹנִי
1 cs	נְכוּנוֹתִי	1 cs	אֶכּוֹן		
3 cp	נָכוֹנוּ	3 mp	יִכּוֹנוּ		
		3 fp	תִּכּוֹנָה		
2 mp	נְכוּנוֹתֶם	2 mp	תִּכּוֹנוּ	2 mp	הִכּוֹנוּ
2 fp	נְכוּנוֹתֶן	2 fp	תִּכּוֹנָה	2 fp	הִכּוֹנָה
1 cp	נְכוּנוֹנוּ	1 cp	נִכּוֹן		

Infinitive Construct	הִכּוֹן	Participle Passive	ms	נָכוֹן
Infinitive Absolute	הִכּוֹן		mp	נְכוֹנִים
			fs	נְכוֹנָה
			fp	נְכוֹנוֹת

(A) The linking vowel placed before consonantal afformatives in the Nifʿal perfect is וֹ.

(B) When consonantal afformatives are added to Nifʿal perfect forms of ʿAyin Vav/ʿAyin Yod verbs, the accent shifts away from the stem vowel וֹ. This causes וֹ to be replaced by וּ. Example: 2 ms נְכוּנוֹתָ becomes נְכוּנוֹתָ.

(C) The dagesh forte in the initial stem consonant of the Nifʿal imperfect, imperative, and infinitive forms is what one would expect in the Nifʿal stem.

(D) Because כּוּן has a נ as its final root consonant, this נ is assimilated before נָה endings. Example: Imperfect 3 fp תִּכּוֹנֶנָה becomes תִּכּוֹנָה.

74.5 *The Hif'il Inflection of Representative 'Ayin Vav/'Ayin Yod Verbs*

(1) [כּוּן], which in the Hif'il signifies "to establish, set up, prepare, make ready, arrange"

	Perfect		Imperfect		Imperative
3 ms	הֵכִין	3 ms	יָכִין		
3 fs	הֵכִינָה	3 fs	תָּכִין		
2 ms	הֲכִינוֹתָ	2 ms	תָּכִין	2 ms	הָכֵן
2 fs	הֲכִינוֹת	2 fs	תָּכִינִי	2 fs	הָכִינִי
1 cs	הֲכִינוֹתִי	1 cs	אָכִין		
3 cp	הֵכִינוּ	3 mp	יָכִינוּ		
		3 fp	תְּכֶנָּה		
2 mp	הֲכִינוֹתֶם	2 mp	תָּכִינוּ	2 mp	הָכִינוּ
2 fp	הֲכִינוֹתֶן	2 fp	תְּכֶנָּה	2 fp	הָכֵנָּה
1 cp	הֲכִינוֹנוּ	1 cp	נָכִין		

Infinitive Construct	הָכִין	Participle Active	ms	מֵכִין
Infinitive Absolute	הָכֵן		mp	מְכִינִים
			fs	מְכִינָה
			fp	מְכִינוֹת

(A) The linking vowel inserted before consonantal afformatives in the Hif'il perfect is וֹ.

(B) The accent shifts away from the stem vowel יִ. whenever the linking vowel is inserted in the perfect forms. This causes the performative vowel ṣere (the nearest changeably long vowel in an open syllable) to volatilize. It becomes ḥaṭef-pataḥ, since it stands beneath the guttural ה.

(C) Final נ of the verb root is combined with the נ of נָה endings by doubling. Example: Imperfect 3 fp תְּכֶנְנָה becomes תְּכֶנָּה.

(2) בּוֹא, "to come, go, enter," which in the Hif'il means "to bring, to cause to go"

	Perfect		Imperfect		Imperative
3 ms	הֵבִיא	3 ms	יָבִיא		
3 fs	הֵבִיאָה	3 fs	תָּבִיא		
2 ms	הֵבֵאתָ	2 ms	תָּבִיא	2 ms	הָבֵא
2 fs	הֵבֵאת	2 fs	תָּבִיאִי	2 fs	הָבִיאִי
1 cs	הֵבֵאתִי	1 cs	אָבִיא		
3 cp	הֵבִיאוּ	3 mp	יָבִיאוּ		
		3 fp	תְּבִיאֶינָה		
2 mp	הֲבֵאתֶם	2 mp	תָּבִיאוּ	2 mp	הָבִיאוּ
2 fp	הֲבֵאתֶן	2 fp	תְּבִיאֶינָה	2 fp	הָבֶאנָה
1 cp	הֵבֵאנוּ	1 cp	נָבִיא		

Infinitive Construct	הָבִיא	Participle Active	ms	מֵבִיא
Infinitive Absolute	הָבֵא		mp	מְבִיאִים
			fs	מְבִיאָה
			fp	מְבִיאוֹת

(A) This doubly weak verb is unique in its rejection of the linking vowel before consonantal afformatives in the Hifʿil perfect. The change that is apparent before consonantal afformatives throughout the Hifʿil perfect is the alteration of the stem vowel from ḥireq-yod to ṣere. This change does not take place, however, before vocalic afformatives.

(B) Accented sᵉgol-yod (ֶי) is inserted as a linking vowel before נָה endings in the Hifʿil imperfect. This causes the preformative vowel qameṣ (the nearest changeably long vowel in an open syllable) to volatilize.

(C) The imperative 2 fp is based on an alternate form of the imperfect 2 fp.

74.6 *The Hofʿal Inflection of* מות, *"to die," which in the Hofʿal stem means* "to be killed" ("to be caused to die")

	Perfect		Imperfect
3 ms	הוּמַת	3 ms	יוּמַת
3 fs	הוּמְתָה	3 fs	תּוּמַת
2 ms	הוּמַתָּ	2 ms	תּוּמַת
2 fs	הוּמַתְּ	2 fs	תּוּמְתִי
1 cs	הוּמַתִּי	1 cs	אוּמַת

	Perfect		Imperfect
3 cp	הוּמְתוּ	3 mp	יוּמְתוּ
		3 fp	תּוּמַתְנָה
2 mp	הוּמַתֶּם	2 mp	תּוּמְתוּ
2 fp	הוּמַתֶּן	2 fp	תּוּמַתְנָה
1 cp	הוּמַתְנוּ	1 cp	נוּמַת

Infinitive Construct	הוּמַת	Participle Passive ms	הוּמָת
Infinitive Absolute	הוּמֵת		

(A)   When the final **ת** of the verb root (מות) stands before a consonantal afformative beginning with **ת**, the two are combined by means of a dagesh forte (cf. XXIX.74.3[3], [B], p. 320).   Example: Perfect 1 cs הוּמַתְתִּי becomes הוּמַתִּי.
(B)   The preformative vowel is šureq throughout the Hofʿal stem of ʿAyin Vav/ʿAyin Yod verbs.

74.7   *The Intensive and Reflexive Stems of ʿAyin Vav/ʿAyin Yod Verbs*

There are no Piʿel, Puʿal, or Hitpaʿel forms for ʿAyin Vav/ʿAyin Yod verbs, except in a few instances in late Biblical Hebrew.   Normally, the characteristic sign of these stems is the doubling of the middle consonant of the verb root.   However, since the middle consonant of ʿAyin Vav/ʿAyin Yod verbs either drops out or becomes a long vowel, it becomes impossible to double it.

Substitute forms for these three stems were created by the repetition of the final root consonant and the supplying of appropriate vowels.   The resultant stems are designated as Polel (for Piʿel), Polal (for Puʿal), and Hitpolel (for Hitpaʿel).

(1)   The Polel inflection of [כון], "to set up, establish, make"

	Perfect		Imperfect		Imperative
3 ms	כּוֹנֵן	3 ms	יְכוֹנֵן		
3 fs	כּוֹנְנָה	3 fs	תְּכוֹנֵן		
2 ms	כּוֹנַנְתָּ	2 ms	תְּכוֹנֵן	2 ms	כּוֹנֵן
2 fs	כּוֹנַנְתְּ	2 fs	תְּכוֹנְנִי	2 fs	כּוֹנְנִי
1 cs	כּוֹנַנְתִּי	1 cs	אֲכוֹנֵן		

	Perfect		Imperfect		Imperative
3 cp	כּוֹנְנוּ	3 mp	יְכוֹנְנוּ		
		3 fp	תְּכוֹנֵנָּה		
2 mp	כּוֹנַנְתֶּם	2 mp	תְּכוֹנְנוּ	2 mp	כּוֹנְנוּ
2 fp	כּוֹנַנְתֶּן	2 fp	תְּכוֹנֵנָּה	2 fp	כּוֹנֵנָּה
1 cp	כּוֹנַנּוּ	1 cp	נְכוֹנֵן		

Infinitive Construct	כּוֹנֵן	Participle Active	ms	מְכוֹנֵן
Infinitive Absolute	כּוֹנֵן			

(A) Note the doubling of נ, the final root consonant, before consonantal afformatives beginning with נ. Example: Perfect 1 cp כּוֹנַנְנוּ becomes כּוֹנַנּוּ.

(B) The unchangeably long stem vowel ḥolem is repeated in every form of this stem.

(2) The Polal inflection of שׁוּב, "to turn, return," which in the Polal stem means "to be restored, returned"

	Perfect		Imperfect
3 ms	שׁוֹבַב	3 ms	יְשׁוֹבַב
3 fs	שׁוֹבְבָה	3 fs	תְּשׁוֹבַב
2 ms	שׁוֹבַבְתָּ	2 ms	תְּשׁוֹבַב
2 fs	שׁוֹבַבְתְּ	2 fs	תְּשׁוֹבְבִי
1 cs	שׁוֹבַבְתִּי	1 cs	אֲשׁוֹבַב
3 cp	שׁוֹבְבוּ	3 mp	יְשׁוֹבְבוּ
		3 fp	תְּשׁוֹבַבְנָה
2 mp	שׁוֹבַבְתֶּם	2 mp	תְּשׁוֹבְבוּ
2 fp	שׁוֹבַבְתֶּן	2 fp	תְּשׁוֹבַבְנָה
1 cp	שׁוֹבַבְנוּ	1 cp	נְשׁוֹבַב

Infinitive Construct	שׁוֹבַב	Participle Passive	ms	מְשׁוֹבָב
Infinitive Absolute	שׁוֹבַב			

(3) The Hitpolel inflection of בִּין, "to understand, discern," which in the Hitpolel stem means "to show oneself attentive, to have understanding, discernment"

327

	Perfect		Imperfect		Imperative
3 ms	הִתְבּוֹנֵן	3 ms	יִתְבּוֹנֵן		
3 fs	הִתְבּוֹנְנָה	3 fs	תִּתְבּוֹנֵן		
2 ms	הִתְבּוֹנַנְתָּ	2 ms	תִּתְבּוֹנֵן	2 ms	הִתְבּוֹנֵן
2 fs	הִתְבּוֹנַנְתְּ	2 fs	תִּתְבּוֹנְנִי	2 fs	הִתְבּוֹנְנִי
1 cs	הִתְבּוֹנַנְתִּי	1 cs	אֶתְבּוֹנֵן		
3 cp	הִתְבּוֹנְנוּ	3 mp	יִתְבּוֹנְנוּ		
		3 fp	תִּתְבּוֹנֵנָּה		
2 mp	הִתְבּוֹנַנְתֶּם	2 mp	תִּתְבּוֹנְנוּ	2 mp	הִתְבּוֹנְנוּ
2 fp	הִתְבּוֹנַנְתֶּן	2 fp	תִּתְבּוֹנֵנָּה	2 fp	הִתְבּוֹנֵנָּה
1 cp	הִתְבּוֹנַנּוּ	1 cp	נִתְבּוֹנֵן		

Infinitive Construct	הִתְבּוֹנֵן	Participle Reflexive	מִתְבּוֹנֵן
Infinitive Absolute	הִתְבּוֹנֵן		

The doubling of נ occurs before consonantal afformatives beginning with נ.
   Example:
            Perfect 1 cp הִתְבּוֹנַנְנוּ becomes הִתְבּוֹנַנּוּ.

EXERCISES

1.   Each of the following entries contains an ʿAyin Vav/ʿAyin Yod verb form.
Supply the proper translation for the form. In the space marked (a) give its stem, in
(b) the identification of the form (perfect, imperfect), in (c) its person, gender, and
number, and in (d) its root. Supply this information only for verbs that are ʿAyin
Vav/ʿAyin Yod.

(1)   יְהוָה בַּשָּׁמַיִם הֵכִין כִּסְאוֹ   The LORD has _____ his throne in the
      heavens. (Ps. 103:19)

            (a) _____ (b) _____ (c) _____ (d) _____

(2)   וְכֹנַנְתִּי אֶת־כִּסְאוֹ עַד־עוֹלָם   And I will _____ his throne forever.
      (1 Chr. 17:12)

            (a) _____ (b) _____ (c) _____ (d) _____

(3)   לְמַעַן תֵּבִינוּ כִּי־אֲנִי הוּא   In order that you may _____ that I am he.
(Isa. 43:10)

    (a) _____ (b) _____ (c) _____ (d) _____

(4)   שִׁירוּ לַיהוָה בָּרֲכוּ שְׁמוֹ   _____ to the LORD; bless his name.
(Ps. 96:2)

    (a) _____ (b) _____ (c) _____ (d) _____

(5)   וְשַׂמְתִּי עֵינִי עֲלֵיהֶם לְטוֹבָה   And I will _____ my eye upon them
for good. (Jer. 24:6)

    (a) _____ (b) _____ (c) _____ (d) _____

(6)   וַיַּךְ אֶת־הַפְּלִשְׁתִּי וַיְמִיתֵהוּ   And he smote the Philistine and _____
him. (2 Sam. 21:17)

    (a) _____ (b) _____ (c) _____ (d) _____

(7)   וְאֵין אֱלֹהִים עִמָּדִי אֲנִי אָמִית וַאֲחַיֶּה   And there is no god beside me;
I _____ and I make alive. (Deut. 32:39)

    (a) _____ (b) _____ (c) _____ (d) _____

(8)   אִם־יָמוּת גֶּבֶר הֲיִחְיֶה   If a man _____, shall he live (again)?
(Job. 14:14)

    (a) _____ (b) _____ (c) _____ (d) _____

(9)   הֲרִימֹתִי קוֹלִי וָאֶקְרָא   I _____ my voice and cried out.
(Gen. 39:15)

    (a) _____ (b) _____ (c) _____ (d) _____

(10)   נַפְשִׁי יְשׁוֹבֵב   He _____ my soul. (Ps. 23:3)

    (a) _____ (b) _____ (c) _____ (d) _____

(11)   וַיָּקָם קַיִן אֶל־הֶבֶל אָחִיו וַיַּהַרְגֵהוּ   And Cain _____ against Abel
his brother and killed him. (Gen. 4:8)

    (a) _____ (b) _____ (c) _____ (d) _____

(12)   יָבֵשׁ חָצִיר נָבֵל צִיץ וּדְבַר־אֱלֹהֵינוּ יָקוּם לְעוֹלָם   The grass withers,
the flower fades; but the word of our God shall _____ for ever.
(Isa. 40:8)

    (a) _____ (b) _____ (c) _____ (d) _____

(13) בֹּשְׁנוּ מְאֹד כִּי־עָזַבְנוּ אָרֶץ We are utterly _____, for we have forsaken the land. (Jer. 9:18)

        (a) _____ (b) _____ (c) _____ (d) _____

(14) הֵבִיא לָנוּ אִישׁ עִבְרִי לְצַחֶק בָּנוּ He has _____ to us a Hebrew man to make sport of us. (Gen. 39:14)

        (a) _____ (b) _____ (c) _____ (d) _____

(15) בָּא אֵלַי לִשְׁכַּב עִמִּי He _____ to me to lie with me. (Gen. 39:14)

        (a) _____ (b) _____ (c) _____ (d) _____

2. Each of the following entries contains an imperative form of an ʻAyin Vav/ʻAyin Yod verb. Supply the proper translation for the form. In the space marked (a) give its stem, in (b) its person, gender, and number, and in (c) its root.

(1) קוּמִי כִּי בָא אוֹרֵךְ

_____, for your light has come. (Isa. 60:1)

    (a) _____
    (b) _____
    (c) _____

(2) וַיֹּאמֶר יְהוָה לְנֹחַ בֹּא־אַתָּה וְכָל־בֵּיתְךָ אֶל־הַתֵּבָה

And the LORD said to Noah, "_____ the ark, you and all your household." (Gen. 7:1)

    (a) _____
    (b) _____
    (c) _____

(3) בֹּאוּ שְׁעָרָיו בְּתוֹדָה

_____ his gates with thanksgiving. (Ps. 100:4)

    (a) _____
    (b) _____
    (c) _____

(4) קוּמוּ בָּרֲכוּ אֶת־יְהוָה אֱלֹהֵיכֶם

_____, bless the LORD your God. (Neh. 9:5)

    (a) _____
    (b) _____
    (c) _____

(5) וַיֹּאמֶר לוֹ עֲלֵה הָקֵם לַיהוָה מִזְבֵּחַ

And he said to him, "Go up, _____ an altar to the LORD." (2 Sam. 24:18)

    (a) _____
    (b) _____
    (c) _____

(6) וַיֹּאמֶר לֹא־קָרָאתִי בְנִי שׁוּב שְׁכָב

And he said, "I did not call, my son; _____, lie down!" (1 Sam. 3:6)

    (a) _____
    (b) _____
    (c) _____

(7) שׁוּבִי בְּתוּלַת יִשְׂרָאֵל

_____, O virgin Israel. (Jer. 31:21)

    (a) _____
    (b) _____
    (c) _____

(8) שֻׁבוּ עָדַי בְּכָל־לְבַבְכֶם
_____ to me with all your heart. (Joel 2:12)

(a) _____
(b) _____
(c) _____

(9) הָשִׁיבָה לִי שְׂשׂוֹן יִשְׁעֶךָ
_____ to me the joy of your salvation. (Ps. 51:14;
Eng. 51:12)

(a) _____
(b) _____
(c) _____

(10) כַּשּׁוֹפָר הָרֵם קוֹלֶךָ
_____ your voice like the trumpet. (Isa. 58:1)

(a) _____
(b) _____
(c) _____

(11) הָרִימִי בַכֹּחַ קוֹלֵךְ
_____ your voice with strength. (Isa. 40:9)

(a) _____
(b) _____
(c) _____

(12) שִׂימָה־לָנוּ מֶלֶךְ לְשָׁפְטֵנוּ
_____ for us a king to judge (govern) us.
(1 Sam. 8:5)

(a) _____
(b) _____
(c) _____

(13) כִּי שָׁם שְׁאֵלוּנוּ שִׁירוּ לָנוּ מִשִּׁיר צִיּוֹן
For there they requested us, "_____ for us from
the song (one of the songs) of Zion." (Ps. 137:3)

(a) _____
(b) _____
(c) _____

(14) וְהָבִיאוּ אֶת־אֲחִיכֶם הַקָּטֹן אֵלַי
And _____ your youngest brother to me.
(Gen. 42:19, 20)

(a) _____
(b) _____
(c) _____

(15) הָשִׁיבֵנִי וְאָשׁוּבָה כִּי אַתָּה יְהוָה אֱלֹהָי
_____ me that I may be restored, for you are
the LORD my God. (Jer. 31:18)

(a) _____
(b) _____
(c) _____

3. Supply the proper translation for the pronouns in the following entries.

(1) וַיִּשָּׂאֵהוּ וַיְבִיאֵהוּ אֶל־אִמּוֹ And _____ lifted _____ up and
brought _____ to _____ mother. (2 Kgs. 4:20)

(2) מִי אַתֶּם וּמֵאַיִן תָּבֹאוּ _____ are _____, and where do
_____ come from? (Josh. 9:8)

(3) וַתָּבוֹא בָהֶם הָרוּחַ וַיִּחְיוּ וַיַּעַמְדוּ עַל־רַגְלֵיהֶם חַיִל גָּדוֹל מְאֹד־מְאֹד
And the spirit (breath) entered _____, and _____ lived, and stood
upon _____ feet, an exceedingly great army. (Ezek. 37:10)

(4)   בָּאנוּ־בָאֵשׁ וּבַמַּיִם _____ have come through the fire and through the water. (Ps. 66:12)

(5)   וְאַתָּה תָּבוֹא אֶל־אֲבֹתֶיךָ בְּשָׁלוֹם And _____ shall go to _____ fathers in peace. (Gen. 15:15)

(6)   וַיְבִאֶהָ אֶל־הָאָדָם And _____ brought _____ to the man. (Gen. 2:22)

(7)   וַיְבִיאֻהוּ יְרוּשָׁלַםִ וַיָּמָת שָׁם And _____ brought _____ to Jerusalem, and _____ died there. (Judg. 1:7)

(8)   לָמָּה תָּבִיאוּ אֹתוֹ אֵלָי Why have _____ brought _____ to _____? (1 Sam. 21:15)

(9)   וַהֲקִימֹתִי אֶת־בְּרִיתִי אִתְּכֶם And _____ will establish _____ covenant with _____. (Lev. 26:9)

(10) כִּי־עָפָר אַתָּה וְאֶל־עָפָר תָּשׁוּב For _____ are dust, and unto dust _____ shall return. (Gen. 3:19)

(11) וַהֲשִׁבֹתִים עַל־הָאָרֶץ הַזֹּאת And _____ will bring _____ back to _____ land. (Jer. 24:6)

(12) מְבַקֵּשׁ שָׁאוּל אָבִי לַהֲמִיתֶךָ Saul _____ father is seeking to kill _____. (1 Sam. 19:2)

(13) הֶעֱלִיתָנוּ מֵאֶרֶץ זָבַת חָלָב וּדְבַשׁ לַהֲמִיתֵנוּ בַּמִּדְבָּר _____ brought _____ up from a land flowing with milk and honey to slay _____ in the wilderness. (Num. 16:13)

(14) בַּהֲכִינוֹ שָׁמַיִם שָׁם אָנִי When _____ established the heavens, _____ was there. (Prov. 8:27)

(15) עַד־עוֹלָם אָכִין זַרְעֶךָ _____ will establish _____ seed (descendants) forever. (Ps. 89:5; Eng. 89:4)

4. Underscore the correct participial form in each of the following entries.

   (1)   מָה אֵלֶּה (בָּא / בָּאִים) לַעֲשׂוֹת
         What are these coming to do? (Zech. 2:4; Eng. 1:21)

   (2)   וְהִנֵּה רָחֵל בִּתּוֹ (בָּאָה / בָּאָה) עִם־הַצֹּאן
         And behold, Rachel his daughter is coming with the flock. (Gen. 29:6)

(3) וַיַּרְא וְהִנֵּה גְמַלִּים (בָּאוֹת / בָּאִים)

And he saw, and behold, camels were coming. (Gen. 24:63)

(4) הִנֵּה יָמִים (בָּאוֹת / בָּאִים)

Behold, the days are coming. (1 Sam. 2:31)

(5) מִי־זֶה (בָּא / בָּאָה) מֵאֱדוֹם

Who is this coming from Edom? (Isa. 63:1)

(6) הִנְנִי (מְבִיאִים / מֵבִיא) רָעָה עַל־יְרוּשָׁלָ͏ִם

Behold, I am bringing evil against Jerusalem. (2 Kgs. 21:12)

(7) וְלָמָה יְהוָה (מְבִיאָה / מֵבִיא) אֹתָנוּ אֶל־הָאָרֶץ הַזֹּאת

Why is the LORD bringing us to this land? (Num. 14:3)

(8) הִנֵּה (מֵתָה / מֵת) שָׁאוּל

Behold, Saul is dead. (2 Sam. 4:10)

(9) כִּי אָמְרוּ כֻּלָּנוּ (מֵתִים / מֵתוֹת)

For they said, "We are all dead (men)." (Exod. 12:33)

(10) (נָכוֹן / נְכוֹנָה) יִהְיֶה הַר בֵּית־יְהוָה בְּרֹאשׁ הֶהָרִים

The mountain of the house of the LORD shall be established at the head of the mountains. (Isa. 2:2)

5. Identify each of the verb sequences in the spaces marked (a). In (b) give the stems of the verbs, and in (c) their roots. (Review Lesson XXI.)

Example:

עֲלוּ הָהָר וַהֲבֵאתֶם עֵץ Go up to the mountain and bring wood. (Hag. 1:8)

(a) <u>Imperative</u> + <u>Perfect</u> sequence (b) <u>Qal</u> , <u>Hif‘il</u>

(c) <u>בּוֹא</u> , <u>עָלָה</u>

(1) אָבוֹא אֵלֶיךָ וּבֵרַכְתִּיךָ I will come to you, and I will bless you. (Exod. 20:24)

(a) _____ + _____ sequence (b) _____ , _____

(c) _____ , _____

(2) בֹּאוּ וְנָבוֹא יְרוּשָׁלָ͏ִם Come, and let us go up to Jerusalem. (Jer. 35:11)

(a) _____ + _____ sequence (b) _____ , _____

(c) _____ , _____

(3) לְמַעַן תִּזְכְּרִי וָבֹשְׁתְּ In order that you may remember and be put to shame (confounded). (Ezek. 16:63)

        (a) _____ + _____ sequence (b) _____ , _____

                 (c) _____ , _____

(4) וַיֹּאמְרוּ נָקוּם וּבָנִינוּ And they said, "Let us arise and (let us) build." (Neh. 2:18)

        (a) _____ + _____ sequence (b) _____ , _____

                 (c) _____ , _____

(5) הִנְנִי נֹתֵן בּוֹ רוּחַ וְשָׁמַע שְׁמוּעָה Behold, I will put a spirit in him, so that he shall hear a rumor (report). (2 Kgs. 19:7)

        (a) _____ + _____ sequence (b) _____ , _____

                 (c) _____ , _____

(6) הֲשִׁיבֵנִי וְאָשׁוּבָה כִּי אַתָּה יְהוָה אֱלֹהָי Restore me, that I may be restored, for you are the LORD my God. (Jer. 31:18)

        (a) _____ + _____ sequence (b) _____ , _____

                 (c) _____ , _____

(7) גַּדְּלוּ לַיהוָה אִתִּי וּנְרוֹמְמָה שְׁמוֹ יַחְדָּו Magnify the LORD with me, and let us exalt his name together. (Ps. 34:4; Eng. 34:3)

        (a) _____ + _____ sequence (b) _____ , _____

                 (c) _____ , _____

(8) וְהָבִיאוּ אֶת־אֲחִיכֶם הַקָּטֹן אֵלַי וְאֵדְעָה כִּי לֹא מְרַגְּלִים אַתֶּם And bring your youngest brother to me, that I may know you are not spies. (Gen. 42:34)

        (a) _____ + _____ sequence (b) _____ , _____

                 (c) _____ , _____

(9) שִׂים לֶחֶם לִפְנֵיהֶם וְיֹאכֵלוּ Set bread before them, that they may eat. (2 Kgs. 6:22)

        (a) _____ + _____ sequence (b) _____ , _____

                 (c) _____ , _____

(10) יָדֶיךָ עָשׂוּנִי וַיְכוֹנְנוּנִי Your hands made me and established me. (Ps. 119:73)

        (a) _____ + _____ sequence (b) _____ , _____

                 (c) _____ , _____

6. Practice pronouncing the Hebrew, noting especially ʿAyin Vav/ʿAyin Yod verb forms. Cover the translation and practice translating the Hebrew from sight.

(1) וַיֹּאמֶר דָּוִד אֶל־הַפְּלִשְׁתִּי אַתָּה בָּא אֵלַי בְּחֶרֶב וְאָנֹכִי בָא־אֵלֶיךָ בְּשֵׁם יְהוָה צְבָאוֹת

And David said to the Philistine, "You come to me with a sword, but I come to you in the name of the LORD of hosts." (1 Sam. 17:45)

(2) וְהִנֵּה רוּחַ גְּדוֹלָה בָּאָה מֵעֵבֶר הַמִּדְבָּר וַיִּגַּע בְּאַרְבַּע פִּנּוֹת הַבַּיִת וַיִּפֹּל עַל־הַנְּעָרִים וַיָּמוּתוּ

And behold, a great wind came from across the desert, and struck the four corners of the house, and it fell upon the young people, and they died. (Job 1:19)

(3) בָּרוּךְ הַבָּא בְּשֵׁם יְהוָה בֵּרַכְנוּכֶם מִבֵּית יְהוָה

Blessed is the one who comes in the name of the LORD; we bless you from the house of the LORD. (Ps. 118:26)

(4) שְׂאוּ שְׁעָרִים רָאשֵׁיכֶם וְיָבוֹא מֶלֶךְ הַכָּבוֹד

Lift up your heads, O gates, that the King of glory may enter. (Ps. 24:7)

(5) כִּי אַתָּה תָּבִיא אֶת־בְּנֵי יִשְׂרָאֵל אֶל־הָאָרֶץ אֲשֶׁר־נִשְׁבַּעְתִּי לָהֶם וְאָנֹכִי אֶהְיֶה עִמָּךְ

For you shall bring the children of Israel to the land which I swore to them; and I will be with you. (Deut. 31:23)

(6) וְלֹא־קָם נָבִיא עוֹד בְּיִשְׂרָאֵל כְּמֹשֶׁה

And there has not arisen a prophet since in Israel like Moses. (Deut. 34:10)

(7) מִי־יַעֲלֶה בְהַר־יְהוָה וּמִי־יָקוּם בִּמְקוֹם קָדְשׁוֹ

Who shall go up to the mountain of the LORD, and who shall stand in his holy place? (Ps. 24:3)

(8) עַל־כֵּן לֹא־יָקֻמוּ רְשָׁעִים בַּמִּשְׁפָּט

Therefore, the wicked shall not stand in the judgment. (Ps. 1:5)

(9) וַיֹּאמֶר אֱלֹהִים אֶל־נֹחַ זֹאת אוֹת־הַבְּרִית אֲשֶׁר הֲקִמֹתִי בֵּינִי וּבֵין כָּל־בָּשָׂר אֲשֶׁר עַל־הָאָרֶץ

And God said to Noah, "This is the sign of the covenant which I have established between me and (between) all flesh that is upon the earth." (Gen. 9:17)

(10)   נָבִיא אָקִים לָהֶם מִקֶּרֶב
אֲחֵיהֶם כָּמוֹךָ וְנָתַתִּי דְבָרַי
בְּפִיו וְדִבֶּר אֲלֵיהֶם אֵת
כָּל־אֲשֶׁר אֲצַוֶּנּוּ

I will raise up for them a prophet like you from among their brethren; and I will put my words in his mouth, and he shall speak to them all that I command him. (Deut. 18:18)

(11)   כִּי עֶזְרָא הֵכִין לְבָבוֹ לִדְרוֹשׁ
אֶת־תּוֹרַת יְהוָה וְלַעֲשֹׂת
וּלְלַמֵּד בְּיִשְׂרָאֵל חֹק וּמִשְׁפָּט

For Ezra set his heart to seek the law of the LORD, and to do (it), and to teach in Israel statue(s) and judgment(s). (Ezr. 7:10)

(12)   שִׁירוּ לַיהוָה שִׁיר חָדָשׁ
תְּהִלָּתוֹ מִקְצֵה הָאָרֶץ

Sing to the LORD a new song, his praise from the end of the earth. (Isa. 42:10)

(13)   וַיִּהְיוּ הַמֵּתִים אֲשֶׁר הֵמִית
בְּמוֹתוֹ רַבִּים מֵאֲשֶׁר הֵמִית
בְּחַיָּיו

And the dead whom he killed at his death were more than those whom he had killed during his life. (Judg. 16:30)

(14)   וְנָתַתָּ לְעַבְדְּךָ לֵב שֹׁמֵעַ
לִשְׁפֹּט אֶת־עַמְּךָ לְהָבִין
בֵּין־טוֹב לְרָע

And give to your servant an obedient mind (heart) to govern (judge) your people, to discern between good and evil. (1 Kgs. 3:9)

(15)   כִּי־אֶרְאֶה יָרֵחַ וְכוֹכָבִים
אֲשֶׁר כּוֹנָנְתָּ מָה־אֱנוֹשׁ
כִּי־תִזְכְּרֶנּוּ וּבֶן־אָדָם
כִּי תִפְקְדֶנּוּ

When I look at the moon and the stars that you have set in place, what is man that you remember him or a son of man that you visit him? (Ps. 8:4,5)

(16)   וּמֵעֵץ הַדַּעַת טוֹב וָרָע לֹא
תֹאכַל מִמֶּנּוּ כִּי בְּיוֹם אֲכָלְךָ
מִמֶּנּוּ מוֹת תָּמוּת

But from the tree of the knowledge of good and evil you shall not eat, for in the day that you eat from it you shall surely die. (Gen. 2:17)

(17)   וַיֹּאמְרוּ אֶל־מֹשֶׁה דַּבֶּר־אַתָּה
עִמָּנוּ וְנִשְׁמָעָה וְאַל־יְדַבֵּר
עִמָּנוּ אֱלֹהִים פֶּן־נָמוּת

And they said to Moses, "You speak to us, and we will obey; but let not God speak to us, lest we die." (Exod. 20:19)

(18)   וַיִּקַּח יְהוָה אֱלֹהִים אֶת־
הָאָדָם וַיַּנִּחֵהוּ בְּגַן־עֵדֶן
לְעָבְדָהּ וּלְשָׁמְרָהּ

And the LORD God took the man and he placed him in the garden of Eden to tend it and to keep it. (Gen. 2:15)

VOCABULARY

(1) גוּר to sojourn

(2) גִּיל to rejoice

(3) דִּין to judge

(4) חוּל/חִיל to whirl, dance, writhe

(5) לוּן/לִין to lodge, pass the night, abide

(6) מוּל to circumcise

(7) נוּחַ to rest, come to rest

(8) נוּס to flee

(9) נוּעַ to quiver, stagger, tremble

(10) עוּר to arouse oneself

(11) פּוּץ to be scattered

(12) רוּץ to run

(13) רִיב to strive, contend

(14) שִׁיר to sing

(15) שִׁית to put, place, set

(16) כָּשַׁל he stumbled

(17) לָכַד he seized, captured

(18) שָׁבַת he ceased, rested

337

LESSON XXX

75. Weak Verbs: Pe Vav/Pe Yod Verbs*

75.1 *Definition*

Pe Vav/Pe Yod verbs include all verbs whose initial root consonant as it now stands is yod. In their root forms, therefore, all Pe Vav/Pe Yod verbs look alike. For example יָבֵשׁ, "he dried up, withered, was dry," and יָטַב, "he was good," have similar root forms (Qal perfect 3 ms), yet the first is to be classified as Pe Vav and the second as Pe Yod. The two can be distinguished not by their Qal forms but by their forms in other stems, particularly in the Nif'al and Hif'al stems.

75.2 *Distinguishing Characteristics of Pe Vav Verbs*

(1) Some Pe Vav verbs have yod as their initial root consonant in most forms of the Qal stem. Another distinguishing characteristic of verbs in this group is that they have pataḥ as the stem vowel in the Qal imperfect. The group includes:

(a)	יָבֵשׁ	"he was dry"		(e)	יָרֵא	"he feared"
(b)	יָגַע	"he grew weary"		(f)	יָרֵשׁ	"he possessed, drove out"
(c)	יָעַץ	"he advised"		(g)	יָשֵׁן	"he fell asleep, slept"
(d)	יָקַץ	"he awoke"				

(a) The initial root consonant appears as yod in all forms of the Qal perfect in these and all other Pe Vav verbs. The Qal perfect is inflected in the customary manner, allowing of course for the necessary changes in doubly weak verbs.

Qal Perfect of יָבֵשׁ and of the doubly weak יָרֵא

3 ms	יָבֵשׁ	יָרֵא
3 fs	יָבְשָׁה	יָרְאָה
2 ms	יָבַשְׁתָּ	יָרֵאתָ
2 fs	etc.	etc.

(b) The initial root consonant appears as yod in all Qal imperfect forms of this group of Pe Vav verbs. Note also that the stem vowel is pataḥ. Since yod is preceded by the preformative vowel ḥireq, it combines with ḥireq to form ḥireq-yod, an unchangeably long vowel.

---

*Refer to Verb Chart 10, pp. 420f., for the conjugation of the Pe Vav/Pe Yod verb.

338

Qal Imperfect of יָבֵשׁ and יָרֵא

3 ms	יִיבַשׁ	יִירָא
3 fs	תִּיבַשׁ	תִּירָא
2 ms	תִּיבַשׁ	תִּירָא
2 fs	תִּיבְשִׁי	תִּירְאִי
1 cs	אִיבַשׁ	אִירָא
3 mp	יִיבְשׁוּ	יִירְאוּ
3 fp	תִּיבַשְׁנָה	תִּירֶאנָה
2 mp	תִּיבְשׁוּ	תִּירְאוּ
2 fp	תִּיבַשְׁנָה	תִּירֶאנָה
1 cp	נִיבַשׁ	נִירָא

(c) The two verbs listed here illustrate the different forms of the Qal imperative that one encounters in this group of Pe Vav verbs. Some of these verbs retain the vav (as yod) in the Qal imperative, while others drop it altogether, resulting in forms that resemble those of many Pe Nun verbs (cf. XXVIII.73.2[4], pp. 303ff.).

Qal Imperative of יָבֵשׁ and יָרַשׁ, "he possessed, inherited"

2 ms	יְבַשׁ	רֵשׁ
2 fs	יְבְשִׁי	רְשִׁי
2 mp	יְבְשׁוּ	רְשׁוּ
2 fp	יְבַשְׁנָה	רֵשְׁנָה

(d) Two variations are also evident in the Qal infinitive forms of this group of Pe Vav verbs. Some form the Qal infinitive construct by retaining the vav (as yod), while others drop vav (yod) from the beginning of the form and add ת to the end of the form, thus producing a segholate form.

Qal Infinitive forms of יָבֵשׁ and יָרַשׁ

Qal Infinitive Construct	יְבשׁ	רֶשֶׁת
Qal Infinitive Absolute	יָבוֹשׁ	יָרוֹשׁ

(e) Qal participles of these and other Pe Vav verbs are formed in the normal manner.

Examples:

	ms	mp	fs
Active:	יוֹרֵשׁ	יוֹרְשִׁים	
	יוֹעֵץ	יוֹעֲצִים	
	יָרֵא	יְרֵאִים	יְרֵאָה
Passive:	יָעוּץ	יְעוּצִים	יְעוּצָה

339

(2)   A second group of Pe Vav verbs consists of those that drop the initial root consonant in the Qal imperfect, Qal imperative, and Qal infinitive construct.   These verbs retain yod as the initial root consonant in all other Qal forms.   In this group of verbs the preformative vowel of the Qal imperfect forms is raised from ḥireq to ṣere.   The stem vowel is also ṣere, which may be volatilized before vocalic afformatives or changed to pataḥ before נָה endings.

The following verbs are among those included in this group:

יָדַע	"he knew"	יָצָא	"he went out"
יָלַד	"he begot"	יָרַד	"he went down"
יָסַף	"he added, increased"	יָשַׁב	"he sat, dwelt"

The verb הָלַךְ, "he went, walked," must also be included here, since in the Qal imperfect, Qal imperative, Qal infinitive construct, and throughout the Hifʿil stem it is treated as a Pe Vav verb.   It is also likely that the verbs [יכח], "he judged, corrected, rebuked," [ישׁע], "he saved, delivered," and [יתר], "he was left over, remained" belong in this group, although they are not found in the Qal stem.

(a)   Qal Imperfect of הָלַךְ, יָצָא, יָשַׁב, and יָדַע

These verbs drop the initial root consonant in the Qal imperfect. In all Qal imperfect forms the preformative vowel is ṣere.   The stem vowel is also ṣere except in the case of יָדַע, which because of its final guttural requires a pataḥ rather than a ṣere.   Because יָצָא is doubly weak, it reflects some of the characteristics of Lamed ʾAlef verbs (cf. XXVI.71, pp. 275ff.).

	יָשַׁב	יָצָא	הָלַךְ	יָדַע
3 ms	יֵשֵׁב	יֵצֵא	יֵלֵךְ	יֵדַע
3 fs	תֵּשֵׁב	תֵּצֵא	תֵּלֵךְ	תֵּדַע
2 ms	תֵּשֵׁב	תֵּצֵא	תֵּלֵךְ	תֵּדַע
2 fs	תֵּשְׁבִי	תֵּצְאִי	תֵּלְכִי	תֵּדְעִי
1 cs	אֵשֵׁב	אֵצֵא	אֵלֵךְ	אֵדַע
3 mp	יֵשְׁבוּ	יֵצְאוּ	יֵלְכוּ	יֵדְעוּ
3 fp	תֵּשַׁבְנָה	תֵּצֶאנָה	תֵּלַכְנָה	תֵּדַעְנָה
2 mp	תֵּשְׁבוּ	תֵּצְאוּ	תֵּלְכוּ	תֵּדְעוּ
2 fp	תֵּשַׁבְנָה	תֵּצֶאנָה	תֵּלַכְנָה	תֵּדַעְנָה
1 cp	נֵשֵׁב	נֵצֵא	נֵלֵךְ	נֵדַע

(b) Qal Imperative

	יָשַׁב	יָצָא	הָלַךְ	יָדַע
2 ms	שֵׁב	צֵא	לֵךְ	דַּע
2 fs	שְׁבִי	צְאִי	לְכִי	דְּעִי
2 mp	שְׁבוּ	צְאוּ	לְכוּ	דְּעוּ
2 fp	שֵׁבְנָה	צֶאנָה	לֵכְנָה	דַּעְנָה

(c) Qal Infinitive Construct

יָשַׁב	יָצָא	הָלַךְ	יָדַע

(לָדַעַת) דַּעַת (לָלֶכֶת) לֶכֶת (לָצֵאת) צֵאת (לָשֶׁבֶת) שֶׁבֶת

(3)   A third group of Pe Vav verbs consists of those that have צ (or occasionally another sibilant) as their middle root consonant (cf. I.1.13, p. 3). These verbs are formed on the analogy of Pe Nun verbs (cf. XXVIII.73, pp. 301–307). When vav (yod) stands at the end of the preformative syllable, it drops out and a dagesh forte is placed in the following consonant (in this case the sibilant). Thus יִיצֹק (Qal imperfect 3 ms from יָצַק, "he poured out") becomes יִצֹק; הִיצִית (Hif‘il perfect 3 ms from יָצַת, "he kindled, set on fire") becomes הִצִּית; and יַיְצִיג (Hif‘il imperfect 3 ms from יָצַג, "he set, placed") becomes יַצִּיג.

(4)   The verb יָכֹל, "he has power, is able," which occurs only in the Qal stem, has a peculiar characteristic in the Qal imperfect. There it retains the vav of the verb root as šureq after each of the imperfect preformatives. Grammarians theorize that the Qal imperfect of this verb may have originally been based on the imperfect of either the Pu‘al or the Hof‘al.

The Qal imperfect forms of יָכֹל attested in the Hebrew Bible are these:

3 ms	יוּכַל	3 mp	יוּכְלוּ
3 fs	תוּכַל	3 fp	------
2 ms	תוּכַל	2 mp	תוּכְלוּ
2 fs	תוּכְלִי	2 fp	------
1 cs	אוּכַל	1 cp	נוּכַל

341

(5) Pe Vav verbs in the Nifʿal stem

The initial vav of Pe Vav verbs acts as a regular consonant in all Nifʿal forms except those of the Nifʿal perfect and Nifʿal participle. It combines with the vowel of the nun preformative in all Nifʿal perfects and participles to form a ḥolem (וֹ). This applies to all classes of Pe Vav verbs.

(a) יָלַד, "he begot"

	Perfect		Imperfect		Imperative
3 ms	נוֹלַד	3 ms	יִוָּלֵד		
3 fs	נוֹלְדָה	3 fs	תִּוָּלֵד		
2 ms	נוֹלַדְתָּ	2 ms	תִּוָּלֵד	2 ms	הִוָּלֵד
2 fs	נוֹלַדְתְּ	2 fs	תִּוָּלְדִי	2 fs	הִוָּלְדִי
1 cs	נוֹלַדְתִּי	1 cs	אִוָּלֵד		
3 cp	נוֹלְדוּ	3 mp	יִוָּלְדוּ		
		3 fp	תִּוָּלַדְנָה		
2 mp	נוֹלַדְתֶּם	2 mp	תִּוָּלְדוּ	2 mp	הִוָּלְדוּ
2 fp	נוֹלַדְתֶּן	2 fp	תִּוָּלַדְנָה	2 fp	הִוָּלַדְנָה
1 cp	נוֹלַדְנוּ	1 cp	נִוָּלֵד		

Infinitive Construct	הִוָּלֵד	Participle Passive	ms	נוֹלָד
Infinitive Absolute	הִוָּלֵד			

(b) [יָשַׁע], "he saved, delivered," a doubly weak verb which in the Nifʿal stem means "he was saved, liberated, delivered"

	Perfect		Imperfect		Imperative
3 ms	נוֹשַׁע	3 ms	יִוָּשַׁע		
3 fs	נוֹשְׁעָה	3 fs	תִּוָּשַׁע		
2 ms	נוֹשַׁעְתָּ	2 ms	תִּוָּשַׁע	2 ms	הִוָּשַׁע
2 fs	נוֹשַׁעְתְּ	2 fs	תִּוָּשְׁעִי	2 fs	הִוָּשְׁעִי
1 cs	נוֹשַׁעְתִּי	1 cs	אִוָּשַׁע		

3 cp	נוֹשְׁעוּ	3 mp	יִוָּשְׁעוּ			
		3 fp	תִּוָּשַׁעְנָה			
2 mp	נוֹשַׁעְתֶּם	2 mp	תִּוָּשְׁעוּ	2 mp	הִוָּשְׁעוּ	
2 fp	נוֹשַׁעְתֶּן	2 fp	תִּוָּשַׁעְנָה	2 fp	הִוָּשַׁעְנָה	
1 cp	נוֹשַׁעְנוּ	1 cp	נִוָּשַׁע			

Infinitive Construct	הִוָּשַׁע	Participle	ms	נוֹשָׁע
Infinitive Absolute	הִוָּשֵׁעַ			

(6) Pe Vav verbs in the intensive stems (Pi‘el, Pu‘al, Hitpa‘el)

Pe Vav verbs normally have a yod as the initial root consonant in the intensive stems, although they occasionally have a vav in the Hitpa‘el stem.
Examples:

יְיַסֵּר   (Pi‘el imperfect 3 ms from יָסַר, "he chastened, corrected")

יְיַשֵּׁר   (Pi‘el imperfect 3 ms from יָשַׁר, "he made straight, smooth")

יִתְיַצֵּב   (Hitpa‘el imperfect 3 ms from יָצַב, "he stationed himself, took his stand")

(7) Pe Vav verbs in the causative stems (Hif‘il, Hof‘al)

Pe Vav verbs retain the vav as ḥolem throughout the Hif‘il stem, and as šureq throughout the Hof‘al stem.

(a) יָשַׁב, "he sat, dwelt," which in the Hif‘il stem means "he caused to sit or to dwell"

	Perfect		Imperfect		Imperative
3 ms	הוֹשִׁיב	3 ms	יוֹשִׁיב	2 ms	הוֹשֵׁב
3 fs	הוֹשִׁיבָה	3 fs	תּוֹשִׁיב	2 fs	הוֹשִׁיבִי
2 ms	הוֹשַׁבְתָּ	2 ms	תּוֹשִׁיב	2 mp	הוֹשִׁיבוּ
	etc.		etc.	2 fp	הוֹשֵׁבְנָה

Infinitive Construct	הוֹשִׁיב	Participle Active	ms	מוֹשִׁיב
Infinitive Absolute	הוֹשֵׁב			

(b) הָלַךְ, "he went, walked," which in the Hif'il stem means "he led or brought"

	Perfect		Imperfect		Imperative
3 ms	הוֹלִיךְ	3 ms	יוֹלִיךְ	2 ms	הוֹלֵךְ
3 fs	הוֹלִיכָה	3 fs	תּוֹלִיךְ	2 fs	הוֹלִיכִי
2 ms	הוֹלַכְתָּ	2 ms	תּוֹלִיךְ	2 mp	הוֹלִיכוּ
	etc.		etc.	2 fp	הוֹלֵכְנָה

Infinitive Construct	הוֹלִיךְ	Participle Active	ms		מוֹלִיךְ
Infinitive Absolute	הוֹלֵךְ		mp		מוֹלִיכִים
			fs		מוֹלִיכָה
			fp		מוֹלִיכוֹת

(c) יָצָא, "he went out" (a doubly weak verb), which in the Hif'il stem means "he brought out or led out"

	Perfect		Imperfect		Imperative
3 ms	הוֹצִיא	3 ms	יוֹצִיא	2 ms	הוֹצֵא
3 fs	הוֹצִיאָה	3 fs	תּוֹצִיא	2 fs	הוֹצִיאִי
2 ms	הוֹצֵאתָ	2 ms	תּוֹצִיא	2 mp	הוֹצִיאוּ
2 fs	הוֹצֵאת	2 fs	תּוֹצִיאִי	2 fp	הוֹצֵאנָה
1 cs	הוֹצֵאתִי	1 cs	אוֹצִיא		
3 cp	הוֹצִיאוּ		etc.		
2 mp	הוֹצֵאתֶם				
	etc.				

Infinitive Construct	הוֹצִיא	Participle Active	ms		מוֹצִיא
Infinitive Absolute	הוֹצֵא		mp		מוֹצִיאִים
			fs		מוֹצִיאָה
			fp		מוֹצִיאוֹת

(d) יָרַד, "he went down," which in the Hof'al stem means "he was brought down"

	Perfect		Imperfect
3 ms	הוּרַד	3 ms	יוּרַד
3 fs	הוּרְדָה	3 fs	תּוּרַד
2 ms	הוּרַדְתָּ	2 ms	תּוּרַד
	etc.		etc.

Infinitive Construct	הוּרַד	Participle Passive	ms	מוּרָד
Infinitive Absolute	הוּרֵד			

75.3 *Distinguishing Characteristics of Pe Yod Verbs*

The number of true Pe Yod verbs in the Hebrew Bible is very limited. A true Pe Yod verb is one that retains the yod as its initial root consonant in all forms. In forms without prefixes, yod is retained as a regular consonant. In forms with prefixes, it is retained either as ḥireq-yod (in the Qal imperfect), or as ṣere-yod (throughout the Hif'il stem).

(1) Six verbs have traditionally been classified as Pe Yod verbs. They are as follows:

יָטַב	"he was good"	יָנַק	"he sucked"
יָלַל	"he wailed, howled"	יָקַץ	"he awoke"
יָמַן	"he went to the right"	יָשַׁר	"he was straight, straightforward, upright"

(2) The occurrences of these verbs are limited to the Qal and/or Hif'il stems, except for the verb יָשַׁר, which has forms not only in these two stems but also in the Pi'el and Pu'al stems.

(a) יָטַב, "he was good"

	Perfect		Imperfect	Imperative
3 ms	יָטַב	3 ms	יִיטַב	(not used)
3 fs	יָטְבָה	3 fs	תִּיטַב	
2 ms	יָטַבְתָּ	2 ms	תִּיטַב	
	etc.		etc.	

(Because יָטַב is a stative verb, its stem vowel in Qal imperfect is pataḥ.)

| Infinitive Construct | יְטֹב | Participle Active | ms | יֹטֵב |
| Infinitive Absolute | יָטוֹב | | | |

(b) יָטַב, "he did well, was good," which in the Hifʻil stem means "he made (a thing) right, good, beautiful"

	Perfect		Imperfect		Imperative
3 ms	הֵיטִיב	3 ms	יֵיטִיב	2 ms	הֵיטֵב
3 fs	הֵיטִיבָה	3 fs	תֵּיטִיב	2 fs	הֵיטִיבִי
2 ms	הֵיטַבְתָּ	2 ms	תֵּיטִיב	2 mp	הֵיטִיבוּ
	etc.		etc.	2 fp	הֵיטֵבְנָה

Infinitive Construct	הֵיטִיב	Participle Active	ms	מֵיטִיב
Infinitive Absolute	הֵיטֵב		mp	מֵיטִיבִים
			fs	מֵיטִיבָה
			fp	מֵיטִיבוֹת

EXERCISES

1. Each of the following entries contains a Pe Vav/Pe Yod verb form. Supply the proper translation for the form. In the space numbered (a) give its stem, in (b) the indentification of the form (perfect, imperfect, imperative), in (c) its person, gender, and number, and in (d) its root.

(1)   שׁוּב וְשֵׁב עִם־הַמֶּלֶךְ Return and _____ with the king. (2 Sam. 15:19)

      (a) _____ (b) _____ (c) _____ (d) _____

(2)   כִּי־אֵשֵׁב בַּחֹשֶׁךְ יְהוָה אוֹר לִי When I _____ in darkness, the LORD is a light to me. (Mic. 7:8)

      (a) _____ (b) _____ (c) _____ (d) _____

(3)   וְאָנֹכִי יְהוָה אֱלֹהֶיךָ עֹד אוֹשִׁיבְךָ בָאֳהָלִים I am the LORD your God;
once again I will cause you to _____ in tents. (Hos. 12:10)

    (a) _____ (b) _____ (c) _____ (d) _____

(4)   אָנֹכִי אֵרֵד עִמְּךָ מִצְרַיְמָה I will _____ _____ with you
to Egypt. (Gen. 46:4)

    (a) _____ (b) _____ (c) _____ (d) _____

(5)   וְיוֹסֵף הוּרַד מִצְרָיְמָה Now Joseph was _____ _____ to Egypt.
(Gen. 39:1)

    (a) _____ (b) _____ (c) _____ (d) _____

(6)   כְּעוֹף הַשָּׁמַיִם אוֹרִידֵם Like a bird of the heavens, I will _____
them _____. (Hos. 7:12)

    (a) _____ (b) _____ (c) _____ (d) _____

(7)   הוֹרֵד אוֹתָם אֶל־הַמַּיִם _____ them _____ to the water.
(Judg. 7:4)

    (a) _____ (b) _____ (c) _____ (d) _____

(8)   אַבְרָהָם הוֹלִיד אֶת־יִצְחָק Abraham _____ Isaac. (Gen. 25:19)

    (a) _____ (b) _____ (c) _____ (d) _____

(9)   דְּעוּ כִּי־יְהוָה הוּא אֱלֹהִים _____ that the LORD, he is God.
(Ps. 100:3)

    (a) _____ (b) _____ (c) _____ (d) _____

(10)   וְיֵדְעוּ כָּל־הָאָרֶץ כִּי יֵשׁ אֱלֹהִים לְיִשְׂרָאֵל That all the earth may
_____ that there is a God for (in) Israel. (1 Sam. 17:46)

    (a) _____ (b) _____ (c) _____ (d) _____

(11)   לֹא־אִירָא רָע כִּי־אַתָּה עִמָּדִי I will _____ no evil, for you are
with me. (Ps. 23:4)

    (a) _____ (b) _____ (c) _____ (d) _____

(12)   הִתְיַצְּבוּ וּרְאוּ אֶת־יְשׁוּעַת יְהוָה _____ _____ and see
the salvation of the LORD. (Exod. 14:13)

    (a) _____ (b) _____ (c) _____ (d) _____

(13)   וַיֹּאמֶר אֵלַי יְהוָה לֵךְ הִנָּבֵא אֶל־עַמִּי יִשְׂרָאֵל And he said to me,
"_____, prophesy to my people Israel." (Amos 7:15)

    (a) _____ (b) _____ (c) _____ (d) _____

(14) וְהוֹשִׁיעַ אֶת־עַמִּי מִיַּד פְּלִשְׁתִּים And he shall _____ my people from the hand of the Philistines. (1 Sam. 9:16)

(a) _____   (b) _____   (c) _____   (d) _____

(15) אֶזְעַק אֵלֶיךָ חָמָס וְלֹא תוֹשִׁיעַ I cry out to you, "Violence!" but you do not _____. (Hab. 1:2)

(a) _____   (b) _____   (c) _____   (d) _____

2. Two Pe Vav verbs, יָכֹל, "he was able," and יָסַף, "he added, repeated," are frequently followed by infinitives construct, normally prefixed with an inseparable preposition. The forms of יָכֹל followed by the infinitive construct express the notion of being able to do (or not to do) something. The forms of יָסַף followed by the infinitive construct express the notion of repeating an action. In the following examples various infinitives construct occur in conjunction with forms of these two Pe Vav verbs. Copy the infinitive construct in the space marked (a), give its stem in the space marked (b), and list its verb root in the space marked (c). An example containing more than one infinitive construct will have additional spaces provided. Note that the infinitives construct are not necessarily derived from Pe Vav/Pe Yod roots.

וְלֹא־יָסַף שְׁמוּאֵל לִרְאוֹת אֶת־שָׁאוּל עַד־יוֹם מוֹתוֹ   (a) **לִרְאוֹת**

And Samuel did not see Saul again until the day   (b) Qal

of his death. (1 Sam. 15:35)   (c) **רָאָה**

(1) וַיֹּאמֶר יְהוָה אֶל־לִבּוֹ לֹא־אֹסִף עוֹד לְהַכּוֹת   (a) _____

אֶת־כָּל־חַי כַּאֲשֶׁר עָשִׂיתִי   (b) _____

And the LORD said in his heart, "I will never again   (c) _____

destroy (kill) every living creature as I have done." (Gen. 8:21)

(2) לָכֵן לֹא־אוֹסִיף לְהוֹשִׁיעַ אֶתְכֶם   (a) _____

Therefore I will deliver you no more. (Judg. 10:13)   (b) _____

(c) _____

(3) לֹא אֹסֵף לִשְׁמֹעַ אֶת־קוֹל יְהוָה אֱלֹהָי   (a) _____

Let me not hear again the voice of the LORD my God.   (b) _____

(Deut. 18:16)   (c) _____

(4) לֹא אוֹסִיף לִהְיוֹת עִמָּכֶם   (a) _____

I will be with you no more. (Josh. 7:12)   (b) _____

(c) _____

(5) לֹא־תוֹסִיפוּ לִשְׁתּוֹתָהּ עוֹד   (a) _____

You shall not drink it again. (Isa. 51:22)   (b) _____

(c) _____

(6) וַיְשַׁלַּח אֶת־הַיּוֹנָה וְלֹא־יָסְפָה שׁוּב־אֵלָיו עוֹד

And he sent out the dove, but she did not return to him

again. (Gen. 8:12)

(a) _____

(b) _____

(c) _____

(7) וַיֹּסִפוּ בְּנֵי יִשְׂרָאֵל לַעֲשׂוֹת הָרַע בְּעֵינֵי יְהוָה

And the sons of Israel again did what was evil in the eyes

of the LORD. (Judg. 3:12)

(a) _____

(b) _____

(c) _____

(8) וְלֹא־יָכֹל מֹשֶׁה לָבוֹא אֶל־אֹהֶל מוֹעֵד

And Moses was not able to enter the tent of meeting.

(Exod. 40:35)

(a) _____

(b) _____

(c) _____

(9) דָּוִד לֹא יָכֹל לִבְנוֹת בַּיִת לְשֵׁם יְהוָה אֱלֹהָיו

David was not able to build a house to the name

of the LORD his God. (1 Kgs. 5:17)

(a) _____

(b) _____

(c) _____

(10) לֹא־אוּכַל עוֹד לָצֵאת וְלָבוֹא

I am no longer able to go out or

to come in. (Deut. 31:2)

(a) _____

(b) _____

(c) _____

(a) _____

(b) _____

(c) _____

(11) מִי יוּכַל לַעֲמֹד לִפְנֵי יְהוָה הָאֱלֹהִים הַקָּדוֹשׁ הַזֶּה

Who is able to stand before the LORD, this holy God?

(1 Sam. 6:20)

(a) _____

(b) _____

(c) _____

(12) מְלָאכָה גְדוֹלָה אֲנִי עֹשֶׂה וְלֹא אוּכַל לָרֶדֶת

I am doing a great work, and I am not able to come

down. (Neh. 6:3)

(a) _____

(b) _____

(c) _____

(13) לֹא נוּכַל דַּבֵּר אֵלֶיךָ רַע אוֹ־טוֹב

We are not able to speak to you evil or good.

(Gen. 24:50)

(a) _____

(b) _____

(c) _____

(14) וְלֹא יָכְלוּ בְּנֵי מְנַשֶּׁה לְהוֹרִישׁ אֶת־הֶעָרִים הָאֵלֶּה

But the sons of Manasseh were not able to take possession

of those cities. (Josh. 17:12)

(a) _____

(b) _____

(c) _____

(15) כִּי מִי יוּכַל לִשְׁפֹּט אֶת־עַמְּךָ

For who is able to judge your people? (1 Kgs. 3:9)

(a) _____

(b) _____

(c) _____

3. Fill in the correct translation for the pronouns in each of the following entries.

(1) וִירַשְׁתָּ אֹתָם וְיָשַׁבְתָּ בְּאַרְצָם And _____ shall take possession of _____, and _____ shall dwell in _____ land. (Deut. 12:29)

(2) לוֹ אֶהְיֶה וְאִתּוֹ אֵשֵׁב I will be _____, and with _____ I will dwell (remain). (2 Sam. 16:18)

(3) בָּתֵּי גָזִית בְּנִיתֶם וְלֹא־תֵשְׁבוּ בָם _____ have built houses of hewn stone, but _____ shall not dwell in _____. (Amos 5:11)

(4) וַיּוֹשִׁיבֵנִי עַל־כִּסֵּא דָוִד אָבִי And _____ caused _____ to sit on the throne of David _____ father. (1 Kgs. 2:24)

(5) וַתֹּאמֶר אֶל־עֲבָדֶיךָ הוֹרִדֻהוּ אֵלַי וְאָשִׂימָה עֵינִי עָלָיו And _____ said to _____ servants, "Bring _____ down to _____, that _____ may set _____ eyes upon _____." (Gen. 44:21)

(6) אָמַר אֵלַי בְּנִי אַתָּה אֲנִי הַיּוֹם יְלִדְתִּיךָ _____ said to _____, "_____ are _____ son, today _____ have begotten _____." (Ps. 2:7)

(7) יְדַעְתִּיךָ בְשֵׁם וְגַם־מָצָאתָ חֵן בְּעֵינִי _____ know _____ by name, and _____ have also found favor in _____ eyes. (Exod. 33:12)

(8) וְאֶת־שֵׁם קָדְשִׁי אוֹדִיעַ בְּתוֹךְ עַמִּי יִשְׂרָאֵל And _____ holy name _____ will make known in the midst of _____ people Israel. (Ezek. 39:7)

(9) וַיֹּאמְרוּ לִי עֲשֵׂה־לָנוּ אֱלֹהִים אֲשֶׁר יֵלְכוּ לְפָנֵינוּ And _____ said to _____, "Make for _____ gods who may go before _____." (Exod. 32:23)

(10) כִּי־אִתְּךָ אֲנִי לְהוֹשִׁיעֶךָ וּלְהַצִּילֶךָ For _____ am with _____ to save _____ and to deliver _____. (Jer. 15:20)

(11) וּמַלְאַךְ פָּנָיו הוֹשִׁיעָם And the angel of _____ presence saved _____. (Isa. 63:9)

(12) אָנֹכִי יְהוָה אֱלֹהֶיךָ אֲשֶׁר הוֹצֵאתִיךָ מֵאֶרֶץ מִצְרַיִם _____ am the LORD _____ God, who brought _____ up from the land of Egypt. (Exod. 20:2)

(13) וַנִּצְעַק אֶל־יְהוָה וַיִּשְׁמַע קֹלֵנוּ וַיִּשְׁלַח מַלְאָךְ וַיֹּצִאֵנוּ מִמִּצְרָיִם And
_____ cried out to the LORD, and _____ heard _____ voice,
and _____ sent an angel and _____ brought _____ up from
Egypt. (Num. 20:16)

(14) וַיֹּאמֶר אֶת־קֹלְךָ שָׁמַעְתִּי בַּגָּן וָאִירָא כִּי־עֵירֹם אָנֹכִי וָאֵחָבֵא And
_____ said, "_____ heard _____ voice in the garden, and
_____ was afraid because _____ was naked, and _____ hid
_____." (Gen. 3:10)

(15) יְהוָה אוֹרִי וְיִשְׁעִי מִמִּי אִירָא The LORD is _____ light and
_____ salvation; of _____ should _____ be afraid? (Ps. 27:1)

(16) וְאָזְנֶיךָ תִּשְׁמַעְנָה דָבָר מֵאַחֲרֶיךָ לֵאמֹר זֶה הַדֶּרֶךְ לְכוּ בוֹ And
_____ ears shall hear a word behind _____ saying, "_____
is the way, walk in _____!" (Isa. 30:21)

(17) וְאֶת־נְבִיאֶיךָ הָרְגוּ בְחֶרֶב וָאִוָּתֵר אֲנִי לְבַדִּי וַיְבַקְשׁוּ אֶת־נַפְשִׁי לְקַחְתָּהּ
And _____ have slain _____ prophets with the sword, and
_____ alone was left, and _____ sought _____ life
to take _____. (1 Kgs. 19:10)

(18) כִּי יְהוָה שֹׁפְטֵנוּ יְהוָה מְחֹקְקֵנוּ יְהוָה מַלְכֵּנוּ הוּא יוֹשִׁיעֵנוּ For the LORD is _____
judge; the LORD is _____ king; _____ will save _____.
(Isa. 33:22)

4. Underscore the correct participial form in each of the following entries.

(1) וְהִיא (יוֹשֶׁבֶת / יוֹשֵׁב) בַּשָּׂדֶה
And she was sitting in the field. (Judg. 13:9)

(2) וּבְתוֹךְ עַם־טְמֵא שְׂפָתַיִם אָנֹכִי (יוֹשֵׁב / יוֹשְׁבִים)
And I am dwelling in the midst of a people of unclean lips. (Isa. 6:5)

(3) וְהִנֵּה מַלְאֲכֵי אֱלֹהִים (יֹרְדִים / יֹרְדוֹת) בּוֹ
And behold, the angels of God were descending on it! (Gen. 28:12)

(4) (יוֹרֵד / יוֹרְדֵי) הַיָּם בָּאֳנִיּוֹת הֵמָּה רָאוּ מַעֲשֵׂי יְהוָה
They that go down to the sea in ships, they see the works of the LORD.
(Ps. 107:23, 24)

(5)   שָׂרָה אִשְׁתְּךָ (יֵלֵד / יֹלֶדֶת) לְךָ בֵּן

Sarah your wife shall bear you a son. (Gen. 17:19)

(6)   הִנֵּה־בֵן (נוֹלָד / נוֹלְדִים) לְבֵית־דָּוִד

Behold, a son shall be born to the house of David. (1 Kgs. 13:2)

(7)   וִהְיִיתֶם כֵּאלֹהִים (יֹדְעֵי / יֹדְעוֹת) טוֹב וָרָע

And you shall be as God, knowing good and evil. (Gen. 3:5)

(8)   מַדּוּעַ אַתְּ (הֹלֵךְ / הֹלֶכֶת) אֵלָיו הַיּוֹם

Why are you going to him today? (2 Kgs. 4:23)

(9)   וַיֹּאמֶר עֵשָׂו הִנֵּה אָנֹכִי (הֹלֵךְ / הֹלֶכֶת) לָמוּת

And Esau said, "Behold, I am going to die." (Gen. 25:32)

(10)   הָעָם (הַהֹלְכוֹת / הַהֹלְכִים) בַּחֹשֶׁךְ רָאוּ אוֹר גָּדוֹל

The people who walk in darkness have seen a great light. (Isa. 9:1)

5. Identify each of the verb sequences by filling in the space marked (a). In (b) give the stems of the verbs, and in (c) supply their roots. (Review Lesson XXI).

(1)   בְּנֵה־לְךָ בַיִת בִּירוּשָׁלַםִ וְיָשַׁבְתָּ שָׁם Build for yourselves a house in Jerusalem, and dwell there. (1 Kgs. 2:36)

   (a) _____ + _____ sequence (b) _____ , _____

   (c) _____ , _____

(2)   קוּם וְיָרַדְתָּ בֵּית הַיּוֹצֵר Arise, and go down to the potter's house. (Jer. 18:2)

   (a) _____ + _____ sequence (b) _____ , _____

   (c) _____ , _____

(3)   שָׂרָה אִשְׁתְּךָ יֹלֶדֶת לְךָ בֵּן וְקָרָאתָ אֶת־שְׁמוֹ יִצְחָק Sarah your wife shall bear you a son, and you shall call his name Isaac. (Gen. 17:19)

   (a) _____ + _____ sequence (b) _____ , _____

   (c) _____ , _____

(4)   וְאֶת־בְּנוֹתֵיכֶם תְּנוּ לַאֲנָשִׁים וְתֵלַדְנָה בָּנִים וּבָנוֹת And give your daughters to men, that they may bear sons and daughters. (Jer. 29:6)

   (a) _____ + _____ sequence (b) _____ , _____

   (c) _____ , _____

(5)   כֵּן אוֹשִׁיעַ אֶתְכֶם וִהְיִיתֶם בְּרָכָה So will I save you and you shall be a blessing. (Zech. 8:13)

   (a) _____ + _____ sequence (b) _____ , _____

   (c) _____ , _____

(6)   וַיֹּאמֶר צֵא וְעָמַדְתָּ בָהָר לִפְנֵי יְהוָה And he said, "Go forth and stand on the mountain before the LORD." (1 Kgs. 19:11)

   (a) _____ + _____ sequence (b) _____ , _____

   (c) _____ , _____

(7)   אֶחָד הָיָה אַבְרָהָם וַיִּירַשׁ אֶת־הָאָרֶץ Abraham was one, and he took possession of the land. (Ezek. 33:24)

   (a) _____ + _____ sequence (b) _____ , _____

   (c) _____ , _____

(8)   עָלֹה נַעֲלֶה וְיָרַשְׁנוּ אֹתָהּ "Let us go up at once and (let us) possess it." (Num. 13:30)

   (a) _____ + _____ sequence (b) _____ , _____

   (c) _____ , _____

(9)   לְמַעַן יִיטַב לְךָ וְיָרַשְׁתָּ אֶת־הָאָרֶץ הַטֹּבָה In order that it may be well with you, and that you may inherit the good land. (Deut. 6:18)

   (a) _____ + _____ sequence (b) _____ , _____

   (c) _____ , _____

(10)   פֶּן־יָבוֹא וְהִכַּנִי lest he should come and smite (kill) me (Gen. 32:12)

   (a) _____ + _____ sequence (b) _____ , _____

   (c) _____ , _____

(11)   וְאָנֹכִי אֶהְיֶה עִם־פִּיךָ וְהוֹרֵיתִיךָ And I will be with your mouth and I will teach you. (Exod. 4:12)

   (a) _____ + _____ sequence (b) _____ , _____

   (c) _____ , _____

(12)   אִם־תֵּלְכִי עִמִּי וְהָלָכְתִּי "If you go with me, I will go." (Judg. 4:8)

   (a) _____ + _____ sequence (b) _____ , _____

   (c) _____ , _____

6. Practice pronouncing the Hebrew, noting especially Pe Vav/Pe Yod verbs. Cover the English translation and practice translating from sight.

(1) אַחַת שָׁאַלְתִּי מֵאֵת־יְהוָה אוֹתָהּ
אֲבַקֵּשׁ שִׁבְתִּי בְּבֵית־יְהוָה
כָּל־יְמֵי חַיַּי

One thing have I asked of the LORD, that will I seek after; my dwelling in the house of the LORD all the days of my life. (Ps. 27:4)

(2) אַךְ טוֹב וָחֶסֶד יִרְדְּפוּנִי
כָּל־יְמֵי חַיָּי

Surely goodness and mercy shall pursue me all the days of my life. (Ps. 23:6)

(3) וַיֵּרֶד יְהוָה לִרְאֹת אֶת־הָעִיר
וְאֶת־הַמִּגְדָּל אֲשֶׁר בָּנוּ בְּנֵי
הָאָדָם

And the LORD came down to see the city and the tower that the children (sons) of men had built. (Gen. 11:5)

(4) כִּי־יֶלֶד יֻלַּד־לָנוּ בֵּן נִתַּן־לָנוּ

For a child has been born to us; a son has been given to us. (Isa. 9:5)

(5) כִּי־יוֹדֵעַ יְהוָה דֶּרֶךְ צַדִּיקִים
וְדֶרֶךְ רְשָׁעִים תֹּאבֵד

For the LORD knows the way of the righteous, but the way of the wicked shall perish. (Ps. 1:6)

(6) כִּי לֹא־תֵדַע מַה־יֵּלֶד יוֹם

For you do not know what a day may bring forth. (Prov. 27:1)

(7) וַיֹּאמֶר אָכֵן יֵשׁ יְהוָה בַּמָּקוֹם
הַזֶּה וְאָנֹכִי לֹא יָדָעְתִּי

And he said, "Surely the LORD is in this place, but I did not know." (Gen. 28:16)

(8) וַיָּקָם מֶלֶךְ־חָדָשׁ עַל־מִצְרָיִם
אֲשֶׁר לֹא־יָדַע אֶת־יוֹסֵף

And there arose a new king over Egypt, who did not know Joseph. (Exod. 1:8)

(9) וּמִי יוֹדֵעַ אִם־לְעֵת כָּזֹאת
הִגַּעַתְּ לַמַּלְכוּת

And who knows if for a time like this you have come to the kingdom? (Est. 4:14)

(10) וַיִּיקֶץ נֹחַ מִיֵּינוֹ וַיֵּדַע אֵת
אֲשֶׁר־עָשָׂה־לוֹ בְּנוֹ הַקָּטָן

And Noah awoke from his wine, and he knew what his youngest son had done to him. (Gen. 9:24)

354

(11) וָאֵרָא אֶל־אַבְרָהָם אֶל־יִצְחָק
וְאֶל־יַעֲקֹב בְּאֵל שַׁדָּי וּשְׁמִי
יְהוָה לֹא נוֹדַעְתִּי לָהֶם

And I appeared to Abraham, Isaac, and Jacob as El Shaddai (God Almighty), but by my name the LORD I was not known to them. (Exod. 6:3)

(12) פְּנוּ־אֵלַי וְהִוָּשְׁעוּ כָּל־אַפְסֵי־
אָרֶץ כִּי אֲנִי־אֵל וְאֵין עוֹד

Turn to me and be saved, all the ends of the earth, for I am God and there is no other. (Isa. 45:22)

(13) כֵּן יִהְיֶה דְבָרִי אֲשֶׁר יֵצֵא
מִפִּי לֹא־יָשׁוּב אֵלַי
רֵיקָם

So shall my word be that goes forth from my mouth; it shall not return to me fruitless. (Isa. 55:11)

(14) יָבֵשׁ חָצִיר נָבֵל צִיץ וּדְבַר־
אֱלֹהֵינוּ יָקוּם לְעוֹלָם

The grass dries up, the flower fades; but the word of our God will stand forever. (Isa. 40:8)

(15) וַיֹּאמֶר אֲלֵיהֶם עִבְרִי אָנֹכִי
וְאֶת־יְהוָה אֱלֹהֵי הַשָּׁמַיִם אֲנִי
יָרֵא אֲשֶׁר־עָשָׂה אֶת־הַיָּם
וְאֶת־הַיַּבָּשָׁה

And he said to them, "I am a Hebrew, and the LORD, the God of heavens, I fear (worship), who made the sea and the dry land." (Jon. 1:9)

(16) וְהָלְכוּ גּוֹיִם רַבִּים וְאָמְרוּ
לְכוּ וְנַעֲלֶה אֶל־הַר־יְהוָה
וְאֶל־בֵּית אֱלֹהֵי יַעֲקֹב וְיוֹרֵנוּ
מִדְּרָכָיו וְנֵלְכָה בְּאֹרְחֹתָיו כִּי
מִצִּיּוֹן תֵּצֵא תוֹרָה וּדְבַר־
יְהוָה מִירוּשָׁלָ͏ִם

And many nations shall come and shall say, "Come, and let us go up to the mountain of the LORD, and to the house of the God of Jacob, that he may teach us hisways and that we may walk in his paths." For from Zion shall go forth the law, and the word of the LORD from Jerusalem. (Mic. 4:2)

(17) וַיֹּאמֶר מֹשֶׁה אֶל־הָאֱלֹהִים
מִי אָנֹכִי כִּי אֵלֵךְ אֶל־פַּרְעֹה
וְכִי אוֹצִיא אֶת־בְּנֵי
יִשְׂרָאֵל מִמִּצְרָיִם

And Moses said to God, "Who am I that I should go to Pharaoh and that I should bring out the children (sons) of Israel from Egypt?" (Exod. 3:11)

(18) בֹּאוּ שְׁעָרָיו בְּתוֹדָה חֲצֵרֹתָיו
בִּתְהִלָּה הוֹדוּ־לוֹ בָּרְכוּ שְׁמוֹ

Enter his gates with thanksgiving, his courts with praise! Give thanks to him, and bless his name! (Ps. 100:4)

VOCABULARY

(1) יָבֵשׁ   he dried up, was dry

(2) יָגַע   he labored, grew weary

(3) [ידה]   (Hifʿil) he praised, confessed, gave thanks

(4) יָטַב   he did well, was good

(5) [יכח]   (Hifʿil) he reproved, rebuked

(6) יָנַק   he sucked

(7) יָסַד   he founded, established

(8) יָסַר   he admonished, chastised

(9) יָעַץ   he counseled, advised

(10) [יצב]   (Hitpaʿel) he stationed himself, took his stand

(11) יָצַק   he poured out

(12) יָצַת   he kindled, set on fire

(13) יָשַׁר   he was straight, straightforward, upright

(14) [יתר]   (Nifʿal) he (it) was left over, remained

(15) קָטַר   he burned (offered) incense, caused a sacrifice to smoke

(16) [שרת]   (Piʿel) he ministered, served

(17) סָגַר   he shut, closed

(18) [שכם]   (Hifʿil) he arose early

356

LESSON XXXI

76. Weak Verbs: Double ʿAyin Verbs*

76.1 *Definition*

Double ʿAyin verbs are those in which the second root consonant has been duplicated. They are also known as "Geminate" verbs.

The dictionary form for Double ʿAyin verbs is Qal perfect 3 ms, which is usually written in its full form (e.g., סָבַב, "he surrounded," קָלַל, "he was swift, light, insignificant," and תָּמַם, "he was finished, completed.") In the Hebrew Bible, however, many Double ʿAyin verbs are found in monosyllabic form. Thus סָבַב is written as סַב, קָלַל as קַל, and תָּמַם as תַּם. Suffixes and prefixes are added to these short forms to determine the inflection of the various stems.

Many verbs whose second and third consonants are identical are inflected in the same manner as strong verbs. Our concern in this lesson is not with this group of verbs, but with those that show such divergence from the pattern of strong verbs that they must be classified as weak.

76.2 *The Qal Stem of Double ʿAyin Verbs*

The Qal stem of Double ʿAyin verbs is complicated in its formation. The principal reason for this is that transitive and intransitive (stative) verbs are inflected differently in the Qal perfect and imperfect. To complicate matters even further, transitive verbs are not always inflected in a consistent manner in the Qal perfect and imperfect. Their Qal perfect third person forms are sometimes written full (3 ms, סָבַב; 3 fs סָבְבָה; 3 cp סָבְבוּ), while at other times they are written defectively (3 ms, סַב; 3 fs, סַבָּה; 3 cp, סַבּוּ). These transitive verbs may also have two different forms in the Qal imperfect, one form analogous to that of ʿAyin Vav/ʿAyin Yod verbs and the other analogous to that of Pe Nun verbs.

(1) The following Double ʿAyin verbs are among those classified as transitive. (Transitive verbs are those that take direct objects.)

(a)	אָרַר	he cursed	(d)	מָדַד	he measured
(b)	בָּלַל	he mixed, confounded	(e)	סָבַב	he surrounded
(c)	גָּלַל	he rolled	(f)	שָׁדַד	he devastated, destroyed

---

*Refer to Verb Chart 11, pp. 422f., for the conjugation of the Double ʿAyin verb.

(2) The peculiarities of these verbs in the Qal stem can be illustrated in the Qal inflection of סָבַב, "he surrounded."

	Perfect			Imperfect			Imperative
3 ms	סַב (סָבַב)		3 ms	יָסֹב יִסֹב			
3 fs	סָבָה (סָבְבָה)		3 fs	תָּסֹב תִּסֹב			
2 ms	סַבּוֹתָ		2 ms	תָּסֹב תִּסֹב		2 ms	סֹב
2 fs	סַבּוֹת		2 fs	תָּסֹבִּי תִּסֹבִּי		2 fs	סֹבִּי
1 cs	סַבּוֹתִי		1 cs	אָסֹב אֶסֹב			
3 cp	סַבּוּ (סָבְבוּ)		3 mp	יָסֹבּוּ יִסֹבּוּ			
			3 fp	תְּסֻבֶּינָה תִּסֻבֶּינָה			
2 mp	סַבּוֹתֶם		2 mp	תָּסֹבּוּ תִּסֹבּוּ		2 mp	סֹבּוּ
2 fp	סַבּוֹתֶן		2 fp	תְּסֻבֶּינָה תִּסֻבֶּינָה		2 fp	סֻבֶּינָה
1 cp	סַבּוֹנוּ		1 cp	נָסֹב נִסֹב			

Infinitive Construct	סֹב	Participle Active	ms	סוֹבֵב
Infinitive Absolute	סָבוֹב	Participle Passive	ms	סָבוּב

(A) A linking vowel is inserted before consonantal afformatives in this and all other stems of Double ʿAyin verbs. This will be holem-vav (וֹ) before consonantal afformatives of the perfect (all stems), and sᵉgol-yod (ֶי) before consonantal afformatives of the imperfect and the imperative (all stems). Holem-vav draws the accent to itself except before the heavy consonantal afformatives תֶּם and תֶּן. Sᵉgol-yod is always accented when it stands as the linking vowel before consonantal afformatives of the imperfect and imperative.

(B) Vocalic afformatives in the Qal perfect, imperfect, and imperative are not accented as in other classes of verbs. Instead, the accent remains on the preceding stem vowel and therefore must be marked.

(C) The addition of any afformative, either vocalic or consonantal, requires the doubling (by dagesh forte) of the preceding root consonant.

(D) The Qal imperfect 3 fp and 2 mp form תְּסֻבֶּינָה came from the addition of ֶינָה to תָּסֹב. This resulted in תָּסֹבֶּינָה. Because of the shift in accent, two changes took place. The nearest vowel in an open syllable was volatilized: תָּ became תְּ. Then holem, left in an unaccented closed syllable, was shortened to qibbuṣ. This resulted in תְּסֻבֶּינָה.

(E) One set of Qal imperfect forms of Double ʿAyin verbs is built on the analogy of Pe Nun verbs (3 ms, יִסֹב; 3 fs, תִּסֹב; etc.). For example, יִדֹּם (Qal imperfect 3 ms, from דָּמַם, "he was silent, speechless"), found in Amos 5:13, is identical in structure to יִפֹּל (Qal imperfect 3 ms, from נָפַל, "he fell"), found in 1 Samuel 14:45. The beginning student may be confused by these two forms, not knowing if they are Pe Nun verbs or Double ‹Ayin verbs. The best way to be certain about the location and translation of verbs forms like these is to consult a reliable Hebrew lexicon or concordance.

(3) The following Double ‹Ayin verbs are included among those that are classified as intransitive (stative). (Intransitive verbs are those that do not take direct objects.)

(a)	חָתַת	he was shattered, dismayed	(e)	רָבַב	he was numerous, many
			(f)	רָעַע	he was bad, evil
(b)	מָרַר	he was bitter	(g)	שָׁמֵם	he was appalled, devastated
(c)	צָרַר	he was in distress			
(d)	קָלַל	he was swift, light, insignificant, (Pi‹el) he cursed	(h)	תָּמַם	he was completed, finished

(4) תָּמַם, "he was finished, completed," illustrates the peculiarities of Double ‹Ayin verbs that are intransitive.

	Perfect		Imperfect		Imperative
3 ms	תַּם	3 ms	יֵתַם		
3 fs	תַּמָּה	3 fs	תֵּתַם		
2 ms	תַּמּוֹתָ	2 ms	תֵּתַם	2 ms	תַּם
2 fs	תַּמּוֹת	2 fs	תֵּתַמִּי	2 fs	תַּמִּי
1 cs	תַּמּוֹתִי	1 cs	אֵתַם		
3 cp	תַּמּוּ	3 mp	יֵתַמּוּ		
		3 fp	תֵּתַמֶּינָה		
2 mp	תַּמּוֹתֶם	2 mp	תֵּתַמּוּ	2 mp	תַּמּוּ
2 fp	תַּמּוֹתֶן	2 fp	תֵּתַמֶּינָה	2 fp	תַּמְנָה
1 cp	תַּמּוֹנוּ	1 cp	נֵתַם		

Infinitive Construct	תֹּם	Participle Active	ms	תַּם
Infinitive Absolute	תֹּם		mp	תַּמִּים
			fs	תַּמָּה
			fp	תַּמּוֹת

(A)   The preformative vowel in Qal imperfect is ṣere, lengthened from ḥireq, by virtue of the fact that it stands in an open unaccented syllable.

(B)   The stem vowel in the Qal imperfect and imperative is pataḥ rather than ḥolem, which is found in the inflection of transitive verbs of this class.

(C)   The rules for the addition of afformatives and for accentuation are the same as in the Qal inflection of transitive verbs.

76.3 *The Nifʿal Stem of Double 'Ayin Verbs*

All Double 'Ayin verbs are inflected alike in the Nifʿal stem.   The peculiarities of these forms can be seen in the Nifʿal inflection of סָבַב , "he surrounded," which in the Nifʿal stem means "he turned himself, he turned around."

	Perfect		Imperfect		Imperative
3 ms	נָסַב	3 ms	יִסַּב		
3 fs	נָסַבָּה	3 fs	תִּסַּב		
2 ms	נְסַבּוֹתָ	2 ms	תִּסַּב	2 ms	הִסַּב
2 fs	נְסַבּוֹת	2 fs	תִּסַּבִּי	2 fs	הִסַּבִּי
1 cs	נְסַבּוֹתִי	1 cs	אֶסַּב		
3 cp	נָסַבּוּ	3 mp	יִסַּבּוּ		
		3 fp	תִּסַּבֶּינָה		
2 mp	נְסַבּוֹתֶם	2 mp	תִּסַּבּוּ	2 mp	הִסַּבּוּ
2 fp	נְסַבּוֹתֶן	2 fp	תִּסַּבֶּינָה	2 fp	הִסַּבֶּינָה
1 cp	נְסַבּוֹנוּ	1 cp	נִסַּב		

Infinitive Construct	הִסַּב	Participle Passive ms	נָסָב
Infinitive Absolute	הִסּׂב		

(A)   All Nifʿal forms of Double 'Ayin verbs are shortened forms.

(B)   The final stem consonant is doubled before all afformatives, both consonantal and vocalic.

(C)   The linking vowels before consonantal afformatives are the same as in the Qal stems (וֹ before perfect afformatives, and ֶי before imperfect and imperative afformatives).

(D)   The linking vowels draw the accent to themselves except before תֶּם and תֶּן.

(E)   Vocalic afformatives are never accented.

(F)   The preformative vowel of the Nifʿal perfect and participial forms is qameṣ rather than ḥireq (which occurs in the strong verb).   Qameṣ is volatilized whenever the accent shifts away from the stem vowel.

(G) The stem vowel of the Nifʿal imperfect, imperative, and infinitive construct is pataḥ rather than ṣere (which occurs in the strong verb).

(H) The dagesh forte in the initial root consonant of the Nifʿal imperfect, imperative, and infinitive forms is the result of the assimiliation of the nun of the Nifʿal stems (יִנָּסֵב becomes יִסֵּב; יִנָּסְבוּ becomes יִסַּבּוּ; etc.).

76.4 The intensive stems (Piʿel, Puʿal, and Hitpaʿel) of most Double ʿAyin verbs are inflected like strong verbs. Occasionally, however, a Double ʿAyin verb will have alternate intensive forms built on the analogy of ʿAyin Vav/ʿAyin Yod verbs. For instance, there may be Poʿel forms in addition to Piʿel forms, Poʿal forms in addition to Puʿal forms, and Hitpoʿel forms in addition to Hitpaʿel forms. A prime example of this occurs with the intensive forms of הָלַל, "he was boastful, he praised."

Synopsis of הָלַל in the Intensive Stems

	Piʿel	Poʿel	Puʿal	Poʿal	Hitpaʿel	Hitpoʿel
Perf. 3 ms	הִלֵּל	הוֹלֵל	הֻלַּל	הוֹלַל	הִתְהַלֵּל	הִתְהוֹלֵל
Impf. 3 ms	יְהַלֵּל	יְהוֹלֵל	יְהֻלַּל	יְהוֹלַל	יִתְהַלֵּל	יִתְהוֹלֵל
Impv. 2 ms	הַלֵּל	הוֹלֵל			הִתְהַלֵּל	הִתְהוֹלֵל
Inf. Const.	הַלֵּל	הוֹלֵל	הֻלַּל	הוֹלַל	הִתְהַלֵּל	הִתְהוֹלֵל
Inf. Abs.	הַלֵּל	הוֹלֵל		הוֹלַל	הִתְהַלֵּל	הִתְהוֹלֵל
Part. Act.	מְהַלֵּל	מְהוֹלֵל			מִתְהַלֵּל	מִתְהוֹלֵל
Part. Pass.			מְהֻלָּל	מְהוֹלָל		

76.5 *The Hifʿil Stem of Double ʿAyin Verbs*

The peculiarities of the Hifʿil stem of Double ʿAyin verbs can be illustrated from the Hifʿil inflection of סָבַב, "he surrounded."

	Perfect		Imperfect		Imperative
3 ms	הֵסֵב	3 ms	יָסֵב (יָסֹב)		
3 fs	הֵסַבָּה	3 fs	תָּסֵב		
2 ms	הֲסִבּוֹתָ	2 ms	תָּסֵב	2 ms	הָסֵב
2 fs	הֲסִבּוֹת	2 fs	תָּסֵבִּי	2 fs	הָסֵבִּי
1 cs	הֲסִבּוֹתִי	1 cs	אָסֵב		

361

3 cp	הֵסַבּוּ	3 mp	יָסֵבּוּ (יִסְבּוּ)				
		3 fp	תְּסֻבֶּינָה				
2 mp	הֲסִבּוֹתֶם	2 mp	תָּסֵבּוּ		2 mp	הָסֵבּוּ	
2 fp	הֲסִבּוֹתֶן	2 fp	תְּסֻבֶּינָה		2 fp	הֲסִבֶּינָה	
1 cp	הֲסִבּוֹנוּ	1 cp	נָסֵב				

Infinitive Construct	הָסֵב	Participle Active ms	מֵסֵב
Infinitive Absolute	הָסֵב		

(A) The preformative vowel is ṣere in the perfect and participial forms.

(B) The linking vowel before consonantal afformatives is ḥolem-vav in the perfect and sᵉgol-yod in the imperfect and imperative.

(C) Linking vowels draw the accent to themselves except before תֶּם and תֶּן. This causes the preformative vowel, which is the nearest preceding vowel in an open syllable, to volatilize. This vowel is reduced to sheva under non-gutturals and ḥatef-pataḥ under gutturals (הֲ). In addition to this, since the stem syllable is a closed syllable and no longer bears the accent before linking vowels, its long vowel, ṣere, must be shortened to ḥireq. The rule applied here is that a closed unaccented syllable ordinarily must have a short vowel.

(D) The stem vowel is ṣere in all Hifʿil forms. It is shortened to ḥireq whenever it loses the accent (before all consonantal afformatives).

(E) The stem vowel ṣere is accented before all vocalic afformatives.

(F) The final stem consonant is doubled before all afformatives, vocalic as well as consonantal.

76.6 *The Hofʿal Stem of Double ʿAyin Verbs*

The Hofʿal stem of Double ʿAyin verbs is formed on the analogy of that of ʿAyin Vav/ʿAyin Yod verbs. A comparison of the Hofʿal synopses of סָבַב, "he surrounded," and קוּם, "to arise," will illustrate the parallels between these two classes of weak verbs. (סָבַב in the Hofʿal means "he or it was turned, was surrounded." The Hofʿal of קוּם means "he or it was raised up.")

Hof'al Synopsis

	סָבַב	קוּם
Perf. 3 ms	הוּסַב	הוּקַם
Impf. 3 ms	יוּסַב	יוּקַם
Impv. 2 ms	----	----
Inf. Const.	הוּסַב	הוּקַם
Inf. Abs.	הוּסַב	הוּקַם
Part. Pass.	מוּסָב	מוּקָם

76.7 *Qal and Hif'il Occurrences of* רָעַע, *"to be evil, bad," which in the Hif'il stem means "he injured, hurt, acted wickedly."*

This is a doubly weak verb (Double 'Ayin and 'Ayin Guttural), which explains the patah (or patah-furtive) before 'ayin whenever it is final in a form. Note that only those forms that actually occur in the Hebrew Bible are included here.

Qal Perfect		Qal Imperfect	
3 ms	רַע	3 ms	יֵרַע
3 fs	רָעָה	3 fs	תֵּרַע
		3 mp	יֵרְעוּ

Hif'il Perfect		Hif'il Imperfect	
3 ms	הֵרַע	3 ms	יָרַע
2 ms	הֲרֵעוֹתָ	2 ms	תָּרַע
1 cs	הֲרֵעוֹתִי	1 cs	אָרַע
3 cp	הֵרֵעוּ	3 mp	יָרֵעוּ
2 mp	הֲרֵעוֹתֶם	2 mp	תָּרֵעוּ
		1 cp	נָרַע

Hif'il Inf. Const.	הָרֵעַ
Hif'il Inf. Abs.	הָרֵעַ

Hif'il Participle ms	מֵרַע
Hif'il Participle mp	מְרֵעִים

EXERCISES

1. Each of the following entries contains a perfect form of a Double 'Ayin verb. In the space marked (a) give its stem, in (b) its person, gender, and number, and in (c) its root.

(1) בַּיּוֹם הַשְּׁבִיעִי סָבְבוּ אֶת־הָעִיר שֶׁבַע פְּעָמִים   (a) _____

On the seventh day they marched around the city   (b) _____

seven times. (Josh. 6:15)   (c) _____

(2) תַּמּוּ דִּבְרֵי אִיּוֹב   (a) _____

The words of Job are completed (ended). (Job 31:40)   (b) _____

(c) _____

(3) וְשַׁדַּי הֵרַע לִי   (a) _____

And the Almighty (Shaddai) has brought evil (calamity)   (b) _____

upon me. (Ruth 1:21)   (c) _____

(4) לָמָה הֲרֵעֹתָ לְעַבְדֶּךָ   (a) _____

Why have you caused evil to your servant? (Num. 11:11)   (b) _____

(c) _____

(5) וְלֹא־הֵסֵב יֹאשִׁיָּהוּ פָנָיו מִמֶּנּוּ   (a) _____

But Josiah would not turn away his face from him.   (b) _____

(2 Chr. 35:22)   (c) _____

(6) חַתּוּ וַיֵּבֹשׁוּ   (a) _____

They are dismayed and confounded (ashamed).   (b) _____

(2 Kgs. 19:26)   (c) _____

(7) נָשַׁמָּה כָּל־הָאָרֶץ   (a) _____

All the earth is made desolate. (Jer. 12:11)   (b) _____

(c) _____

(8) וְנָשַׁמּוּ הַכֹּהֲנִים   (a) _____

And the priests shall be appalled. (Jer. 4:9)   (b) _____

(c) _____

(9) וַהֲשִׁמֹּתִי אֲנִי אֶת־הָאָרֶץ   (a) _____

And I will devastate the land. (Lev. 26:32)   (b) _____

(c) _____

(10) שֶׁבַע בַּיּוֹם הִלַּלְתִּיךָ   (a) _____

Seven times in the day I praise you. (Ps. 119:164)   (b) _____

(c) _____

2. An imperfect form of the Double 'Ayin verb is included in each of the following entries. In the space marked (a) give its stem, in (b) its person, gender, and number, and in (c) its root.

(1) וַיָּסֹבּוּ אֶת־הָעִיר בַּיּוֹם הַשֵּׁנִי פַּעַם אַחַת   (a) _____

And they circled the city once (one time) on the second   (b) _____

day. (Josh. 6:14)   (c) _____

(2) הַיַּרְדֵּן יִסֹּב לְאָחוֹר   (a) _____

The Jordan turned back. (Ps. 114:3)   (b) _____

(c) _____

(3) אָקוּמָה נָּא וַאֲסוֹבְבָה בָעִיר   (a) _____

I will arise and I will go about in the city.   (b) _____

(Song of Sol. 3:2)   (c) _____

(4) וַיַּסֵּב חִזְקִיָּהוּ פָּנָיו אֶל־הַקִּיר   (a) _____

And Hezekiah turned his face to the wall. (Isa. 38:2)   (b) _____

(c) _____

(5) וַתִּתְפַּלֵּל חַנָּה   (a) _____

And Hannah prayed. (1 Sam. 2:1)   (b) _____

(c) _____

(6) לֹא תָאֹר אֶת־הָעָם   (a) _____

You shall not curse the people. (Num. 22:12)   (b) _____

(c) _____

(7) בַּמִּדְבָּר הַזֶּה יִתַּמּוּ וְשָׁם יָמֻתוּ   (a) _____

In this wilderness they shall be brought to an end   (b) _____

(finished), and there they shall die. (Num. 14:35)   (c) _____

(8) וַיַּרְא יְהוָה וַיֵּרַע בְּעֵינָיו   (a) _____

And the LORD saw, and it was evil in his eyes.   (b) _____

(Isa. 59:15)   (c) _____

(9) וְהָיָה מִסְפַּר בְּנֵי־יִשְׂרָאֵל כְּחוֹל הַיָּם אֲשֶׁר לֹא־יִמַּד
וְלֹא יִסָּפֵר

(a) _____
(b) _____
(c) _____

And the number of the children of Israel shall be as the
sand of the sea which can not be measured and can not
be counted. (Hos. 2:1; Eng. 1:10)

(10) וְלֹא־יִירְאוּ עוֹד וְלֹא־יֵחַתּוּ

(a) _____
(b) _____
(c) _____

And they shall not fear any more and they shall not be
dismayed. (Jer. 23:4)

(11) וַיַּרְא כָּל־הָעָם וַיָּרֹנּוּ

(a) _____
(b) _____
(c) _____

And all the people saw and they cried out. (Lev. 9:24)

(12) יָשֹׁמּוּ יְשָׁרִים עַל־זֹאת

(a) _____
(b) _____
(c) _____

The upright ones are appalled at this. (Job 17:8)

(13) וָאֶתְפַּלְלָה לַיהוָה אֱלֹהָי

(a) _____
(b) _____
(c) _____

And I prayed to the LORD my God. (Dan. 9:4)

(14) וַיֹּאמֶר יְהוָה אֵלַי אַל־תִּתְפַּלֵּל בְּעַד־הָעָם הַזֶּה לְטוֹבָה

(a) _____
(b) _____
(c) _____

And the LORD said to me, "Do not pray on behalf of
this people for good." (Jer. 14:11)

(15) וַיַּעֲמֹד פִּינְחָס וַיְפַלֵּל

(a) _____
(b) _____
(c) _____

And Phinehas stood up and prayed. (Ps. 106:30)

(16) אֲהַלְלָה שִׁמְךָ לְעוֹלָם וָעֶד

(a) _____
(b) _____
(c) _____

I will praise your name for ever and ever. (Ps. 145:2)

(17) וַיֹּאמְרוּ כָל־הַקָּהָל אָמֵן וַיְהַלְלוּ אֶת־יְהוָה

(a) _____
(b) _____
(c) _____

And all the congregation said, "Amen!" And they praised
the LORD. (Neh. 5:13)

(18) בַּיהוָה תִּתְהַלֵּל נַפְשִׁי

(a) _____
(b) _____
(c) _____

My soul boasts in the LORD. (Ps. 34:3; Eng. 34:2)

3. Each of the following entries includes an imperative form of a Double 'Ayin verb. In the space marked (a) give its stem, in (b) its person, gender, and number, and in (c) its root.

(1) עִבְרוּ וְסֹבּוּ אֶת־הָעִיר

Pass over and march around the city. (Josh. 6:7)

(a) _____
(b) _____
(c) _____

(2) הָקֵל מִן־הָעֹל אֲשֶׁר־נָתַן אָבִיךָ עָלֵינוּ

Lighten the yoke that your father placed (gave) upon us.
(1 Kgs. 12:9)

(a) _____
(b) _____
(c) _____

(3) רָנִּי בַּת־צִיּוֹן הָרִיעוּ יִשְׂרָאֵל

Sing aloud, O daughter of Zion; Shout, O Israel!
(Zeph. 3:14)

(a) _____
(b) _____
(c) _____

(4) שֹׁמּוּ שָׁמַיִם עַל־זֹאת

Be appalled, O heavens, at this! (Jer. 2:12)

(a) _____
(b) _____
(c) _____

(5) הִתְפַּלֵּל בַּעֲדֵנוּ אֶל־יְהוָה אֱלֹהֵינוּ

Pray on our behalf to the LORD our God. (Jer. 42:20)

(a) _____
(b) _____
(c) _____

(6) הַלְלוּ אֶת־יְהוָה מִן־הַשָּׁמַיִם

Praise the LORD from the heavens. (Ps. 148:1)

(a) _____
(b) _____
(c) _____

(7) הַלְלוּהוּ שֶׁמֶשׁ וְיָרֵחַ

Praise him, sun and moon. (Ps. 148:3)

(a) _____
(b) _____
(c) _____

(8) הַלְלוּ־אֵל בְּקָדְשׁוֹ

Praise God in his sanctuary! (Ps. 150:1)

(a) _____
(b) _____
(c) _____

(9) הַלְלוּ־יָהּ

Praise the LORD! (Ps. 104:35)

(a) _____
(b) _____
(c) _____

(10) הַלְלִי נַפְשִׁי אֶת־יְהוָה

Praise the LORD, O my soul! (Ps. 146:1)

(a) _____
(b) _____
(c) _____

4. A participial form of a Double ʿAyin verb is included in each of the following entries. In the space marked (a) give its stem, in (b) its gender and number, and in (c) its root.

(1)   וּמְקַלֵּל אָבִיו וְאִמּוֹ מוֹת יוּמָת   (a) _____

And the one who makes light of (curses) his father or   (b) _____

his mother shall surely be put to death. (Exod. 21:17)   (c) _____

(2)   כִּי מְבֹרָכָיו יִירְשׁוּ אָרֶץ וּמְקֻלָּלָיו יִכָּרֵתוּ   (a) _____

For those blessed by him shall possess the land, but   (b) _____

those cursed by him shall be cut off. (Ps. 37:22)   (c) _____

(3)   וַאֲבָרֲכָה מְבָרְכֶיךָ וּמְקַלֶּלְךָ אָאֹר   (a) _____

And I will bless the ones blessing you, but the one   (b) _____

cursing you I will curse. (Gen. 12:3)   (c) _____

(4)   אָרוּר הַיּוֹם אֲשֶׁר יֻלַּדְתִּי בּוֹ   (a) _____

Curse be the day on which I was born. (Jer. 20:14)   (b) _____

(c) _____

(5)   וְצֹרֲרֵי יְהוּדָה יִכָּרֵתוּ   (a) _____

And the oppressors of (the ones oppressing) Judah   (b) _____

shall be cut off. (Isa. 11:13)   (c) _____

(6)   וּמִתְפַּלְלִים אֶל־אֵל לֹא יוֹשִׁיעַ   (a) _____

and those who pray to a god who can not save   (b) _____

(Isa. 45:20)   (c) _____

(7)   גָּדוֹל יְהוָה וּמְהֻלָּל מְאֹד   (a) _____

Great is the LORD, and one to be praised profusely.   (b) _____

(Ps. 145:3)   (c) _____

5. Supply the correct pronouns in the translation of each of the following entries.

(1)   יְהַלְלוּ אֶת־שֵׁם יְהוָה כִּי הוּא צִוָּה וְנִבְרָאוּ   Let _____ praise the

name of the LORD, for _____ commanded and _____ were

created. (Ps. 148:5)

(2)   וַנִּתְפַּלֵּל אֶל־אֱלֹהֵינוּ   And _____ prayed to _____ God.

(Neh. 4:3)

(3) **וּקְרָאתֶם אֹתִי וַהֲלַכְתֶּם וְהִתְפַּלַּלְתֶּם אֵלָי וְשָׁמַעְתִּי אֲלֵיכֶם** And
_____ shall call upon _____, and _____ shall come, and
_____ shall pray to _____, and _____ will hear
_____. (Jer. 29:12)

(4) **וְיִתְפַּלֵּל אֵלָיו וְיֹאמַר הַצִּילֵנִי כִּי אֵלִי אָתָּה** And _____ prays to it
and _____ says, "Deliver _____, for _____ are _____
god!" (Isa. 44:17)

(5) **הֵמָּה יִשְׂאוּ קוֹלָם יָרֹנּוּ** _____ lift up _____ voices, _____
shout aloud. (Isa. 24:14)

(6) **וָאֹמַר אָנָה אַתָּה הֹלֵךְ וַיֹּאמֶר אֵלַי לָמֹד אֶת־יְרוּשָׁלָ͏ִם** And _____
said, "Where are _____ going?" And _____ said to _____,
"To measure Jerusalem." (Zech. 2:6)

(7) **וַיֵּרְדוּ אֲבֹתֵינוּ מִצְרַיְמָה וַנֵּשֶׁב בְּמִצְרַיִם יָמִים רַבִּים וַיָּרֵעוּ לָנוּ מִצְרַיִם וְלַאֲבֹתֵינוּ**

And _____ fathers went down to Egypt, and _____ dwelt in Egypt
many day, and the Egyptians dealt harshly with _____ and with
_____ fathers. (Num. 20:15)

(8) **הֵרֵעוּ מֵאֲבוֹתָם** _____ did more evil than _____ fathers.
(Jer. 7:26)

(9) **בְּפִיהֶם יְבָרֵכוּ וּבְקִרְבָּם יְקַלְלוּ** With _____ mouths _____ bless,
but inwardly _____ curse (belittle). (Ps. 62:5; Eng. 62:4)

(10) **חֶבְלֵי שְׁאוֹל סַבֻּנִי** The cords of Sheol encircled _____. (2 Sam. 22:6)

6. In the following clauses and sentences, identify (a) the verb sequence (cf. XXI.63,
pp. 213ff.), (b) the verb stems, and (c) the verb roots.

Example:

אָנֹכִי עָשִׂיתִי אֶת־הָאָרֶץ וּנְתַתִּיהָ לַאֲשֶׁר יָשַׁר בְּעֵינָי I have made the
earth and have given it to the one who is suitable in my sight. (Jer. 27:5)

(a) __Perfect__ + __Perfect__ sequence (b) __Qal__ , __Qal__
(c) __נָתַן__ , __עָשָׂה__

369

(1)   בָּקַע יָם וַיַּעֲבִירֵם   He divided (split open) the sea, and caused them to pass over. (Ps. 78:13)

       (a) _____ + _____ sequence (b) _____ , _____

           (c) _____ , _____

(2)   וְאֶת־מִשְׁפָּטַי תִּשְׁמְרוּ וַעֲשִׂיתֶם אֹתָם   You shall keep my ordinances (judgments) and you shall perform them. (Lev. 25:18)

       (a) _____ + _____ sequence (b) _____ , _____

           (c) _____ , _____

(3)   הַאֵלֵךְ וְקָרָאתִי לָךְ אִשָּׁה מֵינֶקֶת מִן הָעִבְרִיֹּת   Shall I go and call you a nursing woman from the Hebrew women? (Exod. 2:7)

       (a) _____ + _____ sequence (b) _____ , _____

           (c) _____ , _____

(4)   לְמַעַן תִּזְכְּרוּ וַעֲשִׂיתֶם אֶת־כָּל־מִצְוֹתָי   in order that you may remember and do all my commandments (Num. 15:40)

       (a) _____ + _____ sequence (b) _____ , _____

           (c) _____ , _____

(5)   שְׁמֹר מִצְוֹתַי וֶחְיֵה   Keep my commandments, and live. (Prov. 4:4)

       (a) _____ + _____ sequence (b) _____ , _____

           (c) _____ , _____

(6)   הֲרִימֹתִי קוֹלִי וָאֶקְרָא   I lifted up my voice and cried. (Gen. 39:15)

       (a) _____ + _____ sequence (b) _____ , _____

           (c) _____ , _____

(7)   הַאֶעֱלֶה עַל־פְּלִשְׁתִּים וּנְתַתָּם בְּיָדִי   Shall I go up against the Philistines, and will you give them into my hand? (1 Chr. 14:10)

       (a) _____ + _____ sequence (b) _____ , _____

           (c) _____ , _____

(8)   שׁוּבוּ אֶל־הַמֶּלֶךְ וְדִבַּרְתֶּם אֵלָיו   Return to the king and speak to him. (2 Kgs. 1:6)

       (a) _____ + _____ sequence (b) _____ , _____

           (c) _____ , _____

(9)   שְׂאוּ שְׁעָרִים רָאשֵׁיכֶם וְיָבוֹא מֶלֶךְ הַכָּבוֹד   Lift up your heads, O gates, that the King of glory may come in. (Ps. 24:7)

       (a) _____ + _____ sequence (b) _____ , _____

           (c) _____ , _____

(10) שִׁמְעוּ וּתְחִי נַפְשְׁכֶם Hear, that your soul may live. (Isa. 55:3)

(a) _____ + _____ sequence (b) _____ , _____

(c) _____ , _____

7. Practice reading the Hebrew aloud, noting especially occurrences of Double ʿAyin verbs. Cover the English translation and practice translating from sight.

(1) סֹבּוּ צִיּוֹן סִפְרוּ מִגְדָּלֶיהָ

Go round about Zion, count her towers. (Ps. 48:13; Eng. 48:12)

(2) וַתָּבֹא אֵלָיו הַיּוֹנָה לְעֵת עֶרֶב וַיֵּדַע נֹחַ כִּי־קַלּוּ הַמַּיִם מֵעַל הָאָרֶץ

And the dove came to him at the time of evening, and Noah knew that the waters had diminished from upon the earth. (Gen. 8:11)

(3) וַיֹּאמֶר יְהוָה אֶל־לִבּוֹ לֹא־ אֹסִף לְקַלֵּל עוֹד אֶת־הָאֲדָמָה בַּעֲבוּר הָאָדָם וְלֹא־אֹסִף עוֹד לְהַכּוֹת אֶת־כָּל־חַי כַּאֲשֶׁר עָשִׂיתִי

And the LORD said in his heart, "I will never again curse the ground on man's account, and I will never again smite every living creature as I have done." (Gen. 8:21)

(4) וַיֵּרַע הַדָּבָר אֲשֶׁר־עָשָׂה דָוִד בְּעֵינֵי יְהוָה

But the thing that David had done was evil (displeasing) in the eyes of the LORD. (2 Sam. 11:27)

(5) וְהַכֹּהֲנִים נֹשְׂאֵי הָאָרוֹן עֹמְדִים בְּתוֹךְ הַיַּרְדֵּן עַד תֹּם כָּל־ הַדָּבָר אֲשֶׁר־צִוָּה יְהוָה אֶת־ יְהוֹשֻׁעַ לְדַבֵּר אֶל־הָעָם

And the priests bearing the ark were standing in the midst of the Jordan until everything was completed which the LORD commanded Joshua to speak to the people. (Josh. 4:10)

(6) וְעַתָּה לְכָה־נָּא אָרָה־לִּי אֶת־ הָעָם הַזֶּה כִּי־עָצוּם הוּא מִמֶּנִּי אוּלַי אוּכַל נַכֶּה־בּוֹ וַאֲגָרְשֶׁנּוּ מִן־הָאָרֶץ כִּי יָדַעְתִּי אֵת אֲשֶׁר־תְּבָרֵךְ מְבֹרָךְ וַאֲשֶׁר תָּאֹר יוּאָר

Come now, curse for me this people, for they (he) are mightier than I; perhaps I shall be able to smite them (him) and drive them (him) from the land; for I know that he whom you bless is blessed, and he whom you curse is cursed. (Num. 22:6)

371

(7)   וַתִּתְּנֵם בְּיַד צָרֵיהֶם וַיָּצֵרוּ
לָהֶם וּבְעֵת צָרָתָם יִצְעֲקוּ
אֵלֶיךָ וְאַתָּה מִשָּׁמַיִם תִּשְׁמַע
וּכְרַחֲמֶיךָ הָרַבִּים תִּתֵּן לָהֶם
מוֹשִׁיעִים וְיוֹשִׁיעוּם מִיַּד
צָרֵיהֶם

Therefore you gave them into the hand
of their oppressors, and they oppressed
them; and in the time of their oppression
they cried to you and you heard from
heaven; and according to your great
mercies you gave them deliverers, and
they delivered them from the hand of
their oppressors. (Neh. 9:27)

(8)   וּכְכַלּוֹת שְׁלֹמֹה לְהִתְפַּלֵּל
וְהָאֵשׁ יָרְדָה מֵהַשָּׁמַיִם
וַתֹּאכַל הָעֹלָה וְהַזְּבָחִים
וּכְבוֹד יְהוָה מָלֵא אֶת־
הַבָּיִת

When Solomon finished praying, fire came
down from the heavens and devoured
the burnt offering and the sacrifices,
and the glory of the LORD filled
the house. (2 Chr. 7:1)

(9)   וְעַתָּה הָשֵׁב אֵשֶׁת־הָאִישׁ
כִּי־נָבִיא הוּא וְיִתְפַּלֵּל
בַּעַדְךָ וֶחְיֵה וְאִם־אֵינְךָ
מֵשִׁיב דַּע כִּי־מוֹת תָּמוּת
אַתָּה וְכָל־אֲשֶׁר־לָךְ

Now then restore the man's wife; for he
is a prophet, and he will pray for you that
you may live. But if you do not restore
(her), know that you shall surely die,
you, and all that are yours. (Gen. 20:7)

(10)   וַיֹּאמְרוּ כָל־הָעָם אֶל־שְׁמוּאֵל
הִתְפַּלֵּל בְּעַד־עֲבָדֶיךָ אֶל־
יְהוָה אֱלֹהֶיךָ וְאַל־נָמוּת
כִּי־יָסַפְנוּ עַל־כָּל־חַטֹּאתֵינוּ
רָעָה לִשְׁאֹל לָנוּ מֶלֶךְ

And all the people said to Samuel,
"Pray for your servants to the LORD your
God, that we may not die; for we have
added to all our sins (this) evil, to ask
for ourselves a king." (1 Sam. 12:19)

(11)   וְדִרְשׁוּ אֶת־שְׁלוֹם הָעִיר אֲשֶׁר
הִגְלֵיתִי אֶתְכֶם שָׁמָּה
וְהִתְפַּלְלוּ בַעֲדָהּ אֶל־יְהוָה
כִּי בִשְׁלוֹמָהּ יִהְיֶה
לָכֶם שָׁלוֹם

Seek the welfare of the city where I
have taken you into exile, and pray
to the LORD on its behalf; for in its
welfare (properity) you shall have welfare
(prosperity). (Jer. 29:7)

(12)   אַל־יִתְהַלֵּל חָכָם בְּחָכְמָתוֹ
וְאַל־יִתְהַלֵּל הַגִּבּוֹר בִּגְבוּרָתוֹ
אַל־יִתְהַלֵּל עָשִׁיר בְּעָשְׁרוֹ

Let not a wise man boast of his wisdom;
let not the mighty man boast of his
might; let not a rich man boast of his
riches. (Jer. 9:22; Eng. 9:23)

(13)   אַל־תִּתְהַלֵּל בְּיוֹם מָחָר כִּי
לֹא־תֵדַע מַה־יֵּלֶד יוֹם

Do not boast about tomorrow, for you do not know what a day may bring forth (give birth to). (Prov. 27:1)

(14)   בַּיהוָה תִּתְהַלֵּל נַפְשִׁי יִשְׁמְעוּ
עֲנָוִים וְיִשְׂמָחוּ

My soul will glory in the LORD; the humble (afflicted ones) shall hear and be glad. (Ps. 34:3; Eng. 34:2)

(15)   בָּרֲכִי נַפְשִׁי אֶת־יְהוָה
הַלְלוּ־יָהּ

Bless the LORD, O my soul! Hallelujah! (Ps. 104:35)

VOCABULARY

(1)   בָּזַז   he plundered, destroyed

(2)   בָּלַל   he mixed, confounded

(3)   דָּמַם   he was silent, speechless

(4)   [הלל]   (Piʿel, Hitpaʿel) he praised

(5)   [חלל]   (Nifʿal) he was polluted (Hifʿil) he began

(6)   חָנַן   he was gracious, showed favor

(7)   חָתַת   he was shattered, dismayed

(8)   מָדַד   he measured

(9)   נָדַד   he fled

(10)   סָבַב   he surrounded, turned about, went around

(11)   צָרַר   he was in distress

(12)   רָנַן   he shouted for joy, cried out

(13)   שָׁדַד   he devastated, destroyed

(14)   שָׁמַם   he was appalled, devastated

(15)   תָּמַם   he (it) was finished, completed

(16)   גְּבוּל   boundary, border

(17)   גִּבּוֹר   hero, mighty one

(18)   קֶשֶׁת   (f) bow

373

VOCABULARY

[Brackets indicate verb roots that do not usually occur in the Qal stem.]

אָב	father (אֲבִי, const.)	אֶחָד	one, אַחַת (f)
אָבַד	he perished	אָחוֹת	(f) sister
אָבָה	he was willing	אָחַז	he seized, took possession
אָבִיב	ears (of corn); month of year (Mar./Apr.)	אַחֵר	another, other
אֶבְיוֹן	the poor	אַחַר	behind, after
אָבַל	he mourned	אָחוֹר	hind part, back part
אֶבֶן	(f) stone	אַחֲרֵי	after, behind
אָדָם	man, mankind, people	אַחֲרִית	(f) latter part, end, residue
אֲדָמָה	(f) ground, earth	אִי	coast, border, region
אָדוֹן	lord, master, head	אַי	(אֵי) where?
אֲדֹנָי	Lord (pronounced ʾădō-nāy)	אַיֵּה	where?
		אֵיךְ	how?
אָהַב	he loved	אָיַב	he was hostile
אַהֲבָה	(f) love	אוֹיֵב	enemy
אֹהֶל	tent	אַיִל	ram
אוֹ	or	אַיִן	nothing, nought
[אוה]	he desired, longed for, lusted after	אֵין	there is not (construct of אַיִן)
אוֹי	woe! alas!	אֵיפָה	(f) ephah (grain-measure)
אוּלַי	perhaps, peradventure	אִישׁ	man, husband
אָוֶן	trouble, sorrow, wickedness	אֵיתָן	(adj) perennial, ever-flowing
אוֹצָר	treasure, treasury, storehouse	אַךְ	surely, only
אוֹר	to be light, to give light, to shine	אָכַל	he ate
אוֹר	light	אָכֵן	surely
אוֹת	sign	אֵל	God
אָז	then, at that time	אֶל	to, into, toward
אֹזֶן	(f) ear	אַל	not
[אזן]	he listened, heard	אֵלָה	(f) terebinth
אָח	brother (אֲחִי, const.)		

374

אֵלֶּה	these	אֵצֶל	beside, near
אָלָה	(f) oath	אָרַב	he lay in wait, ambushed
אֵלוֹן	(f) terebinth (= אֵלָה)	אֲרֻבָּה	(f) lattice, window, sluice
אֱלֹהִים	God	אַרְבַּע	four, אַרְבָּעָה (f)
אַלּוֹן	oak	אַרְגָּמָן	purple, purple thread or cloth
[אלם]	he was dumb, unable to speak		
אַלְמָנָה	(f) widow	אֲרוֹן	chest, ark
אֶלֶף	ox, thousand	אֶרֶז	cedar
אֵם	(f) mother	אֹרַח	way, path
אִם	if	אֲרִי	lion
אָמָה	(f) maid, handmaid	אַרְיֵה	lion
אַמָּה	(f) cubit	אָרַךְ	he prolonged
אֱמוּנָה	(f) faithfulness, fidelity	אֹרֶךְ	length
[אמן]	(Nif'al) he was faithful (Hif'il) he believed	אַרְמוֹן	citadel, castle, palace
אָמֵץ	he was strong, firm, bold	אֶרֶץ	(f) earth
אָמַר	he said	אָרַר	he cursed
אֱמֶת	(f) truth	אֶשֶׂר	ten
אָנַשׁ	he was sick, weakly	אֵשׁ	(f) fire
אֱנוֹשׁ	man, mankind	אִשָּׁה	(f) woman, wife
אָנֹכִי, אֲנִי	I	אָשֵׁם	he committed a wrong, was guilty
אֲנַחְנוּ	we	אָשָׁם	guilt, offense, trespass, trespass offering
אָסַף	he gathered, removed	אַשְׁמָה	(f) wrong-doing, guilt
אָסַר	he bound, imprisoned	אֲשֶׁר	who, which, what
אַף	nostril, nose, face, anger	אֶשֶׁר (אַשְׁרֵי)	(only pl const) happiness, blessedness
אַף	yea, also, indeed		
אָפָה	he baked	אֲשֵׁרָה	(f) Ashera, sacred tree or pole
אֵפוֹד	ephod (priestly garment)		
אֵפֶר	ashes	אֵת	with
		אֵת	sign of direct object (not to be translated)
אֶצְבַּע	(f) finger	אַתְּ	you (f)

375

אָתָה	he came (poet); (Hif'il) he brought	בִּין	to understand, discern
אַתָּה	you (m)	בִּינָה	(f) understanding
אַתֶּם	you (m pl)	בַּיִת	house (בֵּית, const.)
אֶתְמוֹל	formerly	בָּכָה	he wept
אַתֵּן	you (f pl)	בְּכִי	weeping
		בְּכוֹר	first-born, oldest
בְּאֵר	(f) well	בִּכּוּרִים	first-fruits
בָּאַשׁ	he stank, smelled bad	בַּל	not
בָּבֶל	Babylon	בָּלָה	it became old, wore out
בָּגַד	he dealt treacherously	בְּלִי	without, for lack of
בֶּגֶד	garment	בְּלִיַּעַל	worthlessness
בַּד	separation (always with לְ)	בָּלַל	he mixed, confounded
[בדל]	he separated, divided	בָּלַע	he swallowed, consumed
בֹּהוּ	emptiness	בִּלְעֲדֵי	apart from, except, without
[בהל]	he hastened, acted precipitately, he terrified	בָּמָה	(f) high place
בְּהֵמָה	(f) cattle	בֵּן	son
בּוֹא	to come, go	בָּנָה	he built
בּוּז	to despise	בַּעַד	out from, away from, on behalf of
בּוּס	to tread down, trample	בַּעַל	husband, owner, lord, Baal
בּוֹר	pit, cistern, well	בָּעַר	he (it) burned
בּוֹשׁ	to be ashamed, confounded	בָּצַר	he cut off, made inaccessible, enclosed
בָּזָה	he despised	בָּקַע	he split open
בָּזַז	he plundered, destroyed	בִּקְעָה	(f) valley, plain
בַּז	plunder, spoil, booty	בָּקָר	herd, cattle
בָּחַן	he tested, tried, examined	בֹּקֶר	morning
בָּחַר	he chose	[בקשׁ]	(Pi'el) he sought
בָּטַח	he trusted	בָּרָא	he created
בֶּטֶן	(f) belly, body, womb	בָּרָד	hail
בֵּין	between	בְּרוֹשׁ	cypress or fir
		בַּרְזֶל	iron

בָּרַח   he fled

בְּרִיחַ   bar (to secure a door or gate)

בְּרִית   (f) covenant

[בּרך]   he blessed

בָּרָק   lightning

בֶּרֶךְ   (f) knee

בְּרָכָה   (f) blessing

בָּרַר   he purged, purified, polished

בֹּשֶׂם   spice, balsam

[בשׂר]   (Pi‘el) he bore tidings, preached

בָּשָׂר   flesh

בָּשַׁל   he boiled, seethed

בֹּשֶׁת   (f) shame, shameful thing

בַּת   (f) daughter

בְּתוֹךְ   in the midst of

בְּתוּלָה   (f) virgin

גָּאַל   he redeemed

גּוֹאֵל   redeemer

גָּאוֹן   majesty, excellence

גָּבַהּ   he was high, proud

גְּבוּל   boundary, border

גָּבַר   he was strong, mighty; he prevailed

גִּבּוֹר   hero, mighty one

גִּבְעָה   (f) hill

גָּדַל   he was (became) great

גָּדוֹל   great, large

גָּדַע   he hewed down, hewed off

גּוֹי   nation, people

גּוּר   to sojourn

גֵּר   sojourner

גָּזַז   he sheared (sheep

גָּזַל   he tore away, seized, robbed

גַּיְא   valley (גֵּיא or גֵּי, const.)

גִּיל   to rejoice

גָּלָה   he uncovered, revealed

גּוֹלָה   (f) exile, exiles

גַּל   a heap, wave, billow

גָּלַל   he rolled, rolled away

גִּלּוּלִים   (only pl) idols

גַּם   also, moreover, yea

גָּמַל   he dealt generously with, repaid, recompensed

גְּמוּל   a recompense, benefit

גָּמָל   camel

גַּן   garden

גָּנַב   he stole

גָּעַר   he rebuked

גֶּפֶן   (f) vine

[גרה]   he stirred up strife, engaged in strife

גּוֹרָל   (m and f) lot (as in "casting lots")

גָּרוֹן   neck, throat

גֹּרֶן   threshing-floor

גָּרַע   he diminished, restrained, withdrew

גָּרַשׁ   he drove out, cast out

גֶּשֶׁם   rain, shower

גַּת   (f) wine-press

דֹּב   (m and f) bear

דָּבַק	he cleaved, clung to, kept close	הֶבֶל	vapor, breath, vanity
דָּבָר	word	הָגָה	he moaned, growled, spoke, muttered
[דבר]	(Pi‘el) he spoke	הֲדַס	myrtle (tree)
דְּבַשׁ	honey	הָדַף	he thrust, pushed, drove
דָּג	fish, דָּגָה (f)	הָדַר	he honored, adorned
דָּגָן	corn, grain	הָדָר	splendor, honor, adornment
דּוֹד	beloved, loved one, uncle	הוּא	he
דּוֹר	generation, period	הוֹד	splendor, majesty, splendor
דּוּשׁ	tread, thresh	הַוָּה	(f) desire (usually evil), ruin, destruction
דָּחָה	he pushed, thrust	הוֹי	Ah! Alas! Ha!
דַּי	sufficiency, enough (דֵּי, const.)	הִים, הוּם	to murmur, roar
דִּין	to judge	הוֹן	wealth, sufficiency
[דכא]	he crushed	הָיָה	he was, became
דַּל	(adj) low, weak, poor, helpless	הַיּוֹם	today (lit. "the day")
דָּלַל	he was brought low, languished	הֵיכָל	temple
דֶּלֶת	(f) door	הַיִל	strength, wealth, army
דָּם	blood	הִיא	(f) she
דָּמָה	he was like, resembled	הִין	hin (a measure for liquids)
דְּמוּת	(f) likeness, image	הָלַךְ	he went, walked
דָּמַם	he was silent, speechless	הָלַל	he was boastful, he praised
דַּעַת	(f) knowlege		
דַּק	(adj) thin, small, fine	הֵם, הֵמָּה	they
דָּקַק	he crushed, pulverized, threshed	הֵן, הֵנָּה	(f) they
דָּרַךְ	he treaded, marched	הָמָה	he murmured, growled, roared, was boisterous
דֶּרֶךְ	(m and f) way	הָמוֹן	sound, murmur, roar, crowd, abundance
דָּרַשׁ	he sought, inquired		
דֶּשֶׁא	grass	הָמַם	he made a noise, confused, vexed
דָּשֵׁן	he was fat, grew fat		
דָּת	(f) decree, law	הִנֵּה, הֵן	behold
		הֵנָּה	hither
		הַס	hush! keep silent!

הָפַךְ he overturned, changed, (Nif'al) he was changed, overthrown

הַר mountain

הָרַג he killed, slew

הָרָה to conceive, become pregnant

הָרַס he broke down, destroyed

זְאֵב wolf

זֹאת (f) this

זָבַח he sacrificed, slew

זֶבַח sacrifice

זֵד (adj) insolent, presumptuous

זָדוֹן insolence, presumptuousness

זֶה this

זָהָב gold

[זהר] he instructed, taught, warned

זוּב to flow, gush out

זוּד, זִיד to boil up, seethe, to act proudly, presumptuously

זַיִת olive-tree, olive (זֵית, const.)

זָכָר male

זָכַר he remembered

זִכָּרוֹן memorial, remembrance

זִמָּה (f) plan, device, wickedness

זָמַם he considered, purposed, devised

[זמר] he made melody, made music, sang

זָנָה he committed adultery, fornication

זוֹנָה (f) harlot

זָנַח he rejected, spurned

זָעַם he was indignant

זַעַם indignation

זָעַק he cried out

זְעָקָה (f) cry, outcry

זָקֵן he was old, became old

זָקָן (m and f) beard

זָקֵן (adj) old (of persons only)

זָר a stranger, foreigner; (adj) strange, foreign

זָרָה he scattered, fanned, winnowed

זָרַח he arose, came forth, appeared

זָרַע he sowed

זֶרַע seed, offspring

זְרֹעַ (f) arm, strength

זָרַק he tossed, threw, scattered

[חבא] he hid, withdrew

חָבָה he hid, withdrew

חָבַל (1) he bound, pledged; (2) he acted corruptly, ruined, destroyed

חֶבֶל rope, band, measuring-cord, measured portion, lot

חָבַק he clasped, embraced

חָבַר he united, was joined

חֶבֶר company, association

חָבֵר associate, companion

חָבַשׁ he bound up, harnessed, restrained

חַג feast, festival

חָגַג he made a pilgrimage, attended a religious festival

חָגַר he bound, girded

חָדַל he ceased

חֶדֶר chamber, room

חָדָשׁ (adj) new

[חדשׁ] (Pi'el) he renewed, repaired

חֹדֶשׁ new moon, month

חוֹל sand

חוֹמָה (f) wall

חוּץ a place outside the house, the outdoors, a street

חוּשׁ to hurry, make haste

חָזָה he saw (as in a vision)

חֹזֶה seer, prophet

חָזוֹן vision, oracle, prophecy

חָזַק he was (became) strong

חָזָק (adj) strong, stout, mighty

חָטָא he sinned, missed the mark

חֵטְא sin

חַטָּאת (f) sin

חִטָּה (f) wheat

חִידָה (f) riddle, enigmatic saying or question

חַי (adj) living, alive

חָיָה he lived, revived

חַיָּה (f) living thing, animal

חַיִּים life

חַיִל strength, ability, wealth, army (חֵיל, const.)

חוּל, חִיל to whirl, dance, writhe

חֵךְ palate, roof of mouth, gums

חָכַם he was wise

חָכָם (adj) wise, skillful

חָכְמָה (f) wisdom

חָלָב milk

חֵלֶב fat

חָלָה he was sick, weak

חֳלִי sickness

חֲלוֹם dream

חַלּוֹן (m and f) window

[חלל] (Nif'al) he was polluted (Hif'il) he began

חָלַף he passed away, swept past, changed, exchanged

חָלַץ (1) he took off, withdrew, rescued; (2) he was prepared, equipped (for war)

חָלַק he divided, apportioned, assigned

חֵלֶק portion, tract, territory

חֶלְקָה (f) portion of ground

חָמַד he desired, took pleasure in

חֵמָה (f) heat, rage

חֲמוֹר ass

חָמַל he spared, had compassion on

חָמָס violence

חָמֵץ that which is leavened

חֹמֶר (1) cement, mortar, clay; (2) a dry measure (for grain)

חָמֵשׁ five, חֲמִשָּׁה (f)

חָנָה he encamped

חֲנִית (f) spear

חֲנֻכָּה (f) dedication, consecration

חָנַן	he was gracious, showed favor	חָרַד	he trembled, was terrified
חֵן	favor, grace, acceptance	חָרָה	he (anger) was hot, burned
חִנָּם	in vain, without purpose, freely, gratis	חָרוֹן	fierce, burning anger
חָנֵף	he was polluted, profaned, godless	[חרם]	(Hifʻil) he banned, exterminated, dedicated to destruction
חֶסֶד	goodness, kindness	חֵרֶם	something banned, destined to be destroyed
חָסִיד	kind, pious, godly	חָרַף	he reproached, taunted
חָסָה	he sought refuge	חָרַץ	he cut, sharpened, decided
חָסֵר	he lacked, needed, decreased, diminished		
חָפֵץ	he took delight in, desired	חֶרְפָּה	(f) reproach, taunt
חֵפֶץ	delight, pleasure	חֹרֶף	harvest-time, autumn
חָפַר	he dug, searched for	חָרַשׁ	he cut, engraved, plowed
חָפֵר	he was abashed, ashamed	חָרָשׁ	engraver, carpenter, metalworker
חָפַשׂ	he searched	חָרֵשׁ	he was silent, deaf, speechless
חֵץ	arrow		
חָצֵב	he hewed out	חֵרֵשׁ	(adj) deaf
חָצָה	he divided, halved	חָשַׂךְ	he withheld, refrained
חֲצִי	half	חָשַׂף	he stripped off, made bare
חָצֵר	(m and f) enclosure, court, settlement, village	חָשַׁב	he thought, devised, reckoned
חָצִיר	green grass, herbage	חָשָׁה	he was silent, inactive, still
חֵק, חֵיק	bosom	חָשַׁךְ	it was dark, grew dark
חָקַק	he carved, inscribed, decreed	חֹשֶׁךְ	darkness, obscurity
חֹק	statute	חָתַם	he sealed, attested by sealing, sealed up
חֻקָּה	(f) enactment, decree, statute	חֹתָם	seal, signet-ring
חָקַר	he searched out, examined	חֹתֵן	a wife's father, hence father-in-law
חֶרֶב	(f) sword		
חָרֵב	he was dry, dried up, waste, desolate	חָתַר	he dug, rowed
חָרְבָּה	(f) waste, desolation, ruin	חָתַת	he was shattered, dismayed

טָבַח   he slaughtered, butchered, killed ruthlessly

טָבַל   he dipped, moistened, bathed

טָבַע   he sank down

טַבַּעַת   (f) signet, signet-ring

טָהֵר   he was clean, pure

טָהוֹר   (adj) clean, pure

טוֹב   (adj) good

[טוּל]   to hurl, cast

טוּר   row (of jewels), course (of building stones)

טַל   night-mist, light rain, dew

טָמֵא   he was unclean

טָמֵא   (adj) unclean, defiled

טָמַן   he hid, concealed

טָעַם   he tasted, perceived

טַף   (collective) children, little ones

טֶרֶם   not yet, before that

טָרַף   he tore, rent, plucked

טֶרֶף   food, prey

[יָאל]   (Hif'il) he showed willingness, was pleased, resolved to do (something)

יְאוֹר, יְאר   stream, canal, River Nile

[יבל]   (Hif'il) he led, bore, carried away

יָבֵשׁ   he dried up, was dry

יַבָּשָׁה   (f) dry ground

יָגַע   he labored, grew weary

יְגִיעַ   toil, product of toil

יָד   (f) hand

[יָדָה]   (Hif'il) he praised, confessed, gave thanks

יָדַע   he knew

יָהַב   he gave, ascribed (glory)

יְהוָה   LORD (pronounced ʾădō-nāy)

יָבֵל, יוֹבֵל   ram, ram's horn, cornet

יוֹם   day

יוֹמָם   daily, by day

יוֹנָה   (f) dove

יוֹצֵר   potter

יוֹשֵׁב   inhabitant

יַחְדָּו   together

[יחל]   he waited, tarried

יָטַב   he did well, was good

יַיִן   wine

[יכח]   (Hif'il) he reproved, rebuked

יָכֹל   he was able, he endured

יָלַד   he begot (children)

יֶלֶד   child

[ילל]   (Hif'il) he howled (in distress)

יָם   sea

יָמִין   (f) right hand, right side, south

יָנָה   he oppressed, mistreated

יָנַק   he sucked (as an infant)

יָסַד   he founded, established

יָסַף   he added

יָסַר   he admonished, chastised

יָעַד   he appointed, met at an appointed place

יָעַץ	he counseled, advised	יָשָׁר	(adj) straight, right, upright
יַעַר	wood, forest, thicket	יִשְׂרָאֵל	Israel
יָפֶה	(adj) beautiful, fair, handsome, יָפָה (f)	יָתֵד	(f) tent-peg, pin
יָצָא	he went out	[יתר]	(Nif‘al) he (it) was left over, remained
יָצַב	(Hitpa‘el) he stationed himself, took his stand	יֶתֶר	remnant, remainder, excess
[יצג]	(Hif‘il) he set, placed	כַּאֲשֶׁר	according as, as, when
יִצְהָר	fresh olive oil	כָּבֵד	he was (became) heavy (Pi‘el) he was honored, glorified
יָצַק	he poured out		
יָצַר	he formed		
יָצַת	he kindled, set on fire	כָּבוֹד	glory, honor
יָקַר	he was precious, prized, highly esteemed	כָּבָה	it (he) was quenched, extinguished
יָקָר	(adj) precious, rare, splendid, costly	[כבס]	he washed
		כֶּבֶשׂ	lamb
יָרֵא	he feared	כָּבַשׁ	he subdued, brought into bondage
יִרְאָה	(f) fear		
יָרַד	he went down	כֹּה	thus
יָרָה	he taught	כָּהָה	he grew dim, fainted
יָרֵךְ	(f) thigh, loin, side	כֹּהֵן	priest
יְרוּשָׁלַיִם,		כּוֹכָב	star
יְרוּשָׁלַם	Jerusalem	[כּוּל]	to comprehend, contain, support, nourish
יָרַשׁ	he possessed, inherited, subdued		
		[כּוּן]	to be fixed, firm, established
יֵשׁ	there is, there are	כּוֹס	(f) cup
יָשַׁב	he sat, dwelt	כָּזַב	he lied, was a liar
		כָּזָב	lie, falsehood, deceptive thing
יָשֵׁן	he slept, went to sleep		
[ישׁע]	(Hif‘il) he saved, delivered	[כחד]	he hid, destroyed, effaced
		כֹּחַ, כּוֹחַ	strength, power
יְשׁוּעָה	(f) salvation	כָּחַשׁ	he (it) was disappointing, deceived, failed
יָשַׁר	he was straight, straight-forward, upright		

כִּי for, that, because, when

כִּיּוֹר, כִּיֹר pot, wash-basin

כָּכָה thus

כֹּל all (כָּל־, const.)

כָּלָא he shut up, restrained, withheld

כֶּלֶב dog

כָּלָה he (it) was completed, finished

כָּלָה (f) completion, complete, destruction, annihilation

כַּלָּה (f) daughter-in-law, bride

כְּלִי tool, weapon, vessel

כְּלָיוֹת, כִּלְיָה (f) (only pl) kidneys (כִּלְיוֹת, const.)

כָּלַל he completed, perfected

[כּלם] he was humiliated, put to shame

כְּלִמָּה (f) insult, reproach, ignominy

כֵּן thus, so

כִּנּוֹר lyre (stringed instrument)

[כנע] he humbled himself, was humbled, subdued

כָּנָף (f) wing, skirt, extremity

כִּסֵּה, כִּסֵּא seat of honor, throne

כָּסָה he covered, concealed

כֶּסֶף silver, money

כָּעַס he was vexed, angry

כַּעַס vexation, anger

כַּף (f) hollow of the hand, palm, sole of the foot

כְּפִיר young lion

[כפר] (Pi‘el) he covered, made atonement

כָּרָה (1) he dug; (2) he got by trading, bought

כְּרוּב cherub, a celestial being

כֶּרֶם vineyard

כַּרְמֶל plantation, garden-land

כָּרַע he knelt, bowed down

כָּרַת he cut, cut off

כָּשַׁל he stumbled, staggered

כָּתַב he wrote

כֻּתֹּנֶת (f) tunic, robe

כָּתֵף (f) shoulder, shoulder-blade, side

כָּתַת he beat, hammered, crushed

לֹא not

לְאוֹם, לְאֹם people

לֵב heart, mind, will

לֵבָב heart, mind, will

לְבַד alone, by oneself (בַּד plus לְ)

לְבִלְתִּי so as not, in order not

לָבָן white

לָבַשׁ he put on, wore

לַהַב flame, לֶהָבָה (f)

לָהַט it blazed up, flamed

לוּא, לוּ if, if only, would that!

לוּלֵא if not, unless

לוּחַ tablet, board, plank, plate

לְחִי jaw, cheek

[לחם] he fought

לֶחֶם bread, food

לַיְלָה night

384

לוּן, לִין	to lodge, pass the night, abide
לִין	to scorn
לָכַד	he seized, captured
לָכֵן	therefore
לָמַד	he learned
לָעַג	he mocked, derided, scorned
לַפִּיד	torch, lightning–flash
לִפְנֵי	before, in the presence of
לָקַח	he took
לָשׁוֹן	tongue
מְאֹד	very, exceedingly
מֵאָה	(f) hundred
מֵאַיִן	whence? (מִן plus אַיִן)
[מאן]	(Pi'el) he refused
מָאַס	he rejected, despised
מַבּוּל	flood
מִבְצָר	fortress, fortification
מִגְדָּל	tower, fortress
מָגֵן	(m and f) shield, buckler
מִגְרָשׁ	common–land, open range
מִדְבָּר	wilderness, desert
מָדַד	he measured
מִדָּה	(f) measure, measurement
מָדוֹן	strife, contention
מַדּוּעַ	why? on what account?
מָה	what?
[מהר]	he hastened
מוּג	to melt
מוֹט	to totter, shake, slip

מוֹל, מוּל	in front of
מוּל	to circumcise
מוּסָר	discipline, chastening, correction
מוֹעֵד	appointed time, place
מוֹפֵת	wonder, sign, portent
מוֹקֵשׁ	a bait, lure
מוּר	to change
מִישׁ, מוּשׁ	to depart, remove
מוֹשָׁב	seat, dwelling, dwelling–place
מוֹשִׁיעַ	savior, deliverer
מוּת	to die
מָוֶת	death
מִזְבֵּחַ	altar, place of sacrifice
מְזוּזָה	(f) door-post, gate-post
מְזִמָּה	(f) purpose, discretion, device
מִזְמוֹר	melody, psalm
מִזְרָח	place of sunrise, east
מָחָה	he wiped, wiped out, blotted out
מְחִיר	price, hire
מַחֲנֶה	(m and f) camp, encampment
מָחַץ	he smote, wounded, shattered
מָחָר	tomorrow, in time to come
מָחֳרָת	(f) the following day, the day after
מַחֲשָׁבָה	(f) thought, device, plan, purpose
מַטֶּה	staff, rod, branch, tribe

מִטָּה (f) couch, bed

מָטָר rain

מָטַר it rained, hailed

מִי who?

מַיִם water

מִין species, kind

מַכָּה (f) blow, wound, slaughter

מָכַר he sold

מִכְשׁוֹל a stumbling, stumbling-block

מָלֵא he was full

מָלֵא (adj) full (מְלֵא, const.)

מְלֹא, מִלּוֹא fulness, contents, that which fills

מַלְאָךְ angel, messenger

מְלָאכָה (f) occupation, work

מִלָּה (f) word, speech, utterance

מֶלַח salt

מִלְחָמָה (f) war, battle

[מלט] he escaped

מָלַךְ he reigned, became king

מֶלֶךְ king

מַלְכָּה (f) queen

מַלְכוּת (f) kingdom

מַמְלָכָה (f) kingdom, dominion, reign

מֶמְשָׁלָה (f) rule, dominion, realm

מִן from, out of

מְנָחָה, מְנוּחָה (f) resting-place, rest

מְנֹרָה, מְנוֹרָה (f) lampstand

מִנְחָה (f) offering, gift, tribute

מָנַע he withheld, held back

מַס (collective) laborers, slave-gangs, conscripted, laborers

מָסָךְ covering, screen

מַסֵּכָה (f) molten metal, image, libation

מְסִלָּה (f) highway

מִסְפֵּד wailing

מִסְפָּר number, sum total

מָעַט he became small, diminished

מְעַט a little, few

מֵעִים (only pl) inward parts, intestines, bowels, belly (מְעֵי, const.)

מַעְיָן spring, fountain of water

מָעַל he acted unfaithfully, was treacherous

מַעַל (1) with מִן, above, on the top of; (2) מַעְלָה upwards, forward (in time)

מֵעַל (עַל plus מִן) from upon, from over, from off

מַעֲלָה (f) step, stair

מַעַן (only with לְ) for the sake of, on account of, in order that

מַעֲשֶׂה work, deed

מַעֲשֵׂר tenth part, tithe

מָצָא he found

מַצֵּבָה (f) pillar, sacred stone, stump

מְצוּדָה (f) fortress, stronghold

מַצָּה (f) unleavened bread

מָצוֹר seige-works, entrenchment, seige (מְצוּרָה [f])

מִצְוָה (f) commandment (מִצְוֹת, const.)

מִצְרַיִם Egypt

מָקוֹם place

מַקֵּל rod, staff, stick

מִקְנֶה cattle

מִקְרָא convocation, reading

מַר (adj) bitter, מָרָה (f)

מַרְאֶה sight, appearance, vision

מָרַד he rebelled, revolted

מָרָה he was disobedient, rebellious, stubborn

מָרוֹם height, elevation

מָרַט he made smooth, bare, he scoured, polished

מֶרְכָּבָה (f) chariot

מִרְמָה (f) deceit, treachery

מַרְפֵּא, מַרְפָּא a cure, healing, health

מָרַר he was bitter

מַשָּׂא utterance, oracle

מַשְׂאֵת (f) uprising, utterance, burden, portion

מָשׂוֹשׂ exultation, joy

מֹשֶׁה Moses

מָשַׁח he anointed

מִשְׁכָּב a couch, bed

מִשְׁכָּן dwelling-place, tabernacle

מָשִׁיחַ anointed (one), Messianic prince

מָשַׁךְ he drew out, led, dragged along

מָשַׁל (1) he was like, similar; (2) he spoke in parables; (3) he ruled

מָשָׁל proverb, parable

מִשְׁמֶרֶת (f) a guard, watch, function

מִשְׁפָּחָה (f) family, clan

מִשְׁפָּט judgment, justice

מִשְׁקָל weight (of something)

מִשְׁתֶּה (1) a feast, banquet; (2) a drink

מָתַי when?

מְתִים (only pl) males, men (מְתֵי, const.)

מַתָּנָה (f) gift

מָתְנַיִם (dual) loins

מָתַק it was sweet, pleasant

מָתוֹק (adj) sweet

נָא particle of entreaty, exhortation

נְאֻם utterance, oracle

נָאַף he committed adultery

[נבא] he prophesied

[נבט] (Hifʻil) he saw, looked upon

נָבִיא prophet

נֵבֶל (1) wine-skin, bottle; (2) harp, lute, guitar

נָבָל (adj) foolish, senseless

נָבֵל he sank, dropped down, languished, faded

נְבֵלָה (f) carcass, corpse

נָבַע it flowed, bubbled up, poured out

נֶגֶב Negev, dry country, south

[נגד] (Hifʻil) he told, declared

נֶגֶד in front of, in sight of, opposite to

נָגַע he touched, smote

נֶגַע stroke, plaque, mark, wound

נָגַף he smote, struck

נָגַשׂ he pressed, drove, oppressed

נָגַשׁ he approached, drew near

נָדַב he incited, impelled

נְדָבָה (f) voluntariness, freewill offering

נָדַד he fled, retreated, wandered

נָדַח he drove out, banished, expelled

נָדַר he vowed

נֵדֶר ,נֶדֶר vow

נָהַג he drove, conducted, led off, guided

[נהל] (Piʿel) he led, guided, refreshed

נָהָר river, stream

נוּד to move to and fro, wander, flutter, show grief

נָוֶה abode of shepherd, abode of sheep, meadow, pasture, נָוָה (f)

נוּחַ to rest, come to rest

נוּס to flee, escape

נוּעַ to quiver, stagger, tremble

נוּף to move to and fro, wave, shake

נָזָה he (it) spurted, spattered; (Hifʿil) he sprinkled

נָזִיר one consecrated, devoted, a Nazirite

נָזַל it flowed, trickled down, dropped

[נזר] he dedicated, consecrated

נֶזֶר consecration, crown, Naziriteship

נָחָה he led, guided

נַחַל torrent valley, wadi

נָחַל he took possession, inherited

נַחֲלָה (f) possession, inheritance, property

[נחם] he was sorry, had compassion, suffered grief, repented

נָחָשׁ serpent

[נחשׁ] he practiced divination, observed signs

נְחֹשֶׁת copper, bronze

נָחֵת it went down, descended

נָטָה he stretched out, extended, bent down, turned aside

נָטַע he planted

נָטַף it dropped, dripped; he preached, prophesied

נָטַשׁ he left, forsook

[נכה] (Hifʿil) he struck, killed

נֹכַח front, in front of, opposite to

[נכר] he regarded, recognized, observed

נָכְרִי foreign, alien, strange, unfamiliar

נֵס standard, ensign, signal, sign

[נסה] (Piʿel) he tested, tried

נָסַךְ he poured out, poured an offering

נֶסֶךְ drink-offering

388

נָסַע   he set out, departed, journeyed

נַעַל   (f) sandal, shoe

נָעַר   he shook, shook off, shook out

נַעַר   lad, youth

נַעֲרָה   (f) maiden, young woman

נְעוּרִים   youth, early years of life

נָפַח   he breathed upon, blew

נָפַל   he fell, lay

נֶפֶשׁ   (f) soul, living being, desire, appetite

[נצב]   (Nif'al) he stationed himself, took his stand; (Hif'il) he stationed, set, caused to stand

נֵצַח   eminence, perpetuity, endurance (לָנֶצַח, for ever)

[נצל]   (Hif'il) he delivered

נָצַר   he watched, guarded, kept

נָקַב   he pierced, bored through

נְקֵבָה   (f.) female

[נקה]   he was clean, innocent, guiltless

נָקִי   (adj) innocent, clean, free from, exempt

[נקם]   he avenged, took vengeance

נָקָם   vengeance, נְקָמָה (f)

נָקַף   he went around, encompassed, surrounded, completed a circuit

נֵר   lamp

נָשָׂא   he lifted, carried

[נשג]   (Hif'il) he reached, overtook, attained

נָשָׁא   (1) he lent at interest; (2) (Hif'il) he beguiled, deceived

נָשָׁה   (1) he lent at interest, was a creditor; (2) he forgot

נָשַׁךְ   he (it) bit

נְשָׁמָה   (f) breath

נָשַׁק   he kissed

נֶשֶׁר   vulture, eagle

נָתִיב   path, pathway, נְתִיבָה (f)

נָתַךְ   he poured out, poured forth

נָתַן   he gave, set, placed

נָתַץ   he pulled down, broke down

נָתַק   he pulled apart, tore away, pulled off

נָתַשׁ   he uprooted, plucked up

סָבַב   he surrounded, turned about, went around

סָבִיב   around, surrounding

סָגַר   he shut, closed

סוּג (שׂוּג)   to turn away, depart, backslide

סוֹד   council, assembly, company, counsel

סִיךְ, סוּךְ   (1) to pour, anoint; (2) to hedge, fence in

סוּס   horse

סוּף   to come to an end, cease

סוּפָה   (f) storm-wind

סוּף   reeds, rushes

סוּר   to turn aside, depart; (Hif'il) remove, take away

389

[סוּת] (Hif'il) to incite, allure, instigate

סָחַר he went about, went to and fro, journeyed

סִינַי Sinai

סִיר (m and f) pot

סֻכָּה (f) thicket, booth

סָכַךְ he overshadowed, screened, covered

סָלַח he forgave

סָלַל he lifted up, cast up

סֶלַע craig, cliff

סֹלֶת (f) fine flour

סָמַךְ he leaned, rested, supported

סָעַד he supported, sustained, upheld

סָעַר it stormed, raged

סַעַר tempest, storm-wind, סְעָרָה (f)

סַף (1) basin, goblet; (2) threshold, sill

סָפַד he wailed, lamented

סָפָה he (it) was swept away, snatched away, destroyed

[סָפַר] (Pi'el) he told, related, counted

סוֹפֵר, סֹפֵר scribe, secretary

סֵפֶר book, document, writing

סָקַל he stoned to death

סָרִיס eunuch

סֶרֶן tyrant, official, lord (Philistine official)

סָרַר he was stubborn, rebellious

סָתַם he stopped up, shut up, kept closed

[סָתַר] he concealed, hid

סֵתֶר covering, hiding-place, secrecy

עָב dark cloud, cloud mass, thicket

עָבַד he worked, served

עֶבֶד servant, slave

עֲבֹדָה (f) labor, service

עָבַר he passed over, through

עֶבְרָה (f) overflow, arrogance, fury

עִבְרִי Hebrew

עֲבוּר (only as בַּעֲבוּר) for the sake of, on account of, in order that

עֲבֹת (m and f) cord, rope

עֻגָה (f) cake of bread

עֵגֶל calf, עֶגְלָה (f)

עֲגָלָה (f) cart

עַד (1) until, unto; (2) perpetuity, for ever (see לָעַד)

[עוּד] (Hif'il) to bear witness

עֵד a witness, testimony, evidence

עֵדָה (f) congregation

עֵדוּת (f) testimony

עֵדֶר flock, herd

עוֹד again, yet, still

עָוֶל injustice, unrighteousness, עַוְלָה (f)

עֹל yoke

עוֹלָל, עוֹלֵל   child

עוֹלָם   eternity, long duration, antiquity

עָוֹן   iniquity, guilt, punishment for iniquity

עוּף   to fly

עוֹף   bird(s)

עוּר   to arouse oneself, awake

עוֹר   skin

עִוֵּר   (adj) blind

עָזַב   he abandoned, left, forsook

עַזָּה   Gaza

עָזַז   he was strong

עוֹז, עֹז   strength, might

עַז   (adj) strong

עֵז   (f) she-goat

עָזַר   he helped

עֵזֶר   help, assistance

עֶזְרָת, עֶזְרָה, עֶזְרָתָה   (f) help, assistance

עָטָה   he wrapped himself, enveloped himself with

עָטַף   he was feeble, faint

עֲטָרָה   (f) crown, wreath

עַיִן   (f) eye, fountain (עֵין const.)

עָיֵף   (adj) faint, weary

עִיר   (f) city

עַל   upon, above, about

עַל-פְּנֵי   over, above, upon the face of

עָלָה   he went up, climbed

עֹלָה   (f) whole burnt offering

עֲלִיָּה   (f) roof-chamber, upper story

עֶלְיוֹן   Most High (as in אֵל עֶלְיוֹן, God Most High)

עָלַם   he concealed

עַלְמָה   (f) young woman

עִם   with

עַם   people

עָמַד   he stood

עַמֻּד, עַמּוּד   pillar, column

עָמָל   trouble, labor, toil

עָמֹק   it was deep; (Hif'il) he made deep

עֵמֶק   vale, valley, lowland

עֵנָב   grape(s)

עָנָו   (noun) poor, afflicted, humble, meek

עָנִי   (adj) poor, afflicted, humble

עֳנִי   affliction, poverty

עָנָה   (1) he answered, responded; (2) he was bowed down, afflicted; (3) he sang

עָנָן   cloud

עָפָר   dust

עֵץ   tree, trees, wood

עָצַב   he hurt, was pained, grieved

עֵצָה   (f) counsel, advice

עָצוּם   (adj) mighty, numerous

עֶצֶם   (f) bone, substance, self

עָצַר   he restrained, hindered, detained

עָקֵב   heel, footprint

עֵקֶב   as a consequence of, because

עֶרֶב   evening

עָרַב (1) he took or gave in pledge, exchanged; (2) it was sweet, pleasing

עֲרָבָה (f) desert, steppe

[ערה] he (it) lay naked, was bare, poured out

עֶרְוָה (f) nakedness, indecency

עָרַךְ he arranged, set in order

עֵרֶךְ order, row, estimate

עָרֵל (adj) having foreskin, uncircumcised

עָרְלָה (f) foreskin

עָרוֹם , עָרֹם naked, nakedness

עֹרֶף back of neck, neck

עֲרָפֶל cloud, heavy cloud

עָרַץ he caused trembling, inspired awe

עָרִיץ awe-inspiring, terrifying

עֵשֶׂב herb, herbage

עָשָׂה he did, made

עֶשֶׂר ten, עֲשָׂרָה (f)

עָשַׁק he oppressed, wronged, practiced extortion

עֵישֹׁם , עֵשֹׁם naked, nakedness

עָשָׁן smoke

עָשַׁר he was rich, became rich

עָשִׁיר (adj) rich

עֵת (f) time

עַתָּה now

עָתַר he prayed, entreated, made supplication

פֵּאָה (f) corner, side

[פאר] he beautified, glorified

פָּגַע he met, interceded, made entreaty

פֶּגֶר corpse, carcass

פָּגַשׁ he met, encountered

פָּדָה he ransomed, redeemed

פֹּה here

פֶּה mouth

פּוּחַ to breathe, blow

פּוּץ to be scattered

פַּח bird-trap, snare

פָּחַד he was in dread, stood in awe

פַּחַד dread, trembling

פֶּחָה governor

פָּטַר he removed, set free

[פלא] it was extraordinary, wonderful, hard to comprehend

פֶּלֶא wonder, marvel

פִּלֶגֶשׁ (f) concubine

פָּלַט he escaped, caused to escape, delivered

פָּלִיט escaped one, fugitive

פְּלֵיטָה (f) escape, deliverance

[פלל] (Hitpa'el) he prayed, interceded

פֶּן lest

פִּנָּה (f) corner

פָּנָה he turned towards, faced, prepared

פָּנִים face (faces) (פְּנֵי, const.)

פֶּסַח Passover

פִּסֵּחַ (adj) lame

פֶּסֶל idol, image

פָּעַל he did, made

פֹּעַל doing, deed, work

פַּעַם (f) foot, footstep, time, occurrence

פָּצָה he (it) opened, parted

פָּקַד he visited, appointed

פְּקֻדָּה (f) visitation (for the purpose of punishing), oversight, charge, overseer

פָּקִיד commissioner, deputy, overseer

פָּקַח he opened (the eyes or the ears)

פַּר young bull

פָּרַד he divided, separated

פֶּרֶד mule, פִּרְדָה (f)

פָּרָה he (it) was fruitful, bore fruit

פְּרִי fruit

פָּרַח it budded, sprouted, sent out shoots

פֶּרַח bud, sprout

(פָּרַשׂ) פָּרַס it broke in two, divided into two

פָּרַץ he broke or burst out, broke through, broke open

פֶּרֶץ a bursting forth, a breach, an outburst

פָּרַק he tore off, tore apart

[פרר] he broke, frustrated

פָּרַשׂ he spread, spread out

פָּרָשׁ (1) horse, steed; (2) horseman, rider

פְּרָת Euphrates (river)

פָּשַׁט he stripped off, raided, attacked

פָּשַׁע he rebelled, transgressed

פֶּשַׁע rebellion, transgression

פַּת (f) fragment, bit, morsel

פָּתָה he was simple, simple-minded

פֶּתִי (adj) simple, simple-minded

פָּתַח he opened

פֶּתַח opening, doorway, entrance

פִּתְאֹם suddenly

צֹאן flock, sheep

צָבָא army, way, warfare

צְבָאוֹת hosts, armies (יְהוָה צְבָאוֹת LORD of hosts)

צְבִי (1) beauty, honor; (2) gazelle

צַד side

צָדַק, צָדֵק he was just, righteous

צַדִּיק righteous one

צֶדֶק righteousness

צְדָקָה (f) righteousness

צָהֳרַיִם (only pl) midday, noon

צַוָּאר neck, back of neck

צוּד to hunt

[צוה] (Pi'el) he commanded

צוּם he fasted, abstained from food

צוֹם fasting, a fast

צוּר he confined, bound up, beseiged

393

צוּר	rock, cliff	קֶדֶם	front, east, ancient times
צָחַק	he laughed	[קדם]	he confronted, met, went before, preceded
צִיּוֹן	Zion		
צֵל	shadow, shade	קָדִים	east, east wind
צָלַח	(1) he rushed; (2) he advanced, prospered	קָדֵשׁ	he was holy, consecrated, set apart
צֶלֶם	image, likeness	קָדוֹשׁ	(adj) holy, sacred
צֵלָע	(f) rib, side	קֹדֶשׁ	holiness, apartness, sacredness
צָמֵא	he was thirsty		
צָמַח	it sprouted, sprang up	קָהָל	assembly, convocation, congretation
צֶמַח	sprout, shoot, growth	[קהל]	he assembled, summoned an assembly
צֶמֶר	wool		
צִנָּה	(f) large shield	קַו	line, measuring-line
צָעִיר	(adj) little, insignificant, young	קָוָה	he waited for, looked eagerly for
צָעַק	he cried out	קוֹל	voice
צְעָקָה	(f) cry, outcry	קוּם	to arise, stand
צָפָה	(1) he kept watch, spied; (2) he overlaid	קוֹמָה	(f) height
צָפַן	he hid, treasured up	קָטֹן	(adj) small, young, unimportant
צָפוֹן	(f) north	קָטָן	(adj) small, insignificant
צָפּוֹר, צִפּוֹר	(f) bird	[קטר]	he burned (offered) incense, caused a sacrifice to smoke
צַר	(1) straits, distress, צָרָה (f); (2) adversary, foe		
צוֹר, צֹר	Tyre	קְטֹרֶת	(f) smoke (of sacrifice), incense
צָרַעַת	(f) leprosy	קִינָה	(f) elegy, dirge
צָרַף	he smelted, refined, tested	[קיץ]	(Hifʻil) to awake
צָרַר	(1) he bound up, was restricted; (2) he distressed, was hostile toward	קִיר	wall
		קָלַל	it was light (not heavy), trifling, lightly esteemed
קָבַץ	he collected, gathered	קְלָלָה	(f) curse
קָבַר	he buried	[קנא]	(Piʻel) he was jealous, zealous
קֶבֶר	grave, burial-place		

קִנְאָה	ardor, zeal, jealousy
קָנֶה	reed, stalk
קָנָה	he took possession, acquired, bought
קָסַם	he practiced divination
קֶסֶם	divination
קֵץ	end
קָצֶה	end, extremity
קָצָה	(m and f) end
קָצַף	he was angry, in a rage
קֶצֶף	wrath, anger
קָצַר	(1) it was short; (2) he reaped, harvested
קָצִיר	harvest, time of harvest
קָרָא	(1) he called, proclaimed, read; (2) he met, encountered
קֶרֶב	midst, inward part
קָרַב	he drew near, approached, (Hif'il) he offered
קָרְבָּן	offering, gift
קָרָה	he encountered, met
קָרוֹב	near
קָרַח	he made bald
קִרְיָה	(f) town, city
קֶרֶן	(f) horn
קָרַע	he tore
קָשַׁב	he inclined (his ears), paid attention
קָשָׁה	he was hard, severe, fierce
קָשֶׁה	(adj) hard, difficult, קָשָׁה (f)
קָשַׁר	he joined forces, conspired
קֶשֶׁר	conspiracy
קֶשֶׁת	(f) bow

רָאָה	he saw
רֹאשׁ	head
רִאשׁוֹן	(adj) former, first, chief
רֵאשִׁית	(f) beginning, chief
רָבַב	he became many, much
רָבָה	he became many, multiplied
רַב	(adj) many, much, great, רַבָּה (f)
רֹב	multitude, abundance, greatness
רָבַץ	he stretched himself out, lay down
רָגַז	he was agitated, excited, perturbed, he quivered
רָגַל	he walked on foot, went about (as an explorer, or spy)
רֶגֶל	(f) foot
רֶגַע	a moment
רָדָה	he had dominion over, ruled, dominated
רָדַף	he pursued, persecuted
רוֹאֶה	seer, prophet
רָוָה	he was saturated, drank his fill
רוּחַ	(f) spirit, wind
רוּם	to be high, exalted
[רוּעַ]	(Hif'il) to shout, to sound a signal or an alarm
רוֹעֶה	shepherd
רוּץ	to run
רָחַב	he was large, he enlarged, widened
רֹחַב	breadth, width

רָחָב	(adj) wide, broad, רְחָבָה (f)
רְחוֹב	(f) broad open space, plaza
רַחַם ,רֶחֶם	womb
רַחֲמִים	(pl only) compassion
[רחם]	(Piʾel) he had compassion, was compassionate
רָחַץ	he washed, bathed
רָחַק	he was distant, far away
רָחוֹק	(adj) far, distant
רִיב	to strive, contend
רִיב	strife, dispute, contention
[רִיק]	(Hifʾil) to empty, make empty
רֵק	(adj) empty, vain
רָכַב	he mounted, rode upon
רֶכֶב	chariotry, chariot
רָמַס	he trampled
רָנַן	he shouted for joy, cried out
רִנָּה	(f) a ringing cry
רֵעַ	friend, compassion
רַע	(adj) evil, bad, רָעָה (f)
רַע	evil, distress, misery, calamity, רָעָה (f)
רֹעַ	badness, evil
רָעֵב	he was hungry
רָעָב	famine, hunger
רָעֵב	(adj) hungry, רְעֵבָה (f)
רָעָה	he pastured, tended (flocks)
רַעֲנָן	(adj) luxuriant, fresh
רָעַע	(1) he was evil, bad; (2) he broke
רָעַשׁ	it quaked, trembled, shook

רַעַשׁ	an earthquake, a shaking or trembling
רָפָא	he healed, cured
רָפָה	he sank down, became limp, relaxed
רָצָה	he was gracious, took delight in, was pleased with
רָצוֹן	goodwill, favor, acceptance
רָצַח	he killed, murdered
רָצַץ	he crushed
רַק	(1) (adj) thin; (2) (adv) only, altogether, surely
רָקִיעַ	expanse, firmament
רָקַע	he beat out, stamped, spread out
רָשַׁע	he was wicked, acted wickedly
רָשָׁע	(adj) wicked, guilty
רֶשַׁע	wickedness, רִשְׁעָה (f)
רֶשֶׁת	(f) net
שָׂבַע	he was satisfied, sated
שָׂגַב	he was set on high, exalted
שָׂדֶה	field (שְׂדֵה, const.)
שֶׂה	(m and f) a sheep or a goat
שִׂים ,שׂוּם	to put, place
שִׂישׂ ,שׂוּשׂ	to exult, rejoice
שָׂחַק	he laughed, played
שָׂטָן	adversary, Satan
שֵׂיבָה	(f) gray hair, old age
שִׂיחַ	to complain, muse, meditate upon

שִׂיחַ a complaint, meditation, שִׂיחָה (f)

שָׂכַל he was prudent, clever, successful

שָׂכַר he hired

שָׂכָר wages, reward

שָׂכִיר (adj) hired

שְׂמֹאול ,שְׂמֹאל the left (as opposed to the right), the north (on the left hand as one faces east)

שָׂמַח he rejoiced, was glad

שָׂמֵחַ (adj) glad, joyful, merry, שִׂמְחָה (f)

שִׂמְחָה (f) joy, gladness, mirth

שִׂמְלָה (f) garment, mantle, clothes

שָׂנֵא he hated

שֵׂעָר hair

שָׂעִיר he-goat, buck

שְׂעֹרָה (f) barley

שָׂפָה (f) lip, speech, edge

שַׂק sack, sackcloth

שַׂר chieftain, ruler, official, prince, שָׂרָה (f)

שָׂרִיד survivor

שָׂרַף he burned

שָׂשׂוֹן exultation, joy

שָׁאוֹן a roar, crash, uproar

שְׁאוֹל ,שְׁאֹל (f) Sheol, underworld

שָׁאַל he asked

שָׁאַף (1) he gasped, panted after, longed for; (2) he crushed, trampled upon

שָׁאַר he was left, left over

שְׁאָר residue, remnant, remainder, שְׁאֵרִית (f)

שָׁבָה he took captive, led captive

שְׁבִי captivity, captives, שְׁבוּת ,שְׁבִית (f)

שְׁבוּעָה (f) oath, curse

שֵׁבֶט rod, staff, scepter, tribe

[שבע] (Nif'al) he swore

שֶׁבַע seven, שִׁבְעָה (f)

שָׁבַר he broke in pieces

שֶׁבֶר a breaking , crushing, fracture, breach

שָׁבַת he ceased, rested

שַׁבָּת (m and f) sabbath

שָׁגָה he went astray, erred, wandered off

שָׁדַד he devastated, destroyed

שׁוֹד ,שֹׁד violence, destruction

שָׁוְא emptiness, vanity, worthlessness

שׁוּב to turn, return, repent

שׁוֹפֵט judge

שׁוֹפָר ram's horn, trumpet

שׁוֹר ox, bullock, a head of cattle

[שחה] (Hitpa'lel) he bowed down, worshipped

שָׁחַח he bowed down, crouched

שָׁחַט he killed, slaughtered

שַׁחַר dawn

[שחת] he destroyed, corrupted

שַׁחַת (f) pit, grave

שָׁטַף it overflowed, washed away

שִׁיר to sing

שִׁיר a song

397

שִׁית	to put, place, set	שֶׁמֶשׁ	sun
שָׁכַב	he lay down	שֵׁן	(f) tooth, ivory
שָׁכַח	he forgot	שָׁנָה	(1) he (it) changed; (2) he repeated, did again
שָׁכַל ,שָׁכֹל	he was bereaved, made childless	שָׁנָה	(f) year (שְׁנַת, const.)
[שכם]	(Hif‘il) he arose early	שְׁנֵיהֶם	the two of them
שְׁכֶם	shoulder	שְׁנַיִם	two, שְׁתַּיִם (f)
שָׁכַן	he settled, dwelt	שָׁעָה	he gazed, looked
שָׁכַר	he was drunk, became drunk	[שען]	(Nif‘al) he leaned upon, supported himself
שֶׁלֶג	snow	שַׁעַר	gate
שֻׁלְחָן	table	שִׁפְחָה	(f) maid, hand–maid
שָׁלוֹם	peace	שָׁפַט	he judged, delivered
שָׁלַח	he sent	שָׁפַךְ	he poured out
[שלך]	(Hif‘il) he cast, threw	שָׁפֵל	he became low, was abased
שָׁלַל	he spoiled, plundered	[שקה]	(Hif‘il) he watered, caused to drink
שָׁלָל	prey, spoil, plunder, booty	שִׁקּוּץ	a detestable thing
שָׁלֵם	he was whole, complete	שָׁקַט	he was quiet, undisturbed
שָׁלֵם	(adj) complete, full, perfect, שְׁלֵמָה (f)	שָׁקַל	he weighed, weighed out money
שֶׁלֶם	peace–offering	שֶׁקֶל	shekel, a standard weight of money
שָׁלֹשׁ	three, שְׁלֹשָׁה (f)	[שקף]	he leaned over, looked down
שָׁם	there	שֶׁקֶר	deception, falsehood
שֵׁם	name	שֹׁרֶשׁ	root, stock
[שמד]	he was annihilated, exterminated	[שרת]	(Pi‘el) he ministered, served
שָׁמַיִם	heavens, sky	שֵׁשׁ	six, שִׁשָּׁה (f)
שָׁמֵם	he was appalled, devastated	שָׁתָה	he drank
שְׁמָמָה	(f) a devastation, waste		
שֶׁמֶן	oil, fat		
שְׁמֹנֶה	eight, שְׁמֹנָה (f)		
שָׁמַע	he heard	תְּאֵנָה	(f) fig, fig–tree
שָׁמַר	he kept		

תֹּאַר   outline, form, shape, appearance

תֵּבָה   (f) ark

תְּבוּנָה   (f) produce, yield, income

תֵּבֵל   (f) world

תֶּבֶן   straw

תַּבְנִית   (f) pattern, figure, image

תֹּהוּ   formlessness, confusion, unreality, emptiness

תְּהוֹם   (f) great deep, abyss

תְּהִלָּה   (f) praise, song of praise

תּוֹדָה   (f) thanksgiving

תָּוֶךְ   midst (תּוֹךְ, const.)

תּוֹלְדוֹת   (f) generations

תּוֹלַעַת, תּוֹלֵעָה   (f) worm

תּוֹעֵבָה   (f) abomination

תּוּר   to seek out, spy out, explore

תּוֹרָה   (f) law, instruction (תּוֹרַת, const.)

תְּחִלָּה   (f) beginning

תְּחִנָּה   (f) favor, supplication for favor

תַּחַת   under, instead of

תַּחְתִּי   (adj) lower (parts), lowest (places)

תֵּימָן   (f) south, southern quarter (of the sky)

תִּירוֹשׁ   new wine

תְּכֵלֶת   (f) violet thread or fabric

תָּלָה, תָּלָא   he hung (something)

תֹּם   completeness, integrity, innocence

תְּמֹל, תְּמוֹל (אֶתְמוֹל .cf)   yesterday, recently, formerly

תָּמַךְ   he grasped, upheld, supported

תָּמִיד   continuously

תָּמִים   (adj) perfect, complete, whole

תַּמַּם   he (it) was finished, completed

תְּנוּפָה   (f) a swinging, waving, wave-offering

תַּנּוּר   stove, fire-pot, oven, furnace

[תעב]   he despised, abhorred, made abominable

תָּעָה   he erred, went astray, misled

תֹּף   timbrel, tambourine

תִּפְאָרָה   (f) beauty, glory (תִּפְאֶרֶת, const.)

תְּפִלָּה   (f) prayer (תְּפִלַּת, const.)

תָּפַשׂ   he seized, laid hold of, grasped, wielded

תָּקַע   he struck, thrust (a weapon into someone), pitched (a tent), blew (a trumpet)

תּוֹר, תֹּר   (f) turtle-dove

תְּרוּמָה   (f) contribution, offering

תְּרוּעָה   (f) shout of war, alarm, or joy

תְּרָפִים   (plural only) idols, household gods

תְּשׁוּעָה   (f) deliverance, salvation

תֵּשַׁע   (f) תִּשְׁעָה ,nine

VERB CHART 1
Strong Verb

	Qal	Nif'al	Pi'el	Pu'al	Hitpa'el	Hif'il	Hof'al
			Perfect				
3 ms	שָׁמַר	נִשְׁמַר	שִׁמֵּר	שֻׁמַּר	הִשְׁתַּמֵּר	הִשְׁמִיר	הָשְׁמַר
3 fs	שָׁמְרָה	נִשְׁמְרָה	שִׁמְּרָה	שֻׁמְּרָה	הִשְׁתַּמְּרָה	הִשְׁמִירָה	הָשְׁמְרָה
2 ms	שָׁמַרְתָּ	נִשְׁמַרְתָּ	שִׁמַּרְתָּ	שֻׁמַּרְתָּ	הִשְׁתַּמַּרְתָּ	הִשְׁמַרְתָּ	הָשְׁמַרְתָּ
2 fs	שָׁמַרְתְּ	נִשְׁמַרְתְּ	שִׁמַּרְתְּ	שֻׁמַּרְתְּ	הִשְׁתַּמַּרְתְּ	הִשְׁמַרְתְּ	הָשְׁמַרְתְּ
1 cs	שָׁמַרְתִּי	נִשְׁמַרְתִּי	שִׁמַּרְתִּי	שֻׁמַּרְתִּי	הִשְׁתַּמַּרְתִּי	הִשְׁמַרְתִּי	הָשְׁמַרְתִּי
3 cp	שָׁמְרוּ	נִשְׁמְרוּ	שִׁמְּרוּ	שֻׁמְּרוּ	הִשְׁתַּמְּרוּ	הִשְׁמִירוּ	הָשְׁמְרוּ
2 mp	שְׁמַרְתֶּם	נִשְׁמַרְתֶּם	שִׁמַּרְתֶּם	שֻׁמַּרְתֶּם	הִשְׁתַּמַּרְתֶּם	הִשְׁמַרְתֶּם	הָשְׁמַרְתֶּם
2 fp	שְׁמַרְתֶּן	נִשְׁמַרְתֶּן	שִׁמַּרְתֶּן	שֻׁמַּרְתֶּן	הִשְׁתַּמַּרְתֶּן	הִשְׁמַרְתֶּן	הָשְׁמַרְתֶּן
1 cp	שָׁמַרְנוּ	נִשְׁמַרְנוּ	שִׁמַּרְנוּ	שֻׁמַּרְנוּ	הִשְׁתַּמַּרְנוּ	הִשְׁמַרְנוּ	הָשְׁמַרְנוּ
			Imperfect				
3 ms	יִשְׁמֹר	יִשָּׁמֵר	יְשַׁמֵּר	יְשֻׁמַּר	יִשְׁתַּמֵּר	יַשְׁמִיר	יָשְׁמַר
3 fs	תִּשְׁמֹר	תִּשָּׁמֵר	תְּשַׁמֵּר	תְּשֻׁמַּר	תִּשְׁתַּמֵּר	תַּשְׁמִיר	תָּשְׁמַר
2 ms	תִּשְׁמֹר	תִּשָּׁמֵר	תְּשַׁמֵּר	תְּשֻׁמַּר	תִּשְׁתַּמֵּר	תַּשְׁמִיר	תָּשְׁמַר
2 fs	תִּשְׁמְרִי	תִּשָּׁמְרִי	תְּשַׁמְּרִי	תְּשֻׁמְּרִי	תִּשְׁתַּמְּרִי	תַּשְׁמִירִי	תָּשְׁמְרִי
1 cs	אֶשְׁמֹר	אֶשָּׁמֵר	אֲשַׁמֵּר	אֲשֻׁמַּר	אֶשְׁתַּמֵּר	אַשְׁמִיר	אָשְׁמַר
3 mp	יִשְׁמְרוּ	יִשָּׁמְרוּ	יְשַׁמְּרוּ	יְשֻׁמְּרוּ	יִשְׁתַּמְּרוּ	יַשְׁמִירוּ	יָשְׁמְרוּ
3 fp	תִּשְׁמֹרְנָה	תִּשָּׁמַרְנָה	תְּשַׁמֵּרְנָה	תְּשֻׁמַּרְנָה	תִּשְׁתַּמֵּרְנָה	תַּשְׁמֵרְנָה	תָּשְׁמַרְנָה
2 mp	תִּשְׁמְרוּ	תִּשָּׁמְרוּ	תְּשַׁמְּרוּ	תְּשֻׁמְּרוּ	תִּשְׁתַּמְּרוּ	תַּשְׁמִירוּ	תָּשְׁמְרוּ
2 fp	תִּשְׁמֹרְנָה	תִּשָּׁמַרְנָה	תְּשַׁמֵּרְנָה	תְּשֻׁמַּרְנָה	תִּשְׁתַּמֵּרְנָה	תַּשְׁמֵרְנָה	תָּשְׁמַרְנָה
1 cp	נִשְׁמֹר	נִשָּׁמֵר	נְשַׁמֵּר	נְשֻׁמַּר	נִשְׁתַּמֵּר	נַשְׁמִיר	נָשְׁמַר

	Qal	Nif'al	Pi'el	Pu'al	Hitpa'el	Hif'il	Hof'al
Imperative							
2 ms	שְׁמֹר	הִשָּׁמֵר	שַׁמֵּר		הִשְׁתַּמֵּר	הַשְׁמֵר	
2 fs	שִׁמְרִי	הִשָּׁמְרִי	שַׁמְּרִי		הִשְׁתַּמְּרִי	הַשְׁמִירִי	
2 mp	שִׁמְרוּ	הִשָּׁמְרוּ	שַׁמְּרוּ		הִשְׁתַּמְּרוּ	הַשְׁמִירוּ	
2 fp	שְׁמֹרְנָה	הִשָּׁמַרְנָה	שַׁמֵּרְנָה		הִשְׁתַּמֵּרְנָה	הַשְׁמֵרְנָה	
Infinitive Construct							
	שְׁמֹר	הִשָּׁמֵר	שַׁמֵּר	(שֻׁמַּר)	הִשְׁתַּמֵּר	הַשְׁמִיר	(הָשְׁמַר)
Infinitive Absolute							
	שָׁמוֹר	הִשָּׁמֹר	שַׁמֹּר	שֻׁמֹּר	הִשְׁתַּמֵּר	הַשְׁמֵר	הָשְׁמֵר
		Alt. נִשְׁמֹר	*Alt.* שַׁמֵּר				
Active Participle							
ms	שֹׁמֵר		מְשַׁמֵּר		מִשְׁתַּמֵּר	מַשְׁמִיר	
mp	שֹׁמְרִים		מְשַׁמְּרִים		מִשְׁתַּמְּרִים	מַשְׁמִירִים	
fs	שֹׁמְרָה		מְשַׁמְּרָה		מִשְׁתַּמְּרָה	מַשְׁמִירָה	
fp	שֹׁמְרוֹת		מְשַׁמְּרוֹת		מִשְׁתַּמְּרוֹת	מַשְׁמִירוֹת	
Passive Participle							
ms	שָׁמוּר	נִשְׁמָר		מְשֻׁמָּר			מֻשְׁמָר
mp	שְׁמוּרִים	נִשְׁמָרִים		מְשֻׁמָּרִים			מֻשְׁמָרִים
fs	שְׁמוּרָה	נִשְׁמָרָה		מְשֻׁמָּרָה			מֻשְׁמָרָה
fp	שְׁמוּרוֹת	נִשְׁמָרוֹת		מְשֻׁמָּרוֹת			מֻשְׁמָרוֹת

VERB CHART 2
Pe Guttural

	Qal (Active)	Qal (Stative)	Nif'al	Hif'il	Hof'al
			Perfect		
3 ms	עָמַד	חָזַק	נֶעֱמַד	הֶעֱמִיד	הָעֳמַד
3 fs	עָמְדָה	חָזְקָה	נֶעֶמְדָה	הֶעֱמִידָה	הָעֳמְדָה
2 ms	עָמַדְתָּ	חָזַקְתָּ	נֶעֱמַדְתָּ	הֶעֱמַדְתָּ	הָעֳמַדְתָּ
2 fs	עָמַדְתְּ	חָזַקְתְּ	נֶעֱמַדְתְּ	הֶעֱמַדְתְּ	הָעֳמַדְתְּ
1 cs	עָמַדְתִּי	חָזַקְתִּי	נֶעֱמַדְתִּי	הֶעֱמַדְתִּי	הָעֳמַדְתִּי
3 cp	עָמְדוּ	חָזְקוּ	נֶעֶמְדוּ	הֶעֱמִידוּ	הָעֳמְדוּ
2 mp	עֲמַדְתֶּם	חֲזַקְתֶּם	נֶעֱמַדְתֶּם	הֶעֱמַדְתֶּם	הָעֳמַדְתֶּם
2 fp	עֲמַדְתֶּן	חֲזַקְתֶּן	נֶעֱמַדְתֶּן	הֶעֱמַדְתֶּן	הָעֳמַדְתֶּן
1 cp	עָמַדְנוּ	חָזַקְנוּ	נֶעֱמַדְנוּ	הֶעֱמַדְנוּ	הָעֳמַדְנוּ
			Imperfect		
3 ms	יַעֲמֹד	יֶחֱזַק	יֵעָמֵד	יַעֲמִיד	יָעֳמַד
3 fs	תַּעֲמֹד	תֶּחֱזַק	תֵּעָמֵד	תַּעֲמִיד	תָּעֳמַד
2 ms	תַּעֲמֹד	תֶּחֱזַק	תֵּעָמֵד	תַּעֲמִיד	תָּעֳמַד
2 fs	תַּעֲמְדִי	תֶּחֱזְקִי	תֵּעָמְדִי	תַּעֲמִידִי	תָּעֳמְדִי
1 cs	אֶעֱמֹד	אֶחֱזַק	אֵעָמֵד	אַעֲמִיד	אָעֳמַד
3 mp	יַעֲמְדוּ	יֶחֱזְקוּ	יֵעָמְדוּ	יַעֲמִידוּ	יָעֳמְדוּ
3 fp	תַּעֲמֹדְנָה	תֶּחֱזַקְנָה	תֵּעָמַדְנָה	תַּעֲמֵדְנָה	תָּעֳמַדְנָה
2 mp	תַּעֲמְדוּ	תֶּחֱזְקוּ	תֵּעָמְדוּ	תַּעֲמִידוּ	תָּעֳמְדוּ
2 fp	תַּעֲמֹדְנָה	תֶּחֱזַקְנָה	תֵּעָמַדְנָה	תַּעֲמֵדְנָה	תָּעֳמַדְנָה
1 cp	נַעֲמֹד	נֶחֱזַק	נֵעָמֵד	נַעֲמִיד	נָעֳמַד

	Qal (Active)	Qal (Stative)	Nifʻal	Hifʻil	Hofʻal
Imperative					
2 ms	עֲמֹד	חֲזַק	הֵעָמֵד	הַעֲמֵד	
2 fs	עִמְדִי	חִזְקִי	הֵעָמְדִי	הַעֲמִידִי	
2 mp	עִמְדוּ	חִזְקוּ	הֵעָמְדוּ	הַעֲמִידוּ	
2 fp	עֲמֹדְנָה	חֲזַקְנָה	הֵעָמַדְנָה	הַעֲמֵדְנָה	
Infinitive Construct					
	עֲמֹד		הֵעָמֵד	הַעֲמִיד	
Infinitive Absolute					
	עָמוֹד		נַעֲמֹד	הֵעָמֵד	הַעֲמֵד	הָעֳמֵד
Active Participle					
ms	עֹמֵד			מַעֲמִיד	
mp	עֹמְדִים			מַעֲמִידִים	
fs	עֹמֶדֶת			מַעֲמִידָה	
fp	עֹמְדוֹת			מַעֲמִידוֹת	
Passive Participle					
ms	עָמוּד		נֶעֱמָד		מָעֳמָד
mp	עֲמוּדִים		נֶעֱמָדִים		מָעֳמָדִים
fs	עֲמוּדָה		נֶעֱמָדָה		מָעֳמָדָה
fp	עֲמוּדוֹת		נֶעֱמָדוֹת		מָעֳמָדוֹת

VERB CHART 3
Pe 'Alef

	Qal Perfect		

3 ms	אָכַל	אָמַר	
3 fs	אָכְלָה	אָמְרָה	
2 ms	אָכַלְתָּ	אָמַרְתָּ	
2 fs	אָכַלְתְּ	אָמַרְתְּ	
1 cs	אָכַלְתִּי	אָמַרְתִּי	
3 cp	אָכְלוּ	אָמְרוּ	
2 mp	אֲכַלְתֶּם	אֲמַרְתֶּם	
2 fp	אֲכַלְתֶּן	אֲמַרְתֶּן	
1 cp	אָכַלְנוּ	אָמַרְנוּ	

	Qal Imperfect		

3 ms	יֹאכַל	יֹאמַר	(וַיֹּאמֶר)
3 fs	תֹּאכַל	תֹּאמַר	(וַתֹּאמֶר)
2 ms	תֹּאכַל	תֹּאמַר	(וַתֹּאמֶר)
2 fs	תֹּאכְלִי	תֹּאמְרִי	(וַתֹּאמְרִי)
1 cs	אֹכַל	אֹמַר	(וָאֹמֶר)
3 mp	יֹאכְלוּ	יֹאמְרוּ	(וַיֹּאמְרוּ)
3 fp	תֹּאכַלְנָה	תֹּאמַרְנָה	(וַתֹּאמַרְנָה)
2 mp	תֹּאכְלוּ	תֹּאמְרוּ	(וַתֹּאמְרוּ)
2 fp	תֹּאכַלְנָה	תֹּאמַרְנָה	(וַתֹּאמַרְנָה)
1 cp	נֹאכַל	נֹאמַר	(וַנֹּאמֶר)

Qal Imperative

2 ms	אֱכֹל	אֱמֹר
2 fs	אִכְלִי	אִמְרִי
2 mp	אִכְלוּ	אִמְרוּ
2 fp	אֲכֹלְנָה	אֱמֹרְנָה

Qal Infinitive Construct

אֱכֹל	אֱמֹר

Qal Infinitive Absolute

אָכוֹל	אָמוֹר

Qal Active Participle

ms	אֹכֵל	אֹמֵר
mp	אֹכְלִים	אֹמְרִים
fs	אֹכְלָה	אֹמְרָה
	or אֹכֶלֶת	or אֹמֶרֶת
fp	אֹכְלוֹת	אֹמְרוֹת

Qal Passive Participle

ms	אָכוּל
mp	אֲכוּלִים
fs	אֲכוּלָה
fp	אֲכוּלוֹת

VERB CHART 4
ʿAyin Guttural

	Qal	Nifʿal	Piʿel	Puʿal	Hitpaʿel	Hifʿil	Hofʿal
				Perfect			
3 ms	גָּאַל	נִגְאַל	בֵּרֵךְ	בֹּרַךְ	הִתְבָּרֵךְ	הִגְאִיל	הָגְאַל
3 fs	גָּאֲלָה	נִגְאֲלָה	בֵּרְכָה	בֹּרְכָה	הִתְבָּרְכָה	הִגְאִילָה	הָגְאֲלָה
2 ms	גָּאַלְתָּ	נִגְאַלְתָּ	בֵּרַכְתָּ	בֹּרַכְתָּ	הִתְבָּרַכְתָּ	הִגְאַלְתָּ	הָגְאַלְתָּ
2 fs	גָּאַלְתְּ	נִגְאַלְתְּ	בֵּרַכְתְּ	בֹּרַכְתְּ	הִתְבָּרַכְתְּ	הִגְאַלְתְּ	הָגְאַלְתְּ
1 cs	גָּאַלְתִּי	נִגְאַלְתִּי	בֵּרַכְתִּי	בֹּרַכְתִּי	הִתְבָּרַכְתִּי	הִגְאַלְתִּי	הָגְאַלְתִּי
3 cp	גָּאֲלוּ	נִגְאֲלוּ	בֵּרְכוּ	בֹּרְכוּ	הִתְבָּרְכוּ	הִגְאִילוּ	הָגְאֲלוּ
2 mp	גְּאַלְתֶּם	נִגְאַלְתֶּם	בֵּרַכְתֶּם	בֹּרַכְתֶּם	הִתְבָּרַכְתֶּם	הִגְאַלְתֶּם	הָגְאַלְתֶּם
2 fp	גְּאַלְתֶּן	נִגְאַלְתֶּן	בֵּרַכְתֶּן	בֹּרַכְתֶּן	הִתְבָּרַכְתֶּן	הִגְאַלְתֶּן	הָגְאַלְתֶּן
1 cp	גָּאַלְנוּ	נִגְאַלְנוּ	בֵּרַכְנוּ	בֹּרַכְנוּ	הִתְבָּרַכְנוּ	הִגְאַלְנוּ	הָגְאַלְנוּ
				Imperfect			
3 ms	יִגְאַל	יִגָּאֵל	יְבָרֵךְ	יְבֹרַךְ	יִתְבָּרֵךְ	יַגְאִיל	יֻגְאַל
3 fs	תִּגְאַל	תִּגָּאֵל	תְּבָרֵךְ	תְּבֹרַךְ	תִּתְבָּרֵךְ	תַּגְאִיל	תֻּגְאַל
2 ms	תִּגְאַל	תִּגָּאֵל	תְּבָרֵךְ	תְּבֹרַךְ	תִּתְבָּרֵךְ	תַּגְאִיל	תֻּגְאַל
2 fs	תִּגְאֲלִי	תִּגָּאֲלִי	תְּבָרְכִי	תְּבֹרְכִי	תִּתְבָּרְכִי	תַּגְאִילִי	תֻּגְאֲלִי
1 cs	אֶגְאַל	אֶגָּאֵל	אֲבָרֵךְ	אֲבֹרַךְ	אֶתְבָּרֵךְ	אַגְאִיל	אֻגְאַל
3 mp	יִגְאֲלוּ	יִגָּאֲלוּ	יְבָרְכוּ	יְבֹרְכוּ	יִתְבָּרְכוּ	יַגְאִילוּ	יֻגְאֲלוּ
3 fp	תִּגְאַלְנָה	תִּגָּאַלְנָה	תְּבָרֵכְנָה	תְּבֹרַכְנָה	תִּתְבָּרֵכְנָה	תַּגְאֵלְנָה	תֻּגְאַלְנָה
2 mp	תִּגְאֲלוּ	תִּגָּאֲלוּ	תְּבָרְכוּ	תְּבֹרְכוּ	תִּתְבָּרְכוּ	תַּגְאִילוּ	תֻּגְאֲלוּ
2 fp	תִּגְאַלְנָה	תִּגָּאַלְנָה	תְּבָרֵכְנָה	תְּבֹרַכְנָה	תִּתְבָּרֵכְנָה	תַּגְאֵלְנָה	תֻּגְאַלְנָה
1 cp	נִגְאַל	נִגָּאֵל	נְבָרֵךְ	נְבֹרַךְ	נִתְבָּרֵךְ	נַגְאִיל	נֻגְאַל

	Qal	Nif'al	Pi'el	Pu'al	Hitpa'el	Hif'il	Hof'al
			Imperative				
2 ms	גְּאַל	הִגָּאֵל	בָּרֵךְ		הִתְבָּרֵךְ	הַגְאֵל	
2 fs	גַּאֲלִי	הִגָּאֲלִי	בָּרְכִי		הִתְבָּרְכִי	הַגְאִילִי	
2 mp	גַּאֲלוּ	הִגָּאֲלוּ	בָּרְכוּ		הִתְבָּרְכוּ	הַגְאִילוּ	
2 fp	גְּאַלְנָה	הִגָּאַלְנָה	בָּרֵכְנָה		הִתְבָּרֵכְנָה	הַגְאֵלְנָה	
			Infinitive Construct				
	גְּאֹל	הִגָּאֵל	בָּרֵךְ	בֹּרַךְ	הִתְבָּרֵךְ	הַגְאִיל	הָגְאַל
			Infinitive Absolute				
	גָּאוֹל	נִגְאֹל	בָּרֵךְ		הִתְבָּרֵךְ	הַגְאֵל	הָגְאֵל
			Active Participle				
ms	גֹּאֵל		מְבָרֵךְ		מִתְבָּרֵךְ	מַגְאִיל	
mp	גֹּאֲלִים		מְבָרְכִים		מִתְבָּרְכִים	מַגְאִילִים	
fs	גֹּאֲלָה		מְבָרְכָה		מִתְבָּרְכָה	מַגְאִילָה	
fp	גֹּאֲלוֹת		מְבָרְכוֹת		מִתְבָּרְכוֹת	מַגְאִילוֹת	
			Passive Participle				
ms	גָּאוּל	נִגְאָל		מְבֹרָךְ			מֻגְאָל
mp	גְּאוּלִים	נִגְאָלִים		מְבֹרָכִים			מֻגְאָלִים
fs	גְּאוּלָה	נִגְאָלָה		מְבֹרָכָה			מֻגְאָלָה
fp	גְּאוּלוֹת	נִגְאָלוֹת		מְבֹרָכוֹת			מֻגְאָלוֹת

VERB CHART 5
Lamed Guttural

	Qal	Nif'al	Pi'el	Pu'al	Hitpa'el	Hif'il	Hof'al
				Perfect			
3 ms	שָׁלַח	נִשְׁלַח	שִׁלַּח	שֻׁלַּח	הִשְׁתַּלַּח	הִשְׁלִיחַ	הָשְׁלַח
3 fs	שָׁלְחָה	נִשְׁלְחָה	שִׁלְּחָה	שֻׁלְּחָה	הִשְׁתַּלְּחָה	הִשְׁלִיחָה	הָשְׁלְחָה
2 ms	שָׁלַחְתָּ	נִשְׁלַחְתָּ	שִׁלַּחְתָּ	שֻׁלַּחְתָּ	הִשְׁתַּלַּחְתָּ	הִשְׁלַחְתָּ	הָשְׁלַחְתָּ
2 fs	שָׁלַחַתְּ	נִשְׁלַחַתְּ	שִׁלַּחַתְּ	שֻׁלַּחַתְּ	הִשְׁתַּלַּחַתְּ	הִשְׁלַחַתְּ	הָשְׁלַחַתְּ
1 cs	שָׁלַחְתִּי	נִשְׁלַחְתִּי	שִׁלַּחְתִּי	שֻׁלַּחְתִּי	הִשְׁתַּלַּחְתִּי	הִשְׁלַחְתִּי	הָשְׁלַחְתִּי
3 cp	שָׁלְחוּ	נִשְׁלְחוּ	שִׁלְּחוּ	שֻׁלְּחוּ	הִשְׁתַּלְּחוּ	הִשְׁלִיחוּ	הָשְׁלְחוּ
2 mp	שְׁלַחְתֶּם	נִשְׁלַחְתֶּם	שִׁלַּחְתֶּם	שֻׁלַּחְתֶּם	הִשְׁתַּלַּחְתֶּם	הִשְׁלַחְתֶּם	הָשְׁלַחְתֶּם
2 fp	שְׁלַחְתֶּן	נִשְׁלַחְתֶּן	שִׁלַּחְתֶּן	שֻׁלַּחְתֶּן	הִשְׁתַּלַּחְתֶּן	הִשְׁלַחְתֶּן	הָשְׁלַחְתֶּן
1 cp	שָׁלַחְנוּ	נִשְׁלַחְנוּ	שִׁלַּחְנוּ	שֻׁלַּחְנוּ	הִשְׁתַּלַּחְנוּ	הִשְׁלַחְנוּ	הָשְׁלַחְנוּ
				Imperfect			
3 ms	יִשְׁלַח	יִשָּׁלַח	יְשַׁלַּח	יְשֻׁלַּח	יִשְׁתַּלַּח	יַשְׁלִיחַ	יָשְׁלַח
3 fs	תִּשְׁלַח	תִּשָּׁלַח	תְּשַׁלַּח	תְּשֻׁלַּח	תִּשְׁתַּלַּח	תַּשְׁלִיחַ	תָּשְׁלַח
2 ms	תִּשְׁלַח	תִּשָּׁלַח	תְּשַׁלַּח	תְּשֻׁלַּח	תִּשְׁתַּלַּח	תַּשְׁלִיחַ	תָּשְׁלַח
2 fs	תִּשְׁלְחִי	תִּשָּׁלְחִי	תְּשַׁלְּחִי	תְּשֻׁלְּחִי	תִּשְׁתַּלְּחִי	תַּשְׁלִיחִי	תָּשְׁלְחִי
1 cs	אֶשְׁלַח	אֶשָּׁלַח	אֲשַׁלַּה	אֲשֻׁלַּח	אֶשְׁתַּלַּח	אַשְׁלִיחַ	אָשְׁלַח
3 mp	יִשְׁלְחוּ	יִשָּׁלְחוּ	יְשַׁלְּחוּ	יְשֻׁלְּחוּ	יִשְׁתַּלְּחוּ	יַשְׁלִיחוּ	יָשְׁלְחוּ
3 fp	תִּשְׁלַחְנָה	תִּשָּׁלַחְנָה	תְּשַׁלַּחְנָה	תְּשֻׁלַּחְנָה	תִּשְׁתַּלַּחְנָה	תַּשְׁלַחְנָה	תָּשְׁלַחְנָה
2 mp	תִּשְׁלְחוּ	תִּשָּׁלְחוּ	תְּשַׁלְּחוּ	תְּשֻׁלְּחוּ	תִּשְׁתַּלְּחוּ	תַּשְׁלִיחוּ	תָּשְׁלְחוּ
2 fp	תִּשְׁלַחְנָה	תִּשָּׁלַחְנָה	תְּשַׁלַּחְנָה	תְּשֻׁלַּחְנָה	תִּשְׁתַּלַּחְנָה	תַּשְׁלַחְנָה	תָּשְׁלַחְנָה
1 cp	נִשְׁלַח	נִשָּׁלַח	נְשַׁלַּח	נְשֻׁלַּח	נִשְׁתַּלַּח	נַשְׁלִיחַ	נָשְׁלַח

	Qal	Nifʿal	Piʿel	Puʿal	Hitpaʿel	Hifʿil	Hofʿal
			Imperative				
2 ms	שְׁלַח	הִשָּׁלַח	שַׁלַּח		הִשְׁתַּלַּח	הַשְׁלַח	
2 fs	שִׁלְחִי	הִשָּׁלְחִי	שַׁלְּחִי		הִשְׁתַּלְּחִי	הַשְׁלִיחִי	
2 mp	שִׁלְחוּ	הִשָּׁלְחוּ	שַׁלְּחוּ		הִשְׁתַּלְּחוּ	הַשְׁלִיחוּ	
2 fp	שְׁלַחְנָה	הִשָּׁלַחְנָה	שַׁלַּחְנָה		הִשְׁתַּלַּחְנָה	הַשְׁלַחְנָה	
			Infinitive Construct				
	שְׁלַח	הִשָּׁלַח	שַׁלַּח	שֻׁלַּח	הִשְׁתַּלַּח	הַשְׁלִיחַ	הָשְׁלַח
			Infinitive Absolute				
	שָׁלוֹחַ	נִשְׁלוֹחַ	שַׁלֵּחַ	שֻׁלַּח	הִשְׁתַּלֵּחַ	הַשְׁלֵחַ	הָשְׁלֵחַ
		הִשָּׁלֵחַ					
			Active Participle				
ms	שֹׁלֵחַ		מְשַׁלֵּחַ		מִשְׁתַּלֵּחַ	מַשְׁלִיחַ	
mp	שֹׁלְחִים		מְשַׁלְּחִים		מִשְׁתַּלְּחִים	מַשְׁלִיחִים	
fs	שֹׁלְחָה		מְשַׁלְּחָה		מִשְׁתַּלְּחָה	מַשְׁלִיחָה	
fp	שֹׁלְחוֹת		מְשַׁלְּחוֹת		מִשְׁתַּלְּחוֹת	מַשְׁלִיחוֹת	
			Passive Participle				
ms	שָׁלוּחַ	נִשְׁלָח	מְשֻׁלָּח				מֻשְׁלָח
mp	שְׁלוּחִים	נִשְׁלָחִים	מְשֻׁלָּחִים				מֻשְׁלָחִים
fs	שְׁלוּחָה	נִשְׁלָחָה	מְשֻׁלָּחָה				מֻשְׁלָחָה
fp	שְׁלוּחוֹת	נִשְׁלָחוֹת	מְשֻׁלָּחוֹת				מֻשְׁלָחוֹת

VERB CHART 6
Lamed ʾAlef

	Qal	Nifʿal	Piʿel	Puʿal	Hitpaʿel	Hifʿil	Hofʿal
				Perfect			
3 ms	מָצָא	נִמְצָא	מִצָּא	מֻצָּא	הִתְמַצָּא	הִמְצִיא	הֻמְצָא
3 fs	מָצְאָה	נִמְצְאָה	מִצְּאָה	מֻצְּאָה	הִתְמַצְּאָה	הִמְצִיאָה	הֻמְצְאָה
2 ms	מָצָאתָ	נִמְצֵאתָ	מִצֵּאתָ	מֻצֵּאתָ	הִתְמַצֵּאתָ	הִמְצֵאתָ	הֻמְצֵאתָ
2 fs	מָצָאת	נִמְצֵאת	מִצֵּאת	מֻצֵּאת	הִתְמַצֵּאת	הִמְצֵאת	הֻמְצֵאת
1 cs	מָצָאתִי	נִמְצֵאתִי	מִצֵּאתִי	מֻצֵּאתִי	הִתְמַצֵּאתִי	הִמְצֵאתִי	הֻמְצֵאתִי
3 cp	מָצְאוּ	נִמְצְאוּ	מִצְּאוּ	מֻצְּאוּ	הִתְמַצְּאוּ	הִמְצִיאוּ	הֻמְצְאוּ
2 mp	מְצָאתֶם	נִמְצֵאתֶם	מִצֵּאתֶם	מֻצֵּאתֶם	הִתְמַצֵּאתֶם	הִמְצֵאתֶם	הֻמְצֵאתֶם
2 fp	מְצָאתֶן	נִמְצֵאתֶן	מִצֵּאתֶן	מֻצֵּאתֶן	הִתְמַצֵּאתֶן	הִמְצֵאתֶן	הֻמְצֵאתֶן
1 cp	מָצָאנוּ	נִמְצֵאנוּ	מִצֵּאנוּ	מֻצֵּאנוּ	הִתְמַצֵּאנוּ	הִמְצֵאנוּ	הֻמְצֵאנוּ
				Imperfect			
3 ms	יִמְצָא	יִמָּצֵא	יְמַצֵּא	יְמֻצָּא	יִתְמַצֵּא	יַמְצִיא	יֻמְצָא
3 fs	תִּמְצָא	תִּמָּצֵא	תְּמַצֵּא	תְּמֻצָּא	תִּתְמַצֵּא	תַּמְצִיא	תֻּמְצָא
2 ms	תִּמְצָא	תִּמָּצֵא	תְּמַצֵּא	תְּמֻצָּא	תִּתְמַצֵּא	תַּמְצִיא	תֻּמְצָא
2 fs	תִּמְצְאִי	תִּמָּצְאִי	תְּמַצְּאִי	תְּמֻצְּאִי	תִּתְמַצְּאִי	תַּמְצִיאִי	תֻּמְצְאִי
1 cs	אֶמְצָא	אֶמָּצֵא	אֲמַצֵּא	אֲמֻצָּא	אֶתְמַצֵּא	אַמְצִיא	אֻמְצָא
3 mp	יִמְצְאוּ	יִמָּצְאוּ	יְמַצְּאוּ	יְמֻצְּאוּ	יִתְמַצְּאוּ	יַמְצִיאוּ	יֻמְצְאוּ
3 fp	תִּמְצֶאנָה	תִּמָּצֶאנָה	תְּמַצֶּאנָה	תְּמֻצֶּאנָה	תִּתְמַצֶּאנָה	תַּמְצֶאנָה	תֻּמְצֶאנָה
2 mp	תִּמְצְאוּ	תִּמָּצְאוּ	תְּמַצְּאוּ	תְּמֻצְּאוּ	תִּתְמַצְּאוּ	תַּמְצִיאוּ	תֻּמְצְאוּ
2 fp	תִּמְצֶאנָה	תִּמָּצֶאנָה	תְּמַצֶּאנָה	תְּמֻצֶּאנָה	תִּתְמַצֶּאנָה	תַּמְצֶאנָה	תֻּמְצֶאנָה
1 cp	נִמְצָא	נִמָּצֵא	נְמַצֵּא	נְמֻצָּא	נִתְמַצֵּא	נַמְצִיא	נֻמְצָא

	Qal	Nifʻal	Piʻel	Puʻal	Hitpaʻel	Hifʻil	Hofʻal
Imperative							
2 ms	מְצָא	הִמָּצֵא	מַצֵּא		הִתְמַצֵּא	הַמְצֵא	
2 fs	מִצְאִי	הִמָּצְאִי	מַצְּאִי		הִתְמַצְּאִי	הַמְצִיאִי	
2 mp	מִצְאוּ	הִמָּצְאוּ	מַצְּאוּ		הִתְמַצְּאוּ	הַמְצִיאוּ	
2 fp	מְצֶאנָה	הִמָּצֶאנָה	מַצֶּאנָה		הִתְמַצֶּאנָה	הַמְצֶאנָה	
Infinitive Construct							
	מְצֹא	הִמָּצֵא	מַצֵּא	מֻצָּא	הִתְמַצֵּא	הַמְצִיא	הֻמְצָא
Infinitive Absolute							
	מָצוֹא	נִמְצֹא	מַצֵּא	מֻצָּא	הִתְמַצֵּא	הַמְצֵא	הֻמְצֵא
Active Participle							
ms	מֹצֵא		מְמַצֵּא		מִתְמַצֵּא	מַמְצִיא	
mp	מֹצְאִים		מְמַצְּאִים		מִתְמַצְּאִים	מַמְצִיאִים	
fs	מֹצֵאת		מְמַצֵּאת		מִתְמַצֵּאת	מַמְצִיאָה	
			מְמַצְּאָה		מִתְמַצְּאָה		
fp	מֹצְאוֹת		מְמַצְּאוֹת		מִתְמַצְּאוֹת	מַמְצִיאוֹת	
Passive Participle							
ms	מָצוּא	נִמְצָא		מְמֻצָּא			מֻמְצָא
mp	מְצוּאִים	נִמְצָאִים		מְמֻצָּאִים			מֻמְצָאִים
fs	מְצוּאָה	נִמְצֵאת		מְמֻצָּאָה			מֻמְצָאָה
		נִמְצָאָה					
fp	מְצוּאוֹת	נִמְצָאוֹת		מְמֻצָּאוֹת			מֻמְצָאוֹת

VERB CHART 7
Lamed Hê

	Qal	Nif'al	Pi'el	Pu'al	Hitpa'el	Hif'il	Hof'al
Perfect							
3 ms	גָּלָה	נִגְלָה	גִּלָּה	גֻּלָּה	הִתְגַּלָּה	הִגְלָה	הָגְלָה
3 fs	גָּלְתָה	נִגְלְתָה	גִּלְּתָה	גֻּלְּתָה	הִתְגַּלְּתָה	הִגְלְתָה	הָגְלְתָה
2 ms	גָּלִיתָ	נִגְלֵיתָ	גִּלִּיתָ	גֻּלֵּיתָ	הִתְגַּלִּיתָ	הִגְלִיתָ	הָגְלֵיתָ
2 fs	גָּלִית	נִגְלֵית	גִּלִּית	גֻּלֵּית	הִתְגַּלִּית	הִגְלִית	הָגְלֵית
1 cs	גָּלִיתִי	נִגְלֵיתִי	גִּלִּיתִי	גֻּלֵּיתִי	הִתְגַּלִּיתִי	הִגְלֵיתִי	הָגְלֵיתִי
3 cp	גָּלוּ	נִגְלוּ	גִּלּוּ	גֻּלּוּ	הִתְגַּלּוּ	הִגְלוּ	הָגְלוּ
2 mp	גְּלִיתֶם	נִגְלֵיתֶם	גִּלִּיתֶם	גֻּלֵּיתֶם	הִתְגַּלִּיתֶם	הִגְלִיתֶם	הָגְלֵיתֶם
2 fp	גְּלִיתֶן	נִגְלֵיתֶן	גִּלִּיתֶן	גֻּלֵּיתֶן	הִתְגַּלִּיתֶן	הִגְלִיתֶן	הָגְלֵיתֶן
1 cp	גָּלִינוּ	נִגְלֵינוּ	גִּלִּינוּ	גֻּלֵּינוּ	הִתְגַּלִּינוּ	הִגְלִינוּ	הָגְלֵינוּ
Imperfect							
3 ms	יִגְלֶה	יִגָּלֶה	יְגַלֶּה	יְגֻלֶּה	יִתְגַּלֶּה	יַגְלֶה	יָגְלֶה
3 fs	תִּגְלֶה	תִּגָּלֶה	תְּגַלֶּה	תְּגֻלֶּה	תִּתְגַּלֶּה	תַּגְלֶה	תָּגְלֶה
2 ms	תִּגְלֶה	תִּגָּלֶה	תְּגַלֶּה	תְּגֻלֶּה	תִּתְגַּלֶּה	תַּגְלֶה	תָּגְלֶה
2 fs	תִּגְלִי	תִּגָּלִי	תְּגַלִּי	תְּגֻלִּי	תִּתְגַּלִּי	תַּגְלִי	תָּגְלִי
1 cs	אֶגְלֶה	אֶגָּלֶה	אֲגַלֶּה	אֲגֻלֶּה	אֶתְגַּלֶּה	אַגְלֶה	אָגְלֶה
3 mp	יִגְלוּ	יִגָּלוּ	יְגַלּוּ	יְגֻלּוּ	יִתְגַּלּוּ	יַגְלוּ	יָגְלוּ
3 fp	תִּגְלֶינָה	תִּגָּלֶינָה	תְּגַלֶּינָה	תְּגֻלֶּינָה	תִּתְגַּלֶּינָה	תַּגְלֶינָה	תָּגְלֶינָה
2 mp	תִּגְלוּ	תִּגָּלוּ	תְּגַלּוּ	תְּגֻלּוּ	תִּתְגַּלּוּ	תַּגְלוּ	תָּגְלוּ
2 fp	תִּגְלֶינָה	תִּגָּלֶינָה	תְּגַלֶּינָה	תְּגֻלֶּינָה	תִּתְגַּלֶּינָה	תַּגְלֶינָה	תָּגְלֶינָה
1 cp	נִגְלֶה	נִגָּלֶה	נְגַלֶּה	נְגֻלֶּה	נִתְגַּלֶּה	נַגְלֶה	נָגְלֶה

	Qal	Nif‘al	Pi‘el	Pu‘al	Hitpa‘el	Hif‘il	Hof‘al
			Imperative				
2 ms	גְּלֵה	הִגָּלֵה	גַּלֵּה		הִתְגַּלֵּה	הַגְלֵה	
2 fs	גְּלִי	הִגָּלִי	גַּלִּי		הִתְגַּלִּי	הַגְלִי	
2 mp	גְּלוּ	הִגָּלוּ	גַּלּוּ		הִתְגַּלּוּ	הַגְלוּ	
2 fp	גְּלֶינָה	הִגָּלֶינָה	גַּלֶּינָה		הִתְגַּלֶּינָה	הַגְלֶינָה	
			Infinitive Construct				
	גְּלוֹת	הִגָּלוֹת	גַּלּוֹת	גֻּלּוֹת	הִתְגַּלּוֹת	הַגְלוֹת	הָגְלוֹת
			Infinitive Absolute				
	גָּלֹה	נִגְלֹה	גַּלֹּה	גֻּלֹּה	הִתְגַּלֹּה	הַגְלֵה	הָגְלֵה
			Active Participle				
ms	גֹּלֶה		מְגַלֶּה		מִתְגַּלֶּה	מַגְלֶה	
mp	גֹּלִים		מְגַלִּים		מִתְגַּלִּים	מַגְלִים	
fs	גֹּלָה		מְגַלָּה		מִתְגַּלָּה	מַגְלָה	
fp	גֹּלוֹת		מְגַלּוֹת		מִתְגַּלּוֹת	מַגְלוֹת	
			Passive Participle				
ms	גָּלוּי	נִגְלֶה		מְגֻלֶּה			מָגְלֶה
mp	גְּלוּיִים	נִגְלִים		מְגֻלִּים			מָגְלִים
fs	גְּלוּיָה	נִגְלָה		מְגֻלָּה			מָגְלָה
fp	גְּלוּיוֹת	נִגְלוֹת		מְגֻלּוֹת			מָגְלוֹת

413

VERB CHART 8
Pe Nun

	Qal	Qal	Qal	Qal	Nif'al	Hif'il	Hof'al
	נָפַל	נָגַשׁ	נָתַן	לָקַח	נִגַּשׁ	נָגַשׁ	נָגַשׁ

Perfect

	Qal	Qal	Qal	Qal	Nif'al	Hif'il	Hof'al
3 ms	נָפַל	נָגַשׁ	נָתַן	לָקַח	נִגַּשׁ	הִגִּישׁ	הֻגַּשׁ
3 fs	נָפְלָה	נִגְּשָׁה	נָתְנָה	לָקְחָה	נִגְּשָׁה	הִגִּישָׁה	הֻגְּשָׁה
2 ms	נָפַלְתָּ	נִגַּשְׁתָּ	נָתַתָּ	לָקַחְתָּ	נִגַּשְׁתָּ	הִגַּשְׁתָּ	הֻגַּשְׁתָּ
2 fs	נָפַלְתְּ	נִגַּשְׁתְּ	נָתַתְּ	לָקַחְתְּ	נִגַּשְׁתְּ	הִגַּשְׁתְּ	הֻגַּשְׁתְּ
1 cs	נָפַלְתִּי	נִגַּשְׁתִּי	נָתַתִּי	לָקַחְתִּי	נִגַּשְׁתִּי	הִגַּשְׁתִּי	הֻגַּשְׁתִּי
3 cp	נָפְלוּ	נִגְּשׁוּ	נָתְנוּ	לָקְחוּ	נִגְּשׁוּ	הִגִּישׁוּ	הֻגְּשׁוּ
2 mp	נְפַלְתֶּם	נִגַּשְׁתֶּם	נְתַתֶּם	לְקַחְתֶּם	נִגַּשְׁתֶּם	הִגַּשְׁתֶּם	הֻגַּשְׁתֶּם
2 fp	נְפַלְתֶּן	נִגַּשְׁתֶּן	נְתַתֶּן	לְקַחְתֶּן	נִגַּשְׁתֶּן	הִגַּשְׁתֶּן	הֻגַּשְׁתֶּן
1 cp	נָפַלְנוּ	נִגַּשְׁנוּ	נָתַנּוּ	לָקַחְנוּ	נִגַּשְׁנוּ	הִגַּשְׁנוּ	הֻגַּשְׁנוּ

Imperfect

	Qal	Qal	Qal	Qal	Nif'al	Hif'il	Hof'al
3 ms	יִפֹּל	יִגַּשׁ	יִתֵּן	יִקַּח	יִנָּגֵשׁ	יַגִּישׁ	יֻגַּשׁ
3 fs	תִּפֹּל	תִּגַּשׁ	תִּתֵּן	תִּקַּח	תִּנָּגֵשׁ	תַּגִּישׁ	תֻּגַּשׁ
2 ms	תִּפֹּל	תִּגַּשׁ	תִּתֵּן	תִּקַּח	תִּנָּגֵשׁ	תַּגִּישׁ	תֻּגַּשׁ
2 fs	תִּפְּלִי	תִּגְּשִׁי	תִּתְּנִי	תִּקְּחִי	תִּנָּגְשִׁי	תַּגִּישִׁי	תֻּגְּשִׁי
1 cs	אֶפֹּל	אֶגַּשׁ	אֶתֵּן	אֶקַּח	אֶנָּגֵשׁ	אַגִּישׁ	אֻגַּשׁ
3 mp	יִפְּלוּ	יִגְּשׁוּ	יִתְּנוּ	יִקְּחוּ	יִנָּגְשׁוּ	יַגִּישׁוּ	יֻגְּשׁוּ
3 fp	תִּפֹּלְנָה	תִּגַּשְׁנָה	תִּתֵּנָּה	תִּקַּחְנָה	תִּנָּגַשְׁנָה	תַּגֵּשְׁנָה	תֻּגַּשְׁנָה
2 mp	תִּפְּלוּ	תִּגְּשׁוּ	תִּתְּנוּ	תִּקְּחוּ	תִּנָּגְשׁוּ	תַּגִּישׁוּ	תֻּגְּשׁוּ
2 fp	תִּפֹּלְנָה	תִּגַּשְׁנָה	תִּתֵּנָּה	תִּקַּחְנָה	תִּנָּגַשְׁנָה	תַּגֵּשְׁנָה	תֻּגַּשְׁנָה
1 cp	נִפֹּל	נִגַּשׁ	נִתֵּן	נִקַּח	נִנָּגֵשׁ	נַגִּישׁ	נֻגַּשׁ

	Qal	Qal	Qal	Qal	Nifʻal	Hifʻil	Hofʻal
	נָפַל	נְגַשׁ	נָתַן	לָקַח	נָגַשׁ	נָגַשׁ	נָגַשׁ

Imperative

	Qal	Qal	Qal	Qal	Nifʻal	Hifʻil	Hofʻal
2 ms	נְפֹל	גַּשׁ	תֵּן	קַח	הִנָּגֵשׁ	הַגֵּשׁ	
2 fs	נִפְלִי	גְּשִׁי	תְּנִי	קְחִי	הִנָּגְשִׁי	הַגִּישִׁי	
2 mp	נִפְלוּ	גְּשׁוּ	תְּנוּ	קְחוּ	הִנָּגְשׁוּ	הַגִּישׁוּ	
2 fp	נְפֹלְנָה	גַּשְׁנָה	תֵּנָּה	קַחְנָה	הִנָּגַשְׁנָה	הַגֵּשְׁנָה	

Infinitive Construct

	Qal	Qal	Qal	Qal	Nifʻal	Hifʻil	Hofʻal
	נְפֹל	גֶּשֶׁת	תֵּת	קַחַת	הִנָּגֵשׁ	הַגִּישׁ	הֻגַּשׁ

Infinitive Absolute

	Qal	Qal	Qal	Qal	Nifʻal	Hifʻil	Hofʻal
	נָפוֹל	נָגוֹשׁ	נָתוֹן	לָקוֹחַ	הִנָּגֵשׁ	הַגֵּשׁ	הֻגֵּשׁ

Active Participle

	Qal	Qal	Qal	Qal	Nifʻal	Hifʻil	Hofʻal
ms	נֹפֵל	נֹגֵשׁ	נֹתֵן	לֹקֵחַ		מַגִּישׁ	
mp	נֹפְלִים	נֹגְשִׁים	נֹתְנִים	לֹקְחִים		מַגִּישִׁים	
fs	נֹפְלָה	נֹגְשָׁה	נֹתְנָה	לֹקְחָה		מַגִּישָׁה	
fp	נֹפְלוֹת	נֹגְשׁוֹת	נֹתְנוֹת	לֹקְחוֹת		מַגִּישׁוֹת	

Passive Participle

	Qal	Qal	Qal	Qal	Nifʻal	Hifʻil	Hofʻal
ms	נָפוּל				נִגָּשׁ		מֻגָּשׁ
mp	נְפוּלִים				נִגָּשִׁים		מֻגָּשִׁים
fs	נְפוּלָה				נִגָּשָׁה		מֻגָּשָׁה
fp	נְפוּלוֹת				נִגָּשׁוֹת		מֻגָּשׁוֹת

	Qal	Qal	Qal	Qal	Qal
	Perfect				
	קוּם (שׂוּם, שִׂים)		בּוֹא	בּוֹשׁ	מוּת
3 ms	קָם	שָׂם	בָּא	בּוֹשׁ	מֵת
3 fs	קָמָה	שָׂמָה	בָּאָה	בּוֹשָׁה	מֵתָה
2 ms	קַמְתָּ	שַׂמְתָּ	בָּאתָ	בֹּשְׁתָּ	מַתָּה
2 fs	קַמְתְּ	שַׂמְתְּ	בָּאת	בֹּשְׁתְּ	מַתְּ
1 cs	קַמְתִּי	שַׂמְתִּי	בָּאתִי	בֹּשְׁתִּי	מַתִּי
3 cp	קָמוּ	שָׂמוּ	בָּאוּ	בּוֹשׁוּ	מֵתוּ
2 mp	קַמְתֶּם	שַׂמְתֶּם	בָּאתֶם	בָּשְׁתֶּם	מַתֶּם
2 fp	קַמְתֶּן	שַׂמְתֶּן	בָּאתֶן	בָּשְׁתֶּן	מַתֶּן
1 cp	קַמְנוּ	שַׂמְנוּ	בָּאנוּ	בּוֹשְׁנוּ	מַתְנוּ
	Imperfect				
3 ms	יָקוּם	יָשִׂים	יָבוֹא	יֵבוֹשׁ	יָמוּת
3 fs	תָּקוּם	תָּשִׂים	תָּבוֹא	תֵּבוֹשׁ	תָּמוּת
2 ms	תָּקוּם	תָּשִׂים	תָּבוֹא	תֵּבוֹשׁ	תָּמוּת
2 fs	תָּקוּמִי	תָּשִׂימִי	תָּבוֹאִי	תֵּבוֹשִׁי	תָּמוּתִי
1 cs	אָקוּם	אָשִׂים	אָבוֹא	אֵבוֹשׁ	אָמוּת
3 mp	יָקוּמוּ	יָשִׂימוּ	יָבוֹאוּ	יֵבוֹשׁוּ	יָמוּתוּ
3 fp	תְּקוּמֶינָה	תְּשִׂימֶינָה	תָּבוֹאנָה	תֵּבוֹשְׁנָה	תְּמוּתֶינָה
2 mp	תָּקוּמוּ	תָּשִׂימוּ	תָּבוֹאוּ	תֵּבוֹשׁוּ	תָּמוּתוּ
2 fp	תְּקוּמֶינָה	תְּשִׂימֶינָה	תָּבוֹאנָה	תֵּבוֹשְׁנָה	תְּמוּתֶינָה
1 cp	נָקוּם	נָשִׂים	נָבוֹא	נֵבוֹשׁ	נָמוּת

	Qal	Qal	Qal	Qal	Qal
			Imperative		
	קוּם (שִׂים, שׂוֹם)	שִׂים	בּוֹא	בּוֹשׁ	מוּת
2 ms	קוּם	שִׂים	בּוֹא	בּוֹשׁ	מוּת
2 fs	קוּמִי	שִׂימִי	בּוֹאִי	בּוֹשִׁי	מוּתִי
2 mp	קוּמוּ	שִׂימוּ	בּוֹאוּ	בּוֹשׁוּ	מוּתוּ
2 fp	קֹמְנָה	שֵׂמְנָה	בֹּאנָה	בֹּשְׁנָה	מֹתְנָה
			Infinitive Construct		
	קוּם (שִׂים, שׂוֹם)	שִׂים	בּוֹא	בּוֹשׁ	מוּת
			Infinitive Absolute		
	קוֹם	שׂוֹם	בּוֹא	בּוֹשׁ	מוֹת
			Active Participle		
ms	קָם	שָׂם	בָּא	בּוֹשׁ	מֵת
mp	קָמִים	שָׂמִים	בָּאִים	בּוֹשִׁים	מֵתִים
fs	קָמָה	שָׂמָה	בָּאָה	בּוֹשָׁה	מֵתָה
fp	קָמוֹת	שָׂמוֹת	בָּאוֹת	בּוֹשׁוֹת	מֵתוֹת

	Nif‘al	Polel	Hif‘il	Hof‘al
		Perfect		
	כּוּן	כּוּן	קוּם	מוּת
3 ms	נָכוֹן	כּוֹגֵן	הֵקִים	הוּקַם
3 fs	נָכוֹנָה	כּוֹנְנָה	הֵקִימָה	הוּקְמָה
2 ms	נְכוּנוֹתָ	כּוֹנַנְתָּ	הֲקִימוֹתָ	הוּקַמְתָּ
2 fs	נְכוּנוֹת	כּוֹנַנְתְּ	הֲקִימוֹת	הוּקַמְתְּ
1 cs	נְכוּנוֹתִי	כּוֹנַנְתִּי	הֲקִימוֹתִי	הוּקַמְתִּי
3 cp	נָכוֹנוּ	כּוֹנְנוּ	הֵקִימוּ	הוּקְמוּ
2 mp	נְכוּנוֹתֶם	כּוֹנַנְתֶּם	הֲקִימוֹתֶם	הוּקַמְתֶּם
2 fp	נְכוּנוֹתֶן	כּוֹנַנְתֶּן	הֲקִימוֹתֶן	הוּקַמְתֶּן
1 cp	נְכוּנוֹנוּ	כּוֹנַנּוּ	הֲקִימוֹנוּ	הוּקַמְנוּ
		Imperfect		
3 ms	יִכּוֹן	יְכוֹגֵן	יָקִים	יוּמַת
3 fs	תִּכּוֹן	תְּכוֹגֵן	תָּקִים	תּוּמַת
2 ms	תִּכּוֹן	תְּכוֹגֵן	תָּקִים	תּוּמַת
2 fs	תִּכּוֹנִי	תְּכוֹנְנִי	תָּקִימִי	תּוּמְתִי
1 cs	אֶכּוֹן	אֲכוֹגֵן	אָקִים	אוּמַת
3 mp	יִכּוֹנוּ	יְכוֹנְנוּ	יָקִימוּ	יוּמְתוּ
3 fp	תִּכּוֹנָה	תְּכוֹגֵנָּה	תָּקֵמְנָה	תּוּמַתְנָה
2 mp	תִּכּוֹנוּ	תְּכוֹנְנוּ	תָּקִימוּ	תּוּמְתוּ
2 fp	תִּכּוֹנָה	תְּכוֹגֵנָּה	תָּקֵמְנָה	תּוּמַתְנָה
1 cp	נִכּוֹן	נְכוֹגֵן	נָקִים	נוּמַת

	Nif‘al	Polel	Hif‘il	Hof‘al
		Imperative		
	כּוֹן כּוּן	כּוּן	קוּם	מוּת
2 ms	הִכּוֹן	כּוֹנֵן	הָקֵם	
2 fs	הִכּוֹנִי	כּוֹנְנִי	הָקִימִי	
2 mp	הִכּוֹנוּ	כּוֹנְנוּ	הָקִימוּ	
2 fp	הִכּוֹנָה	כּוֹנֵנָּה	הָקֵמְנָה	
		Infinitive Construct		
	הִכּוֹן	כּוֹנֵן	הָקִים	הוּמַת
		Infinitive Absolute		
	הִכּוֹן	כּוֹנֵן	הָקֵם	הוּמֵת
		Active Participle		
ms		מְכוֹנֵן	מֵקִים	
mp		מְכוֹנְנִים	מְקִימִים	
fs		מְכוֹנְנָה	מְקִימָה	
fp		מְכוֹנְנוֹת	מְקִימוֹת	
		Passive Participle		
ms	נָכוֹן			מוּמָת
mp	נְכוֹנִים			מוּמָתִים
fs	נְכוֹנָה			מוּמָתָה
fp	נְכוֹנוֹת			מוּמָתוֹת

VERB CHART 10
Pe Vav/Pe Yod

	Qal	Qal	Nif‘al	Hif‘il	Hof‘al	Qal	Hif‘il
				Perfect			
	יָשַׁב	יָרֵא	יָשַׁב	יָשַׁב	יָשַׁב	יָטַב	יָטַב
3 ms	יָשַׁב	יָרֵא	נוֹשַׁב	הוֹשִׁיב	הוּשַׁב	יָטַב	הֵיטִיב
3 fs	יָשְׁבָה	יָרְאָה	נוֹשְׁבָה	הוֹשִׁיבָה	הוּשְׁבָה	יָטְבָה	הֵיטִיבָה
2 ms	יָשַׁבְתָּ	יָרֵאתָ	נוֹשַׁבְתָּ	הוֹשַׁבְתָּ	הוּשַׁבְתָּ	יָטַבְתָּ	הֵיטַבְתָּ
2 fs	יָשַׁבְתְּ	יָרֵאת	נוֹשַׁבְתְּ	הוֹשַׁבְתְּ	הוּשַׁבְתְּ	יָטַבְתְּ	הֵיטַבְתְּ
1 cs	יָשַׁבְתִּי	יָרֵאתִי	נוֹשַׁבְתִּי	הוֹשַׁבְתִּי	הוּשַׁבְתִּי	יָטַבְתִּי	הֵיטַבְתִּי
3 cp	יָשְׁבוּ	יָרְאוּ	נוֹשְׁבוּ	הוֹשִׁיבוּ	הוּשְׁבוּ	יָטְבוּ	הֵיטִיבוּ
2 mp	יְשַׁבְתֶּם	יְרֵאתֶם	נוֹשַׁבְתֶּם	הוֹשַׁבְתֶּם	הוּשַׁבְתֶּם	יְטַבְתֶּם	הֵיטַבְתֶּם
2 fp	יְשַׁבְתֶּן	יְרֵאתֶן	נוֹשַׁבְתֶּן	הוֹשַׁבְתֶּן	הוּשַׁבְתֶּן	יְטַבְתֶּן	הֵיטַבְתֶּן
1 cp	יָשַׁבְנוּ	יָרֵאנוּ	נוֹשַׁבְנוּ	הוֹשַׁבְנוּ	הוּשַׁבְנוּ	יָטַבְנוּ	הֵיטַבְנוּ
				Imperfect			
3 ms	יֵשֵׁב	יִירָא	יִוָּשֵׁב	יוֹשִׁיב	יוּשַׁב	יִיטַב	יֵיטִיב
3 fs	תֵּשֵׁב	תִּירָא	תִּוָּשֵׁב	תּוֹשִׁיב	תּוּשַׁב	תִּיטַב	תֵּיטִיב
2 ms	תֵּשֵׁב	תִּירָא	תִּוָּשֵׁב	תּוֹשִׁיב	תּוּשַׁב	תִּיטַב	תֵּיטִיב
2 fs	תֵּשְׁבִי	תִּירְאִי	תִּוָּשְׁבִי	תּוֹשִׁיבִי	תּוּשְׁבִי	תִּיטְבִי	תֵּיטִיבִי
1 cs	אֵשֵׁב	אִירָא	אִוָּשֵׁב	אוֹשִׁיב	אוּשַׁב	אִיטַב	אֵיטִיב
3 mp	יֵשְׁבוּ	יִירְאוּ	יִוָּשְׁבוּ	יוֹשִׁיבוּ	יוּשְׁבוּ	יִיטְבוּ	יֵיטִיבוּ
3 fp	תֵּשַׁבְנָה	תִּירֶאנָה	תִּוָּשַׁבְנָה	תּוֹשֵׁבְנָה	תּוּשַׁבְנָה	תִּיטַבְנָה	תֵּיטֵבְנָה
2 mp	תֵּשְׁבוּ	תִּירְאוּ	תִּוָּשְׁבוּ	תּוֹשִׁיבוּ	תּוּשְׁבוּ	תִּיטְבוּ	תֵּיטִיבוּ
2 fp	תֵּשַׁבְנָה	תִּירֶאנָה	תִּוָּשַׁבְנָה	תּוֹשֵׁבְנָה	תּוּשַׁבְנָה	תִּיטַבְנָה	תֵּיטֵבְנָה
1 cp	נֵשֵׁב	נִירָא	נִוָּשֵׁב	נוֹשִׁיב	נוּשַׁב	נִיטַב	נֵיטִיב

420

	Qal	Qal	Nif'al	Hif'il	Hof'al	Qal	Hif'il
Imperative							
	יָשֵׁב	יְרָא	יָשֵׁב	יָשֵׁב	יָשֵׁב	יָטַב	יָטֵב
2 ms	שֵׁב	יְרָא	הִוָּשֵׁב	הוֹשֵׁב		יֵטַב	הֵיטֵב
2 fs	שְׁבִי	יִרְאִי	הִוָּשְׁבִי	הוֹשִׁיבִי		יֵטְבִי	הֵיטִיבִי
2 mp	שְׁבוּ	יִרְאוּ	הִוָּשְׁבוּ	הוֹשִׁיבוּ		יֵטְבוּ	הֵיטִיבוּ
2 fp	שֵׁבְנָה	יְרֶאנָה	הִוָּשַׁבְנָה	הוֹשֵׁבְנָה		יֵטַבְנָה	הֵיטַבְנָה
Infinitive Construct							
	שֶׁבֶת	יִרְאָה	הִוָּשֵׁב	הוֹשִׁיב	הוּשַׁב	יְטֹב	הֵיטִיב
Infinitive Absolute							
	יָשׁוֹב		הִוָּשֵׁב	הוֹשֵׁב	הוּשֵׁב	יָטוֹב	הֵיטֵב
Active Participle							
ms	יֹשֵׁב	יָרֵא		מוֹשִׁיב		יֹטֵב	מֵיטִיב
mp	יֹשְׁבִים			מוֹשִׁיבִים		יֹטְבִים	מֵיטִיבִים
fs	יֹשְׁבָה			מוֹשִׁיבָה		יֹטְבָה	מֵיטִיבָה
fp	יֹשְׁבוֹת			מוֹשִׁיבוֹת		יֹטְבוֹת	מֵיטִיבוֹת
Passive Participle							
ms			נוֹשָׁב		מוּשָׁב		
mp			נוֹשְׁבִים		מוּשָׁבִים		
fs			נוֹשָׁבָה		מוּשָׁבָה		
fp			נוֹשָׁבוֹת		מוּשָׁבוֹת		

VERB CHART 11
Double ʿAyin

Perfect

	Qal	Nifʿal	Polel	Polal	Hitpolel	Hifʿil	Hofʿal
3 ms	סֹב סַב	נָסַב	סוֹבֵב	סוֹבַב	הִסְתּוֹבֵב	הֵסֵב	הוּסַב
3 fs	סַבָּה	נָסַבָּה	סוֹבְבָה	סוֹבְבָה	הִסְתּוֹבְבָה	הֵסַבָּה	הוּסַבָּה
2 ms	סַבּוֹתָ	נְסַבּוֹתָ	סוֹבַבְתָּ	סוֹבַבְתָּ	הִסְתּוֹבַבְתָּ	הֲסִבּוֹתָ	הֲסַבּוֹתָ
2 fs	סַבּוֹת	נְסַבּוֹת	סוֹבַבְתְּ	סוֹבַבְתְּ	הִסְתּוֹבַבְתְּ	הֲסִבּוֹת	הוּסַבּוֹת
1 cs	סַבּוֹתִי	נְסַבּוֹתִי	סוֹבַבְתִּי	סוֹבַבְתִּי	הִסְתּוֹבַבְתִּי	הֲסִבּוֹתִי	הֲסַבּוֹתִי
3 cp	סַבּוּ	נָסַבּוּ	סוֹבְבוּ	סוֹבְבוּ	הִסְתּוֹבְבוּ	הֵסַבּוּ	הוּסַבּוּ
2 mp	סַבּוֹתֶם	נְסַבּוֹתֶם	סוֹבַבְתֶּם	סוֹבַבְתֶּם	הִסְתּוֹבַבְתֶּם	הֲסִבּוֹתֶם	הוּסַבּוֹתֶם
2 fp	סַבּוֹתֶן	נְסַבּוֹתֶן	סוֹבַבְתֶּן	סוֹבַבְתֶּן	הִסְתּוֹבַבְתֶּן	הֲסִבּוֹתֶן	הוּסַבּוֹתֶן
1 cp	סַבּוֹנוּ	נְסַבּוֹנוּ	סוֹבַבְנוּ	סוֹבַבְנוּ	הִסְתּוֹבַבְנוּ	הֲסִבּוֹנוּ	הוּסַבּוֹנוּ

Imperfect

	Qal(1)	Qal(2)	Nifʿal	Polel	Polal	Hitpolel	Hifʿil	Hofʿal
3 ms	יָסֹב	יִסֹב	יִסַּב	יְסוֹבֵב	יְסוֹבַב	יִסְתּוֹבֵב	יָסֵב	יוּסַב
3 fs	תָּסֹב	תִּסֹב	תִּסַּב	תְּסוֹבֵב	תְּסוֹבַב	תִּסְתּוֹבֵב	תָּסֵב	תּוּסַב
2 ms	תָּסֹב	תִּסֹב	תִּסַּב	תְּסוֹבֵב	תְּסוֹבַב	תִּסְתּוֹבֵב	תָּסֵב	תּוּסַב
2 fs	תָּסֹבִּי	תִּסֹבִּי	תִּסַּבִּי	תְּסוֹבְבִי	תְּסוֹבְבִי	תִּסְתּוֹבְבִי	תָּסֵבִּי	תּוּסַבִּי
1 cs	אָסֹב	אֶסֹב	אֶסַּב	אֲסוֹבֵב	אֲסוֹבַב	אֶסְתּוֹבֵב	אָסֵב	אוּסַב
3 mp	יָסֹבּוּ	יִסֹבּוּ	יִסַּבּוּ	יְסוֹבְבוּ	יְסוֹבְבוּ	יִסְתּוֹבְבוּ	יָסֵבּוּ	יוּסַבּוּ
3 fp	תָּסֻבֶּינָה	תִּסֹבְנָה	תִּסַּבֶּינָה	תְּסוֹבַבְנָה	תְּסוֹבַבְנָה	תִּסְתּוֹבַבְנָה	תְּסֻבֶּינָה	תּוּסַבֶּינָה
2 mp	תָּסֹבּוּ	תִּסֹבּוּ	תִּסַּבּוּ	תְּסוֹבְבוּ	תְּסוֹבְבוּ	תִּסְתּוֹבְבוּ	תָּסֵבּוּ	תּוּסַבּוּ
2 fp	תָּסֻבֶּינָה	תִּסֹבְנָה	תִּסַּבֶּינָה	תְּסוֹבַבְנָה	תְּסוֹבַבְנָה	תִּסְתּוֹבַבְנָה	תְּסֻבֶּינָה	תּוּסַבֶּינָה
1 cp	נָסֹב	נִסֹב	נִסַּב	נְסוֹבֵב	נְסוֹבַב	נִסְתּוֹבֵב	נָסֵב	נוּסַב

	Qal	Nifʻal	Polel	Polal	Hitpolel	Hifʻil	Hofʻal
Imperative							
2 ms	סֹב	הִסַּב	סוֹבֵב		הִסְתּוֹבֵב	הָסֵב	
2 fs	סֹבִּי	הִסַּבִּי	סוֹבְבִי		הִסְתּוֹבְבִי	הָסֵבִּי	
2 mp	סֹבּוּ	הִסַּבּוּ	סוֹבְבוּ		הִסְתּוֹבְבוּ	הָסֵבּוּ	
2 fp	סֻבֶּינָה	הִסַּבֶּינָה	סוֹבֵבְנָה		הִסְתּוֹבֵבְנָה	הֲסִבֶּינָה	
Infinitive Construct							
	סֹב	הִסַּב	סוֹבֵב	סֹבַב	הִסְתּוֹבֵב	הָסֵב	הוּסַב
Infinitive Absolute							
	סָבוֹב	הִסֹּב	סוֹבֵב	סֹבַב	הִסְתּוֹבֵב	הָסֵב	הוּסַב
Active Participle							
ms	סֹבֵב		מְסוֹבֵב		מִסְתּוֹבֵב	מֵסֵב	
mp	סֹבְבִים		מְסוֹבְבִים		מִסְתּוֹבְבִים	מְסִבִּים	
fs	סֹבְבָה		מְסוֹבְבָה		מִסְתּוֹבְבָה	מְסִבָּה	
fp	סֹבְבוֹת		מְסוֹבְבוֹת		מִסְתּוֹבְבוֹת	מְסִבּוֹת	
Passive Participle							
ms		נָסַב	מְסוֹבָב				מוּסָב
mp		נְסַבִּים	מְסוֹבָבִים				מוּסַבִּים
fs		נְסַבָּה	מְסוֹבָבָה				מוּסַבָּה
fp		נְסַבּוֹת	מְסוֹבָבוֹת				מוּסַבּוֹת

GLOSSARY

Absolute State: the simple, ordinary form of nouns, the form under which they are listed in dictionaries. Nouns often have an altered form when placed in the construct state, due mainly to their loss of stress.

Accented Syllable: the syllable carrying the major accent in a word, sometimes referred to as the tone syllable. The accented syllable will normally be the final syllable in a word. A munaḥ (֑) will be used throughout this grammar to mark any accented syllable that is not final in a word.

Accents: the non-vowel marks placed above and below words to indicate the primary accented syllable and to mark other secondarily accented syllables in multi-syllable words. Accents also serve as a guide to the chanting of the text in synagogue settings and as marks of punctuation to indicate the smaller syntactical segments that may be found within a verse (sentence). About two-thirds of the accents are disjunctive (separating) and about one-third conjunctive (joining). There are separate systems of prose and poetic accents, although they sometimes overlap. The latter are found primarily in Psalms, Job, and Proverbs. The inserting of accents into the consonantal text of the Hebrew Bible was the work of the Masoretes, who were active between A.D. 500 and 1000.

Active Voice: the classification of a verbal inflection in which the subject of the verb is represented as performing the action of the verb. Its opposite is the passive voice.

Adjective: see **Attributive Adjective; Predicate Adjective**

Adverb: a word that modifies or describes a verb, an adjective, or another adverb. It may specify where, when, how, or why a certain action has occurred or a certain condition exists. Hebrew adverbs are few in number in comparison with modern languages. These include adverbs of *location* (פֹּה, "here," שָׁם, "there," חוּץ, "outside," etc.); adverbs of *degree* (מְאֹד, "very," מְעַט, "few, a little," תָּמִיד, "continually," עוֹד, "again," etc.); adverbs of *time* (עַתָּה, "now," אָז, "then," טֶרֶם, "before, not yet," עוֹלָם, "forever," הַיּוֹם, "today," etc.); and adverbs of *manner* (פִּתְאֹם, "suddenly," יַחְדָּו, "together," חִנָּם, "in vain, for nothing," etc.).

Afformative: see **Suffix**

Agreement: the sharing of common grammatical features by two different parts of speech. Attributive adjectives, for example, agree in gender, number, and definiteness (both adjectives and modified nouns appearing as either definite or indefinite) with the nouns they describe or modify. Predicate adjectives (used in verbless sentences) agree with their subject nouns in gender and number but never take the definite article, even when a subject noun is definite. Inflected verb forms will also agree with their subjects in person, gender, and number (participles in gender and number only).

(1) Agreement of attributive adjective and modified noun:

אִשָּׁה טוֹבָה   "a good woman"

הָאִשָּׁה הַטּוֹבָה   "the good woman"

(2) Agreement of predicate adjective and subject noun:

זָקֵן הָאִישׁ   "the man (was) old"

הָאֲנָשִׁים טֹבִים   "the men (were) good"

(3) Agreement between inflected verb forms and their subjects:

בָּרָא אֱלֹהִים   "God created"

אָמְרָה הָאִשָּׁה   "the woman said"

Alphabet: the twenty-two letters of Biblical Hebrew in their proper order. This number is arrived at by considering שׁ and שׂ as variant forms of the same letter. All Hebrew alphabetical letters are consonants; the vowels were invented later. A purely consonantal text is known as an unpointed or unvocalized text. Offical synagogue scrolls are written in unpointed Hebrew. Five of the letters of the alphabet are classified as gutturals (א, ה, ח, ע, and sometimes ר). Five are classified as sibilants (ז, ס, צ, שׁ, and שׂ). Five have alternate forms when they are final in words (כ → ך, מ → ם, נ → ן, פ → ף, צ → ץ).

Apocopation: the shortening of a verb form and the subsequent changes in vocalization and syllable structure. Apocopation occurs most frequently with imperfect forms of Lamed He verbs when they are used as jussives or are prefixed with the vav consecutive.

יִהְיֶה   Qal imperfect 3 ms of הָיָה, "he was," translated "he will be"

יְהִי   Jussive, or shortened form of the above, translated "let him (it) be"

וַיְהִי   Apocopated form of וַיִּהְיֶה, translated "and he (it) was"

Aramaic: a Semitic language sharing a common script and a close structural relationship with Biblical Hebrew. Certain sections of the Bible are actually written in Aramaic, including Ezra 4:8–6:18; 7:12–26; Dan. 2:4b–7:28; and Jer. 10:11. A number of isolated Aramaic words appear elsewhere in the Bible. The Targums to biblical books, as well as Syriac versions of the Bible, are also written in Aramaic. The Masoretic notes appearing along the side margins (Masorah Parva) and at the top and bottom of manuscript pages (Masorah Magna) are

425

written in a form of abbreviated Aramaic, since Aramaic was the working language of the scholars who prepared these notes.

Ashkenazi, pl. Ashkenazim: a term applied to Jews who migrated to Germany and other Eastern European countries after the period of the Crusades. Ashkenazi is also the term used to describe their system of spoken Hebrew, a system that differed from that of the Sephardim, a term applied to Jews who migrated to Spain and surrounding regions.

Assimilation: the process by which the letter נ, when positioned as the final consonant in a closed syllable (other than the final syllable of a word), is absorbed or assimilated into the following consonant by means of a dagesh forte.

נָתַתָּ (from נָתַן) → נָתַנְתָּ   יִפֹּל → (נָפַל from) יִנְפֹּל

Assimilation also occurs when ת of the Hitpaʿel preformative (הִת) precedes ד, ט, or another ת. In such instances the ת of the prefix is assimilated into the following consonant by means of a dagesh forte.

הִתְטַמֵּא, "he defiled himself," becomes הִטַּמֵּא

ʾAtnaḥ: a major disjunctive accent that generally appears on the accented syllable of the last word in the first half of a verse, thus dividing the verse into two syntactical units. It is found, for example, on the word אֱלֹהִים in Genesis 1:1, indicating that this word marks the syntactical end of the first half of the verse. Silluq performs a similar function on the accented syllable of the final word in each verse. Because both ʾatnaḥ and silluq are heavy disjunctive accents, the words that carry them are always in pause and so must have a long vowel in their accented syllables.

Attributive Adjective: an adjective that directly describes an attribute of a noun. It usually follows the noun it modifies and agrees with it in gender (masculine or feminine), number (singular or plural), and definiteness (definite or indefinite).

מֶלֶךְ גָּדוֹל   "a great king"

הָעִיר הַגְּדוֹלָה   "the great city"

הַמְּלָכִים הַגְּדוֹלִים   "the great kings"

ʿAyin Guttural (II-Guttural) Verb: a verb classified as weak by virtue of the fact that its middle root consonant is a guttural. The various peculiarities of gutturals affect the conjugation of ʿAyin Gutturals.

ʿAyin Vav/ʿAyin Yod (II-Vav/II-Yod) Verb: a verb rendered weak by virtue of the fact that its middle root consonant was originally either vav or yod, but the middle consonant has now combined with a preceding vowel to form a diphthong, either **יְ**, **וֹ**, or **וּ**. The resultant verb roots are essentially biliteral (consisting of only two consonants) and are always cited in dictionaries in their Qal infinitive construct forms.

BeGad KeFaT Consonants: a mnemonic device for remembering the six consonants that may take a dagesh lene when not preceded by a full vowel or a vocal sheva. The presence of dagesh lene serves to harden the pronunciation, while its omission serves to soften it, although in Modern Hebrew only three consonants without dagesh lene (**ב**, **כ**, and **פ**) are given a softer sound.

Biconsonantal Root (also referred to as diconsonantal root): a verb root composed of only two consonants, thus making it monosyllabic. Since biconsonantal verb roots originally had as their middle consonant either vav or yod, they are classified as ʿAyin Vav/ʿAyin Yod (II-Vav/II-Yod) verbs.

שִׂים "to put, place"   קוּם "to arise"

Cardinal Numerals: those used in counting, as *one*, *two*, *three*, etc. An ordinal numeral is one that expresses consecutive order or rank, or relative position in a series, as *first*, *second*, *third*, etc.

Causative: see **Hifʿil**

Cohortative: a first person imperfect verb form, either singular or plural, often with a **הָ** suffix, used to express the speaker's desire, determination, or self-encouragement to perform a certain action, sometimes referred to as the "first person imperative." The cohortative suffix **הָ** draws the accent to itself, causing the preceding vowel (now left in an open, unaccented syllable) to volatilize. The particle **נָא** may appear after a cohortative verb form for emphasis.

Collective Nouns: nouns that are singular in form but capable of being either singular or plural in meaning. Thus **עַם** may refer to "a people," requiring singular modifiers and singular verbs, or it may refer to a body of individual persons, "the people," in which case it requires plural modifiers and plural verbs.

Comparative Degree: the degree (expressed in English by such phrases as "greater than," "better than," "younger than," etc.) expressed by the preposition **מִן** (the so-called "comparative *min*") prefixed to a noun or a pronoun that is preceded by an adjective or some form of a stative verb. This Hebrew construction sometimes expresses a meaning similar to the English superlative.

טוֹבִים הַשְּׁנַיִם מִן־הָאֶחָד   "Two are better than one."

יָרוּם מִמֶּנִּי   "It is too high for me."

וַיִּגְדַּל שְׁלֹמֹה מִכֹּל מַלְכֵי הָאָרֶץ   "And Solomon was greater than all the kings of the earth."

Compensatory Lengthening of Vowels: the lengthening that occurs when short vowels are left in open, unaccented syllables before gutturals that have refused a dagesh forte. Such lengthening is not required before ה and ח since they are doubled by implication (virtually doubled). The pattern of compensatory lengthening is as follows:

      patah to qames (_ to ָ)

      hireq to sere (. to ׃)

      qibbus to holem (ֻ to ֹ)

Composite Sheva: see **Compound Sheva**

Compound Sheva: the form of the sheva that replaces a simple (vocal) sheva after a guttural. Compound shevas consist of a simple sheva (׃) combined with a short vowel from either the "a" class (_), the "e" class (׃.), or the "o" class (ָ). The resultant forms are hatef-patah (ֲ), hatef-s^egol (ֱ), and hatef-qames (ֳ). These are used mainly in the inflection of weak verbs having one or more gutturals in their root forms. Compound shevas must always be treated as vocal shevas.

Conjugation: the orderly presentation of all the inflected forms of a verb according to person, gender, and number. The only conjugations covering the full range of person, gender, and number are the perfect (or suffix) conjugation and the imperfect (or prefix) conjugation. To conjugate a verb means to list in order all its inflected forms in all stems.

Conjunction: see **Vav Conjunction; Vav Consecutive**

Conjunctive Dagesh Forte (also referred to as euphonic dagesh forte): a dagesh forte placed in the initial consonant of a word in order to link it to the preceding word.

      זֶה־שְּׁמִי   "This (is) my name."

      מַה־יַּעֲשֶׂה־לִּי   "What will he do to me?"

Consonant: see **Alphabet**

Consonantal Suffix: a verb suffix that begins with a consonant rather than a vowel. Consonantal suffixes are not accented, except for תֶּם and תֶּן, the suffixes for the perfect 2 mp and 2 fp.

Construct Relationship: the joining together of two (occasionally three, but rarely four) nouns within a sentence. The joining may be by a maqqef or by simple juxtaposition. The final noun remains in the absolute state while the noun (or nouns) preceding it must be in the construct state. Nouns so joined are treated as a single speech unit, with only the final noun (the absolute noun) receiving a major accent. The construct relationship functions to express genitival relationship and nuances of meaning associated with the preposition "of."

Construct State: the state of a noun placed in a construct relationship to a noun in the absolute state. A noun must also be written in its construct form when it is supplied with a pronominal suffix. The basic reason nouns are placed in the construct state is to express genitival relationships of the possessed/possessor type, and to convey the various nuances of meaning associated with the preposition "of."

בַּיִת   "house" (absolute state)

בֵּית   "house" (construct state)

בֵּית־דָּוִד   "the house of David" (construct relationship)

בֵּיתוֹ   "his house" (construct state with pronominal suffix)

Coordinate Relationship: a linking of two or more verb forms by means of vav conjunction or vav consecutive. The first word in such a sequence acts as the governing verb and controls both the time frame (past, present, or future) and the mode (indicative, subjunctive, imperative, or hortatory) of the verbs linked to it. A perfect may govern another perfect or an imperfect, the latter having the distinction of always being linked to its governing perfect by means of a vav consecutive. An imperfect may govern another imperfect or a perfect. An imperative may govern a perfect, an imperfect, or another imperative. An infinitive absolute may govern a perfect, and a participle may also govern a perfect. The list given here is not meant to be exhaustive but covers the most frequently occurring verb sequences.

Dagesh Forte: a dot placed inside a non-guttural consonant to indicate the doubling of the consonant or the assimilation of a preceding consonant (usually נ or ת). The consonant doubled by dagesh forte or containing an assimilated letter must be preceded by a consonant pointed with a full vowel.

Dagesh Lene: a dot placed in six consonants (ב, ג, ד, כ, פ, ת – BeGaD KeFaT) when they stand at the beginning of a word or a new syllable within a word and are not immediately preceded by a full vowel or a vocal sheva, either in the preceding syllable or (under certain circumstances) in the preceding word. The presence of dagesh lene serves to harden the pronunciation of the BeGaD KeFaT letters, while its absence serves to soften their pronunciation, although in modern usage (and throughout this grammar) only the letters ב, כ, and פ are given a softer sound when they are written without dagesh lene.

Definite Article: a prefixed particle placed on a noun and/or its modifying adjective to indicate that it is a definite noun. The table for writing definite articles is as follows:

429

(1) הּ · (he plus paṭaḥ plus dagesh forte) before non–gutturals

    (a) הַבֵּן "the son"

    (b) בְּנוֹ הַקָּטָן "his youngest son"

    (c) הַסֵּפֶר הַגָּדוֹל "the large book"

(2) הָ (he plus qameṣ) before א, ר, and (generally) ע

    (a) הָעִיר "the city"

    (b) הָרוּחַ "the spirit"

(3) הַ (he plus paṭaḥ) before ה and ח (doubled by implication)

    (a) הַחֹשֶׁךְ "the darkness"

    (b) הַהוּא "that" (demonstrative pronoun plus article)

(4) הֶ (he plus sᵉgol) before חָ and before unaccented הָ or עָ

    (a) הֶחָכָם "the wise"

    (b) הֶהָרִים "the mountains"

    (c) הֶעָרִים "the cities"

Defective Writing: see **Scriptio Plena**

Definite/Indefinite Noun: Hebrew has no indefinite article. A Hebrew noun is indefinite if it has no definite article prefixed to it. A noun is definite if it has the definite article prefixed to it, if it is a proper name, if it is in the construct state and stands in construct relationship to a definite noun, or if it has a pronominal suffix.

(1) Indefinite nouns

    בֵּן "a son"   בַּיִת "a house"

(2) Definite nouns

    (a) הַבַּיִת "the house"

    (b) יִשְׂרָאֵל "Israel"

    (c) בֵּית יִשְׂרָאֵל "the house of Israel"

    (d) בְּנוֹ הַקָּטָן "his youngest son"

Demonstrative Pronouns: pronouns that specify or single out someone or something. These have a function parallel to that of adjectives in that they may be used in either an attributive sense (*"this* house") or in a predicative sense (*"this* is the house").

Denominative Verb: a verb derived from a noun. For example, [נבא], "he prophesied," is derived from נָבִיא, "a prophet."

Diphthong: a gliding speech sound made up of two originally separate sounds, as the *oi* sound in *boy* or *boil*. Hebrew diphthongs originated from the juxtaposition of a vowel letter or vowel indicator (א, ה, י, or ו, otherwise known as *matres lectionis*) and a preceding short vowel of a homogeneous class. The diphthongs that resulted from the merger of these two formerly independent elements include: יָ (יַ, pausal form), יְ, יֶ, יֵ, וֹ, וּ. Diphthongs are classified as unchangeably long vowels, which means that they cannot be shortened or volatilized. The value of a diphthong is represented in transliteration by the circumflex accent.

בּוֹ *bô*, בֵּין *bên*, בִּין *bîn*

Direct Object: a person or thing that receives the action of a transitive verb. A direct object may be a noun (either definite or indefinite), a proper name, or a pronominal suffix attached either to the end of a verb form or to the particle אֵת. אֵת functions as the direct object indicator and is not to be translated. When used before a definite noun, it may stand alone, or it may be joined to the noun by a maqqef. When the latter occurs, אֵת ceases to be accented and ṣere must be shortened to sᵉgol.

אֵת הַשָּׁמַיִם "the heavens" (Gen. 1:1)

אֶת־הַשָּׁמַיִם "the heavens" (Exod. 20:11)

Double ʿAyin Verb (Geminate Verb): a verb classified as weak by virtue of the fact that its second and third root consonants are the same.

Examples: סָבַב, "he surrounded," קָלַל, "he was swift, light (not heavy), insignificant," and תָּמַם, "he was finished, complete."

Euphonic Dagesh Forte: see **Conjunctive Dagesh Forte**

Full Vowel: any vowel except a vocal sheva (simple or compound). Vocal shevas are treated as half–vowels.

Full Writing: see **Scriptio Plena**

Geminate Verb: see **Double ʿAyin Verb**

Gender: the determination of nouns, adjectives, pronouns, pronominal suffixes, and all verb forms (except infinitives) as either masculine or feminine. Verb forms that do not have separate masculine and feminine endings are said to be common in gender. Thus שָׁמְרוּ, "they kept," is a Qal perfect third *common* plural from שָׁמַר. The subject "they" could consist of either males or females, or a mixture of the two.

Gentilic Adjective: an adjective formed by a special ḥireq–yod (יִ) ending added to the name of a country to designate the citizens of that country, as in the

modern use of "Israeli" and "Saudi." Biblical examples include: מוֹאָבִי ,
"Moabite," עִבְרִי , "Hebrew," יִשְׂרָאֵלִי (fem. יִשְׂרְאֵלִית), "Israelite."

Gutturals: five consonants (א, ה, ח, ע, and sometimes ר) so designated by their
having been pronounced in the throat. They have three distinctive characteristics
that set them apart from other consonants:

    (1)   They cannot be doubled by receiving a dagesh forte, which often
           necessitates the compensatory lengthening of the preceding short vowel.

    (2)   They tend to take "a" class vowels both immediately before and after
           them.

    (3)   They take compound shevas instead of simple shevas.

[א is always quiescent at the end of a syllable. ה is quiescent at the end of the
final syllable in a word, unless it is pointed with a mappiq (הּ).]

Half-Vowel: any vocal sheva, whether simple (ְ) or compound (ֱ , ֲ , ֳ).
A half-vowel always stands beneath a consonant that begins a word or a new
syllable within a word.

Hapax Legomenon: a Greek phrase meaning "read once," which in the context of
the study of the Hebrew Bible is used to describe a particular form of a word or a
particular combination of words that occurs in a given context but is not found
elsewhere. The plural of *Hapax Legomenon* is *Hapax Legomena*. A Hapax
Legomenon is often marked in the Masorah Parva of the Masoretic Text by a
lamed with a point placed above it (ל). Approximately 2000 of the 8000 or so
words in the Hebrew Bible are Hapax Legomena. See וְלַהֲבִיאֲךָ in Exodus 23:20.

He-Directive: a ָה ending added to nouns or directional adverbs to indicate
"direction toward" or "motion toward" a thing or a place (never toward a person).
The He-Directive ending never takes the accent.

He (ה) Interrogative: a particle prefixed to the initial word in a question, and thus
functioning somewhat like a question mark in modern languages. The He
Interrogative is written as follows:

    (a)   הֲ before a non-guttural pointed with a full vowel

    (b)   הַ before a guttural pointed with any full vowel except qameṣ or
           qameṣ-ḥatuf

    (c)   הֶ before a guttural pointed with qameṣ or qameṣ-ḥatuf

    (d)   הַ before any consonant (guttural or non-guttural) pointed with a vocal
           sheva (simple or compound)

Hebrew Language: language of the Semitic family of languages, which includes
Akkadian, Syriac-Aramean, Canaanite, Moabite, Phoenician, Arabic, Ethiopic, etc.
Evidence suggests that the ancestors of the Hebrews were Arameans (cf. Gen.

31:47; Deut. 26:5). They apparently learned the Hebrew language after they migrated to the land of Canaan. The Ugaritic tablets, excavated in 1929 and following, clearly demonstrate that the Hebrew language, even including its poetic structures, was largely taken over from the Canaanites. In fact, the biblical designation for the language is not "Hebrew" but "the language of Canaan" (cf. Isa. 19:18). The Hebrews continued to shape and expand the language they had borrowed from the Canaanites through their contacts with other peoples.

Hif'il: the sixth verb stem, normally functioning as the causative counterpart to Qal verb forms.

> Qal perfect 3 ms שָׁמַע, "he heard"
>
> Hif'il perfect 3 ms הִשְׁמִיעַ, "he caused (another) to hear"

Hitpa'el: the fifth verb stem, characterized by the longer preformative (הִת in perfect, יִת in imperfects, etc.) and the doubling of the middle consonant of the verb root. Hitpa'el verbs are intransitive and usually have a reflexive force (הִתְחַבֵּא, "he hid himself"). Some Hitpa'el forms are only indirectly reflexive and are translated much like Qal forms (הִתְהַלֵּךְ, "he walked").

Hof'al: the seventh verb stem, functioning as the causative passive, the counterpart to the causative active (Hif'il).

> הוֹרִיד, Hif'il perfect 3 ms (from יָרַד, "he went down"), translated "he brought down"
>
> הוּרַד, Hof'al perfect 3 ms (also from יָרַד), translated "he was brought down"

Hollow Verb: see 'Ayin Vav/'Ayin Yod Verb

Hortatory Mode: the mode of the verb used to exhort or motivate someone to act in a certain way, or to express the speaker's desire, determination, or self-encouragement to undertake a certain action. It involves the use of both jussive and cohortative forms of verbs.

> יַעֲזֹב רָשָׁע דַּרְכּוֹ   "Let the wicked forsake his way."
>
> נִבְנֶה־לָּנוּ עִיר   "Let us build for us a city."

Imperative: the verb conjugation used to express commands. Its occurrences are limited to second person forms and to positive commands. Prohibitions are expressed by לֹא with the imperfect or אַל with the jussive. Imperatives may occur in any stem except Pu'al or Hof'al.

Imperative Mode: the mode of the verb used in expressing commands or prohibitions.

> קוּם לֵךְ "Arise, go!"   לֹא תִגְנֹב "You shall not steal!"

433

Imperfect: the incomplete or non–perfective conjugation of the verb. It is also referred to as the prefix conjugation, since abbreviated subject pronouns are prefixed to its forms.

Independent Pronoun (also referred to as a subject pronoun): a free-standing personal pronoun that functions as the subject of a verb but never as the object. An independent pronoun will often appear in a verbless clause or sentence, with some form of the verb "to be" understood [אֲנִי יְהוָה, "I (am) the LORD"].

Indicative Mode: the mode of the verb reflected in ordinary statements of fact, statements that are declaratory in nature, and not contingent upon other factors, either expressed or unexpressed.

בָּרָא אֱלֹהִים   "God created."

וַיִּקְרָא אֶל־מֹשֶׁה   "And he called to Moses."

Infinitive Absolute: one of two infinitives (see **Infinitive Construct**) expressing the basic idea of the verb root without the limitations of person, gender, and number. Unlike the infinitive construct, the infinitive absolute never takes prepositional prefixes or pronominal suffixes. Infinitives absolute sometimes function like English gerunds ("eating," "drinking," etc.). In a few instances they serve as alternate forms of the imperative. Usually, however, they stand either before or after a conjugated form of a cognate verb, thus serving to intensify or reiterate the verbal statement, as in מוֹת תָּמוּת, "You shall surely die."

Infinitive Construct: one of the two infinitives (see **Infinitive Absolute**) expressing the bare idea of a verb root without the specification of person, gender, and number. Infinitives construct may take prepositional prefixes and/or pronominal suffixes. In the case of ʿAyin Vav/ʿAyin Yod verbs, it is the Qal infinitive construct that is cited as the verb root, as in מוּת, "to die."

Interrogative Adverb: an adverbial particle designed to elicit information about direction, origin, location, duration, intention, etc.

(a)   אֵי, אַיֵּה, אֵיפֹה   "Where?"

(b)   אֵי־מִזֶּה, מֵאַיִן   "Whence?"

(c)   אָנָה   "Whither?"

(d)   אֵיךְ   "How?"

(e)   עַד־מָתַי, עַד־אָנָה   "How long?"

(f)   מַדּוּעַ, לָמָּה   "Why?"

Interrogative He: see He (ה) Interrogative

Interrogative Pronoun: a pronoun used to introduce a question. The interrogative pronoun מִי ("Who?") refers to persons, while מָה ("What?") refers to things. They are unchangeable in form, regardless of the gender or number of their referents. Both may function as subject or as object of a verb. מִי may also be used to show possession when prefixed by the preposition לְ (לְמִי, "to whom?" or "whose?"). מִי is invariable in form either with or without a prefix, or regardless of whether it stands alone or is joined to the following word by a maqqef. The vocalization of מָה, however, shows the following variations:

(a) מָה whenever it is free-standing or when it is joined by a maqqef to a word beginning with א, ה, or ר

(b) מַה־ when joined by maqqef to a word beginning with a non-guttural (in which case a dagesh forte will be placed in the non-guttural consonant following maqqef), מַה־זֹּאת, "What is this?"

(c) מֶה (or מֶה־) before ה or ע

Intransitive Verb: a verb which cannot take a direct object. A transitive verb, on the other hand, is one that requires a direct object to complete its meaning.

קוּם אֱכָל־לֶחֶם "Arise (intransitive), eat bread (transitive)." (1 Kgs. 21:7)

Jussive: a third person imperfect verb form used to express a wish, desire, or command in the third person. There is no difference in form between jussives and imperfects in strong verbs. In weak verbs, however, jussives often appear as shortened forms of third person imperfects, especially in the case of Lamed He verbs. The particle נָא may be added after jussives for emphasis.

Lamed 'Alef (III-'Alef) Verb: a verb rendered weak by virtue of the fact that its third root consonant is א. Since final א is always quiescent (ceases to function as a consonant), it will affect the vocalization of verb forms in which it stands.

Lamed Guttural (III-Guttural) Verb: a verb classified as weak by virtue of the fact that its final root consonant is either ה (rarely used), ח, or ע. Final ר behaves not as a guttural but as a strong consonant. Verbs whose roots end in א or ה behave so differently that they constitute separate classes of weak verbs. The conjugation of Lamed Gutturals is determined by the various rules governing the use of gutturals.

Lamed He (III-He) Verb: a verb rendered weak by virtue of the fact that its third root consonant is ה. In some inflected forms the ה of the verb root is replaced by an original י (yod).

Lengthening of Vowels: see **Compensatory Lengthening of Vowels**

435

Location (sometimes referred to as parsing): the systematic analysis of an inflected form of a verb according to stem, form (perfect, imperfect, etc.), person, gender, number, root (plus its meaning), and its resultant translation.

יִשְׁמֹר Qal (stem), Imperfect (form), 3 ms (Person, gender, number), from שָׁמַר (root), "he kept," translated: "he will keep, guard"

Locative ה: see **He–Directive**

Mappiq: a dot that can be inserted in a final ה (גָּבַהּ) to indicate that it functions as a strong guttural and not merely as a vowel letter. Final ה without a mappiq becomes quiescent (ceases to function as a consonant) and is therefore unable to make the syllable in which it stands a closed syllable. This rule applies only to a ה that is final in a word and not to one that occupies an initial or an intermediate position. While הּ (he + mappiq) sometimes occurs as the final consonant in the root form of a verb, its most common occurrence is as the 3 fs pronominal suffix to a noun, verb, or preposition. Examples are: סוּסָהּ, "her horse," לְשָׁמְרָהּ, "to keep it," לָהּ, "for her."

Maqqef: a short horizontal stroke (resembling a hyphen in modern languages) used to join two or more words into a single speech unit. All words in such a unit lose their primary accents, except the word that closes the unit. When a closed syllable with a long vowel loses its primary accent because of maqqef, the long vowel, unless unchangeably long, must be shortened. וְאֶת־כָּל־הַדָּם is a single speech unit with two maqqefs and the first two words have had their vowels shortened (וְאֵת becoming וְאֶת־, and כֹּל becoming כָּל־).

Masorah: see **Masoretic Text**

Masoretes: Jewish scholars active from about A.D. 500 to 1000. They took up the earlier work of the scribes. Because Hebrew had largely ceased to be a spoken language in their time, the Masoretes invented a system of vowel pointings and superimposed it on the fixed consonantal text. They also devised a system of accents and superimposed it on the text. Vowels and accents were written under, within, and above the existing text. The Masoretes also made textual annotations and placed them on the side of the page (Masorah Parva), at the top and bottom of the page (Masorah Magna), and at the end of individual books (Masorah Finalis). Some notes contained statistical information about the frequency of occurrence of words, groups of words, or special forms. Others represented early attempts to improve the Hebrew text and clarify its meaning. The text that resulted from the efforts of the Masoretes came to be known as the Masoretic Text (MT). The Masoretic Text is the text represented in modern printed editions of the Hebrew Bible.

Masoretic Text (abbreviated as MT): the name given to the fixed consonantal text with its accompanying system of vowels and accents and its various types of Masorah (Masorah Parva, Masorah Magna, Masorah Finalis). The text was perfected toward the end of the ninth or the beginning of the tenth century A.D. and since then has replaced all other textual traditions. The primary witnesses to this textual tradition are the Aleppo codex (A), containing the entire Hebrew Bible and dating from the first half of the tenth century A.D.; the Leningrad Codex (L), containing the entire Hebrew Bible and, according to its colophon, copied in A.D. 1008; the Cairo Codex (C), containing the Former and Latter Prophets and copied and pointed, according to its colophon, in A.D. 895; and the British Museum Codex (OR.4445), a pointed and accented manuscript of the Pentateuch dated c. A.D. 820–850.

Matres Lectionis (*mothers of reading*): a Latin phrase coined by early grammarians to designate certain consonants that served as vowel indicators before the full system of vowel points was invented. א and ה represented "a" class vowels, י, "i" and "e" class vowels, and ו, "o" and "u" class vowels. Writing that contained vowel letters was called *scriptio plene*, while writing that omitted them was called *scriptio defectiva*.

Meteg: a small vertical stroke ordinarily placed to the left of a vowel (sometimes printed to the right in *BHS*, cf. וַיְהִ֫י in Gen. 1:7). It functions as a secondary accent. Its uses include the following:

(a) to stress the pronunciation of long vowels standing two or more syllables before the accented syllable of a word

(b) to stress full vowels standing immediately before consonants with half-vowels

(c) to stress unchangeably long vowels standing in syllables that immediately precede a maqqef

Modal Auxiliary: one of a group of "helping" verbs used with other verbs to express the various distinctions of mode. Included here are such verbs as "could," "should," "may," "must," "dare," "will," "shall," etc.

Mode (also called **Mood**): the characterization of a verb which defines a speaker's attitude toward an action taken or a state expressed. This involves such attitudes as certainty (indicative mode), uncertainty (subjunctive mode), command (imperative mode), and wish or desire (jussive or hortatory mode).

Munah: one of the accents supplied by the Masoretes to the pointed text, classified as a conjunctive accent. In this Grammar, however, it has been adopted as the standard accent for words accented on any syllable other than their final syllable.

אֵ֫לֶּה, "these," גֶּ֫פֶן, "vine"

437

Nif'al: the second of the verb stems, generally identifiable by a nun (נ) prefix, whether actually present or assimilated. Nif'al often stands as the passive counterpart to the Qal. At other times it may be translated in an active sense, much like the Qal. It may also express a reflexive action, where the subject becomes the object of the action performed.

Noun: a word used to denote a person, place, or thing. The name of a person or place is classified as a proper name. Participles often function as nouns. Nouns may occur in either the absolute or the construct state, in either the masculine or the feminine gender, and in either the singular, plural, or dual number. They may appear either with or without the definite article, and be prefixed with prepositions or conjunctions. They may end with a pronominal suffix or with a He–Directive.

Number: the property of a word which indicates whether it has one or more referents. Hebrew distinguishes three possible numbers for nouns (singular, plural, and dual) and two (singular and plural) for pronouns, adjectives, and all verb forms except infinitives.

Object of a Preposition: a noun or pronoun that follows a preposition.

Object Pronouns: pronominal suffixes that may be added to verbs and prepositions to function as objects of these two parts of speech. Object pronouns, like independent (subject) pronouns, include in their structure the elements of person, gender, and number.

Ordinal Numerals: numerals used to express consecutive order or rank, or relative position in a series, as *first*, *second*, *third*, etc. Cardinal numerals are those used in counting, as *one*, *two*, *three*, etc.

Paradigm: a table showing the way a verb can be conjugated or a noun declined. The verb charts at the end of this Grammar provide examples of paradigms of both strong and weak verbs.

Participles: verb forms sharing the properties and performing the functions of adjectives, verbs, and nouns. By their endings they display both gender (masculine/feminine) and number (singular/plural), but not person. They are also classified according to voice, as either active, passive, or reflexive. Only the Qal stem exhibits both active and passive participial forms. Nif'al participles may be either passive or reflexive in voice. Qal participles alone occur without prefixes. Nif'al participles are prefixed with נ, and participial forms of all remaining stems are prefixed with מ.

Particle: a class of short, undeclinable words consisting of such forms as the definite article, the ה directive, the נָא particle of entreaty, particles of existence (אַיִן, יֵשׁ), prepositions, conjunctions, interjections and exclamations (הִנֵּה הוֹי), etc.

Passive Voice: the classification of a verbal inflection in which the subject is the recipient rather than the performer of the action. Its opposite is the active voice.

Pataḥ Furtive: a pataḥ inserted before ה (he with mappiq), ח, and ע when they stand as the final consonants in words and are immediately preceded by long vowels not of the "a" class. Pataḥ furtive is actually inserted *between* the final strong guttural and the vowel that precedes it. It does not have the value of a full vowel and therefore does not increase the number of syllables in the word in which it stands.

וְרוּחַ (Gen. 1:2), נֹחַ (Gen. 6:9), רָקִיעַ (Gen. 1:6), גָּבֹהַּ (1 Sam. 9:2)

Pausal Forms: the altered forms that words ordinarily take when they are marked with a major disjunctive accent within a sentence (verse). A pausal form may differ from the ordinary form of a word by having a long vowel in place of a short vowel or by having a shift in the location of the major accented syllable within the word.

Ordinary Forms	Pausal Forms
אֶרֶץ	אָרֶץ
אֲנִי	אָנִי
יִכָּרְתוּ	יִכָּרֵתוּ
בִּיתְךָ	בִּיתֶךָ

Pe 'Alef (I-'Alef) Verb: a verb rendered weak by virtue of the fact that its initial root consonant is א. However, not all verbs with initial א are conjugated alike. Most are treated simply as Pe Gutturals. Those that are genuinely Pe 'Alef include אָבַד, "he was lost, perished," אָכַל, "he ate," אָמַר, "he said."

Pe Guttural (I-Guttural) Verb: a verb classified as weak by virtue of the fact that its initial root consonant is either ה, ח, ע, or ר. A verb whose initial root consonant is א may also belong to the Pe Guttural class, or it may differ so widely in form from other verbs of this class that it must be treated separately, as a Pe 'Alef verb. The various pecularities of gutturals affect the conjugation of Pe Guttural verbs.

Pe Nun (I-Nun) Verb: a verb rendered weak by virtue of the fact that its initial root consonant is נ. When in the inflection of a Pe Nun verb the initial nun is supported by a syllable divider (silent sheva), the נ is dropped, along with its silent sheva, and the following consonant is doubled (by a dagesh forte).

Pe Vav/Pe Yod (I-Vav/I-Yod) Verbs: verbs rendered weak by virtue of the fact that in non-prefixed forms they have yod as their initial root consonant, except where this consonant is omitted altogether. In prefixed forms, verbs properly Pe Yod still retain the yod, although in the form of a diphthong; verbs properly Pe Vav, on the other hand, have a vav after the prefix, again in the form of a diphthong. This is one of the most complicated of all the classes of weak verbs.

Perfect: one of the verb conjugations, sometimes referred to as the "affix" conjugation, since its primary characteristic is the affixing of the subject pronoun to the end of the verb root. It describes a completed action in past, present, or future time, the time being determined by the context.

Pi'el: the third of the verb stems, characterized by a doubling of the middle consonant of the verb root. Pi'el may function as the intensification of the Qal, as the transitive counterpart to verbs normally intransitive in the Qal, or as the causative active (similar in meaning to the Hif'il).

Pointed Text: a text supplied with vowels, also known as a vocalized text. An unpointed text is one consisting only of consonants without vowel points. Synagogue scrolls are unpointed scrolls and are pronounced according to a longstanding oral tradition.

Predicate Adjective: an adjective that functions as predicate to a subject noun or pronoun. Predicate adjectives are usually found in verbless sentences (the verb "to be" understood), or following an inflected form of the verb הָיָה, "he was." A predicate adjective usually stands before its subject but may sometimes follow it. It agrees with its subject in gender and number but never takes the definite article, even though its subject may be definite.

טוֹב הַדָּבָר	"The word (is) good."
טוֹבָה הָאָרֶץ	"The land was good."
וְהָיָה הַמִּזְבֵּחַ קֹדֶשׁ	"And the altar shall be holy."

Prefix (also referred to as preformative): something added to the beginning of a verb root to help to determine the remaining inflected forms of the verb in all stems.

Preformative: see **Prefix**

Pronominal Suffix: a shortened form of a personal pronoun that may be added to the end of prepositions, particles, nouns, or verbs. When affixed to a preposition, it becomes the object of the preposition. When attached to a particle, its meaning will be determined by the nature of the particle. When placed at the end of a noun (always the construct form of the noun), it will function as a possessive pronoun. When affixed to a verb it will normally function as object of the verb, but may occasionally function as subject, if its accompanying verb is an infinitive construct.

Proper Noun: the name of a person (Noah), a people (Moabites), or a place (Egypt). Hebrew proper nouns, unlike their counterparts in English, do not begin with capital letters, since Hebrew has none.

Puʻal: the fourth verb stem, characterized by the doubling of the middle root consonant. It functions as the passive counterpart to the Piʻel.

Qal: the basic stem of the verb, from which the other six stems are derived. Qal (קַל) is derived from קָלַל, "he (it) was light (not heavy), insignificant." It is classified as the simple active stem, although it has a passive participle, perhaps the only surviving remnant of an old Qal passive conjugation.

Radical: another name for a verb root consonant. While it is common practice to speak, for example, of the verb root שָׁמַר as having three consonants, it is also acceptable to say that it has three radicals.

Reflexive: the description of an action which the subject of the verb performs upon himself/herself. A reflexive action is ordinarily expressed by verb forms of either the Nifʻal or the Hitpaʻel stem.

Relative Pronoun: a pronoun that refers back to its antecedent and introduces a clause that modifies the antecedent. The most common relative pronoun is אֲשֶׁר, equivalent in meaning to the English relative pronoun "who," "which," "that." It is fixed in its form and unaffected by the gender or number of its antecedent.

מִי־הָאִישׁ אֲשֶׁר בָּנָה בַיִת־חָדָשׁ "Who is the man who has built a new house?" (Deut. 20:5)

הָאִשָּׁה אֲשֶׁר נָתַתָּה עִמָּדִי "the woman whom you gave to me" (Gen. 3:12)

Root: see **Verb Root**

Scriptio Defectiva (*defective writing*): see **Scriptio Plena**

Scriptio Plena (*full writing*): a Latin term coined by early grammarians to designate a text supplied with extra consonants (*Matres Lectionis*) that served as vowel indicators during the period before the text itself was pointed. The Dead Sea scroll of Isaiah (1QIsᵃ), for example, is such a text. *Scriptio Defectiva* (*defective writing*) refers to a text, or a word within a text, written without the use of vowel letters or vowel indicators. The same word may sometimes be written full and sometimes defective.

טֹב or טוֹב, קָדֹשׁ or קָדוֹשׁ

Semitic Languages: the family of languages to which Hebrew belongs. It is usually divided into three groups: (1) East Semitic (Akkadian); (2) Northwest Semitic (Canaanite, Moabite, Phoenician, Punic, Hebrew, Ugaritic, Aramaic, Syriac, Samaritan, and Nabatean); (3) Southwest Semitic (Arabic, Sabean, Minean, and Ethiopic).

The common features shared by this family of languages include the following: (1) All are basically consonantal in character, the addition of vowel signs being a late development in most. (2) All are written from right to left, except Akkadian and Ethiopic. (3) All show a decided preference for tri-consonantal verb roots. (4) The third person singular form of the verb is usually cited as the verb root. (5) In each of these languages there is a wide range of verb stems, with Akkadian, Ethiopic, and Arabic having more than a dozen, and Hebrew and Aramaic each having seven.

Sephardi, pl **Sephardim:** a term applied to Jews who migrated to Spain and surrounding regions. Sephardi (or Sephardic) is also used to describe the system of pronunciation used by this particular Jewish community, which is the system adopted by this grammar.

Shortening of Vowels: A long vowel standing in a closed accented syllable must be changed to a short vowel if the syllable loses its accent. If qameṣ, it is changed to pataḥ; if ṣere, to seˢgol; if ḥolem, to qameṣ-ḥaṭuf. The most common occurrences of such shortening is when an absolute noun is placed in the construct state, or when the particle נָא is added to either the jussive or the imperative form of a verb.

(1)	יָד	"hand" (absolute state)
	יַד־אֱלֹהִים	"the hand of God" (construct state)
(2)	יִזְכֹּר	"he will remember"
	יִזְכָּר־נָא	"let him remember"
(3)	דַּבֵּר	"Speak!"
	דַּבֶּר־נָא	"Pray, speak!"

Sibilants: the term used to describe letters of the alphabet that have an "s" sound. These include ז, ס, צ, שׁ, and שׂ.

Sign of the Direct Object: the particle אֵת, which is placed before a definite noun to indicate that the noun receives the action of the verb. It may stand alone before a noun or be joined to it by a maqqef. It is never translated.

Silent Sheva: identical in form to the simple sheva, but differing from it in its function. Whereas the simple sheva stands beneath a non-guttural consonant at the beginning of a word or a new syllable within a word and is always vocal, the silent sheva stands beneath a non-guttural consonant that closes a syllable within a word and is therefore silent (often described as a "syllable divider"). When two shevas stand beneath adjacent consonants within a word, the first will be a silent sheva marking the end of a closed syllable, and the second will be a simple (vocal) sheva marking the beginning of a new syllable.

יִשְׁמְרוּ The first sheva (שְׁ) is silent, the second (מְ) is vocal.

Silluq: a major disjunctive accent that resembles a meteg in form but is placed on the accented syllable of the final word in each verse, the word that is immediately followed by sof passuq (׃), the Hebrew equivalent of a period. Silluq is found, for example, on the final syllable of אֶחָד in Genesis 1:5. A word accented by silluq is always in pause and the syllable carrying silluq must have a long vowel.

Simple Sheva: a sheva placed beneath a non-guttural consonant at the beginning of a word or at the beginning of a new syllable within a word. Simple shevas are therefore to be treated as vocal shevas.

בְּרִית, "covenant," begins with בּ supported by a simple (vocal) sheva (בְּ).

Sof Passuq: the sign (׃) that indicates the end of a verse or sentence. It is equivalent to the period in other languages.

Stative Verb: a verb that describes a condition, quality, or state of being of its subject. Since no action is involved, it is to be classified as an intransitive verb. The root form of triliteral stative verbs normally follows the pattern seen in such verbs as גָּדֵל, "he was great," and קָרֵב, "he was near." However, there are some roots that have either sere or holem in the second syllable, as זָקֵן, "he was old," and יָכֹל, "he was able."

Stems: see **Verb Stems**

Strong Verbs (also known as sound verbs): verbs that have three strong consonants in their root form (Qal perfect 3 ms). The consonants that do not render a verb "weak" are ב, ג, ד, ז, ט, כ, ל, מ, נ (except when נ stands as the initial or the final consonant in a verb root), ס, פ, צ, ק, ר (only when ר is the final consonant in a verb root), שׂ, שׁ, and ת. A strong verb must be made up entirely of strong consonants.

Strong verbs: בָּקַשׁ, קָטַל, מָלַךְ, etc.

Weak Verbs: יָצָא, עָשָׂה, נָפַל, etc.

Subject: the noun or pronoun that performs the action of the verb or exists in a state or condition described by the verb. When the subject is a pronoun, it may be expressed by the verb itself, without having to be written as a separate form.

443

Subject Pronoun: see **Independent Pronoun**

Subjunctive Mode: the mode of the verb that reflects an action or a state of being not yet realized in the time of the context, or about which there is an element of doubt or uncertainty.

אִם־יִהְיֶה אֱלֹהִים עִמָּדִי "If God will be with me."

פֶּן־נָמוּת "Lest we should die."

Substantive: see **Noun**

Suffix (also referred to as afformative): generally used to describe the pronominal endings added to perfect, imperfect, and imperative forms of the verb to indicate the person, gender, and number of each. Suffix may also be used to designate the object pronouns added to verbs and the possessive pronouns added to nouns and prepositions. These suffixes are also distinguished according to person, gender, and number.

Syllable: a unit of pronunciation initiated by a consonant supported by a vocal sheva (simple or compound) or by a full vowel (short or long). If the initial consonant is supported by a vocal sheva, it cannot by itself constitute a syllable, but must be paired with the following consonant and its full vowel in order to be classified as a syllable. Thus there will be as many syllables as there are full vowels within a word. Thus בִּין and בְּרִית are both one-syllable words, since each has only one full vowel.

Syllables are either open or closed. An open syllable is one ending in a vowel. A closed syllable is one ending in a consonant (except א or final ה). An open syllable will normally have a long vowel, although the vowel may be short if the syllable is accented. A closed syllable will normally have a short vowel, although the vowel may be long if the syllable is accented. These changes are most likely to occur when words are placed in pause by a heavy disjunctive accent.

Syntax: an advanced branch of Hebrew grammar. Waltke and O'Connor describe their *Introduction to Biblical Hebrew Syntax* as "an intermediary grammar of the language of the Hebrew Bible." But while an introductory grammar aims primarily at giving students a grasp of the basic fundamentals of the language, a treatise on syntax deals with such matters as the formation of grammatical sentences and the arrangement and relationship of various parts of speech within a phrase, clause, or sentence. Grammar focuses attention on the form of isolated words; syntax deals with the function and meaning of words in context.

TANAKH: an acronym formed from the initial letters of the three words used to describe major divisions of the Hebrew Bible. These are:

> **(T)** Torah (Law)
>
> **(N)** Nebhi'im (Prophets)
>
> **(K)** Kethubhim (Writings)

The Hebrew Bible is commonly referred to simply as the Tanakh.

Tone Syllable: an alternate name for the syllable carrying the main accent in a word, otherwise known as the accented syllable. The tone syllable will normally be the final syllable in a word. A munaḥ (ˎ) will be used throughout this Grammar to mark any accented syllable that is not final in a word.

Transitive Verb: a verb which requires a direct object to complete its meaning. An intransitive verb, on the other hand, is one which cannot take a direct object.

וַיֵּלֶךְ אַבְרָהָם וַיִּקַּח אֶת־הָאַיִל

"And Abraham went [intransitive] and took the ram [transitive]." (Gen. 22:13)

Transliteration: the process whereby the individual letters of a word written in one language are transcribed into their phonetical equivalents in another language. Shalom, for example, is the transliteration of שָׁלוֹם; its translation is "peace."

Transposition of Sibilants: when the ת of the Hitpaʻel preformative is placed before one of the sibilants ס, צ, שׂ, or שׁ, the ת of the preformative and the following sibilant are transposed. This change in the sequence of sounds is also referred to as metathesis.

> הִתְשַׁמֵּר, "he took heed to himself," becomes הִשְׁתַּמֵּר
>
> הִתְסַתֵּר, "he hid himself," becomes הִסְתַּתֵּר

A further change becomes necessary when ת is followed by the sibilant צ. After ת and צ are transposed, ת is changed to ט.

> הִתְצַדֵּק, "he justified himself," first becomes הִצְתַּדֵּק, which in turn becomes הִצְטַדֵּק

Unchangeably Long Vowels: see **Diphthong**

445

Vav Conjunction: the conjunction "and," used to connect words, phrases, clauses, and sentences. The rules for writing vav conjunction:

(a) וְ before consonants with full vowels (except בּ, מ, and פּ)

(b) וּ before בּ, מ, and פּ and before consonants pointed with a simple sheva (except before יְ)

(c) וִ before יְ (וִיהִי) instead of (וְיִהִי)

(d) וַ, וֶ, וָ before consonants pointed with a compound sheva
(וַחֲלִי, וֶאֱמֶת, וָאֲנִי)

Vav Consecutive (also described as vav conversive): a form of the conjunction "and" found only on imperfect forms of the verb. A verb prefixed with vav consecutive must be translated in past time and in the indicative mode. It may be either sequential ("and then") or consequential ("and so") in meaning. Vav consecutive is usually written vav + pataḥ + dagesh forte in the following consonant (וַ). However, before an imperfect 1 cs form, which has א as its prefix, the dagesh forte cannot be placed in the guttural א, and therefore the preceding vowel pataḥ must be lengthened to qames. When vav consecutive is prefixed to imperfect forms of Lamed He verbs, these are often shortened or apocopated.

Verb Root: the base form of the verb from which other forms evolve. It is the form listed in lexicons. For triliteral verbs found in the Qal stem, it is the Qal perfect 3 ms form. For triliteral verbs not found in the Qal, it is normally listed in brackets without vowels, as in [בקשׁ]. For ʿAyin Vav/ʿAyin Yod verbs, it is the Qal infinitive construct, as in מוּת, "to die," שִׂים, "to put or place."

Verb Sequences: see **Coordinate Relationship**

Verb Stems (also referred to as conjugations, or as *binyan*, Hebrew for "building"): the seven major conjugation patterns of Hebrew verbs. The first of these, the Qal (קַל) stem (from קָלַל, "he was light, insignificant"), is often described as the "basic" or "pure" stem, and the remaining six as "derived" stems. The latter are formed by such devices as the internal modification of vowels, the doubling of middle root consonants, and the addition of stem preformatives.
The Qal stem is the simple active stem. The second, the Nifʿal (נִפְעַל) may be either reflexive or simple passive. The Piʿel (פִּעֵל) stem is intensive active; the Puʿal (פֻּעַל), intensive passive; and the Hitpaʿel (הִתְפַּעֵל), reflexive. The two causative stems are Hifʿil (הִפְעִיל), causative active, and Hofʿal (הָפְעַל), causative passive. Rarely will one encounter a verb that has conjugated forms in all seven of these stems, or even in a majority of them.

Vocalic Suffix: a verb suffix that begins with a vowel. Vocalic suffixes will draw the accent to themselves, except where they occur in the Hifʻil stem and are preceded by ḥireq-yod.

Volatilization (also referred to as vowel reduction): the process whereby a full vowel is reduced to a half vowel (vocal sheva). Reduction occurs when an originally accented syllable loses its accent to a new syllable added to the end of the word. The new syllable may represent a pronominal suffix, a person, gender, and number ending of a verb form, or a plural ending of a noun. In verb forms, a shift in accent causes the nearest preceding vowel in an open syllable to volatilize. Volatilization in nouns involves vowels left in open syllables two or more syllables before the accented syllable (tone syllable). This includes nouns that lose their accent by being placed in construct relationship to other nouns.

(1) 3 fs suffix הָ added to שָׁמַר, "he kept"

שָׁמְרָה → שָׁמַרָה → שָׁמַר + הָ

(2) mp ending ִים added to נָבִיא, "prophet"

נְבִיאִים → נָבִיאִים → נָבִיא + ִים

(3) דָּבָר "word," הָאִישׁ "the man"

דְּבַר הָאִישׁ "the word of the man"

447

SUBJECT INDEX